Praise for

JEFFERSON'S TREASURE

"Gregory May's masterful new biography restores Albert Gallatin to his rightful place in the history of the new republic. Gallatin was the indefatigable and indispensable Republican, the Treasury Secretary who made Hamiltonian finance serve Jeffersonian ends. May achieves the rare balance between sympathetic engagement and critical detachment that can make good biography into illuminating history. *Jefferson's Treasure* will be recognized as an important contribution to our understanding of the American founding."

> —PETER S. ONUF, University of Virginia, coauthor (with Annette Gordon-Reed) of *"Most Blessed of the Patriarchs": Thomas Jefferson and the Empire of the Imagination*

"'A real Treasure,' wrote James Madison to his friend Jefferson early in his acquaintance with the proud Genevan, then an even-tempered congressman, who would go on to manage the national economy during their two presidencies. As Treasury Secretary, Albert Gallatin pointed the modest young republic to a debt-free condition, and founding era history remains incomplete without him. His admiring biographer Henry Adams knew that in 1879. But until Gregory May's expansive new life of Gallatin, no scholar had ever fully plumbed the depths of his mind and fleshed out his personality, nor conveyed his politics in such lively prose. At last, he emerges from the shadow of presidents."

> —ANDREW BURSTEIN AND NANCY ISENBERG, coauthors of *Madison and Jefferson*

"*Jefferson's Treasure* provides a masterful portrait of one of America's least likely founding players, Swiss-born Albert Gallatin, America's longest-serving Treasury Secretary, who balanced the Jeffersonian crusade for debt reduction and small budgets with the needs of the emerging American nation. Gregory May's compelling account employs Gallatin's financial wizardry, statesmanship, and deep humanity as a powerful lens for viewing the nation's formative decades."

> —DAVID O. STEWART, author of *Madison's Gift: Five Partnerships That Built America* and *The Summer of 1787: The Men Who Invented the Constitution*

"*Jefferson's Treasure* is the fascinating story of Albert Gallatin and his struggle to unwind the protectionist and debt-dependent central banking scheme with which Alexander Hamilton had financed the new government of the United States. Hamilton's centralized American economy enriched the money class on the coast at the expense of ordinary Americans. Gallatin had faith in free trade and debt-free public finance—not only to spread prosperity to all, but also to guarantee political liberty. Greg May serves up a solid contribution to the history of the early Republic and a wealth of wisdom for our times."
—**GEORGE GILDER**, author of *Wealth and Poverty*

"From the 1790s through the 1840s Albert Gallatin, an immigrant from Europe who became a congressman, Treasury Secretary, and diplomat, was a leading player in American affairs. Gregory May's deeply researched and engagingly written book is much more than a biography. Via the long life of Gallatin, May gives us an insightful account of the major political, economic, and financial problems the young United States faced from the Washington administration through the Mexican War. Greg May's *Jefferson's Treasure* is a tour de force!"

—**RICHARD SYLLA**, author of *Alexander Hamilton: The Illustrated Biography*; Professor Emeritus of Economics, New York University; and Chairman, Museum of American Finance

"With careful research, keen insights, and clear writing, Gregory May recovers the extraordinary life of Albert Gallatin, a resourceful immigrant, canny politician, and financial wizard of the early republic. A worthy rival to Alexander Hamilton, Gallatin is now overdue for his own Broadway musical."

—**ALAN TAYLOR**, author of *American Revolutions: A Continental History, 1750-1804*

Jefferson's Treasure

Jefferson's
TREASURE

How Albert Gallatin
Saved the New Nation
from Debt

GREGORY MAY

REGNERY
HISTORY

Regnery® is a registered trademark of Salem Communications Holding Corporation

Regnery History™ is a trademark of Salem Communications Holding Corporation

Cataloging-in-Publication data on file with the Library of Congress

ISBN 978-1-62157-645-7

Published in the United States by
Regnery History
An imprint of Regnery Publishing
A Division of Salem Media Group
300 New Jersey Ave NW
Washington, DC 20001
www.RegneryHistory.com

Manufactured in the United States of America

10 9 8 7 6 5 4 3 2 1

Books are available in quantity for promotional or premium use. For information on discounts and terms, please visit our website: www. Regnery.com.

To Anna

Why should we celebrate
These dead men more than the dying?
It is not to ring the bell backward
Nor is it an incantation
To summon the spectre of a Rose.
We cannot revive old factions
We cannot restore old policies
Or follow an antique drum.
These men, and those who opposed them
And those whom they opposed
Accept the constitution of silence
And are folded in a single party.
Whatever we inherit from the fortunate
We have taken from the defeated
What they had to leave us—a symbol:
A symbol perfected in death.

—T. S. Eliot, "Little Gidding"
　　Four Quartets

CONTENTS

ILLUSTRATIONS

5.2   Joseph Hopper Nicholson by C. B. J. F. de Saint-Mémin, engraving, 1806. Maryland Historical Society, Saint-Mémin Collection.

5.3   Robert Smith by C. B. J. F. de Saint-Mémin, engraving, 1803. Maryland Historical Society, Saint-Mémin Collection.

5.4   Samuel Smith by Rembrandt Peale, oil on canvas, 1818. Maryland Historical Society, Baltimore City Life Museum Collection.

6.1   Albert Gallatin by Rembrandt Peale, oil on canvas, 1805. Independence National Historical Park, no. INDE 11875 (SN 13.078).

6.2   Silhouettes of Hannah and Albert Gallatin, anon., c. 1806. Albert and Shirley Small Special Collections Library, University of Virginia, Gallatin Family Papers.

7.1   Albert Gallatin by William H. Powell, oil on canvas, 1843. New-York Historical Society, obj. no. 1844.1 (gift of the artist).

7.2   Albert Gallatin by Anthony, Edwards, and Co., daguerreotype, c. [1842?]. New-York Historical Society, Albert Gallatin Papers.

7.3   John Badollet by Charles Alexandre Lesueur, sketch, c. 1833. Indiana Historical Society, M0219.

8.1   *Signing of the Treaty of Ghent, Christmas Eve, 1814* by Sir Amédée Forestier, oil on canvas, 1914. Smithsonian American Art Museum, no. 1922.5.2 (gift of the Sulgrave Institution of the United States and Great Britain).

8.2   *Broadway Tabernacle, New York, 24 December 1847* by Tompkins H. Matteson, American Art Union lithograph, 1848. U. S. National Park Service, "Gaslight in America: A Guide for Historic Preservation," Plate 16, https://www.nps.gov/parkhistory/online_books/hcrs/myers/plate2.htm.

INTRODUCTION

When Thomas Jefferson appointed Albert Gallatin to be Secretary of the Treasury in 1801, Federalists expected the worst. They had just lost the presidency for the first time, in an election so sharply contested that it took thirty-six ballots in the House of Representatives to make Jefferson president. They had also lost their majority in Congress. Now Jefferson was putting the man who had led the Republican Congressional opposition in charge of the largest and most powerful department of government. They knew this man Gallatin all too well. He was a foreigner, a tax rebel, and a dangerously clever man. For the last six years, he had been the ablest and most vocal critic of the federal financial system. His objections to taxes, federal spending, and public debt were relentless. Now he would turn those objections into policies that would endanger the fragile federal regime. At the least, he would starve the embryonic military establishment in order to repay the debt.

Their vision of an American nation-state vigorous enough to win deference from its people and respect from other nations would collapse.[1]

Gallatin had come to national attention only six years earlier when
the Pennsylvania backcountry rose against Alexander Hamilton's tax on
distilled spirits in what later would be called the Whiskey Rebellion.
Gallatin was then thirty-three years old—a lean man of just above average height with bushy black hair, a prominent forehead, and a long
curved nose. He had come to America from Geneva in 1780, about a
year before the British surrender at Yorktown signaled American victory
in the Revolutionary War. After struggling for a few years in New England, he had settled on the remote frontier in the southwestern corner of
Pennsylvania, where he speculated in land, kept a store, and raised a few
crops. Nothing quite worked; nothing had put him on the path to the
fortune he sought. But his talents had not gone unnoticed. Local worthies
in the backcountry sent Gallatin to the Pennsylvania Constitutional
Convention in 1790 and then to the state legislature in 1791. There he
showed a rare aptitude for public finance, a prodigious appetite for work,
and a knack for getting along with men of different political persuasions.
An aristocrat by birth, he had become an outspoken republican by conviction. He made friends among the emerging Republican opposition in
Philadelphia, and he married Hannah Nicholson, the daughter of a leading Republican partisan in New York. Gallatin had taken a lead in the
early protests against Hamilton's whiskey excise, but he opposed the
protesters' turn toward violence. His moderation earned him respect and
an unexpected election to Congress.

Violent protests against the whiskey tax got national attention
because they stabbed at the heart of federal power. No government can
survive without money and credit. No government can get credit unless
potential lenders believe it can collect taxes. And no government can
collect taxes effectively unless its citizens think they are fair. Those truths
were painfully plain in the 1790s. The old government under the Articles
of Confederation had run up $54 million of debt during the Revolution-
ary War because it had no power to tax. The states—which had run up

$25 million in war debts of their own—failed to pay their shares of the common expenses, and the Confederation effectively defaulted on its obligations. It was unclear when or even whether the national government could pay what it owed. The American economy, damaged by war, uncertainty, and British trade restrictions, had fallen into a severe depression a few years after the fighting ended. Unpaid interest on federal and state obligations had mounted to more than $4 million. By 1788, debt claims against the federal government were worth only 10 to 20 cents on the dollar.[2]

Necessity forced many cash-strapped Revolutionary veterans, farmers, and small merchants to sell their claims against the government at those heavy discounts. Speculative trading concentrated the claims into the hands of a relative few, and trading grew rampant when the ratification of the Constitution—which gave the national government broad taxing powers—increased the chances of repayment. By 1790, an estimated two-thirds of the government debt for which accounts survive belonged to about 300 to 500 men. Most of them were in Philadelphia, New York, and other mercantile cities along the coast. They were wealthier and more influential than most other citizens, and they stood to reap enormous profits if the new federal government undertook to repay the debt at face value. This posed a serious political problem. More than a few Americans bridled at the idea of collecting taxes from ordinary people to deliver a windfall to a few rich men. They thought speculators should receive no more than the market value of their claims.[3]

Alexander Hamilton had confronted the political problem boldly when he became the first Secretary of the Treasury in 1789. He was convinced that the nation's strength depended on its credit. As a young army officer on George Washington's staff, Hamilton had watched the fiscal failures of the Confederation government undermine the war effort. He began to study public finance, and he observed how Great Britain and France borrowed the money they needed to wage the wars that made them great powers. He sent unsolicited financial reform proposals to public officials and published his ideas in the newspapers.

Credit was power, and Hamilton wanted the United States to have great power. He was determined to use the fiscal powers in the new Constitution to create confidence—a regime's essential currency—in the new American nation.[4]

Hamilton told Congress that two measures were essential to confidence. The federal government must promise to pay the Confederation's debts at face value. And to make that promise credible, the government must promise to fund the payments with revenues from specifically identified taxes. Hamilton conceded that those measures would enrich the speculators who had bought debt cheaply, but he claimed it would give much greater benefits to the whole nation. First, funding the payments from an identified stream of revenue would allow the government to borrow more easily, and borrowing would allow taxpayers to spread the extraordinary cost of wars and other emergencies over prosperous periods of peace and stability. Second, funded debt would increase the capital available for investment in the nation's developing economy. Confidence that the debt could be repaid would raise and stabilize its price. Higher prices would give the debt holders more capital, and price stability would encourage them to put that capital to more productive uses than speculation.[5]

Hamilton knew that paying the debt at face value would be controversial, but he had an even more controversial proposal. He wanted the federal government to assume the wartime debts of the individual states. Hamilton claimed that assumption would cost taxpayers nothing because the amount to be paid was the same no matter which government paid it. And without assumption, he argued, the states would compete with the federal government for tax revenues to the detriment of both the governments and the people. State and national creditors would quarrel with one another rather than uniting in support of the new federal regime. Hamilton left the obvious corollary unspoken: assumption would increase the power and importance of the federal government.[6]

To accomplish his objectives, Hamilton refinanced the entire public debt. He repaid foreign creditors from the proceeds of new foreign loans, and he gave domestic creditors an exchange offer. The terms of the exchange offer were complicated, perhaps unnecessarily, by his desire to lower the interest rates on the domestic debt. Creditors who surrendered their old Confederation claims got a basket of new federal bonds that could be traded in the securities markets. Two-thirds of the bonds paid interest at the old 6 percent rate. The other third also paid 6 percent interest, but only after ten years. For back interest on the old claims, creditors got additional bonds bearing 3 percent interest. State creditors received a somewhat less attractive mix of the same bonds.[7]

The plan reduced the effective interest rate on the federal debt from 6 percent to 4 percent and made a comparable dent in the rate on state debts. But Hamilton gave creditors two important inducements to accept that reduction in interest rates. First, payments on the new federal bonds would have first claim on most of the federal government's tax revenues. The holders of the old claims would get only what was left over. Second, the new bonds would have long stated maturities. The government could redeem the old obligations at any time, and it probably would redeem them as soon as it could borrow fresh money at lower rates. By exchanging their old claims for new bonds, creditors could lock in a return on their money that was likely to be attractive over the long run.[8]

Hamilton believed that relatively moderate taxes would produce enough revenue to pay the reduced interest on the federal debt and the ordinary costs of government. He embraced the prevailing assumption that the federal government could raise substantially all of the money it needed from duties on imported goods. The duties he had in mind ranged from 5 to 15 percent of the value of the goods. Duties increased the price of imported goods, but they were effective taxes for several reasons. The government could collect them at the ports, and the merchants who paid them had better access to cash than other citizens did. The indirect tax burden passed on to the buyers of the goods in the form of higher prices was less apparent, and therefore less painful, than a direct tax. And the burden fell more heavily on wealthier citizens because most of the dutiable consumer goods apart from salt were nonessentials such as distilled spirits, wine, beer, tea, spices, and fine leather products. But Hamilton recognized that the assumption of state debts would require the federal government to raise some additional revenue. He could not get all of the money he needed from higher import duties because duties that high would encourage smuggling. So he reluctantly proposed an excise tax on whiskey and other spirits distilled within the United States.[9]

Excise taxes on alcoholic beverages and other manufactured products were a significant part of the British tax base, but the people detested them. The collection of excise taxes required an extensive internal system of inspection—an intrusion that heightened resentment over the cash exaction. Hamilton nevertheless preferred an excise on whiskey to a direct tax on land and houses. The new Constitution required the federal government to apportion direct taxes among the states in proportion to their populations. So the amount of land tax apportioned to a heavily populated state would be greater than the amount apportioned to a thinly populated state even if the heavily populated state had less land than the thinly populated state. The direct tax per acre therefore would be higher in the more densely populated Northern states. Direct taxes also could be hard to collect from cash-strapped farmers and householders. Whiskey distillers, on the other hand, had a product readily reducible to cash, and a tax that raised the price of their product would keep it from undercutting the spirits subject to import duties.[10]

Just months after Congress passed his debt plan, Hamilton made another audacious financial recommendation. He proposed to charter a national bank explicitly modeled on the Bank of England. This Bank of the United States would have a capital of $10 million, more than four times the combined capital of the four existing American banks and probably as much as all of the gold and silver specie then circulating in the country. Hamilton claimed that the national bank would accomplish three things. It would make more money available because bank notes backed by the bank's large capital could substitute for specie. Better monetary circulation would make it easier for the government to collect taxes, which the government would deposit with the bank. And the concentration of deposits in the bank would make it easier for the government to borrow large amounts quickly in emergencies.[11]

Hamilton wanted the federal government to have a significant stake in the national bank, but he believed that private shareholders could manage it more effectively. Therefore he proposed to make the new bank's shares an attractive investment. The bank would get a charter for twenty years, and the federal government would promise not to charter a competing bank. Shareholders could pay for three-quarters of their shares with the new federal bonds. That would give control of the bank to the same sort of wealthy men who had engrossed the federal bonds. It also would allow them to leverage the value of those bonds into an even larger amount of bank credit. These were enormous advantages in a young nation where capital was scarce and large companies virtually nonexistent. Despite objections to the concentration of privilege and power, Congress accepted Hamilton's recommendation. Within two months, it had adopted his bank plan almost verbatim.[12]

Hamilton's bank bill went down hard with Thomas Jefferson. Jefferson's friend and confidant James Madison had opposed parts of Hamilton's fiscal plan in the House of Representatives from the beginning. Madison was appalled by the excessive speculation in government claims, and he wanted to compensate the original holders for the losses they had suffered when default forced them to sell their claims for pennies on the dollar. He also resisted federal assumption of the states' debts because he believed it would disadvantage Virginia and other states that had reduced their war debts. Jefferson, recently installed as Secretary of State and disposed to support his cabinet colleague at the Treasury, had talked Madison into accepting a compromise on assumption. But the bank proposal convinced Jefferson that Madison had been right all along. Jefferson was a brilliant man, but he had little experience with finance. Like most farmers mired in debt, he distrusted merchants and bankers. His inexperience with finance combined with that distrust to raise concerns that he could not shake. It seemed to him that the national bank offered the people very little.[13]

Most Americans were farmers. They needed credit, but land was their only collateral. A bank generally would not lend against land, as Hamilton had acknowledged, because land was too illiquid. So the bank would benefit a small group of wealthy men, most of them merchants in Northern cities. And the Bank's own shareholders probably would receive preferential treatment. Thus self-interest would draw those men to the federal regime—and to Hamilton's administration. The concentration in private hands of wealth ultimately backed by tax revenues distressed Jefferson. Its political implications positively alarmed him. He and Madison tried to block the bank bill by arguing that the Constitution had not given the federal government any express power to charter a bank. Hamilton convinced George Washington that the Constitution authorized the bank and any other measure that the federal government needed in order to exercise its constitutional responsibilities. Washington signed the bank bill in early 1791.[14]

Within the next year, Madison and Jefferson moved ever so gingerly into opposition against the administration in which Jefferson still served as Secretary of State. Jefferson wrote letters to political friends throughout the country to elicit their concerns about the tendency of federal measures and to insinuate that he and others might share those concerns. Madison recruited a college friend named Philip Freneau to start an opposition newspaper in Philadelphia, and Jefferson gave Freneau a salary for an undemanding job at the State department. In an anonymous and increasingly hard-hitting series of essays for the new newspaper, Madison denounced the faction that was taking control of the federal government. Those who "pamper[ed] the spirit of speculation," he declared, were not the true friends of the Union. Their measures had increased "the causes of corruption in the government, and the pretexts for new taxes," which undermined confidence in the Union and alienated the people's affections. The man who had professed in Federalist No. 10 that an extensive republic would dilute the power of factions now believed that a faction was seizing power. About half of the members of the House of Representatives gradually fell into one of two coteries. One coterie generally resisted Madison's positions, and the other supported them. The division foreshadowed the emergence of a Federalist party committed to the administration and a Republican party opposed to it.[15]

Madison's supporters were a disparate bunch, ranging from back-country Pennsylvania farmer William Findley through slaveholding Virginia planter William Branch Giles to discontented Massachusetts merchant Elbridge Gerry. But they had something in common. They believed that the American Revolution had been an escape not only from British domination of colonial Americans, but also from the British style of government in which factions used collusion, corruption, and consanguinity to grasp political power. Building on the thinking of English republicans and British liberals, they developed an abiding suspicion of government authority and government interference in the private sphere.[16]

What Madison and his supporters saw in Hamilton's financial system alarmed them. Not content with the centralization of power accomplished by the Constitution, Hamilton seemed bent on consolidating even greater power by administration. It was not just that the federal government was sweeping the country's fiscal resources under its control. It was that the connections between the federal government, the public debt, and the Bank of the United States would persuade Bank shareholders in Congress to support further consolidation. Hamilton cultivated those men, and his ministerial style of directing legislation shifted power to the executive branch, which he and other unelected men could manipulate. To recent revolutionaries, the most obvious explanation was that Hamilton meant to use collusion, corruption, and perhaps a touch of consanguinity to construct an administration like the British ministries. Hamilton might have been an obscure immigrant, but he had married into the aristocratic Schuyler family in New York and made powerful friends. He had spoken in favor of constitutional monarchy at the Federal Convention. The threat to republican government seemed clear.[17]

Whether they could turn back the threat was less clear. Hamilton was a formidable man, "an host within himself" in the Biblical phrase Jefferson later applied to him. He had the support of Washington, the virtually unassailable embodiment of Revolutionary virtue. And he had a masterful grip on public finance, a subject with which Madison,

Jefferson, and their supporters struggled. Hamilton's Treasury operations bewildered them; they could not escape the feeling that he meant to dupe them.[18]

An early skirmish between Madison's supporters and Hamilton showed how far he overmatched them. They thought they had found an opening when they discovered that Hamilton had shifted proceeds from a Dutch loan earmarked to repay French debts into a domestic account and used the money to bid up the price of the new federal bonds. The maneuver looked illegal, possibly even corrupt. Waiting until Congress was about to adjourn in early 1793, Madison's henchman Giles got the House to call for information about the affected Treasury accounts. He and Madison obviously hoped the insinuation about Hamilton's lack of integrity would metastasize until Congress returned in the autumn. They had miscalculated. Hamilton promptly delivered crisp, detailed reports explaining what he had done, why he had done it, and how it had saved the public money. Claiming that he could not understand the reports, Giles introduced nine resolutions censuring Hamilton's conduct. But the resolutions only confirmed that Giles indeed had not understood the reports, and the House roundly rejected them. Only Madison and six other members stuck with Giles on each vote. Giles's resolutions were a tamer version of drafts that Jefferson himself had prepared. By the end of the year, Jefferson resigned in frustration and returned to his farm in Virginia. About a year later, Hamilton resigned to resume his law practice in New York and left the Treasury in the hands of his protégé Oliver Wolcott. Madison soldiered on as the leader of the minority in the House.[19]

Albert Gallatin was an essential addition to the Republican cadre when he entered the House in 1795. His natural talent with numbers and his experience with public finance in Pennsylvania at last put the Republicans on equal terms with the Treasury. Gallatin demystified Treasury operations, showed how the Washington administration had increased the public debt, and exposed the administration's financial proposals to more open debate. He had an instinct for making shrewd amendments, often—his opponents complained—at the end of the day when they were tired or distracted. His speeches were persuasive, and despite a thick French accent, his delivery was compelling. Madison was soon reporting to Jefferson that Gallatin was "a real Treasure," and at his aerie in Virginia, Jefferson caught Madison's enthusiasm. "If Mr. Gallatin," he wrote, "would undertake to reduce [Hamilton's] chaos to order, present us with a clear view of our finances, and put them into a form as simple as they will admit, he will merit immortal honor. The accounts of the US. ought to be, and may be made, as simple as those of a common farmer, and capable of being understood by common farmers."[20]

Perhaps few farmers read them, but Gallatin wrote two important books on the federal government's finances. The first one appeared just after the 1796 election in which John Adams defeated Jefferson. The second appeared on the eve of the election in which Jefferson beat Adams four years later. Both were partisan productions, but Gallatin did not simply repeat the usual Republican cant about corruption and monarchism. Instead he made reasoned arguments based on the liberal political economic theory explicated in Adam Smith's *Wealth of Nations*.[21]

Gallatin's views on public finance rested on the premise that most government spending retards economic improvement because it consumes capital. Gallatin thought military spending, which together with interest on the public debt accounted for substantially all of the federal government's spending, was particularly wasteful because war destroyed capital. Funded debt did not benefit the public, Gallatin argued, because funding made borrowing easier, borrowing made spending easier, and military spending made the government more likely to get into war. Interest payments on the public debt shifted money from productive taxpayers to wealthy speculators and investors who were more likely to waste it on luxuries. The country could not fulfill its potential, he claimed, unless the government restrained spending and repaid the national debt. Gallatin then marshaled figures—clear, methodical, and just complicated enough to be credible—to prove that the Federalist administrations had spent too much, increased the public debt, and made inadequate arrangements for repayment. Gallatin's books were tough reading. They lacked the verve and lyricism of Hamilton's best prose.

But they demonstrated a mastery of federal finance. Some readers thought that, in fact, was the main point.[22]

The month after Jefferson appointed Gallatin to the Treasury, James McHenry sent Charles Carroll of Carrollton his copy of Gallatin's first book and his assessment of the author. McHenry was a prosperous Baltimore merchant, a signer of the Constitution, and a recent Secretary of War. Carroll was one of the wealthiest men in Maryland, a signer of the Declaration of Independence, and a strong Federalist. In the letter accompanying Gallatin's book, McHenry described its author as a *"political adventurer"* driven by his thirst for public office. He said that Gallatin had set his eye on the Treasury from the time he came to Congress, and Madison, who was once "the opposition Lord of the Treasury domain," had yielded it up to Gallatin—who had "reigned over it, ever since without a rival among his party."[23]

McHenry claimed that Gallatin had paved his way to popularity by his steady insistence on taking and spending as little as possible of the people's money, and he expected Gallatin to secure his power by continuing to insist on those principles. Because finance affected "almost every measure of government," McHenry predicted that Gallatin would weaken the army and the navy and leave the country ill prepared for war. One could only hope, said McHenry, that Gallatin's desire for popularity would lead him to yield a bit to the wisdom of "virtuous men of property and talents." Coming so soon after a bitter election, McHenry's assessment was reasonably fair. Perhaps McHenry remembered it thirteen years later when bombs burst in air over the fort that bears his name.[24]

Some doctrinaire Republicans also worried about Gallatin. One of them was John Taylor of Caroline. Taylor was a stalwart Virginia Republican who had served in the Senate and written a number of hard-hitting political pamphlets against the Bank of the United States. He complained to his successor in the Senate that Gallatin's first book had left him "greatly disappointed and chagrined." The book had "indeed detailed and ascertained a series of important facts," he said, "but what use has it made of these facts?" Instead of striking at Hamilton's corruptive financial system, Gallatin had invented "some ingenious excuses for

Hamilton, which Hamilton never thought of himself." Gallatin had even countenanced the taxes needed to support Hamilton's scam. Good Republicans were not obliged, Taylor thundered, to provide the "ways & means to feed" Hamilton's "system of monopoly" just "because there is law for it."[25]

Some months after Gallatin took office, a venerable Virginia Republican named Edmund Pendleton—friend and mentor of both Taylor and Jefferson—published a long newspaper piece headlined "The Danger Not Over." He reminded the faithful that true republicanism would require "some check on the abuse of *public credit*." John Taylor no doubt remembered this when he summed up some Republicans' disappointment with the Jefferson administration twelve years later. A number of people, he told James Monroe, "soon thought, and said to one another, that Mr: Jefferson did many good things, but neglected some better things." To them it seemed that Jefferson's policies in office had been "very like a compromise with Mr: Hamilton's."[26]

Jefferson knew that Gallatin was controversial, but he did not hesitate to appoint him. Jefferson believed that Gallatin was the only man in their party who understood Hamilton's financial system well enough to reform it. And Jefferson never swerved from that conclusion. The year after he left the presidency, he urged Gallatin to remain at the Treasury. Repayment of the public debt was "vital to the destinies of our government," he reminded the Treasury secretary, and "that great hope" would be lost without him. But public finance was a difficult subject for Jefferson, and the two men had their differences along the way. Gallatin hesitated to dismantle Hamilton's internal revenue system too abruptly because he feared that might leave the Treasury short of money. And Gallatin believed that the Bank of the United States was an important agent for Treasury operations, so he first calmly ignored and then patiently resisted Jefferson's suggestions to undermine it.[27]

Jefferson had moments of deep frustration. "We can pay off [Hamilton's] debt," he lamented to a French economist, "but we can never get rid of his financial system. It mortifies me to be strengthening principles which I deem radically vicious. But the vice is entailed on us by the first error." What was troubling Jefferson? Was it old Pendleton's stern warning against the abuse of public credit? Was it Gallatin's defense of the Bank? Had Hamilton's commitments and Gallatin's pragmatism stopped Jefferson from adopting some truly republican financial solution? Or was this optimistic man who carefully wrote down his expenses but rarely added them up simply unwilling to accept fiscal reality—to believe that republican grace could not expiate government's original sin?[28]

Henry Adams, who relished the irony of Jefferson's situation, published the first biography of Albert Gallatin in 1879, ten years before he began issuing his formidable *History of the United States during the Administrations of Thomas Jefferson and James Madison*. Adams had found Gallatin's papers soon after starting to work on the Republican administrations. He was the first historian to study them, and he keenly appreciated Gallatin's significance. "After a long study of the prominent figures in our history," he told Samuel Tilden years later, "I am more than ever convinced" that Gallatin "was the most fully and perfectly equipped statesman we can show.... I cannot say as much for his friends Jefferson, Madison and Monroe." The biography's 678 pages brim with transcriptions woven together by just enough commentary to make them coherent. The Gallatin described in Adams's book is a noble leader undaunted by conflict, a remote character of forbidding integrity suspended against sketchy political scenery that Adams had not yet fully constructed. His biography of Gallatin was not meant to be read alone, Henry Adams told his brother. He conceived it as a source book, a compilation on which he could draw—along with three volumes of Gallatin's selected papers—when he turned to his larger project. It served Adams's purpose, it remains an invaluable resource, and it leaves readers as unsatisfied as Adams knew they would be.[29]

Not until the late 1950s did Gallatin get a readable treatment. The Gallatin portrayed in Raymond Walters's useful biography is a believable person. His personal problems and the toll they exacted become clearer. The period in which he lived takes on shape. Newspapers, contemporary letters, and more financial data now furnish the set. But the scene is a tableau painted in the mid-twentieth-century Consensus style, and

Gallatin plays the wonted roles. He is a freedom-loving immigrant drawn to the unpeopled American wilderness, a struggling businessman pursuing the American dream, and a democratic politician hewing the way toward American hegemony. The reader is left wondering whether Gallatin could really have been so exemplary. The year after Walters published his book, the economist Alexander Balinky gave a harsh answer to that question. In a book about Gallatin's fiscal policies, Balinky blasted the Jeffersonian Republicans' adherence to what he called a backward-looking agrarian political economy, and he leveled the heaviest fire at Gallatin for his counter-productive frugality and his diversion of resources into accelerated repayment of the national debt. The critique was Keynesian and—despite Balinky's best efforts—ahistorical. Balinky recognized that Gallatin and his contemporaries thought most government spending was unproductive, but he felt obliged to discredit the practical conclusions they derived from that premise.[30]

Balinky's failure demonstrates something important about Gallatin's place in our historical memory. Modern democracies have a strong bent toward deficit spending, as Gallatin once told Lafayette, because the people at large see an immediate benefit from public spending for which they do not have to pay. Balanced budgets are difficult to swallow, and debt repayment is harsh medicine. If responsible deficit spending can indeed facilitate economic growth and ameliorate social conditions, austerity is poison. If national strength and public welfare require perpetual debt, light doses of deficit reduction can take the place of purgative debt repayment. The fiscal responsibility on which Gallatin insisted becomes a quaint aspiration. So most modern Americans find it easier to appreciate a man like Hamilton, who adapted European methods to the management of American debt. Gallatin—to the extent we remember him—becomes a rallying figure for the small government fiscal opposition.[31]

Gallatin deserves a properly historicized treatment. The politics and economics of another time were more complicated than they appear in retrospect, and the fiscal policies of the past often turned on factors that elude us in hindsight. We cannot understand the Jeffersonian Republicans' strident objections to Alexander Hamilton's financial system unless we look closely at what they actually did about the system when they came to power. We cannot understand what they did about it until we re-encounter their choices. It is not enough to look at the taxes they repealed and the debt they repaid, the troops they disbanded and the national bank they closed. Nor is it enough to generalize about their economic and social aspirations, their agrarian bias, and their views on political economy. We need to watch the actors struggle over practical decisions and deal with unwanted contingencies. Instead of simply quoting their rhetoric, we must ask what they accomplished and why they failed. We must get to know the man who was in charge of the Treasury.

Earlier debates about liberal and classical republican influences on Jeffersonian Republican political economy cast some light in Gallatin's direction. Yet curiously, he remains in shadow. We have enormously important new knowledge about political economic theories, but little about fiscal policies. A leading monograph on Jeffersonian political economy relegates Republican fiscal policy to footnote, and the index entry for "financial systems" in another important monograph on the subject contains nothing but a cross-reference to "Hamiltonian finance." Synthesis amalgamates Gallatin with Jefferson and Madison or loses him entirely. A fascination with theory crowds out analysis of action. This rich body of work nevertheless provides a context in which we can begin to recover Gallatin's importance and to bring him forward in a role that he and his contemporaries would have recognized.[32]

New studies of the liberal democratic state as an active force in American life raise the lights brighter by showing how early Americans relied on the federal government whether or not they chose to admit it. These studies also remind modern Americans that people in an emerging economy expect more from their government than we imagine and that a liberal government competing with mercantile regimes has fewer choices than it would hope. This important new body of work demythologizes the dichotomy between statists and anti-statists in the Early Republic. It shows that their political rhetoric commonly disguises more than it discloses. Against this background, we can more clearly assess the accommodations that Jeffersonian Republican leaders made once they came to power. And we can begin to appreciate the inescapable importance of a practical man like Albert Gallatin.[33]

No one doubts that Albert Gallatin was a central figure in the Early Republic. "What Hamilton was to Washington, Gallatin was to Jefferson," wrote Henry Adams. If the "historical Jefferson hardly would have been possible without a Madison," as another historian has said, then neither of them would have been possible without Gallatin. All three men rejected Hamilton's vision for America, but only Gallatin was capable of undoing the fiscal system through which Hamilton had hoped to implement it. Gallatin was Treasury secretary for twelve years, longer than anyone else would lead an executive department for the next century. He put the country's finances on a bold new republican course. He abolished internal revenue taxes in peacetime, slashed federal spending, and repaid half of the national debt. He stoutly resisted military spending because he thought a well-armed government was more likely to waste the country's resources in war. His frugality became the hallmark of American public finance for more than a hundred years. His statue on a tall pedestal in front of the Treasury building bears witness to his hold on the American imagination well into the twentieth century.[34]

If we have lost sight of Gallatin, it is because we have lost sight of the pragmatic, liberal republicanism he practiced. He insisted on keeping the federal government small so that it could be cheap. He wanted the government to be cheap so that it could devote more of its revenue to repayment of the public debt. He wanted to get rid of the public debt in order to free the government from the temptation to spend and to liberate the people from the burden of debt service. He thought both goals were critical. If the government funded its spending with borrowed money, its debts would keep growing larger because the people would not understand how much it was spending. And if the government had large debts, it would become more beholden to its creditors than to the rest of the people. A nation deeply in debt—as an eloquent senator would put it half a century later—was not wholly free.[35]

But Gallatin believed in the state. He reformed the federal government's finances in order to make it stronger. He thought revenues freed

from debt service should be used to build roads and canals and to promote domestic manufacturing. For all of his resistance to military spending, he looked forward to the day when the United States could afford
to build a credible navy to defend its international trade. He never shared
the orthodox Republican antipathy toward banking, and he always supported the Bank of the United States. Gallatin nevertheless believed that
the state should keep within limits. While he wanted the federal government to do things the people could not do for themselves, he thought the
nation's destiny ultimately depended on what we today call private
enterprise. He believed that a frugal government should leave most of
the nation's capital in the hands of its citizens. Yet he was never dogmatic.
He thought Americans left entirely to their own devices could become
too selfish, and as he reconciled himself to the unwanted consequences
of his failures in the War of 1812, he welcomed the nationalism he saw
rising from the ashes.

CHAPTER 1

BECOMING
REPUBLICAN

Albert Gallatin came to America in 1780 as a youth of nineteen. He landed in an unexpected place. The American merchant ship *Katty*, which he and his boyhood friend Henri Serre had boarded in Nantes, was bound for Boston. But dense fog drove it into Cape Anne on the northern tip of Massachusetts Bay. Too impatient to wait for the weather to lift, the two young men hired horses and set off down the thirty-mile coastal road to Boston. The rocky dirt road followed a high ridge about three or four miles back from the sea. It was July, and the thin-soiled countryside looked poor and arid. At Lynn, the road descended into salt marshes where tides through the low places had bared underlying rocks and insects were more aggressive. The road ended at Winnisimmet, where they took places on the ferry to Boston. As the ferry crossed the Mystic River, they could see off to the right the charred ruins of Charlestown—burned by British troops in the battle for Bunker Hill five years earlier.[1]

Gallatin and Serre had left their native Geneva on a cool day in April with a few clothes and no word to their families. Gallatin brought along what he hoped would be enough money for both of them. They spent about half of it on their way across France and their passage to Boston. While their ship to Boston waited for the winds, they wrote home to tell their families where they were going, and they spent much of their remaining money on nine boxes of tea. They hoped to make a quick profit on the tea when they landed because they knew no one in Boston and they had no other prospects.[2]

Gallatin never explained why he came to America. In 1780, the country's prospects seemed almost as uncertain as his own. The newly United States were still fighting their long war for independence from Great Britain. The war had devastated the economy, and the military situation was unstable. George Washington's dwindling Continental Army was stuck in New Jersey keeping watch on the stronger British force in New York. Another British army had captured the key Southern port of Charleston, and Lord Cornwallis was leading it north through the Carolinas. The main French army sent to aid the American rebels reached Newport only three days before Gallatin and Serre reached Cape Anne, but the French troops would stay there for a year before joining Washington's march to defeat Cornwallis at Yorktown in October 1781.[3]

Some of Gallatin's biographers have speculated that he was a republican or a romantic drawn to the United States by sympathy for the American Revolution. There is some evidence to support that claim. A family story says Gallatin refused his grandmother's offer to help him get a commission in the Hessian army. She knew the Landgrave of Hesse-Kassel from his student days in Geneva. But Hessian troops were fighting for the British in North America, and Gallatin declared that he would not serve a tyrant—a response impertinent enough to earn him a cuff on the ear. Some of Gallatin's close friends at school in Geneva had dissident ideas. Two of them, François d'Ivernois and Étienne Dumont, later agitated for political reforms and ultimately went to England where they joined the liberal circle around Lord Shelburne, a Whig politician who lost power for making a generous peace with the United States after the

Revolution. Gallatin's closest friends were Serre, who was a romantic young boy from a poor family, and Jean Badollet, a boy of modest background with smoldering republican sensibilities. One of Gallatin's earliest letters from America gives a surprisingly detailed description of Massachusetts's revolutionary constitution, and Gallatin's political supporters later tried to burnish his reputation by hinting that he came to America to join the great struggle for freedom. But a hard look at Gallatin's early years shows that the young man who left Geneva in 1780 was not yet the republican he would become.[4]

A republic in form, the Geneva of Gallatin's youth was an aristocracy in fact. The ancient stone walled city and its small agricultural hinterland had become an independent city-state in the sixteenth century, when supporters of the Protestant Reformation renounced its feudal ties to the Catholic bishop and the Catholic duke of neighboring Savoy. The self-governing city adopted John Calvin's austere ecclesiastical ordinances. But encrusted distinctions between the old political classes remained. Only a quarter of the city's 25,000 inhabitants were citizens, and only adult male citizens had the right to vote and to follow whatever occupation they chose. Fewer than 6 percent of the inhabitants were patricians, and only the approximately four hundred adult male patricians could serve on the two self-perpetuating councils that governed the city. The Council of Two Hundred chose the members of an executive Council of Twenty-Five, which in turn elected the members of the larger council. The small council also nominated from among its own members the four syndics who served as leaders of the government. A General Council of all citizens could disapprove the candidates, but it had no right to nominate alternatives or to pass legislation. The rest of the population had no political rights. Peasants who lived outside the city were subjects of the state or their masters. Workers who lived in the city had more freedom, but they could not enter the professions or the more lucrative occupations. They had the right to buy citizenship, but scarcely any of them could afford it.[5]

What justified the patricians' political prerogatives were their achievements. Calvin's ordinances proscribed ostentation and high living, and patricians were expected to live with the same austerity as everyone else. But they were expected to accomplish more than anyone else. First, they had to be wealthier. A citizen was not a patrician unless he owned taxable property worth at least 105,000 Genevese florins, more than the best-paid craftsman could earn in a lifetime. Calvin had taught that God had elected those whom he would save from damnation and that men and women could do nothing to save themselves. But through great earthly success, a believer could assure himself and those around him that he was among the elect. Second, patricians had to give exemplary service to the state. All Christian believers had to strive to live virtuously, but those who served the community most visibly were most evidently upright. Just as success marked patricians with God's favor, service justified their privileges to their fellow citizens. That the same families continued to be blessed from generation to generation was an expression of God's imponderable will.[6]

This sclerotic system survived because Genevans were anxious about the survival of their state. Calvin's exhortations to duty and hard work had driven them to prosper. By the 1760s, their city was an important European center for watchmaking and finance. But the small city's location left them exposed. Geneva was a vulnerable Protestant enclave of a few square miles squeezed between Catholic France, Catholic Savoy, and a loose Swiss Confederation weakened by differences between its Catholic and Protestant members. Annual celebrations of the city's bravery in L'Escalade, when Genevans had stopped a Savoyard army from scaling the walls in 1602, reminded the Genevans of their vulnerability. Civil disturbance within the city had prompted military intervention by France, Bern, and Zurich in 1738, and those powers remained guarantors of the established constitutional order. The arrangement made political change difficult. But as the secularizing influence of the French Enlightenment led some of the wealthiest patricians to freer thinking and more comfortable living, both puritanical patricians and middle class citizens grew restive. The Francophile patricians who befriended Voltaire when he took refuge in Geneva and attended his theatrical performances at Ferney, just outside the city-state's borders, alienated the conservative

Calvinists who feared France, shunned extravagance, and supported Geneva's ban on theaters. Albert Gallatin's parents and paternal grand-parents were among the patricians who flocked to Voltaire.[7]

Challenges to the aristocratic order caused civil commotion through-out Gallatin's youth. In 1762, the year after his birth, simmering middle class resentment broke into the open when the small council banned Jean-Jacques Rousseau's *Émile* and *Social Contract*. Rousseau was a Genevan citizen from a poor family who had left home at sixteen, emerged as a litterateur in Paris, and then blossomed into a social critic and thinker. His support for representative government resonated with many aspiring middle class citizens in Geneva, and his renunciation of extravagant living appealed to their austere sensibilities. They took the ban on his books as an affront. Middle class reformers sent the patrician small council a representation claiming that the ban was illegal and ask-ing the council to refer the matter to the citizens' General Council.[8]

The small council refused to send questions about the ban to the General Council, and the reformers—now calling themselves *represent-ants*—began agitating for greater civil rights. In *Letters Written from the Country*, a prominent member of the small council defended its right to negate citizens' representations (the *droit négatif*). In response, leading *representants* denounced the patricians who claimed that right—the *négatifs*—as usurpers. In several of the following years, the General Council refused to accept candidates nominated by the small council—one of whom was a Gallatin. In 1768, the *representants* began to arm themselves, and to avoid bloodshed, the *négatifs* accepted reforms. The settlement added fifty members to the large patrician council and gave citizens the right to elect half of them. It allowed citizens to reject up to four of the patricians' candidates for the small council. The disenfran-chised majority of the population, the so-called *natifs*, got some com-mercial privileges and permission to enter the medical professions.[9]

A leading historian of revolution has called the upheaval of 1768 the first modern democratic revolution, but it simply set the stage for decades of conflict. The old class distinctions survived, and the *natif* majority remained utterly disenfranchised. When the *natifs* demonstrated for greater civil rights in 1770, the patricians and the middle class citizens united to put them down by force. The General Council overwhelmingly approved the death penalty for anyone who advocated enfranchising the *natifs*. Political agitation nevertheless continued throughout the 1770s, and leading *representants* began to sympathize with the *natifs* in a wider critique of the aristocratic order. In 1781 and 1782, just after Gallatin left Geneva, there were armed uprisings, and *representant* leaders, including Gallatin's friend d'Ivernois, took over the city government. Frightened patricians called on France, Bern, and Zurich to make good their guarantee of the established order. The French government—which found republicanism on its own borders less convenient than republicanism in Britain's North American colonies—laid siege to the city for three weeks. The reform government collapsed, the leading *representants* fled, and the French revoked the 1768 reforms. The established patrician order would hold on for another decade until violent tumult sparked by the French Revolution brought it down in 1792–94.[10]

Gallatin became an orphan when he was nine years old, two years after the upheaval of 1768. The boy named Abraham Alphonse Albert Gallatin had been born January 29, 1761, into a comfortable patrician family. He was a ninth-generation descendant of a Savoyard gentleman named Jean Gallatini who had helped establish Geneva's independence, and both of his parents belonged to the city's elite. But his father, a watch merchant named Jean, died when the boy was four. His mother, Sophia Albertine Rolaz du Rosey, took over the family's business, but she was overwhelmed by the burden of a baby son and an emotionally troubled nine-year-old daughter. She sent her daughter for treatment at a distinguished French medical facility in Montpellier. She kept her son in Geneva, but sent him to live with a close friend named Catherine Pictet, who was also a distant cousin of her late husband. Gallatin's mother died five years later. His sister, whom he scarcely remembered, died in Montpellier a few years afterwards.[11]

The orphaned boy Albert was not left alone. Catherine Pictet had embraced him as her own child from the time he went to live with her.

She was an unmarried middle-aged woman in a community where most women married, and the boy was very important to her. His grandparents, who lived in country houses outside the city, helped support him, and the extended Gallatin family was a great protector. Although the Gallatins' relative wealth had declined significantly during the half century before Albert's birth, their standing and influence were unquestioned. A senior member of the family became the guardian of the boy's modest inheritance, and a seventeenth-century trust for the relief of family members advanced money for his early education.[12]

In 1774, after preparatory education with tutors, Gallatin entered the Geneva Academy, a college that educated the city's young male citizens at state expense. It was one of the leading Protestant educational institutions in Europe, and it was well known in the United States. Thomas Jefferson recommended the Academy to American parents when he was the American minister to France, and when the revolutionary uprisings in Geneva during 1792–94 threatened it, Jefferson and John Adams solicited George Washington's support for an unpropitious proposal to bring it to the United States. Genevan boys typically attended the Academy's preparatory school for a few years before undertaking the rigorous classical program in the lower school of the college. After four years in the lower school, those who chose to continue in theology or law spent an additional four years in the college's upper school.[13]

Gallatin attended the Academy for a final preparatory year and then spent four years in the lower school. The curriculum focused on classical literature, but there was rigorous instruction in geometry, algebra, and calculus. The faculty's attitudes toward religion were relaxed, and there was little religious training in the lower school. Gallatin later would confess that he "never exactly knew the extent of Calvin's opinions" until he learned them from the Presbyterians in America. But a decade of civil strife had hardened political attitudes, and the faculty saw themselves as defenders of the tenuously established political order. They recognized that the patricians' political legitimacy depended on their superior ability and achievements, so instruction at the Academy was traditional and exacting.[14]

Within a year of leaving the Academy, Gallatin had left for America. He recalled on more than one occasion that almost every young man of good family went on to study law in the Academy's upper school. He did not. He went home to tutor Catherine Pictet's young nephew. He later explained to his guardian that he had left Geneva because his situation made him feel dependent. But he had declined his maternal uncle's offer of a position that would have supported what his guardian called an "upright ordinary life."[15]

Gallatin's real reasons for leaving Geneva ran deeper than he could say. He was a proud young man. Like other young men of his class, he understood that his future standing would depend on his achievements—on the wealth he could accumulate and the contribution he could make to the legitimacy of the standing order. But the path before him in Geneva seemed unpromising. He could not see how to distinguish himself. If he was to be more than a poor cousin in a great family, he needed to look elsewhere. The earliest letters that he sent to his close friend Jean Badollet after he left Geneva were full of adolescent confidence about making his own fortune. The young Gallatin claimed there were rich prospects in arms trading and land speculation. He was reaching beyond his limited prospects in Geneva because they threatened his self-worth, but he was too proud and too shy to say so.[16]

Gallatin never saw Catherine Pictet again. She died twenty years before he first returned to Geneva in 1815. But he never escaped her influence. Despite her consternation over his unannounced departure, Pictet sent him money and arranged introductions for him in America. She continually reproved him for passivity and idleness, by which she meant his tendency to lose himself in reading and study rather than more productive endeavors. A friend with whom Gallatin stayed in Philadelphia had told her, she wrote in 1787, that "you have retained your former indolence" and "he could not get you to socialize or to dress up." Reading and study "are not interests likely to lead to great enterprise, or for which a large fortune is of any use," she scolded, "and you could have pursued them without leaving home." Gallatin internalized the criticism, and in letters throughout his life he often reproached himself for being "idle," "indolent," and "lazy" when left to his own devices.[17]

As he matured and Pictet declined, Gallatin increasingly regretted how he had left her. "I trust, I hope at least," he wrote when he heard of her death in 1795, that the comfort she must have taken in knowing he had not entirely disappointed her expectations would "in some degree have made amends for my unpardonable neglect" of her. Late in life, Gallatin spoke of Pictet with tearful emotion in a circle of close friends, and in autobiographical notes that he made shortly before he died, he calculated the expenses she had borne to raise him as if reckoning an unsettled debt to the last penny.[18]

The land of promise was not a land of plenty, and Gallatin and Serre struggled to find footing in America. The Revolutionary War had destroyed a great deal and disrupted everything else. Armies ruined farms, houses, and commercial property. Independence upended the traditional American trade with Britain and its colonies, and wartime inflation evaporated purchasing power. American incomes had fallen by 20 to 30 percent since the war began. Boston was a dull city of unadorned brick buildings and plain frame houses. Gallatin and Serre found its inhabitants to be dour people with little respect for strangers. The Bostonians' settled prejudice against Frenchmen—rooted in centuries of Anglo-French conflict and watered by the New England blood shed in the French and Indian War—easily extended to two young French speakers from Geneva. Not only did most ordinary Bostonians speak no French, reported another Francophone visitor at the time, they turned "peevish" with anyone who could not speak good "American." The man in the street disapproved of most types of recreation, particularly on Sundays. A French priest on his way to join the army in Newport called Sundays in Boston a "day of melancholy." Gallatin and Serre pronounced the place to be a drab, provincial version of the Calvinist city they had left behind, and they found no buyers for their tea.[19]

The young men were glad to meet a Genevan couple named Gideon and Mary Madelon Delesdernier. The Delesderniers were headed for a remote outpost near the small port of Machias on the downeast coast of

Maine, where their son Lewis was serving in the Continental Army. Happy to be in the company of French speakers, the young men decided to go along and try their hand at the fur trade. They exchanged their tea (and some more of their money) for sugar, tobacco, and rum to barter with Native American hunters and headed north. Although they found trade prospects in Machias no better than in Boston, the pair reveled in the surrounding forests and their contact with the Abenaki people. Here was the America of woods, wilds, and Indians, of mystery and possibility. Gallatin and Serre wrote enthusiastic letters to Jean Badollet about the Natives' wonderfully light birch-bark canoes and the curious rackets that they used to walk on top of the snow. Most of the Natives wore European clothes, they reported, "except for the women who—but [we] want to leave you curious" so that you will be "eager to join us as soon as possible."[20]

Maine was intriguing, but the prospect of chopping wood through another cold winter there drove the men back to Boston in the autumn of 1781. There, amid the plain buildings, dour residents, and Sunday melancholy, they tried to support themselves by giving French lessons. A letter from the Philadelphia merchant and financier Robert Morris—the powerful Superintendent of Finance for the Confederation Congress—reached them the following spring. Morris wrote to say that their families wanted to hear from them, and Gallatin replied with adolescent candor. He confessed that he and Serre were suffering certain "Inconveniences," the greatest of which, he explained, "was not the want of Money" but "the want of suitable acquaintances." Excuse "my broken English," he begged in a postscript, "as I did like better to [treat] your Indulgence than to have it corrected by any body" and "Mr Serre writes worse English yet than I do."[21]

With the help of an introduction from Pictet, Gallatin arranged to give French lessons to students at Harvard College the following year. Among them were boys from well-established Boston families who must have found Gallatin's appearance as strange as his broken English. He was a lean, thin-faced young fellow of about 5'10" with a gawky manner and sallow complexion. His coarse, bushy black hair framed a prominent forehead that accentuated his long curved nose. He was negligent about his clothes. Harrison Gray Otis, a student who would become one of Gallatin's political opponents in the next decade, later claimed rather cruelly that the young teacher had only one shirt to his name. But whatever his disadvantages of appearance, no one would have mistaken Gallatin for an uncultivated man. His manners were good, his dark eyes radiated intelligence, and his understanding was quick. He lived a rather meager life, but he dreamed of better fortune.[22]

Like many who sought their fortunes in America at the time, Gallatin dreamed of the unsettled land. This field for dreams was vast, but rutted by conflict and uncertainty. Most of the unsettled land lay in a contested area west of the Appalachian Mountains. Vigorous Native American nations possessed the region, and they defended their territories with diplomacy, menace, and war. Britain's coastal colonies had competing and overlapping state claims to this largely unmapped backcountry, and European and colonial speculators had spent decades staking private claims that further complicated the situation. In 1763, the British government had prohibited colonial settlement west of the mountains in order to avoid expensive conflict with the Natives. Although both colonists and colonial officials widely disregarded the ban, settlements in the region had remained scattered until the Revolution. The Revolution unleashed restraints, and migrants coursed into choice areas in Kentucky and southwestern Pennsylvania. But in the early 1780s, prospects in the backcountry were still uncertain. The American states were only starting to resolve their competing claims, and Britain would not finally recognize American independence and relinquish its own claims in the West until late 1783. Many of the recent backcountry settlers were squatters who interfered, sometimes aggressively, with legal settlement. And Native Americans, faced with diminished support from the British, were preparing themselves to resist increased European American incursions.[23]

Gallatin's dream—described in his letters to Badollet and a now fragmentary memorandum—was a settlement of European peasants who would sharecrop a large tract of land for him and a group of investors until they could earn land for farms of their own. They would also use the wood so plentiful in America to make clocks. He proposed to put the settlement in Pennsylvania or Virginia. The more Southern states were too hot for Europeans, he thought, and New England was too backward and inhospitable. Gallatin looked down on rural New Englanders for their "rigid Calvinism," "Superstition," and "sedentary pursuits of Agriculture." Only in the coastal towns "where Commerce has kept [the people] closely tied to the Mother County…since the war" had he met educated men. And even there, he found the Revolution had driven away the "richest, most enlightened, most virtuous families" and replaced them with "foreign adventurers" and "commoners born in America." Since New England's "indifferently educated" leaders had "little superiority over anyone else," he found the social order "quite confused." He had heard better things of the people in Pennsylvania and Virginia. It was the pipedream of an urban aristocrat suspended between two worlds.[24]

In the late spring of 1783, Gallatin struck a partnership with a young Frenchman who shared his dream. Jean Savary de Valcoulon had come to America as an agent to collect payment from the state of Virginia for French loans made during the war. He had some capital and some access to Virginia's political leaders, and he hoped to use them to buy backcountry land for his own account. But he spoke no English. Gallatin agreed to translate and to help Savary buy land in exchange for a partnership interest. In July, they headed to Philadelphia.[25]

Philadelphia had a booming market in Virginia land claims, most of them in the form of warrants. These warrants were simply rights to acquire a specified quantity of land in a loosely designated area. Since the start of the Revolution, Virginia had issued warrants for hundreds of thousands of acres in an effort to pay its soldiers and settle its debts. Speculation in those warrants was rife, and they were now irresistibly cheap. By autumn of 1783, Savary and Gallatin had bought warrants for extensive tracts in the Virginia backcountry south of the Ohio River (now West Virginia), including about 120,000 acres in the area between the Little Kanawha River and the place where the Kanawha River enters the

Ohio River. They set off for Richmond to collect the French loans and begin to make good on their land claims.[26]

Savary and Gallatin's land warrants were a risky investment. The land they had the right to claim was in a wooded wilderness hundreds of miles from settled communities. To exercise the warrants, they had to locate particular tracts, survey them, and then patent or register their title. Surveying trips into the wilderness would be strenuous and dangerous. Surveying parties often attracted hostile attention from Native Americans who understood that they were harbingers of destructive white incursion. Savary and Gallatin also would have to deal with the competing claims of other speculators and the physical presence of squatters. Many warrant holders never managed to obtain a patent. Even if they did, they could find it difficult to recruit settlers or to sell the land in a market where other sellers competed aggressively—often driven by the need to repay debts they had incurred to buy their claims in the first place. Bringing their venture to fruition would require months of dogged work in the wilderness and years of skillful deal making. Serre, who had caught up with Savary and Gallatin in Philadelphia, preferred to try his luck in Jamaica where—like so many unseasoned Europeans—he died within a year. Gallatin learned to survey, and for the next two years he would spend the summers surveying in the West and the winters dealing in Richmond and Philadelphia.[27]

He was becoming a new man. The difficult years in America had chastened him. And news that his boyhood friends d'Ivernois and Dumont were among the *representants* who had fled repression in Geneva jolted him into recognizing how much he had changed. "From 1200 leagues away," he wrote in a remarkable letter to Badollet, "one sees more clearly." He had still supported the aristocratic government when he left Geneva because "surrounded by people who think a certain way, one begins to think as they do." But his enthusiasm for the republican regimes he saw in America had "produced a gradual change in my opinion." He had "moved much closer to [Dumont's] way of thinking," and he now believed that Geneva's aristocratic regime was "based on false principles." What a difference, he exclaimed, between the Genevan system controlled by small councils and the American system "where separate legislative and executive bodies are elected for one year, where judges who simply interpret the laws are elected for life and are thus outside the influence of the sovereign...and where one is not judged by a titleholder, but by twelve men chosen from among the citizens whom either side can remove." He had decided to stay. "America seems to me the best country in which to settle because of its constitution, its climate and the resources that I find here."[28]

Gallatin's description of the settlement that he and Savary projected in western Virginia reflected the change in his outlook. Now, instead of asking Badollet to help him find peasants to work the land on shares, he proposed a settlement where *representant* refugees from Geneva could become independent farmers and small capitalists. He touted the high quality of the land and urged Badollet to join him. But his appeal was not sentimental. Settling in the woods, he told Badollet, "one should expect a life of hardship without the refinements of the city. I feel brave enough for that, but I never would advise anyone to do it without being well prepared." There was no hint of the romantic pastoral sensibility so gracefully expressed in J. Hector St. John Crèvecoeur's recently published *Letters from an American Farmer*. And there was none of the agrarian bias against cities found in the famous passage about sturdy yeomen from Thomas Jefferson's *Notes on the State of Virginia*. Gallatin had embraced republicanism and enterprise, but not the idea of rustic virtue.[29]

Gallatin first entered the Appalachian backcountry in the spring of 1784 to locate and survey land in Monongalia County, Virginia. This promising area was on a beautiful high plateau west of the Allegheny Mountains, just south of Virginia's recently negotiated western boundary with Pennsylvania (in what is now northern West Virginia). The land looked reasonably fertile, and there was talk that a canal connecting the Potomac River with the Ohio might pass through the area. George Washington, a Potomac River landowner who backed the canal, was among the prominent men who already had claimed land in Monongalia County. Gallatin later would tell of meeting Washington one evening in a rude cabin near the county surveyor's office. Washington was interrogating hunters and taking careful notes in a tedious effort to identify the best passage through the mountains. Unable to curb his natural impatience, Gallatin exclaimed that the best choice was obvious. Washington put down his pen, gave Gallatin a withering stare, and then continued his inquiries. But a short while later, according to Gallatin's account, the great man conceded that the young surveyor was right. Gallatin told the story to bolster the criticism of Washington that he and other opponents of Washington's administration voiced in the 1790s, but he must also have found it a comforting reminder that he was not the only prominent man who had invested his hopes in the Allegheny highlands.[30]

As the 1784 surveying season ended, Gallatin decided to establish a base just across the Pennsylvania line at the place where he guessed the Potomac canal might meet the headwaters of the Ohio. Gallatin leased a few acres there in Fayette County, where Georges Creek empties into the Monongahela River, and made plans to open a store. Fayette was the rawest county on the frontier, formed just a year earlier at what one settler petition called the "Ends of the American earth." To Ephraim Douglass, a former Continental officer, the tiny county seat of Uniontown seemed "the most obscure spot on the face of the globe." The only place Douglass could find to live was a room above a small distillery, where even the open gables failed to draw out the smoke. He thought the surrounding country "very poor in everything but its soil." "[M]oney we have not," he wrote, "nor any practicable way of making it."[31]

The following season, Savary and Gallatin led an expedition even deeper into the wilderness to survey their 120,000-acre claim between the Kanawha rivers. From Georges Creek, they floated down the Monongahela to meet the Ohio at Ft. Pitt (Pittsburgh) and then continued another 250 miles down the Ohio to the mouth of the Little Kanawha. Their next few months in the wilderness were hard. The expedition felled great swaths of undergrowth to open lines of sight through the forests. They fed themselves by hunting bison, which were plentiful in the region. They treated their cuts, bruises, and snakebites with rye whiskey, and they collapsed at night into dirty cotton tents pitched beneath the trees.[32]

Their surveys were successful, but their labor was lost. Native American nations had now banded together to resist spreading white incursions, and during the summer of 1785 they began widespread attacks against surveying parties and scattered settlers. By August, reports of the lethal attacks frightened Savary, Gallatin, and other surveyors out of the backcountry. False reports of Gallatin's death at the hands of a much-feared white renegade named Simon Girty eventually reached his family in Geneva, prompting a diplomatic inquiry to Jefferson in Paris and requiring Gallatin to identify himself to a lawyer in Philadelphia as "the same man who had been killed by the Savages in the Fredericksburg Gazette." In the meantime, Savary and Gallatin shifted their attention back to Fayette County. They signed a formal lease with Thomas Clare for the store on Georges Creek and focused on land claims closer to the Pennsylvania state line. In a testament to his decision to stay in America and his connection to his Virginia land, Gallatin took a Virginia citizenship oath at the October 1785 session of the Monongalia County court.[33]

Gallatin came of age under Genevan law when he turned twenty-five in January 1786, and he used a small inheritance from his parents to purchase a 370-acre farm just south of Georges Creek on a bluff above the Monongahela River. He called the place Friendship Hill. He built a cabin there sometime during the first year, and by 1789 he had begun a brick house on a knoll near the river with the finest view across his land. It was a plain two-story building with a side hall and one room on each floor. It remained unfinished for years. The interior woodwork was not added until 1791, and the interior of the brick walls probably remained unplastered until 1794. Rude though it was, the new establishment marked Gallatin as a wealthy man by the undemanding standards of the frontier county.[34]

Gallatin, Savary, and an irregular band of Genevans and Frenchmen lived at Friendship Hill. The Native American resistance that began in 1785 continued to keep surveyors out of the deep backcountry, so the men farmed, distilled spirits, and tended store. Gallatin spent the winters traveling to Richmond, Philadelphia, New York, and Boston—finding potential land buyers, trading in claims, watching for the main chance.

Badollet finally joined the band in the middle of 1786. He complained about the commotion at Friendship Hill and moved nearby to a place of his own, but he and Gallatin remained closest friends. It was in letters they exchanged for the rest of their lives that Gallatin, who rarely exposed his feelings, often unburdened himself. In one of the letters written years later, he reflected on their hardships during those early years in Fayette County. "I do not know in the United States any spot," he wrote to Badollet, "which afforded less means to earn a bare subsistence for those who could not live by manual labor, than the sequestered corner in which accident...first placed us."[35]

To a restless and politically observant young man, the controversy over the ratification of the new federal constitution that erupted during Gallatin's second year at Friendship Hill was irresistible. The debate in Pennsylvania reflected a fairly clear division in state politics. Most of the opposition to ratification came from the rural counties in the northern and western parts of the state—from Fayette County and places like it where voters tended to be from relatively humble backgrounds. Their notion of true republican government centered on self-determination for their own communities and reduction of the burdens that government imposed on ordinary people. They were suspicious of a centralized government and the power it could give to their creditors, wealthy merchants, and other outside interests. For most of the previous decade, their representatives to the Pennsylvania Assembly had been fighting a rearguard action against the rising influence of a band of men drawn from the professional and mercantile classes of Philadelphia and the regional commercial towns. Everyone who had represented Pennsylvania at the Federal Convention which drafted the new Constitution belonged to that band. And the document seemed designed to give them and propertied men like them a stronger grip on power. Their eagerness to call a ratifying convention more quickly than Pennsylvania law allowed seemed to confirm that suspicion.[36]

David Redick, a backcountry lawyer who happened to be in Philadelphia just as the push for ratification began, put his concerns succinctly in a letter to a Western friend. Why, he asked, should Congress get the power to levy taxes directly on the people, keep standing armies in peacetime, and meddle with state laws and election procedures? Why did the constitution fail to guarantee freedom of the press and jury trials in debt collection cases? If the proposed constitution "be a good one or even a tollorable one," he wrote, "the Necessities and the good Sense of America will lead us to adopt it. if otherwise give us time and it will be amended...but I think the measures pursued here is a Strong evidence that these people know it will not bear an examination." There, in embryo, were the objections that the constitution's opponents would elaborate as the ratification debate unfolded. To a man from a small city-state so recently converted to republicanism, the arguments for keeping power closer to the people were compelling.[37]

Pennsylvania's ratifying convention was in fact the first to meet. Federalist members outnumbered Antifederalists by almost two to one because the hasty call to convention had outrun efforts to organize dissent in the backcountry. The Federalists dominated the convention so effectively that the Antifederalists' proposed amendments did not even appear in its official journal. Alexander James Dallas, a promising young lawyer who edited a Philadelphia newspaper, lost his job for publishing the Antifederalist speeches. This heavy-handed management had consequences. Just days after the convention ratified the constitution in December 1787 by a lopsided vote of 46–23, the minority published a protest that would become one of the most widely republished Antifederalist pamphlets.[38]

The "Dissent of the Minority of the Convention" was a radical democratic critique of stronger national government. It called for amendments to guarantee press freedom, jury trials in civil cases, and other individual rights. But those were not its main point. The protest's main thrust was a fundamental attack on the consolidation of power in a government insufficiently accountable to the people. It was a direct challenge to the elitist, centralizing views in pseudonymous newspaper essays by Alexander Hamilton and James Madison that soon reappeared in a book called *The Federalist*. A truly republican constitution, the dissenters argued, would provide for smaller Congressional districts so that voters could elect representatives from their own communities. The elite men who would win election in large districts could not represent the ordinary people's interests. A truly republican constitution also would not allow the federal government to tax the people directly, to maintain standing armies in peacetime, to change state election procedures, or to call out state militia. Those powers, so central to the Federalist constitution, threatened the people's rights and weakened the state governments that were more responsive to their wishes.[39]

Ratification did not end the constitutional debate in Pennsylvania. Federalists had insisted that the states not make amendments to the Constitution a condition for ratification because ratification would fail if states offered different amendments. They had also resisted calls for a new national convention to consider amendments because they thought it would postpone and weaken the new government. But by the time the Constitution took effect in late June 1788, on ratification by nine of the thirteen states, Massachusetts had recommended specific amendments. Some thought the New York convention, which had an overwhelming Antifederalist majority, would make amendments a condition for ratification. Although the Pennsylvania legislature had tabled calls for amendments during the spring, a conditional ratification in New York might force it to reconsider. Pennsylvania Antifederalists decided to prepare for this possibility. They called for a convention in Harrisburg to propose constitutional amendments and nominate candidates for Congress.[40]

The Harrisburg convention gave Gallatin an opportunity to join the fray. The ratification controversy had aroused his new political aspirations; he told Badollet that he had thought about standing for a seat in the Virginia ratification convention. Now a local committee in Fayette County sent him to Harrisburg along with John Smilie, an Irish-born farmer, member of the state's executive council, and dissenting member of the Pennsylvania ratification convention. It is not clear how Gallatin won the committee's attention. The frontier gave foreigners like Gallatin and Smilie opportunities that they would not have had in more settled areas. But even on the frontier, a young newcomer with a heavy French accent was not an obvious candidate for office. Perhaps Gallatin had developed a constituency among men who came to his store. Perhaps local worthies thought the young surveyor and land speculator shared their economic interests. Perhaps they just thought the Harrisburg meeting would be a good trial for a well-educated fellow who might turn out to be useful. Indeed, by the time the committee picked Gallatin in mid-August, there was little chance that the Harrisburg convention could accomplish anything. New York had just ratified the Constitution unconditionally, and the Pennsylvania Assembly was almost certain to ignore the New York convention's simultaneous call for a national convention to consider amendments.[41]

The changed circumstances prompted Gallatin to take a radical stance in Harrisburg. Because he believed the Pennsylvania legislature would ignore New York's call, Gallatin wanted the Harrisburg convention itself to call on the people throughout the Union to elect delegates to a new constitutional convention. But most of the thirty-three delegates assembled in Harrisburg—about two-thirds of them from the eastern counties—were not prepared to take that extra-constitutional leap. They recommended a set of constitutional amendments, but rather than call for a national convention, they simply drafted a petition asking the Pennsylvania Assembly to invoke the amendment procedure in the Constitution. They also nominated a slate of reasonably moderate candidates for the Congressional election to be held the following month.[42]

Newspapers throughout the country published the Harrisburg convention's petition, but the convention apparently never actually sent it to the Assembly. That would have been useless, and the majority knew it. By showing restraint, they signaled their intention to cooperate with the new regime. Although amendments were the meeting's ostensible purpose, observed one local Federalist, "the real one seems to be to let themselves down as easy as possible and to come in for a share of the good things the new government may have to bestow." The convention "was a mere Election Jobb," another Pennsylvania Federalist assured George Washington, and even if Antifederalist candidates got elected to Congress, he thought they would be harmless. Once "warm in their Seats they will, as it always happens in such Cases, find it their Interest to support a

Government in which they are Sharers tho' they may make a little Bustle ad captandum [to appeal to the masses]." Washington's correspondent was right not to worry. Only two of the Harrisburg convention's eight candidates won election. The Harrisburg convention's moderation had not earned the Antifederalists political rehabilitation.[43]

As the first federal Congress tried to assemble a quorum in March 1789, Gallatin had his mind on a more consuming affair. He had just heard from Savary that the woman he loved was refusing to accept his latest letter. Her name was Sophia Allegre, and she was the twenty-two-year-old daughter of the landlady with whom Gallatin boarded when he stayed in Richmond. Her father, the son of a Huguenot refugee, had died when she was eight or nine. Her mother, left to support two daughters and a son, had taken up needlework and taken in boarders. Gallatin had been attracted to Sophie—as the younger daughter was called—for years, but he was a bashful suitor. The news that she had refused his letter set him in action.[44]

Gallatin rushed to Richmond and then on into the piney flatlands of New Kent County, where Sophia Allegre was staying with her recently married sister. He spent more than two weeks of the next month visiting her there. "She never played the coquette," Gallatin reported to Badollet at the beginning of May, "but from the second day gave me her complete acceptance and told me that…she believed she had always loved me." She had declined his letter only because she had been "surprised"—and no doubt hurt—"to have heard nothing of me for more than a year." But her mother, Gallatin told Badollet, was "furious." "She did not want her daughter to be led into the wilds of Pennsylvania by a man without connections, without money, who speaks English like a Frenchman who had been a school teacher in Cambridge."[45]

With her mother still obdurate, Sophia Allegre eloped to marry Albert Gallatin on May 14. She then begged her mother's forgiveness in a letter brimming with emotion: "forgive Dear mamma, and generously accept again your poor Sophia who feels for the uneasiness she is sure she has occasioned you." She said she had eloped only because Gallatin was essential to her happiness. "He is perhaps not a very handsome man," she conceded, "but he is possessed of more assensual qualities which, I shall not pretend to numerate—as coming from me they might be supposed to be partial."[46]

Neither a response from her mother nor anything else about Sophia Gallatin survives. Her summer in the cool, clean air of the Allegheny highlands must have seemed startlingly different from hot, humid summers in Richmond, and the long quiet days near the forest a dreamlike contrast to the muffled din of carts, horses, and clanging pots in a small city. But within a few months Sophia Gallatin fell ill, and by October she lay buried a short walk from the house at Friendship Hill. Her grieving husband left her grave unmarked. "She said that I would know where she laid," he remembered many years later, "and to the rest of the world it was of little importance." Her death shook his confidence; he even considered returning to Geneva. But politics gradually revived him and set him on a path he would follow for the next twenty-six years.[47]

CHAPTER 2

POLITICAL
PROMISE

G allatin always remembered the Pennsylvania Constitutional Convention of 1789 with a touch of awe. It was the first official assembly in which he served, and he thought it was "one of the ablest bodies"
to which he ever belonged. Setting aside the exceptionally talented James
Madison and John Marshall, he thought the convention had "embraced
as much talent and knowledge." as any United States Congress during
his public life. But what most distinguished the convention in his memory
was the absence—in those "more favorable times"—of party bitterness.
The delegates differed over matters of principle, but they showed "less
prejudice and more sincerity" and greater willingness to make "mutual
concessions." For a sorrowful young widower, the convention was a
heady glimpse at the promise of political life.[1]

Gallatin came to Philadelphia for the convention two weeks late,
distraught by the recent death of his wife. A stranger who saw him take
his seat in early December would have found him an interesting character.

Now within a month of his twenty-ninth birthday, he had the same lean figure that he had brought to America almost a decade earlier. But his coarse black hair was beginning to recede, accentuating his prominent forehead, and he had a quiet reserve born of sadness. His French accent was pronounced enough to draw him into occasional mispronunciations, but listeners found his speech otherwise idiomatic. Although awkward in mixed company, he was comfortable and even convivial among men. He soon bonded with the other western Pennsylvania delegates who shared lodgings at Major Alexander Boyd's boarding house on Sixth Street.[2]

Philadelphia was the largest and most sophisticated city in America in 1789. Even European visitors remarked on the attractive regularity of the city plan and the simple appeal of the city's best brick buildings. Philadelphia had always been the capital of Pennsylvania, it had been the national capital until Congress moved to New York earlier that year, and it remained the financial center of the country. But the city as Gallatin experienced it was busy, noisy, and unwelcoming. Its roughly 42,000 people lived in less than a square mile, making the city more crowded than even the most crowded modern American cities. Virtually every block was home to bustling commercial activity, and even polite houses often contained a business and multiple households. The old Quaker elite, culturally conservative and politically emasculated by the Revolution, had retreated into itself. Brash parvenus enriched by war and speculation dominated the social scene. And neither the old nor the new elite had much time for poor fellows from the backcountry.[3]

Gallatin had not expected to attend the Constitutional Convention at all. He and other Antifederalists were opposed to changing the state constitution, and they had urged the people to boycott the election for convention delegates. They accepted their own elections to the convention only after the boycott failed. Fayette County sent Gallatin and John Smilie, the same two men it had sent to the Antifederalist meeting in Harrisburg. Neighboring Westmoreland County also sent two Antifederalists, including the bright and articulate Irish-born farmer William Findley. Although a few Western counties with budding trade centers sent Federalists, the elections confirmed that—despite a poor showing in the first elections to the United States Congress—the Antifederalists still held sway in the backcountry. The Pennsylvania Constitutional Convention gave them another chance to prove that they could be politically effective. But the majority of the convention delegates were Federalists, so the Antifederalists' effectiveness would depend on their ability to compromise.[4]

The Federalist majority in the Pennsylvania Assembly had called the convention in order to drive a stake through the heart of the state's 1776 constitution. Their objections to it were longstanding. Like other Revolutionary state constitutions, Pennsylvania's gave the legislature greater power than any other branch of government. But it had gone even further than most in removing checks on the popular will. All free adult male taxpayers and their adult sons could vote for members of the legislature. The members met in a single body, and they served for only one year. The bills they passed could not become law until the next legislature approved them. Executive power rested with a large council rather than a single governor. And judges were elected to serve for only seven years. A special Council of Censors had the power to block constitutional changes. Loyalty oaths disenfranchised most of the Quakers and many of the wealthy Tories who had dominated government before the Revolution.[5]

These radical constitutional arrangements had brought men from humbler backgrounds into power. Most of them represented rural interests, and many of them came from the Western counties. This more democratic faction had lost control of the Assembly in 1780 because of rising popular discontent with the economic dislocation caused by the Revolutionary War, and they had remained in the minority during all but one of the following years. But they had enough votes in the Council of Censors to stop the majority from calling a new constitutional convention. In the debate over ratification of the federal constitution, substantially all of the majority (who called themselves Republicans in state politics) became Federalists. And substantially all of the defenders of the radical state constitution (the Constitutionalists) became Antifederalists. When ratification of the federal constitution weakened the Antifederalists, the Federalist majority in the Assembly pressed their advantage by calling a state constitutional convention without the consent of the Council of Censors.[6]

The Federalists wanted the Pennsylvania Constitutional Convention to adopt a constitutional framework for the state based on the federal model. They sought a bicameral legislature, a single governor with veto power, and judges who would serve during good behavior. Some Federalists also wanted to restrict the franchise to men of property. But James Wilson, a Philadelphia lawyer who had taken a leading role at the Federal Convention, and other liberal-minded Federalists understood that they had as much reason to compromise as the Antifederalists. Their heavy-handed management of the Pennsylvania ratifying convention and their peremptory call for the state constitutional convention had made them vulnerable to popular claims that they were authoritarian, "monarchical" elitists. To hold onto power in a state where popular feeling could run high, they needed to prove that they were good republicans. So when William Findley approached Wilson with an offer to cooperate, Wilson listened.[7]

To the great dismay of conservative Federalists, a working majority of liberal Federalists and Antifederalists took control of the convention. The Federalists got a bicameral legislature, single executive, and tenured judges, but the Antifederalists got to keep a broad franchise and annual direct elections. Given the Antifederalists' relative weakness, the outcome was a significant achievement. And it was a preliminary step toward the emergence of a durable affiliation between the Antifederalists and liberal Federalists that came to be called "the republican interest." Although the Antifederalists "had been completely laid upon their backs" in the post-ratification elections, one of the conservatives later complained, they soon "turned on their sides, and were in a fair way of being very soon on top of their antagonists."[8]

By his own account, Gallatin "took but a subordinate share" in the convention debates. Findley and Smilie—experienced men twenty years his senior—were the principal Antifederalist spokesmen, and the most active men of Gallatin's generation were the promising young lawyers James Ross from Pittsburgh and Alexander Addison from nearby Washington County. But Gallatin did argue tenaciously for three points close to the heart of the Antifederalist conception of true republican government.[9]

Gallatin first rose to oppose a reduction in the size of the assembly. The core principle of free government, he told the convention, is that the people themselves should exercise as much power as they can. Although representation was necessary for practical reasons, a truly representative assembly must include "every class of people." If the legislature was too small, the electoral districts would be larger than the communities where people know each other. "Poor honest Farmers" and men of modest abilities therefore could not win seats. Only rich and prominent men were well enough known to win votes outside their own communities. This "natural Aristocracy" of worthy men, Gallatin argued, could not represent the people because its members did not share "the same feelings" as "the mass of the people." Gallatin's argument echoed the Antifederalist claim that the federal Congress could not "actually represent" the people because ordinary men would not get elected from the large Congressional districts. And it squarely contradicted the elitist views of Federalists like James Madison, who had grown disgusted with the unreliability of state legislatures full of ordinary men. Madison claimed the federal system was better precisely because only the enlightened elite could win seats in Congress. But at the Pennsylvania convention, the attempt to reduce the size of the lower house failed.[10]

Gallatin's second objective was the popular election of state senators. Some Federalists wanted to have state senators chosen by electors rather than a direct vote of the people. They thought electors would make better choices, and they thought the state needed rich and worthy senators to balance the excesses of the ordinary folk in the lower house. James Madison and Thomas Jefferson had made similar arguments against the direct election of state senators in Virginia. The Federalists at the Pennsylvania convention thought that, at the least, wealthier districts should get proportionately greater representation in the senate and candidates for the senate should meet higher property qualifications. These were the most contentious issues at the convention. Gallatin acknowledged that the "attempts of power against wealth" could be dangerous in a representative government, but he strongly supported direct election. He thought that ordinary people were less likely to attack property rights if they lived under a government they themselves had elected. The convention's working majority of Antifederalists and liberal Federalists agreed.[11]

Gallatin's third objective was to extend the franchise to all long-term residents of the state. (The presumption that only men should vote ran so deep that no one mentioned a gender requirement.) Most states gave the vote only to men who owned a house, land, or other significant property. Madison had supported that restriction on the right to vote at the Federal Convention, and Jefferson had included it in his draft of a constitution for Virginia. But broad suffrage was one of the key liberal features in the Pennsylvania constitution, and the Antifederalists were determined to keep it. They managed to stop the Federalists from adding property qualifications, but they failed in their attempt to broaden the franchise. Gallatin also made a motion to provide for the election of Congressmen by districts rather than at large. Election at large favored candidates from the more heavily populated, southeastern part of the state, and it had given Federalist candidates a clear advantage in the first Congressional election. But the issue was contentious, and Gallatin agreed to withdraw his motion. Like the legislatures in other states, the Pennsylvania Assembly would continue to switch between election at large and election by district as political factions jockeyed for advantage.[12]

In the first election under the new Pennsylvania constitution, Gallatin won one of Fayette County's two seats in the House of Representatives. Two-thirds of the voters supported him, almost as many of them as voted to return the Federalist-leaning incumbent James Finley as their other representative. Gallatin would win reelection to the House overwhelmingly in 1791 and without contest in 1792.[13]

Philadelphia was even busier and more crowded when Gallatin returned for the Pennsylvania Assembly in December 1790. The federal government had just moved back to Philadelphia for the ten years that it would take to build a new national capital on the Potomac River in

Maryland. So Philadelphia was filling up with senators, Congressmen, government officials, and foreign ministers. Gallatin again took lodgings at Major Boyd's with the other Antifederalist representatives from the backcountry. Most influential people in town looked down on these men from the backcountry, so they tended to hang together. When William Maclay—one of Pennsylvania's federal senators—needed to talk to them on a cold winter evening a few months later, he knew where to find them. Gallatin's elite background and excellent education distinguished him from most of the others, but he was too poor, too unaccomplished, and too shy to mingle in Philadelphia society. The influential might not dismiss him as a rube, but they did not invite him to their parties.[14]

William Bingham, the Federalist speaker of the lower house in which Gallatin served, was an extreme yet telling example of the kind of men who held sway. Bingham had grown up in a fairly prosperous Philadelphia family, but made his fortune from privateering and profiteering during the Revolution. He lived in an 18,000-square-foot neoclassical house on half a block in the middle of town, where he and his celebrated wife gave large parties each week. President Washington, leading government officials, and distinguished foreign visitors were invited. Bingham's poor backcountry colleagues from the Assembly generally were not. Even a clever, handsome, and successful young merchant like John Swanwick—a business partner of Bingham's father-in-law—was left fluttering on the periphery. He and other men like him found company in voluntary associations and political clubs—gatherings where republican political ideas blended with stymied personal aspirations to inspire criticism of the Federalist regime.[15]

Gallatin's closest friends in Philadelphia were other Antifederalists involved in the emerging Republican opposition. The most prominent of them was James Hutchinson, a Quaker doctor, chemistry professor, and leading organizer of opposition forces throughout the state. Falstaffian in more than girth, Hutchinson was not to everyone's taste. William Maclay, annoyed when Hutchinson stopped by Major Boyd's while Maclay was there on that winter evening in 1791, described him as "a greasy Skin of Oyle...puffing like a porpoise" who indulged in the disgusting habit of talking about other people's health. But Hutchinson had the gift of making friends. A prominent Philadelphian with Federalist sympathies called him "one of the best of men." Hutchinson sent Gallatin convivial, news-filled letters that drew him into the older man's political orbit. Hutchinson was secretary of the American Philosophical Society, and it almost certainly was he who arranged Gallatin's election into that select company soon after Gallatin took his seat in the Assembly. Alexander Hamilton was elected the same month. Hutchinson's involvement in the Pennsylvania Society for the Promotion of the Abolition of Slavery also may have encouraged Gallatin to join that society a few years later. Gallatin was saddened when Hutchinson died in 1793 from yellow fever caught while treating the poor.[16]

Alexander James Dallas, a young lawyer on the threshold of a promising career, soon became Gallatin's closest friend in Philadelphia. The two of them were ambitious young immigrants of about the same age, and they would remain close friends for most of their lives. Dallas had been born into a respectable Scottish family in Jamaica, educated in England, and drawn to Philadelphia in 1783 for a better living than he could find in the West Indies. While waiting for his law practice to grow large enough to support him and his English wife, Dallas edited law reports and then a newspaper—until the paper's owner dismissed him for reporting the Antifederalist speeches at the Pennsylvania ratifying convention. After ratification, Dallas collaborated with Hutchinson to remake the Antifederalists into a viable republican force in state politics. Governor Thomas Mifflin—perhaps more impressed by his ability and his elegant appearance than his politics—appointed Dallas to be Secretary of the Commonwealth early in 1791. This was an important administrative post in the newly strengthened executive branch of the state government, and Dallas's diligence combined with Mifflin's increasing alcoholism soon made it a very powerful position.[17]

Gallatin proved himself an effective legislator. He gained, as he later put it, "an extraordinary influence" in the House—"the more remarkable, as I was always in a *party* minority." He attributed his influence to "my great industry and to the facility with which I could understand and carry on the current business." Gallatin worked and studied hard. He confessed to his close friend John Badollet that he had spent the money he needed for new winter clothes on Hume's *History of England*, Gibbon's *Decline and Fall of the Roman Empire*, and a new edition of Blackstone's *Commentaries on the Laws of England*. But Gallatin owed at least a part of his success to the rather modest abilities of other members of the House. A few distinguished themselves, but the rest were content to let an eager young man like Gallatin do most of the work. In an assembly that formed a separate committee to prepare each bill, Gallatin served on more committees than anyone else.[18]

Gallatin immediately showed an aptitude for public finance. Within a few months of joining the House, he had prepared the Ways and Means committee's report on a proposal to refinance the state debt. The proposal was not entirely his own, but his report made the complex recommendations clear and credible. He began with the proposition that the state must do justice to its creditors by paying them what it had promised. Since the state did not have enough money to do that, he proposed consolidating all of the state's debt into a huge bank loan. The state could pay interest on the bank loan from existing tax revenues, increased land sales, and interest on the federal bonds that it had received when it assumed debts that the Confederation government could not pay. And it could repay the principal as soon as its fiscal situation improved. The report also recommended reducing the state's war debt by encouraging the debt holders to exchange their claims for the new federal bonds offered under Hamilton's assumption plan. Some of the state's creditors had balked at accepting Hamilton's offer because the federal bonds carried a lower interest rate than the state debt. So Gallatin proposed to pay creditors who accepted the offer an amount equal to the difference in interest.[19]

The house adopted the refinancing plan in April 1791 without significant change. Votes on some parts of the plan were close. But the following year, the Ways and Means committee reported that the plan had worked. The state's revenues had exceeded its expenses, the value of federal bonds had risen, and the state could repay the bank loan from surplus revenues and sales of the federal bonds. The cornerstone of the governor's house laid that spring proudly proclaimed that "PENNSYLVANIA was happily out of debt."[20]

The refinancing report was a bravura performance for a young man, and it laid the foundation of Gallatin's reputation. It was not original in concept, and it must have disappointed some members of Gallatin's own party because of the concessions that it made to wealthy speculators. But it demonstrated three qualities that begin to explain Gallatin's success in public life. The first was a gift for numbers. Gallatin had an active and quantitative mind. Numbers helped him think, and thinking made him happy. His surviving papers are full of numbers—accounts, revenue figures, trade estimates, debt computations, and random calculations scattered across the margins of other documents and the backs of old letters. Chance reports about multiple sightings of a meteor prompted him to calculate its height and trajectory. Minor inaccuracies in a debt amortization calculation spurred him to work out a new formula. And a visitor to his sickbed at the end of his life found him with a slate and pencil solving algebra problems for his own amusement. His rigorous education in higher mathematics had cultivated this quantitative gift, but the talent itself was innate.[21]

The second quality was a remarkable ability to assimilate complex information into a simple, cogent presentation. Extensive handwritten tables that Gallatin prepared for the Ways and Means report are only one of the examples in his papers of his careful organization of masses of information into systematic, almost intuitive formats. That was how he solved problems. "I can lay no claim to either originality of thinking or felicity of expression," he wrote when immersed in another large project years later. "If I have met with any success... it has been exclusively through patient and most thorough investigation of all the attainable facts, and a cautious application of these to the questions under discussion."[22]

The third quality shown by the refinancing report was a knack for finding practical solutions to problems that others tended to politicize. It was not that Gallatin compromised his political principles. Indeed, his principles kept him in the political minority for most of the decade he spent as a legislator. It was simply that he recognized when problems— even if they had become politically contentious—were not really matters of principle. He saw that fiscal affairs, in particular, had an internal logic of their own that often got lost in political rhetoric. His bent toward finding practical solutions was almost instinctive. He long remembered being "quite astonished" by the praise he won for the Ways and Means report because he had not been "at all aware that I had done so well." The report had succeeded, he thought, because it gave creditors "strict justice, without the slightest regard to party feelings or popular preju- dices." He had just done what needed to be done. If the payment of some additional interest could convince the state's creditors to accept Hamil- ton's assumption offer, that was a reasonable price for the state to pay for relief from the rest of the debt.[23]

Refinancing the state debt was not Gallatin's only important con- tribution to Pennsylvania's public finances. He also helped to create the Bank of Pennsylvania. Pennsylvania had chartered the country's first major commercial bank—the Bank of North America—in 1782, but the democratic faction in the Assembly had repeatedly attacked it as a government-sponsored monopoly that enriched a few merchants and refused loans to farmers. Similar agrarian criticism of banking had resurfaced in the debates over Hamilton's controversial Bank of the United States. By 1793, however, sentiment in Pennsylvania was chang- ing. Other states had chartered nine banks in the previous three years. Some of the Antifederalists now believed that a state bank could help Pennsylvania manage its finances and counteract the influence of the Federalist-dominated Bank of the United States.[24]

In a report for the Ways and Means committee, Gallatin advocated chartering a state bank much like the Bank of the United States. The state would buy a third of the bank's shares with the profits it was mak- ing from public lands and federal bonds. Gallatin thought that the invest- ment would keep the legislature from squandering those profits on current spending, and he claimed that future dividends on the bank shares would significantly reduce the need for taxes. The bank could also act as the state's fiscal agent and its principal lender. To win support from the rural counties, Gallatin's proposal required the bank to lend the state enough money to establish a land bank that could make mortgage loans to farmers. The bank charter passed, and the Bank of Pennsylvania largely lived up to Gallatin's expectations. Although the land bank did not last long, the Bank of Pennsylvania itself increased access to credit by opening branches around the state. The striking neoclassical building on Second Street that the bank commissioned from architect Benjamin Henry Latrobe five years later became a visible symbol of its success. And the dividends that the state received from the bank were large enough to cover a substantial portion of the state's expenses during the next several decades.[25]

Credit was important to Gallatin's Western constituents, but he understood they had more basic problems. High mountains to the east, Native American resistance to the west, and Spanish control of the southwest restricted their economic opportunities. To thrive, they needed access across the mountains to Philadelphia and down the Mississippi River to the port of New Orleans. They needed protection from Native raids, and they needed freer access to good land. The letters Gallatin received from his constituents were full of these concerns, and Gallatin himself shared in their economic hardship. He tried to be philosophical about the difficulty of making any money in the backcountry. At least, he told Badollet one winter, the two of them had not "gone backwards" in the previous year as they had in the five years before that. And at least living in the backcountry had kept them from being "trampled upon" and "hurt by the ostentatious display of wealth" in the seaport cities. There was not much that Gallatin could do about Indian relations or Mississippi navigation—those were federal affairs—but he did push the state legislature to improve transportation and land policies.[26]

Because improved transportation would help the port of Philadelphia as well as the hinterland, there was fairly general support for building roads and canals. But they were expensive. The demand for improvements in well-settled areas tended to crowd out the needs of the backcountry. Gallatin and other backcountry representatives therefore were strong supporters of alternative funding arrangements for Eastern improvements. In 1792, Gallatin helped to prepare a bill that authorized private toll road companies to improve four major roads into Philadelphia. The Philadelphia-Lancaster toll road opened just two years later, and it set an important precedent. Gallatin later claimed it was "the first extensive turnpike...in the United States." Heavy traffic made the road profitable, and the profits helped attract private investment for other turnpikes. The use of private capital for the Lancaster road freed public funds for new roads further west, and Gallatin saw to it that reliable men like his friends Thomas Clare and John Badollet were appointed to the commissions that set the routes for those roads.[27]

Land policy was more controversial because it involved the conflicting interests of speculators and settlers. The land act that Gallatin saw to passage in 1792 allowed purchasers to buy as few as 100 acres. It also limited land claims to 400 acres, and it required buyers to settle the land promptly and keep it occupied. Those provisions favored actual settlers over absentee investors, and they drew strong objections from speculators. The speculators argued that the state should sell vacant land in large tracts to developers who could organize compact and defensible settlements. They also claimed that sales of large tracts would produce more income for the state. Some men in the Eastern part of the state raised even more basic objections. They thought the land act made it too easy for young farmers and laborers to buy land in the West. Western migration would decrease the value of land in the East and raise the price of labor. Gallatin's response was both political and practical. "The happiness of a country," he said, depended "on the poorer class of people having it in their power to become freeholders" and to live comfortably on their own "industry and exertions." Besides, he pointed out, the failure to open land on good terms simply drove settlers to other states.[28]

While Gallatin was trying to be practical, politics were becoming more partisan. The events surrounding Gallatin's own election to the United States Senate reflected the partisan tensions. By February 1793, Pennsylvania had been without one of its two federal senators for almost two years because the Assembly could not decide how to fill the vacancy.

Philadelphia financier Robert Morris had one seat, so there was general agreement that the other seat should go to someone from a rural county. But the two houses of the Assembly could not agree on how to select that person. Gallatin helped broker a deal, and he emerged from the negotiations as the consensus candidate for the seat. Although he belonged to the minority party, the majority respected him for his even temper and unremitting energy. Gallatin warned them that he might not have been a citizen for the nine years that the Constitution required, but the Assembly elected him anyway.[29]

The national political climate heated up sharply soon after Gallatin's election as Americans got news that the French Revolution had turned more radical. When the French people rose against unrestrained monarchy in 1789, American enthusiasm for what appeared to be a sister republican revolution had been widespread. But as domestic violence escalated within France and France declared war on Britain in 1793, American opinions began to diverge. Most Federalists saw the continuing turbulence in France and the senseless execution of the deposed king as evidence that radical thinking and popular commotion could easily undermine responsible republican government. Many of those in the emerging opposition, on the other hand, thought the fate of republican government everywhere turned on the French revolutionary government's ability to defend itself from Britain and the other monarchies in Europe. The arrival of young Citizen Genêt as minister from France in April sparked an outburst of celebration among partisan republicans, who began forming political clubs to build on enthusiasm for the French republic and to develop resistance against "monarchical" tendencies in the federal government. The largest and most important of those Democratic Republican societies was in Philadelphia, and Gallatin's friends Hutchinson and Dallas were founding members.[30]

Two months after Gallatin took his Senate seat in December, Federalist senators moved to expel him for failure to satisfy the citizenship requirement. Senators Aaron Burr and John Taylor, unabashed partisans from the Republican seedbeds in New York and Virginia, scrambled to defend him. Although Senate debates had never before been opened to the public, Burr and Taylor got the public admitted to hear the debate on Gallatin's exclusion. In that debate, Burr claimed Gallatin had been a citizen since 1781 because he was living in Massachusetts when the Articles of Confederation gave national citizenship to all "free inhabitants" of the states. Gallatin's later naturalization oath in Virginia, said Burr, simply reconfirmed his status. The Federalists contended that no one could become a citizen of the United States unless he was first the citizen of a state, and they said that Gallatin had never satisfied the citizenship requirements of any state. Whatever the merit of those conflicting arguments, partisanship determined the outcome. The expulsion vote became a test of party loyalty, and Gallatin lost 14–12. Even Robert Morris, who had promised to stay neutral in deference to the wishes of his own state, voted against him.[31]

By the time he was expelled from the Senate, Gallatin himself had joined the partisan republican attacks on Treasury secretary Alexander Hamilton. Hamilton's fiscal policies had been the focus of opposition to the Federalist regime from the start, and now—with Hamilton's funding and assumption plans in place—the opposition turned to personal attacks on Hamilton himself. Hamilton's decisive response to William Branch Giles's clumsy attempts to investigate the Treasury had raised a serious doubt whether anyone in the republican opposition could bring Hamilton to account. Gallatin must have thought he could. Shortly after he took his seat in the Senate, Gallatin made a motion for a new and more complete Treasury accounting. When the Senate passed it, Hamilton popped. He sent the Senate two testy letters complaining that "desultory" calls for information distracted him from business, increased his already enormous workload, and endangered his health. Hamilton never provided the information that the Senate requested, but Gallatin had landed a blow.[32]

The summer before he took his Senate seat, Gallatin met Hannah Nicholson. He had stayed in Philadelphia during the summer recess to work on a legislative investigation. The weather was hot, the work was tedious, and the strain showed. His friend Alexander Dallas invited him to join Dallas and his wife Maria on an excursion up the Hudson River.

As the three of them passed through New York in June, they called on a retired naval commander named James Nicholson. Commodore Nicholson—as everyone called him—was a prominent republican organizer, and the two young republicans from Pennsylvania wanted to meet him. He and his wife Frances lived in a fine house on William Street in the good part of town. Republican partisans were always welcome there, and two of the Nicholsons' daughters had married republican-leaning members of Congress when the federal government was in New York. The oldest daughter still living at home was named Hannah. By the time Gallatin and the Dallases left New York a few days later, they had persuaded her to accompany them on their trip up the Hudson.[33]

Hannah Nicholson was an intelligent, well-educated woman with a lively sense of humor. She was twenty-six at the time, older than her two sisters had been when they married and about four years older than the mean age at which elite women of the time married. No full portrait of her survives. But a silhouette made years later suggests she resembled her older sister Catherine, a handsome woman with long brown hair, a round face, and a pert nose. Albert at thirty-two was a lean, dark-haired, bright-eyed young man—a senator and a good republican. The two of them made an immediate connection, and Albert began visiting the Nicholson family as frequently as he could. By late July, he was writing—as carefully as his terrible penmanship permitted—for Commodore Nicholson's permission to marry Hannah.[34]

The warm and candid letters that the couple exchanged after their engagement reveal their compatibility. Each of them was clever, insightful, and direct. To Hannah's suggestion that she had much to learn from him, Albert demurred. "I am but a child, and will have to receive instruction from you," he wrote, "for most of my life has been spent very far indeed from anything like the polite part of the world." So while he would teach her "history, French, or anything else" that he knew, he had far more important things to learn from her. "You must polish my manners, teach me how to talk to people I do not know, and how to render myself agreeable to strangers,—I was going to say, to ladies,—but as I pleased you without any instructions, I have become very vain on that head." They wrote to each other about current events and their political views. Albert confessed opinions that he knew Hannah's highly partisan father would find too moderate, so he cautioned her (since even quite personal letters got passed around) that "my politics are only for you." As yellow fever swept through Philadelphia late that summer, he admitted to her the fears that he tried to hide from others. When he fell ill in New York three weeks later, she nursed him at home so that he would not have to go to the public hospital for fever patients. Finding themselves already so much together, they moved up their wedding date to November 11, 1793.[35]

For Albert, the marriage was a good match. James Nicholson came from an established Maryland family, and although he had served without particular distinction, he was the senior officer in the American navy during the Revolution. His wife Frances was the only child of a wealthy Bermuda merchant named Thomas Witter who had settled in New York before the Revolution. The two of them had reared six children on James's small profits as a merchant and Frances's ample income from her inheritance. Commodore Nicholson was a stout, resolute, sometimes blustering man who did not hesitate to express himself emphatically. He had excellent political connections, and politics were an important part of the family's life. Four of the five Nicholson daughters would eventually marry members of Congress. The only son, twenty-year-old James Witter Nicholson, had just graduated from Columbia College in New York. All eight members of the family were—making some allowance for the Commodore—quite amiable, and they quickly became the family that Albert Gallatin had lacked.[36]

In letters to Badollet, Gallatin was characteristically plainspoken about his marriage. "I know you will be happy in hearing," he wrote soon after the engagement, "that I am contracted with a girl about 25 years old, who is neither handsome nor rich, but sensible, well informed, good natured & belonging to a respectable & very amiable family, who I believe are satisfied with the intended match." He was equally direct in a letter three months after the wedding. "Her person is…far less attractive than either her mind or her heart," he reported, "and yet I do not wish her to have any other...for I think I can read in her face the expression of her soul and as to her shape and size you know my taste....Her understanding is good, she is as well informed as most young ladies, she is perfectly simple and unaffected, she loves me, and"—he ended—"she is a pretty good democrat (and so by the bye are all her relations)." Hannah Gallatin was in short a good republican wife—the kind of sensible and intelligent woman commended by the contemporary literature on companionate marriage. There was only one problem. "She is what you will call a city belle," Gallatin told Badollet, with habits "not very well adapted to a country life and specially to a Fayette County life."[37]

It was a problem that would plague the couple for many years. But as they considered where to spend their first summer, Hannah and Albert Gallatin had more pressing concerns. They did not know how Albert would support them. He knew that farming would not be enough. He thought about increasing his mercantile business, getting back into land speculation, or perhaps even studying the law. But neither of them questioned whether he would remain in politics. Gallatin had taken his election to the Senate as a validation of his political ambition and his partisan exclusion from the Senate as a call to arms. As he worried about bringing Hannah to Fayette County for the first time, getting his house plastered, and selling land claims to raise cash, he always assumed he would return to the Pennsylvania Assembly in the autumn.[38]

CHAPTER 3

GALLATIN'S INSURRECTION

G allatin returned to the Pennsylvania Assembly in the autumn of 1794, but he came through a whirlwind. Protests against Alexander Hamilton's excise tax on whiskey had sparked an armed uprising in western Pennsylvania during the summer. The troops sent to suppress it counted Gallatin among the chief rebels. The Assembly wanted to invalidate his election, and the federal courts demanded his testimony. The Whiskey Rebellion—known to contemporaries as the Western Insurrection—was the first aggressive challenge to the scarcely established federal regime, and the leaders of the new government made it an object lesson. They claimed that the insurrection demonstrated the dangers of popular dissent, and their claim forced Gallatin and other opposition leaders to justify what they had done.

Prejudice against excise taxes ran deep in British and American political culture. Excise tax collection required a government official to inspect, quantify, and mark the items subject to tax. Taxpayers perceived the whole process as a governmental intrusion into their private sphere. Although excises were an important part of the British tax base, popular hatred of them and the excisemen who collected them had never abated. Hamilton had admitted that the "genius of the people will ill brook the inquisitive and peremptory spirit of excise laws," but the need for additional revenue to support federal assumption of the states' war debts in 1791 forced him to reconsider. He believed that raising import duties high enough to fund assumption would encourage smuggling and reduce overall collections. He also believed that direct taxes on persons or real estate would be even more unpopular than a targeted excise on domestic whiskey production. Most people in the predominantly agrarian nation had little ready cash to pay taxes; distillers at least had a reliably marketable product to sell. Imported spirits already bore duties, so a tax on cheaper domestic alternatives seemed fair, and it also could discourage over-consumption.[1]

Hamilton's excise proposal excited particular attention in Pennsylvania because the Western Country was full of distillers. The Western Country—composed of Fayette, Westmoreland, Washington, and Allegheny counties—lay in the mountainous southwestern corner of the state. It had changed significantly since Gallatin first came there. The free population had grown to about 63,500 persons, including 13,000 adult men. The social and economic structure had become more stratified, and the number of landless workers was rising. The market needs of the region, however, continued to be severely restricted by high mountains to the east and unsettled conditions to the west. The settlers distilled a higher proportion of their surplus grain than most Americans because whiskey was easier to transport than the grain from which they made it. But the settlers could not make as many cash sales as eastern distillers, and they resented the proposition that they must use what meager cash came their way to pay taxes into the pockets of the well-to-do Easterners who held most of the federal debt.[2]

Popular opposition to Hamilton's excise proposal presented a problem for political leaders in the Western Country. Most of them shared their constituents' opposition to the tax. Some joined the opposition to improve their political standing. Others simply believed it was right to represent the people's view—and self-destructive to do otherwise. But it was not clear to any of them how they should go about opposing a federal measure. The Constitution gave the new federal government broad powers to tax the people directly. Although the Federalists had claimed that the federal government would not need to impose internal taxes during peacetime, Antifederalists never doubted that the Constitution allowed Congress to impose them any time. It was not even clear whether the state legislature had the right to instruct the state's United States senators to oppose the measure. During Gallatin's first session in the Pennsylvania legislature, he and other Western representatives had put their weight behind resolutions advising Pennsylvania's senators to vote against the excise. But they had accomplished very little. The lower house passed the resolutions 40–16, but the Senate rejected them, and by the time the Assembly adjourned in the summer of 1791, the federal tax on domestic whiskey was law.[3]

William Maclay, who opposed the tax but feared a leader of the Western tax opposition might take his seat in the Senate, took a caustic view of the Assembly's debates on the issue. "I can already plainly see," he noted in his diary, "That all this Matter will vanish in Air[,] Finley Gallatin Smiley...in fact all the Conductors of the Business having nothing further in View than the securing themselves Niches in the Six dollar Temple of Congress." The legislative protest against the excise was "only meant as the Step-lather to facilitate their ascent." Maclay would not be the last one to say so, but he and others who blamed the Western politicians failed to see the full dimensions of their dilemma.[4]

If the government did not redress the people's grievances, then what were the people to do? Some citizens took the Revolution as proof that crowd action and organized disobedience were the answers. If the people were sovereign, it seemed to follow that nothing should prevent them from bringing an errant government to heel. And the Revolution had weakened the culture of deference that enabled elite members of the community to moderate crowd violence. But many other citizens and most political leaders in the new regime thought that government by the people had undercut the case for direct action. With British imperial authorities gone and republican institutions in place, the people's own representatives controlled the government, and the government's measures were the products of majority decision-making. The people could petition for redress and vote for different representatives in the next election. But if the majority was to rule, what gave the people the right to do more? Popular resistance to the new regime seemed anti-republican, even seditious.[5]

Popular protests against the federal excise had not yet broken out in early 1791. Writing to his son-in-law Williams Stephens Smith, who had just been appointed to be the federal revenue superintendent for New York, John Adams was almost ebullient about the national government's prospects. He thought the government had "given more general satisfaction than I expected ever to live to see," and he congratulated his son-in-law on his new position. But John Nevill, who had resigned from the Pennsylvania Assembly to become the federal revenue inspector for the Western Country, was less sanguine. In a letter currying favor with Gallatin, he expressed only the modest confidence that excise revenue would "grow into Satisfaction at least as far as to be tollerabile." Nevill had reason to be cautious. He had been a general officer in the Continental Army, he was a prominent landowner, and his family and their connections held lucrative governmental positions around Pittsburgh. Appointees like him were meant to lend the federal regime prestige and to help it command the people's deference. But in the Assembly's debates on the excise resolutions, Nevill had spoken against the very tax he now undertook to collect. It therefore seemed to his neighbors and even some of his political friends that he had compromised himself for a federal salary. That made his appointment an example of the very sort of corruption that Hamilton's opponents feared: the use of federal patronage to silence dissent and consolidate federal power.[6]

Just weeks after he got the letter from Nevill, Gallatin joined a small group of Western leaders at Redstone Old Fort (now Brownsville) to organize popular opposition to the excise. Hamilton later would call this meeting the first step toward insurrection. Gallatin had been invited to the meeting by a Washington County lawyer and court official named James Marshel, who had argued against repealing Pennsylvania's own excise on whiskey sales and then lost his seat in the Assembly to Thomas Ryerson, the only Western representative to oppose the resolutions against the federal excise. Marshel probably saw an opportunity to ride popular discontent over the federal excise to his own political redemption. Others who attended the meeting may have had their eyes on similar political advantages. The meeting put Edward Cook—a prominent Fayette County landowner who had helped to draft Pennsylvania's Revolutionary constitution—into the chair and elected Gallatin as clerk. They then resolved that the federal excise was "unequal in its operation, immoral in its effects, dangerous to liberty, and especially oppressive and injurious to the inhabitants of the western country." They called on voters in the Western counties to send delegates to a September meeting at Pittsburgh.[7]

The Pittsburgh meeting gave the excise protest a sharper edge. Gallatin and other legislators were not there because the Assembly was meeting in Philadelphia at the time, and the eleven delegates who came to Pittsburgh did not show moderation. The petition they sent to Congress instead showed how easily opposition to the whiskey excise could connect to other popular grievances against the federal government. After denouncing the excise as the "base offspring" of Hamilton's funding system, the petition went on to deplore the failure to discriminate between speculators and original holders of the federal debt, the high interest rate on the new federal bonds, the exorbitant salaries paid to federal officials, and the unconstitutionality of the national bank. And the meeting did not stop there. In a separate address to the people, the delegates urged them to nullify the excise law by putting pressure on their fellow citizens not to become tax collectors. Without excisemen, they said, "the law cannot be carried into effect and it will be the same as if it did not exist."[8]

The appeal for popular nullification of a contested law was rooted in past practice. Pennsylvania's own whiskey excise had been a dead letter in the Western Country for years. The Pittsburgh meeting remonstrated

against it, and the Assembly repealed it shortly afterward. But the roots
of the appeal reached further down into the potentially destabilizing localism of rural communities, especially those on the frontier. Frontier communities were relatively isolated from commercial activity in the rest of the
country, so they defined their interests from a more parochial perspective.
They rejected the authority of elected representatives who failed to reflect
the local community's will, and they believed they had a considerable right
to regulate their own affairs. The Antifederalism of men like Findley,
Smilie, and Gallatin bore features of this localism, and Federalist leaders
like Washington and Hamilton understood that it posed a threat to the
national regime's authority. Many distillers in the Western Country simply
did not register their stills, and similar disobedience appeared in Kentucky
and the western reaches of Virginia and the Carolinas.[9]

The appeal for popular nullification also raised the possibility of
more active resistance. On the day before the Pittsburgh meeting and
perhaps unbeknown to the delegates there, sixteen men with blackened
faces had abducted the newly appointed revenue collector for Washington and Allegheny counties, basted him with hot tar, covered him with
loose feathers, and made him promise to publish his resignation in the
Pittsburgh newspaper. Tarring and feathering was an intimidation ritual
that folk communities traditionally used to regulate the behavior of
errant members, and cultural understandings generally kept its inherent
violence within bounds. But other traditional forms of resistance involved
greater violence. Since colonial times, militant citizens had taken up arms
to "regulate" governments they believed to be corrupt or unresponsive.
Regulations continued after the Revolution. The incidents in Massachusetts in 1786 and 1787 known as Shays's Rebellion—in which regulators
exchanged fire with the troops sent to disperse them—were the most
notable example. But regulators from the backwoods of Maine to the
farmlands of Pennsylvania had detained officials, closed courts to prevent
prosecutions or foreclosures, and meted out their own rough justice.[10]

A second meeting at Pittsburgh about a year after the first one
attempted to marshal continued resistance to the excise without
inciting violence. This time, Gallatin and other minority members

of the Assembly attended. The delegates declared it their duty "to persist in our remonstrances to Congress, and in every other legal measure that may obstruct the operation of the Law until we are able to obtain its total repeal." But they went further. They appointed committees of correspondence like those that had been used during the Revolution. And since Nevill had managed to appoint tax collectors notwithstanding the first Pittsburgh meeting's plea, the delegates called on their fellow citizens to shun them. Describing the excisemen as "lost to every sense of virtue and feeling for the distresses of the country," the delegates urged the people to consider the tax collectors "unworthy of our friendship; have no intercourse or dealings with them; withdraw from them every assistance, and withhold all the comforts of life which depend upon those duties that as men and fellow citizens we owe to each other." As clerk of the meeting, Gallatin signed those resolutions.[11]

The second Pittsburgh meeting had immediate consequences. The next day, Nevill reported to his superiors that he could not collect the excise without resorting to force. Two days later, disguised men ransacked the private house where Nevill had his Washington County collection office. Reports of this resistance in the Western Country hit Hamilton at a bad time. He had grown increasingly sensitive to the criticism of his Treasury administration, and he was coming to believe that his critics were dangerous men. A few months earlier, he had denounced press criticism of the excise as evidence of "a serious design to subvert the government." And at the time when he got the disturbing reports from the West, he happened to be writing Washington a letter that accused Thomas Jefferson of undermining the administration. Hamilton promptly sent the revenue supervisor for Pennsylvania to investigate the Western commotion, asked Attorney General Edmund Randolph to indict the men who had attended the Pittsburgh meeting, and mailed Washington the draft of a proclamation against the tax resistance. Hamilton also pressed Washington to send troops to the Western Country. Washington thought troops were inexpedient, but he did sign the proclamation. Washington and Hamilton worried that Jefferson might not give the proclamation the customary attestation from the State department, but Jefferson signed without comment.[12]

Hamilton's letter asking Randolph to indict Gallatin and the other delegates to the Pittsburgh meeting has been lost, but a letter Hamilton sent to Chief Justice John Jay at the same time lays out the line he must have taken with Randolph. The letter to Jay claimed that there was no such thing as a "legal measure [to] obstruct the operation of the Law." Obstructing the law was illegal, Hamilton argued, and therefore resolutions advocating obstruction were criminal. Randolph disagreed. In a response suffused with the strain he was evidently feeling, Randolph first made what he took to be obvious points: citizens had the right to assemble, to remonstrate, and to invite others to do the same. He agreed that shunning tax collectors went a step further, but he did not think it was a crime. Although Randolph conceded that the "artfull language" of the Pittsburgh resolutions might be a mask for criminal sedition, he refused to prosecute.[13]

Gallatin soon understood that he and the others at Pittsburgh had tested the government's tolerance. The revenue supervisor's report to Hamilton had named Gallatin, Smilie, and Findley along with more violent Washington County agitators James Marshel and David Bradford as leaders of the protest. Even a Philadelphia newspaper not uncritical of the administration questioned a minority's right "to insult the civil authority." Gallatin began to reposition himself, but he was more matter of fact than repentant. Back in Philadelphia for the December 1792 meeting of the legislature, he found "our friends as kind and even our opponents as polite as ever." Apprehensions about the danger that he and other Western protest leaders might encounter when they appeared in Philadelphia had proved "altogether groundless." Still, Gallatin tried to relieve tension by admitting that the Pittsburgh resolutions were "perhaps too violent, & undoubtedly highly impolitick." He nevertheless insisted that they "contained nothing illegal," and he said that the government's failure to indict anyone proved the fuss about the meeting had been just a play for advantage in the October 1792 elections.[14]

The Pittsburgh meeting did affect the October elections. Federalist and Republican contingents had organized opposing statewide Congressional tickets. About half of the candidates were the same on both tickets—not so much because of their moderation as because of their overwhelming popularity. The contest for the remaining six seats, however, was heated.

Gallatin was an opposition organizer in the Western Country. "The apprehensions of our opponents are raised to the highest degree," Alexander Dallas told him in September; "it will be our own fault and not their ability, if we fail." When opposition candidates managed to win only three of the six seats, there was disappointment. The convivial Doctor Hutchinson was as hearty as ever. "[Y]our Western Counties have done nobly," he told Gallatin. But even he admitted that "your excise meeting lost us the majority...for the most of our ticket" in two counties where "the arts of our opponents together with the President's proclamation...detached many of our honest but credulous friends."[15]

Gallatin struck a brave pose two months later when he told his friend and neighbor Thomas Clare that Smilie's victory in the election had so dismayed the Federalist "high flyers" that they no longer talked about the Pittsburgh meeting—though he did concede that the meeting had "hurt our general interest throughout the State." To Badollet, Gallatin was more candid. "[W]e are generally blamed by our friends for the violence of our resolutions at Pittsburgh," he wrote, "& they have undoubtedly tended to render the Excise law more popular than it was before."[16]

However views might have moderated elsewhere, the excise remained deeply unpopular in the Western Country. William Findley, who had also been elected to Congress, assured Pennsylvania's governor that he and other Western leaders did not countenance the abuse of revenue officers, but he said they could not change the popular mood. He believed that the people would not impede judicial enforcement of the tax unless the accused were taken "out of the proper Counties for trial." In that case, he would "not undertake for the consequences." Findley did not need to explain. He and the governor both understood that local juries were likely to nullify the excise law by refusing to convict those prose-cuted for flouting it. Gallatin apparently agreed with Findley about the necessity of local trials. He suggested to Badollet that the two men indicted for ransacking Nevill's Washington County office should "keep out of the way & not be found" when the federal marshal came to sum-mon them to trial in York. Gallatin believed they were innocent, and he thought that "drag[ging] people at such a distance" for trial set a danger-ous precedent.[17]

Gallatin stayed out of the Western Country from late 1792 until May 1794. During those eighteen months, he attended the legislature, spent the recess on a legislative investigation, married Hannah Nichol-son, and tried to defend his seat in the Senate. He later claimed that he had been too busy even to talk about the protests against the excise. "Neither during [my] absence," he would tell the Pennsylvania legisla-ture, "nor after my return to the western country...until the riots began, had I the slightest conversation that I can recollect, much less any delib-erate conference or correspondence, either directly or indirectly, with any of its inhabitants, on the subject of the excise law." His denial is too categorical to be believed—and in fact, Gallatin had advised men indicted for vandalizing the revenue collector's office to evade service of process. Gallatin's denial also hints that his long absence from home may have been part of a deliberate strategy to distance himself from the protests. But no other surviving evidence refutes Gallatin's denial, and it may have represented his honest recollection.[18]

Whether or not he talked about the excise protests while he was away, Gallatin must have caught whiffs of trouble distilling at home. The president had issued a proclamation in February 1794 against men who had attacked the excise collector in Gallatin's home county, and the Pittsburgh newspaper was still reprinting it when Gallatin returned home. The collector was corrupt and personally unpopular, but the spring of 1794 had seen other collectors attacked, barns burned, and registered stills "mended." To relieve one poor Washington County citizen from harassment, Nevill published a notice in the Pittsburgh paper declaring that the man had never asked or been asked to be a revenue officer. "Besides," Nevill added, he could use no more revenue officers in that county "unless the people would be better tempered, which I hope will soon be the case."[19]

About a month after Gallatin came home, Nevill's hope vanished in flames. The insurrection had begun. The flash point came—as Findley had predicted—when Nevill accompanied a federal marshal to serve writs summoning delinquent distillers to federal court in Philadelphia. A cry that the "Federal Sheriff" was taking men out of the Western Country for trial reached a militia company that happened to be drilling nearby. Members of the company belonged to one of the Democratic Republican Societies formed earlier that year when the advance of the French Revolution had stoked partisan republican fervor. By morning, the company had surrounded Nevill's large house on the bluff of a hill overlooking his fine property. Nevill fired on them, mortally wounding a militiaman. After an exchange of shots that shattered windows and wounded several more militiamen, the company withdrew. But they returned in force the next day and burned Nevill's house to the ground. Insurgents arrested the federal marshal and robbed the mails. Within two weeks, thousands of militiamen from the Western counties had assembled on a large drill field just outside Pittsburgh. To save the town, intimidated townspeople banished Nevill's son and a few other prominent citizens known to be hostile to the insurgents.[20]

It was clear to Hamilton that the administration's political opponents in western Pennsylvania were responsible for the uprising. In a report to Washington, he claimed there had been no spontaneous popular resistance to the tax laws. Resistance arose, he said, only after "formal public meetings of influential individuals" adopted resolutions meant "to render the laws odious, to discountenance a compliance with them, and to intimidate individuals from accepting and executing Offices under them." Hamilton named names (and in a later letter to support his contention that Pennsylvania officials were involved, he named even more). Among them was Gallatin's.[21]

The insurrection intensified the dilemma with which Gallatin and other Western leaders had struggled since Hamilton first proposed the excise. These men sympathized with their constituents, and they believed the people had a right to protest against the tax. They were even prepared to overlook occasional attacks on revenue officers and destruction of property that followed traditional intimidation rituals. But armed opposition to law enforcement was an altogether different matter. Armed resistance to the government, as they understood it, was treason. Whatever they might have intended when the protests began years earlier, all but the most extreme of the Western leaders now wanted to pull back. But opposing an armed and hostile crowd was difficult and risky business.[22]

A meeting called by the insurgents for Parkinson's Ferry (now Monongahela) in the middle of August 1794 forced the Western leaders to take a stand. Over two hundred delegates came to the meeting from the four western Pennsylvania counties and two neighboring Virginia counties, and even more men came to watch. The delegates gathered beneath a grove of trees on a high hill overlooking the Monongahela River. The onlookers—many of them armed—sat on felled trees and stumps in a half circle around them. The delegates again elected Edward Cook as chairman and Gallatin as secretary. The meeting set the pattern for dissident behavior over the next few months. David Bradford, James Marshel, and a few others from Washington County where protest had been strongest advocated armed resistance to federal law enforcement. There was a liberty pole and even talk of regional independence. Most of the delegates were not prepared to go that far, but they equivocated out of fear, sympathy, or strategy. Hugh Henry Brackenridge, a Pittsburgh lawyer and former member of the legislature who meant well enough, was prominent among the temporizers. William Findley also kept his head down.[23]

Gallatin, in contrast, spoke out against armed resistance and violence. He told the insurgents they should not resist the courts, and he condemned the destruction of property. In their accounts of the Parkinson's Ferry meeting, Brackenridge, Findley, and others applauded Gallatin's courage—if not his good sense—in confronting the insurgents. Brackenridge explained that he had tried to cajole the angry men because he found it difficult to speak out against them directly. But even Gallatin was not immune to pressure from the crowd. Challenged for denouncing the burning of a man's barn, he too may have equivocated. "If you had burned him in it," Brackenridge reported Gallatin saying, "it might have been something; but the barn had done no harm." In the margin of his copy of Brackenridge's book, Gallatin denied this. It was, he noted there, what Brackenridge would have said in his place.[24]

As the meeting at Parkinson's Ferry was ending, word came that President Washington had called out the militia and sent commissioners to negotiate with the insurgents. The delegates at Parkinson's Ferry appointed Gallatin and fourteen others to meet the commissioners and report back to a standing committee. The meeting proved futile. The commissioners offered a blanket amnesty in exchange for full submission to the law. Gallatin and the other conferees urged the standing committee to accept the offer, but a substantial minority of the committee refused. Confronted with this continuing show of resistance, the commissioners demanded a written declaration of submission from each voter in the four Western counties. They set September 11 as the submission date.[25]

Behind the confrontation between the insurgents and the federal authorities lay incompatible views on the role of popular dissent under a republican government. On the day the Parkinson's Ferry conferees met the federal commissioners, a western Pennsylvania newspaper published resolutions that succinctly summarized the insurgents' position. "[E]very law made by the [people's] representatives not agreeable to the voice of those from whom they derive their authority," the resolutions declared, "is tyrannical and unjust." Because republican government rests on virtue rather than power, "the laws should recommend themselves to the affections of the people." If they did not, the people must protect their rights by resisting the unjust laws.[26]

Writing as "Tully" in a Philadelphia newspaper, Hamilton took a nearly opposite position. A "sacred respect" for the laws made by the majority, he said, was "the vital principle, the sustaining energy of free government." The question therefore was plain: "shall the majority govern or be governed?...shall there be government, or no government?"

Contempt for the law was the road to anarchy, and anarchy was the road to despotism. Except in "great and urgent cases," resistance to law was "treason against society, against liberty, against every thing that ought to be dear to a free, enlightened, and prudent people." A few months later, a western Pennsylvania judge tried to describe to a grand jury how the insurgents had gone astray. Their problem, he explained, was that their understanding of self-government was too parochial. It rested on *"a mistaken use of the word people."* The insurgents misunderstood the word to mean only those in "their own neighborhood" rather than the "whole people of the Union."[27]

The September 11 date set by the federal commissioners came quickly. Many voters bridled at signing the prescribed form of submission. They believed that it implied they had broken the law and that it cut off their right to petition for repeal of the excise law. The day before the submission deadline, Fayette County's leaders decided to let the county's citizens cast a vote for submission without signing the form. They issued a long declaration—which appears to have been Gallatin's work—explaining themselves to both the voters and the federal authorities.[28]

The Fayette County declaration recited grievances, justified past protests, and then urged submission. Although it showed embarrassment about the second Pittsburgh meeting's call to shun revenue officers, it still vowed to give the excise no more support "than what is required by law" and to seek repeal through "every legal & constitutional means." But having established common ground with the people, the declaration changed tone. It made the case for submission in majoritarian language not so different from Hamilton's. Violent resistance to the excise law, the document declared, was simply "the attempt of a minority to overrule & to oppress the majority," and it would "destroy every principle of constitutional & rational liberty which we now enjoy." If "any one part of the Union" could use force to oppose "the determination of the whole, there is an end to Government itself and of course to the Union." Force was never justified unless the people had "no legal & constitutional remedy" and the evils being resisted far surpassed "those that must ensue from resistance." The Fayette County declaration showed sympathy for the protests, but it reflected more sober thinking. Gallatin and other Western Republicans, a newspaper correspondent sharply observed, "too late...begin to see their error" and "are trying to make their peace."[29]

The submission in Fayette and the other counties was far from unanimous, and it failed to convince federal authorities that resistance had ended. Washington ordered the militia to assemble in late September, and by late October an army had entered the Western Country. The overwhelming force of about 13,000 men roughly equaled the region's adult male population. It met no resistance. David Bradford and other extremists fled down the Mississippi into Spanish territory. Troops began to arrest suspects and witnesses in the middle of the night on November 13. Six days later, they started back to Philadelphia with about twenty prisoners in tow.[30]

Hamilton came west with the army to direct investigations, and his list of suspects included Gallatin, Findley, Smilie, and Brackenridge. He showed particular interest in Gallatin and Findley, two of the more vocal critics of his Treasury policies. Friends warned Gallatin in early October that he would be safer in Philadelphia. Others later reported that Hamilton was browbeating witnesses for testimony that could implicate Gallatin in treason. And Alexander Dallas, who came west with the Pennsylvania militia, saw Gallatin's name on a list handed around the army of "persons who were to be destroyed at all counts." Just days before the army started making arrests, Albert and Hannah Gallatin headed east, passing—presumably unrecognized—through troops who had started to turn back suspicious travelers. When Thomas Clare, their closest neighbor in Fayette County, had not heard from them a month later, he worried that something was wrong. "There Never Was More industry made by any Set of men," he wrote to Gallatin, "than there Was by Some that Was hear to get Holt of You."[31]

Voters in the Western Country went to the polls on the regular election day in October before the army entered the area, and Gallatin's constituents returned him to the Pennsylvania Assembly. To Gallatin's complete surprise, voters in the adjacent Congressional district made up of Washington and Allegheny counties also elected him to the federal

House of Representatives. Brackenridge was the leading Republican candidate in that district. But John McMillan, an influential Presbyterian minister, had nominated Gallatin at the last minute because Gallatin's bold stand against the insurgents impressed him more than Brackenridge's equivocations. The voters gave Gallatin a small margin over Brackenridge and three other candidates. Gallatin first got word of the election as he prepared to leave the Western Country.[32]

The winter was full of recriminations. Washington's annual address to Congress blamed the insurrection on men who had stoked popular prejudice against the excise law in order to gain power. They had led the Western people astray, he said, through the concerted action of "certain self-created societies." Washington's reference to self-created societies was a clear allusion to the opposition Democratic Republican Societies, and the fact that the renegade militiamen who had burned Nevill's house belonged to one of them made his charge plausible. But Washington's more fundamental claim, equally clear to all who heard him, was that political organizations other than the elected organs of government were illegitimate. A furious long sentence in a personal letter he had written two months earlier revealed the depth of his feeling on this subject. "[F]or can any thing be more absurd—more arrogant—or more pernicious to the peace of Society," he had fumed, "than for selfcreated bodies, forming themselves into *permanent* Censors, & under the shade of Night in a conclave...to declare that *this* act is unconstitutional—and *that act* is pregnant of mischief."[33]

The Senate's reply to the president's speech adopted his allusion to the Democratic Republican Societies, but Washington's denunciation of the societies sparked debate in the House. James Madison—who thought the president was aiming to tar the societies with the insurrection and the Congressional opposition with the societies—ignored the subject in his draft of the House's reply, but the administration's supporters objected. After five days of debate and several close votes, the House adopted a reply that blamed the uprising on unspecified "individuals or combinations of men"—a phrase more accurate than the one Washington had used. Many Western opposition leaders blamed for the insurrection had never joined a Democratic Republican Society. Gallatin, Findley, and Brackenridge, for example, were not members. But any improvement in accuracy was a byproduct of the House's efforts to patch over still unreconciled differences about the legitimacy of popular dissent.[34]

Partisan recriminations continued when the Pennsylvania Assembly convened in early December. Both houses of the Assembly invalidated the elections of members from the four Western counties on the ground that "terror" had kept the "friends to government and good order" away from the polls. The point of this action, Gallatin and his friends suspected, was to establish grounds for excluding Gallatin from his new seat in Congress. Madison—the Republican leader in Congress—shared their suspicion, and some Federalists in Congress seem to have been aware of the strategy. In a letter written just before the Pennsylvania legislature took its first steps to invalidate the elections, arch-Federalist Congressman Fisher Ames expressed his hope that the people—having seen the "pit open"—would not approach it again by sending to Congress those "who led them blindfold to its brink!" Whatever their motives may have been, the majority legislators in the Pennsylvania Assembly were greatly disappointed when a new Western election in early February returned all of the same members, except for one who had chosen to stand down.[35]

Gallatin's speech to the Pennsylvania legislature in defense of the Western elections became the first published account of the Western Insurrection. Gallatin argued that the violence had ended before the elections and that, in any event, the procedure adopted to exclude the Western members was unconstitutional. But his speech had a much deeper purpose than the defense of the Western elections. Gallatin aimed to defend the people's right to protest. He refuted the claim that "intemperate resolutions" by "combinations of influential characters" had provoked the uprising. The lower house of the Assembly itself, he said, had adopted the first resolutions against the excise law. How could it be criminal for citizens directly affected by the law to adopt their own resolutions? Even if they were wrong, the people had a right to express their opinions.[36]

Gallatin admitted that the Pittsburgh resolutions urging the people to treat revenue officers with contempt were "reprehensible" because they had diminished the "respect for the execution of the laws...essential to the maintenance of a free government." But he claimed that his support for those resolutions was "*my only political sin.*" And he insisted that the resolutions were not illegal and had not provoked violence. The violence, he said, was a spontaneous expression of popular outrage. Once violence erupted, he and other good citizens had a duty to participate in the public meetings that followed. Only the participation of good citizens could keep the crowd under control. The election of known "friends of order and government," like Gallatin himself, showed that most of the voters had been peaceful citizens who favored submission.[37]

Federal grand juries in Philadelphia indicted about thirty alleged insurgents for treason. They indicted others for various misdemeanors, some of them for nothing more than rebellious statements. Merely attending the Parkinson's Ferry meeting was among the acts called treasonable. Gallatin was in Philadelphia during May 1795 as a witness for the government and several of the defendants. He wrote home that almost all of the members of the grand juries were Federalists from Philadelphia. The trial jury pool included a few more residents of the Western counties because the law required it, but Gallatin emphasized that jurors from the Philadelphia area predominated. Perhaps he need not have worried. Only two defendants were convicted of treason, and the president pardoned them. Gallatin seems never to have worried that he would be prosecuted, unlike Brackenridge who—with his flair for a good story—remembered that his Philadelphia landlady had tried to evict him so that he could not be hanged out of her house.[38]

In his late-life correspondence with Thomas Jefferson, John Adams pointedly referred to the Whiskey Rebellion as "Gallatins Insurrection." The aspersion on Gallatin was Adams's rhetorical response to Jefferson's claim that only the Republican opposition had suffered from "the terrorism" of the 1790s, but the aspersion was not new. For those who wanted to blame Western opposition leaders for the insurrection, Gallatin was an irresistible scapegoat. His visible role at the protest meetings and his defense of the Western elections brought him to national attention, and his emergence as a leader of the Republican opposition in Congress shortly afterwards made him the focus of political controversy.[39]

Branding their Francophone leader as a rebel was a delicious way for the Federalists to deride the Francophile Republicans. But the aspersion was not just a slur. Gallatin had confessed his political sin. With the violent excesses of the French Revolution swirling in the background, Federalists could point to the Western Insurrection as unassailable proof that popular dissent and those who condoned it were a threat to republican government. Organizing popular opposition could destabilize the new regime, bring chaos, and—to continue the litany of the time—invite tyranny. In the charged political atmosphere of the 1790s, a sin like that would not be forgotten.[40]

CHAPTER 4

OPPOSITION
LEADER

The summer before Gallatin entered the House of Representatives, crowds up and down the country lit bonfires and burned John Jay in effigy. George Washington had sent Jay to London the previous year in the hope that he could resolve differences with Britain that were threatening to bring on a war that the infant federal government could not afford. Somewhat chagrined by the treaty Jay sent home in the spring of 1795, Washington kept it secret. He got the Senate to consent by a bare two-thirds vote without releasing the treaty's terms to the public. Washington's secrecy fed Republican suspicions that the Federalist Jay had betrayed American interests, so by the time the Republican Philadelphia *Aurora* published a leaked copy of the treaty in July, only terms more favorable than Americans had a right to expect could have prevented popular outcry. When Alexander Hamilton tried to address an angry outdoor crowd of treaty protesters in New York, they stoned him.[1]

Hamilton had retired from the Treasury earlier in 1795 to resume his law practice in New York, but he remained an outspoken government advisor and a focus of Republican abuse. To blacken Hamilton's reputation, Gallatin's aggressively partisan father-in-law James Nicholson had spread a rumor that Hamilton had accumulated a portfolio of British bonds while he headed the Treasury. Hamilton had not challenged Commodore Nicholson to retract that story, and when Nicholson saw Hamilton trying to duck away from the leaders of the angry crowd, he proclaimed Hamilton a coward. The insult left Hamilton little choice but to challenge Nicholson to a duel. By the time Hannah Gallatin, who was staying with her parents that summer, heard about the affair, the parties' seconds had patched it up. But her embattled husband, who was off in Fayette County on business, took the occasion to warn her that complaining about the abuse that the Federalists had heaped on him "with as much warmth as you usually do" could lead to more such affairs of honor.[2]

The British Treaty put a match to partisan tinder laid during years of controversy over Hamilton's financial policies. By the time Hamilton resigned, he had used a bold adaptation of the British fiscal and monetary system to resolve the new American regime's financial crisis. He had established a tax system, financed the new government's operations, and refinanced the disorganized and depreciated national debt. With the federal government's assumption of the states' Revolutionary War debts, he had both nationalized the loyalties of the moneyed debt holders and eliminated the need for heavy state taxes. He had created a national bank through which the government could raise loans, manage its debt, and pay its bills. And in a valedictory flourish, he had left behind a plan to repay much of the debt over the next twenty-four years.[3]

But Hamilton's policies had a heavy political cost. Madison, Jefferson, and others who now called themselves Republicans had coalesced in opposition to it. They thought Hamilton's heavy reliance on import duties kept the country in thrall to British merchants, they said the government spent too much money, and they criticized Hamilton for adopting the British government's practice of paying off old debt by issuing new debt that the government could not redeem for many years. They claimed that Hamilton's assumption plan had needlessly increased the national debt. They believed the national bank was an unconstitutional monopoly that corrupted members of Congress. They insisted that the public debt must be repaid as promptly as possible, and they dismissed Hamilton's long-term debt repayment plan as nothing but a confidence trick to raise the price of government bonds.[4]

Although Federalists often spoke of the Republican opposition as the Virginia faction or Southern party, sectionalism was only one dimension of a complex democratic movement that was beginning to form throughout the country. Its adherents—rich, poor, but mostly middling—typically were men with aspirations for advancement that conflicted with the Federalists' traditional notions of deference and social stability. The movement's strength in Gallatin's Pennsylvania was particularly important to its early success. There, in what one historian has called the "crucible of American democracy," democratic elements in a diverse population had begun to affiliate earlier than in other states. Smallholders and modest farmers led the effort in the countryside, while in Philadelphia a new generation of businessmen and professionals and a growing workforce of craftsmen and laborers joined the cause. Some of these men had been Antifederalists in 1787, a few had been Federalists, but many of them were new to political action. As their objections to the Federalist regime accumulated, their affiliation strengthened. They organized popular meetings, announced party tickets, and distributed campaign broadsides. If they were not a political party in the modern sense, it is because they lived in another time; in their own time, they could hardly be described otherwise.[5]

Albert Gallatin and Alexander Dallas were good examples of the type of men who became leaders of the democratic movement in Pennsylvania. Both were intelligent, well-educated young immigrants. Despite their affiliation with the minority party, both had won some influence in state government. But neither belonged to the elite social, business, and political circles around Washington that directed national affairs. They probably never would, and they knew it. That did not make them resentful, but it did leaven their politics. Gallatin's feelings ring out from a letter he sent to his wife as he traveled through the Hudson River manors of the great New York families in the spring of 1795. "The more I see of this State the better I like Pennsylvania," he wrote. Pennsylvania had no Livingstons, no Rensselaers, and—he could have added—no Schuylers (the family into which Hamilton had married). "[F]rom the suburbs of Philadelphia to the banks of the Ohio I do not know a single family that has any extensive influence. An equal distribution of property has rendered every individual independent, and there is amongst us true and real equality.... [A]s I am poor," he concluded, "I like a country where no person is very rich."[6]

The tensions over federal finances had already been exacerbated by foreign policy differences. When France declared war on Britain in 1793, Federalists shocked by the radical turn in the French Revolution sympathized with Britain. Republicans tended to side with France. But those differences—although often expressed in violent terms—were mostly a matter of sentiment. Federalists called their opponents Jacobins, blamed them for the Western Insurrection, and accused them of trying to disorganize the federal government. Republicans—who often were more Anglophobic than truly Francophile—denounced the Federalists as crypto-monarchists and pointed to President Washington's unilateral decree of American neutrality as proof of executive usurpation. Neither party, however, wanted to get involved in the European conflict. And party differences over commercial retaliation were ultimately inconsequential because the European belligerents held the trump cards. Even the popular enthusiasm whipped up by Citizen Genêt's arrival in 1793 had no lasting consequences. Genêt had endangered American neutrality by fitting out French privateers in American ports, and he contemptuously ignored Washington's attempts to enforce the neutrality decree against him. Republican leaders soon found the young man a serious embarrassment, and Thomas Jefferson himself—then Secretary of State—asked the French government to recall him.[7]

It was Britain's wartime interference with American interests in 1793–94 that brought American partisan differences to a flash point.

Britain's enforcement of its mercantile restrictions against American trade with British colonies in the West Indies had disappointed many Americans who expected independence to lead to freer trade. From the beginning of the new government, Madison, Jefferson, and other Republicans had tried repeatedly to get Congress to enact retaliatory measures against British shipping. So when Britain started to seize American ships for trading with France and her colonies in the West Indies, the seizures hit a sore spot. News that the British governor of Canada was stirring up Native American tribes on the frontier hit another sensitive spot. Native American forces had defeated both of the armies sent to assert federal authority in the Northwest, and Britain still held forts on Native territory inside the United States that it had promised to evacuate after the Revolution. Britain's support for the Natives and its grip on the Western fur trade were serious threats to American interests.[8]

Although the new British provocations initially outraged all Americans, partisan differences soon reemerged. Since substantially all of the federal government's revenue came from import duties and 90 percent of the imports came from Britain, the administration leaned heavily toward finding an accommodation. It wanted to raise a standing army to give the country more heft in negotiations and more protection if they failed. Republicans, on the other hand, renewed their call for commercial retaliation against Britain. They thought a standing army would increase federal spending and executive patronage. And they feared the administration would use the army to put down domestic political opposition.[9]

The Republican Congressmen who came to Philadelphia in December 1795 thought they had a small majority and a promising issue. The raucous protesters who burned Jay in effigy had complained that his treaty conceded American maritime rights in exchange for little more than the renewal of promises that the British had failed to keep since the end of the Revolution. The treaty gave up the right to retaliate against British trade restrictions, but it left Britain free to discriminate against the United States. The protesters insinuated that only British influence in the administration could explain this betrayal, and some of them openly criticized Washington for the first time. Republicans saw this as their chance to assert the legislative power that they thought the administration had undermined.[10]

The Republicans expected their opportunity to come when the administration asked the House for the money it needed to implement Jay's treaty. The Constitution gave Congress alone the power to appropriate money, and the Republicans meant to argue that agreements in a treaty made by the president with the consent of the Senate did not obligate the House to spend money. Otherwise, the president could use the treaty power to usurp the legislature's power of the purse. Washington saw the confrontation coming, and he put it off as long as he could. Months passed without a request for the treaty appropriations. In the meantime, the anticipated showdown over the power of the purse made the House more attentive to fiscal affairs.[11]

That attention to fiscal affairs pushed Gallatin into the Republican vanguard. Reduction of government spending and repayment of public debt were party dogmas, but Gallatin—boosted by the success that mastery of finance had given him in the Pennsylvania Assembly—made those issues his particular project. He believed the federal government would not reduce its spending and its debt unless the House took a more direct hand in Treasury administration. Both Hamilton and his successor Oliver Wolcott, Gallatin thought, had spent too much money, and the House's clumsy probes into Hamilton's Treasury management had been little more than political harassment. Gallatin himself had only preliminary ideas about what the House should do, but he knew that reform would require frugality, accountability, and legislative oversight. With the emboldened Republican cadre behind him and the fight over the British Treaty ahead of him, Gallatin began seizing opportunities to build those three footings for Republican fiscal reform.[12]

Gallatin opened his campaign for frugality by blasting an administration proposal to issue more funded debt to repay loans that Hamilton had run up with the Bank of the United States. Hamilton had famously called his system of issuing debt backed by future taxes a "national blessing." He had pointed out two benefits: the government could spread extraordinary costs over longer periods, and the private holders of the government bonds could use them as collateral to borrow money for private investment. Hamilton had been careful to say that the federal government should not use the funding system to pay its ordinary operating expenses, but Republicans routinely derided him for calling debt a blessing under any circumstances. Gallatin now deliberately inverted Hamilton's claim in order to attack the funding system.[13]

Hamilton's funding system was a "public curse," Gallatin told the House, because it made deficit spending "appear so easy." It allowed the government to pay its expenses with bonds that would not come due for decades. The only current cost of funded spending was a small amount of additional interest, so the system effectively masked the real cost of government. Although the Treasury denied it, Gallatin claimed that the new federal government had run up a deficit of $2.8 million since 1791—roughly 10 percent of its total spending. The only way to prevent future deficits was to reduce spending and raise taxes. Since military spending was the main expense, retrenchment had to begin there. Gallatin insisted that he was not making a standard Whig attack on standing armies. He did not think a standing army was "dangerous to the liberties of the people." But he also did not believe that it was "necessary for the support of government." His point was that the government could not afford it. The government therefore should raise troops only when it needed them. Gallatin made a similar point about naval spending. The money spent on the navy was wasted because the few ships the country could afford stood no chance against one of the European navies. The nation would grow stronger, he said, if it paid its debts first and built a credible navy later.[14]

To keep the administration frugal, the House had to make the Treasury more accountable for the money it spent. The House should stop assuming that an expense was reasonable just "because the President of the United States asked for it." Congressmen should not appropriate 30 cents for daily army rations until they understood why the old rate of 15 cents was too low. The House also should stop the Treasury from lumping the military appropriations together and treating the total amount as "a general grant" to the War department. As long as the president could shift money that had been appropriated for one purpose to some other use whenever he saw fit, Congress had no control over spending. The House needed to make its appropriations as specific as practicable, and all spending bills should specify that the amounts appropriated for one thing could not be spent on another. Through persistence, Gallatin got that specific appropriations language added to the military spending bills for the following year—but the House dropped it two years later when the Federalists regained the majority.[15]

To keep the administration accountable over the long term, Gallatin moved for the creation of a standing Committee of Ways and Means. The Republican opposition's previous attempts to establish a standing committee on finance had failed. The Federalist majority in earlier Congresses had allowed Hamilton to set financial policy himself, and the House had not developed the expertise needed to monitor his Treasury operations. But with Hamilton gone and a weaker man in his place, Gallatin's motion passed without opposition. The Speaker of the House put Gallatin and five other Republicans on the committee. Although the chairman and the other eight members were Federalists, the committee nevertheless came to function as Gallatin intended. The House's "appropriations are minute," Wolcott would later complain to Hamilton. "Gallatin to whom they all yield, is evidently intending to break down this Department by charging it with an impracticable detail."[16]

It was in a debate on the Mint that Gallatin staked out his most sweeping claim for legislative fiscal authority. The Mint was notoriously inefficient, and Gallatin wanted to cut its funding. He claimed that the House could withhold appropriations for the Mint even though Congress had already authorized the Mint to spend money. The Constitution gave the House power over the public revenue, he said, so that it could "check the other branches of Government whenever necessary." The administration's supporters stoutly denied that the House had the authority Gallatin was claiming for it. They insisted that one house of Congress could not dishonor spending commitments in a law that had been enacted by both houses. Once the government made a commitment, they said, the House had to fund it. Gallatin conceded that the House should only withhold appropriations on "important occasions," but that was not much of a retreat. Everyone knew that Gallatin was less concerned about the Mint than about blazing a trail to attack the British Treaty.[17]

Seeing the treaty at issue, an emigré British journalist who styled himself Peter Porcupine loosed one of his quills. He reported that "Mr. Gallatin (from *Geneva*)" had said the House could withhold appropriations, *"when they see proper, to stop the wheels of Government."* He chided Gallatin for inciting the Western Insurrection and then wiggling out of responsibility for it. In a rare full-page cartoon, he showed Gallatin standing before a guillotine, sawing the air and ranting "Stop de Wheels of Government." The caption used Gallatin's confession after the insurrection to ridicule him as "A Political Sinner." The connection between Gallatin, French radicalism, and domestic disorder was revealed! At least, growled Porcupine, the man was consistent.[18]

So were the Federalists. For the next six years they derided Gallatin relentlessly. Porcupine even took the Quakers to task for asking Gallatin to present an anti-slavery petition to Congress. Everything Gallatin touches "smack[s] of sedition and insurrection," he wrote, so that "a petition being presented by him would, with me, be a sufficient reason for kicking it *under the table*." Most of the abuse drew on the Federalists' strong streak of nativism. Federalist Congressmen called Gallatin a foreigner and—more bitingly—a Frenchman. They mocked his accent. They claimed he was under foreign influence. And in echoes of Porcupine's pungent phrase, they complained that he and the rest of the Republicans were trying to "stop the wheels of government." A large Federalist cartoon showed Gallatin pulling back on the wheel of Washington's chariot of state while Jefferson shouted directions and a savage swarm of French Revolutionary soldiers invaded in the background.[19]

House debate on the British Treaty began in March 1796 when Edward Livingston made a motion calling on Washington for the diplomatic papers. Livingston was a brilliant but brash young man from a New York manorial family that had drifted into the Republican orbit when Washington failed to give anyone in the family a meaningful federal appointment. His older brother Robert R. Livingston had admonished

Edward that he should take his cues from James Madison, the leading Republican in the House. But as months dragged by and the cold Philadelphia winter limped into spring, the younger Livingston lost patience waiting for Washington to seek funding for the treaty. The House, Livingston declared, should get the diplomatic papers now so that it would be prepared to deal with the funding request when it came.[20]

Livingston's motion took Madison by surprise, but Gallatin entered the debate with vigor because his speech on the Mint had prepared him. The question was whether the House had the right to withhold the appropriations needed to execute a properly ratified treaty. Gallatin claimed that it did because otherwise the president and the Senate could use treaties to exercise the spending power that the Constitution had specifically entrusted to the people's representatives in the House. Reading Gallatin's speech from his retirement in Virginia, Jefferson declared himself "enchanted." It should be "printed at the end of the Federalist," he told Madison, as "the only rational commentary" on the fiscal prerogatives of the House. He acknowledged a few difficulties in Gallatin's constitutional analysis, but he was willing to swallow them down because he thought that any other conclusion would "annihilate the whole of the powers given by the constitution to the legislature." Madison—burdened by his memory of debates on the treaty power in the Federal Convention—was less decisive. In a long speech to the House, which legal scholars still cite for its expedient reference to the state ratifying conventions as the best evidence of original intent, Madison sifted through five alternative views on the question before cautiously concluding that Gallatin was right. Madison's conscience, Federalist Fisher Ames archly observed, "made him a coward."[21]

After weeks of debate, the House passed a resolution calling for the diplomatic papers by a vote of 62–37. Gallatin and Livingston presented it to the president the next day. That was the high-water mark for opposition to Jay's treaty. A few days later, Washington refused to deliver the papers. Federalists around the country organized meetings and petitions in favor of the treaty, and the Republicans' majority in the House began to melt away. "The prevailing party in the House of Representatives,"

John Jay wrote to Washington as he watched the change in sentiment, "appear to me to be digging their political grave."[22]

Gallatin immediately came under pressure from the Western Country. To the Republicans in Congress, Jay's treaty represented a capitulation to British mercantile interests brought on by a Federalist fiscal system that depended on revenue from British trade. But men on the frontier had a very different perspective. Their prospects depended on peace with the Native Americans, land, and access to markets down the great rivers of the interior. Federal troops had finally managed to win a victory over the Natives in the summer of 1794, and some of the tribes had ceded enormous tracts of land to the federal government at the Treaty of Greenville a year later. Those cessions raised hopes that Britain's evacuation of its forts on the frontier could help to fulfill. And just as the House had begun debating the British Treaty, Westerners got word of a new treaty with Spain that gave Americans the right to navigate the Mississippi and land goods at New Orleans. The pieces fitted together so well that it was easy to believe—as Federalists claimed—that the British, Spanish, and Indian treaties depended on each other.[23]

Gallatin soon found himself backed into a corner. Hugh Henry Brackenridge, who had lost to Gallatin in his bid for Congress, got the Presbyterian minister who had nominated Gallatin to organize a petition in favor of the British Treaty. Brackenridge may have honestly thought that a defeat for the treaty would damage the Republican cause, but Gallatin must have sensed political menace in his maneuver. Gallatin dutifully presented Western petitions to the House, and he began to equivocate. He persuaded a Republican caucus—one of the first party caucuses ever held—to limit the party's objective to securing a separate vote on each of the three treaties. He then got the House to fund the Spanish treaty, the one most important to his constituents, without a roll call vote in order to minimize Republicans' embarrassment. But his final speech on the British Treaty showed him still struggling to balance his party's position against his constituents' interests. He first repeated the Republican objections to the treaty, then said he would vote to fund it just to end the standoff, and finally tried to postpone the vote. In the end, he voted against treaty funding when it passed by just three votes. William Findley was caught skulking to avoid the vote.[24]

It was a disheartening performance. Still, Gallatin came off better than he could have expected in the Western press. "Your Gallatin is half a Frenchman," one correspondent wrote to the Federalist *Pittsburgh Gazette.* "I can no other way account for his infatuation in opposing the treaty so interesting to your country." But another writer thought Gallatin was simply a stubborn "enthusiast" like the hapless Anacharsis Cloots, a foreign idealist who had lost his life in the French Reign of Terror. As the autumn 1796 election approach, other writers defended Gallatin. He was indeed half a Frenchman, one resolutely declared, because "he is a friend of liberty and equality." "Why are the Federal faction opposed to GALLATIN?" asked an election broadside. The answer was clear: "Because he is a friend of the People."[25]

Gallatin attracted greater abuse from other quarters. Satirists found his homeliness, French accent, and whiff of sedition irresistible, and they took to stigmatizing the Congressional Republicans as "Gallatin & Co." But implicit in their abuse was the recognition that Gallatin had emerged from the treaty debate as the leading Republican in Congress. Harrison Gray Otis, a well-to-do lawyer who had studied French under Gallatin at Harvard, marveled that such a man could be "the *leader* of the majority in Congress." "Shall we join a vagrant foreigner in opposition to a Washington," he asked a Boston public meeting; "a foreigner who to [my] knowledge ten years ago came to this Country without a *second shirt to his back?* A man who in comparison to Washington is like a Satyre to a Hyperian?" Peter Porcupine was more venomous. "Murderers," he spat, always choose "some preciously ill-looking villain to give the first stab." Then Porcupine pivoted to give his own parting stab to "Citizen Madison." This former chief of the Republican villains, he said, "has so sunk out of sight this campaign that we can look upon him...as no more than an aide-de-camp...without even the hope of repairing his reputation. As a politician he is no more; he is absolutely deceased, cold, stiff and buried in oblivion for ever and ever." A Boston paper dismissed Madison as a mere "file-coverer for an itinerant Genevan."[26]

Gallatin's rapid emergence as a leader of Congress was astonishing, and late in life he still seemed slightly bemused by it. "I was destitute of eloquence," he remembered, "and had to surmount the great obstacles of speaking in a foreign language with a very bad pronunciation." The advantages that paved his way to success, he thought, were "laborious investigation, habits of analysis, thorough knowledge of the subjects under discussion, more intensive general information due to an excellent early education; to which I think I may add quickness of apprehension and a sound judgement." A well-connected young British visitor named David Erskine who met Gallatin at the time made a similar assessment. Erskine was a close observer of American politics, and he later returned as the British minister to the United States. He pegged Gallatin as "an artful, hard headed & ambitious man, well conversant in political knowledge & extremely assiduous in collecting every information that can be useful to him."[27]

But other factors contributed to Gallatin's success. Despite the effort it cost him to speak, his speeches were persuasive. His arguments were clear, and he did not resort to the sharp rhetoric that was becoming increasingly common in partisan debates. He had the benefit of the information, acquaintances, and reputation acquired during five years at the Pennsylvania state house just down the street. The combination of his elite background and his republican lifestyle allowed him to mix with men of all sorts. And apart from Madison, Livingston, and Virginians William Branch Giles and John Nicholas, few other Republican members stood out. Indeed, an embittered newspaper editor later complained that the abuse Gallatin had received from the Federalists actually helped to make him a political celebrity. Whatever its causes, Gallatin's rapid emergence was singular at the time. Not until future chief justice John Marshall emerged as a Federalist leader in 1799–1800 did another freshman Congressman take leadership so quickly.[28]

Madison had quickly recognized the particular importance of Gallatin's financial talent as he watched him at work in the Ways and Means committee. Gallatin was, Madison enthusiastically reported to Jefferson, "sound in his principles, accurate in his calculations &

indefatigable in his researches." The Genevan could grasp matters that Hamilton previously had managed to keep just beyond the Republicans' reach. "Who could have supposed," wrote Madison, "that Hamilton could have gone off in the triumph he assumed, with such a condition of the finances behind him?" Gallatin's ability to show where Hamilton had faltered gave the opposition a vital new advantage. It also gave Gallatin an important opportunity to solidify his leadership position, and he was eager to make the most of it. In the summer recess—spent with his pregnant wife at the Nicholsons' house in New York—Gallatin wrote a two-hundred-page book about public finance.[29]

Gallatin's *Sketch of the Finances of the United States* was an indictment of Hamilton's fiscal policies and a proposal for reform. But the book differed from most other Republican productions of the period in three ways. First, it lacked the partisan cant so typical in Republican literature. It scarcely mentioned federal consolidation, executive aggrandizement, and the corruption of Congress. Gallatin instead stuck to an argument based on conventional liberal theories of political economy. Adam Smith had synthesized those theories in his *Wealth of Nations*, and important passages in Gallatin's *Sketch* paraphrased Smith's book. Gallatin's tone was measured and reasonable. Parts of his book were so anodyne that they left some readers puzzling over his motives. At one point, Gallatin even conceded that the loan misapplication for which Giles had hounded Hamilton was an insignificant technical violation.[30]

Second, Gallatin's book did not embrace standard Republican orthodoxies. It barely mentioned hobbyhorses such as the failure to discriminate between public creditors and the corruptive potential of the Bank of the United States. Rather than carp about unjust windfalls to rich men who speculated in federal bonds, for example, it deplored the overall economic cost of diverting scarce capital into speculation.[31]

Finally, Gallatin's book was an unusual exercise in quantitative analysis. It exhausted over half of its two hundred pages—and perhaps most of its readers—with facts and figures and discussions of those facts and figures before coming to its main argument. The book aimed to explain the administration's fiscal shortcomings to the attentive and the numerate, not to sling slogans to excite the indignant.[32]

Hamilton's claim that a funded debt can produce public benefits, Gallatin argued, was simply mistaken. The funding system made it easier for the government to borrow money, borrowing led to greater government spending, and government spending consumed capital that the people could have used for more productive purposes. The federal bonds were not a sound medium for exchange or savings because their value would sink as the public debt increased. Bond ownership might make moneyed men more loyal to the federal government, but their self-interested support was as likely to harm the rest of the people as to help them. Mounting debt benefited wealthy debt holders and speculators at the expense of the ordinary taxpayers who had to pay the interest. Reducing the debt would leave taxpayers more money for their own businesses and government more money to make internal improvements.[33]

Hamilton's contrary view on public debt, Gallatin continued, had led to expensive mistakes. The most obvious was the careless assumption of the states' war debts before anyone knew the amount of those debts. If offsetting obligations had been identified and canceled, the federal government could have saved about $11 million—15 percent of its original debt of $74 million. Almost as egregious, Gallatin claimed, was the inadequacy of Hamilton's arrangements for debt repayment. The law passed shortly after Hamilton left the Treasury dealt with only a part of the federal debt, and the nominal repayments made under that law had not actually reduced the debt because the government still spent more money than it got. A less obvious but more profound problem with Hamilton's system was the encouragement it gave to speculation. Rising debt made bond prices unstable, and price fluctuations encouraged the wealthy to trade bonds instead of investing their money in trade, manufacturing, roads, and canals.[34]

Having delivered his critique, Gallatin turned to reform proposals. His book made three. First, the federal government must reduce spending, particularly military spending. As long as the European nations were locked in enervating wars of their own, Gallatin said, there was little chance that the United States would have to defend itself. The United States would grow stronger by improving its public finances than by building a military establishment because the incommensurate army and navy that it could afford would be useless against the larger forces that European nations could deploy.[35]

Second, the government must reform its tax system to increase revenues. The nation's wealth was in land and commerce, not in manufacturing. Excise taxes on manufactured products were therefore misdirected and self-defeating. They also were expensive to collect. Import duties were appropriate and productive, but their revenue potential was limited because higher rates of duty increased the incentive to smuggle. Import duties also fell more heavily on the Southern states because they manufactured fewer goods than the Northern states. Direct taxes on land were the solution, and they could also resolve an existing tax inequity. The Constitution required direct taxes to be apportioned among the states in proportion to their populations. The amount of land tax apportioned to the heavily populated Northern states would therefore be higher per acre than the amount apportioned to the thinly populated Southern states. That would help to offset the disproportionate tax burden that Hamilton's reliance on import duties had thrown onto the Southern states.[36]

Third, the government must sell more public land and use the money to repay the Revolutionary War debt. It was appropriate to use the national patrimony to pay the price of national liberty, and well-managed land sales would expand settlement and promote national development. But federal land law would have to be reformed in order to increase sales. The current price per acre was too high to attract land speculators, and the credit terms were too tight to accommodate actual settlers.[37]

⚬⚬⚬

By the time Congress reconvened in December 1796, important changes were taking place. John Adams had just been elected president in the first contested presidential election, and he was set to take office in March. Thomas Jefferson, who had come within three electoral votes of beating Adams, was going to be vice president. James Madison was planning to retire to Virginia with his new wife Dolley Todd, the buxom young widow of a Philadelphia lawyer. Hannah Gallatin was at her parents' house in New York awaiting the birth of her first child. Albert Gallatin had been reelected to Congress by a wide margin despite complaints that he lived outside his Congressional district and seldom visited the Western Country. But some of the other Republican Congressmen had not been so lucky, and the Republicans expected to find themselves in a clear minority.[38]

Washington condescended to invite Gallatin for dinner on a cold winter evening about a month before he stepped aside for John Adams. Albert reported to Hannah that he had donned "my new, or rather my only good coat, my new jacket, and my pair of black silk inexpressibles" for the occasion. It was the first time he had seen Washington all year, and he thought the president looked "more than usually grave, cool, and reserved." Washington's dinners with members of Congress were notoriously solemn affairs—sometimes eaten almost in silence—and this one was no exception. Mrs. Washington continued to be "a very good-natured and amiable woman," Albert told Hannah. "Not so her husband, in your husband's humble opinion; but that between you and me, for I hate treason, and you know that it would be less sacrilegious to carry arms against our country than to refuse singing" praises to "the best and greatest of men." He knew Hannah and her feisty father would smile at that. Although Washington had been a formidable obstacle for the Republicans, Gallatin and many of the others now saw him as the plodder Gallatin remembered from their first encounter in the wilderness a dozen years earlier.[39]

Shortly after he took office, John Adams called the new Congress into an early spring session. Both Britain and France had been disrupting trade and seizing American ships in order to starve each other into submission, but France had grown particularly hostile. The French Directory saw the American rapprochement with Britain as a threat, and they claimed that the new American treaty with Britain violated American obligations to France under the treaty that the two countries had made during the American Revolution. The Directory had meddled in the American presidential election to support Jefferson, sent agents to promote old French territorial claims in the Mississippi country, and escalated seizures of American ships on the Atlantic. Now, miffed over the Washington administration's substitution of the Federalist Charles Cotesworth Pinckney for the Republican James Monroe as the American minister to France, the Directory had expelled Pinckney. Adams proposed to send a special diplomatic mission to France, but he also asked Congress to let American merchant ships arm themselves, to enlarge the navy, and to form a provisional army. All of this threatened to make the new Congress even more contentious than the last one.[40]

For the next year, Gallatin and the Republican minority kept up a steady opposition to the administration's military buildup. They condemned the attempt to parlay the foreign crisis into muscular measures, and Gallatin hammered away with the arguments he had made in the last Congress and in his book. He professed to believe that a standing army posed less danger to the people than to government itself. Nothing so weakened a government as "the want of money," he said, and "nothing consumed so much of it as a large military establishment." The young American nation's reputation in the world depended more on its fiscal strength than its military pretensions. Money spent projecting hollow power now would retard development of the resources needed to project real power later. Gallatin even opposed funding for military contracts with businesses in his own Congressional district.[41]

"The house is almost equally divided," a Federalist senator grumbled, and the minority "under the *controul* of the Genevese, are a well organized & disciplined Corps, never going astray, or doing right even by mistake." But the intensity of the legislative battle began to take its toll on the Republicans. Gallatin was uncommonly anxious, he told his wife. Nicholas was almost in a fever, Livingston kept running off to New York, and others fell ill. As relations with France degenerated into an undeclared naval fight known as the Quasi-War, the Republican position was not sustainable. Commodore Nicholson—writing with his usual bluster—berated "those irritating fellows who say all they can devise to provoke the french to war with us, & are themselves, I have no doubt Cowards, but [say] not [a] word against their friends the English." Jefferson's letters expressed similar frustration with the Federalists' willingness to overlook continued British interferences with American trade. But Gallatin had no illusions about the real problem. The French, he wrote to his wife, "behave even worse than I was afraid from their haughtiness they would. May God save us from war!"[42]

When the administration reported the failure of its peace mission to France in March 1798, the Republican opposition faltered. Livingston, Giles, and Nicholas allowed themselves to be trapped into a call for the diplomatic papers, which Adams promptly delivered. The papers revealed that French agents designated as X, Y, and Z had sought bribes from the American envoys as a predicate for negotiations. The revelation sparked widespread outrage against France. The outrage sharpened anxieties about the infiltration of political radicals into the United States, and those anxieties fueled nativist reactions to the flow of refugees from the revolution in France, repression in Ireland, and slave revolt in Saint-Domingue. Men wearing Federalist black cockades clashed in the streets with men wearing Republican tricolors, and some of the French émigrés in Philadelphia prepared to flee again. "*He who is not with us, is against us,*" trumpeted the pro-administration *Gazette of the United States.* Because the French boasted that they had a party in the United States, said Abigail Adams, the men in the Republican opposition "ought to be carefully marked."[43]

The Federalist majority in Congress began adopting repressive measures. A new Naturalization Act extended the period for citizenship from five to fourteen years. Two Alien Acts authorized the president to deport all enemy aliens and any other alien he deemed dangerous. And a Sedition Act criminalized any collaboration to oppose government measures and any false statements intended to bring government officials into disrepute. Gallatin and other Republicans tried to defeat those measures, but they had lost their footing. The "Jesuit Gallatin is as subtle and as artfull and designing as ever," wrote Abigail Adams, "but meets with a more decided opposition."[44]

The abuse hurled at Gallatin on the floor of the House grew much sharper. References to American Jacobins and the Western Insurrection were painfully pointed. A "Frenchman is a Frenchman," Gallatin's former student Harrison Gray Otis told him in one debate. Naturalization "does not alter his character; he is still called, and known to be a Frenchman." Robert Goodloe Harper, a Federalist who chaired the Ways and Means committee, declared that persons born outside the United States should not be allowed "to take part in the Government." Some New England legislatures took a similar tack, proposing a federal constitutional amendment to exclude from Congress anyone who had not been a citizen for at least fourteen years when he was elected. The amendment targeted Gallatin, who had been a citizen for only thirteen years at the last election.[45]

Gallatin was dismissive about the amendment's chance of success, but in a long letter to James Witter Nicholson—the brother-in-law who managed his affairs in Fayette County—he confessed to feeling isolated. Livingston, Nicholas, and Giles had all gone home. "I remain almost alone to bear the irksome burden of opposition," he wrote, "but I consider it a sacred duty to remain firm to the post." One of Hamilton's confidants gloated that Gallatin could now only "clog" the wheels of government. Jefferson stayed in Philadelphia to preside over the Senate, and the political persecution that he and Gallatin shared during what Jefferson later called the "reign of witches" welded a firm bond between them. Late in life, Jefferson vividly remembered that "mr Gallatin alone remain[ed] in the H. of R. and myself in the Senate…bidding defiance to the brow beatings and insults with which they assailed us."[46]

Gallatin's unusually even disposition helped him weather the storm. He refused to rise to Federalist taunts, and he rarely even mentioned them in public. He kept up a dogged opposition without resorting to the invective that he heard from all sides. "Your papa has not yet answered my last political letter," he wrote to his wife during one particularly tense period. "I am afraid he thinks me too moderate and believes that I am going to trim. But moderation and firmness have ever been and ever will be my motto." Yet despite his apparent equanimity, Gallatin was not entirely impervious to the abuse. He could not resist telling the House that Ways and Means chairman Robert Goodloe Harper simply did not understand the revenue figures. And in a witty and extended display of his own quantitative acuity, he lampooned Harper for miscalculating the supermajority vote needed to pass a constitutional amendment. Harper gracefully conceded Gallatin's wit on that occasion, but Gallatin's biting comment about his failure to understand the revenue figures so rankled Harper that he mentioned it in a debate almost two years later.[47]

Gallatin took more than his share of verbal abuse because he was the very incarnation of Federalist anxieties. Federalist Congressmen who quoted the second Pittsburgh meeting's resolutions and derided Gallatin for "preaching up the rights of man" were afraid that disorderly democratic forces could undermine the American republic just as they had subverted the republican experiment in France. Uneasiness about identity, hierarchy, and social order was pervasive. Even Edward Livingston revealed more than he intended when he stood up for Gallatin against Harrison Gray Otis, a haughty man from origins far less exalted than Livingston's. Livingston was almost tempted to smile, he told Otis, at the arrogant pretensions of some men who mistreated members who were their equals in the House "whatever they might be out of doors." What one historian has called the "once tight braid of social, economic, and political authority" was visibly unraveling. Thomas Paine's *Rights of Man* and the writings by other foreign radicals who had fled to America tugged on the loosened strands, attacking traditional institutions and criticizing measures that Federalists believed necessary to social order. External threats to the weak nation's shipping and commercial interests increased the sense of anxiety. A foreigner with intelligent black eyes was just the sort of man that the Federalist novelist Charles Brockden Brown had fashioned into his villain Carwin, an artful ventriloquist who projected subversive ideas that brought murder and disorder to a peaceful family in the American Eden.[48]

The Quasi-War with France allowed Congress and the administration to increase military preparations. Without adequate naval protection, American shipping lay open to new French spoliations. The cost of maritime insurance spiked, commerce slowed, and national pride suffered. The resulting sense of vulnerability made irrational fears of a French invasion seem plausible. Federalists exploited those fears to establish a Navy department, a Provisional Army, an Additional Army, and finally an Eventual Army. They recalled Washington to command, and Hamilton scrambled over his seniors in military service to get himself appointed as second in command. To argue—as Gallatin did— for balancing the actual cost of lost shipping against the much greater cost of war ran counter to the national mood. No "American," sneered Porcupine, would think of making such things *"a mere matter of calculation."* Robert Goodloe Harper belittled Gallatin's arguments as "the calculation of a schoolboy, not a statesman; of the countinghouse, not the cabinet." All nations, Harper said, had to borrow to pay for war. "We also must submit to the common necessity, or submit to the power of those who assail us." Even commercially minded Republicans such as Congressman Samuel Smith, a successful merchant from Baltimore, clashed with Gallatin because they too supported the creation of a larger navy.[49]

Increased military spending drove Congress to pass the first direct tax, a one-time $2 million assessment on real property and slaves. The House had approved a direct tax on land and slaves in the previous Congress, but then dropped it in favor of other measures. Necessity now drove Congress back to the idea. Direct taxes were unpopular. Indirect taxes such as import duties and excises only raised the price of the goods subject to tax, and since most of those goods were not necessities, cash-strapped farmers and workers could avoid most of the tax burden by avoiding luxury goods. Direct taxes, on the other hand, required all property owners to come up with money to pay the tax. Direct taxes also required assessment and collection throughout the country rather than simply at the ports or places of production. And as Gallatin had pointed out in his book, a land tax would hit farmers in densely populated Northeastern states more heavily than farmers elsewhere.[50]

Gallatin, Madison, and many other Republicans had supported direct taxes in principle for several reasons. They thought a revenue base that was less vulnerable to trade disruptions could free the government from its dependence on British trade. That would give the United States a freer hand in foreign policy. They also thought that ordinary people were more likely to resist government spending if the tax cost of that spending was more obvious to them. And they thought the heavier burden thrown on farmers in the North was a fair offset for the heavier burden that import duties threw on farmers in the South and West. Republicans also may have believed, as one insightful historian has argued, that heavier taxes on Northern farmers would help to alienate them from the Federalist administration. But by the time Congress passed the $2 million direct tax, the Federalists had found a twist to solve that problem. The direct tax law required houses to be assessed separately from land and taxed first, so farm land in a densely populated state would bear no tax at all if the amount raised from houses and slaves was enough to satisfy the state's quota. This arrangement spread among all householders the burden that otherwise would have fallen disproportionately on farmers.[51]

Gallatin helped to amend the direct tax bill so that the tax rates were more progressive, but he ultimately voted against it. He claimed that the separate assessment of houses would increase the tax on modest farmhouses, which added very little to the taxable value of the land on which they stood. He also thought the administration would waste the tax money. It seemed clear that the threat of a French invasion was a pure delusion, and it would be almost impossible for the navy to build new ships in time to be useful. When the people finally saw through the Federalist scaremongering, they would turn on the men who had taxed them to pay for this useless military buildup. "I cannot believe," Gallatin wrote, "that the system of deception upon the people, which has brought this country to its present state, can last long." Jefferson, as usual, said it with more flair. The war fever will soon pass, he assured his friend John Taylor; "the Doctor is now on his way to cure it, in the guise of a taxgatherer."[52]

But the war fever was still raging in the autumn of 1798 when Gallatin spent a night in Reading, Pennsylvania, on his way home. Bells rung to honor his arrival prompted a Federalist crowd to retaliate by serenading him through the night. The next morning, the crowd burned him in effigy as he was helping Hannah Gallatin and her youngest sister Adden Nicholson into a carriage in front of their lodgings. But the crowd was disappointed, an unfriendly chronicler related, when the "old fox" himself gave them the slip by decamping "down the *back* alley as fast as his horse would carry him."[53]

Electioneering in Gallatin's Congressional district was more complicated than ever. Brackenridge—who had a longstanding personal grudge against Gallatin's Federalist opponent—feared Gallatin would lose. He first tried to set up John Nevill's son as a third candidate to split the Federalist vote, and when that failed he threw his own hat into the ring. Gallatin wrote electioneering letters to the newspapers for the first time. The local Republican paper covered its entire front page with an anonymous letter (almost certainly from William Findley) sharply distinguishing Gallatin's native Geneva from belligerent France and lauding Gallatin's past political service. In the end, Gallatin won the election with about the same margin he had two years earlier. But he and his party remained an embattled minority in Congress. The Federalist majority continued to expand the military establishment, and the Republicans found themselves unable to resist domestic repression. When Gallatin—armed with petitions from more than 18,000 Pennsylvania voters—began to rally support for repealing the Alien and Sedition Acts, Federalist members silenced further debate by shuffling, coughing, and making other disruptive noises.[54]

Although Gallatin opposed the military buildup, it brought him a business opportunity. Through his friend Alexander Dallas, Pennsylvania's chief administrative officer, Gallatin got a contract to make muskets for the Pennsylvania militia. He and his partners had established a small manufacturing village on the Monongahela River across Georges Creek from Gallatin's farm. They called the place New Geneva. It had begun to take shape in 1795 when Gallatin, his friend John Badollet, his brother-in-law James Witter Nicholson, and two Genevan émigrés formed a partnership to develop the 650-acre site, build mills and houses, and sell house lots. They launched the venture just as Gallatin entered Congress, and it soon became an additional worry for the absent entrepreneur. The work did not proceed smoothly, the partners bickered with each other, and the risks they assumed back in New Geneva troubled a careful man who was not there to hear their explanations. A glassworks was running up debts that would grow for years before it started producing glass in profitable quantities. The musket contract drew the partners into yet another risky endeavor. Should they fail to deliver the muskets, Gallatin fretted, they would lose $26,000—more than either he or the partnership was worth.[55]

The partnership's debt gave Gallatin particular anxiety. "To be in debt is to me the worst of all possible situations," he told Maria Nicholson, the sister-in-law with whom he was closest. As long as he remained in debt, he told her, he would have "no rest and no peace of mind." To his wife Gallatin confided that he had always viewed debt "with a kind of horror," and he bemoaned the "egregious folly" of giving others the power to put him in debt. He confessed that he worried about all of this much more than he ought to. The whole partnership business, he lamented to Maria Nicholson early in 1800, was "extremely disagreeable" and "still more distressing to my feelings on account of its consequences." He did not know whether he could end the arrangement on honorable terms without ruining himself and her brother James.[56]

Later that year, Gallatin did buy out his partners and entrust management of the New Geneva venture to James Witter Nicholson. The young man liked living in the West. He married a woman from a locally prominent family and settled down in New Geneva. He eventually proved to be a reasonably sound manager, but Gallatin remained apprehensive about the business for many years. "The fact is," he explained to an old friend, "I am not well calculated to make money,—I care but little about it, for I want but little myself, and my mind pursues other objects with more pleasure than mere business."[57]

The collapse of other prospects doubtless heightened Gallatin's anxiety about the business in New Geneva. Gallatin had sold most of his Western land claims to Robert Morris shortly after he married Hannah

Nicholson, but Morris fell into debtors' prison in February 1798, leaving most of his note for the purchase price unpaid. It soon became clear that Morris was insolvent, and his note—one of Gallatin's principal financial assets—became worthless. The settlement of Gallatin's grandfather's estate in Geneva later that year brought another disappointment. It left Gallatin with a small debt rather than the modest additional inheritance he had expected. The real property sold for less than half, he thought, of what it would have brought before the French Revolution unleashed a revolution in Geneva. "You may see," he explained to Hannah, "that the French revolution has cost me exactly 16,000 dollars. . . . Yet the Federals call me a Frenchman, in the French interest and forsooth in the French pay. Let them clamor. I want no reward but self-approbation,—and yours, my beloved, too."[58]

CHAPTER 5

REPUBLICAN
TRIUMPH

In October 1799, the Republicans in Pennsylvania managed to get
Thomas McKean elected governor. It was an important show of their
growing popular strength and a portent—they hoped—of Thomas Jefferson's prospects in the presidential election of 1800.[1]

The Federalist regime had weakened in 1799. The $2 million direct
tax provoked the sort of popular complaints many had predicted. President Adams heard them himself as he traveled home to Massachusetts.
Ham-fisted tax assessment in rural counties just outside Philadelphia had
sparked armed resistance from German-speaking communities there that
had been reliably Federalist. Republican leaders worried that Fries's
Rebellion—as this latest tax uprising came to be called—could swing
public opinion back toward the administration, but the administration's
heavy-handed use of troops against the tax resisters had just the opposite
effect. The expensive military buildup that had prompted Congress to
impose the direct tax in the first place also lost support when French

naval defeats revealed the threat of a French invasion as the delusion it always had been. Prosecutions of several Republican newspaper editors under the Sedition Act—including the rowdy Matthew Lyon who got himself reelected to Congress while he was locked in jail—provoked relatively little popular outcry, but they did cement the commitment of Republican partisans.[2]

The Federalists failed to respond with the necessary unity. In a show of political courage, recklessness, or both, President Adams had surprised the members of his own administration early in the year by announcing a new peace mission to France. The peace mission dented the justification for the military buildup, the cabinet opposed it, and many leading Federalists lost confidence in Adams. Alexander Hamilton was aghast over Adams's decision. Hamilton had maneuvered to have Southern Federalist Thomas Pinckney elected instead of Adams in 1796, and now—with his own ego and political prospects bound up in the new army—Hamilton again tried to undercut Adams's presidential candidacy. By the end of 1799, prominent Federalists were already musing in their private letters about the possibility that the presidential election might go to the House of Representatives.[3]

The first few months of 1800 put the Federalists' apprehensions on display. The Senate took up a bill that would have given a Congressional select committee the power to decide which presidential electoral votes to count when the states sent their returns to Congress. James Ross, a Federalist senator from Pennsylvania who had just lost the gubernatorial election to McKean, introduced the bill. The two houses of the Pennsylvania legislature had failed to agree on a procedure for choosing the state's presidential electors, and Ross's bill appeared to be a transparent attempt to let the Federalist majority in Congress award Pennsylvania's electoral votes to Adams if the state failed to come up with a single slate. When William Duane published a leaked copy of Ross's bill in his Philadelphia *Aurora*, the Senate tried to cover their embarrassment by hauling him before them for breach of senatorial privilege. Then they capped off this comedy of political errors by refusing to hear Duane's main defense—a blunder that allowed Duane's politically savvy lawyers,

Alexander Dallas and radical English émigré Thomas Cooper, to stage a theatrical withdrawal from the case.[4]

While Federalists in the Senate were taking this characteristically authoritarian approach, Aaron Burr and his small cadre of Republican organizers in New York were pioneering urban democracy. Their goal was to elect a Republican majority to the New York legislature, which would choose New York's presidential electors. Many thought that New York's electoral votes could decide the presidential election and that New York City's votes would determine who controlled the state legislature. Burr rose to this challenge with energy and imagination. He wrangled the city's leading Republicans onto the party's ticket, and—using methods that were unprecedented at the time—he and his team of aides spent months systematically identifying and canvassing the city's voters. Their headquarters was Burr's house on the northern edge of the city, but they often worked and ate at Commodore Nicholson's house in the center of town. Matthew Livingston Davis, a devoted lieutenant whom Burr had scooped up from far down the social scale, kept Gallatin informed through a stream of letters. Stuffed with sedulous praise for Burr and smarmy chatter about the Nicholsons, the letters were meant to make it impossible for Gallatin to deny Burr the reward he had in mind. "Republicanism Triumphant," Davis crowed at midnight after the polls had closed. "To Col Burr we are indebted for everything."[5]

Letters from Albert Gallatin and Commodore Nicholson soon crossed in the mail. Congress was about to recess for the summer, and the Republican members had caucused to choose a vice presidential candidate. They agreed that the candidate should come from New York, and they asked Gallatin to find out whether the New York Republicans preferred George Clinton or Aaron Burr. Albert relayed the question to New York in a long letter to Hannah. He knew that she would handle the matter discreetly, and he probably thought a snoopy Federalist postmaster was less likely to open a personal letter to her than a franked letter from a member of Congress addressed to her father.[6]

The question was a delicate one. Clinton and Burr led different political factions in a state where party affiliations remained fluid. Clinton was a sixty-year-old Revolutionary hero who had served as the state's governor for eighteen years before retiring in 1795. He possessed great influence, but he claimed to be tired of politics. He had clung to retirement until Burr persuaded him to lend luster to the Republican ticket in this critical election by running for a seat in the legislature. Burr was a handsome, dark-haired man seventeen years younger than Clinton. He too had fought in the Revolution, after which he had gone into law and politics. Burr had defeated Alexander Hamilton's father-in-law for a seat in the Senate, where he had led the unsuccessful fight to save Gallatin's seat in 1794. Nakedly ambitious, Burr had managed to position himself—despite his relative youth—as the Republican vice presidential candidate in 1796. But while Jefferson came within three electoral votes of beating Adams in that election, Burr finished far behind all of the other candidates because electors in Virginia and other Southern states abandoned him. He was now an influential member of the New York legislature.[7]

The letter that Nicholson had already sent to Gallatin anticipated the delicate question about the vice presidential nomination. "I cannot inform You what either Burr or [Clinton's] expectations are," Nicholson wrote. He promised to write again as soon as he had spoken with his "friend & neighbor Govr Clinton," but he made his own sympathies clear. The result of the city election was so "Miraculous," he said, "that I cannot account for it but from the intervention of A Supreme Power & our friend Burr the Agent." Burr is "a General far superior to your Hambletons, as much so, as A Man is to A Boy," and he "deserves any thing & every thing of His Country."[8]

The next day, Nicholson reported that Clinton wanted to stay in retirement and therefore would endorse Burr. Other New York Republicans' confidence in Burr was, he said, "universal & unbounded." But there was a problem. Burr would not agree to run again without assurances that the party's Southern electors would not dishonor him this time. "I confidently hope," Nicholson told Gallatin, "you will be able to Smooth over the business of the last Election." A separate letter from Hannah Gallatin was more explicit. "Burr says he has no confidence in the Virginians," she told her husband; "they once deceived him, and they are not to be trusted." A few days later, Albert reported back to Hannah that the Republicans in Congress had "unanimously agreed to support Burr for Vice-President." He said that the Virginians and the New Yorkers, at least, had pledged to cast their votes equally for Jefferson and Burr. The deal had been struck, the seeds of a tied presidential election planted.[9]

Gallatin spent the early summer at the Nicholsons' house producing a short campaign book. *Views of the Public Debt, Receipts and Expenditures of the United States*—which Matthew Livingston Davis and his brother printed in August—had two objectives. It aimed to show voters that the Federalist administrations had increased the public debt by $6.7 to $9.5 million—9 to 12 percent of the total debt now outstanding. By giving a confident explanation of those estimates, the book also aimed to demonstrate its author's mastery of federal finance. The *Aurora* touted Gallatin's book, and Republican organizers distributed copies up and down the coast. But Federalist partisans focused on the message between the lines and took direct aim at the author's pretensions. It was clear, wrote Fisher Ames, that "Gallatin pants for Wolcott's place." How on earth, a Boston newspaper asked its readers, could anyone possibly think of replacing a good Treasury secretary like Oliver Wolcott with a "whiskey-patriot"?[10]

Assembled in the City of Washington for the first time, Congress got confirmation of earlier reports that Jefferson and Burr had received the same number of electoral votes. "This has produced great dismay and gloom on the republican gentlemen here," Jefferson wrote to Madison, "and equal exultation on the federalists, who openly declare they will prevent an election" and name the president *pro tempore* of the Senate to be chief executive. In the case of a tied electoral vote, the Constitution directed the House to choose a president from among the contenders, with each state delegation casting one vote. There were sixteen states in the Union, so it would take nine states to elect Jefferson. But in the House, which had been elected during the war scare of 1798, Republicans controlled only eight delegations. Federalists controlled six, and Maryland and Vermont were evenly split. There were rumors, Jefferson told Madison, that a Federalist in one of the split delegations would vote for Jefferson to avert a crisis. Although no one could be sure of that, Jefferson conceded, he had already contacted the man he wanted as his Secretary of the Navy. "The person proposed for the T[reasury]," however, had "not come yet."[11]

Gallatin arrived a month later. He had been in Fayette County since late summer. He had contested and won his seat in the next Congress. But business and reluctance to leave Hannah Gallatin alone had detained him. This would be Hannah's second winter in the West, and the couple had agreed it would be her last. Although they had enlarged the house at Friendship Hill about two years earlier, she found life there uncongenial. Her letters to Albert after he left for Washington described her loneliness, fears, and frustrations. She loved her sons—four-year-old James and a one-year-old named Albert Rolaz—but she missed adult companionship. It was difficult to find help, so she had to rehire a man who often showed up only for meals. Because she had refused to pay the higher price a farmer demanded for a steer he had fed longer than they agreed, she was without meat for the rest of the winter. She hinted at a new pregnancy. "I am fully convinced," Albert reassured her, "that you cannot live happy where you are." They would move as soon as he could find a way to support them "this side of the mountain." Perhaps to protect himself from disappointment or in recognition that political disappointment might require a change in plans, he mulled over the possibility of moving to New York and studying to practice law.[12]

Albert's letters to his wife contain some of the best early descriptions of Washington. He arrived through cold rain and snow and took lodgings with Jefferson and other leading Republicans at Conrad and McMunn's boardinghouse just south of the unfinished Capitol. "The situation" in Washington, he reported to Hannah, "is far from pleasant or even convenient." Besides seven or eight boardinghouses, "the whole of the Federal city as connected with the Capitol" consists of "one tailor, one shoemaker, one printer, a washing-woman, a grocery store, a pamphlets and stationery shop, a small dry-good shop, and an oyster house." Nearby on the Potomac's Eastern Branch (now called the Anacostia) were "half a dozen houses, a very large but perfectly empty warehouse & a wharf graced by not a single vessel." What others called "magnificent distances" beyond the Capitol heights caught his attention less than an intervening swamp fed by a small stream "with the profuse appellation of Tyber." The President's House was elegant, and he thought the part of the federal district around it might one day become a pleasant town like Lancaster or Annapolis. "The company is good enough," he said, "but it is always the same." The cosmopolitan Federalist senator Gouverneur Morris was more caustic. All that Washington needed to be a perfect city, he told a friend in Europe, was "houses, wine cellars, kitchens, educated men, amiable women, and a few other such trifles."[13]

By the time Gallatin arrived, the gloom Jefferson had described to Madison seemed more menacing. Imprudent as it seemed to Hamilton and most of the other Federalists who were not cooped up in Washington, the Federalist Congressmen had decided to keep Jefferson out by putting Burr in. Burr's reputation as an ambitious man with flexible principles made the strategy seem plausible. If Burr depended on them to get elected, the Federalist members convinced themselves, he would have to depend on them once he took office. And if Burr was as ambitious as they thought, he would be willing to do that. All they had to do was entice a few Republicans in the split delegations to join them or intimidate a few into believing that Burr's election was safer than an interregnum, a new election, or giving executive power to a Federalist president *pro tempore* of the Senate. This much of the story seems clear enough. But contemporaries and historians alike have agreed on little else. The most contentious questions surround Burr. Did he want the House to elect him president or did he support Jefferson? Did he or his friends actively work for either outcome? Or did he simply keep all possibilities open by failing to say that he would not serve as president even if he were elected?[14]

It took Gallatin about two weeks to get a grasp on the situation. Perhaps willfully ignoring some contrary indications, he initially reported to his wife that Burr *"sincerely* opposed" the Federalist designs to elect him and would "go *any length*" to stop them. Leading Federalists in Philadelphia and "almost every leading federalist out of Congress in

Maryland & Virginia," he wrote, also wanted the House to accept Jefferson. Maryland feared any president other than Jefferson would let the government decamp from the unpleasant new capital, so someone in the Maryland delegation would swing the state's vote to Jefferson. Or perhaps Delaware's sole member, Federalist James Bayard, would vote for Jefferson to end the crisis. "In every possible case," Gallatin concluded, "I think we have nothing to fear." Gallatin's confidence at this stage was not singular. Nathaniel Macon, the levelheaded North Carolina Republican who would become Speaker of the House in the next Congress, sent similar assurances to Andrew Jackson, a rough fellow whom he had befriended when Jackson was the Congressman from Tennessee a few years earlier.[15]

A week later, Gallatin was beginning to understand the depths of the problem. "[B]eing all thrown together in a few boarding-houses, with hardly any other society than ourselves," he wrote to his wife, the members of Congress "are not likely to be…very moderate politicians." "A few drink, & some gamble, but the majority drink nought but politics, and by not mixing with men of different or more moderate sentiments, they inflame one another." He now saw "some danger in the fate of the election, which I had not before contemplated." Gallatin was "certain" that "our friends" would not vote for Burr, and he was beginning to doubt whether any of the Federalists would vote for Jefferson. That would leave the government with no executive and no clear constitutional provision for electing one. Rather than usurp power by appointing a president, he thought, the Federalist majority was likely to call a new election. He would oppose that. Unwittingly proving his own point about the absence of moderation, he declared that the Republicans should not yield "an inch of ground to the federal faction, when we are supported by the Constitution & by the people." Tensions emerged on all sides. Sorry to have encountered some Republican members at a ball, Federalist Harrison Gray Otis decided to attend no more parties. "I confess," he told his wife, "I do not enjoy myself with these people."[16]

Within another week, Gallatin had found the plot. He gave Jefferson and Virginia Congressman John Nicholas a long memorandum that outlined the two parties' strategic objectives, their tactical alternatives, and the likely outcomes. Doing the methodical analysis made him feel confident again. A letter to his wife explained why. Since the Republicans would control the next Congress, he said, they could end any Federalist usurpation of executive authority when Congress met in the autumn. So the Federalists in the current House of Representatives had little to gain unless they seized permanent executive power unconstitutionally. He was sure that the majority of them would not go that far. Their insistence on Burr was therefore a bluff. The Republican minority could call the bluff by insisting on Jefferson. As long as no Republican voted for Burr, the odds for Jefferson were "one hundred to one."[17]

The odds of Jefferson's election may have seemed worse once the House began voting. The Federalist majority upped the ante by adopting a rule that the House would not adjourn until it had chosen a president. The rule was meant to put pressure on the Republican minority, but at least it showed—Albert told Hannah Gallatin—"that they mean to cho[o]se." The night before the balloting began, rowdy Jefferson supporters paraded and broke windows. The first vote, at one o'clock on February 11, found the expected eight states for Jefferson and six states for Burr. Maryland and Vermont were still evenly divided. Nineteen hours and twenty-seven ballots later, no state had budged. Hannah Gallatin's cousin Joseph Hopper Nicholson—carried to the Capitol because he was too sick to walk through the falling snow—voted from his litter throughout the night to keep the Maryland delegation from going to Burr. His wife, born into what had been a Federalist family, sat beside him.[18]

The Federalists flinched and postponed the next vote until noon, but the count remained the same. "Our hopes of a change on their part are exclusively with Maryland," Albert wrote to Hannah. He and other members had heard that the Republican governors in Pennsylvania and Virginia were prepared to use force to prevent the Federalists from seizing power if the House could not make an election. The end came more quietly than that five days later in the way Gallatin had predicted. Federalist abstentions on the thirty-sixth ballot gave Maryland and

Vermont to Jefferson. James Bayard of Delaware, who had broken the deadlock by telling his party that he would vote for Jefferson rather than risk the failure of the election, cast a blank ballot. "Thus has ended," Gallatin wrote home, "the most wicked & absurd attempt ever tried by the Federalists."[19]

The Republicans had prevailed, but the election had spun a thread in what would become a web of differences between Gallatin and Samuel Smith. Smith was a Baltimore merchant, militia general, and Republican Congressman about ten years older than Gallatin. He was a big, bold, handsome man—nearly six feet tall with broad shoulders, thick dark hair, and a pugnacious nose a bit big for his face. His family had come to Baltimore before the Revolution when it was a small village, and they had prospered mightily as the city grew into a major port for wheat exports and privateering. Smith had built a large fortune, and prosperity had made him a proud and decisive man.[20]

A month before Gallatin got to Washington, Smith had met with Burr to sound out his intentions. Smith meant well, but he was ill suited to the task. A bluff man of business, Smith wanted Burr to settle things by declaring that he would not serve as president. A subtle and ambitious man with a nuanced sense of honor, Burr would not do that. He had already said that he was not seeking the presidency, and he felt insulted by importunate suggestions that he should preemptively refuse to accept the office if the House elected him. Smith discredited Burr's subtle distinction and came to suspect Burr's intentions. Smith's suspicions made him overestimate the Federalist threat, and—as successive ballots in the House increased tension—Smith began responding to requests from key Federalist members who wanted assurances about what Jefferson would do if he were elected. Smith later denied having committed Jefferson, but James Bayard apparently believed that Smith spoke for Jefferson when he said the new administration would honor federal debt obligations, maintain the navy, and keep certain officeholders in their places.[21]

Gallatin thought Smith's discussions with the Federalists had unnecessarily compromised Jefferson's position. Gallatin also may have worried that Jefferson—wary of Gallatin's connections to Burr—had chosen to work through Smith rather than to confide in Gallatin. Gallatin and Smith had already clashed over naval spending during the Quasi-War, so Gallatin was particularly sensitive to Smith's attempts to get a commitment from Jefferson on that issue. Gallatin's recollection when asked about the affair many years later—after his breach with Smith undoubtedly had colored his memory—suggests that he resented what he regarded as Smith's interference.[22]

Jefferson's widely anticipated nomination of Gallatin as Secretary of the Treasury drew criticism. Federalist newspapers complained that Gallatin was a tax rebel and a foreigner with a bad accent and radical principles. Federalist senators prepared to oppose his confirmation. But some Federalists were more discerning in private letters. Former War secretary James McHenry complained that Gallatin would weigh "the national honor and security" against "the number of dollars and cents" it would take to maintain them. He feared that many things "which ought to be done" would "be left undone, under colour of a regard to economy." But as long as the country remained at peace, McHenry grudgingly admitted, he had "no glaring causes for extraordinary alarm or complaint." Indeed, he conceded that Gallatin's insistence on the reduction of the public debt might—by reducing the annual interest expense—"augment the *disposable* revenue of the U. S." Some months later, Bayard gave a more buoyant assessment. "Mon. Gallatin," he thought, was "among the best" of Jefferson's nominees.[23]

Despite the anticipated opposition, Gallatin's nomination was never in doubt. Jefferson and Madison—who was to be Secretary of State—had agreed on the nomination when Jefferson stopped at Madison's house on his way to Washington in November, and Jefferson proposed it to Gallatin shortly after the final ballot in the House. Albert then sent Hannah the letter she had been expecting. Among Mr. Jefferson's nominees, he told her, was "a certain friend of yours." But this man was so "obnoxious to the other party" that Jefferson would not send his nomination to the Senate until more of the new Republican members arrived in the autumn. In the meantime, he wrote, her friend would accept a recess appointment. Albert said he was sure that she would prefer Washington to Fayette

County. But he asked her to make a resolution. "[W]hatever may be our station this side of the mountain, it will be essentially necessary that we should be extremely humble in our expenses." He thought that would be "a little harder than you expect, for the style of living here is Maryland-like, and it requires more fortitude to live here in a humble way than it did in Philadelphia."[24]

Gallatin stayed in Washington a few weeks longer to see Jefferson inaugurated, attend a cabinet meeting, and look for a house. He set out for home in the middle of March, leaving Jefferson a sketch of the next federal budget. He was eager to start to work. "We had another deep fall of snow in the mountains last Tuesday," Gallatin wrote to Jefferson at the end of April. But he had strong horses, he would leave home the day after tomorrow, and he would be in Washington within ten days.[25]

CHAPTER 6

DEBT AND DEMOCRACY

W hen Gallatin took charge of the Treasury in the spring of 1801, it was by far the largest department of the federal government. Seventy-three of the 127 executive officials in Washington worked for the Treasury, and the 1,200 revenue officers in the rest of the country were the government's largest civilian work force. The Treasury also managed the Mint, public lands, harbors and lighthouses, hospitals for seamen, and—through the autonomous Postmaster General—the 900-man postal service. The Treasury secretary and his Washington staff worked in a brick building just east of the President's House, where the vastly larger Treasury building stands today. The two-story structure had sixteen rooms on each floor, laid out along intersecting central hallways. Put up in the rush to construct the capital city, it had few embellishments, and it already felt crowded. A fire that began in the wood framing behind a shoddily constructed fireplace had destroyed some records a few months earlier. Republicans muttered that the Federalists had set the fire to stop an inquiry into the outgoing administration's misuse of federal money, and the House had investigated. But because the flames had destroyed the relevant account books, evidence about the shoddy construction did not dispel suspicion.[1]

The Republican opposition to the Federalist regime had arisen from more fundamental suspicions about what went on at the Treasury, and fiscal reforms stood at the head of the now triumphant party's agenda. Gallatin's books and his speeches in Congress had charted a program for reform, and Jefferson epitomized the new administration's objectives in his call for "a government rigorously frugal & simple, applying all the possible savings of the public revenue to the discharge of the public debt." Jefferson's inaugural address promised that a "wise and frugal" Republican government would "not take from the mouth of labor the bread it has earned." Whether the new administration could keep those promises depended on Gallatin. He was the only leading Republican with demonstrated expertise in public finance. And although Federalists and even some Republicans criticized him for jockeying his way into the Treasury post, none of them doubted his ability or offered an alternative candidate.[2]

It was clear that Gallatin would play a central role in the new government. Although he was the youngest member of the cabinet, no one but James Madison, the new Secretary of State, had more political experience or a wider reputation. And Madison had been out of Congress during the previous four years while Gallatin was leading the Republican opposition in the House. Edward Thornton, the British *chargé d'affaires*, confidently reported to London that Gallatin and Madison would be Jefferson's principal advisors. Should they become rivals, Thornton predicted that Gallatin would predominate because he was more artful and more decisive than Madison and more capable of achieving results. Jefferson could handle foreign affairs by himself, but he could not manage fiscal affairs without Gallatin.[3]

In fact, there was never any rivalry between Gallatin and Madison. Jefferson, Gallatin, and Madison worked well together from the start. Gallatin was different from the other two men in many ways. He was eighteen years younger than Jefferson and ten years younger than Madison. He was a small manufacturer rather than a farmer. His experience in the egalitarian scramble of Pennsylvania politics bore little resemblance to their experience as members of the lesser gentry that took control of Virginia during the Revolution. But Madison and Jefferson had come to know Gallatin well during their dark days in opposition, and they treated him as a political equal. The three of them were not a triumvirate, as Henry Adams and others have imagined. Jefferson made his own decisions, Madison and Gallatin conferred only on occasion, and the three of them rarely met as a separate group. But Jefferson put special confidence in both men. He consulted them earlier and more frequently than he consulted anyone else, and it was apparent to everyone that they had outsized influence. By the time the War of 1812 revealed deep fissures in Republican policy, it was plausible for a Federalist Congressman from Boston to lay the blame on a cabinet "composed, to all efficient purposes, of two Virginians and a foreigner."[4]

Albert and Hannah Gallatin found it difficult to locate suitable housing for themselves and their two young sons in the raw city of Washington. The family lived briefly on Capitol Hill near Margaret Bayard Smith and her husband Samuel Harrison Smith, a moderate young Philadelphian whom Jefferson and Gallatin had encouraged to launch a Republican newspaper called the *National Intelligencer*. The Gallatin family then moved to a row house adjoining James and Dolley Madison's house on the road west of the President's House. But the fevers of their first Washington summer and their concern for the child that Hannah was expecting soon drove them back to higher ground.[5]

In August, the Gallatins rented a two-story brick house on Capitol Hill, where they would live for the next twelve years. It stood at the foot of the road to Bladensburg, within sight of the freshly completed north wing of the Capitol. The annual rent was relatively high—$500, or 10 percent of Gallatin's $5,000 salary at the Treasury—but the house had ample space. Its front door opened into a wide center hall with two large rooms on each side, and the back door opened out into an enclosed yard containing a separate kitchen, carriage house, and stable. The family kept several servants, who probably were enslaved African Americans leased from their owners, and one or both of Hannah Gallatin's unmarried sisters, Maria and Adden Nicholson, often stayed with the family during the winter social season. But the Gallatins lived a relatively quiet and thrifty life, as Albert had told Hannah their modest means would require.[6]

The Gallatins' choice of a quiet life on Capitol Hill turned out to have advantages. Their house became an evening resort for leading members of the new Republican majority in Congress. This gave Gallatin the opportunity to act as an executive liaison to Congress without offending Republican notions of legislative supremacy. An admiring Pennsylvania Congressman of the next generation later gave Hannah Gallatin much of the credit for the success of these evening gatherings. "She was a reading woman, & a politician," he remembered, "unspoil'd by wealth."[7]

Among the Gallatins' most frequent visitors was Nathaniel Macon, a stocky, avuncular North Carolina planter whose plain manners matched his resolute insistence on Republican simplicity in government. He was Speaker of the House during the first six years of Jefferson's administration. John Randolph, a Congressman from Southside Virginia, was another frequent visitor. Randolph was Macon's opposite in everything but Republican fervor. A thin and sometimes acerbic man with a boyish face and a fragile ego, Randolph dominated the House during the early years of the Jefferson administration with his nimble intellect and stunning rhetorical gifts. Macon made him chairman of the Ways and Means committee, and Randolph's close cooperation with Gallatin boosted the administration's financial measures through the House.[8]

A third important visitor was Joseph Hopper Nicholson, the Maryland Congressman who had had himself carried to the Capitol on his sickbed so that he could cast his vote for Jefferson. Joseph Nicholson was Hannah Gallatin's first cousin. He was an erect, handsome man with dark eyes, a full shock of curly brown hair, and manly good graces. Everyone liked him, and he was a particular favorite of his female cousins.

Hannah Gallatin's niece Frances Few was so smitten by her "handsome Cousin Joe" that the phrase became a private joke in the family. Nicholson had married into one of the wealthiest families in Maryland and established himself as a Baltimore lawyer and Eastern Shore planter. He was a persuasive speaker with a natural flair for legislative business. Gallatin respected his judgment, and the two men regularly confided in each other.[9]

Nicholson, Randolph, and Macon were close friends, and they formed the Republican vanguard in the House during Jefferson's first term. Gallatin's friendship with them and other men in Congress gave him considerable influence on legislation. He often commented on bills, sometimes drafted them himself, and regularly lobbied in support of the administration's measures. "I will loiter today about Congress to attend to some bills," read one of his routine notes to Jefferson. In this discreet way, Gallatin gave Congress the same kind of ministerial direction that he and other Republicans had criticized when Alexander Hamilton furnished it more openly.[10]

On most days, Gallatin was hard at work in his office at the Treasury. The Treasury building was about a mile and half from his house on Capitol Hill, and the ride took him twenty minutes. The "straight causeway...(called the Pennsylvania Avenue)" that cut through the swamp below Capitol Hill often was soggy, so he probably kept to a road along the ridge to the north (F Street). As he descended the ridge, a large office building called Blodgett's Hotel appeared on his right and the features of the Treasury building gradually emerged on the horizon against the taller profile of the President's House. Gallatin arrived early, and he usually stayed late by the standards of the time. He left home before the rest of the household had breakfast and returned in time for a late dinner at four or five o'clock. After dinner, he often worked at home late into the night.[11]

Gallatin's physical appearance did not impress anyone. He was growing bald and a bit stooped. A Federalist senator who knew him reasonably well thought that he was "very inattentive & negligent of his person & dress—his linen is often soiled, & his clothes tattered." That may have been an exaggeration. The senator was one of the many Federalists who disapproved of the studied plainness and informality on which Jefferson, Macon, and other leading Republicans insisted. But Gallatin's homeliness and his reputation for thrift encouraged exaggeration. "Mr. Gallatin is a little man with a monstrous nose and large black piercing eyes," a Charleston newspaper reported. He ties back his hair in an unfashionable "queue of great length; he is as brown as a man of colour, and has lost most of his teeth." He "does not go into society…and is said to be constantly in his office smoking and writing." Even Gallatin's smoking habits became the stuff of fable. He stopped buying cigars in bulk, the admiring young Pennsylvania Congressman recalled, because he found that he smoked fewer and spent less if he bought only a quarter's worth at a time.[12]

Gallatin's thrift became legendary because he slashed federal spending to find the money he needed to repay the national debt. He had long ago dismissed Hamilton's plan for repaying the debt as inadequate. Hamilton's plan appropriated revenue from specific taxes to the repayment of particular bonds, all subject to a variety of contingencies. It also allocated surpluses, which probably had never existed and which no one had ever bothered to calculate, to a sinking fund that could repurchase bonds in the market. The plan was complicated and—perhaps intentionally—confusing. Jefferson described it colorfully as "a number of scraps & remnants many of which were nothing at all" applied to "different objects in reversion and remainder until the whole system was involved in impenetrable fog."[13]

Gallatin believed that Hamilton's plan could not effectively reduce the debt because the payments were provisional, they did not apply to all of the bonds, and—most important—they were smaller than the new debts the government had incurred to pay its expenses. The sinking fund was merely an accounting device designed to leave the false impression that the government had set aside money to repay the debt. The whole thing, Gallatin concluded, was just "a matter of discretion with the Secretary of the Treasury." Its purpose was not so much to extinguish the debt as to manipulate repayments and repurchases in order to support the government's credit and increase the price of its bonds. Gallatin had fundamentally different intentions. The only way the government could reduce its debt, he had repeated many times, was to spend less than it received. In the flush of the Republican triumph, he set out to make it do that.[14]

As he went to work on the Republican administration's first budget during the summer and autumn of 1801, Gallatin used straightforward arithmetic. He estimated that federal revenues for the following year would amount to $10.6 million. He liquidated the various appropriations for principal and interest on the debt into a definite annual sum of $7.3 million. He determined (with a bit of algebra that both he and Jefferson found difficult) that fixed annual payments of that amount could repay the entire federal debt within sixteen years. Since the terms of some of the bonds prevented the government from repaying them any earlier, he adopted the $7.3 million annual debt payment as the foundation for his budget, and he gave it priority over all other claims on the federal revenue. That left him $3.3 million to pay for the rest of the government's expenses.[15]

Those expenses had averaged $5.8 million over the previous four years, and the cuts in military spending at the end of the Quasi-War would not produce the $2.5 million annual spending reduction that Gallatin needed. Gallatin and the other Republicans had carped about high federal salaries and wasteful civil administration when they were in opposition. But total civilian spending made up only $1.25 of the $5.8 million total, and Gallatin now confessed to Jefferson that he did not think he could reduce it by more than a few hundred thousand dollars. The savings he needed would have to come from deep cuts in military spending—just as the Federalists had predicted. Gallatin was not reluctant to make those cuts. A standing army was anathema to good Republicans, and Gallatin had argued for years that money spent on the small navy that the government could afford was simply wasted. To balance the budget, he proposed to cut the army's appropriation from $1.7 to $1.4 million and the navy's from $2.1 to $1.1 million.[16]

Gallatin soon found that political pressure to repeal the whiskey excise and the other internal taxes would require even larger cuts in spending. Gallatin himself wanted to repeal internal taxes. They were unpopular, they were expensive to collect, and they probably would raise only about $650,000 in the following year. He thought the people would pay internal taxes more willingly in wartime if they did not have to pay them in peacetime. Repeal also would allow him to abolish the 500-man internal revenue service, which he found bloated with inefficient layers of reporting and supervision. But Gallatin hesitated to repeal internal taxes immediately. Debt repayment was his first priority, and he wanted to retain all of the taxes until he was sure that import duties alone could produce enough revenue to meet his debt repayment schedule. Jefferson disagreed. Convinced of the political importance of sweeping away the only federal taxes that touched most ordinary people directly, he pushed for immediate repeal.[17]

Gallatin agreed to repeal internal taxes on the understanding that repeal would not reduce the fixed annual payments on the debt, and Jefferson's first annual message to Congress assured them that import duties alone could pay for a leaner, more frugal Republican government. There was grumbling. "The Genevan & American Philosophers you will find more bold in experiment than wise & intelligent as statesmen," one Federalist dryly observed. "In their visionary brains the amount of our revenues by import is calculated even to a cent for preceding years. Its surplus is to astonish the citizens." But Gallatin and Jefferson knew that the Republican majorities in Congress would support them. Through John Randolph, Gallatin brokered the necessary additional spending cuts in the War and Navy departments. And after a long debate—in which Federalists pointed out that import duties on necessities such as salt were more burdensome than internal taxes on luxuries such as whiskey—the Republican majorities abolished internal taxes. A few weeks later, they replaced Hamilton's vague debt repayment plan with a $7.3 million fixed annual appropriation that took priority over all other federal spending.[18]

To keep government spending within his tight new limits, Gallatin pushed for the same measures he had advocated when he was in opposition—specific appropriations and greater accountability. At Gallatin's urging, Jefferson asked Congress to make its appropriations as specific as possible, to prohibit money appropriated for one purpose from being spent for related purposes, and to require the army and navy to account directly to the Treasury rather than to their own separate auditors. Those measures would give Congress more control over spending and increase the Treasury's ability to monitor it. Congress took the cue. It restored specific appropriations language to the annual military spending bills, and it made civilian appropriations even more specific. Using questions supplied by Gallatin, Joseph Nicholson launched an investigation into whether the previous administration had misspent public money. Nicholson's investigation report criticized laxity in the army and navy, and he introduced a bill to require the direct accounting to Treasury that Gallatin had recommended. Although the bill languished amid partisan bickering over Nicholson's findings, he and Gallatin had made their point. The report prompted former Treasury secretary Oliver Wolcott to defend himself in a long *Address to the People of the United States.* Meanwhile, Gallatin's insistence on cost control began to elicit polite complaints from the new Secretary of the Navy, Robert Smith, who was Congressman Samuel Smith's brother.[19]

The new administration's fiscal reforms provoked a diatribe from Hamilton that lasted almost as long as it took Congress to enact them. Thinly disguised as Lucius Crassus—a Roman consul remembered for proscribing foreigners who claimed to be Roman citizens—Hamilton published essay after essay denouncing the repeal of internal taxes and claiming that only the great success of his own fiscal administration made such a profligate decision possible. He excoriated Jefferson for pandering to the people by invoking the "bewitching tenets of that illuminated doctrine, which promises man, ere long, an emancipation from the burdens and restraints of government." Leaving the people to their own devices would not lead to national prosperity, he argued. "[P]ractical politicians" knew that governments had to encourage prosperity. The Jefferson administration's obsession with repaying debt and repealing taxes would "sink the government" by cutting off the money essential to "its respectability," "the accomplishment of its most salutary plans," and "its power of being useful." If the government's revenues exceeded its current expenses, it should use the excess to strengthen the military establishment and build internal improvements. Gallatin's insistence on specific appropriations and greater account-ability was nothing but "a deliberate design...to arraign the former administrations." It was ridiculous to appropriate (as Jefferson had put it to Congress) "'a specific sum for each specific purpose, *susceptible of definition*.'" These were the measures of "LITTLE POLITICIANS, who now...enjoy the benefits of a policy, which they had neither the wi[s]dom to plan nor the spirit to adopt."[20]

The Republicans' views on debt and democracy could not have been more different. They believed that repayment of Hamilton's funded debt was essential to freedom and republican government. That belief rested on interlocking economic and political foundations.

The economic foundation for the belief was the orthodox liberal premise—elaborated by Adam Smith and others—that government spending on everything except public improvements consumes a nation's investment capital. As long as a government could spend no more than the people were willing to pay in taxes, there was a salutary natural limit on this consumption. Credit made that limit flexible, though only to the extent that lenders believed the people ultimately would accept higher taxes. But the British funding system that Hamilton had adopted demol-ished the natural limit on government spending. The government could borrow far more than the people were willing to pay in taxes because the people had to pay only enough to cover the annual interest. The funding system, therefore, was a snare. It prevented the people from understanding how much money the government was actually spending, and it allowed the government to go deeper and deeper into debt. The annual payments on the federal debt already consumed about 70 percent of the government's revenue, and the taxes needed to fund continuing debt payments would shift more and more capital from ordinary people into the hands of wealthy creditors. Until the government freed its rev-enues from this burden, it could not afford to do much of anything without borrowing even more.[21]

That economic analysis supported the Republicans' political critique of funded debt. Hamilton had argued that the public debt would strengthen national government because the public creditors' self-interest would lead them to support the federal regime. The Republicans accepted that prediction, but they thought it was a malediction. True republican government required the participation of the people, and the people could participate more effectively in state and local governments where they were more directly represented. Consolidating power in a distant federal government shifted political control away from the people. Shifting capital into the hands of wealthy men reduced the influence of ordinary citizens. And designing men could use—and had used, the Republicans thought—the self-interest of public creditors to corrupt Congress into accepting greater consolidation.[22]

Embedded in the Republicans' economic and political thinking were more visceral beliefs about debt and democracy. Like Adam Smith and other liberal political economists, Republicans thought about public debt in the same way they thought about private debt. They believed that the failure to pay it would bring ruin. If a private debtor did not pay his debts, lenders would cut off his credit and foreclose on his property. This was a painful personal concern of more than a few Republicans, particularly the farmers—and small producers like Gallatin himself—whose mounting debts sometimes kept them awake at night. They understood that government debtors were different from private debtors because economic growth could increase the government's revenues, bolster its credit, and delay the final reckoning. But they believed the reckoning would ultimately come unless the government exercised fiscal restraint.[23]

These notions about debt interlocked with equally visceral Republican ideas about democracy. A republican government gave sovereignty to the people, but true popular sovereignty depended on the people's independence, their freedom to act in their own best interests. Economic arrangements that made voters dependent on others—creditors, landlords, or employers—compromised their independence. A contemporary American play entitled *Independence* caught the theme exactly. "I am an independent farmer," declared the main character, "don't owe five guineas in the world." Public debt compromised the government's independence in the same way that debt compromised an individual's independence. A government beholden to its creditors was not truly under popular control. Its people were not wholly free. True freedom depended on frugal government uncorrupted by debt.[24]

Republicans believed that public debt jeopardized not only freedom, but peace. Montesquieu, Rousseau, and other Enlightenment thinkers had maintained that monarchies were more warlike than republics because they could shift the physical and economic burdens of war to their subjects. Republics were inherently peaceful because people who bore the awful burdens of war would avoid armed conflict. Were all nations to become republics, destructive warfare would end and universal peace would usher in an era of unparalleled prosperity. Hamilton had dismissed this vision as a utopian dream. He said there had been "almost as many popular as royal wars" and it was dangerous to believe otherwise. The best way to avoid war, he wrote in *The Federalist*, was to prepare for it.[25]

But Madison, Jefferson, and other Republicans embraced the vision of republican peace, and they thought Hamilton's system for funding the public debt threatened it. If one generation could pass the cost of war to another generation, Madison argued, republican government would never fulfill the promise of "Universal Peace." John Taylor, whose faith in the pure republicanism of the 1790s never wavered, called public borrowing itself a type of warfare through which one generation plundered another. Nathaniel Macon claimed that modern wars never really ended because "the war of killing, prepared the way for a war of taxes," which were raked in by a troop of tax collectors almost "as destructive to the human race as so many Alexanders." And Jefferson spoke of "peace, economy, and riddance of public debt" as a composite objective—each interlocking element dependent on the others. He thought that the best way to keep a country at peace was to deny it the means for waging war. In peacetime, the government should disband its armed forces and rely on the militia for public defense. If it could do without internal taxes, it should repeal them. A government that had the means for waging war, he said, was more likely to use them.[26]

Gallatin believed in the link between fiscal policy and peace. Perhaps it was a "visionary dream," he had told Congress during the Quasi-War, but he hoped America's distance from Europe could allow Americans to avoid conflict and live in peace "without armies and navies, and without being deeply involved in debt." He thought Americans should strive to "become a happy, and not a powerful nation; or at least, no way powerful, except for self-defence." An increase in public debt to fund military spending would be a confession that Americans meant to join the great nations of Europe in their wasteful careers of war and destruction. "I agree most fully with you," Gallatin had confirmed to Jefferson as they set about their fiscal reforms, "that pretended tax-preparations, treasury-preparations, and army-preparations against contingent wars tend only to encourage wars."[27]

Whatever the merits of the Republicans' political economic theories, their repeal of the Federalists' internal taxes was popular. A crowd in the town soon to be Ohio's capital celebrated the expiration of those "oppressive and odious internal taxes" by consigning the laws to a bonfire and toasting the health of "the present œconomical administration." Stalwart John Taylor had never doubted the political importance of tax repeal. While Gallatin and Jefferson were still discussing it, Taylor had assured another Virginia Republican that a "rigid economy will enable the administration to repeal some of the most obnoxious tax laws, and this will acquire a confidence." Jefferson had correctly judged the political situation when he insisted on sweeping away internal taxes, and Republicans took to heart the people's outpouring of gratitude.[28]

Debt repayment and tax reduction were popular, but the administration pursued those reforms with a single-mindedness that liberal European political economists could scarcely have imagined when they wrote about the fiscal reforms needed in their own countries. Although Hamilton had copied some of the British fiscal arrangements, Hamilton's regime placed a far lighter burden on the American economy than the burdens that had sparked the liberal economic critiques in Europe. Britain and France had a complex variety of taxes on trade, consumption, land, and even incomes, and they had accumulated large public debts over almost a century of expensive warfare. Rough estimates suggest that their taxes extracted 7 to 12 percent of national income during the late eighteenth century and that their national debts were ten to fifteen times larger than their annual tax revenues. America's situation was different. The Revolutionary War and Hamilton's refinancing had saddled the federal government with a debt that was thirty times its annual tax revenue, but the government itself was far smaller, and the federal taxes amounted to only about 2 percent of national income. State taxes probably accounted for another 2 percent. The relatively undeveloped country already showed great potential for rapid expansion of population and economic output. So when Jefferson complained that the United States was the most indebted nation in the Atlantic world, he was misjudging the effective burden. Gallatin's sweeping fiscal reforms were—even from the liberal economic perspective—overkill.[29]

Taking stock as his first Congress prepared to adjourn, Jefferson expressed satisfaction with Gallatin's reforms. The new fiscal program, he told a friend, "will pretty completely fulfil all the desires of the people." Reductions in spending had allowed the administration to repeal internal taxes and still have enough money to repay the debt. A few months later, Jefferson assured a thoughtful Republican that the public finances were "now under such a course of application as nothing could derange them but war or federalism." Adversaries might carp, he said in a swipe at Hamilton, that the administration was indebted to them for the means of paying the debt, but "[w]e never charged them with the want of foresight in providing money," only "with the misapplication of it." In fact, he said, the Federalists had raised too much money. After giving back the surplus, "we [can] do more with a part than they did with the whole." The path ahead of us is "so quiet," he rhapsodized, "that we have nothing scarcely to propose to our Legislature."[30]

But the financial path ahead of the Administration actually diverged in one important respect from the path Jefferson himself would have chosen. He had conceded long ago that the federal government must keep its promises to the holders of the public debt. But he had not reconciled himself to the Bank of the United States. He still believed that it was an unconstitutional monopoly bent toward the corruption of republican government. And as he prepared his first annual message to Congress, he had pored over the Bank's financial statements—statements that he admitted he did not understand—searching, probing, wishing for a way to get at the Bank. He had not found one, and Gallatin had not helped him.[31]

Gallatin, in fact, had assured the Bank of his confidence and asked it to open a branch in Washington to help handle the government's money. A few months later, circumstances forced Gallatin to mention the subject to Jefferson. The Bank of the United States had put pressure on the Bank of Pennsylvania to repay some of its notes. Gallatin had sponsored the Pennsylvania bank when he was in the state legislature, and he decided to help it defend itself from the Bank of the United States by giving it an advance payment on a federal foreign exchange contract. It was proper for the federal government to help a state bank, he assured Jefferson, but—he added—it would not be proper to "displease" the Bank of the United States. The Bank was important to the government for two reasons, he said. Since it was the only bank with branches throughout the country, it was the only bank that could use deposits taken from the government in one place to make payments for the government in another. And since it was the best-capitalized bank in the country, it was the lender to which the government would have to turn in an emergency.[32]

Jefferson grudgingly accepted Gallatin's judgment at the time, but a year later he came back to Gallatin with a proposal for shifting the government's deposits to friendly Republican state banks. Gallatin ignored the idea until, a few months after that, Jefferson went on to propose that the government should keep its money in an "independent" bank owned and operated by the Treasury. This time, Gallatin patiently repeated the advantages of using the Bank of the United States as the government's fiscal agent. He also pointed out that allowing the government's money to circulate within the banking system made it easier for merchants to get the funds they needed to pay federal import duties. Set against those advantages, he told Jefferson, "there are none but political objections." And Gallatin thought those were overblown. The Bank of the United States could not overbear the federal government, he said, because the Bank needed the government—its principal depositor—more than the government needed the Bank. Without the government's deposits, the Bank would not have enough money to meet its obligations to its customers and the other banks. "Whenever [the Bank] shall appear to be really dangerous," he assured Jefferson, "they are completely in our power and may be crushed."[33]

Gallatin said nothing at the time about the Bank's gradually emerging power over the other banks and the national money supply. State bank notes were the most widely used type of currency, and the Bank received a large proportion of those notes as federal deposits because merchants typically used them to pay import duties. By forcing state banks to pay off their notes, the Bank could reduce the money supply to some extent. While that helped to curb currency-driven inflation, it also curtailed the amount of credit that banks could offer to their customers. Gallatin probably did not mention those powers to Jefferson because Gallatin, like almost everyone else at the time, had not yet consciously embraced the concept of central banking—though he intuitively understood the Bank's central-banking potential well enough to give it additional government funds during a liquidity squeeze in 1804, to pressure it into giving other banks liquidity in the following year, and to warn it against putting too much pressure on other banks three years later.[34]

Jefferson let Gallatin have the last word on the Bank. He made no more proposals to undercut it, but he never changed his mind about it. "I often pressed [Gallatin] to divide the public deposits among all the respectable banks," Jefferson later confided to a Virginia Republican, "but his repugnance to it prevented my persisting." Forty years later, Gallatin could say without qualification that "Mr. Jefferson...lived and died a decided enemy of our banking system generally, and specially to a bank of the United States."[35]

⟿

Patronage presented an even more urgent problem than the government's finances during Gallatin's first year in office, and it consumed much of his energy. Washington and Adams had given federal jobs to very few Republicans, so Jefferson's election unleashed an intense demand from the Republican faithful for appointment to office. With that demand came widespread calls to remove Federalist officeholders in order to make room. Nothing gave more difficulty, Jefferson complained, than this "business of removal and appointment," and his notes from the first meeting of his cabinet mention almost nothing else. The stakes for the leaders of the new administration were high. They, like their Federalist predecessors, needed to have likeminded officials on whom they could rely to execute their policies. They also needed to recognize their political followers' claims for reward and influence. But they had a competing objective born of their grand conception of the Republican electoral victory. They believed their victory was the first rush of a great wind that would part the political waters, bring ordinary people once perverted by Federalism across to the Republican side, and sweep the implacable Federalist leadership into oblivion. If they wanted ordinary Federalists to accept this deliverance, they could not remove worthy men from office simply because they were Federalists.[36]

Many members of both parties thought the famous palliative in Jefferson's inaugural address—"We are all republicans: we are all federalists"—promised restraint in removals. But most Federalists knew the situation was unstable. "We are all tranquil as they say at Paris after a Revolution," one Federalist leader quipped to another. And important Republicans were quick to point out that it would take extensive removals to make enough room for the deserving. Virginia Congressman William Branch Giles told Jefferson that "one of the benefits expected by the friends of the new order of things" was a "pretty general purgation of office." Jefferson had already decided to remove the men John Adams had appointed during his last weeks in office, cleanse the judiciary of Federalist district attorneys and marshals, and sweep out Federalists who had been derelict in their duties. The pressure to do more than that put him in a painful situation, and he played for time. The administration, he told Giles, would decide what to do when Madison and Gallatin got to Washington: "that some ought to be removed from office, & that all ought not, all mankind will agree. but where to draw the line perhaps no two will agree."[37]

As a practical matter, Gallatin shouldered most of the burden of Republican patronage because more than 90 percent of the federal civilian jobs were in the Treasury (30 percent of them were in the autonomous Postal Service). He therefore saw almost every respectable request for a federal civilian position. Throughout the spring and summer of 1801, job-seeking letters from friends, acquaintances, and strangers poured into his office.[38]

David Gelston, a prosperous New York merchant, solid Republican, and close friend of the Nicholsons, confidently reached for the plum appointment as customs collector of the Port of New York. Major Boyd, Gallatin's old landlord in Philadelphia, sent a stream of letters pleading that a steady public salary could rescue his family from want. James Madison's brother-in-law John G. Jackson wrote from western Virginia to ask for a contract to carry the mail. A friend of Isaac Griffin, who was the father-in-law of Gallatin's brother-in-law, asked Griffin to help him get Gallatin's ear. And an Irishman in Philadelphia named John M. Taylor sent Gallatin a letter asking to be, as Gallatin whimsically noted on the back, "one thing or an other." Aaron Burr sent a list of loyal supporters for whom he wanted jobs in New York. Jefferson repeatedly sought Gallatin's advice on the patronage requests that he received, such as the one in which inveterate Pennsylvania office-seeker Tench Coxe explained why he was suitable for any one of seven offices. "God knows...others will serve you as I do by emptying their pockets into your Sack," former Congressman Matthew Lyon told Gallatin, as he proceeded to stuff in another four pages of recommendations.[39]

Gallatin handled patronage with his characteristic thoroughness. He ordered up the first comprehensive roster of federal officeholders ever made, and he solicited advice from reliable Republicans around the country. Years of administrative experience in Pennsylvania gave his friend Alexander Dallas valuable insight. It was "visionary" to expect the Federalist party to collapse, Dallas told him, but restraint in removals could win the Republican party enough converts to keep it firmly in power. Dallas predicted that the administration could get Republicans into half of the federal offices within a few years simply by dismissing delinquents, turning out anyone who actively campaigned for the Federalists, and appointing only Republicans. But nothing the administration could do, predicted Dallas, would silence Republican dissatisfaction because Republicans would complain almost as much about selections from among themselves as they did about keeping Federalists in office. "[Y]ou can tell me, whether the cry of 'turn *him* out,' is not forever closed with the prayer of 'put *me* in.' Acquiesce in the cry, but reject the prayer, will the clamor be diminished?" "The task of nominating a successor," warned Dallas, "must always…be a restraint upon the power of removal."[40]

As pressure from Republican office-seekers mounted, Jefferson seized on a remonstrance from the merchants in New Haven as an opportunity to announce his position. The situation in New Haven was highly charged. John Adams had appointed Elizur Goodrich to be the new customs collector just as he was leaving office, and Jefferson had turned Goodrich out along with Adams's other "midnight" appointees. Goodrich's appointment was especially obnoxious to Republicans because both he and his brother had been sitting members of Congress when Adams appointed him. But Samuel Bishop—the man Jefferson chose to replace Goodrich—was too old for the job, and his son Abraham, whom everyone expected to succeed him, was a strident Republican partisan who had made himself unpopular in Federalist Connecticut. The merchants' complaint insinuated that replacing Goodrich with Bishop was a departure from the conciliatory statement in Jefferson's inaugural address.[41]

Jefferson's reply was artful but firm. Was it reasonable, he asked the merchants, to treat his statements "in favor of *political tolerance*" as assurances that Federalist officeholders could stay in place? Was it not political *intolerance* that had kept Republicans out of federal office for the last twelve years? So how could it be tolerant to perpetuate the Federalists' monopoly of an office after a solemn election had put the people's party in power? Surely Republicans had a right to participate in the administration of their own government. And if they had that right, Jefferson continued, "how are vacancies to be obtained? Those by death are few; by resignation, none. Can any other mode than...removal be proposed?" Removing men to make way for new appointments is "a painful office," he concluded, "but it is made my duty." That, of course, was not the last word. A bitter rejoinder berated Jefferson for taking bread from the mouths of true patriots and giving it to men such as Madison, an apostate to the Constitution he had helped to create, and Gallatin, "a hateful FOREIGNER" who ought to have been hanged for "HIGH TREASON."[42]

Gallatin took his own stab at political tolerance a few weeks later. The customs collectors were the best-remunerated federal officeholders outside Washington (some of them earned more than cabinet members until Congress capped their income the following year), and they had the right to name subordinate officers. This gave them considerable political influence, and since most of them were still Federalists, Gallatin thought he should warn them not to abuse it. He proposed to send the collectors two directives. The first would instruct them to drop political tests for nominations to office. "[T]he Door of Office," Gallatin wrote, was no longer shut against any man "merely on account of his political Opinions." The customs collectors should choose men solely for their "Integrity, and Capacity suitable to the Station." The second directive would tell the collectors not to use their positions to influence elections. Federal officers were free to vote as they chose just like any other citizen, he assured them, but the use of "official influence to restrain or controul the same rights in others" violated republican principles. Gallatin's proposed directives directly contradicted the traditional Federalist understanding that elite officeholders should use their prestige and patronage to consolidate support for the regime. At the same time, of course, they renounced any Republican intention to use those same powers for their own partisan advantage.[43]

Jefferson no longer felt so tolerant, and with a gentleness that his enemies often saw as evasion, he rejected Gallatin's proposals. "Mr. Madison happened to be with me when I opened your circular to the

Collectors," began his reply. Although they both applauded Gallatin's sentiments, he said, they thought Gallatin should reserve them until Jefferson's own response to the New Haven merchants had more time to shape public opinion. Then Jefferson came to the real point. Some "particular considerations" had kept him from issuing his own proclamation against electioneering by public official, and before the collectors dropped political tests, he thought they should give at least half of the customs positions to Republicans.[44]

Gallatin resisted this more partisan approach. He reported to Jefferson a few weeks later that Jefferson's response to the New Haven merchants was having "a greater effect" than intended because now "the Republicans hope for a greater number of removals [and] the Federals also expect it." He thought the administration should dampen both the hopes and the fears. Only wide popular support for the Republican party could ensure the "permanent establishment of those republican principles of limitation of power & public economy, for which we have successfully contended." Gallatin therefore thought it would be better "to displease many of our political friends" than to antagonize "the mass of the Federal citizens" by making unpopular removals from office. "The sooner we can stop the ferment the better."[45]

Jefferson acknowledged that his letter to New Haven had increased the clamor for removals from "Sweeping republicans," but he insisted that "moderate & genuine republicans" and "Republican federalists" were satisfied. And on the political test for future appointments, he was unyielding. His administration would appoint no more Federalists, he told Gallatin, until Republicans had "a due proportion" of the public offices. Gallatin understood; he dropped his proposed directives. He and Jefferson gradually forced more and more Federalists out of federal jobs and replaced them with Republicans. Three years later, when Jefferson suggested that they ought to discourage federal officeholders from electioneering, Gallatin gently suggested that they had missed their chance.[46]

Nowhere was the Republican clamor for patronage louder than in Pennsylvania. Thomas McKean had swept the Federalists out of state offices when he became governor in 1799, and many Pennsylvania

Republicans expected Jefferson to do the same thing in national offices. They brought their hopes and claims to Gallatin, the only Pennsylvanian in the administration. William Duane was among the most importunate of them, and he was impossible to ignore. Duane was the editor of the Philadelphia *Aurora,* the country's leading Republican newspaper. He was a committed republican of Irish extraction, hardened by the persecution he had suffered as an opposition journalist in Great Britain and British India. He came to work at the *Aurora* in 1798, and when yellow fever felled its editor that summer, Duane took over his paper and married his widow. A band of Federalist troopers enraged by the *Aurora*'s reports on their violent behavior during Fries's Rebellion beat Duane senseless the next year. The beating made him a political martyr. The *Aurora* had been outspoken for Jefferson in 1800, and Duane had set up a printing office in Washington to reap his reward.[47]

By the time Duane got to Gallatin's office in August 1801, he was spoiling for action. A federal district court had jailed him for contempt, and he had accumulated other grievances against the administration. Most of the government printing was going to Samuel Harrison Smith, the respectable moderate who ran the *National Intelligencer.* And although Gallatin had responded to Duane's complaints about that, his response had been tardy and unencouraging. But rather than simply vent his personal grievances, Duane chose to blend them with what he thought were more principled claims. He brought along a dossier in which he had listed the government clerks in Washington, their salaries, and his views on their fitness. He identified a few of them as "Republican" in politics or at least "Modest" in ability. He had even found one "Good man." Among the rest of them, however, he found "Hamiltonians," "Execrable Aristocrats," "Complete Picaroons," a total "0," and "Wolcott's dear Nephew." These men had to go, and true Republicans—starting with two former Treasury clerks who had given Duane copies of the suspicious government accounts that had disappeared in the Treasury fire—should replace them.[48]

Gallatin ignored Duane's bluster. He fired no Treasury clerks for their political views, and even when Jefferson intimated that he should give one of Duane's informants a job, Gallatin refused. He thought that would undercut the Treasury official who had quite properly fired the man for leaking official documents. Gallatin did give Duane some Treasury printing, and he was appalled when the clerk of the House—a Republican operative who should have known better—failed to give Duane a share of the House's printing. But in the end Gallatin offered Duane little.[49]

Gallatin's reluctance to help Duane was a symptom of the uneasy relationship between middle and working class factions in Pennsylvania's Republican party. Their affiliation had served their common interests while the Federalists held power, but the Republican victory focused attention on their differences. Gallatin's friend Dallas was a leader of the more prosperous Republicans. These men were professionals, merchants, and landowners. Although they were not part of the traditional elite, they moved in respectable circles. Their republicanism was moderate, and Republican success tended to make it more so. Governor McKean favored them in his appointments to state offices, so they could accept restraint in removals from federal offices. Jefferson was comfortable with men like this. They had adequate incomes, good sense, and respectable reputations. At the very first cabinet meeting, he had signaled his intention to make Dallas the United States attorney for eastern Pennsylvania, and he arranged to replace some of the income that Dallas would lose from his private law practice by giving him a supplemental appointment as the federal commissioner in bankruptcy. McKean plumped Dallas's cushion a bit more by appointing him to be the recorder for one of the state courts in Philadelphia.[50]

The more discontented working class Republicans—many of them ethnically German or Irish—looked to Duane and his friend Michael Leib for leadership. Leib was a doctor from Philadelphia's German community who had won election to Congress from a working class district in 1798, and the excessive attention he gave to his clothes, hair, and perfume betrayed his social anxiety and edgy aspirations. Some mixture of calculation and conviction made him a spokesman for the common man. He and Duane shared a certain class bitterness against their more comfortable Republican allies, and that bitterness gained bite as they watched those men receive the patronage they craved. They did not turn their resentment on Jefferson—he was too important, too charismatic, and too gentle with them—but it did affect their dealings with the moderate Republicans. Not long after Duane visited Gallatin, he and Leib went to court to challenge the legality of Dallas's simultaneous appointments to federal and state offices. And when the Pennsylvania courts rejected the challenge, they got the state legislature to change the law over McKean's veto. It was a direct blow at what Duane and Leib were coming to see as the Dallas-Gallatin wing of the party. Dallas and Gallatin brushed it aside, but it was a harbinger of more to come.[51]

Another unwelcome visitor came to see Gallatin in September, and at the time his visit worried Gallatin more than Duane's. Matthew Livingston Davis was one of the hardworking acolytes who had helped Burr deliver New York's electoral votes to Jefferson. He was a poor boy who had become a printer, a political organizer, and—thanks to Burr—a bank clerk. During the New York City electioneering, he had frequented the Nicholsons' house and sent Gallatin a stream of ingratiating letters. Davis was prominent on Burr's list of New Yorkers to be rewarded, but Jefferson—who appointed most of the others—had ignored him. When the slight became painfully obvious because the patrician Edward Livingston could not resist talking about it, Davis was chagrined. Throwing off the advice of his friends, he decided to take his case to Jefferson in person.[52]

What Davis brought through Gallatin's door was a problem more complicated than one man's disappointed expectations. The Republicans in New York were an essential part of the national coalition that had elected Jefferson, but the Republican party in New York was an uneasy alliance of prominent men whose supporters were more loyal to them than to the party. Although Burr had a considerable popular following in his New York City bastion, George Clinton—who had abandoned his retirement to become governor again—and the Livingston family controlled appointments to state offices because they had stronger backing in other parts of the state. Burr therefore needed federal patronage for his supporters. But ambitious younger members of the Clinton and Livingston factions quickly saw that Burr's ambiguous behavior during the presidential election crisis had made him vulnerable, and they seized the opportunity to undercut his recommendations—or at least to show those Burrites who did get federal jobs that they owed them to the sufferance of others. John Armstrong, a Continental Army officer from Pennsylvania who had married one of the Livingstons and moved to the Hudson Valley, pointedly warned Gallatin not to appoint Matthew Livingston Davis. He even hinted at doubts about David Gelston, the friend of the Nicholsons who had asked to be named customs collector for New York, and he suggested that Gallatin and the president should vet their New York appointments with Governor Clinton.[53]

The situation in New York worried Gallatin for both political and personal reasons. He had long disliked the influence of the great families, which made politics in New York undemocratic and unstable. While he thought the collective interests of ordinary citizens would hold the Republicans together in Pennsylvania, he feared the self-interest of a few influential men could split the party in New York. And a split that allowed the Federalists to regain control of New York would cost Jefferson the next presidential election. Gallatin's personal reasons for concern were less weighty, but awkward. Commodore Nicholson had backed Burr in 1800, Gallatin had brokered Burr's vice presidential nomination, and Nicholson—whose Revolutionary service, social standing, and support for the Republican cause gave him a claim as good as anyone's—had let it be known to friends in New York that he wanted a federal job. Nicholson was careful to gather recommendations from the Clinton faction as well as from Burr, but the Nicholson family's relationship with Burr was closer. The appearance of nepotism made Gallatin uncomfortable, but the chance of getting sidewise with the New York factions was even worse.[54]

Unable to talk Davis out of going to Monticello, Gallatin sent Jefferson candid letters about the situation in New York. He made three points. First, he thought the administration should not remove the Federalist who held the office Davis wanted. The Republicans in New York were turning Federalists out of state offices indiscriminately, and Gallatin believed that the administration would only disgrace itself by yielding to the same "spirit of persecution." But if the administration did decide to remove the incumbent, Gallatin thought Davis should get the job. He conceded that Davis did not move in "a very elevated sphere," and he had to apologize for Davis's rude intrusion on Jefferson's privacy. But Gallatin nevertheless believed the administration should prefer Davis to other candidates because the Burrites represented the real popular majority in New York. This brought Gallatin to the heart of the matter. Rejecting Davis would alienate Burr, and Gallatin thought that was a bad idea. If the Republicans dropped Burr as the vice presidential candidate at the next election, to whom could they turn? Madison was the only obvious alternative, but the Constitution did not allow the president and the vice president to come from the same state. If the party was not going to accept Burr as Jefferson's successor, said Gallatin, it ought not to have nominated him to be vice president in the first place. Until the presidential succession was settled, Gallatin concluded, they needed to keep Burr on their side.[55]

Gallatin's earnest letters were a mistake. Jefferson preferred to duck this sort of political conflict whenever he could—something the more forthright Gallatin never completely understood. Jefferson told Davis that nothing had been decided. He left the Federalist incumbent in place, he turned to Governor Clinton and the Livingstons rather than Burr for advice on New York appointments, and a few years later when everyone's attention had drifted elsewhere, he gave the post that Davis wanted to a respectable Clintonian. The Federalist press jeered that the Republican "liberty and *equality* gentry" were putting federal offices in New York into the hands of "TWO families to keep them...out of the reach of the aristocrats."[56]

Respectability remained as much a requirement for senior federal appointment under Jefferson as it had been under Washington and Adams. The hundreds of patronage letters that passed through Gallatin's hands consistently mentioned not only a man's politics but also his military or public service, his means, and his social standing. Jefferson did appoint more men from modest backgrounds, but they were men who had bettered themselves. They were the striving, self-fashioning achievers who had tended to become Republicans because their achievements were not enough to win them acceptance from the Federalist elite. There was room in the Republican civil service for new men like that, but there was no room for men like Davis who had bad manners and lowly occupations.[57]

There also was no room for African Americans or women. Postmaster General Gideon Granger, a Connecticut man, fired the free blacks he found in the postal service because he feared their travel with the mail would give them the opportunity to promote slave revolts. It would never have occurred to anyone to consider a woman for a senior post, but Gallatin did venture to propose a woman as keeper of the lighthouse off Cape Fear in North Carolina. Rebecca Long was the former keeper's widow, and her case was sympathetic. Her son-in-law had killed her husband in a hunting accident a few months earlier, and she probably had been tending the lighthouse by herself ever since. The customs collector in Wilmington vouched for her, and Gallatin was prepared to give her the job. But Jefferson was not. "The appointment of a woman to office," he told Gallatin, "is an innovation for which the public is not prepared, nor am I." He chose a Revolutionary War veteran and former revenue officer instead.[58]

෴

The trans-Appalachian West assumed great importance in American life during the early years of Jefferson's administration. The populations of western Pennsylvania, upstate New York, Vermont, Kentucky, and Tennessee had grown dramatically, and a new wave of American settlers was pushing into the public lands north of the Ohio River. Jefferson and Madison understood the economic and political significance of those developments. They envisioned the West as a place where sturdy yeomen farmers could extend the material foundations for stable republican government. And they expected those men to be the sort of virtuous agrarian citizens who would defend freedom, democracy, and the ascendency of the Republican party. But Jefferson and Madison had never been in the West, and Gallatin—who had lived there—personified a more complicated reality. He was not the sturdy yeoman farmer of Republican daydreams. He had started a town, and glass from his small factory glazed windows along the Ohio. What he brought to bear on Western problems was not just a political persuasion, but an instinctive pragmatism annealed in the furnace of frontier experience.[59]

The Treasury had administered the public lands since the beginning of the federal government because land sales were expected to be an important source of revenue. When Gallatin took office, most of the lands available for sale were in four extensive districts laid out above the Ohio River from the western border of Pennsylvania to a line beyond Cincinnati. Several states and groups of speculators owned other districts above the river, but the bulk of the enormous territory between the Ohio and the Great Lakes still belonged to Native American peoples. In the 1790s, both Hamilton and Gallatin had looked to the public lands for money needed to pay the national debt, and both of them had supported the federal government's efforts to wrest more land from Natives and sell it to white men. But their approaches to land sales were profoundly different. Hamilton wanted to sell the land to speculators in large tracts to raise the money as quickly as possible. Gallatin conceded that bulk sales would raise money more quickly, but he thought they would jeopardize a more important objective.[60]

What was at stake in the public domain, as Gallatin and other Republicans saw it, was nothing less than who would own the Western country. Would it be rich speculators and landlords with mobs of tenants? Or would it be settlers working their own land? Since land ownership gave men the independence they needed to be good citizens, easy access to land was an essential part of the Republican vision. The nation's welfare, Gallatin had told Congress, depended as much on the people's access to land as it did on the nation's political institutions. The country was happy, he said, "because the poor man has been able always to attain his portion of the land." To keep speculators from engrossing the public lands, Gallatin had proposed to sell land in tracts as small as 320 acres at a minimum price high enough to prevent speculators from earning a quick profit on resale. But the land law that Congress adopted in 1796 was an unsatisfactory compromise. Its minimum price of $2 per acre was too high for speculators, but its minimum purchase of 640 acres was more than most settlers could afford. The resulting sales were vanishingly small.[61]

A more liberal land law in 1800 cut the minimum tract size in half—to the 320 acres that Gallatin had proposed. It kept the minimum price at $2 per acre, and it allowed buyers to pay for their land in installments over four years. Treasury officials in the Ohio territory held the first public auctions under the new land law in the month Gallatin took office. The auctions were an important test of whether the law could increase sales, and on the face of things, the results were encouraging. The government sold more land than it ever had under the prior law. In a report to Congress, Gallatin congratulated himself that the new arrangements had effectively "destroyed the monopoly of lands, and [thrown] the land exclusively in the hands of actual settlers." But the real situation was knottier than it appeared. Wealthier settlers and other investors had bought large quantities of land at the minimum price, ordinary settlers complained that the minimum price was too high, and the presence of squatters made the sale of some tracts quite difficult. The new credit system also presented risks. By 1803, buyers' obligations to the Treasury had mounted to $1.1 million, and ordinary settlers began to default because their land was not producing enough income to cover the installments due on their purchases. Defaulting settlers lost their land and most of the payments they already had made.[62]

As indebted settlers began calling for relief, Gallatin realized that credit sales were a trap. He knew from his own hard experience that it was "almost impossible" to earn enough money from newly settled land to pay for it in four years. Sales on credit to settlers who had no other resources were therefore unsound, and they were creating a class of people hostile to the federal government. In an 1804 report to the House, Gallatin proposed new terms of sale. He did not want to reduce the price per acre very much because he thought that would attract speculators and prevent the "gradual and equal distribution of property." He thought a large reduction in the minimum tract size, on the other hand, would give ordinary settlers the chance to buy a homestead at a price they could afford to pay in cash. He therefore proposed to offer tracts as small as 160 acres, reduce the price to $1.50 per acre, and eliminate sales on credit.[63]

Congress adopted the smaller tract size, but it left the minimum price unchanged and it continued to offer credit—even eliminating interest charges as long as buyers made their payments on time. The number of land sales increased sharply during the next two years. Average receipts from land sales during Gallatin's remaining years at the Treasury ran about 50 percent higher than they had been during the best year under the earlier law. But despite the large increase in the number of sales, the actual cash receipts remained relatively modest—about $640,000 annually—and incessant cries from delinquent purchasers led Congress to enact five separate relief measures.[64]

A modern historian has called the survey and sale of the public lands "the largest and most difficult administrative tasks of the Republican era," and the spike in sales during Gallatin's years at the Treasury put an enormous burden on the Treasury's immature bureaucracy. Land administration was complicated. The Treasury could not offer a district for sale until surveyors working in wilderness conditions had divided it into townships six miles square and then platted each township into thirty-six saleable tracts of one square mile—640 acres. The laws that reduced the minimum tract size required additional surveys, plat revisions, and further delays. Once the land had been surveyed, the Treasury needed to establish local land offices to handle sales. The eighteen land offices—fourteen of them established under Gallatin's direction—were remote and thinly staffed. Each office employed a land register to keep track of the land records and a receiver to collect money from the buyers. Some of the offices also had special commissioners to sort out competing claims under old land grants. As land sales rose, these officials often floundered, and the only person at the Treasury to whom they could turn was the Treasury secretary himself.[65]

The problems in the land offices were endless. A new chief surveyor insisted that the plats should be more precise, which brought surveys to a crawl. The receiver in Cincinnati needed authorization to hire guarded wagons so he could send $150,000 in specie—which weighed about four tons—to Pittsburgh. The register in Chillicothe, Ohio, wanted to know whether he could charge the same fee for recording land sold at auction as he had charged for recording land sold over the counter. Buyers at the auctions colluded to prevent competitive bidding, and land officers found no good way to stop them. The order of the day, a chief surveyor complained, was "speculation, Surveying Jobbing, Pettyfogging, Fakery, Electioneering for public places, & everything except labor & industry." John Badollet—whom Gallatin in an unusual act of favoritism had appointed to be the register at Vincennes in the Indiana territory—complained that governor William Henry Harrison was conniving to infiltrate slavery into the free territory. Problems also appeared back in Washington. "I know this business is very troublesome to you," a friend acknowledged, but some of the Treasury clerks handling the land records had their hands out for extra fees. Gallatin urged Congress to create a separate bureau within the Treasury to supervise public lands, but it was not until 1812 that Congress finally responded by creating the General Land Office.[66]

The summer of 1803 brought to Washington the electrifying news that American negotiators in Paris had purchased Louisiana from France and extended the American West beyond the Mississippi River. The purchase was an unexpectedly sweeping solution to a problem presented two years earlier when the administration heard that Spain was returning Louisiana to France, its original colonial master. The master of Louisiana controlled the Mississippi, and the Mississippi was a vital outlet for the agricultural surplus produced by American settlers in the trans-Appalachian West. Settlers could float down the river bulky agricultural commodities that they could not afford to carry east over the mountains. Foreign interference with Mississippi navigation therefore jeopardized Westerners' income and the value of their land. Spain had conceded American rights to use the river and the port of New Orleans by treaty in 1795, but Spanish authorities had not always observed the treaty and French intentions were unclear. The post-revolutionary French government, dominated by a brash young Corsican general named Napoleon Bonaparte, was aggressive. Reports received in Washington said that he was sending a large army to America to recover the sugar colony of Saint-Domingue (Haiti) from the former slaves who now ruled it and then to establish large garrisons on the lower Mississippi. Past doubts about the federal government's ability to protect Western interests had prompted Western settlers to flirt with regional independence and even allegiance to Spain, so French control of the Mississippi raised fresh fears of disunion.[67]

The administration had offered France $2 million for the port of New Orleans and the region called West Florida, which ran east from New Orleans along the coast of the Gulf of Mexico. But Bonaparte had ignored the offer until the costly failure of his expedition to Saint-Domingue and the prospect of an expensive new war with Britain changed his mind. He decided to cash his chips on the American table so he could resume play in Europe, and he offered to sell the entire Louisiana territory to the United States for 80 million francs. This vast region of more than 825,000 square miles spread northwest from the mouth of the Mississippi across the Great Plains to the Rocky Mountains. The American negotiators in Paris, James Monroe and Robert R. Livingston, had no authority to make such a grand purchase, but they knew the seller was mercurial and the offer too good to refuse. Within weeks they agreed to buy Louisiana for 60 million francs and the assumption of 20 million francs in claims that American citizens had made against France for shipping seized during the 1790s—a total price of about $15 million.[68]

The administration was delighted with the purchase, but Jefferson spent the summer fretting about the constitutional questions it presented. Could the federal government acquire new territory? Who would govern it? Could its inhabitants become American citizens as the purchase treaty required, and could states formed from it join the Union? The Constitution gave no express answers to those questions, and that made them difficult for a man who had claimed that the federal government could not charter a bank in the absence of express constitutional authorization. Jefferson concluded that he could not ratify the purchase treaty without a constitutional amendment, but since the treaty gave the United States only six months for ratification, he convinced himself that an amendment after the fact would suffice.[69]

Gallatin and other members of the cabinet took a less complicated position. All nations, Gallatin assured Jefferson, had an inherent right to acquire territory. The constitutional provisions that gave the president and the Senate power to make treaties therefore gave them all of the authority they needed to buy Louisiana. And the constitutional provisions that empowered Congress to regulate territories and to admit new states applied to new territories as well as the original ones. Gallatin had given Jefferson the same sort of pragmatic advice on the expedition Jefferson was sending to explore the Louisiana territory. Jefferson had been planning to send Meriwether Lewis and William Clark into Louisiana even before France agreed to sell it, and he had assured the French and Spanish governments that the expedition's objectives were purely scientific. His draft instructions to Lewis and Clark would have borne that out because they dwelt on plants and animals, indigenous peoples, and a possible water passage to the Pacific Ocean. Gallatin prepared a more practical set of instructions. He reminded Jefferson that the United States might have to occupy the French territory in order to prevent Britain from seizing it during a war with France, and he thought it was certain that Americans eventually would settle there. Gallatin's instructions therefore focused on soil fertility and the region's capacity to support settlement.[70]

Gallatin's problem during the summer of 1803 was how to pay for Louisiana. Fifteen million dollars was an enormous amount of money, especially for an administration that had committed most of its resources to repaying public debt, and the Louisiana treaty was distressingly specific about how the money had to be paid. The main $11.25 million payment had to be made with new federal bonds paying 6 percent interest. Gallatin had specifically objected to delivering bonds because he thought he could raise the same amount in cash in the United States on better terms. The treaty's provision for paying the $3.75 million of private American claims was not much better. It let corruptible French officials decide which claims to pay, and it created unpredictable demands for money because the American Treasury had to pay the claims in cash whenever they happened to settle.[71]

Although he never quite said so in writing, it is clear that Gallatin thought the French negotiators had duped the Americans on the payment arrangements. Events in Europe had already proven him right. The French government—eager to get its hands on the cash it needed to renew war with Britain—sold the $11.25 million of American bonds to the Baring family's bank in London and their partners in Amsterdam for what amounted to less than $9 million. The hefty discount on the bonds gave the bankers room for a big profit, and it suggested to other lenders that American government bonds must be a risky investment. The rich opportunities for French officials to get kickbacks from the bankers and bribes from the private claimants were obvious. Madison mentioned Gallatin's concern to James Monroe in only a vague way, so it was left to John Taylor—who had taken the absent Monroe under his wing—to tell him plainly that some people in Washington thought the treaty would let the French officials who had made it "be paid rich by it."[72]

Whatever his misgivings about the payment terms, Gallatin worked amicably with Alexander Baring—the young banker who came to Washington to complete his firm's bond purchase—and he began to adjust his overall plan for repaying the public debt to take account of the new obligations. Since swelling trade had increased federal revenue from import duties, Gallatin thought the government could afford to increase its annual payment on the debt from $7.3 million to $8 million. That would allow the government to repay the Louisiana bonds only eighteen months later than the date by which Gallatin had planned to repay all of the other debt. Congress adopted Gallatin's plan, but two years later a flood of cash demands from the American claimants almost forced

Gallatin to borrow money for the first time. He and Jefferson were greatly relieved when he managed to pay off the claimants without taking a loan. Republican borrowing would have given the Federalists a propaganda victory. In his annual message to Congress a few months later, Jefferson took pains to emphasize that the Treasury had paid both the Louisiana purchase claims and $9 million on the public debt from revenues collected during the current year.[73]

Questions about roads and canals most clearly revealed the fundamental difference between the approaches that Gallatin and Jefferson took toward Western development. Gallatin was an enthusiastic supporter of those internal improvements. He knew from firsthand experience that Americans in the West could not prosper unless they could send their products to market in more populated places. He also had seen how the settlers' political loyalty could shift when they believed the United States government did not support their economic efforts. Although Adam Smith and other liberal political economists thought private toll companies should build most transportation improvements, Gallatin knew from his experience in Pennsylvania that traffic in the backcountry was simply too light to attract the necessary private investment. He thought that public spending on roads and canals was—unlike military spending—a productive use of capital that could increase the value of public and private land, expand production, and grow public revenues. He therefore believed that the federal government should support the major interstate improvements needed to connect the American interior with the Atlantic coast and the waters of the Mississippi.[74]

Jefferson agreed that the federal government should support internal improvements, and his second inaugural address celebrated the day when repayment of the national debt would "liberate" federal revenues to be used for that purpose. But Jefferson's insistence that the federal government stay within the literal language of the Constitution profoundly compromised his commitment to internal improvements. The law admitting Ohio to the Union in 1802 dedicated 5 percent of the receipts from public land sale in the state to the federal construction of roads linking Ohio with other regions. Gallatin had anticipated questions about this arrangement, and his outline for the law carefully provided that the federal government could not build the roads without getting the consent of the states through which they would pass. But as Jefferson thought about it, he decided that that limitation on federal authority was insufficient. He worried that the federal government did not even have the constitutional authority to spend money on light-houses and piers in the Delaware River, and he predicted that federal public works would lead to "bottomless expense," excessive executive patronage, and corruption.[75]

By the time Jefferson endorsed federal spending on internal improvements in his second inaugural address, he was saying that it would require a constitutional amendment and a just repartition of federal money among the states. Jefferson further complicated the whole issue by broadening the improvements that he mentioned to include "arts, manufactures, education, and other great objects within each state." Two years later, when Jefferson specifically invited Congress to develop a policy for internal improvements, Gallatin convinced him to give priority to roads and canals and to drop the reference to proportional spending within each state. But the dissonance in Republican thinking that ultimately would drown out Gallatin's call for transportation improvements was already audible.[76]

The money set aside from land sales in Ohio paid for preliminary work on the first national road in 1806 and 1807. The Cumberland Road, as it was called at the time, was to run from Cumberland, Maryland, on the Potomac River to Wheeling, Virginia (now West Virginia), on the Ohio River along a route that went through Gallatin's old Congressional district in southwestern Pennsylvania. Gallatin took charge of the project, but his experience with it soon confirmed Jefferson's fear that internal improvements could easily become jobs in the worst sense of the word. The Pennsylvania legislature conditioned its consent to construction of the road on deviations that took it through the principal towns in Fayette and Washington counties. This local interference deeply annoyed Jefferson, but Gallatin counseled accommodation. Since a road across the Appalachians was "a national object of great importance (particularly as a bond of union)," he said, "I think it more useful to remove local and State opposition than to adhere too strictly" to the original plan, however correct it might have been. Jefferson stonewalled for a few months and then grudgingly accepted the deviations after Gallatin pointed out that the loss of the affected counties could swing Pennsylvania's electoral votes to the Federalists in the next presidential election. This groundbreaking federal road project advanced slowly, and fights about its cost and the constitutional basis for funding it continued for years. The road did not reach Wheeling until 1818.[77]

The dangers of federal internal improvements became even more apparent early in 1807 when senators from Kentucky and Delaware started logrolling to get federal money for canals in those states. The collusion between senators from the states that would benefit appalled John Quincy Adams, a forty-year-old Federalist senator from Massachusetts and the son of John and Abigail Adams. He denounced the senators for sacrificing the public good to their own parochial interests, and he called on the Treasury to prepare an overall plan showing which roads and canals would provide the most benefit to the whole nation. Adams's proposal failed at the time. But when the logs set in motion for the two canal projects later jammed, the Senate adopted a virtually identical proposal from Thomas Worthington of Ohio—a close friend of Gallatin and a supporter of public improvements.[78]

The Report on Roads and Canals that Gallatin delivered to the Senate in 1808 was a towering appeal for an immense program of transportation improvements. Gallatin began the report by tipping his hat to the value of privately funded toll roads, but he quickly came to his essential point. Private enterprise, he said, could not build the great roads and canals needed to unleash the nation's economic potential because capital was too scarce and most of the country was too sparsely settled to generate an adequate short-term return on the necessary investment. Only the federal government could "remove these obstacles," and its "early and efficient" aid would produce interlocking economic and political advantages. Good roads and canals would increase personal and commercial interaction among the American people, and increased interaction would unite the people into a "community of interest." Government spending on roads and canals, in other words, would give the free market wider scope to build natural bonds of national union. "No other single operation, within the power of government," Gallatin declared, "can more effectually tend to strengthen and perpetuate that union, which secures external independence, domestic peace, and internal liberty."[79]

The improvements that Gallatin proposed were breathtaking. They included an inland waterway stretching along the Atlantic coast, a road from Maine to Georgia, five great road and canal systems linking major Atlantic coastal rivers to corresponding rivers and lakes on the other side of the Appalachians, three new roads running deeper into the West, and a clutch of canals around the falls on major waterways. His report included a preliminary engineering analysis by Benjamin Henry Latrobe and Robert Fulton, the best-known engineers in the country, and it estimated the projects proposed would cost $16.6 million. Geography determined the location of the major improvements, so Gallatin proposed to do "justice" by committing another $3.4 million to local improvements in other parts of the country. The total investment therefore would be $20 million.[80]

The government could make this $20 million investment over ten years, Gallatin explained, out of the surplus he expected to generate as he paid down the public debt and reduced the interest burden on the annual revenues. The government could undertake the projects itself— the approach Gallatin clearly favored because it would prevent "local interests" from altering the routes—but it also could purchase shares and make loans to private companies formed to undertake them. The federal government had the constitutional authority, Gallatin maintained, to build roads and canals with the consent of the states through which they passed. In order to prevent states from imposing "impediments" and suggesting "modifications," however, Congress should consider a constitutional amendment that eliminated the need for consent.[81]

Gallatin's 1808 report stands as one of the greatest government planning documents of the Early Republic, but Congress never acted on it. By the time Gallatin delivered the report, Jefferson was in his last year as president and Congress was preoccupied by the threat of war. When two Western members tried to get most of Gallatin's recommendations adopted two years later, their bill died amid concerns about its cost and constitutionality. An engineer who had worked on coastal surveys lamented to Gallatin that the "failure of this wise and provident measure...presents an astonishing picture of our political inconsistency!" The Republicans were really no better at getting on with improvement than the Federalists had been, complained William Duane in the *Aurora*. "T[h]e federalists had so much to borrow, the democrats so much to pay, that neither could afford money, for the proper business of the country." When war with Britain grew imminent in 1812, Gallatin himself had to tell Congress that the Treasury could no longer spare the money for internal improvements.[82]

After the War of 1812, Henry Clay, John C. Calhoun, and other young nationalists who had taken control of the Republican party used Gallatin's report as the template for their own bold program of federal internal improvements, and by the mid-nineteenth century, substantially all of the roads and canals that Gallatin had proposed actually were constructed. But the federal government built only one of them— the Cumberland Road—and funded only a part of three others. The states and private companies built the rest. Why was that? Why did a federal plan for improvements so obviously important to the nation's economic development and political cohesion fail to win Congressional support? The answer points to an essential impasse in Republican political thought.[83]

Jefferson and other members of the Republican gentry believed it was appropriate for governments—sometimes even the federal government—to help open opportunities for private enterprise. But they viewed the construction of federal public works within the states as a suspect extension of federal power. They were willing to consider a few particular projects, but absent a constitutional amendment, they shied away from almost all of them and they opposed an overall program of improvements. Although Jefferson in retirement continued his rhetorical celebrations of the day when the federal government would be able to use

revenues "liberated" from debt service for internal improvements, he
clung to those constitutional concerns. And toward the end of his life,
Jefferson flatly denounced the federal construction of roads and canals
as an unconstitutional federal intrusion into the states. Rock-ribbed
Republicans such as Nathaniel Macon and John Randolph—who eventually made an express connection between their opposition to federal
internal improvements and their fear of federal interference with domestic slavery—had come to the same conclusion. For them, keeping the
federal government small and frugal was ultimately more important than
developing the material basis for prosperity in the American West.[84]

Albert Gallatin's commitment to his mission at the Treasury was
unremitting, and as he worked through hot summers in Washington, he
was often alone. Congress was in recess. Hannah Gallatin and their
children were at her parents' house in New York City or their country
house in a nearby village called Greenwich. She found both places health-
ier and more congenial than Washington—a city that she predicted
*"never will be of any consequence even if the national government
should remain there."* The child Hannah had been expecting when she
moved to Washington had died within eight months, and two of the three
children she had during her remaining years in Washington died within
their first year. Only a daughter named Frances, born in 1803, survived.
By July, as the risk of mosquito-borne illness in Washington increased,
Jefferson and other cabinet members left town. Jefferson flatly refused
to risk his health by staying in the capital, and he urged Gallatin to follow
his example. But Gallatin thought the Treasury required "constant
superintendence," and he remained until late summer when he joined his
family in New York or Greenwich for a few weeks. A Federalist newspaper in Boston turned the old taunt about Gallatin "stopping the wheels
of government" into a jeer that he now was "the only one of our *Rulers*
who keeps the wheels going."[85]

The summers in Washington took their toll. Gallatin frequently ran fevers and sometimes found himself too exhausted to work. "If my health does not improve," he confided to his brother-in-law late one summer, "I must resign." And loneliness deepened his discontent. "I want you and miss you every way," he wrote to Hannah Gallatin one evening. "I really do not know what I should or could do without you." She had poured her own longing into a letter the previous day. "I am...distressed at the idea of being so long without you, and your situation so forlorn," she told him; "there is not an evening passes but I accompany you in imagination in your solitary walks with your seegar, on the pavement before the door, or backward & forwards in one of the rooms....I will kiss the children for you," she reassured him. "I will be good, I will love you, with all my heart and I will spend no money."[86]

CHAPTER 7

FRUGALITY'S PRICE

The man in Rembrandt Peale's portrait of Albert Gallatin looks confident and comfortable. When Peale painted the picture in February 1805 for his father's museum in Philadelphia, Gallatin had reason to be both. His family was back in Washington for the winter, his children seemed healthy, and even his long-neglected business in New Geneva was doing better than expected. He had repaid $13.6 million of the national debt over the previous four years, financed the purchase of Louisiana, and accumulated $4.8 million of cash in the Treasury. The Republican regime had grown stronger. The Republican caucus in Congress chose New York governor George Clinton to replace Aaron Burr as the vice presidential candidate in 1804, and Burr hastened his descent into political oblivion by killing Alexander Hamilton in a duel five months later. Jefferson and Clinton won the 1804 presidential election in a landslide that expanded Republican majorities in both houses of Congress. Jefferson's second inaugural address celebrated his administration's fiscal

achievements. "The suppression of unnecessary offices, of useless establishments and expenses, enabled us to discontinue our internal taxes," he
exalted. Since only import duties remained, "it may be the pleasure and
pride of an American to ask, What farmer, what mechanic, what laborer
ever sees a taxgatherer of the United States?" It was a beguiling narrative,
and prospects for the next four years seemed good.[1]

But a second look at Peale's portrait reveals a slight wariness in
Gallatin's expression, a tense circumspection so thoroughly under control
that the gifted painter barely caught it. There was reason for that too.
Gallatin's children were healthy, but he worried that he could not give
them a proper education in a backward place like Washington. His fiscal
accomplishments over the previous four years were impressive, but he
had not achieved them in the way he had intended. Although the government was spending about $2 million less each year than it had spent
under John Adams, the actual reductions in military spending were too
small to balance Gallatin's budgets. Only an unanticipated spike in
import duties had saved him from embarrassment, and much of that
bonanza came from the temporary opportunities that trade disruption
during the Napoleonic wars had given to American merchants.[2]

Gallatin was also beginning to sense that his immersion in his
work, his resistance to partisan patronage, and his relentless insistence
on frugal government could carry a heavy price. He found little time
to return to Pennsylvania except to visit Alexander Dallas on his way
to and from New York, and both his absence and his close friendship
with Dallas exposed him to attacks from the dissatisfied Republicans
around William Duane and Michael Leib. His resistance to widespread
removals of Federalists from office made enemies of those who wanted
the places, and—just as Dallas had warned him—his selections among
Republican office-seekers for places that came open made as many
enemies as friends. Scrimping to repay the public debt carried a particularly heavy price because he found himself objecting to almost
everything.[3]

Gallatin's frugality drew criticism from both political parties. Federalists took it as confirmation that there was little more to Republicanism

than opposition to the central government and the measures necessary to sustain it. The real danger to the Republican administration, wrote the perceptive Federalist senator John Quincy Adams, lay not on the rocky coast of Federalist New England but in "the shallowness of their [own] waters." He predicted that "[t]heir system is so short sighted, and so contracted, that it will never stand a popular test even of twelve years." Some Republicans also believed Gallatin had gone too far. John Taylor— an early and inveterate critic of Hamilton's financial system—thought the administration was obsessed with fiscal affairs. He thought structural reforms, such as term limits and permanent reductions in presidential patronage, would invigorate the Republican cause far more than redeeming the debt and financing the purchase of Louisiana. For "brilliant as [those things] are," he told a friend, there is a certain "counting:house duskishness" about them that "will rapidly consign them to oblivion."[4]

A certain narrowness had crept into Gallatin's financial management after the bold fiscal reforms of the administration's early years. He knew his reforms would not work unless he restrained spending, and cost overruns in the early years had redoubled his determination to do that. Within his own department, Gallatin could be positively parsimonious. He refused to reimburse officials in the land offices for their rent, furniture, and firewood, for example, because the law made no specific appropriation for those things. The land officers found that galling. "I love frugality and economy in the Management of public Money," one told his son, "but I view Parsimony & extravagance as extremes that are Equally productive of Evil." Gallatin even went so far as to close the lighthouse at Sandy Hook, which guided ships into New York harbor, because of an expensive property dispute. That may have had more calamitous consequences. David Gelston, the customs collector for New York and intimate friend of the Nicholson family, wrote to warn him that local citizens thought the closure had caused three shipwrecks.[5]

Outside his department, Gallatin had two levers by which he could control spending. The first was his review of the other executive departments' annual spending estimates. The law establishing the Treasury required the Treasury secretary to make annual reports to Congress on the government's projected revenues and expenditures. Alexander Hamilton had stretched that responsibility into a mandate to supervise government spending, and Gallatin made it clear to Jefferson from the outset that he meant to do the same thing. Gallatin assured Jefferson that he would collaborate with him (something Hamilton had not always done with Washington), but he left no doubt that he thought the law made the estimates his responsibility.[6]

Gallatin's second lever was the settlement of government accounts. This power was crucial because the Treasury had little direct control over what the government spent day to day. Civilian and military officers throughout the country and naval and diplomatic officers abroad spent the money on their own responsibility and then submitted accounts of what they had done. Responsibility for reviewing the accounts fell to the auditor of the Treasury or—in the case of military spending—the separate auditors in the War and Navy departments. The Comptroller of the Treasury settled disputes and resolved difficult legal questions. The settlement of accounts was an unwieldy tool because the process was tedious and the Treasury secretary had no formal role in it. As a practical matter, however, the comptroller often consulted the Treasury secretary on large or contentious matters, and the heads of other executive departments came directly to the Treasury secretary for large or urgent advances.[7]

Asking Gallatin for money could be a trying experience, as even Jefferson discovered in the case of Edward Stevens. Stevens was a doctor from Philadelphia, a native of St. Croix, and a childhood friend of Alexander Hamilton. The Adams administration had sent him to Saint-Domingue in 1799 to open relations with the government established by François Dominique Toussaint Louverture and the former slaves who had taken over the French colony. Stevens was designated as a consul rather than a minister because Toussaint's government had not yet declared independence from France. But Jefferson was stating the obvious when he reported to Madison at the time that Stevens "may be considered our Minister to Touissant." When Stevens claimed reimbursement for his expenses after he came home, he ran into a problem. Consuls were not entitled to reimbursement, and he had no official documents proving that the Adams administration had promised otherwise in his case. The Comptroller of the Treasury therefore denied Stevens's claim. Madison thought Stevens deserved to be paid, and Jefferson asked Gallatin to intervene. Jefferson recognized there was no specific appropriation for Stevens's expenses, but he thought the Treasury should pay them out of a general appropriation for foreign relations. He said that Congress— aware that it should not make its appropriations "too minute"—had entrusted that lump sum to the State department's discretion.[8]

Gallatin promised to look into the matter, but he bristled at Jefferson's expedient dismissal of the need for a specific appropriation. With "perfect respect and great deference to your judgment," he replied, "[p]ermit me...to say that...the Secretary of the Treasury is, in the nature of things, left sole judge" of whether a specific payment is proper. It therefore seemed just, he continued, that "he should be permitted to act in conformity with his own view on the subject." Surely, came Jefferson's soothing response, the question of legal responsibility for the decision would never arise because "we shall ultimately come to a result in which we can all harmonize." Jefferson was wrong about that. Gallatin rejected Stevens's claim, and detailed memoranda from Madison and Jefferson did not change his mind. Jefferson finally had to play his trump card. Because the Constitution created a single rather than a plural executive, he told Gallatin, "I presume I must decide between the [different] opinions, however reluctantly." He instructed the comptroller to approve Stevens's claim.[9]

No one had suffered more from Gallatin's frugality than Robert Smith, the Secretary of the Navy. He was an admiralty lawyer from the port city of Baltimore and the brother of Baltimore merchant Samuel Smith, who had clashed with Gallatin over naval spending ever since the Quasi-War with France. The Navy secretary looked like his older brother—same bold body, same big nose—but he lacked his brother's intelligence and self-confidence. He was sociable and he and his wife entertained generously, but what in his brother appeared to be pride seemed only vanity in him. Robert Smith nevertheless carried political weight because he had important connections in the Senate.

His brother was now a senator from Maryland, and his brother-in-law Wilson Cary Nicholas, a neighbor and friend of Jefferson, was a senator from Virginia.[10]

The navy post was not a plum appointment, and Robert Smith had not been Jefferson's first (or even his second) choice for the job. The navy had grown to thirty-three ships during the Quasi-War, but Congress kept only six large frigates in service when the conflict ended and everyone had expected the economy-minded Republican administration to make additional cuts. In fact, deteriorating relations with Tripoli had given the navy new life. Tripoli and other North African states made a practice of seizing the merchant ships of nations that failed to pay them tribute. The United States had initially agreed to pay, as other nations did, because the amount demanded was less than the cost of resistance. But Tripoli's increasing demands led to misunderstandings and late payment. The resulting naval war in the Mediterranean began shortly after Jefferson took office and lasted four years.[11]

Given the war, Smith found it impossible to operate his department within the pinched estimates on which Gallatin had insisted when the administration repealed internal taxes. But Gallatin soon concluded that Smith's shortcomings as an administrator were part of the problem. "I cannot discover any approach towards reform" in the navy, he told Jefferson after two years of experience. "[A]lthough I am sensible that in the opinion of many wise & good men, my ideas of expenditures are...too contracted," he continued, "yet I feel a strong confidence that on this particular point I am right." The situation made Jefferson uncomfortable. He supported Gallatin's drive to reduce spending and he had an instinctive Republican aversion to navies, but he flinched from confronting Smith directly. So he and Gallatin took to hammering out the Navy department's estimates between themselves before "opening them" to Smith.[12]

A navy might not present the hazard to popular liberty that Republicans saw in a standing army, but Republicans believed a navy could oppress a nation just as surely by swelling its public debt. The enormous debt that Britain had incurred in its naval wars with France was a clear demonstration of the danger, and the Republicans had made it an object lesson in their attacks on Hamilton's funding system. Gallatin had argued during the Quasi-War that Congress should limit naval spending until the United States could afford to build a competitive navy. He recognized that the war with Tripoli was a special situation, but Smith's inability to contain spending confirmed Gallatin in his belief that the United States was not yet ready to begin building a larger navy. It seemed to him that tribute to the North African states was cheaper, easier to quantify, and therefore better than a naval war.[13]

Jefferson himself was ambivalent. On one day, his Republican reflexes told him that a shortfall in revenue would require a further cut in naval spending. But a week later, he found himself ordering another frigate into the Mediterranean even though the Navy department had no money left in its appropriation. In 1804, Gallatin bowed to reality by asking Congress for an additional 2.5 percent duty on imports to pay for Mediterranean naval operations. He meant the special Mediterranean Fund to be not so much "a protest against loose expenditure" (as Henry Adams would have it), but a demonstration of the Republican conviction that raising taxes was the best way to focus the people's attention on how much money the government spent.[14]

As the Tripolitan War wound down early in 1805, tensions within the administration over the navy's spending finally erupted. Gallatin complained to Jefferson that naval spending continued relatively unabated despite the decline in hostilities and—more pointedly—that the large amounts spent during the war had failed to strengthen the navy. "On this subject," he said, "I have, for the sake of preserving perfect harmony in your councils, however grating to my feelings, been almost uniformly silent; and I beg that you will ascribe what I now say to a sense of duty and to the grateful attachment I feel for you." Gallatin's complaint prompted a frank conversation between Jefferson, Gallatin, and Robert Smith. What Gallatin must have said in that conversation came echoing back in a letter that Smith sent to him the next week. A boy whom Gallatin had proposed as a midshipman would have to wait for a vacancy, wrote Smith. "As we are woefully constrained to spend a 'confounded sight of money' upon objects indespensably necessary, *I do not like to incur the expense of a cent that can possibly be avoided.*"[15]

Like most things that happened in the small capital city, the conflict between Gallatin and Robert Smith became a subject of gossip. "I do not understand your manoeuvres at head quarters," John Randolph wrote to Gallatin, "nor should I be surprised to see the navy department abolished, or, in more appropriate phrase, swept by the board, at the next session of Congress." But the talk—or at least Randolph's rendition of it—missed the mark. Gallatin was not against the navy; he was only against wasting money on an ineffectual navy. His estimates for the next Congress proposed to continue the Mediterranean surtax and to commit the surtax revenue to a multi-year program of naval construction. He hoped to postpone most of the spending for three or four years so that he could first get rid of more debt, but he told Jefferson that he had "had no doubt for a long time that the United States would ultimately have a navy." He thought a competitive navy was a necessary incident of national sovereignty and a vital protection for the trade that produced the import duties on which the federal government depended. Without a navy, he said, American commerce would suffer perpetual "injuries and insults" whenever there was a war in Europe.[16]

The tension between Gallatin and Smith boiled over in the autumn of 1805 when Gallatin discovered that Smith had ignored or hidden significant deficits in the Navy department. The problem came to light when Smith abruptly announced that he needed $170,000 more than the navy had left in its appropriation in order to pay off the crews of several returning frigates. Gallatin bridled at Smith's suggestion that he could just cover the shortfall by taking an unauthorized loan from the Bank of the United States, and he began probing the dimensions of the problem. As best he could determine, he told Smith, the navy's total deficit for the year was going to be $250,000. Actually, Smith replied, the deficit would run to $600,000 because he had used a chunk of his current appropriation to pay overruns from the previous year. He had, in other words, overspent his appropriation by 50 percent. The disclosure was a turning point in the two men's relationship. Gallatin began sending Smith long didactic letters about the limits on his spending authority, and Jefferson started to sit in on Gallatin's meetings with Smith to ensure—he told Gallatin—that Smith would "modify his estimate to our mutual liking." When Smith again overspent his budget two years later, Gallatin underscored the overrun by asking Congress for a special appropriation.[17]

Jefferson supported Gallatin's efforts to control naval spending, but his own enthusiasm for building a fleet of gunboats significantly increased costs in the Navy department. The navy had used gunboats effectively in the shallow shore waters of the Mediterranean during the Tripolitan War, but the gunboats built for American waters after the war were not meant to be frugal substitutes for larger ships. They were instead a cheap, flexible, rapidly constructed substitute for expensive harbor fortifications. The gunboat construction program therefore shifted costs from the War department, which was in charge of fortifications, to the Navy department, which was responsible for vessels. But if the relative speed with which gunboats could be built was a strong argument in their favor, it was from Gallatin's point of view an argument for deferring construction of most of the gunboats until the eve of war. He agreed with Jefferson that some of the boats could be used to stop smuggling during peacetime, but given how easy the boats were to construct, he thought the annual cost of maintaining more of them than he needed for law enforcement was a waste of money. Gallatin also predicted that these small boats would deteriorate faster than large ships, making many of them useless by the time they were needed.[18]

Jefferson sharply rejected Gallatin's arguments against building a fleet of gunboats. He thought it would take too long to build a sufficient number during a crisis, and he claimed it would be easy to maintain the light boats in dry docks. By 1807, Jefferson and Robert Smith had convinced Congress to spend $852,000 on 188 additional gunboats, almost doubling the navy's peacetime spending estimate. Jefferson also toyed with engineer Robert Fulton's proposal to substitute a newly invented weapon called the torpedo for expensive harbor defenses. Although Jefferson never implemented Fulton's idea, his flirtation with it gave the writer Washington Irving and his jolly band of Federalist satirists a delicious chance to lampoon the administration's policy. For "to do our government justice," they wrote, "it has no objection to injuring and exterminating its enemies in any manner—provided the thing can be done *economically.*"[19]

◦◦◦◦◦

While Gallatin found it difficult to control spending, his results on the revenue side were more encouraging. The administration's decision to give up internal taxes had succeeded because the rapid expansion of American trade had boosted the revenue from import duties to record levels. Duties that had never before brought in more than $7.5 million in a single year generated $9.1 million in 1800, $10.8 million in 1801, and an average of $11.7 million for the next four years. The receipts rose because the Napoleonic Wars had increased demand for American grain, timber, and other commodities, and the fatter American incomes from rising export sales had swelled the demand for taxable imports.[20]

But part of the increase came from the carrying trade between the belligerent European nations and their sugar colonies in the Caribbean. Britain and France regularly attacked each other's merchant ships, so war had made transatlantic trade between Europe and the colonies risky and expensive for British and French merchants. That opened new opportunities for American ships. British and French mercantile regulations made it illegal for American ships to carry goods directly between the Caribbean colonies and foreign ports, but French authorities waived their regulations in order to get goods through British blockades, and British admiralty courts did not apply the regulations to neutral ships that broke their voyages in their home ports. If a ship unloaded its cargo and paid import duties on the goods at home before carrying them on to a foreign country, the British courts took the view that the re-exported goods were neutral property.[21]

Jefferson's administration insisted that neutral ships had the right to carry even a belligerent's property because free ships made free goods under international law, and Madison wrote a dense pamphlet denouncing Britain's refusal to recognize the maritime rights of neutral nations.

But the United States had no power to enforce those claims to maritime rights, and in practice the British rule already gave American merchants a lucrative opportunity to act as middlemen. Their home ports were near the Caribbean colonies, and federal law let them draw back all but 1 percent of the American import duties when they re-exported the goods they had landed. Federal revenue from broken voyages grew significant as the carrying trade mushroomed. The value of foreign goods re-exported from the United States rose from less than $0.5 million before the European wars erupted to $40 million in 1800 and $60 million in 1806—$20 million more than the value of the American domestic goods exported during that year.[22]

Gallatin knew that the revenue from wartime trade—particularly the carrying trade—was vulnerable. A drop in import duties during a brief period of European peace in 1802–03 showed what could happen, and even when the wars resumed, American trade was exposed to interruption. British merchants complained that Americans were using their wartime advantage to take over markets that Britain would find it difficult to reclaim in peacetime. The merchants got support from British politicians who had long believed that Britain should keep Americans out of the colonial trade. And because the British outgunned the French navy, it seemed clear to British leaders that neutral traders were helping France far more than they helped Britain.[23]

By 1805, these threats to neutral trade were coming to a head. American negotiators James Monroe and William Pinkney had been unable to make a new commercial treaty with the British government. The British navy insisted on its right to search American ships and to impress any British subjects found among the crews into the British service. Since the British claimed that Britons remained subject to impressment even if they had become American citizens, and since many native Americans looked and sounded like Britons, press crews often abducted Americans. American merchants' reliance on broken voyages to conduct the colonial trade also collapsed. In a case involving the American ship *Essex*, a British admiralty court declared that broken voyages were frauds unless merchants could prove they had actually intended to import the goods into

the United States at the time they paid the American import duties. This
stiffer interpretation of the law—which allowed the court to condemn
the *Essex*'s cargo of Spanish wine—sent a shock through the American
mercantile community. The British seized scores of American ships
embarked on what their owners had believed to be legal voyages. The
cost of insuring new cargoes quadrupled. Imports began to fall. And
Lord Nelson's destruction of the French fleet at Trafalgar in October
gave the British a free hand to blockade continental Europe, intercept
neutral trade, and impress sailors from American ships.[24]

Jefferson's annual message in December 1805 asked Congress to
respond to the British seizures of American ships, but the United States
had few choices. The American navy was so inconsequential that, although
Jefferson toyed with the idea of raising a naval militia, no one seriously
considered armed resistance. A ban on imports from Britain and its
colonies was an obvious alternative. Trade boycotts had a respectable
pedigree going back to the American patriots' non-importation pacts
during the Revolution, and they played to Jefferson's belief that appeals
to reason and enlightened self-interest would allow nations to settle
disputes without going to war. But excluding British goods would be
expensive. Substantially all of the federal revenues came from import
duties, and the vast majority of American imports still came from Britain
and its colonies. High discriminatory duties on British imports were
another possibility, but duties high enough to harm the British would
also decrease imports and reduce federal revenue.[25]

So Gallatin was horrified when the House took up a resolution
offered by Andrew Gregg—whom Gallatin called the "MisRepresenta-
tive" from Pennsylvania—to ban British imports entirely. Two weeks
later, Joseph Nicholson, who had been out of town when Gregg offered
the resolution, made a more modest proposal to limit non-importation
to a list of British goods that Americans could get from other sources.
Nicholson's bill was full of flaws, but it gathered support because it was
far less likely to reduce import duties to dire levels. To give merchants
ample time to rearrange their affairs, the House deferred the bill's effective date until November 1806. John Randolph, who thought that any

trade sanctions would be self-destructive, derided Nicholson's bill as a "milk-and-water-bill, a dose of chicken broth to be taken nine months hence." But the Republican majorities passed it by lopsided votes of 93–32 in the House and 19-9 in the Senate.[26]

The non-importation debates brought Randolph's simmering resentment against the administration to a boil, and his snide aspersion on his friend Nicholson's bill was benign compared to the damage he thoughtlessly inflicted on Gallatin. Randolph had differed with the administration over its proposal to give New England speculators five million acres to settle corrupt land claims in Georgia's Yazoo backcountry and, more recently, over a secret proposal to pay France $2 million for pressuring Spain to relinquish its territorial claims to West Florida. He thought both proposals were dishonorable, and he criticized the administration for foisting the responsibility for them onto Congress. But the real causes of his resentment ran much deeper. Randolph was at heart an agrarian Antifederalist whose obsession with keeping the federal government small and frugal knew no bounds. He found Jefferson's smooth expediency distasteful, and he thought Madison was drifting back toward the centralizing views he had espoused in that book called *The Federalist*. For his part, Jefferson found Randolph erratic and unreliable as a floor leader for the administration's measures, and he had reached out to other members of the House for legislative leadership. That jabbed Randolph's fragile ego. So when one of those members made a motion to take the non-importation question away from Randolph's Ways and Means committee so that Gregg could offer his resolution, Randolph exploded.[27]

Randolph knew Gallatin would not approve Gregg's proposal, so he looked for a way to throw Gallatin's weight into the balance against it. Whatever his differences with other members of the administration, Randolph admired Gallatin for his frugality, intelligence, and candor. He had turned a blind eye to Gallatin's participation in the Yazoo settlement and the secret $2 million appropriation for West Florida, both of which he chose to blame on Madison and—much more cautiously—Jefferson. Knowing that many Republicans in the House would defer to Gallatin's views on the fiscal consequences of non-importation, Randolph thought he was justified in forcing Gallatin's hand on the subject. So Randolph got the House to call on Gallatin for a special report that would give him the opportunity to explain the cost of Gregg's bill.[28]

But Randolph did not stop there. In a sensational speech on March 5, he insinuated that Madison had sponsored Gregg's proposal without consulting Gallatin. He knew for certain, Randolph told the House, that Madison had withheld important foreign dispatches about West Florida from Gallatin, and under the circumstances he could only conclude (indeed, he had it "from a Cabinet Minister"!) that *There is no longer any Cabinet.* Randolph lambasted Madison for his duplicity and his doctrinaire insistence on maritime rights that the weak American nation could not possibly defend against the British navy. If opposition to these useless policies meant he was no longer a good Republican, Randolph declared, so be it. He was willing to be called a *tertium quid*—the epithet that William Duane had begun to hurl at moderate "third somethings" in Pennsylvania who were neither Federalists nor true Republicans. In an even more flamboyant speech a month later on the West Florida question, Randolph went on to claim (again citing Gallatin) that Madison had tried to draw money out of the Treasury for the secret $2 million payment to France before Congress had approved it.[29]

Randolph was a brilliant speaker, and his very recklessness made these speeches spectacular performances. But the speeches did a great deal of damage in the Washington community. Randolph "has passed the rubicon," observed one of the Federalist senators who had flocked to the House chamber to hear him. "[N]either the President or Secretary of State can after this be on terms with him." That assessment was accurate. Randolph's speeches isolated him and a small coterie of Southern Congressmen who supported him, and Jefferson no longer invited him to dinner at the President's House. The speeches also strained Randolph's relationship with Gallatin. Randolph's insinuations about Gallatin's disclosure of cabinet affairs embarrassed Gallatin and forced him to make painful explanations to Jefferson, Madison, and the House.[30]

Although Gallatin continued to work well with Randolph as chairman of the Ways and Means committee, he quietly dropped their social relationship. "I have no communication with the great folks," Randolph wrote to Joseph Nicholson from his farm in Virginia a year later. "Gallatin used formerly to write to me, but of late our intercourse has dropped. I think it is more than two years since I was in his house. How this has happened I can't tell, or rather I *can*, for I have not been invited there." Nathaniel Macon remained fond of Randolph, but since Randolph no longer spent time at the Gallatins' house, Macon saw him less frequently. The two of them sometimes met a few likeminded Congressmen at Macon's boarding house, and because the woman who ran it was named Hamilton, Randolph wryly referred to these supporters of small and frugal government as "the Hamiltonians." Joseph Nicholson also remained friendly with Randolph, but a month after Randolph broke with the administration, Nicholson retired from the House to take the bench in a Maryland state court. Nicholson was one of the Gallatin family's favorite relatives, and they were downcast over his departure. Others "will tell you what void you have created here," Gallatin told Nicholson at the end of a business letter a few days after he left, but "I confine myself to what relates to your business; for I have contracted the bad habit of expressing nothing when I feel most."[31]

Days after Randolph declared there was no cabinet, Jefferson got a long letter from William Duane. Duane purported to be sharing rumors that Madison was the only member of the administration who still supported Jefferson, but he had a great deal more than that on his mind. Duane, Michael Leib, and their largely working class supporters now stood in open opposition to the moderate middle class Republicans in Pennsylvania—the men Duane derided as Quids. The two groups had quarreled over the plebian faction's demands for patronage and reforms in the state's judicial system, which remained firmly in the hands of Federalists and moderate Republican lawyers such as Dallas. The confrontation between the two factions had split the Republican party in the state, revealed the moderates to be a minority, and forced them to ally with Federalists in order to reelect McKean as governor in 1805. The Quids' alliance with the Federalists in the gubernatorial election hardened Duane's conviction that he and his followers—who called themselves Democrats—were the Republican faithful, and he seized on the quarrels in Washington as an opportunity to win Jefferson's support for his faction.[32]

Getting Gallatin out of the way was one of Duane's important objectives. Duane knew that Jefferson took Gallatin's advice on patronage and other political matters in Pennsylvania. He and other Democrats blamed Gallatin for standing in the way of the removals from office needed to create the additional patronage they demanded. And they believed that Gallatin and Dallas had been behind a Quid attempt to block Leib's reelection to Congress in 1804. Indeed, Duane later claimed that Gallatin had warned Duane that his continued support for Leib would lead to his own political destruction. By the spring of 1806, Duane's *Aurora* had been sniping at Gallatin for months. So it was perhaps with more hope than foundation that Duane's letter to Jefferson mentioned a report "that you have broken with the Secy. of the Treasury, and that he is not consulted by you and that he proposes to resign."[33]

Gallatin had tried to insulate Jefferson from the party conflict in Pennsylvania. When Duane and Leib organized ward meetings in Philadelphia in 1803 to petition for more removals from office, Gallatin advised Jefferson not to send Duane a letter defending the administration's conduct. The quarrel in Pennsylvania, Gallatin told him, was between "the thinking part of the community" and "a violent party" who had "a strong hold on public opinion," and nothing that Jefferson could say would "make converts of men under the influence of passions or governed by self interest." Their clamor for office at a time when Republicans otherwise supported the administration was proof that they were less interested in good republican government than in "a few paltry offices—offices not of a political & discretionary nature, but mere inferior administrative offices of profit.... Either a schism will take place, in which case the leaders of those men would divide from us, or time and the good sense of the people will...cure the evil." He thought the "malcontents" were relatively few and good sense would prevail. Jefferson took Gallatin's advice at the time and withheld the letter.[34]

But Gallatin's prediction about political developments in Pennsylvania had been wrong, and Jefferson now decided to follow his own instincts. He was not surprised that Republicans had begun to divide after they defeated the Federalists. Earlier jostling between Burrites, Clintonians, and Livingstons in New York had shown what could happen. Jefferson believed, though, that he could hold the factions together at the national level as long as he held on to a loyal majority in Congress and kept himself clear of the infighting. His reply to Duane's letter played on those themes. "That Mr. R. has openly attacked the administration is sufficiently known," he acknowledged. But the overwhelming majority in the House for the measure that Randolph had opposed showed "which side retains its orthodoxy." Any suggestion that the cabinet had divided, he continued, was "totally unfounded. There never was a more harmonious, a more cordial administration, nor ever a moment when it has been otherwise." It was equally false "in every tittle," he purred on, that he had ever shown any "predilection for those called the third party or Quids." If only Duane would come to Washington, he would see for himself how smoothly everything was going. But perhaps these "short facts"—and here Jefferson gently placed a barb—would "suffice to inspire you with caution until you can come."[35]

Jefferson's reply to Duane was a masterful effort to mollify a strong-willed man, but it failed. Almost everyone expected Jefferson to retire when his second term ended in 1809, and Madison seemed positioned to be his successor. But many Republicans—including Randolph and his minority—questioned Madison's leadership ability and were suspicious of his Federalist past. Duane shared those doubts, but he had been cautious about expressing them in the absence of any consensus around the alternative presidential candidates, George Clinton and James Monroe. The insinuations about Madison that Randolph had attributed to Gallatin now gave Duane an irresistible opening. By the autumn of 1806, his *Aurora* was using attacks on "the *evil genius...Gallatin*" as a vehicle to repeat accusations about Madison. These attacks led a writer to the Richmond *Enquirer*, the leading Republican paper in Virginia, to question Gallatin's Republican orthodoxy and his loyalty to the administration. And the *Enquirer*'s influential editor, Thomas Ritchie, agreed that Gallatin's "mysterious" involvement with the Republican minority was ample cause "for *suspicion*."[36]

The newspaper criticism prompted Jefferson to assure Gallatin of his continued "affections & confidence." He wanted "no doubts or jealousies" to "find a moment's harbor in either of our minds," Jefferson told Gallatin, and he continued to believe that "our administration now drawing towards a close" would be remembered as much for its "harmony" as for "the great operations by which it will have advanced the well-being of the nation." Gallatin responded with gratitude. He regretted that his "long and confidential intercourse" with Republican Congressmen—and particularly his "free communications of facts & opinions to Mr Randolph"—might have given rise to honest misunderstandings about his intentions. But he saw no excuse for "the Philadelphia attacks" on his personal integrity. All that he and the other members of the administration could do, Gallatin stoically concluded, was to persevere in their efforts "to preserve peace abroad" and "to improve and invigorate our republican institutions" at home. He omitted from the letter, however, a passage in his draft that had pledged his support for Madison's presidential candidacy. He must have thought the pledge was inappropriate, excessive, or at least premature.[37]

"Peace, economy, and riddance of public debt"—Jefferson's longing for that consummation was almost poignant by the spring of 1807. He was nearly sixty-four, he had grown tired in office, and—though he had two more years to serve—he was already sending furniture home to Virginia. He needed to believe in the success of his great republican experiment. "[W]ars & contentions indeed fill the pages of history," he mused to a friend in Europe, "but more blest is the nation whose silent course of happiness furnishes nothing for history to say. this is what I ambition for my own country, and what it has fortunately enjoyed now upwards of 20. years, while Europe has been in constant Volcanic eruption." The truth was bleaker. Even the small Tripolitan War had taxed the country's austere fiscal system, and the United States lacked the muscle to stop the European belligerents from interdicting American trade. Napoleon had issued a decree from Berlin in December 1806 that barred neutral traders from bringing goods to continental Europe from Britain and its colonies. The British navy was still seizing American ships and impressing American sailors. And the treaty with Britain that Monroe and Pinkney had finally managed to negotiate a few months earlier was so unsatisfactory that Jefferson had not even sent it to the Senate. Peace had a price in the war-torn Atlantic world, and America's frugal Republican government had scarcely begun to pay it.[38]

Gallatin was on his way to New York at the end of June 1807 when a messenger caught up with him in Philadelphia and summoned him back to Washington. Six days earlier, the British warship *Leopard* had attacked the American naval frigate *Chesapeake* as it was leaving Norfolk, seized four crewmembers who were deserters from the British navy, and left the American ship to limp back to Norfolk in disgrace with three dead, eighteen wounded, tattered rigging, and twenty-two cannon balls in its hull. The attack was not the first British outrage off the American coast. The previous summer, HMS *Leander* had killed a man in New York harbor when it fired a warning shot to stop an American merchant ship. But the attack on the *Chesapeake* was the first British action against an American naval ship, and it seemed to set the two countries on the path toward war.[39]

An exhausted Gallatin reported to Jefferson that he was returning to Washington as quickly as possible. It "will save a day...if I can see you soon after your arrival," Jefferson responded. "If you arrive before half after three, come and take a family dinner with me." The cabinet began meeting the day after Gallatin reached Washington, and over the next five days it sent messages to London demanding satisfaction, ordered all British warships out of American waters, deployed gunboats to protect the harbors, and called on state governors to prepare their militia. Tempers ran high throughout the country, and many expected war to follow quickly. But the cabinet decided to give the British ample time to explain, and they agreed not to recall Congress until late October. Only Robert Smith, Jefferson recorded in his notes, "wished an earlier call." Smith thought the British outrage demanded a prompt response.[40]

"War will be a most calamitous event," Albert wrote to Hannah, who was in New York. "Our commerce will be destroyed and our revenue nearly annihilated." And he feared war might break out soon. If British warships attacked New York harbor, he said, she should take the family to Greenwich. "There seems but one sentiment" here, came Hannah's spirited response: "*We cannot submit to be degraded.*" War was indeed "a dreadful thing" she said, but peace "was impossible with a Nation of pirates." Convinced there was no time to lose, Albert began making war plans. Just "between ourselves," he confided to Hannah a week later, "I doubt...whether everything shall be done which ought to be done." He privately wished Congress had been recalled sooner, and he thought it would have been called sooner if Washington were not so unhealthy in late summer. He was not very well himself. "I think I increased my sickness by intensity of thinking and not sleeping at nights," he wrote, but he felt himself getting better as he "digested" his plans.[41]

It was difficult for an administration that had depended on peace to prepare itself for war. The army consisted of a few thousand men, the navy had seven warships and a defensive fleet of small gunboats, and the Treasury got substantially all of its revenue from taxes on foreign trade. But Gallatin brought just enough realism to the task to make Republican policy seem plausible. He was "not very sanguine" about American military exploits, he admitted to Joseph Nicholson, and he expected the people to find the privations of war "very irksome....We will be poorer both as a nation and as a Government, our debt & taxes will increase; and our progress in every respect be interrupted." But he thought the nation could defend its "independence & honor," and he expected that a "very few years of peace" would repair the economic and fiscal damage. Indeed, he said, war might awaken "nobler feelings & habits than avarice & luxury" and keep Americans from degenerating "into a nation of mere calculators." The political damage from war was another matter.

He predicted that war would increase executive power, embolden speculators to interfere in government decisions, and introduce a standing army and a permanent navy. For those things, he foresaw no remedy.[42]

However much Gallatin regretted the financial consequences of war, he had a strategy for dealing with them. The Treasury would pay for the costs of the war itself with borrowed money because taxes heavy enough to cover war costs would hurt an economy already weakened by unavoidable wartime damage to trade. But to maintain its ability to borrow, the Treasury would need to show that its current revenue could cover the normal costs of peacetime government and all of the interest on the public debt, including the interest on money borrowed to conduct the war. Since wartime disruption of trade would reduce the taxable imports on which federal revenue now depended, the Treasury would need to raise additional revenue.[43]

Gallatin expected to find that additional revenue in two places. He thought Congress could double the rate of import duties because smuggling would be more difficult in wartime and scarcity would force consumers to accept higher prices. He also thought that the people, who had been relieved of internal taxes in peacetime, would be willing to bear them when war made the need for them apparent. He had about $8–10 million in the Treasury that he could use to cover expenses during the year it would take to enact new taxes, rebuild the internal revenue system, and begin collections. He estimated he would need to borrow $10 million to pay for each year of war. Borrowings that large would cause interest rates to rise. "People will fight," he told Joseph Nicholson, "but they never give their money for nothing." He began to sound out bankers about how much they would lend, and he directed the Bank of the United States to start buying government bonds to support their price. As long as the nation could find the means, he told Nicholson, expense "must never be an objection" to needed war measures.[44]

Worried that others were not doing enough, Gallatin did not confine his planning to financial matters. As Jefferson left Washington for the summer, Gallatin gave him a nineteen-page memorandum on the country's military situation. It was more comprehensive than anything Jefferson got from the War or Navy departments (which appear to have given him only lists of the available forces and some advice on specific issues). Gallatin's memorandum surveyed the country's overall military resources, flagged the most essential preparations, and projected a military strategy. He thought the British would attack New York, Norfolk, Charleston, and New Orleans. He also predicted they would come to Washington, not only to destroy the main navy yard but also to deliver "a stroke which would give [them] reputation and attach disgrace to us." They would approach the capital overland through Maryland, he said, rather than coming up the Potomac River. Gallatin also made the case for American attacks on Upper Canada (southern Ontario), Montreal, Quebec, and the British naval base at Halifax. He thought those attacks could disrupt Britain's trade with its Native American allies, put British forces on the defensive, and hamper British blockades of the American coast. He now thought the first year of war would cost $13 million, which, when added to the costs of civil government and payments on the public debt, would require $22.5 million—half of which he would have to borrow.[45]

Parts of Gallatin's memorandum found their way into the war plans Jefferson sent to Secretary of War Henry Dearborn from Monticello a week later. Meanwhile, Robert Smith was tussling with Gallatin over Gallatin's proposal to send a naval ship to warn American merchants in the Indian Ocean, and Smith—who thought the appearance of an American naval ship would spark British ships there into action—gave Gallatin a dose of his own medicine by pointing out that the Navy had no appropriation to pay for the voyage. This time it was Gallatin who suggested they could get the money by arranging an unauthorized loan through one of the customs collectors.[46]

By the time Congress returned in October 1807, the Republican instinct for peace and frugality was stifling the quick resentments of early summer. "Peace is every thing to us in this part of the Union," Nathaniel Macon had written to Gallatin from North Carolina during the break. The last three crops in his district had been bad, forcing even the "careful and industrious to go in debt for bread." If the executive could avoid war, said Macon, that would add as much to its reputation as the purchase of

Louisiana. Joseph Nicholson had predicted there would be no war unless it came before the merchants began "to calculate" and let "Considerations of Profit and Loss" trump "their Resentment," and what Gallatin heard when he finally reached New York late in the summer confirmed that prediction. "The people of this city do not appear to me to be in favor of war," he wrote to Madison, "and they fear it so much, that they have persuaded themselves that there is no danger" of it.[47]

Jefferson's draft of his message to the returning Congress took a belligerent attitude, but Gallatin convinced him to tone it down. There was no advantage in declaring war before spring anyway, Gallatin told him, because the country needed at least that long to prepare. Gallatin was glad he had "neutralized" the message, he confided to his wife a few days later, because "Congress is certainly peaceably disposed." And as Jefferson revised his message, he told Gallatin to drop the "odious idea" of borrowing money for the current year since events might make that unnecessary.[48]

Jefferson's "neutralized" message left Congress adrift. For almost two months, Congress talked about everything from harbor fortifications and gunboats to militia organization and trade sanctions. The administration also drifted. Although the non-importation measure enacted in 1806 (and twice deferred) was going to take effect in the middle of December, Gallatin could not get Jefferson and Madison to focus on the measures that would have to be adopted in order to enforce it. While Congress and the administration drifted, events began to overtake them. The protracted war in Europe was causing Britain and France to toughen their treatment of neutral nations. Two days after the non-importation law took effect, Washington got word that the British government had ordered its navy to step up the impressment of sailors from neutral ships. With that report came news that Napoleon was aggressively enforcing his Berlin decree, which closed the European continent to goods from Britain and its colonies, against American ships. As the need for decisive action became inescapable, Jefferson and Madison decided to embrace a bold idea—a complete embargo on American exports to the rest of the world.[49]

What Jefferson and Madison had in mind was an embargo of indefinite duration. The United States and other governments had used brief embargoes to retaliate against the hostile acts of other nations, to keep their own merchant ships out of harm's way, and to bring resources home in preparation for war. In 1794, Congress had declared a thirty-day embargo in response to the British seizure of American ships suspected of trading with France. But the thinking behind an open-ended embargo was grander. Jefferson and Madison had long believed that the United States should use trade sanctions as an instrument of foreign policy. Since the 1790s, they had argued that European manufacturers and consumers needed American grain, naval stores, and other commodities more than American consumers needed European manufactured goods. They pointed out that European colonies in the West Indies relied on American supplies to feed the large enslaved workforce they used to produce sugar. And they thought sustained American insistence on open trade could eventually break down European mercantile restrictions and increase American agricultural and commercial prosperity.[50]

Jefferson and Madison thought that the case for trade sanctions had grown stronger over the previous decade. The growth of industrialized cloth manufacturing in Britain and the beginning of American cotton production were weaving new commercial connections between the two countries. The increasing importance of those connections made it seem possible that trade sanctions could achieve wider foreign policy objectives, such as stopping the impressment of sailors. The fundamental Republican belief that war tended to undermine democratic government—by increasing public debt and executive power—predisposed them to pursue that possibility. And the administration's frugality had left few other choices. The American army and navy were almost nonexistent, the federal revenues were heavily committed to repaying debt from the last war, and good Republicans hated to borrow money. The European belligerents' interference with American trade and American sailors demanded a response, and trade sanctions seemed to be the only response the frugal Republican regime could afford.[51]

Although Gallatin had insisted on the frugality that eliminated other options, he opposed an open-ended embargo. How could he do otherwise? An embargo on exports would reduce imports dramatically because American ships could not sail to get them and any foreign ships that brought them would have to return in ballast. And the collapse in imports would tear a gaping hole in federal revenues. But the disturbing new reports about increased impressment and wider trade exclusions forced the administration's hand. The day after those reports appeared in the *National Intelligencer,* Jefferson proposed the embargo to the cabinet, the cabinet accepted the idea, and Attorney General Caesar Rodney sent a draft resolution to a friend in Congress.[52]

Gallatin worried through the night. Early the next morning, he gave Jefferson his objections in writing. "In every point of view, privations, sufferings, revenue, effect on the enemy, politics at home, &c., I prefer war to a permanent embargo," he said. "Government prohibitions do always more mischief than...calculated; and it is not without much hesitation that a statesman should hazard to regulate the concerns of individuals as if he could do it better than themselves." He thought the cabinet had reacted too hastily to the news from Europe. An embargo of limited duration would give them room to develop other responses without appearing to back down. In any event, he thought foreign ships caught in American ports when the embargo began should be allowed to depart. As to the hope that the embargo would persuade the British to change their policies, he thought it "entirely groundless." Jefferson's reply was soothing. "I...am clearly for the exception, but come here before half after ten, and let us be together before the message [to Congress] goes out of our hands."[53]

Jefferson's message to Congress mentioned the new dangers awaiting American ships abroad and expressed confidence that Congress would "perceive all the advantages" of keeping them at home. There was no reference to precedents, no further explanation, no exhortation; the message was two sentences long. But the Senate passed the embargo by an overwhelming vote within hours, and the House passed it three days later. On the evening of December 22, Gallatin directed the customs collectors to stop all foreign bound ships from leaving port and to follow the instructions issued during the brief embargo in 1794. He was at a loss to say more; the Embargo Act was only two sections long, and it did not even provide penalties for violations. The following day, Gallatin sent Jefferson the first of many scores of letters about the embargo that they would exchange over the coming months. Unless the embargo statute was amended, Gallatin said, the collectors could not prevent a ship that sailed for another American port from diverting to a foreign port; to enforce the law, they would need to use force. Jefferson agreed amendments were needed, but "in the meantime," he said, "the revenue cutters & armed vessels must use force."[54]

Three essays in the *National Intelligencer* tried to explain to the public what the government had done. These essays, which have been attributed to Madison, justified the embargo as a precaution—"a dignified retirement within ourselves" to avoid the seizures and disgrace facing American ships on the high seas. They also expressed a hope that the loss of American exports would coerce the European belligerents into rescinding their hostile measures. But that coercive effect, the writer insisted, would only be a fortunate "collateral" consequence of a measure aimed at protecting American property. The essays put a brave face on the domestic consequences of the embargo. They promised that the embargo would increase "household manufactures," spark useful industries, and disprove the belligerents' "insulting opinion" that Americans were willing to barter their rights for any chance to make money. Most farmers already had shipped their crops for the year, said the writer, and most honest merchants had brought their property home. All in all, the writer assured his countrymen, the embargo was "the best expedient in its best form." It only remained for the American people to embrace this measure "adopted for their good."[55]

Jefferson put it more plainly in a private explanation to John Taylor. Keeping "our vessels, cargoes & seamen" at home, he wrote, "saves us the necessity of making their capture the cause of immediate war." It "gives [us] time. time may produce peace in Europe. peace in Europe removes all causes of differences till another European war, & by that time our debt may be paid, our revenues clear, & our strength increased."[56]

The embargo was a drastic measure, and the administration's failure to make a strong case for it was striking. Apart from the essays in the *Intelligencer*, the administration said almost nothing in public defense of the embargo. The "wisdom of Washington is so consummate and so exclusive," Alexander Dallas wrote from Philadelphia, "that we never hear anybody being consulted beyond the precincts of the capital." And the *Intelligencer's* patronizing assurance that the government knew best rang hollow to Federalists with commercial interests. They complained that the administration showed solicitude for farmers and manufacturers, but no regard for the merchants and sailors most directly affected by the embargo. "If Mr. J. can prevent the clamours of the farmers and soothe the manufacturers by giving them monopolies," wrote one, what does he care about "the destruction of the navigation of the Northern States?" Would it not be better, asked another, "to expose the surplus of our produce" to the risks of wartime trade than to let it "decay and rot before our eyes?" Some Federalists argued that the Constitution gave the federal government no authority to impose a permanent embargo. And many scoffed at the administration's claim that the embargo treated all nations equally. They thought it was obvious that a ban on American exports did more harm to Britain than to France because the British navy was already hampering French trade, and they deplored this American tilt toward Napoleon's tyrannical regime at a time when Britain was the last remaining bastion of liberty in Europe.[57]

The embargo put many sailors and dockworkers out of work. These hungry men protested, and newspapers in Northern ports predicted there would be mob violence. "In spite of all that can be said," observed Federalist Rufus King, the embargo "cannot be popular; and if continued will shake many men's confidence in the present administration." Gallatin agreed. "From present appearances," he told his wife a few months later, "the Federalists will turn us out" in the next presidential election.[58]

The task of enforcing the embargo fell to Gallatin and his eighty-five customs collectors, and a measure that had seemed expedient in

Washington quickly proved inexpedient in the ports. There were two ultimately insoluble problems. First, the embargo was poorly conceived. Gallatin got the embargo law amended as he identified problems, and by the time Congress recessed in April, it had passed four long supplementary statutes to impose specific penalties, expand Treasury's enforcement powers, regulate coasting voyages between American ports, and prevent exports by land across the Canadian border. Gallatin also sent the customs collectors a stream of directives to settle questions of statutory interpretation, coordinate enforcement practices, and anticipate evasions. They showed, wrote a coastal Massachusetts minister with unintentional irony, "an intimate acquaintance with the facts & the true manners of our Commerce." But as the stream of directives turned into a torrent—584 by the time Congress reconvened in the autumn of 1808—it became plain that no number of statutes and administrative rulings could stop the commerce of an enterprising nation.[59]

The second problem was equally profound. The customs service was simply not up to the task. The customs collectors had never been given enough men and cutters to stop smuggling, so they had learned over the years to administer the revenue laws with flexibility and restraint. Very few of the collectors were corrupt, but virtually all of them were accommodating because they needed the cooperation of merchants in order to do their jobs. Collectors accustomed to this style of administration (with its overtones of what modern scholars have called regulatory capture) found it extremely difficult to bring the export business in their ports to a halt. It seemed reasonable to allow local merchants to relicense their oceangoing vessels for use in the coasting trade, and it seemed only decent to believe returning captains who swore that storms—which relieved them from the embargo's penalties—had driven those relicensed vessels into foreign ports. If the collectors took a harder line, local judges and juries often would not support them, and the collectors were personally liable for damages if the courts found their seizure of a ship or its cargo had been wrongful. A prominent Republican judge in New York repeatedly held Gallatin's friend David Gelston liable for seizures.[60]

Gallatin tried to deal with deficiencies in the customs service by centralizing authority in Washington, but he suffered setbacks. First, the federal courts did not support him. One of the enforcement statutes specifically authorized the collectors to detain any ship they suspected of evading the embargo until the president himself decided whether to release it. But when Gallatin directed the collectors to treat certain types of cargo as sufficient grounds for suspicion, the federal circuit court in Charleston—in an opinion by a judge Jefferson had appointed to the Supreme Court—slapped him down. The court said the statute had given the authority to the collectors themselves, not to the Treasury. And Jefferson himself undercut Gallatin's effort at centralization by authorizing state governors to issue permits for coastal shipments of flour whenever their states' food supplies ran low. Once flour got on board a ship, however, smugglers could easily divert it into the export trade. Gallatin warned Jefferson that some governors would cave in to the smugglers, and one of them did. Within two months, the Republican governor of Massachusetts had issued enough permits to feed the people of his state for a year. Nothing could stop him from issuing even more permits until he died a few months later.[61]

Gallatin's efforts to enforce the embargo were dogged, and as the summer of 1808 wore on, they took an increasingly heavy toll. As early as February, he had asked Jefferson for soldiers and gunboats to help stop smuggling. By May, soldiers and smugglers were shooting each other along Lake Champlain in upstate New York, and August brought news of what was being called an insurrection along Lake Ontario. In Newburyport, Massachusetts, an armed mob stopped customs officials from detaining a suspicious vessel. Smuggling around Passamaquoddy Bay in the boundary waters of Maine became so notorious that Gallatin told one collector "the very act of clearing for Passamaquoddy may be considered as prima facie evidence of an intended fraud!" Gallatin was more respectful when he wrote directly to the collector at Passamaquoddy. Lewis Delesdernier was the soldier son of the Genevan couple with whom Gallatin had spent his first winter in America, and he had been the collector of the small port ever since the Revolution. Smugglers had overwhelmed him long ago, and the embargo made that agonizingly apparent. "[M]y Circumstances as a Public Officer and the Magnitude of the Business I am Concerned in," he confessed to Gallatin, "is so Intricate that I am in the most perplexed and distressed situation that Can possibly be Conceived off." By the time Gallatin went to New York to see his family at the end of July, he felt much the same way.[62]

"I am so much overwhelmed even here with business and interruptions, that I have not time to write correctly," Gallatin wrote to Jefferson from New York. But what Gallatin said to Jefferson was clear enough. A "restrictive measure of the nature of the embargo applied to a nation under such circumstances as the United States cannot be enforced without the assistance of means as strong as the measure itself." The experience of the summer had shown that enforcement would require greater military force as well as "arbitrary powers" of seizure that Gallatin called "dangerous and odious." The prospect of increased force appalled Gallatin. "The very sight of a bayonet to preserve order amongst citizens rouses my indignation," he had told Hannah Gallatin after a sentry stabbed a civilian at the Washington Navy Yard years earlier. Gallatin thought the prospect of violence against civilians would shock Jefferson into a change of policy. He was wrong.[63]

"This embargo law is certainly the most embarrassing one we have ever had to execute," Jefferson acknowledged; but as long as the country preferred embargo to war, "Congress must legalize all *means* which may be necessary to obtain it's *end*." Coming from a man who had castigated his Federalist predecessors for their heavy-handed disregard of civil liberties in the 1790s, it was a chilling response. Jefferson had convinced himself that the country still supported him in the execution of an ineffective policy that was provoking domestic unrest. He was prepared to enforce the law with more force than the federal government had used since the Western Insurrection. And nowhere did he acknowledge the irony of leaving Gallatin—who had opposed the policy—saddled with the responsibility for doing all of this. "Peace, economy, and riddance of public debt" had begun to exact a heavy price, and Jefferson was steeled to pay it.[64]

Other Republicans were growing restive. Ezekiel Bacon, a Congressman from western Massachusetts, wrote to Gallatin about the political effect in his district of the extensive smuggling in upstate New York. It was the "common remark," he reported, that the embargo "should be either enforced or repealed." Discontent over the embargo amplified differences within the Republican party and encouraged those who wanted George Clinton or James Monroe, instead of Madison, to be the party's presidential candidate. Jefferson and Madison had embarrassed their old friend Monroe by rejecting the treaty that he and William Pinkney negotiated with Britain, and Monroe thought that receiving support in the presidential contest would help to vindicate his reputation. When the Congressional Republican caucus chose Madison for president and Clinton as his running mate, Monroe did not withdraw, and dissident Republicans continued to grumble. "I will candidly tell you," Dallas wrote to Gallatin, "that almost every thing that is done, seems to excite disgust. . . . I verily believe, one year more of writing, speaking, and appointing, would render Mr Jefferson a more odious President, even to the Democrats, than John Adams. My only hope is, that Mr Madison's election may not be affected, nor his Administration perplexed, in consequence of the growing dissatisfaction, among the reputable members of the Republican party."[65]

By autumn, Gallatin was fairly confident that Madison would see off the other Republican candidates and defeat Federalist Charles Cotesworth Pinckney in the presidential election despite the unpopularity of the embargo, and he began to work for an urgent change in foreign policy under the new administration. It seemed clear to him that the embargo was a costly failure. It had won no concessions from Britain or France, it had destroyed the American carrying trade and severely damaged the American economy, and it was about to bring down the Treasury. Most of the current year's revenue came from collecting bonds that merchants had given for duties on the previous year's imports, so the Treasury still had some room to maneuver. Indeed, the revenues actually collected during 1808 hit a new high of $16.4 million. But new imports for the fiscal year ending in September 1808 had plummeted to less than half of their level in 1807, and Gallatin knew that the amount collected on merchants' bonds during 1809 would plunge in response. The embargo also was undermining the federal government's authority. When crop prices fell by half, even Republican farmers turned into smugglers. The people, Gallatin told Madison, "view the embargo less as a shield protecting them against the decrees & orders of foreign powers, than as the true if not primary cause of the stagnation of commerce & depreciation of produce." The resulting "disobedience & resistance...sap the very foundation of our institutions. And I had rather to encounter war itself than to display our impotence to enforce our laws." He now thought that war was the only real alternative.[66]

❦

When Congress convened in November, Jefferson's annual message acknowledged that the embargo had failed to induce Britain or France to treat American commerce any better. He expressed confidence that Congress would respond with suitable measures, but he did not say what those should be. Faced with the deteriorating situation at the Treasury, Gallatin pushed for clearer direction. Both he and Madison believed, he told Jefferson, that "it would be eligible to point out to [Congress] some precise and distinct course." Although the three of them might not yet agree on what that course should be, "we must (or rather you must) decide the question absolutely." But Jefferson—tired of office and disillusioned by the failure of peaceful coercion—did nothing. "There never has been a situation of the world before, in which such endeavors as we have made would not have secured our peace," Jefferson sighed to James Monroe. "If we go to war now, I fear we may renounce forever the hope of seeing an end of our national debt." Madison had just won the presidential election, and it seemed best, Jefferson told Monroe and other old friends, to let him decide what to do.[67]

Madison also hesitated to commit himself, so Gallatin seized the initiative. Gallatin had a tendency to grab slack reins when he thought others were doing too little, but his motives in this case ran deeper. He wanted to be Secretary of State. After eight arduous years at the Treasury, he was ready for a change of responsibilities. The expensive failure of the embargo—which he had opposed—made him more eager than ever to lead the government away from trade sanctions toward a more aggressive foreign policy. And although he would never have said so in writing, it must have occurred to him that a man who could move Republican foreign policy in a more successful direction might one day become the party's candidate for president. Madison recognized the need for a change in policy, he had confidence in Gallatin, and he let him take the lead. In consultation with Madison, Gallatin prepared a long policy paper that recited the belligerents' continuing violations of American neutral rights and laid out the possible responses. He arranged for George Washington Campbell of Tennessee, who chaired the House Foreign Relations and the Ways and Means committees, to introduce the paper in the House as a report on the president's annual message. And in the finance report that Gallatin delivered to Congress a few days later, he laid out the fiscal consequences of the foreign policy alternatives in Campbell's report.[68]

Campbell's report declared that the nation's only real alternatives were to go to war with Britain and France or to continue the embargo. A repeal of the embargo without a declaration of war would be a submission to the belligerents' trade restrictions. And with Britain in control of the Atlantic, any trade restriction less restrictive than the embargo would favor France and still leave a gaping hole in federal revenues. The report recommended excluding British and French ships from American waters, banning all imports of British and French goods, and preparing the nation for war. The embargo was to remain in force until war had been declared. In his financial report, Gallatin explained that war and embargo would have equivalent effects on the Treasury. Both would require the federal government to borrow money. But Gallatin thought the Treasury could borrow the necessary money on reasonable terms, and he believed Congress could double the duties collected on the goods imported under war or embargo conditions. War, he said, would not require Congress to reimpose internal taxes.[69]

After debating Campbell's report for most of a month, the House adopted its recommendations and turned to military preparations. In the meantime, Gallatin and Virginia senator William Branch Giles got Congress to enact the draconian new law that Gallatin needed to enforce the embargo. But Gallatin's heart was not in it. He did not think the people would endure the embargo much longer. After an evening at Gallatin's house, Nathaniel Macon—who strongly preferred embargo to war—reported to Joseph Nicholson that Gallatin was "most decidedly for war." But, as Gallatin himself explained to Nicholson, "a great confusion and perplexity reigns in Congress" because Madison remained uncommitted. Federalist James Bayard's assessment of the situation was similar. "It is difficult to conjecture what is the system of the Administration," he told his cousin. "It may be that they find it impossible to execute any system with their unwieldy mass of coadjutors in the House of Reps. . . . They promise to do everything and in the end do nothing." Gallatin did his best to remain optimistic. "Mr. Madison," he told Nicholson, "is, as I always knew him, slow in taking his ground, but firm when the storm arises."[70]

The storm came up quickly. While the Senate was debating measures to enforce the embargo, William Giles and other restive Republican senators passed a bill that required the president to call the entire navy into active service. A week later, the House adopted the same measure. Gallatin was stunned. Full deployment of the navy would cost $6 million and deplete the Treasury reserves on which he was depending to pay for the entire first year of a war. The House ultimately backtracked and persuaded the Senate to reduce the additional deployment to four frigates, but the rebuff to the administration was plain. A week later, the revolt grew wider. A majority in the House rejected the administration's recommendation to keep the embargo in force until Congress had declared war. Despite its earlier support for Campbell's report, the majority now voted to repeal the embargo on March 4—the day of Madison's inauguration.[71]

Campbell voiced dismay, and Macon bewailed this submission to the belligerents' restrictions. But lawlessness in New York and New England had persuaded many Northern Republicans to back down. "The genius and duty of Republican Governments," a Massachusetts Congressman told the House, "is to make laws to suit the people, and not to attempt to make the people suit the laws." Congress folded the embargo repeal into a non-intercourse bill that excluded both British and French ships and goods from the United States. A dispirited Jefferson signed it as one of his last official acts.[72]

No one could mistake the political importance of these developments. The same Congress that had endorsed Gallatin's frugality in its first session opened the spigot for naval spending in its second. The same session of Congress that had enacted draconian measures to enforce the embargo humiliated Jefferson by repealing it just as he left office. What had happened? As he stared at the list of Congressmen who had voted to deploy the entire navy, Gallatin thought he could see a pattern. Prominent among the bill's supporters were the friends of Robert and Samuel Smith. At the head of his private tally of the votes, Gallatin put the Smiths' brother-in-law, Wilson Cary Nicholas. Nicholas had supported the administration when he served in the Senate during Jefferson's first term, but the difference between Gallatin's fiscal policy and the Smiths' views on naval spending had unsettled him. And Madison's indecision about the direction of foreign affairs gave Nicholas, the Smiths, and their other friends—among whom Giles was prominent—a chance to push aside Gallatin's parsimonious policy. This unforeseen rebuff to his fiscal authority stung Gallatin. On his vote tally—the only one from his years at the Treasury that remains in his papers—Gallatin bitterly blamed the "Smith Faction, or Ruling Party" for sacrificing the "Republican cause itself, and the people of the United States" to their "Favoritism, extravagance, parade, and folly."[73]

How had it come to this? The embargo's failure had undermined the administration's political authority, damaged the case for peaceful coercion of the belligerents, and strengthened the argument for a navy capable of protecting American trade. But there was much more at play. Jefferson's stature had once made it difficult for anyone in the Republican party to challenge him. All of the party's quarreling factions had acknowledged his leadership, and the few men around John Randolph who had broken with Jefferson quickly found themselves in the wilderness. But Jefferson was now a lame duck, and the man about to succeed him was an altogether different character. Although Madison had had as much to do with the formation of the Republican party as Jefferson, he did not have Jefferson's political stature. Madison was a small, quiet man. He had no charisma, and he had built few working relationships with members of Congress during his eight years at the State department. Men such as Samuel Smith and William Giles did not defer to him. They had been influential members of Congress for many years. They had supported his presidential candidacy when other Republicans had not, and they thought he owed them something.[74]

When Madison let it be known just before Congress was about to adjourn that he intended to nominate Gallatin as his successor at the State department, Giles was quick to object. The objection came against the background of his alliance with the Smiths, but it had a marked personal element. Giles thought he himself had reason to expect a cabinet appointment. He was the same age as Gallatin, he too had borne a leading share in the Republican opposition of the 1790s, and he had acted as a party leader in the Senate for the last four years. A man of great forensic but quite ordinary intellectual ability, Giles honestly saw no essential difference between Gallatin's capacities and his own. Giles complained to Madison in person about his intention to nominate Gallatin and then sent Madison a long letter that betrayed his own ambition and his pique about having been overlooked.[75]

Giles's opposition to the appointment took Madison by surprise. He thought Campbell's report had showcased Gallatin's foreign policy qualifications, and he had not anticipated opposition. Brought up short, Madison asked Wilson Cary Nicholas to sound out other senators about Gallatin's nomination. He knew Nicholas was close to Giles and the Smiths, and he must have hoped that Nicholas could change their minds. But Nicholas was too deeply entangled in the Smith faction's effort to check Gallatin's influence and remove his curb on naval spending. Relying on Giles and Samuel Smith for part of his information, Nicholas reported to Madison that at least half of the Senate would vote against

Gallatin. Madison tried to quiet the opposition by suggesting he would appoint Robert Smith to replace Gallatin at the Treasury. But Gallatin— confident that Robert Smith could not do the job—rejected the idea. And because he needed to keep Gallatin in the cabinet, Madison now found himself backed into appointing Robert Smith to be Secretary of State instead. It was not a brilliant appointment, and no one pretended other- wise. But as Smith at least *"can spell,"* John Randolph mordantly observed, he "ought to be preferred to G[iles]."[76]

Gallatin had expected to become Secretary of State, and the miscar- riage of his nomination hurt him deeply. He and Hannah Gallatin had put his expectations on display by giving weekly dinner parties and a large reception—a "squeeze"—to show that they were up to the social demands of the job. But Gallatin's pain over the failure of his nomination went beyond disappointed expectations. For eight years he had been the administration's principal link to Congress. He thought he had forged— during countless quiet evenings at home and many long hours in the Capitol—good working relationships with the members of Congress. He knew that some of them believed he was too frugal, but he had not real- ized until the naval deployment bill passed how much his frugality had weakened his position with them. The news that he did not have enough friends in the Senate to win confirmation was a brutal blow, and it made him apprehensive about his ability to shepherd the new administration's fiscal measures through Congress.[77]

Disappointment and apprehension were bad enough, but Gallatin's pain went still deeper. He felt betrayed. Among the frequent visitors to the Gallatins' quiet evenings at home during this session of Congress had been Wilson Cary Nicholas, Samuel Smith, and John Montgomery—a Maryland Congressman sometimes allied with Smith who was wooing Gallatin's sister-in-law Maria Nicholson. These men had shared in the conversations from which Nathaniel Macon, George Washington Camp- bell, and others knew that Gallatin preferred war to peaceful coercion. They knew that Gallatin had written Campbell's report. But that had not stopped them from questioning Gallatin's commitment to national defense in order to put their own man in the State department. Gallatin did not expect that Republicans he befriended would always support him. Macon, one of his closest friends, often did not. But Gallatin did expect his friends to be candid and principled. The Smiths and their faction—he now believed—were neither, and they had maneuvered themselves into a position from which they could do him harm.[78]

Gallatin was not sure what to do next. "I have much to say," he wrote to Joseph Nicholson soon after Madison's inauguration, "and want a long conversation with you before the meeting of Congress." "Mrs G. says vice & intrigue are all powerful.... I tell her that virtue is its own reward; and she insists that that language is mere affectation." In a letter to his friend Thomas Worthington, who had retired from the Senate two years earlier, Gallatin was frank about his situation. "I am not disgusted tho' often disappointed," he said, "but I am fairly tired." He weighed the advantages and disadvantages of retiring to western Pennsylvania. He said he wanted "peace, retirement, and to have nothing to mind but the education of my children & the social intercourse of a few friends." But he knew Hannah could not be happy in the West.[79]

Gallatin might have been talking to himself a month later when he advised John Badollet to keep his federal job in Indiana despite his frustrations with the chicanery around him. "I do not know," he told Badollet, "what you can do yourself without an office.... At what time, or in what country, did you ever hear that men assumed the priviledge of being more honest than the mass of the society in which they lived, without being hated and persecuted?" All we can do is "fulfill our duty without looking at the consequences so far as relates to ourselves." But he confessed, "I preach better than I practice."[80]

CHAPTER 8

REPUBLICANS
AT WAR

In August 1809, Hannah and Albert Gallatin fulfilled what Jefferson called an "antient promise" to visit him and his family at Monticello. They came with Dolley and James Madison from Montpelier, where they had spent the previous week. A warm day's journey on orange clay roads through the countryside brought them to the foot of Jefferson's little mountain in late afternoon. Slowly ascending the rough road through the woods, they burst at last into the top clearing where Jefferson's distinctive villa stood against a sweeping view of twilight blue mountains.[1]

The Gallatin, Madison, and Jefferson families had become good friends in Washington, but this was not a social visit. Albert Gallatin rarely took time to visit anywhere other than New York and Philadelphia, and he had declined earlier invitations to Monticello. He had come this time because he had something on his mind. He was considering whether to resign from the Treasury. He had gone to Baltimore in the spring to discuss that question with Joseph Nicholson and returned undecided.

He had ordered only enough Madeira to last through the next session of Congress. If he meant to stay longer than that, he needed Jefferson and Madison—the leaders of his party—to lock arms with him and demonstrate publicly that he had their unequivocal support. What Gallatin said to them during his visit to Virginia went unrecorded, but a letter from Jefferson that followed Gallatin back to Washington—a letter that Jefferson must have discussed with Madison—gave him the statement of support that he needed.[2]

Jefferson's letter rallied Gallatin to their great project. "I consider the fortunes of our republic as depending, in an eminent degree," he wrote, "on the extinguishment of the public debt, before we engage in any war." If the nation was still saddled with the existing debt when the next war came, "we shall be committed to the English career of debt, corruption & rottenness, closing with revolution." Deliverance from that fate, said Jefferson, depended on Madison and Gallatin. "[W]e shall not see another president & Secretary of the Treasury making all other objects subordinate" to the repayment of debt. Jefferson cherished the belief that Gallatin would embrace the final accomplishment of that great goal as "the measure of your fame." Backbiting from some members of Congress was not a serious problem, Jefferson assured him. No one else in the administration "ever occupied stronger ground in the esteem of Congress than yourself," and everyone expected his standing with Congress to remain high. Gallatin had "nothing therefore to apprehend" from Congress or from the president, who "above all men" was "most interested & affectionately disposed to support you." "I hope," Jefferson concluded, that "you will abandon entirely the idea you expressed to me" and consider the next eight years in office "essential to your political career."[3]

Although Jefferson's letter gave Gallatin what he needed, Gallatin knew the man and the political situation well enough not to take it at face value. He fully expected the United States would go to war before the nation had paid the existing debt, and he could not deceive himself about the rebuffs Congress had dealt him. His reply to Jefferson was grateful, but candid, cautious, and—in places—testy.[4]

Gallatin confessed that the deep disappointments of the past winter had hurt him personally and politically. His said his friendship for Madison and his sense of duty nevertheless would keep him at the Treasury as long as he could be useful. How long that would be he could not tell. "The reduction of the public debt was certainly the principal object in bringing me into office," he wrote, so he would judge his usefulness by whether he could continue to achieve it. He knew that war preparations would make it almost impossible to reduce debt over the next few years and that war would require new loans. "But it seems to me," he said, that he should be able to insist that the government not run up new debt until war began. "I cannot my dear Sir, consent to act the part of a mere financier, to become a contriver of taxes, a dealer of loans, a seeker of resources for the purpose of supporting useless baubles, of encreasing the number of idle & dissipated members of the community, of fattening contractors, pursers and agents, and of introducing, in all its ramifications, that system of patronage, corruption & rotenness which you so justly execrate." The next session of Congress would tell whether he could defend "our old principles." If he could not, he intimated, he would resign.[5]

Gallatin had reason to question the fiscal prospects of the new administration. He already faced a deficit for the current year—the first deficit since the Republicans had come to power—and American relations with Britain continued to deteriorate. The deficit was the result of plunging imports during the embargo, and Gallatin had anticipated it. He had proposed to double the tax rate on the remaining imports in order to cover the shortfall, but higher taxes were too bitter a pill for the Republicans in Congress. The Republicans had opposed John Adams's tax increases during the Quasi-War, they had repealed internal taxes after Jefferson's election, and they believed their party's popularity depended on low taxes. The strong-minded John Taylor summed up the political situation with his usual plainness. "It is extreme folly to suppose that the bulk of the people are influenced by abstract political principles," he told James Monroe. That "was never the case in any nation." It was not the principles of the Adams and Jefferson administrations that caused "their change of places or degrees of popularity. Both was done by taxes imposed and removed." The Republican majority in Congress had ignored Gallatin's call for double duties, replaced the embargo with a non-intercourse measure that would allow more taxable trade, and gambled on an improvement in relations with Britain.[6]

The Republicans' wager seemed canny for a while. The non-intercourse law that replaced the embargo barred imports from whichever of the two nations first dropped its own restrictions on American trade. Shortly after Madison became president, Britain seemed ready to take the offer. The British minister in Washington, David Erskine, was an enthusiastic young man well disposed toward the United States. He had spent time in Philadelphia a decade earlier, married an American, and returned as British minister in 1806 with a sincere desire to improve relations between the two countries. The month after Madison took office, he and Erskine reached an agreement under which Britain would drop its most obnoxious restrictions on American trade in exchange for the readmission of British goods to the American market. Madison immediately proclaimed that he would lift the ban on British imports, and the country breathed a sigh of relief.[7]

But in their eagerness for better relations, Madison and Erskine had gotten ahead of themselves. Both sides were deceived, wrote Federalist Rufus King, based on his long experience as American minister in London. One "rejoices because they think that the Embargo, &c^a has brought England to terms," and the other because they believe domestic opposition to the embargo "has obliged the administration to abandon their [restrictive] system." Britain's foreign minister George Canning had no such delusions. He repudiated Erskine's agreement and published diplomatic dispatches intended to show that Madison had acted in bad faith because he knew the agreement exceeded Erskine's instructions.[8]

News of Canning's repudiation of the agreement reached Washington after Madison had gone home for the summer. Madison insisted he could deal with the crisis by mail, but Gallatin finally persuaded him to return to Washington for an emergency cabinet meeting. The cabinet decided to reinstate non-intercourse with Britain, and—after Madison had scrambled back home—Gallatin and Robert Smith exchanged notes with Erskine in an effort to prove that the United States had negotiated with him in good faith. By the time Gallatin set off to visit Madison and Jefferson in Virginia, he did not think the new administration could avoid war much longer. Although he had advocated war in Campbell's report nine months earlier, it now seemed a dispiriting prospect. "[W]e are not so prepared for resistance as we were one year ago," he wrote. A year ago, American ships were safe at home and the Treasury had enough money to pay for the first year of fighting. Now, he said, "we have wasted our resources," emptied the Treasury, and "must begin any plan of resistance with considerable and therefore unpopular loans."[9]

This dispiriting prospect explained the caution in Gallatin's reply to Jefferson, but the testiness arose from his confrontation with the Smith brothers. The Smiths made their money from transatlantic trade, and Gallatin thought their insistence on excessive naval spending to protect that trade was outrageously self-interested. He also had come to believe they meant to destroy him politically for standing in their way. They had found allies in William Branch Giles, who was jealous of Gallatin, William Duane, whom Gallatin had left hungry, and Michael Leib, the Philadelphia radical who had just clawed his way into the Senate. Milling around in the shadows behind these men was a larger group of malcontent Republicans who disliked Madison's indecisive foreign policy and objected to Gallatin's influence in the government. Those "invisibles," as Nathaniel Macon called them, were not a majority in either house of Congress, and they frequently disagreed with each other on important issues. But as the vote on the navy bill the previous winter had shown, they could combine with the Federalist minority to disorganize administration policy when it suited their purposes. Macon was looking for a "good opportunity" to scatter them, and soon after Madison took office, Gallatin thought he had found one.[10]

A routine Treasury audit revealed that Robert Smith's Navy department had paid his brother Samuel's mercantile firm in Baltimore more than $250,000 for bills of exchange on a firm in the Mediterranean port of Leghorn (Livorno) during the Tripolitan War, and the money had disappeared. The transaction was not patently outrageous. In a world with few banks, the government often gave American merchants cash in exchange for the right to use their credit to make government purchases abroad. And while self-dealing was suspicious, it was not necessarily damning. What had brought the transaction to Gallatin's attention was something worse. Samuel Smith's firm apparently did not have as much credit with the firm in Leghorn as the navy had paid for, and oddly, the navy had never used all of the credit that was available. That left unspent money with the Leghorn firm, and one of the partners in the firm had absconded with it. So while no single part of the transaction conclusively indicted the Smiths, the overall circumstances looked suspicious and played to Gallatin's belief that the Smiths were mercenary men who used political power for selfish purposes.[11]

Gallatin's discovery of the Leghorn transaction was timely because Samuel Smith's term in the Senate was about to end. An attack on Smith's reputation could help his opponents take control of the Maryland legislature and stop it from re-electing Smith. Gallatin had shared his discovery with Joseph Nicholson when they met in Baltimore during the spring, and Nicholson had encouraged Macon to spread the Leghorn accounts before Congress. But Gallatin and Macon came up with a warier approach. They got John Randolph to call for a general investigation into government spending under the prior administration. Randolph's motion for the investigation passed unanimously, and under its guise he began probing into the naval accounts. Congress adjourned before he could complete the investigation, but his committee published preliminary findings—which included a report from Gallatin on the Leghorn transaction.[12]

The Smiths were furious. Robert Smith claimed that the Leghorn transaction was routine and pointedly deplored the committee's failure to ask him for an explanation. Samuel Smith's response was even more forceful. "I believe it impossible," he wrote to Gallatin, "that any man who has the least pretensions to character would commit an act so base as that [you have] charged on me." But Gallatin did not back down. The transaction as it appeared in the accounts, he told Samuel Smith, was "the most extraordinary that has fallen within my knowledge since I have been in this Department." Gallatin said he did not intend to comment on the case, but if the Treasury failed to recover the missing money from the firm in Leghorn, "we might have recourse against [your firm]." Samuel Smith took pains to tell Jefferson, in a letter that reached him shortly before Gallatin visited in August, that he had wiped away the "malicious" aspersion on his character. "[W]ho originated the tale," he wrote Jefferson, "I will not pain you by telling." Smith held on to his Senate seat despite Gallatin's attempt to smear him, but his struggle with Gallatin was far from over and both of them knew it.[13]

⁊⤫⤬

It was a fight over the Bank of the United States that brought Gallatin and the Smiths to a showdown. Gallatin wanted Congress to re-charter the Bank's charter when it expired in 1811, and he sent Congress a report recommending a new charter two days before Madison took office. At first, Samuel Smith did not oppose the charter because he conceded that a national bank could serve useful purposes. But like many commercially-minded Republicans, he believed that the existing Bank was a Federalist-dominated institution that favored insiders and sent most of its profits to British shareholders. (Gallatin had actually played into the hands of Republicans who felt that way when, in order to repay foreign debt, he sold the government's shares in the Bank to the British banker Alexander Baring in 1802.) After an inconclusive debate in which Republicans aired these objections, Congress postponed further discussion of the Bank's charter until the following year.[14]

By then, Smith's simmering hostility to the Bank—and to Gallatin—had begun to change his mind. He told a Washington dinner party in his bluntly outspoken way that the directors of the Bank's Baltimore branch were a bunch of Scots and Englishmen who would not lend money to good Republicans. A Bank director who got wind of the conversation wrote to tell Smith that the Baltimore branch actually had given more credit to "Democrats" than to anyone else during the past

three years. Smith tried to minimize what he had said, but the director—who knew him—would have none of it. "I rather suspect my
General," he wrote back, that "you were on your high horse, & gallop-
ing away like the devil."[15]

Samuel Smith may have been on his high horse, but he had not out-
ridden his own interests. He sat on the board of directors of two Baltimore banks that competed for capital with the Philadelphia-based Bank
of the United States, and he and his brother Robert owned shares in
several other Maryland banks. State-chartered banks had become more
important in the twenty years since Congress had established the Bank
of the United States. Although the nation's population had not quite
doubled, the number of state banks had jumped from five to 117 and
their banking capital had gone from about $4.6 million to $66.3 million.
Republicans had formed quite a few of those banks, which made credit
available to small producers, partisan Republicans, and other borrowers
whom the Bank had ignored. Old Republican objections to the Bank as
an aristocratic institution were now leavened with the middle class yeast
of commercial competition.[16]

Supporters of the state banks resented the Bank's virtual monopoly
on federal deposits, which they thought allowed the Bank to curtail the
amount of credit that the state banks could offer. Most bank loans took
the form of notes issued to the borrower by the lending bank. The borrower used the bank notes as currency to buy goods and services and to
repay other obligations. Merchants used bank notes to pay off the bonds
they had given for federal import duties, so a large portion of the state
banks' notes fell into the hands of the Bank of the United States. Banks
had to pay their notes in gold or silver. So if the Bank required the state
banks to pay the notes it received as deposits, the state banks had to give
the Bank specie they otherwise could have used to back bank notes lent
to their customers. And the Bank—which paid no interest on government
deposits—got more specie that it could use to make interest-bearing loans
to its own customers. Those involved in state banking thought this
arrangement gave the Bank an unfair competitive advantage. Whether

the Bank actually did compete unfairly was difficult to prove, but the political force of the allegation was undeniable.[17]

Gallatin tried to keep the Bank's petition for a new charter from getting caught in the controversy over its relationship with the state banks. His initial report in favor of the charter was vague about the size of the Bank's specie holdings and silent about its calls for the redemption of state bank notes. But those issues were inescapable, and they sparked the first open discussion in the United States about aspects of what later would be called central banking. Opponents of the Bank claimed that its steady calls for payment of state bank notes prevented the state banks from giving the business community as much credit as it needed. The argument resonated in cities like Baltimore where trade had expanded quickly to meet Europe's wartime demand for flour and smuggled goods. Supporters of the Bank, who included established merchants and bankers in the older port cities of Philadelphia and New York, responded that the Bank's calls on the state banks helped control inflation by discouraging the state banks from issuing too many notes. That check on the state banks, supporters argued, helped the federal government fulfill its constitutional mandate to provide a sound and uniform national currency.[18]

This debate about whether the country needed a national bank to regulate the money supply would take on immense political significance when Andrew Jackson set out to destroy the Bank of the United States twenty years later. But when the House asked Gallatin for another report on the Bank's charter in the spring of 1810, he was still at pains to avoid the controversy. He confined himself to the practical case for the Bank as a fiscal agent and lender to the federal government—the same case that he had made privately to Jefferson eight years earlier. But Gallatin did recommend significant changes in the Bank's charter. He proposed to increase the Bank's capital from $10 million to $30 million, require it to pay interest on federal deposits, and commit it to lend up to $18 million to the federal government. Those changes served the government's purposes because they would give the Treasury reliable access to credit in wartime. But they also quietly responded to the Bank's critics. Since the Bank would have a much larger amount of capital to invest during peacetime, it would have a reason to hold more of the state bank notes that it received on deposit. And the sale of new Bank shares to raise the additional $20 million of capital could dilute the interest of the Bank's foreign shareholders. Gallatin proposed to offer up to $15 million of the new shares to the states and to sell the rest to American citizens.[19]

Congressional debate over the Bank of the United States dragged into the winter of 1810 because it severely divided the Republican majority. Many Republicans supported Gallatin's proposal for a new charter, but some—like the Smiths—thought the government should shift its deposits to the state banks. Others simply could not shake their distrust of a Federalist bank with foreign shareholders, and the most orthodox Republicans "conscientiously opposed" the Bank for the same constitutional reasons that Jefferson and Madison had given in 1791. The constitutional argument allowed all of the Bank's opponents to cloak their motives in lofty rhetoric. By the time a House committee presented a bill for re-charter, sentiment was so divided that the committee's chairman opened the debate by opposing the committee's bill.[20]

Madison was thought to favor a new charter along the lines Gallatin proposed, but he never said so publicly. His silence emboldened Gallatin's enemies, and it gave Madison's own enemies a chance to emasculate his administration without criticizing the president directly. William Duane's *Aurora* ran a set of editorials crudely attacking Gallatin, the Bank, and the administration's financial policies. How, Duane insinuated, had Gallatin come to be one of the wealthiest men in the country? Might it have something to do with his support for the Yazoo land speculators and the British shareholders in the Bank of the United States? The Pennsylvania and Virginia legislatures asked their representatives in Congress to vote against re-charter. Without presidential leadership, the divided House drifted into indecision. Finally, in late January, it voted 65–64 to postpone the Bank question indefinitely. Nathaniel Macon, who had always believed that the Bank was unconstitutional, told Joseph Nicholson that he was "really sorry that my best judgment compelled me" to vote with "the invisibles." Their good friend Gallatin, he reported, was "mortified" by the outcome.[21]

Rallying to save the Bank's charter in the Senate, Gallatin found an able ally in William H. Crawford of Georgia. Crawford was a giant of a man—6'3" and well over two hundred pounds—with sharp blue eyes and a square, handsome face. His great intelligence, commanding voice, and winning manner had taken him from a tiny law office in the Georgia backcountry to the Senate of the United States in eight years. Crawford had chaired the Senate committee that reported in favor of the Bank's charter, and he quickly lost patience with the constitutional cant he heard Samuel Smith using to justify his opposition. He got Gallatin to give him a report explicitly stating that the Bank helped the federal government exercise its undoubted constitutional powers to collect revenue and promote the general welfare of the United States, and armed with that report, he took to the Senate floor.[22]

The Bank, Crawford told the Senate, was constitutional if it helped the federal government perform its proper functions. Whether or not the Bank was doing that had to be determined under the actual circumstances. The banking system that had grown up since the nation's founding could not be simply "frowned out of existence." The Bank gave the Treasury credit against the bonds that merchants posted for the payment of import duties, and many of the merchants in turn looked to the Bank for the loans they needed to pay off those bonds. The same merchants who owed the United States $10–12 million also owed the Bank $14 million. If the Bank were liquidated, the merchants would have to pay all of those debts at once. How could they possibly do that without delivering a serious shock to the economy? And what provision of the Constitution required such a crisis? Circumstances could not increase the federal government's constitutional powers, but circumstances did determine the proper means for exercising them. Arguments about original intention were simply irrelevant to questions about the methods for exercising constitutional powers. "[W]hen acting today," he said, we are "not to inquire what means were necessary and proper twenty years ago, not what were necessary and proper at the organization of the Government, but…what means are necessary and proper this day." As to the proper means for exercising the government's powers, he concluded, the Constitution "is an eternal *now*."[23]

A thirty-three-year-old freshman senator from Kentucky named Henry Clay pounced on Crawford's arguments. Clay was a tall man—wiry, active, and gregarious—with a receding hairline, wide mouth, and thin lips. He came from Lexington, one of the vigorous new commercial cities west of the Appalachians. He had built a successful law practice representing Kentucky's powerful state banks. Clay thought they and the other state banks throughout the country were perfectly capable of handling the federal government's business, and he said so. But he also bludgeoned Crawford for his lack of Republican purity. If Crawford had gone over to the enemy, he taunted, was it kind of him "to look back upon his former friends" and rebuke them for fidelity to "their old principles?" Twenty years of an unconstitutional banking system was no excuse for twenty more. Congress was not a court of law; precedent did not matter. "Here no rule exists but the Constitution," Clay said. And having "wandered throughout the whole Constitution in quest of some congenial spot," the "vagrant power to erect a bank" had found none. It was true that the Bank gave merchants the credit they needed to pay federal taxes, but other banks could do the same thing. Indeed, Clay concluded, it would be safer for the government not to depend on a bank dominated by English shareholders when "[w]e are possibly on the eve of a rupture with that nation."[24]

The Senate vote on the Bank's charter was a political watershed for the administration. The Senate rejected the charter on the tie-breaking vote of Vice President George Clinton, Madison's old rival for the presidency. Samuel Smith, Giles, and Leib voted against the Bank. The outcome was no surprise, but the vote highlighted Republican disunity. Men on both sides laid most of the blame on Madison's lack of leadership. Nathaniel Macon, for example, had heard conflicting reports about Madison's position on the Bank. At first he heard that Madison thought the Bank question was *"res adjudicata"*—so there was no need to reconsider the constitutional issue—but rumor later reported that Madison had changed his mind. Men had a right to change their minds, said Macon, but when "great men or rather men in high responsible stations, change their deliberate opinions, it seems to me, that they in some way or other ought to give the reason." If Madison had recommended the Bank's charter, one Federalist Congressman flatly concluded, Congress would have passed it. But Madison instead had let himself be "overawed by a powerful party against the bank.... The truth is as a President he is but little better than a man of straw and has no independence in anything." Rufus King privately rejoiced that the Bank's defeat had "shewn [Madison] such as we know him to be."[25]

The disarray in Congress was only part of the problem. The fight between Gallatin and the Smiths was wrecking Madison's cabinet. Robert Smith had gotten the Comptroller of the Treasury, a fellow Marylander, to sign off on the disputed Leghorn transaction, and Congress had called on Gallatin for another report about it. Gallatin waited until the very day when the Senate was voting on the Bank to deliver a complicated report that effectively exonerated the Smiths without ever saying so. Buried deep in Gallatin's findings was a concession that Samuel Smith's firm would have had the credit it sold to the Navy if one of the cargoes it sent to Leghorn had not been lost. The report, Robert Smith complained to his brother, was "nothing but a labored covert apology" for Gallatin's "former misunderstandings and misrepresentation." Duane's *Aurora* and a Smith-backed Baltimore newspaper insinuated that Gallatin had backed the Bank because he was a British agent and dismissed Madison as "destitute of that energy or 'decision of character'" needed to be president. Robert Smith leaked confidential information from cabinet meetings to his brother and their friends in Congress, and he quietly undercut diplomatic efforts that Madison—who found Smith incompetent—had insisted on directing himself.[26]

"Things as they are cannot go on much longer," John Randolph predicted. "The administration are now in fact aground" and nothing remains "but to lighten the ship." A few days after the Senate rejected the Bank, Macon, Crawford, and some of Gallatin's other friends in

Congress visited Madison and urged him to dismiss Robert Smith. "I do not know what has been the effect of our call at the palace," Crawford reported to Joseph Nicholson. "Some of them are to call [again] tomorrow." Gallatin knew of these visits, and he tightened the pressure on Madison by doing what he had been considering for a long time. He resigned.[27]

Once Madison had to decide between Smith and Gallatin, his choice was never in doubt. He asked Gallatin to stay and prepared to dismiss Robert Smith. Smith's dismissal would make it even harder to get Gallatin confirmed as Secretary of State than it had been two years earlier, but the cabinet vacancy gave the president an opportunity to heal other differences within the Republican party. Madison thought he could reconcile with James Monroe and the old Republicans who had supported Monroe in the presidential election by appointing Monroe to the State department. Gallatin discreetly approached Monroe through one of the Virginia senators and found Monroe open to the appointment. Although many of the old Republicans still suspected Madison of unforgivable Federalist tendencies, Monroe's friend John Taylor encouraged Monroe to go into the administration. The "selfish intriguers" besieging the president, Taylor told him, were trying "to drive off Gallatin who has more real weight of character than the whole together." If Monroe could help Madison to defend Gallatin, that would be "an essential public service."[28]

Madison tried to ease Smith out of the way by offering to appoint him the American minister to Russia, but Smith decided to rebuff Madison's gesture and go noisily. In a contentious *Address to the People of the United States*, he blamed everything that had gone wrong at the State department on Madison's interference. Smith's address did not strike at Gallatin, but Duane's *Aurora* declared that Gallatin had hijacked the whole Administration. His supporters, the paper reported, say Gallatin has more talent than the rest of the administration put together, including Madison himself. What did that mean? "Why clearly that Mr. *Gallatin* is to all intents and purposes the *president*, and even more than the president of the United States." The substitution of Monroe for Robert Smith was indeed "a triumph of the Gallatin over the Smith party," as one Federalist Congressman put it, but the victory gave Gallatin no solace. "Notwithstanding the change," he confided to Joseph Nicholson, "I feel no satisfaction in my present situation." The change left him inextricably committed to an increasingly difficult job.[29]

The foreign policy situation that James Monroe inherited when he became Secretary of State had only grown more complicated since Britain repudiated Erskine's agreement in the summer of 1809. The Republicans' preference for trade sanctions rather than war had kept the nation at peace. But the restrictive system—as the reliance on sanctions was coming to be called—drew the government into endless embarrassments. After a debate that lasted into the spring of 1810, Congress had replaced the non-intercourse law with an inverted arrangement. The non-intercourse law had kept imports from Britain and France out of the United States as long as those countries maintained their restrictions on American trade. The new measure reopened trade with both countries, but promised the first one to recognize American neutral rights that the United States would reinstate non-intercourse against the other.[30]

Several months later, Napoleon invited Madison's administration to believe that he had taken the bait. A crafty letter from his foreign minister, the Duc de Cadore, announced that Napoleon had revoked French restrictions on American trade, but only on the understanding that the United States would cause the British to revoke theirs. Whether Cadore's letter deceived Madison—or whether he simply thought he could use it to deceive the British or to focus American grievances on Britain alone—has never been clear. But Madison decided to take the letter at face value, and he issued a proclamation that imposed non-intercourse on Britain unless it lifted its own restrictions. The British government pointed out that France was in fact continuing to seize American ships and refused to make any concessions to the United States. That left the administration in the awkward position of trading with a country that was preying on American commerce and refusing to trade with the only country that could do anything about it. Monroe, who had hoped for an accommodation with Britain, came to the State department with no diplomatic leverage and few peaceful options.[31]

⟨≈⟩

de restrictions had revived public interest in the question of
her the federal government should encourage American manufactur-
. The question was as old as the republic. Political independence had
ot freed Americans from economic dependence on British manufactured
goods. But the Revolutionary War had demonstrated a need for the
domestic production of weapons, gunpowder, and other military supplies, and the year after Washington became president, Congress asked
Alexander Hamilton for a plan to encourage the domestic manufacture
of essential goods.[32]

The Report on Manufactures that Hamilton delivered two years
later was much more than Congress had requested. It was an extended
argument for encouraging domestic manufactures of all kinds in order
to create a more balanced, self-sustaining national economy. Hamilton
pointedly rejected the arguments for free trade made by Adam Smith and
other liberal political economists. In a world where other nation-states
pursued mercantilist policies designed to protect their own markets, he
said, free trade was an unrealistic aspiration. Mercantile restrictions on
the sale of American agricultural produce in Europe prevented Americans from earning enough foreign exchange to buy all of the European
manufactured goods they needed. The solution was for the United States
to manufacture more of those goods at home. When properly developed,
American factories could supply a wide range of goods and consume a
growing portion of the country's agricultural produce. To encourage
manufacturing, Hamilton proposed protective tariffs, cash subsidies to
large manufacturers, and outright bans on certain imports. Congress did
impose higher import duties on some of the goods that competed with
emerging American manufactures, but nothing came of the rest of Hamilton's ideas.[33]

The embargo and the import restrictions had sparked new demand
for a variety of American-made manufactures even though they were not
as good or as cheap as European comparables. The demand prompted
American merchants to put millions of dollars that had been pushed out

of international trade into new manufacturing ventures. Textile manufacturing was particularly attractive, and the number of cotton mills in the country leaped from fifteen in 1808 to 102 in 1809. The significant new investment in manufacturing brought renewed calls for protection, and in June 1809, the House by a lopsided vote of 93–38 asked Gallatin for a report.[34]

Hamilton's report on manufactures is well known, but the report on manufactures that Gallatin delivered twenty years later is not. Even Gallatin's modern biographers brush by it. The problem is that Gallatin's report can seem anomalous. Jefferson's unforgettable comparison of sturdy yeoman farmers with wretched urban workers haunts historical memory, and although scholars know that Jefferson and Madison did value home manufactures, the notion that the Republicans were agrarians opposed to the development of American manufacturing dies hard. But in fact manufacturers were an important part of the Republican movement from its beginning. In the pivotal states of Pennsylvania and New York, it was striving small producers and ambitious factory owners who gave rural Republicans the boost they needed to gain political control. These emerging manufacturers chafed under the stable, deferential social order that Federalists were trying to preserve, and they saw federal excise taxes on manufactured goods as a direct threat to their economic interests. Their determination to rise and prosper brought them into the Republican opposition, and after the Republican victory in 1800, they delivered a regular drumbeat of petitions to Congress for the protection of American manufacturing.[35]

Gallatin himself was a manufacturer, and by the time Congress asked him to report on American manufacturing, he had already dropped hints about opportunities for encouraging it. Early in Jefferson's administration, he had told Congress that the Treasury needed to collect better information on the domestic consumption of imported goods so that Congress could design import duties "most favorable to the agricultural and manufacturing interests of the country." When he suggested doubling import duties after the *Chesapeake* affair in order to prepare the country for war, he said that the resulting protection for domestic manufacturers would be a "desirable object" in itself. And in the finance report he gave to Congress after a year of embargo, Gallatin recommended a permanent increase in the import duties on goods that Americans could manufacture for themselves in sufficient quantities.[36]

But there were limits on how far Gallatin was willing to go. In opposing the embargo, he had reminded Jefferson that a statesman should hesitate "to regulate the concerns of individuals as if he could do it better than themselves." And Gallatin did not need to look far to know that some agrarian Republicans flatly opposed any protection for domestic manufacturing. More than a few of the Congressmen who voted against asking him for the report on manufacturing were Republicans, and his good friend Nathaniel Macon was one of them. Gallatin repeatedly cautioned Jefferson and Madison not to justify trade sanctions against the European belligerents by claiming that they would encourage domestic manufacturing. Just months after he gave Congress his report on manufactures, Gallatin asked Madison not even to mention protection as a reason for raising import duties. "As I want [the higher] duties for revenue purposes," he told Madison, "I am somewhat apprehensive that a direct demand for protection of manufactures (on which Subject there will be a difference of opinion) may defeat the object."[37]

Gallatin understood that Congress was unlikely to act on the Report on Manufactures that he delivered in 1810, but he nevertheless embraced the opportunity to lay out a liberal Republican program for the development of manufacturing. Gallatin began by sorting American manufactures into three categories: those already developed enough to satisfy domestic demand, those well enough established to supply a good part of the demand, and those not advanced enough to warrant attention. By the time Gallatin wrote, the production of goods in the first two categories had grown much more extensive than it had been at the time of Hamilton's report. Gallatin estimated that the annual output was worth more than $120 million and that the workers and factories responsible for it consumed about as much American food and raw material as the country exported. He attributed this growth to the import duties imposed on foreign goods for revenue purposes, the repeal of federal excise taxes, the absence of domestic regulation, and the protection provided by trade sanctions over the previous two years. The chief impediments to further growth, he reported, were the lure of cheap agricultural land, the high price of labor, and the lack of sufficient capital. He said that lack of capital was the main problem, and he thought that the federal government should tackle it by lending American manufacturers up to $20 million at the rate of $5 million per year.[38]

The difference between Gallatin's proposal for loans and Hamilton's proposals for protective tariffs, subsidies, and import bans reflected not only the economic progress of two decades, but also profound differences in their thinking. Gallatin built his argument on the liberal political economics in Smith's *Wealth of Nations*. High protective tariffs, he wrote, destroyed competition, raised consumer prices, and diverted "capital and industry into channels generally less profitable to the nation" than those private interests would have chosen on their own. He thought the import duties that the federal government used to raise revenue already provided a good deal of protection for domestic industries. He was reluctant to offer more because the higher prices resulting from greater protection taxed all consumers for the benefit of a few manufacturers. He thought subsidies were an equally inefficient way to promote economic development because they too shifted money from all taxpayers to the favored manufacturers. He did not even bother to discuss the obvious economic inefficiency of banning foreign goods entirely.[39]

Gallatin specifically rejected the neo-mercantilist arguments that Hamilton had made in his report. Hamilton had claimed that liberal free market theories did not work in a developing country such as the United States. The American economy was still struggling to outgrow its colonial dependence on commodity exports. The European economies, on the other hand, had already established manufacturing. Since established manufacturers could almost always produce goods more cheaply, said Hamilton, the American economy would not be able to emerge from colonial dependency unless the federal government gave domestic manufacturers protection from foreign competition. Gallatin agreed that the American economy was still emerging, but he did not think that justified higher trade barriers. The "only powerful obstacle" confronting American manufacturers, he said, was Britain's "vastly superior capital," which allowed "her merchants to give very long credits, to sell on small profits, and to make occasional sacrifices." The solution was to give resourceful American manufacturers the capital they needed to compete.[40]

∽

The Republican trade sanctions may have helped American manufacturing, but they did not achieve their foreign policy objective. Britain and France were still interfering with American trade, and Britain was still impressing sailors from American merchant ships. In May 1811, while cruising to protect American ships from the British warships hovering just off the North Carolina coast, the American frigate *President* mistakenly attacked a much smaller British sloop called the *Little Belt*, killed nine men, wounded twenty-three others, and blamed the whole incident on the British commander. The episode was a sensational example of the increasing tension between the two countries, and newspapers on both sides of the Atlantic printed partisan accounts and harsh recriminations throughout the summer. Two months later, Madison issued a proclamation calling the new Congress to an early session in November.[41]

During the summer of 1811, tension also mounted on the northwestern frontier. The federal government's efforts to take more Native American land in the Indiana territory had fanned a Native spiritual and cultural revival. Many of those caught up in the revival gathered around the Shawnee prophet Tenskwatawa and his brother Tecumseh, who were determined to put a stop to land cessions and cultural assimilation. Natives in the region had traded furs with the British in the Canadian provinces for half a century, and as the nativists prepared for conflict with the United States, they naturally turned to the British for support. Scattered violence broke out on both sides. From Indiana, Gallatin's friend John Badollet warned that territorial governor William Henry Harrison would use the violence as an excuse to break the nativists' spirited resistance. In the autumn, Harrison marched on Tenskwatawa's village, burned it, and killed about a hundred inhabitants. Almost 200 of Harrison's 1,000 men died in the attack. Reports of the clash, which came to be called the Battle of Tippecanoe, reached Washington soon after Congress assembled.[42]

Many members of the new Congress were coming to believe that the nation could no longer sidestep the great decision between war and peace. "Peace, economy, and riddance of public debt" were Republican articles of faith, and Republican abhorrence for the expansion of executive power inevitable during wartime was profound. But people throughout the country were losing patience with the disruptions caused by trade restrictions. They also resented what they saw as an arrogant British disregard for the maritime rights of an independent nation. And many from the West, where a wider war with Native Americans seemed certain, claimed that British agents in Canada were stoking the violence to slow American settlement and maintain their grip on the valuable fur trade.[43]

Whether these resentments and grievances would lead Congress to declare war against Britain was not yet clear. In New England, where much of the population made a living from maritime trade, there was more sympathy for the British and more tolerance for the extreme measures to which their long-running war against France had driven them. New Englanders also had no doubt that a war with Britain would devastate what remained of the transatlantic trade damaged by the Republicans' restrictive system. Federalists remained strong in the region, and even the Republican leaders there found it expedient to lean against some of their party's restrictive measures. Republicans elsewhere thought the Federalists in New England were self-interested and disloyal. They claimed that the Republican trade sanctions would have been more effective if this treacherous faction had not condoned smuggling and encouraged the British to think that New England might leave the Union if the two countries came to blows. But they remained unsure what the country should do next. Gallatin reassured his good friend Thomas Worthington, who was preparing to reenter the Senate, that he was "not the only person who feels embarrassed as to the proper course...in the present crisis."[44]

Madison no longer believed that the nation could avoid war with Britain, and his opening message to Congress would have said so more explicitly if Gallatin had not nudged him back toward his customary reticence. But Henry Clay and about a dozen other hawkish young Congressmen from the interior of the country needed no prompting to press for war. Clay had given up his place in the Senate to take a seat in the more vigorous House, and the House promptly elected him to be its speaker. He put other warlike men in control of the key committees, and together they pushed for military preparations.[45]

Outspoken Federalist Josiah Quincy, who had told the previous Congress that the Republican majority "could not be kicked into" war, remained skeptical of the Republicans' real intentions. He thought most of them were just trying to frighten the British ministry into withdrawing its obnoxious measures. Other Federalists claimed the Republican "war hawks" only meant to goad New England maritime interests into opposing war so that they could blame the Federalists for a new extension of the unpopular restrictive system. Most thought taxes would be the true test of the Republicans' intentions. Federalist James Bayard wrote that he would not "believe them in earnest" about war until they agreed to raise the taxes to pay for it. In the meantime, he thought their war talk was just so much "juggling" over whether Madison could win reelection in the autumn of 1812. The mercantile community apparently agreed: insurance rates on transatlantic cargoes remained low for months after Congress met.[46]

Gallatin knew that taxes would test the Republicans' resolve, and he had nudged Madison away from an outright call for war because he was not sure Congress would raise them. In fact, the finance reports he had delivered since 1807 had not prepared Congress to raise taxes. In those reports, Gallatin had expressed confidence that the government could borrow the money needed for war as long as its current revenues covered ordinary peacetime expenses and interest on the public debt. Gallatin had suggested doubling import duties to make up for the revenue lost to trade sanctions, but he had assured Congress that they would not have to impose internal taxes. Now those confident assurances were gone. Gallatin's finance report to the new Congress projected a peacetime deficit of $2.6 million. It said higher import duties might not cover the deficit in wartime, and it explicitly mentioned the possibility of "moderate internal taxes." Gallatin also hinted that wartime borrowing could mount to the enormous sum of $40 million, and—for the first time—he said that circumstances beyond the government's control could make it difficult to borrow.[47]

When the Ways and Means committee asked for a fuller explanation, Gallatin gave a guarded account of his change in position. He said Congress's failure to raise import duties after the embargo had deprived the Treasury of about $20 million in revenue over the past three years and forced it to spend a $14 million cash reserve. The refusal to re-charter the Bank also had eliminated the only lender from which the Treasury could have borrowed $20 million. The $40 million or more lost to those two decisions, Gallatin told the committee, would have paid for four years of war without the need for internal taxes. As it was—now that they had asked him—he felt obliged to recommend $5 million of internal taxes and a $10 million loan. The internal taxes he proposed were the whiskey excise and the other unpopular taxes on which the Federalists had relied.[48]

Gallatin's finance reports were more sobering than the Republicans in Congress had expected, and his critics accused him of standing in the way of war. William Branch Giles, who wanted to raise an army more than twice as large as the 10,000 men Madison had requested, was particularly harsh. If "you deal out your means so sparingly as to fail of your object," Giles told the Senate, you create "prodigal waste and profusion of economy." The half measures of resistance to Britain that had "dishonored the nation" for years, he said, arose from the administration's reluctance "to press on the Treasury Department, and to disturb the popularity and repose of the gentleman at the head of it." Gallatin's friends claimed that he had "the most splendid financial talents." Well, then, Congress should give him "scope for the demonstration" of those talents. Gallatin may have reduced the public debt by half, but what good had that done? Did people ever think about the size of the public debt when they made their own business decisions? Of course not, because a large public debt was "so entirely within [the country's] ability." If proper preparations for war required more debt, said Giles, the Treasury secretary should bestir himself to raise it.[49]

William Duane's *Aurora* took up the cry. Gallatin's report on war finance proved once again, Duane told his readers, that "it *is impossible to repose confidence in any administration in which Mr. Gallatin holds a predominant influence.*" One half of the public, wrote a correspondent to the paper, believes that Gallatin's report "is *all a sham*" by which "the wheels of the government are to be stopped." The other half thinks Gallatin "has actually done his *very best*," but that his vaunted financial talents are better suited to "speculating in lands and banks, than in the concerns of a free people." Re-erecting the internal revenue system, the paper declared, "would be like the creation of *Babel*" to catch "the mites...in the higher regions of the atmosphere." The Treasury should simply issue its own notes for the amount it needed. Using Treasury notes would give the 6 percent interest directly to the public who took the notes rather than to bankers and moneylenders.[50]

Even young Hezekiah Niles's more balanced *Weekly Register* said that Gallatin's report to the Ways and Means committee was seen as "'*a damper*' upon the new army, &c. artfully drawn up for the express purpose of alarming the people, and checking the *decision* of congress." It diminished Gallatin's reputation, Niles reported, "to be able to point out no other means of raising a revenue than those recommended by...Messrs. *Hamilton and Wolcott.*" Other newspapers were no kinder. The Federalist *New-York Evening Post* gleefully disparaged Gallatin for proposing the very same taxes he had opposed in the 1790s. And the London *Times* intoned that Gallatin's budget embarked America on "the same voyage in which so many of the old Governments of Europe have been wrecked,—taxes, loans, public debt, &c."[51]

Whatever his critics claimed, Gallatin was in fact resolved to war. He thought the failure of the restrictive system left no alternative, and he now blamed that failure on the Federalists in New England. Early in March, Madison sent Congress a batch of papers purchased from a

British agent named John Henry that purported to show New England Federalists were plotting treason and secession from the Union. Gallatin had helped Monroe to purchase them from a shady intermediary for the startling sum of $50,000, and the administration hoped the papers would consolidate its own party's resolution for war. But even as he joined the push toward war, Gallatin clung to the hope that war would not destroy the frugal Republican fiscal system he had worked so hard to build.[52]

"You have seen from your retreat," Gallatin wrote to Jefferson soon after the Henry papers became public, "that our hopes and endeavours to preserve peace…have at last been frustrated." Yet despite the evident disloyalty in some quarters, he said, "the mass of the people [would] support their own Government in an unavoidable war." Pennsylvania was "never more firm or united," and the "South & West cannot be shaken." Then he came to his main point. He would endeavor, he assured his old leader, to keep "the evils" that were "inseparable" from war isolated to wartime so that the United States could emerge from the war "with the smallest possible quantity of debt, perpetual taxation, military establishments and other corrupting or anti Republican habits or institutions." However unlikely that outcome might have seemed, it was not yet too much to hope.[53]

As Congress ground its way through war preparations in the spring of 1812, there was even a remnant of hope for peace. Reports from London said British manufacturers were pushing their government to lift its restrictions on American trade. Congress put off the subjects of war and internal taxes in anticipation of official dispatches. "We are waiting here with great impatience for a little insect called a Hornet," Federalist senator James Bayard teased a Republican friend back home in Delaware. "It is supposed it will arrive winged with peace or war." In the meantime, there would be no new taxes. "No war, no taxes, not a bad combination," Bayard wrote. "How results the specific gravity? Will the war float the taxes, or the taxes sink the war?" But when the navy brig *Hornet* returned from London late in May, it brought no news of British concessions. Days later, Henry Clay and a group of Congressional

Republicans had two meetings with Madison. And on June 1, Madison asked Congress to declare war.[54]

Madison's war message recounted the nation's grievances against Britain, and it was not a short document. But the litany of wrongs boiled down to three complaints. First, the British navy was impressing American sailors on the high seas and even off the American coast. Second, the British were seizing American ships engaged in neutral trade with Britain's European enemies—using peremptory Orders in Council and paper blockades of the European coast to justify this gross violation of international law. Finally, the British were encouraging the Native American warriors who attacked civilian men, women, and children on the American frontiers. Thus Britain, declared Madison, was already at war against the United States. After years of forbearance and peaceful resistance, it was time for Congress to determine whether the United States should oppose "force to force in defense of their national rights."[55]

A House committee added Britain's incitement of treason and secession in New England to the country's list of grievances, and the House voted for war just two days after it received Madison's message. The Senate initially voted to limit the war to naval attacks on British ships. Gallatin and Monroe, apparently speaking for the administration, supported this approach. Perhaps they thought it would head off opposition from Northern senators who feared British and Native attacks from Canada, or perhaps they saw naval war as another measured step in a gradual escalation to full hostilities. But after two weeks of debate, the Senate adopted the House's unqualified declaration of war on June 17, 1812.[56]

ॐ

What has come to be called the War of 1812 was not popular when it began. The vote for war was relatively close in both houses. Unanimous opposition from the Federalists had been expected, but significant opposition among the Republicans was cause for concern. The vote in the House was 79–49, and sixteen of the forty-nine opponents were Republicans. Fourteen of them had frequently opposed Madison, and most of them wanted New Yorker DeWitt Clinton—nephew of Madison's recently deceased vice president—to replace Madison as the Republican presidential candidate in the autumn election. The vote for war in the Senate was a much closer 19–13, with seven of the twenty-six Republican senators in opposition. The bill passed the Senate only because the administration's most hawkish critics—such as Giles, Leib, and Samuel Smith—had little choice but to vote for it. Whether the administration could count on their continued support in its prosecution of the war remained to be seen. Whether it could find enough Republican support to raise the enormous amount of money needed to pay for the war already seemed doubtful.[57]

"We have not money enough to last" until January, Gallatin told Joseph Nicholson a week after the declaration of war. "General Smith is using every endeavour to run us aground by opposing everything, Treasury notes, double duties &ª. The Senate is so nearly divided, & the division so encreased by…the War question, that we can hardly rely on carrying any thing." The problem was not confined to the Senate. While the Senate was still debating war, the House Ways and Means committee had asked Gallatin whether they could raise enough additional revenue by lifting the ban on British imports rather than imposing internal taxes. Gallatin responded that they could if British imports returned to previous levels. He almost certainly did not believe that imports actually would rebound to previous levels if the two nations were at war. But insisting on internal taxes could—as James Bayard had put it—sink the war. In the end, the House did nothing. It kept the ban on British imports and postponed the debate on internal taxes until after the November election.[58]

The outcome was not what Gallatin wanted, but he facilitated it. If internal taxes could not pass, then much as he regretted it, Gallatin needed to get them off the table before they weakened support for the Republican party and the war. Shortly before the House voted to postpone internal taxes, Gallatin had sent Congress fresh estimates hinting that they could substitute $5 million of short-term Treasury notes for the $5 million of internal taxes he had originally requested. Short-term

Treasury notes were a new idea. Although the British Exchequer regularly issued short-term notes in anticipation of the year's taxes, the American Treasury had never done that. Gallatin hoped that he could repay the notes within a year, either from new taxes or from the proceeds of new short-term notes. He asked Jonathan Roberts—a Pennsylvania Congressman who often spoke for him—to get the tax debate postponed as soon as Congress had authorized the notes. Congress did double the duties on imports, authorize the Administration to borrow $11 million, and approve the $5 million issue of Treasury notes. But it would do no more.[59]

Republican war finance was not supposed to work that way. Gallatin had been saying for years that the people would be willing to pay unpopular internal taxes when war required them. That time had now come. War would soon disrupt trade and jeopardize the import duties on which the government relied for its revenue. The Treasury therefore would need new sources of revenue simply to pay the government's ordinary peacetime expenses and the interest on the public debt. Unless taxes could cover those basic expenses, Gallatin had said, it would be difficult for the Treasury to borrow the large amounts needed for the extraordinary expenses of war. Events were already proving him right. His nationwide advertisement for subscriptions to the $11 million loan brought in only $6.26 million by the end of June, and he got only $1.15 million more when he advertised a second time in August. The state banks to which the government had moved its money after the Bank of the United States began liquidation provided about two-thirds of the amount raised, and the rest came from individuals. The stated interest rate was 6 percent, and Gallatin was quick to point out that the Treasury had never before raised that much new money at such a low rate without the help of the Bank of the United States. But less than 4 percent of the money came from New England—where opposition to the war ran high—and about a third of the amount offered went unsold.[60]

The postponement of internal taxes and the disappointment on the war loan had begun to expose deep-seated problems in Republican fiscal policy. Gallatin had taken three risks in his reform of Hamilton's system, and the war was now bringing all three of them home.[61]

First, Gallatin had narrowed the tax base down to import duties. A narrow tax base was inherently inflexible, and import duties were notoriously vulnerable in wartime. Gallatin had told Congress that import duties could raise almost enough money in peacetime to pay for a war. But in wartime, he warned, they could raise scarcely enough to pay for the peacetime establishment. That was particularly true when the enemy was a major peacetime trading partner and the world's greatest naval power. Broadening the tax base in wartime, it now appeared, was not going to be as easy as Gallatin had believed. Violent resistance to internal taxes in the Revolution and the tax insurrections that followed it had tainted them. Even if Congress worked up the political courage to reimpose internal taxes, it would take time to reconstruct the collection system and even more time to bring in the revenue.[62]

Second, Gallatin had given repayment of the public debt unquestioned priority over military spending even as one of the largest military conflicts in history roiled the Atlantic world. About 60 percent of the federal revenue for the fiscal years 1802 through 1811 went to pay principal and interest on the public debt. Gallatin had said debt repayment would strengthen the country more than military spending, and it suited most Republicans to believe him. They had an aversion to standing armies and expensive navies. They thought the militia could defend the country from invasion for as long as it took to build up a regular army. They thought harbor defenses were more important than warships. Left unchallenged, Gallatin's frugality became a compulsive disorder. From Jefferson's inauguration until the outbreak of the War of 1812, writes one leading historian of the war, Gallatin's fiscal program was "the most important factor shaping Republican military policy." When the war began, the country had only 7,000 men in the army and seventeen ships in the navy. Because the Republican administrations believed they could not afford a viable military establishment, they never seriously considered how long the nation could go on without one.[63]

Third, Gallatin had decided the Treasury could borrow enough money to pay for war when it came. Borrowing was indeed a sounder way to finance a war than simply issuing government notes—a method that had discredited the old Confederation government when the value of its notes depreciated to almost nothing. Britain had shown that well-managed borrowing could support expensive warfare for decades. And Gallatin's success in repaying the Revolutionary War debt gave him confidence that the federal government would be able to repay new war debt when peace returned again. But the post-Revolutionary American government had never borrowed the large amounts of money it would take to pay for a major war, and the experience of European governments showed that war increased the cost of money and made it more difficult to find lenders. Gallatin had not expected to find money in the exhausted credit markets of Europe, but he had believed he could borrow it in the United States. The tepid response to the $11 million loan offering raised serious doubts about his ability to do that.[64]

The Republican response to the failure of the $11 million loan was divided. Congress had already authorized $5 million of Treasury notes in lieu of internal taxes, and Giles, Duane, and some others pushed for even more short-term notes. But other Republicans thought any form of borrowing would ultimately fail unless Congress provided taxes to support it. And John Taylor gave a more fundamental warning about the corrosive effect that borrowing could have on true republican government. "It will hereafter be said," he warned Monroe, that borrowing unsupported by taxes was "a substitution of the will of money lenders for the public will, a confession of the national disapprobation of war, and an evasion of the constitutional provision for declaring it." The Federalist press was snider. The government had pledged "[n]ot a cent of revenue" on the $11 million loan, said the *New-York Evening Post*, for the very good reason that "they have none to pledge." The fragile Republican fiscal system teetered on the balance between the need for taxes and the political price of raising them—and no one could be sure what would happen when war put its bloody fingers on the scale.[65]

Everyone expected the fighting to begin along the Canadian border. The American navy was far too small to launch a significant attack on the British in the West Indies, so the only way the United States could get at Britain was through Canada. The existing war with Native Americans in the Indiana territory also made countering British influence along the northwestern frontier an important defensive objective. And Britain's Canadian colonies appeared quite vulnerable. They had only half a million European inhabitants compared to the 7.5 million in the United States, so although the regular American army and the British garrison in Canada were roughly equal in size at the start of the war, the United States would soon be able to recruit far more soldiers than the British could muster. Upper Canada—the colony above the Great Lakes—seemed especially vulnerable because it was even more sparsely populated than the rest of the country and it lay hundreds of miles west of the main garrisons in Montreal and Quebec. There was reason to think that some Canadians would welcome an American invasion, and there was talk in Congress about the conquest of Canada. But conquest was not the administration's ultimate objective, and the Republican leadership in Congress agreed. Although Henry Clay acknowledged to an ally back home that it might be difficult to give up conquered territory, he insisted that the "object of the War" was "the redress of injuries"; Canada was only "the instrument."[66]

Whatever their intentions, most Americans underestimated the difficulty of invading Canada. Claims that conquest would be "a mere matter of marching" made too little allowance for the deplorable condition of the American army. It was widely scattered, its senior officers were aging veterans of the Revolution, its junior officers were inexperienced, and its administrative and supply systems had disintegrated. The militia was no better. It was a Republican article of faith that the ordinary citizens in the state militias could defend the nation. But Republican majorities in Congress had rejected Jefferson's attempts to improve militia organization, most states had not properly trained or equipped their militia, and some states—particularly in Federalist New

England—insisted that the president could not call out their militia without the governor's consent. Some militiamen also claimed that, having been mustered for national defense, they were not required to participate in an actual invasion of Canada. Jefferson expected the ill-prepared American forces to blunder, but he thought the "weakness of our enemy" in Canada was great enough to "make our first errors innocent." The land campaigns of 1812 proved otherwise.[67]

The American army launched its first campaign against Canada on the northwestern frontier where war with Native Americans had already begun. Two thousand men under the command of William Hull, governor of the Michigan territory, started working their way from Ohio toward Fort Detroit on the Canadian border several months before Congress declared war on Britain. Hull had been an effective regimental leader in the Revolution, but he was suffering from age and incapacity following a stroke. British forces on the river below Detroit heard about the declaration of war before Hull did, and they seized an American ship carrying papers that revealed Hull's plans. Hull managed to push across the Detroit River into Canada despite the refusal of 200 militiamen to join the invasion, and he issued a proclamation about the liberation of Canada that brought some of the inhabitants to his side. But Native attacks on his supply route drove him back to Fort Detroit, where a reinforced British army besieged him. The siege shook Hull emotionally, and the British played on his fears by threatening to unleash their Native allies on the fort's inhabitants when it fell. Rattled and disabled, Hull surrendered the fort without a fight.[68]

A court martial later convicted William Hull of cowardice. His defenders claimed the British had gotten early notice of war through letters that Gallatin had forwarded to fur traders in Canada for his friend John Jacob Astor. Astor was a shrewd, hardworking German immigrant to New York who was making a substantial fortune in the fur trade. His portrait by John Wesley Jarvis shows a square, stocky man with a steady gaze and a determined set to his mouth. Astor sometimes misspelled the same word in two different ways in the same letter, but he was a highly intelligent man who understood business and finance—and their relationship to politics—exceptionally well. He had begun cultivating Gallatin years earlier with useful information, ingratiating visits, and thoughtful presents for which Gallatin, who liked Astor but understood his motives, at first took pains to reimburse him. Gallatin had indeed shown solicitude for Astor's concern that his significant stocks of weapons, gunpowder, and other supplies in Canada could fall into enemy hands, but Gallatin insisted that he had coordinated Astor's communications to Canada through the War department.[69]

While the army struggled, the perennially underfunded American navy gave a remarkably good account of itself. The seventeen ships with which the navy began the war were stronger and faster than British ships of the same class. The Quasi-War and the Tripolitan War had seasoned a new generation of naval officers who were eager to distinguish themselves. Gallatin objected to their preference for gallant single-ship combat and proposed to organize their ships into squadrons to protect American merchant ships returning with taxable imports. The administration adopted this policy, but one of the navy's more aggressive commanders—determined not to let his five ships get bottled up in New York harbor while they waited for orders—had already taken his squadron into the Atlantic to attack British ships. Commodore John Rodgers's fighting instincts proved correct. The threat he posed forced the British admiral on the American coast to keep his own ships together rather than scatter them to blockade American seaports. Six months later, New York's governor found "more cause of exultation than could reasonably have been expected, considering the pacific structure of our national government.... Nearly as great a proportion of homeward bound merchantmen have escaped capture as has been customary during the last three or four years of peace."[70]

Commodore Rodgers had scored a tremendous naval achievement, but it was three American victories in single combat with British naval ships that got most of the public attention on both sides of the Atlantic. In August, the American frigate *Constitution* sank the British frigate *Guerrière* without suffering any damage to its own hull, earning itself the nickname Old Ironsides. Two months later, the *United States* crippled the *Macedonian* and brought it into Newport as a prize ship. And at the very end of the year, the *Constitution* dismasted and sank the *Java* off Brazil as it was making for India with a new British governor aboard. These dramatic successes boosted American morale, and they shocked the British who had lost only five naval battles in twenty-five years of war with France.[71]

But tactical victories at sea did not compensate for the Madison administration's inability to execute its principal strategy on land. All three of the land campaigns against Canada in 1812 failed. Two months after the initial failure at Detroit, an Anglo-Native force of only 2,000 repulsed an American army three times that size as it tried to cross the Niagara River at Queenstown Heights. A repeat attempt by the same American army about six weeks later also failed when part of the militia refused to enter Canada. In December, a third invading American army under Henry Dearborn, a Revolutionary veteran who had been Jefferson's War secretary, abandoned its march on Montreal after relatively minor fighting. Militia elements had once again refused to cross the border. "The series of misfortunes experienced this year in our military land operations," Gallatin lamented to Jefferson in December, "exceeds all anticipations made even by those who had least confidence in our inexperienced officers and undisciplined men."[72]

The nation did not rally around its wartime president. Madison could not project the resolute personal authority expected of a war leader, and the weakness in his administration's leadership of the war was obvious. War secretary William Eustis was a Boston doctor without fighting experience, and Navy secretary Paul Hamilton was a South Carolinian planter gripped by alcoholism. Neither could deal with the challenges he now confronted, and it fell to Monroe and Gallatin to come up with many of the necessary plans, including plans to create a new general staff for the army.[73]

Gallatin's tendency to overcompensate when he thought others were deficient only highlighted the administration's weaknesses. "You can not have an idea of the weakness and villainy of our Cabinet," wrote

John Adams's old Navy secretary from his perspective as a merchant in Georgetown. "Gallatin who is a French man is everything, rules the Cabinet entirely. This cunning dangerous man has the address to make the Fed[s] believe he is opposed always to every obnoxious measure, altho he dictates them all." The architect and engineer Benjamin Henry Latrobe, who had a particularly keen ear for the buzz around Washington, gave his son a more piquant description. "Mr. Madison, whom your mother, in her way, compared to a little shrivelled spider, in the midst of a large flabby cobweb shaking in the wind, will be nobody at all. Mr. Gallatin has in fact been president for some time." The opinion of the Republican leaders in Congress was not much different. "I have intended...twenty times to write you," Henry Clay told Madison's former attorney general, but "I have not had the courage to pourtray my feelings to you....It is in vain to conceal the fact" that "Mr. Madison is wholly unfit for the storms of War. Nature has cast him in too benevolent a mould."[74]

Madison managed to win the 1812 presidential election, but the vote revealed a significant loss of support for his administration and the Republican party. The dissident Republican candidate DeWitt Clinton, who had discredited himself with many mainstream Republicans by seeking support from the Federalists, took every state northeast of Pennsylvania except Vermont. Madison won the election by only 39 out of 217 electoral votes, the narrowest margin of presidential victory since the Republicans had taken power. Republicans kept control of Congress, but they lost strength in both houses.[75]

It was clear by the end of 1812 that "Mr. Madison's War"—as critics had begun to call it—was going to cost considerably more than Gallatin had expected. Inexperience and incompetence in the War and Navy departments were only part of the problem. Gallatin's own misestimations accounted for the rest. Gallatin had claimed that a year of war would cost about $10 million, but early experience pointed to a figure closer to $20 million. Gallatin had estimated that import duties and land sales could bring in $11.5 million during the first full year of war, but he now projected they would fall to $5 million during the second. Yet instead of taking up the internal tax measures postponed from its last session, Congress spent its time throwing away a revenue windfall worth at least $10 million.[76]

That revenue windfall came from a flood of illegal imports. The prewar reports that the British ministry was about to withdraw its restrictions on American trade had been accurate. When the ministry withdrew them—just days after the United States declared war—American merchants operating in Europe assumed that their government would respond by lifting its ban on British imports. To get the jump on the pent-up American demand for British goods, they quickly shipped large cargoes to the United States. By the time they heard that the United States had declared war, they had shipped goods costing at least $18 million. Unfortunately for these enterprising merchants, the non-intercourse law, which was still in force when their cargoes reached the United States, required the Treasury to impose duties, penalties, and forfeiture of the goods.[77]

Gallatin thought those consequences were draconian under the circumstances, but the law gave him little discretion, and the merchants would earn large windfall profits if he did not enforce the law. He proposed a Solomonic solution: the Treasury would let the merchants keep the goods, but require them to pay full duties and to lend the government an amount equal to the cost of the goods. Federalists from maritime New England were indignant, malcontent Republicans saw another chance to land a blow on Gallatin, and some of the Republican war hawks—who feared the forced loans would make the war more unpopular—joined in the outcry against Gallatin's proposal. Instead of presenting a regular system of taxation to meet the needs of the war, Giles complained, Gallatin had "substituted a miserable impracticable attempt to plunder the merchants." After months of debate, Congress passed a law directing the Treasury to remit penalties and forfeitures on all goods belonging to American merchants who could show that they had purchased the goods before they got news of the war. The House then launched an investigation into Gallatin's use of this new discretion. The whole controversy absorbed an enormous amount of energy that was urgently needed elsewhere.[78]

⟨⟨⟩⟩

By the beginning of 1813, the Treasury was running out of money again. Although Gallatin and Monroe had set limits on military spending, it easily outpaced government receipts. There was still no Congressional majority to raise taxes because the Republicans feared new taxes would make them unpopular. Instead, Congress passed a bill authorizing the Treasury to borrow another $16 million. The loan bill left the Treasury free to offer whatever terms were needed, but raising that much money without support from new taxes was going to be difficult. The war was not going well, the New England lenders were still refusing to finance it, and the banks elsewhere had already lent the government about as much as they could.[79]

Gallatin tried to raise the $16 million by selling 6 percent bonds to a private syndicate in New York led by John Jacob Astor and David Parish, a wealthy German merchant with business in New York and Philadelphia. Astor wanted naval protection for a fur trading settlement called Astoria which he had established at the mouth of the Columbia River in the Oregon territory, and the connection between his concern about the settlement and his interest in the bonds was unmistakable. When the pair decided to pass on the loan, Astor blamed the decision on Parish. Although "he Should Leik to be engagd," Astor told Gallatin, "yet he must Decline b[e]cause he See[s] no provability of a Speedy arrangement for Peace and he is of opinion that not more than 2 or 3 Millions could be raisd in Philadelphia and that at not Less than 7 pct." Without a national bank, said Astor, "it apears to me that…the government must be for ever exposd to inconveneys as to money Matters—." When the public took up only $3.9 million of $16 million in bonds that Gallatin offered at the end of February, it was hard to disagree. "To BORROW— not to TAX—the GOVERNMENT was prone," quipped a Federalist newspaper; "The People, not Subscribing, left it quite ALONE." In early March, Gallatin had to tell Madison that "[w]e have hardly money enough to last till the end of the month."[80]

It was Alexander Dallas who helped Gallatin to syndicate the unsold portion of the bonds. Dallas encouraged David Parish to talk to a wealthy client of Dallas named Stephen Girard, a self-made French immigrant who had grown so rich as a merchant in Philadelphia that he could buy the entire assets of the Bank of the United States when Congress refused to re-charter it. Girard was aggressive and graceless, and members of the Philadelphia establishment held him at arm's length. They thought he was "as sordid and selfish as a cold heart, unsocial habits, a perverse temper, and five millions, can make him." The state legislature had refused to give him a banking charter, so Girard had relied on a legal opinion from Dallas to set up an unincorporated Bank of Stephen Girard. Girard had several reasons to help the Treasury syndicate the remainder of the loan. He thought his bank's participation in the syndicate could raise its commercial standing. He also thought participation would help him settle the Treasury's claim that he owed over $900,000 in penalties for smuggling British goods into the United States. And Girard could scent the distinct probability of a very good return on his money.[81]

After a second attempt to sell the 6 percent bonds to the public came up short at the end of March, Gallatin went to Philadelphia for a meeting with Girard, Parish, and Astor. Girard and Parish offered to buy $8 million of the bonds for themselves and a syndicate in Philadelphia at 88 cents on the dollar. Astor and his group in New York offered to take another $2 million at the same price. Gallatin took both offers and paid the syndicate members a .25 percent commission. Almost twenty years later, a Congressional report on the need for a Bank of the United States would claim that the Treasury actually got far less than 88 cents on the dollar for the bonds because the purchasers paid for them with heavily depreciated state bank notes. It said the actual specie value that the government had received was only 42 cents on the dollar. Gallatin thought that report exaggerated the loss, but he offered no alternative calculation. He had been desperate for the money, and there was little he could have done about the price. He was right when he reported to Congress two months after the syndication that the terms would have been better if "taxes had been previously laid."[82]

While Gallatin was struggling to place $16 million in bonds, Madison and Monroe grasped at an opportunity to end the costly war. They did not believe that the belated British withdrawal of restrictions on American trade was an adequate basis for peace because the British still insisted that they had the right to impress sailors, declare paper blockades, and reimpose restrictions on neutral trade if circumstances changed. But in March 1813, Madison and Monroe saw a chance to settle those issues. Andrei Dashkov, the dashing young Russian minister to the United States, delivered an offer from the Russian emperor to mediate the differences between Britain and the United States at his capital in St. Petersburg.[83]

Emperor Alexander wanted to put an end to the Anglo-American war because it was disrupting Russian trade with the United States. Russia was a commodity-producing nation almost entirely dependent on foreign trade for the goods that its ruling class consumed. The Russian government had twice organized leagues of armed neutrality to protect maritime rights, and as the European wars wore on, it increasingly depended on neutral American ships to carry on its trade. Although military defeat had forced Alexander to accept terms from Napoleon at Tilsit (Sovetsk) in 1807, Russia had always chafed under Napoleon's restrictions on trade. Alexander's widening departures from those restrictions contributed to Napoleon's decision to invade Russia in the summer of 1812. That invasion destroyed Napoleon's principal army, brought Russia into alliance with Britain against France, and pushed Alexander into a costly new land campaign against Napoleon in Germany. But because the British navy kept enemy American ships away, Russia's trade had not revived. Alexander believed that an Anglo-American mediation would allow him to confirm the maritime rights of neutrals and to repair Russian commerce.[84]

Russia's longstanding position on neutral rights made Alexander's offer attractive to the Madison administration. Madison and Monroe accepted it within ten days—without waiting for Britain's reaction—and began to pick candidates for a bipartisan delegation to St. Petersburg. James Bayard's charm and moderation made him a comfortable choice from among the Federalists opposed to the war. Henry Clay was a promising possibility from among the pro-war Republicans. It would not have occurred to Madison and Monroe to send the Treasury secretary, but he volunteered to go. [85]

Gallatin had both patriotic and personal reasons to volunteer for the St. Petersburg mission. The war was going badly, dividing the nation, and costing far more than he had expected. It seemed poised to bring down the Republican administration and entail another staggering war debt on the federal government. The nation's future could be quite different from the one that he, Jefferson, and Madison had envisioned when they took office, and his twelve arduous years at the Treasury would have been for nothing. But it was Gallatin's unhappiness during the last four of those years that gave him the sharpest motive to volunteer. He had remained at the Treasury when Madison took office despite his misgivings. But the incompetence of Eustis and Hamilton at the War and Navy departments had complicated his job, and the partisan opposition to him and Madison had exhausted and embittered him.[86]

The recent appointment of New Yorker John Armstrong to replace Eustis at the War department had made Gallatin's situation even worse. Armstrong was a capable but difficult man whose reputation for "indolence and intrigue" had previously kept him from getting an executive appointment. He also had connections with the administration's critics, and although Gallatin had preferred Armstrong to other, even less satisfactory candidates for the job, he acknowledged that Armstrong might lack "that disinterested zeal...so useful in producing hearty co-operation and unity of action." Many had predicted that Armstrong would "soon set the Cabinet by the ears," and he lost no time in doing just that. In an effort to curry favor with William Duane, whose *Aurora* clearly could be useful to him, Armstrong appointed Duane adjutant general for Pennsylvania. For Gallatin, it was the last straw. The appointment of this man who had maligned him for years was "so obnoxious" to him, he told his brothers-in-law, that he "felt no wish to remain associated with an administration which would employ such a miscreant."[87]

Madison and Monroe were reluctant to lose Gallatin from the Treasury, but Gallatin persuaded them to let him go. He got Dashkov to support his appointment, and he suggested that he might be able to complete the mission and return to the Treasury by the end of the year. Gallatin also got support from Astor and other government lenders who had confidence in him and believed that his appointment would increase the value of their government bonds. So in April 1813, Madison commissioned Gallatin as the senior member of a delegation to the Russian mediation that also included James Bayard and John Quincy Adams. Adams had been in St. Petersburg for four years as the American minister to Russia, a post that Madison had given him after he lost his Senate seat for supporting Jefferson's embargo. Gallatin and Bayard were to leave for Russia immediately. Madison appointed William Jones, a Philadelphia merchant recently confirmed as the new Navy secretary, to be the acting Treasury secretary in Gallatin's absence. Astor sent Gallatin eight silver fox furs— the "finest furrs" available anywhere—to protect him from the Russian cold. "[O]f your Sucess I have Little Doubt," wrote Astor, "as I feel Satisfied that you will do all that can and ought to be done and that nothing will be left to Chance."[88]

Gallatin's last two weeks at the Treasury were a whirl of activity. The war Congress had called the new Congress elected in 1812 to a special session in May so that it could address the country's deteriorating fiscal situation. That made Gallatin's immediate departure awkward, but he was determined to go and equally determined to put all of the necessary arrangements in place before he left. He prepared the annual Treasury report for William Jones's signature. He drafted the tax bills that he wanted to be enacted. And he gave the new secretaries of War and the Navy strict instructions not to spend more than $1.5 million and $0.5 million per month for the remainder of the year. On April 20, he turned over the Treasury department to Jones.[89]

"Few men are so thoroughly men of business as Mr Gallatin," Treasury comptroller Richard Rush told his father's old friend John Adams.

He drew up the necessary tax bills, gave his well-trained clerks "very precise and full instructions," and "left nothing in arrears when he went away....Should he get back" by Christmas, wrote Rush, "all may be well." Adams's reply was knowing. "To be one of the most indefatigable of Men, both in buissness and Studies, has been an acknowledged Character of Mr Gallatin for the twenty odd years that I have known his name," he wrote, but "I cannot expect his return by Christmas." Diplomatic ceremonies, feasts, and parties consume time, and peace negotiations always "meet with unforeseen Embarrassments." Then came a flash of the bitterness that Adams had nursed since his defeat a dozen years earlier. "I must own," he confessed, "a little Sarcastical delight" over Gallatin's revival of the internal taxes that were repealed "in a great measure by [his own] influence."[90]

Jesse Bledsoe, a new Republican senator from Kentucky, was more critical of Gallatin's departure. At "the very moment" when Gallatin's financial skill was needed most, he told his governor, did "this man abandon his post & solicit a foreign Mission," leaving his duties to be performed by clerks "under the mere Signature...(for it is nothing else) of Mr Jones." To top it off, Gallatin had "left a Padlock upon the Treasy & secured it by the terms of his Loan—No More than one Million a Month to be Expended by the Secy of War—." That constricted spending would cripple military operations in Canada. The better-informed Henry Latrobe slipped William Duane more accurate information and a pithier assessment of the situation. "It is asserted," he told Duane, that Gallatin "has left positive orders" that the army cannot spend more than $1.5 million per month—"so that though absent his ghost still governs us."[91]

CHAPTER 9

REDEMPTION

A lbert Gallatin and James Bayard needed British passports to put to sea. The British navy had begun blockading the American coast early in 1813, and by the time they left for St. Petersburg in May, British ships blocked the main ports south of New England. Two days out of New Castle, Delaware, their ship *Neptune* found the British frigate *Spartan* anchored in the mouth of the Delaware Bay. The *Spartan* sent out a boarding party and required the *Neptune*'s captain Lloyd Jones (brother of the Navy secretary in whose care Gallatin had left the Treasury) to row over with his papers. Jones delivered passports that James Monroe had gotten from the British admiral in charge through the good offices of Russian minister Andrei Dashkov. The *Spartan*'s captain accepted them, exchanged courtesies with Jones, and allowed him to sail on the evening ebb tide.[1]

The six-week Atlantic crossing was cold for the season. Temperatures hung in the fifties, and three sustained gales left the passengers seasick most of the time. Gallatin gave up the journal he had started while the ship was in the Delaware Bay, and he kept to himself. Bayard, who weathered the gales better, was disappointed. Although he and Gallatin had known each other since Bayard entered Congress in 1797, differences in their politics and temperaments had kept them from becoming more than acquaintances. Bayard was a portly, convivial man of impeccable appearance and unfailing courtesy whom Republicans had taken to calling "the Chevalier." He found good company, a pack of cards, and plenty of wine to be some compensation for long absences from his family and his law practice back home in Delaware. He was popular in Washington, although a more abstemious Federalist senator thought that he lived "too fast to live long." Bayard had made friendly overtures to Gallatin over the years, and he had hoped they might become friends during the voyage. Gallatin's seasickness and circumspection prevented that. Gallatin "has scarcely ever recovered his spirits and gaiety after one gale, before he was deprived of them by another," Bayard recorded three weeks out. "This is the more unfortunate as he stands in need of the whole stock with which nature has supplied to render him tolerable company."[2]

Not until the *Neptune* anchored off Gothenburg on the west coast of Sweden in late June did Gallatin revive. He and the other passengers scrambled over small coastal islands where flower-strewn patches of grass peppered the bare rocks, and they hired a boat to take them down a ten-mile channel to the austere town of brick buildings plastered in white. There were nine of them besides Gallatin and Bayard—four young secretaries, four black servants, and a Russian named Pflug whom Dashkov had sent along. The secretaries were Gallatin's sixteen-year-old son James, Alexander Dallas's twenty-one-year-old son George, Bayard's friend George Milligan, and Dolley Madison's only surviving child from her first marriage, John Payne Todd. The servants were Peter Brown and Henry Smith (or Smothers), who had worked for the Gallatins in Washington, George Shorter, who worked for Bayard, and a man named Peter who came with Pflug. All of the servants probably were enslaved. In Gothenburg, Gallatin swelled with emotion on meeting merchants from Philadelphia and Georgetown. It was good to see anyone after so long a voyage, he wrote, "but to meet Americans at such distance from home is a feeling to be understood only by those who have experienced it. I could have pressed every one to my bosom as a brother." The tired travellers shared a simple afternoon dinner with "three bottles of good wine" and went to bed without supper. While the others sauntered out after breakfast, Gallatin took up a pen and started to work.[3]

Gallatin's first letter was to Baring Brothers, the federal government's bankers in London. It was a simple message asking them to publish notice of the *Neptune*'s arrival and to provide credit in St. Petersburg, but Gallatin also ventured to ask for "any intelligence connected with our mission which you may deem important, and which you may feel at liberty to communicate." Alexander Baring, the partner in charge of American business, got the point. Baring had known Gallatin since they worked together on the Louisiana purchase, and he could see that Gallatin wanted a back channel to the British government. By the time he responded a month later—just as the *Neptune* reached St. Petersburg—Baring had opened one.[4]

It was clear to "the eyes of a European politician," Baring wrote to Gallatin, that Russian "interference" would offer "no practical benefit." Now that Britain had removed its restrictions on American trade, he said, the issue dividing the two countries was impressment. That was a purely domestic question about a sovereign's claim on his subjects that had arisen between nations only because Britain and the United States were so recently separated. Their differences on the question were therefore "a sort of family quarrel," and "in the present state of Europe," mediation by a foreign government would only complicate things. "These, I have reason to know, are pretty nearly the sentiments of government here," Baring reported, "and before this reaches you, you will have been informed" that it has declined mediation in favor of direct negotiations in London or Gothenburg. Gallatin replied that the United States would be willing to enter into direct negotiations, but he, Bayard, and John Quincy Adams had only been given the power to attend mediation.[5]

In St. Petersburg, everything was complicated. Napoleon's army had not attacked the Russian capital, but the French invasion had reconfigured the political scene there. Alexander's pro-French chancellor Nikolai Rumyantsev had suffered a stroke when Napoleon invaded, and although he had recovered his health, he had lost his credibility. Rumyantsev had supported Russia's treaty with France in 1807, and he had clung to the French alignment despite the damage that Napoleon's trade restrictions inflicted on the Russian economy. Even after the French invaded, Rumyantsev urged Alexander to make a new peace. Rumyantsev hoped the Anglo-American mediation could redeem him by reviving foreign trade. But the emperor had turned his ear to Karl Nesselrode—the foreign secretary who was with Alexander and his army in Germany—and Rumyantsev's standing sank so low that the British minister openly insulted him by coming to his dinner parties shamefully late.[6]

Weeks before Gallatin and Bayard arrived, Rumyantsev privately confessed to John Quincy Adams that the British had rejected his mediation offer. But Rumyantsev insisted on renewing the offer, and there things stalled for the next three months. The American administration had given its envoys no power to enter into direct negotiations with the British, the envoys could not take their leave from St. Petersburg without official notice that Britain had declined mediation, and Rumyantsev lacked the influence to get a straight answer. In late September, Gallatin and Bayard awoke to a dusting of snow on the roofs of the city and the fear of being trapped in Russia for the winter.[7]

A month later came more bad news. Letters and newspapers arriving through London reported that the Senate had rejected Gallatin's nomination to the peace commission. It took a day for the others to work up the courage to tell Gallatin, but he took the news calmly. There had been grumbling before he left Washington that the peace mission was incompatible with his responsibilities at the Treasury. The president did not have authority to appoint an acting Treasury secretary for longer than six months, and Gallatin would not return within that time, even on the airy assumption that he might get home by Christmas. The opportunity for Gallatin's enemies to push him out of the Treasury was obvious. "I am well aware," Gallatin had told his brother-in-law shortly before he left, that "my going to Russia" probably will lead to the appointment of another Treasury secretary and "my returning to private life." He told his friend Senator Worthington that he was fully prepared for "that sacrifice...& will be amply rewarded if I can only be instrumental in extricating our Country from war & disunion, by a peace on honorable terms." As delays in St. Petersburg made his ouster from the Treasury more likely, he had grown fatalistic. He begged Hannah Gallatin not to worry about the inevitable intrigues against him. They were the work, he said, of "little men, who can effect nothing, but what must inevitably take place, by the natural course of events, and without any interference on their part."[8]

The Senate would have confirmed Gallatin's nomination if Madison had appointed another Treasury secretary. But Madison wanted Gallatin to stay at the Treasury, and Gallatin had never told him that he was willing to leave if confirmation to the peace commission depended on it. "The Senate have been sitting for three weeks with closed doors," a young military aide named Thomas Hart Benton had reported to Andrew Jackson in June. "The scuffle is to get Gallatin out of the treasury, and to do that, a strong party...perhaps the majority, require his resignation of Secretaryship before they confirm his nomination of ambassador." A Senate committee went to see Madison on the subject, but he claimed that it was his prerogative to staff executive offices, and he refused to discuss the matter. The Senate then resolved by a vote of 20–14 that the duties of Treasury secretary and peace envoy were incompatible. But despite the clarity of that warning, Madison refused to budge. He was seriously ill at the time, and having taken the position that a cabinet secretary could take a diplomatic assignment, he instinctively defaulted to stubborn consistency.[9]

Forced to a showdown, the Senate rejected Gallatin's nomination on a vote of 17–18 with Gallatin's old enemies Samuel Smith, William Branch Giles, and Michael Leib in the majority. Jesse Bledsoe from Kentucky voted for confirmation despite his strong objection to the dual appointments. But he said he would have done otherwise if Gallatin had not already sailed, and so, he claimed, "Said Nearly Every Republican Senator Who voted with me." The administration's supporters in the

Senate, Madison lamely explained to Gallatin, had miscounted the votes. But Madison's long and labored letter to Gallatin revealed a deeper truth. In an effort to assert his authority and discipline the Republican malcontents, the president had overplayed his hand. Perhaps what Madison had done was right, John Jacob Astor wrote to Gallatin, "but I think I would have Done otherwise....I wonder that you Did not Intrust your Ideas [about leaving the Treasury] to some of your friends. no one but Mᴿ Worthington seemed to know anything about it." Hannah Gallatin's reaction was more vigorous. The triumph of her husband's enemies in his absence was "a trifle," she told Dolley Madison, "for he has a self approving conscience and his peace is within his own breast while theirs are torn with every black and malevolent passion."[10]

Rumyantsev asked Gallatin to remain in St. Petersburg until he got official instructions from Washington, but news of the Senate's rejection of his nomination focused Gallatin and Bayard on the hopelessness of their situation. They had spent four months waiting for the British to change their minds about mediation. They had attended an endless round of dinners, parties, solemn masses, court functions, and balls that lasted through the night. And they had nothing to show for it. Rumyantsev had no further answer from the British government. All of the news about the war came through London, and it took an extra month for it to reach St. Petersburg. Bayard's health was deteriorating. It was time, they concluded, to leave. They ordered the *Neptune* to sail from the Baltic Sea before it froze shut. They wrote to James Monroe that they would go overland to meet the ship as soon as the snow was deep enough for them to travel on it. And they waited another six weeks. Finally, in January 1814, they took leave of the imperial court and set off through the snow in three carriages mounted on runners—Gallatin and his son James in one, Bayard in another, and Peter Brown with the rest of the servants in the rear. The other secretaries had gone ahead.[11]

Gallatin and Bayard had decided to go to London where they could get fresh news and investigate possibilities for peace before Gallatin continued home. It was a prodigious journey—fifteen hundred miles down the Baltic coast and across war-torn Germany to Amsterdam where they hoped to meet the *Neptune* for passage to England. The winter was bitterly cold. It snowed nearly every day for the first four weeks, and the sky remained gray after that. The carriages pitched and swerved along drifted post roads through barren, sparsely populated country where the travellers saw little but a white expanse of snow. It took six horses to keep a carriage moving, eight where the snow was deep. Every six to twelve miles the carriages stopped at a relay station to pick up fresh horses, and while they waited the passengers choked down coarse meals in low rooms smelling of smoke, sweat, and horse manure. They passed a few nights in cold, dirty hostels, but they spent most nights on the road in their frigid carriages. They entered some cities to rest and see the sights. They had to detour around other cities because French troops had occupied them. Thirty-eight days after leaving St. Petersburg, the travellers pulled into Amsterdam without—Bayard reported to Adams—any "material" accident. Bayard claimed that he was feeling better, but violent pains in his chest during the journey had given him a chilling premonition.[12]

The travelers reached London in early April, along with the news that allied armies led by Emperor Alexander had taken Paris and forced Napoleon into exile on the Mediterranean island of Elba. The news cast a shadow over prospects for peace in North America. Gallatin and Bayard had heard that the British and American governments were planning to hold bilateral peace negotiations in Gothenburg. The American administration had ordered Bayard and Adams there, and it was sending Henry Clay and Jonathan Russell, the new American minister to Sweden, to join them. But Napoleon's downfall released a wave of anti-American feeling in Britain. The British people had long seen the American declaration of war as a stab in the back—a craven blow struck at a free nation locked in a life or death struggle with French tyranny—and they now demanded retaliation. Pamphlets damp from the London presses called for territorial and other concessions that sounded extravagant to the Americans. The British government dispatched 12,000 battle-hardened troops from southern France to give the Americans "a good drubbing." "In the intoxication of an unexpected success, which they ascribe to themselves," Gallatin dryly observed, "the English people eagerly wish that their pride may be fully gratified by what they call the 'punishment of America.'" He blamed this anti-Americanism on the Federalists, whose wild speeches nurtured the British impression that American Republicans were Francophiles.[13]

Gallatin soon learned from the newspapers that he was to be more than an observer. In February, Madison had added him to the peace commission. A large group of senators had threatened to declare the Treasury vacant unless Madison appointed someone to take Gallatin's place, and Madison had finally capitulated. He appointed George Washington Campbell of Tennessee to be Treasury secretary, and the Senate—its malcontents pleased to have pushed Gallatin out of the administration—confirmed Gallatin's new appointment to the peace commission.[14]

Happy to be useful again, Gallatin set to work without waiting for official notice. He urged the other American commissioners to move the peace negotiations from Gothenburg to London or a neutral city in Holland closer to the flow of international news. When the British government proposed the Flemish city of Ghent (now in Belgium), he and Bayard promptly agreed even though British and Prussian troops still occupied it. Gallatin sent letters to William H. Crawford, now the American minister to France, and the Marquis de Lafayette asking whether they could help persuade Emperor Alexander to push the British toward peace with the United States. The European peace, Gallatin told America's old friend Lafayette, had created a crisis for the American republic. While "the great part of the civilized world rejoices at the restoration of a general peace," he wrote, "the United States...are placed in a more critical situation than ever they were since the first years of their Revolution." Lafayette arranged for Gallatin to meet Alexander when the emperor came to London in June, and Gallatin sent Alexander a memorandum linking American grievances to broader concerns about the maritime rights of all neutral nations. Alexander listened, but he did little more. Napoleon's defeat had altered his diplomatic calculations. He was the victor of the day. He meant to rebalance power in Europe. A distant war that kept Britain slightly distracted strengthened his hand. The British and the Americans, he told an American consul whom he knew better than Gallatin, would just "have to fight it out."[15]

Fighting it out was not a good prospect for the Americans. Although American forces were more successful in 1813 than they had been during 1812, they had not weakened Britain's grip on its Canadian colonies. British ships were keeping most of the American navy bottled up in port. The cost of the war was spiraling beyond the Treasury's resources. Although Congress had passed most of the internal tax bills that Gallatin had left for them when he departed, Treasury secretary Campbell already needed an additional $29 million to pay for the war. There was no reason to doubt British threats of sharp retaliation during the summer of 1814, and there was every reason to wonder how American forces could withstand it. From London, Gallatin warned Monroe that the British would try to vindicate their pride by capturing Washington and attacking Baltimore. Their aims, he thought, might be to divide the Union, to bring the Federalists back to power, or at least to force the United States to give up territory, fishing rights, and trading rights. At home, Nathaniel Macon saw little but gloom. "Without a change in the management of the war," he predicted, "the republican party must go down." The people "will be disgusted with an administration, who have declared war, without ability to conduct it, to a favorable issue; disgrace & taxes will not suit any nation."[16]

The British government thought time was on their side. By the end of June, a British army had occupied eastern Maine, established a military government there, and exacted loyalty oaths from the population. British ships raided with impunity throughout the Chesapeake Bay. African Americans enslaved on farms around the bay began slipping away to freedom on British ships. The British admiral refused to give Monroe passports for messengers to the American peace commission, forcing the American Secretary of State to send his coded diplomatic messages through the British naval pouches. The British ministry in London kept the American commissioners in Ghent waiting over a month for the arrival of the British negotiators.[17]

☙

Ghent was a manufacturing and trading city at the confluence of the rivers Scheldt and Leie—ancient, prosperous, and dull. And the negotiations at Ghent were a backwater in the swirling diplomacy that engulfed Europe's political leaders after Napoleon's fall. Napoleon had toppled regimes and redrawn borders all over Europe that now had to be restored or recreated. Britain's future peace and prosperity hung in the balance, so Lord Liverpool's Tory ministry segregated the Anglo-American talks in Ghent and focused its energy on the critical European negotiations in Paris, London, and Vienna. Victory over France had confirmed the importance of Britain's naval supremacy. The British could deal with the Americans in due course; in the meantime, they needed to keep maritime issues out of the European discussions. Liverpool and his foreign minister, Lord Castlereagh, left day-to-day responsibility for the American talks with Lord Bathurst, the minister for War and the Colonies, who was no friend of the upstart Americans. He thought the best way to prevent them from threatening British interests was to keep the United States in its place outside the prevailing international order. For all three of them, the peace that Madison's administration so urgently needed was a secondary objective.[18]

The contrast between the teams that the United States and Britain sent to Ghent reflected their governments' different approaches to the negotiations. Four of the five Americans were accomplished men active in public life. Gallatin had been a central figure in every administration since the Republicans took power. Bayard was a respected member of the opposition and one of the longest-serving members of Congress. John Quincy Adams—who had been a senator from Massachusetts and a minister to the Netherlands, Prussia, and Russia—was the country's most experienced diplomat. Henry Clay was the Speaker of the House and a recognized spokesman for a new generation of legislators. Only Jonathan Russell, a Rhode Island merchant who had scrambled into diplomacy a few years earlier, was cut from different cloth; he had been appointed to the commission when the negotiations were slated for Sweden, where he was to be the new American minister. The Madison administration had confidence in these men, and it listened to their advice about how to handle the negotiations.[19]

The three British negotiators were able men, but they were public servants and their government kept them on a short leash. Lord Gambier, the head of the British delegation, was an admiral who had gone to sea at eleven, risen through the ranks, and earned a peerage for bombarding the neutral city of Copenhagen when the Danes refused to surrender their fleet (which the British feared Napoleon would capture). William Adams was a respected admiralty lawyer who had been sent to dispose of the Americans' pretensions to maritime rights. Henry Goulburn, barely thirty, was an undersecretary in Bathurst's Colonial Office. Goulburn was a man of considerable talent who would later become Home Secretary and twice serve as Chancellor of the Exchequer. But Goulburn at Ghent—even in his flashes of contemptuous anti-Americanism—was no more than Bathurst's loyal deputy. The British commissioners sent all of the messages they exchanged with the Americans back to London for instructions. "The extent of their authority," griped Adams after six weeks, "is to perform the service of a Post-Office between us and the British privy-Council."[20]

When the British and American negotiators met in mid-August 1814, the British demands left the Americans gasping. The British declared that the vast territory between the Ohio River and the Great Lakes still held by Native Americans should become a buffer zone closed to white settlement. They wanted to retain the territory British troops had occupied in eastern Maine as a corridor between the important British forts at Quebec and Halifax. They also proposed to keep several forts their troops had captured on the Great Lakes, and they wanted to revise the boundary between the United States and Upper Canada to protect British navigation on the Lakes and ensure British access to the Mississippi River. They claimed war had annulled the American fishing rights off Canada that had been recognized in the peace treaty at the end of the Revolutionary War. And they begrudgingly mentioned impressment, only because they knew the Americans would bring it up.[21]

The British demands showed that the two nations understood the war in deeply different ways. The British believed that impressment and blockade had been essential to their victory in the twenty-year struggle against France. They were affronted when the United States continued the war to contest those practices even after Britain had revoked its restrictions on American trade. And the American war strategy had raised new concerns. Attacks on Canada had incited disloyalty among the civilian population, endangered the valuable fur trade, and threatened to cut off Canadian supplies of food and naval stores, which had become more vital after the United States shut off American supplies. It seemed clear to the British that Americans favored France, coveted Britain's Atlantic commerce, and wanted to conquer Canada.[22]

Considered in that light, the British demands were not as extravagant as the Americans believed. They were security measures to keep the United States out of the Canadian provinces and to improve Britain's hold on them. A British presence in eastern Maine would make the Canadian border more defensible and stop the rampant smuggling in Passamaquoddy Bay. The buffer zone would protect Native tribes on which the British depended to help defend Canada's long interior frontier. The British could even argue that their demands required no territorial concessions from the United States. The treaty ending the Revolutionary War had promised the British access to the Mississippi, and Jay's treaty had recognized that the northwestern boundary might have to be adjusted to provide it. The occupied part of Maine had been disputed territory for decades, and the Native buffer zone was a region that the United States itself had conceded to the sovereign tribes in the 1795 Treaty of Greenville. If the British tone was a bit peremptory, as the American negotiators complained, it was little different from the tone Britain was taking with European governments that the British thought they had saved from Napoleon.[23]

But Americans' long preoccupation with their own grievances had prevented them from anticipating the British demands. Americans had endured twenty years of British interference with neutral trade and repeated bursts of British impressment. British mercantile policies had cut off valuable American trade with the West Indies after the Revolution and challenged American notions about their natural right to trade freely. Those injuries seemed more than enough to justify Americans' attempt to coerce Britain by attacking its Canadian colonies. Even Monroe, who had more sympathy with Britain's perspective than other members of the administration, had not foreseen that American attacks on Canada would proliferate disputes between the two countries. His initial instructions to the peace commissioners said a great deal about impressment and trade, but they mentioned Canada only to argue—in paragraphs later redacted from the version Monroe published—that a complete cession of the Canadian provinces to the United States would be the best way to eliminate friction along the border. Monroe did not mention alternative solutions. Even the opening British position failed to enlighten Monroe, Madison, and the American commissioners, who thought the British were making sweeping demands in order to drag out the negotiations until they had gained military advantage in North America. They were not entirely wrong about that; the British did mean to stall until they were in a stronger position. But the Americans were wrong to treat the British demands as new grievances rather than pragmatic responses to America's conduct of the war.[24]

The American and British commissioners did not have another formal meeting for three and a half months. The Americans rented a house in the center of Ghent known by the misleadingly grand name Hotel d'Alcantara, and their secretaries took rooms in the nearby public Hotel des Pays-Bas. The British commissioners and their entourage moved into part of a converted Carthusian monastery a bit to the north, on the other side of the River Leie. The secretaries carried long, tensely argued notes between the two delegations. Since both sides thought agreement unlikely, the notes tended to be exercises in national self-justification—the sort of things each government could publish to lay blame on the other when the talks collapsed. The two delegations occasionally met for dinner. Although the dinner conversations were rather stiff, they did provide opportunities to nudge things along. The Americans rarely saw the British commissioners at the parties, dinners, concerts, and lectures the Americans attended in the city because—with British troops in residence—the townspeople did not welcome the British commissioners as readily as they did the Americans. When the Americans invited the British commissioners to a large party at the American residence, the British arranged to be out of town on the appointed day so that they could politely decline. Months later, Gambier would confess to Adams that he and the other British commissioners knew scarcely anyone in Ghent.[25]

The Senate's initial rejection of Gallatin's nomination had left the slightly younger Adams as head of the American commission, but he struggled in that role. Adams had enormous intellectual gifts, and he had turned the self-criticism born of his parents' high expectations into absolutely remarkable self-awareness. But he was not a natural leader. He was—as he confessed to himself—dour, relentless, critical, and inclined to inflexibility. The other commissioners, who thought his notes to the British commissioners were too strident, tore them to pieces. At first Adams bristled. "On the general view of the subject we are unanimous," he complained in his diary, "but in my exposition of it, one objects to the form, and another to the substance of every paragraph." Gallatin is for "striking out every expression that may be offensive to the feelings of the adverse party." Clay is "displeased with figurative language." Russell amends "the construction of every sentence," and although Bayard agrees to say "precisely the same thing," he "chooses to say it only in his own language." Adams saw that Gallatin had a knack for achieving consensus, so he started collaborating with him on the commission's papers. That worked better. While the others still struck out "seven eights of what I write," Adams told his wife, they rejected only "one half of what Mr. Gallatin writes." Gallatin was "always perfectly cool," while "I in the judgment of my Colleagues, am often more than temperately warm."[26]

Adams soon acknowledged that Gallatin had become the effective leader of the commission. He admired the man. The British commissioners were able enough, he told his wife early in September, "but for extent and copiousness of information, for sagacity and shrewdness of comprehension, for vivacity of intellect, and fertility of resources there is certainly not among them a man equal to Mr. Gallatin," who "has in his character one of the most extraordinary combinations of stubbornness and...flexibility that I ever met in [a] man." Adams particularly admired the "playfulness of disposition" that allowed Gallatin to defuse anger "with a joke." He could even laugh at himself when Gallatin suggested—with a mischievous smile and "a tone of perfect good humor"—that one of Adams's angry outbursts was nothing but a mistake in logic. "Mr. Gallatin keeps and increases his influence over us all," Adams told his wife at the end of September. "It would have been an irreparable loss, if our Country had been deprived of the benefit of his talents in this Negotiation." But Adams was too critical—of himself and everyone else—to spare Gallatin entirely. The man's great fault, he noted when the negotiations grew tense a few months later, was "an ingenuity sometimes intrenching upon ingenuousness." Gallatin's private assessment of Adams was more trenchant. Although Adams was a "virtuous man," Gallatin told a friend years later, he lacked judgment "to a deplorable degree."[27]

News that the British had burned the public buildings in Washington on August 24 reached Ghent on the first of October. Troops from the British fleet in the Chesapeake Bay had landed in Maryland, scattered American defenders at Bladensburg, and marched down the Bladensburg Road into Washington without encountering further resistance. Madison, his cabinet, and most other federal officials fled, and their clerks scurried behind them with whatever government records they could cram into the available wagons. The commander of the Navy Yard torched it to keep the British from seizing ships and supplies. British troops set fire to the Capitol, the President's House, the Treasury, and the War and Navy Departments. They spared the Patent Office in Blodgett's Hotel only because William Thornton, its polymath superintendent, stayed in town to challenge them. Federal officials scattered throughout the surrounding countryside could see the flames of the other buildings flickering against the night sky. The British troops returned to their ships the next day, and American officials began trickling back into town to resume the government's business in makeshift quarters.[28]

Gallatin's house at the foot of the Bladensburg Road was one of the few private buildings that the British burned. As the British vanguard came down the road, a sniper in the house shot Major General Robert Ross's horse out from under him. The troops retaliated with torches. They had no idea who lived in the house, and in fact the Gallatins no longer did. Hannah Gallatin had left Washington after Albert and James went to Europe. Her younger son Albert Rolaz, who was attending school outside Philadelphia, entered the college at Princeton in the autumn of 1813, and her daughter Frances enrolled in a school next door to Alexander Dallas's house in Philadelphia. Hannah moved between Philadelphia, where she often stayed with Dallas and his wife, and New York, where she stayed with her mother. The owner of the Capitol Hill house took it back, and friends moved the Gallatins' furniture to a smaller brick house near the Treasury building. Two weeks before the British attacked, Hannah asked her friend Dolley Madison to have her silver moved out of town.[29]

The Gallatins lost only a collection of maps that Albert had left at the Treasury building. But the British attack on the house where they had lived for twelve years left an impression. The new house near the Treasury that Hannah had never seen was not home, and the dispersal of her family had already left her feeling—she told her brother—"about as forlorn as you can conceive." The attack on her old house even sparked emotion in others. "Did you feel very, very sorry at hearing that your old House was burnt," Joseph Nicholson asked her when he heard the news. "I did really, I had spent so many happy Hours in it."[30]

Apart from the destruction of the Navy Yard, the British attack on Washington had little military significance. But it handed the British and their negotiators a propaganda victory. Goulburn struck the tone when he sent Clay a newspaper account one Sunday morning along with a sardonic note to say that Clay might find it interesting. Gallatin and the other Americans tried to turn the table by calling the burning of government buildings "an act of vandalism" for which there was "no precedent" in twenty years of European warfare. But the British punctured American outrage with a pointed reminder that American troops had burned Upper Canada's government buildings, and the fiery demonstration of British power spoke for itself. Gallatin solemnly advised his friend Madame de Staël, an exiled French writer and salonnière whom he had met in London, not to dump her American government bonds in the wake of the attack. He admitted that "the taking of Washington may present new obstacles to peace." Yet in the end, he assured her, the United States would prevail and the price of American government bonds would return to par. The country had "pulled out of an even worse situation" after the Revolutionary War.[31]

The tide of war did begin to turn in the weeks after the British burned Washington. Soon after the news about Washington came reports that Baltimore had repulsed a British attack. Troops organized by Samuel Smith in his capacity as a major general of the Maryland militia had turned back a land assault and killed General Ross. The harbor fort named for native son James McHenry—John Adams's War secretary—had withstood a twenty-five-hour naval bombardment. Joseph Nicholson, who had led a company of the fort's defenders, celebrated by publishing the now familiar lines about the fort's endurance written by his brother-in-law Francis Scott Key. The negotiators in Ghent also heard about a more significant American victory near Plattsburgh in upstate New York. On September 11, American ships brilliantly commanded by thirty-year-old Thomas McDonough had demolished the British fleet supporting an invasion down Lake Champlain. Loss of the fleet forced the invading army to return to Canada. With it went the British hope that one season of aggressive retaliation would be enough to defeat the Americans.[32]

In Ghent, the negotiators on both sides were discouraged. If "we had either burnt Baltimore or held Plattsburgh," Goulburn lamented to Bathurst, "I believe we should have had peace" on good terms. "As things appear to be going on in America, the result of our negotiation may be very different." The Americans were equally disheartened because they saw no change in the British negotiators' attitude. "I thought they were waiting for the issue of the campaign in America," Adams wrote to William Crawford in Paris. "But success and defeat there produce the same result upon them." When they heard about British success in eastern Maine and Washington, he said, they increased their demands. But when they heard about British failures in Baltimore and Plattsburgh, they spoke of fighting to "wipe off the disgrace." It was the news from European negotiations in Vienna, he thought, that would ultimately determine "the balance of peace or of war" in America.[33]

Crawford agreed that the outcome at Ghent depended on European affairs, and he thought that dimmed the prospects for peace. "Common report says that the Congress [in Vienna] is likely to arrange nothing," Crawford wrote to Adams. In that case, "our struggle must be continued for several campaigns to come." The American commissioners sent Monroe a dispatch despairing of peace and enclosing the many notes they had exchanged with the British commissioners so that he could see how unreasonable the British had been. Members of Congress guessed the contents of the dispatch long before Monroe published it. "I...imagine that there is no probability of a peace," Nathaniel Macon told Joseph Nicholson; "nor do I believe, that the Congress at Vienna will trouble themselves about our affairs." Macon thought the other European powers would be glad to let Britain "worry herself a while with us, to weaken her and to try whether this Government can support a war, and maintain [our] national rights." But Gallatin remained dogged. He sent Monroe a separate detailed list of the points under discussion at Ghent with specific requests for final instructions. And Clay—who had a canny sense for weakness—sent Monroe a private letter predicting that the British were about to back down.[34]

Clay's intuition was right. Events in Europe had begun to push Liverpool's ministry toward ending the American war. British taxpayers, who had expected relief after Napoleon's downfall, were rumbling about the "prodigious expense" of the war with America, and members of Parliament had begun to question the ministry's handling of the peace talks. Meanwhile, disturbing reports from Vienna said that Emperor Alexander would insist on his plan to resurrect the kingdom of Poland as a Russian satellite and to give Prussia the kingdom of Saxony as compensation for its Polish lands. Castlereagh feared that might compel Britain to ally with Austria against Russia and Prussia and—unthinkable as it would have seemed in the spring—lead to new fighting in Europe.[35]

Liverpool could see that his government's North American strategy had to change. His first instinct was to redouble British military efforts in America, but the Duke of Wellington—the victorious commander of Britain's forces in Europe—cautioned him against it. Victory in America, Wellington told him, would require naval superiority on the Great Lakes. Unless the government was willing to invest the time, men, and money needed to achieve that, Wellington said, Britain should give up its pretensions to American territory and make peace. Protests from taxpayers, complaints in Parliament, saber rattling in Vienna, and the dash of cold water from Wellington were a sobering combination. By the middle of November, Liverpool and his cabinet decided to drop the demands they had been making in Ghent and end the American war as quickly as they could.[36]

Until the Liverpool ministry relented, the negotiators at Ghent had accomplished almost nothing. The only issue they had resolved was the Native American buffer zone. The British had agreed to give up their demand for the buffer zone in exchange for an American promise to restore the Native tribes to the lands they had occupied before the United States went to war with them in 1811. The compromise allowed the British ministry to save face, but it effectively left Britain's Native allies to fend for themselves. The American commissioners had accepted the compromise, Gallatin assured Monroe, only because it was merely "nominal." It did not stop the United States from taking Native lands in the future (and in fact, treaties that the federal government made with Native tribes shortly after the war marked the beginning of more aggressive and sustained white appropriations of Native lands). Resolution of the Native American issue nevertheless was an important step toward peace because the British had threatened to break off negotiations if it was not resolved. But all of the other issues—impressment, blockades, boundaries, occupied territories, fishing rights, and British access to the

Mississippi—remained. Although Monroe's instructions permitted the American commissioners to drop the impressment issue, they had decided not to budge on it unless the British dropped their claims to eastern Maine and the American forts along the Lakes. British claims to American territory were an insuperable barrier to peace.[37]

Just as the Liverpool ministry was rethinking its position, the American negotiators sent the British team a draft treaty proposing a return to the status quo before the war. The draft, largely prepared by Gallatin, was the first full proposal submitted by either side. It called for the return of all territory taken during the war and the creation of bilateral commissions to settle boundary disputes. It also proposed resolutions of the two issues for which the United States had gone to war. It asked the British to give up impressment in exchange for an American promise to keep British subjects from serving on American ships. And it asked the British to agree that neutral ships had the right to enter any port unless a belligerent nation had put blockading ships in place to exclude them. Neutral ships that violated mere paper blockades against trade would not be subject to seizure. The draft said nothing about fishing rights or Mississippi navigation, however, because the Americans themselves could not agree on an acceptable solution. Clay—the defender of Western interests—opposed Gallatin's proposal to let the British navigate the Mississippi in exchange for British recognition of American fishing rights, Adams refused to make any concession on fishing rights, and no one could come up with another solution that the British were likely to accept. In a transmittal note to the British, the Americans claimed that they had put the fisheries issue aside because they believed the war had not altered longstanding American rights.[38]

The British response—which reflected the new mood in London— was a breakthrough. The British agreed to give up all occupied territory "belonging to" the United States and to let commissions settle the boundary disputes. Although the British qualification on the promise to return occupied territory sounded open-ended, the American commissioners understood that it only related to a few islands in Passamaquoddy Bay. The United States had governed those islands since the Revolution, but

British officials claimed they belonged to Nova Scotia and pointed to the notorious smuggling there as proof that American administration had failed. The British commissioners rejected the American proposals on impressment and blockades, but suggested that those practices were not worth fighting about since the British government had stopped them when fighting ended in Europe. Adams bristled to defend the "crumbs and atoms" of territory that the British wanted to keep, but even he was prepared to drop the other points. "We have every thing but Peace in our hands," he exalted. "The [islands] upon which they still insist, and which we cannot yield are in themselves so trifling and insignificant that neither of the two Nations would tolerate a War for them." The negotiators would soon have the satisfaction, he said, of "redeeming our union from a situation of unparalleled danger and deep distress."[39]

The final negotiations took most of December. The British and American commissioners resumed formal meetings and turned to their remaining differences with renewed purpose. The British asked for formal recognition of their right to navigate the Mississippi, and the Americans countered by asking for recognition of their fishing rights. Both points were contentious, and both sides finally agreed to drop them without giving up their claims. The British reluctantly agreed not to carry away the American slaves they had liberated during the war, and the Americans pledged to cooperate with the British to end the Atlantic slave trade. Britain had outlawed the slave trade in 1807, and British reformers wanted their government to use its naval power to stop slave trading by ships of all nations. The United States had outlawed slave trading by Americans in 1794, American investment in the slave trade in 1800, and slave imports to the United States in 1807, so although the American negotiators had no instructions on the point, they were willing to accept the loose pledge of cooperation. The British insisted that the treaty not take effect until the American government had ratified it. Britain's past experience gave them reason for caution. The Senate had rejected a part of Jay's treaty, and Jefferson had never even sent the Monroe-Pinkney treaty to the Senate. Liverpool feared that Madison might "play us some trick" in ratification unless British forces kept his feet to the fire.[40]

The parties signed the peace treaty on Christmas Eve. Shortly after four o'clock, the American commissioners and their secretaries took carriages to the monastery where the British were staying. The British delegation met them in a large reception room hung round with mirrors that caught the waning winter light. The Americans delivered the three copies of the treaty that they had prepared, and the British delivered two of their three copies. Anthony St. John Baker, the senior British secretary, read the third copy aloud while Gallatin, Adams, and the three British commissioners compared the copies they held in their hands. The reading took well over an hour. The light failed and servants lit lamps. The commissioners corrected a few minor errors. They signed the six copies and set their seals in the blood-red wax dropped by their names. Then Gambier and Adams exchanged the two sets and solemn hopes for a lasting peace. At half past six, the Americans took carriages home through the darkness. Another carriage waited in the courtyard to take Baker and the treaty to Ostend for a fast night boat across the English Channel.[41]

That night and the following day were a time for bittersweet reflection and precautious self-justification. The American commissioners had made peace without conceding territory. That was something, but that was all. The treaty said nothing about impressment or paper blockades—the issues for which the United States had gone to war—and it left a list of contentious boundary issues for the future. "Whatever objections may be made to it, and objections there will be," Albert wrote to Hannah, "it is as good as could be obtained" and as good as "we had...a right to expect." For "not having a better peace & six months sooner, the United States are solely indebted to the New England traitors." Adams wrote to his mother in a similar vein. Although the treaty was not as good as it might have been under better circumstances, he thought it was creditable. "We have abandoned no essential right, and if we have left everything open for future controversy, we have at least secured to our country the power at her own option to [end] the war." Russell, who later claimed that Adams would have bargained away Mississippi navigation in exchange for recognition of American fishing rights, thought the American commissioners had done "the best, or nearly the best," they could have done. Clay was more guarded. The treaty, he told Monroe, was not "very unfavorable. We lose no territory, I think no honor." Bayard had no doubt that the Senate would ratify the treaty because it was "certainly as favorable as could be expected under existing circumstances."[42]

Gallatin sent Monroe a long private letter explaining that four things had hampered the American negotiators. The first was the lack of timely information. News about the war in America and the peace negotiations in Vienna reached London first, and that gave the British a distinct advantage. The second was the dissent and disloyalty in New England, which had encouraged the British to believe that delaying the peace might destroy the Union. The third difficulty was the cold calculations of the European powers. While the "*people* of Europe" were "decidedly in our favor," Gallatin wrote, their leaders had been worse than indifferent. They had hoped to benefit from the continuation of a war that could "occupy & weaken" their arrogant British ally. Finally, the British themselves had not been committed to peace. Their attitude "had long fluctuated" based on the latest reports from the American battlefields or the European peace tables. But despite everything, Gallatin wrote, the war and the treaty just concluded would "increase our character & consequence in Europe." The war had shown that the United States could resist one of the most formidable military powers on earth. And the treaty proved that the United States was strong enough "to obtain peace on equal terms" without the foreign assistance that it had needed in the Revolutionary War.[43]

Peace—peace anywhere—was an occasion for celebration in the occupied city of Ghent, and celebrations kept the British commissioners in town for a week longer than Goulburn, at least, wanted to stay. The American anthem "Hail, Columbia" had become popular in Ghent after Gallatin's servant Peter Brown whistled it for a local musician, and musicians now played it along with "God Save the King" at fetes and dinners to celebrate the peace. Adams beamed when a beautiful young Flemish woman seated beside him at dinner told Goulburn that she thought the American tune was far gayer. That only showed, the consummate Englishman told her, that she was not English. The president of the local academy of fine arts made sketches of the American commissioners and a portrait of Adams, perhaps as studies for a commemorative painting that he never accomplished. The sketch of Gallatin shows a tired, serious man with a faint smile and a much fuller face than he wears in other portraits. He had been away from home for twenty months, and it showed.[44]

The American commissioners did not expect to get home for months longer. An Atlantic crossing was risky in winter, and they still had work to do in Europe. Their commissions gave them authority to negotiate a commercial treaty with Britain if they were able to make peace, and they had offered to meet British negotiators in London once both countries ratified the peace treaty. In the meantime, all of them but Gallatin went to Paris. Adams went to await his wife, whom he had rather briskly directed to pack up their St. Petersburg apartment and cross the continent with their seven-year-old son to meet him there. Adams had decided to resign from his post in St. Petersburg, and he was expecting Madison to appoint him as the American minister to Britain. Bayard and Clay went to Paris to wait for word on the ratification and commercial negotiations, and Russell went for a holiday before taking his post in Sweden. Instead of going to Paris, Gallatin and his son James set off on a six-week pilgrimage to Geneva. Adams speculated that Madison might ask Gallatin to take Adams's place in St. Petersburg, but he hoped Gallatin would go somewhere his talents could be more useful. Without disrespect to anyone else, he told his wife, "I consider [Mr. Gallatin] as having contributed the largest and most important share to the conclusion of the Peace."[45]

◦◦◦

The peace came barely in time to redeem the United States from economic and financial disaster. American commerce, banking, and public finance were in shambles. By the end of the war, legal imports had fallen to 24 percent of their level during the last full year of peace and exports had sunk to 11 percent of their pre-war level. The British blockade had disrupted shipping, and Congress had imposed an embargo to prevent trading with the enemy. Although smuggling was rampant, most commercial farmers could not find adequate markets for the grain and other commodities they had exported in peacetime. Law-abiding merchants shifted their capital into privateering or new domestic manufacturing. Wartime scarcity and high wartime duties on imported goods made domestic manufacturing profitable. Textile production made particular progress in New England. But one financially sophisticated Federalist predicted that the artificial boom in American manufacturing would cause problems after the war. Congress would have to lower duties in order to increase taxable imports, and lower duties would leave the new manufacturers exposed to foreign competition. So when "this mad frolic is over," he said, "you must say farewell [to] revenues from trade" or you must invite "the groans and curses of those, who now embark in manufacturing projects." Republican policy was going to "ruin your planters now, and your mechanics by and bye."[46]

Most American banks now refused to pay their obligations in gold or silver coins, and their refusal to pay specie had wrecked the nation's banking and currency systems. The problem began in Washington and Baltimore, where banks stopped payment in order to prevent runs on the banks when the British attacked those cities. But the fear of bank failures quickly spread to other cities because the number of state banks had spiked after the Bank of the United States went out of business and the people were worried that some of the banks did not have enough specie to pay their noteholders and depositors. Within weeks, all of the banks outside New England stopped paying hard money. Banks even stopped taking each other's notes, so farmers, merchants, and the federal government could not send money from one bank to another. The only way to make payment was to deliver bank notes, and no one would accept bank notes at face value. Discounts ran at 15 to 30 percent—even higher when someone had to use the notes of a bank in one region to make payments in another region. The country had no currency of uniform value.[47]

The federal government defaulted on the public debt. The government's financial position had deteriorated sharply throughout 1814, and by November, the Treasury reached the end of its rope. It did not have the money to pay off its short-term notes as they came due, and it could not persuade the New England banks to release specie on deposit with them to pay the interest due on its long term bonds. The Treasury managed to keep the default from spilling over to Europe because Gallatin persuaded Alexander Baring to advance enough money to pay bondholders there. Baring had qualms about making a loan to the enemy, but he agreed to let the United States have the money in order to protect his bank's position with the customers to whom it had sold the bonds. Gallatin had worked the federal debt down to $45 million by the time the war began, but by the time the war ended the debt stood at $120 million.[48]

The failure of the banking system had triggered the Treasury's default, but the basic reasons for it lay in the wider failure of the Republican fiscal system. The British government's fiscal system had paid for another eighteen years of war against France after the British banks stopped making specie payments in 1797. Indeed, the British banks did not resume specie payments until six years after the war ended. The Republican fiscal system was not so resilient. Gallatin had narrowed the tax base and starved the military establishment in order to pay down the public debt, and the Republicans in Congress had destroyed the national bank. When war put the system to the test, it crumbled.[49]

There were three reasons for its failure. First, the Republican majority in Congress did not want to raise taxes. It had been easy to justify tax repeal by saying that people would pay taxes more willingly in wartime, but it was another thing to ask the people for the money when the time came. Even Gallatin shied away from internal taxes in 1812 because he feared they would weaken support for the war. And although Congress passed most of Gallatin's tax bills the next year, they did not raise enough money. The government had to borrow money not only to pay for the war but also to make payments on its existing debts. That dented confidence in the government's ultimate ability to pay its debts and damaged its capacity to borrow. Congress imposed additional taxes in 1814, but they came too late to boost confidence or raise revenue before the war ended.[50]

Second, the administration could not build up military forces quickly enough to execute its war strategy. Because Republicans believed their democratic government was inherently peaceful, they did not think the United States would need soldiers and ships unless another country attacked it. The Republicans' decision to attack Canada required a major adjustment in thinking. The government could not invade another country with militiamen who thought their job was to resist invasions, and the regular army was too small to attack Canada by itself. The more seasoned navy—despite its good showing—could not stop British retaliation along the American coast or keep British ships off the Great Lakes. The administration made progress as the war continued. It raised armies, established a general staff, and promoted more capable commanders. Brilliant young naval officers built fleets on the Great Lakes and scored important victories. But the American defeats at the start of the war had been very costly. They gave the British time to send additional forces to North America, and they warned potential lenders that the war would be long, expensive, and uncertain.[51]

Finally, Gallatin found it difficult to borrow money for a government that could not raise revenue or win battles. He had to accept 88 cents on the dollar for the bonds he sold as he was leaving for St. Petersburg, and federal borrowing got even more difficult after he left. Congress authorized a $25 million bond offering in 1814, but the Treasury could sell only half that amount and the price of the new bonds fell to 80 cents on the dollar. Some of the bond purchasers defaulted. In the end, the Treasury got only $8.3 million—in the form of depreciated state bank notes. A few months later, it got only $2.4 million when it tried to borrow $10 million, and the Treasury ended 1814 with unpaid expenses of more than $11 million. "Our finances are in a deplorable state," Monroe lamented to Jefferson. "With a country consisting of the best materials in the world, whose people are patriotic & virtuous, & willing to support the war; whose resources are greater than those of any other country; & whose means have scarcely yet been touch'd, we have neither money in the treasury [n]or credit."[52]

The fiscal crisis drove Treasury secretary Campbell from office at the end of 1814. His final report to Congress confessed that Gallatin's plan to pay for the war with borrowed money had broken down completely. The current yield on the 6 percent Treasury notes (which had dipped below 6 percent before the war) fluctuated between 7 and 9 percent. Campbell did not see how the government could pay for the war unless it raised taxes yet again and offered even higher interest rates for new borrowing. Madison convinced Gallatin's friend Alexander Dallas to take Campbell's place. Dallas was a commercial lawyer from the country's most important financial center, and he understood finance. Although the populist wing of the Pennsylvania Republicans still hated him, even they grudgingly supported his appointment. "Tell *Doctor* Madison that we are now willing to submit to his Philadelphia lawyer for head of the treasury," one of them reportedly told Madison's private secretary. "The public patient is so sick that we must swallow anything the doctor prescribes, however nauseous the bolus." What Dallas found when he got to Washington in the middle of October—about a month before the Treasury was forced into default—appalled him.[53]

The Ways and Means committee was proposing to pay for the war with paper money. A report by committee chairman John W. Eppes claimed that the government could raise as much money as it needed by issuing short-term Treasury notes backed by new taxes. If the government issued the notes in small denominations that people could use as paper money and accepted the notes in payment for federal taxes, said Eppes, the Treasury notes would hold their face value. People would therefore prefer them to depreciated bank notes, and the demand for them would be high. Eppes's report reflected a plan that his father-in-law, Thomas Jefferson, had begun urging on him as soon as Gallatin left the country. Gallatin had never convinced Jefferson that the government needed banks, and Jefferson took advantage of Gallatin's absence to pursue his own longstanding conviction that the Treasury could simply fund itself. By issuing its own notes directly to the public, Jefferson told

Eppes, the Treasury could keep the spread that banks earned when the Treasury borrowed from them. And once the public saw that Treasury notes did not depreciate like bank notes, Jefferson was convinced, the Treasury could sell as many notes as it liked without paying any interest at all![54]

Dallas tried to say it politely, but he thought the proposal was daft. Everyone remembered how paper money had depreciated to nothing during the Revolutionary War, and even political economists who advocated paper money said that only banks should issue it because governments—driven by politics rather than profit—were sure to issue too much. Three days after he took office, Dallas sent the Ways and Means committee a plan squarely at odds with Eppes's report. Dallas called Treasury notes "an expensive and precarious substitute" for bank notes and urged the committee to establish a new national bank instead. Gallatin emphatically agreed. He had not yet heard about Eppes's report, but he had seen it coming. In a dispatch from Ghent, he sharply warned Monroe against paper money. He acknowledged that it might be too late for a national bank to rescue the government, but he told Monroe that issuing paper money would only make the crisis worse.[55]

Dallas's proposal for a new national bank resembled Alexander Hamilton's proposal for the first Bank of the United States. Dallas envisioned a bank with an enlarged capital of $50 million that would issue bank notes and commit to lend up to $30 million to the Treasury. The government would buy $20 million of the bank's shares in exchange for its own bonds, and the public would buy most of the rest in exchange for Treasury notes and bonds that the government had issued to pay for the war. Dallas believed the plan would increase the value of the government's outstanding debt and make it easier for the government to issue new debt. He also thought the bank's notes would maintain their face value if the bank's charter capped the total amount of notes it could issue and the Treasury accepted the notes in payment for taxes. The new bank's notes could therefore create a currency with uniform value throughout the country. Dallas had no doubt that a national bank was constitutional. If the twenty-year existence of the Bank of the United States had not already settled the question, he said, then the current financial crisis was proof enough that the government needed the bank in order to fulfill its constitutional responsibilities. Dallas did agree with Eppes on the need for new revenue, and he proposed to more than double the internal taxes.[56]

Congress passed Dallas's tax proposals, but it gutted his Hamiltonian bank plan. The bank bill that Congress sent to the president in January—about two months after the Treasury's default and a month before news of the peace treaty—gave Dallas almost nothing. It created a national bank with a capital of only $30 million, required investors to pay for most of their shares with specie or Treasury notes to be issued in the future, and committed the bank to lend the government only $500,000. Dallas was bitter. "I asked for bread," he wrote, "and they gave me a stone. I asked for a Bank to serve the Government during the war; and they have given me a commercial Bank, to go into operation after the war." Madison agreed, and he vetoed the bill. He told Congress that he thought past practice had settled the constitutional question. But he said the bank they had authorized would not be able to revive public credit, provide a uniform currency, or lend the government enough money.[57]

Dallas promptly sent the Ways and Means committee a pointed new report explaining why the Treasury had defaulted and asking them to raise $40 million for the next year of war. Eppes read it aloud to the members of the House who sat huddled together in the Patent Office that had survived the British attack on Washington. When he had finished, reported a Federalist spectator, he threw the report on the table "with expressive violence" and turning to a nearby Federalist member asked "with a bitter levity between jest and earnest: 'Well, sir, will your party take the Government if we will give it up to them?' 'No, sir,'" replied the man, "'not unless you will give it to *us* as we gave it to *you*.'" John Jacob Astor sent Gallatin a plainspoken businessman's assessment of the situation. "I am sorry to say that my fears of your absents have ben too much Realizd," he wrote. "[E]verything has ben more or Less

Mismanagd—and I see no Chanc of bettering but by a Peace which we more than ever wish for."[58]

⌒≫⌒

Gallatin and the other commissioners left Ghent relieved that their country had not lost the war, but by the time Americans at home got news of the peace, it suddenly seemed to them that the United States had won. In January 1815, Andrew Jackson and a hastily assembled force of 4,500 Americans had shattered a veteran British army of 6,000 in a Louisiana canefield and stopped the invasion of New Orleans. News of Jackson's victory reached Washington just ten days before news of the peace, and it was almost impossible not to believe that the two events were related. Madison took news of the peace treaty quietly. Jonathan Roberts, a Pennsylvania senator who was close to Gallatin, found Madison alone with his thoughts in the large house he had borrowed after the British burned the President's House. Madison was sitting by a fireplace at the far end of a long, dim room with a single lamp on the stand beside him. Yes, he told Roberts, the news appeared to be true, but he would have to wait for the documents before he could officially announce it. The rest of the town burst into celebration.[59]

The timing of the news, the relief from anxiety, the confirmation of national aspirations—all of those things coalesced into the thrilling belief that the young American republic had bested one of the greatest monarchies on earth. "Who does not rejoice that he is not an European!" exalted a Pennsylvania Congressman who later wrote a triumphal history of the war. "Who is not proud to feel himself an American—our wrongs revenged—our rights recognized!" Whatever the terms of the peace treaty, he told the House, the victory outside New Orleans had "consecrated the compact beyond the powers of parchment and diplomacy." "Within five and thirty years of our national existence, we have achieved a second acknowledgment of our national sovereignty." Madison himself claimed victory when he sent the treaty to Congress. The treaty was, he assured them, the honorable termination of "a campaign signalized by the most brilliant successes."[60]

Jonathan Roberts agreed. Although the treaty said nothing about impressment or paper blockades, Roberts told his brother, "victory perches on our banner" and "the tyrants of the Ocean" were vanquished. Roberts also saw the treaty as a victory for the Republican party at home. The "triumph over the Aristocrats & Monarchists is equally glorious with that over the enemy," he wrote. "It is the triumph of virtue over vice[,] of republican men & republican principles over the advocates & doctrines of Tyranny." A former Congressional colleague told Gallatin that although he thought the war had begun "in the most child like manner without preparation or any attainable object," it had now "given us great honour & Glory in the Eyes of the World" and instilled "National Confidence" in men at home "who did not know how Justly to Estimate Our power & Resources." With wartime anxieties freshly in mind, even Federalists could rejoice at the return to safety. A Federalist Congressman from Massachusetts thought Madison's message to Congress was "about as false and Jesuitical as usual," but he called the peace "a blessing beyond all price."[61]

Mythical or not, the American victory humiliated the Federalists. They controlled all of the state governments in New England by the end of the war, and their opposition to the war had grown into a steely refusal to support it. They had refused to send troops, refused to lend money, and toyed with the idea of seceding from the Union. In late December 1814 and early January 1815, Federalist delegates from throughout New England had assembled in Hartford to discuss what ought to be done next. Most Republicans believed that Federalist resistance already had dangerously undermined the American war effort, and they now feared something worse. The Hartford Convention stopped short of calling for secession, but it did condemn the administration's conduct of the war and demand changes in the Constitution. Among those changes were amendments to eliminate the three-fifths clause that gave the slave states more votes in federal elections, to require a two-thirds vote of Congress to declare war, and to exclude naturalized citizens from federal office.

The convention sent its resolutions to Washington with a three-man delegation led by Gallatin's old student and political enemy, Harrison Gray Otis.[62]

Imagine Otis's discomfiture when he got to Washington on the very day the city got news of the peace treaty. The Republican newspapers could scarcely contain themselves. One roguishly reported that the Hartford delegation included a man called "*Titus Oates*, or some such name"—cleverly conflating poor Otis with an infamous English traitor of the 1670s. When the diminutive Madison refused to see him, Otis claimed that the "little Pigmy" was shaking in his boots. But he knew better. Victory had discredited the New England Federalists. A pamphlet entitled *The Olive Branch*—which quickly became the most widely read political tract of the time—took New England merchants to task for getting the country into a war over maritime trade and then refusing to support the war in order to gain partisan political advantage. A year later, even Otis was urging the Federalists in Massachusetts to support the Republican presidential candidate. The Federalist party, Jefferson told Gallatin, "was extinguished in the battle of [New] Orleans." It was an exaggeration. The Federalists stumbled on for a few more years. But like many of Jefferson's exaggerations, it was essentially true.[63]

While Republicans at home were celebrating victory, Gallatin and his son James were visiting Geneva. It had been thirty-five years since Gallatin left Geneva determined to make his own way in the world, and although the letters he wrote during his return visit have been lost, it is not difficult to imagine what he thought as his carriage rocked its way south through France, across the Jura Mountains, and into the stone walled city of his youth.[64]

Gallatin was not the wealthy man he had hoped to become when he left Geneva so long ago. He had neglected business because he liked politics better. But his political career—despite its rough patches—had been a success. He was one of the most important men in his adopted country. He and his friends had governed it for fourteen years. Both friend and foe compared him to Jacques Necker, the brilliant Genevan expatriate who had reformed France's fiscal affairs before the French

Revolution. Although the comparison was sometimes meant to insinuate that foreign financial reformers could get a country into trouble, it had a more flattering resonance in post-revolutionary Geneva. Necker had spent the last years of his life in retreat near the city, and his daughter, Gallatin's friend Madame de Staël, had come there when Napoleon exiled her from Paris. Seated across from Gallatin in the carriage as it rocked along was his eighteen-year-old son. To return to Geneva with him—a handsome fellow of about the same age Gallatin had been when he left—must have filled Gallatin with emotion.[65]

The convulsions in Europe over the previous twenty years had not spared Geneva, and Gallatin arrived just as Genevans of his class were beginning to crawl from the wreckage. Popular uprisings had brought down the old republican oligarchy in 1792–94, French troops had occupied the city in 1797, and France had annexed Geneva the following year. Many of the wealthiest Genevans fled. After Napoleon lost his grip late in 1813, conservative elements in the city had tried to recreate the old republican regime. The "old aristocrats are reappearing," Madame de Staël had written to Gallatin, "forgetting...that they are already dead." Her assessment was correct. The old leaders' hopes crumbled before the victorious allies' plan to combine Geneva with the Swiss cantons into a neutral buffer state between France and Austria. When Gallatin arrived in his native city at the end of January 1815, his old friend François d'Ivernois was in Vienna for the final negotiations. Word about formation of the new Swiss Confederation reached Geneva while Gallatin was there.[66]

Gallatin had stayed in touch with his family in Geneva throughout the years of upheaval. He was proud of them. Although the old political order in Geneva had passed away, the Gallatins were still important people. Their standing and what it said about his own origins gratified Gallatin. He no longer believed that men of his class had a right to govern others; he had become thoroughly republican decades ago. But after years of being abused as a foreigner and a poor man, he did take satisfaction in belonging to a family as distinguished as any in the United States. The Gallatins were also proud of him. He was a famous man, and more than that, he was a man of great accomplishments. Accomplishments demonstrated the merit on which social and political authority in Geneva had traditionally depended. The state council's official greeting to Albert Gallatin was a recognition of merit. With the world in flux around them, the Gallatins were glad to welcome their distinguished cousin home.[67]

The European world was fluid indeed. Albert and James Gallatin were on their way from Geneva to Paris in early March when they heard that Napoleon had escaped from exile. As he made his way north toward Paris, large elements of the French army deserted Louis XVIII, the Bourbon king who had been restored by the allied armies, and rallied to Napoleon's banners. Louis fled to Ghent two weeks later, and—while Gallatin was attending the theater in Paris on the night of March 20— Napoleon entered his old capital and resumed power. Britain and its allies declared war against him. It now seemed unlikely that the Liverpool ministry would have time to negotiate a trade treaty with the United States, but after waiting a month in Paris for some indication of British intentions, Gallatin decided to press the subject. He left Adams and Bayard—whose health had taken a sharp turn for the worse—to follow later, and he set off to join Clay, who had gone on to London.[68]

Gallatin and Clay got Castlereagh's attention almost immediately, but on a different subject. At the beginning of April, British guards had killed seven American prisoners of war and wounded over sixty more during a riot at Dartmoor Prison in south Devon. The incident embarrassed the British government, which had been slow to repatriate the thousands of American sailors that it was holding there, and Castlereagh wanted Gallatin and Clay to help lead an investigation. Gallatin and Clay shifted that task to others, but they got Castlereagh's promise that he would arrange to start commercial negotiations within a few days. Castlereagh did nothing, however, until Gallatin and Clay let it be known three weeks later that they intended to leave. So it was not until the middle of May that Gallatin and Clay first met with the British negotiators—Henry Goulburn and William Adams, their counterparts at Ghent, and Frederick John Robinson, a young vice president of the Board of Trade (who later became prime minister as Lord Goderich). John Quincy

Adams arrived ten days later, and negotiations began in early June. James Bayard made it no further than Plymouth where—disabled by fever and coughing from deterioration in his chest—he remained with the *Neptune* to await passage home.[69]

Once meetings began, the British and American negotiators hammered out a new commercial agreement in less than a month. It was a simple document because, as they had done at Ghent, the negotiators dropped the points that they could not resolve. The British government would not give up impressment or limit blockades. It also would not make exceptions to its longstanding mercantile restrictions on trade with British colonies in Canada and the West Indies. The Americans for their part refused to let the British resume the fur trade with Natives on the American side of the Canadian border. The parties did agree to drop discriminatory duties on trade between Britain and the United States, and the British agreed to let Americans trade at their principal ports in the East Indies (in modern India and Malaysia) on terms no less favorable than those given to any other nation. The agreement would expire in four years. Because it resolved so little, Gallatin insisted that the parties call the agreement a convention rather than a treaty. The negotiators signed it on July 3, 1815, two weeks after allied armies defeated Napoleon at Waterloo.[70]

Gallatin made few claims for the trade convention when he sent it to Madison. But since the British would have preferred no agreement at all, he wrote, the convention was at least "evidence of [their] friendly disposition." Madison replied that no one had expected a British government flush with its triumph in Europe to pay much attention to its relations with the United States. Two months later, Gallatin told Monroe that the opportunity for increased American trade with the East Indies was both more significant and more problematic than it appeared to be. The British had made similar concessions in Jay's treaty and the unratified Monroe-Pinkney treaty because the East India Company, which then held a monopoly on British trade with India, was not able to send adequate supplies there. Now that the Indian trade had been opened to all British subjects, Gallatin explained, the concession was more generous because

1. Statue of Albert Gallatin by James Earle Fraser, 1941, at the North Front of the United States Department of the Treasury Building.

2.1 *A Peep into the Antifederalist Club*, 1793. The large central figure is Albert Gallatin's friend James Hutchinson.

2.2 *The Times: A Political Portrait*, about 1796. The two figures in the right foreground are Albert Gallatin and Thomas Jefferson.

3. *A Political Sinner.* This cartoon of Albert Gallatin was the frontispiece in Peter Porcupine's *Political Censor*, April 1796.

4.1 *View of the Capitol of Washington Before It Was Burnt Down by the British* by William Russell Birch, 1800. The unfinished Capitol as seen from a spot near Albert and Hannah Gallatin's house at the foot of the Bladensburg Road.

4.2 *View of Blodgett's Hotel in Washington* by Nicholas King, about 1799–1801. The two structures on the central horizon in this view from the foot of Capitol Hill are the President's House and, to its right, the Treasury building.

5.2 Joseph Hopper Nicholson by C. B.
J. F. de Saint-Mémin, 1806.

5.1 Alexander James Dallas by Gilbert
Stuart, about 1800.

5.3 Robert Smith by C. B. J. F. de Saint-
Mémin, 1803.

5.4 Samuel Smith by Rembrandt Peale,
1818.

6.1 Albert Gallatin by
Rembrandt Peale, 1805.

6.2 Albert and Hannah Gallatin, about 1806.

7.1 Albert Gallatin by William H. Powell, 1843.

7.2 Albert Gallatin by Anthony, Edwards & Co., about 1842.

7.3 John Badollet by Charles Alexander Lesueur, about 1833.

8.1 *Signing of the Treaty of Ghent, Christmas Eve, 1814* by Sir Amédée Forestier, 1914.

8.2 *Broadway Tabernacle* by Tompkins H. Matteson, 1848.

Britain had much less need for it. But because Americans generally had to pay for East Indian goods in specie, Gallatin warned that increased trade with India would exacerbate the specie shortage at home.[71]

Gallatin had a long dinner with Alexander Baring on the day he signed the trade agreement. He had intended to start for home the next morning, but he drank so much that he could not travel. Clay left without him, and Gallatin set out the following day. He was anxious to get back to the United States. William Crawford had resigned as American minister to France, and Gallatin heard while he was in London that Madison had appointed him to be Crawford's successor. Madison also had appointed John Quincy Adams to be the American minister to Britain, as expected, and James Bayard to be minister to Russia. Bayard declined on account of his health. When Crawford reached Plymouth in June to get return passage on the *Neptune*, he found Bayard in dire condition. Crawford ordered the *Neptune* to sail without waiting for Gallatin and Clay in the hope that Bayard could reach home before he died. So the first week of July found Clay and Gallatin bouncing across England to take passage from Liverpool on a merchant ship bound for New York. Whether or not Gallatin was going to accept the appointment as minister to France—and he had not decided—he was determined to go home. He had been away for more than two years. His family was scattered, the house where they had lived was gone, and his wife was so lonely that he had feared she was on her way to London. He sailed on July 22.[72]

The *Neptune* entered the Delaware Bay a week later on its way back to New Castle. Although it came laden with a dying man, there was quiet triumph in its return. Two years earlier a British frigate had blocked its way and the British captain had demanded British passports. Now the *Neptune* sailed unchallenged to let Bayard die in a country at peace. The *Neptune* reached port on the last night of July and docked by the light of a waning moon at three o'clock in the morning. Alexander Dallas, who was in Philadelphia for a summer break from the disasters that war had brought to the Treasury, heard of the ship's arrival and dashed off a note to Hannah Gallatin shortly after daybreak. She was dismayed when she got word that her son and husband were not aboard. But she smothered her disappointment when she learned why. James Bayard died in the arms of his family six days after he landed.[73]

The ship bringing Albert Gallatin and Henry Clay from Liverpool made New York Harbor on the first of September, about a week later than they had expected. The silence surrounding most intimate moments in history embraces Albert and Hannah Gallatin's reunion. But accounts of a large public dinner in honor of the two peacemakers appeared in the newspapers. Prominent New Yorkers of both political parties gave the dinner at the city Republicans' impressive new headquarters in Tammany Hall on City Hall Park. Alexander Dallas came up from Philadelphia for the occasion, and Rufus King, the Federalist senator from New York, came in from his farm on Long Island. There were more than two dozen patriotic toasts—none of them particularly imaginative. But after the public guests went home, Dallas proposed a toast that probably had more bite than he intended. "The lesson of the war—," he said, "preparation in peace."[74]

CHAPTER 10

REPUBLICAN
REBIRTH

Albert Gallatin was fifty-four years old when he returned to the United States in September 1815. He spent most of the next nine months with his family at his mother-in-law's house in Greenwich, about two miles above New York City. Frances Nicholson's large comfortable house sat back from the road on a triangular corner lot at Tenth Street and Sixth Avenue, surrounded by trees and a hand-mown grass dooryard. Greenwich was different from St. Petersburg, Ghent, Geneva, Paris, London, and nearby New York. It was quiet there. Carts and carriages passed in the road, but the more frequent sounds were muffled hoof falls, voices beyond the trees, and bird song. In the winter, the Gallatins moved into a smaller house toward the back of the lot. When it snowed and everyone kept to their fires, there was almost no sound outside the family circle. Quiet was what Albert needed. He was tired, and his prospects were uncertain. He had been at the center of power for fourteen years, but the paths now before him were leading elsewhere. He already sensed that he had left political life. Over the next fifteen years—and not without some wistfulness—he would come to accept that.[1]

James Madison had appointed Gallatin to be the American minister to France, but on the day of the honorary dinner at Tammany Hall, Alexander Dallas found Gallatin undecided. If it were left to him, Dallas told Madison, Gallatin probably would not go to France. But as it "probably depends on Mrs Gallatin, I will not venture a conjecture." Albert asked Madison for some time to consider what he and Hannah could do with their children and business affairs during a long absence. In any case, he said, the Atlantic would be too rough for a crossing until next spring. Writing to Thomas Jefferson two days later, Gallatin admitted his greatest concern. France under a Bourbon king restored by the Duke of Wellington's army would be "a vassal" of Great Britain for years, he said. So "the mission with which I have been honoured is, in a political view, unimportant."[2]

Gallatin's friends saw that he was reluctant to go to France, and he got other offers. A Republican activist married to Dallas's oldest daughter wrote to say that party leaders in Philadelphia wanted Gallatin to run for an empty seat in Congress. Anthony Charles Cazenove, a well-connected Genevan émigré who had been one of Gallatin's partners at New Geneva twenty years earlier, offered to take Gallatin into his trading business in Alexandria, the Potomac River port on the Virginia side of the federal district. "To return to the westward would now suit you nearly as little as Mrs Gallatin or your children," Cazenove wrote, and "the activity of your mind will induce you to follow some steady pursuit." Gallatin also got a strikingly attractive offer from his friend John Jacob Astor. Astor wrote that the capital invested in his fur and Chinese luxury goods business amounted to $800,000, and he offered to give Gallatin a one-fifth share in the business on credit. The "trade is easy & I am well acquainted with it," he wrote. He was confident that they could count on an annual profit after interest on their capital of $50,000–100,000, more than Gallatin's combined earnings from twelve years at the Treasury.[3]

None of these offers appealed to Gallatin, and by late November he had declined them all. He had bruises enough from William Duane and his other enemies in Pennsylvania politics without running for Congress, and he had long ago recognized that he did not care enough about money to keep his mind on business. But he also did not want to go to France. Since an American minister could not accomplish anything there, Gallatin explained in a private letter to Madison, the mission was not worth the personal sacrifices that it would require him to make. He would have to spend more than he earned in order to live as well as diplomats in Paris were expected to live, and his children would return to America with "expensive & foreign habits" that they could not afford. Gallatin thanked Madison for trying to keep him in the Treasury while he was in Europe and said that he and his family would "retire in the Spring to our home on the Monongahela." In a letter to his brother-in-law James Witter Nicholson, Gallatin explained that he was coming back to New Geneva in order to sell his property. He did not know what he would do after that.[4]

Secretary of State James Monroe spent the next two months persuading Gallatin to go to France. Louis XVIII had just appointed a friend of Russian Emperor Alexander, the Duc de Richelieu, to be his chief minister despite the British government's objections, and Monroe predicted that Richelieu would tilt toward the United States. Monroe also promised to press Congress for higher diplomatic salaries. Your decision "has not been made public," he assured Gallatin, so "it is still in your power, to accept the mission." Gallatin agreed to reconsider. Were it not for the need to provide for his family, he said, he would prefer to stay in public life. Finally in February, after more prompting from Monroe, Gallatin agreed to go. But he said that he would come home if he found it impossible to live on his income.[5]

Gallatin had several reasons for changing his mind. "My family cannot be reconciled" to living in "the Western Country," he confessed to his good friend Thomas Worthington, and "my income is altogether insufficient to support them in one of our large cities." He had instructed James Nicholson to sell all of his Western property except for his home farm and his share in the glassworks. "I do not think this is the wisest plan," he told Worthington, "but I cannot help it." He needed the money.

By way of explaining to Jefferson why he had decided to go to France—and why he hoped to return soon—he dropped another hint that he meant Jefferson to share with Madison and Monroe. "I did not feel yet old enough, [n]or had I philosophy enough," he wrote, "to go into retirement and abstract myself altogether from public affairs."[6]

It was a difficult time to be "a statesman out of place." The war with Britain had been a powerful catalyst, and Americans could sense that changes arising from the war were going to transform the nation. The prospect did not please some of the older Republicans. Jefferson wrote that the war had broken "the most remarkable tide of prosperity any nation ever experienced" and closed "such prospects of future improvement as were never before in the view of any people. farewell all hope of extinguishing public debt!" he lamented. "[F]arewell all visions of applying surpluses of revenue to the improvements of peace rather than the ravages of war. our enemy has indeed the consolation of Satan on removing our first parents from Paradise; from a peaceable and agricultural nation he makes us a military & manufacturing one." Some Federalists foresaw the same loss of Eden. Now that Britain had converted Americans "from our peaceful habits...into a Military People," Rufus King warned a son living in London, the United States would grow powerful, and "neither our neighbors on the East, nor the West will remain in security."[7]

But John Quincy Adams—an ardent patriot of the next generation—embraced the bold new prospect. "For my part," he had written to William Crawford from Ghent, "I cannot imagine a possible state of the world...in which the United States shall not be a great naval and military power. Between that and the dissolution of the Union there is no alternative." Because Adams doubted that the American people would ever claim that destiny unless they were pushed to it, he believed the war had created a "favorable opportunity" to "lay the foundation" for future greatness. He thought Congress should reorganize public finance and build a navy capable of resisting blockades. The "surest pledge" of peace, said Adams, was preparation for war. Alexander Hamilton had said the same thing thirty years earlier in *The Federalist*.[8]

James Madison himself struck a similar theme in his annual message to Congress after the war. It was December 1815—three months after Gallatin's return—and Congress was now meeting in a plain brick building hastily put up across the street from the burnt-out Capitol. Madison called attention to the need for a stronger peacetime army and a larger navy. He rejoiced that federal revenues were recovering, but said the country needed a new national bank to stabilize the currency. He suggested imposing higher import duties to protect domestic manufacturers of goods needed for national defense. "However wise the theory" favoring free markets, he said, "there are in this as in other cases exceptions to the general rule." Madison also endorsed the construction of roads and canals to spread commerce and bind the nation together. He did, however, caution Congress that they would need to obtain a constitutional amendment before they could spend federal money on those improvements.[9]

The people had elected this Congress a year earlier when the war's outcome hung in the balance, and its strong Republican majorities were ready for decisive measures. Henry Clay, who had been reelected Speaker of the House, led the way—coming down from the speaker's chair to confess that he had changed his mind about the constitutionality of a national bank. Congress chartered a new Bank of the United States with a capital of $35 million. It continued most of the internal taxes in order to repay the new war debt. It reorganized the army's general staff and authorized seventeen new naval ships. It raised a tariff against foreign competition by increasing the import duties on goods that domestic manufacturers could produce in adequate quantities, particularly wool and cotton textiles of the type made in New England. And it voted funds for roads and canals of national importance, only to see Madison veto that measure because he insisted that federal spending on internal improvements required a constitutional amendment.[10]

The new measures horrified some of Gallatin's friends who clung to their old Republican principles. Nathaniel Macon impugned no one's motives, but he marveled that he seemed to be the only person who still could not find a constitutional basis for a national bank. And he did not think it was right to raise import duties so that American manufacturers could charge everyone else higher prices. How could "a war undertaken for sailors rights & free trade," he wondered, possibly justify "a system to tax all classes for the benefit of the manufacturers"? As Macon pondered these things, he recurred to the old Republican fear that aristocrats had bent the federal government to their own uses. In no other way, he told Joseph Nicholson, "can any one account for the great and almost universal change which has taken place" in what "is now called republican politics." John Randolph was even more scathing. The Republican party's post-war program, he told a close friend, "out-Hamiltons Alexander Hamilton."[11]

Gallatin quietly supported the pragmatic new Republican program. He had fought to re-charter the first Bank of the United States before the war, and he had always insisted—except when politics got in the way—that Congress would have to raise taxes when war came. He and Monroe had begun reforming the army staff during the war, and the war had proven that naval construction was more urgent than Gallatin had previously admitted. Congress had taken Gallatin's 1808 Report on Roads and Canals as the template for its own plan of internal improvement. And although his 1810 Report on Manufactures had proposed to lend domestic manufacturers money rather than to protect them with higher duties, Gallatin now recognized the need for some tariff protection. As soon as the war ended, British manufacturers had dumped cheap goods on the American market in order to regain their market share. The British could afford to dump goods because they had enough capital to cover temporary losses. Since the American manufacturers had too little capital to resist, Gallatin thought they needed moderate tariff protection. But he believed that some of the duties Dallas had proposed were too high; he said that an outright ban on cotton cloth from the British East Indies might work better. A ban would be easier to enforce, and it would reduce the amount of specie exported to pay for the cloth.[12]

Gallatin felt frustrated to be on the sidelines at a time like this, and he focused his frustration on the banks' refusal to resume paying gold and silver. When the banks had stopped paying specie more than a year earlier, they had left the country with no currency—no money that had the same value everywhere. Merchants and farmers struggled to do their business with bank notes of uncertain value. Travellers could not pay for their dinner with the bank notes they had brought from home. Gallatin himself had been reduced to asking Joseph Nicholson if he would be good enough to give young Albert Rolaz Gallatin enough "*Philadelphia* money" to get him back to Princeton. Gallatin thought the banks' "unnecessary violation of the public faith" was outrageous. It "occupies my thoughts more than any other subject," he confessed to Monroe. "I feel as a passenger in a storm, vexed that I cannot assist." And as he had done on previous occasions when he thought others were not doing enough, Gallatin meddled. He believed the Treasury should do more to force the banks back to specie payment, and he could scarcely write a letter to one of his political friends without saying so. He gathered data on the specie balances in the banks around the country, and he warned Madison that most Pennsylvania politicians—including some of "my best friends"—were "paper-tainted."[13]

Gallatin's meddling destroyed his lifelong friendship with Dallas, who had grown touchy under the stress of office. The cordial, open correspondence they had shared for decades stopped; even their occasional business letters lacked the usual complimentary closings. Dallas tried to charge Gallatin and Clay import duties for the goods they had brought home in their baggage from Europe. Gallatin sent Clay a long note explaining that the Treasury in the past had exempted diplomats' baggage. Clay passed along the note to Dallas and declared that he would "*not pay* one cent." After consulting with the president, Dallas said that he was "authorized to state" that no duties applied. By March, Dallas had declined a dinner invitation from Gallatin with a frosty one-liner. Two months later, he dismissed a Treasury clerk who had worked for Gallatin in New Geneva for almost twenty years. Gallatin quickly got the man a new job with the Registrar of the Treasury, and he took the precaution of asking Madison to protect his old friend John Badollet if anyone tried to turn him out of the Land Office.[14]

Despite his frustration with his place on the sidelines, Gallatin was not prepared to return to the Treasury. When Dallas announced in April 1816 that he wanted to leave office by October, Madison invited Gallatin back to his old place. Joseph Nicholson urged him to take it. "For God's sake come into the Treasury again," he wrote; "you can be infinitely more useful there than in France, where you have nothing to gain, and may lose." But in a deeply coded letter to Madison, Gallatin declined. He said that while he felt fit for "the higher duties of office" and believed he could be more useful at home, the Treasury required too much close attention to "mechanical" detail. He had "lost sight of the thread and routine," and given the confused state of the currency, he thought that "an active young man" could do better. He hoped his stay in France would be short, but he would disappoint his family if he did not go.[15]

Gallatin still wanted to be Secretary of State. The autumn presidential election was about six months away. The Congressional Republican caucus had just nominated Virginian James Monroe for president and New Yorker Daniel Tompkins for vice president. Monroe's Secretary of State would therefore have to come from an important Republican state other than Virginia or New York. Gallatin's friend William H. Crawford of Georgia was an obvious candidate. Crawford, who had taken over the War department after he returned from France, was very popular with the Republicans in Congress, and he had received 54 votes in the party presidential caucus against the 65 for Monroe. That gave Crawford a claim to be Secretary of State, the post from which both Madison and Monroe had sought the presidency. But Henry Clay also had his eye on the job, and Monroe did not want to offend Clay because he had wide influence in the House. The hazards of choosing between Crawford and Clay might give Monroe a reason to look for a third choice—perhaps an old cabinet colleague and peacemaker from the Republican bastion of Pennsylvania. Gallatin's hopes may have risen when Madison pushed Crawford into accepting the Treasury post after Gallatin declined it despite Crawford's desire to wait for a new appointment until Monroe took office.[16]

৩২৩

Hannah and Albert Gallatin and their three children sailed for France in June 1816 on the *Peacock*, a Navy sloop refitted for their trip. Gallatin told Monroe that he still expected to be "very useless at Paris," and he kept telling everyone that he hoped to return soon. Yet despite misgivings about his mission, Gallatin struck a celebratory note as he took a parting look at the American scene. The war with Britain had produced both "evil & good," he told an old Congressional colleague, "but I think the good preponderates." It was true that the war had "laid the foundation of permanent taxes & military establishments," which he and other Republicans once thought "unfavorable to the happiness & free institutions of the country." But under the austere old Republican system, it now seemed to him, "we were becoming too selfish, too much attached exclusively to the acquisition of wealth, above all, too much confined in our political feelings to local and state objects." The war had changed all of that. It had "renewed & reinstated the National feelings & character" that had waned since the Revolution. The people are now "more Americans," said Gallatin; "they feel & act more as a Nation, and I hope that the permanency of the Union is thereby better secured."[17]

War also had changed things in France. Louis XVIII—once again restored to his throne after Napoleon's defeat at Waterloo—was gouty, weak, and beholden to Britain and its allies. Allied troops remained in France to keep peace and ensure collection of the war indemnities that the allies had demanded after Waterloo. A severely cold summer in 1816 led to crop failures and fears of popular unrest, so Louis's nervous government was subsidizing food for the volatile masses in Paris. Elite life in Paris, however, had blossomed after the Bourbon restoration. Military officers, politicians, and intellectuals came to the city from all over Europe. French Royalists scattered by the Revolution reclaimed their homeland, and French republicans exiled by Napoleon returned to press their case for a limited constitutional monarchy. Hannah and Albert Gallatin rented a spacious *hôtel particulier* in a quiet district along the Left Bank that had been popular with the lesser nobility before the

Revolution. The house came furnished, and the Gallatins used part of the State department's allowance for their outfit to equip it with an extensive dinner service from the fashionable Nast porcelain factory.[18]

Although he went to Paris insisting that he would not stay long, Gallatin stayed for seven years. Monroe picked John Quincy Adams to be his Secretary of State, giving the nod to the country's most experienced diplomat to avoid choosing between Crawford and Clay. Gallatin did not write about his disappointment at the time, but he alluded to it in a letter to his son Albert Rolaz years later. "Mr Monroe," he wrote then, "is the only person that I have a right to charge with ingratitude, but I am far from being the only one." It was Gallatin who had paved the way for Monroe's advancement by pushing Robert Smith out of the State department. It was Gallatin who had helped Monroe reorganize the army during the war and Gallatin who had helped him win the peace. Crawford and Clay certainly had competing political claims for Monroe's attention; the unlikeable Adams did not. But Gallatin buried those thoughts, established a respectful working relationship with Adams, and found that he liked living in Paris.[19]

Paris after the wars was pleasant and intellectually engaging. Gallatin's friendships with the Marquis de Lafayette and Madame de Staël gave him ready access to liberal republican circles. Although Lafayette himself generally stayed away from town because of his differences with the Bourbon government, de Staël kept an active salon during the season before she died in 1817. But Hannah and Albert Gallatin found many of their closest friends among other expatriates. The acclaimed Prussian scientist Alexander von Humboldt, whom Gallatin had met when Humboldt passed through Washington in the summer of 1804, encouraged him to cultivate his dormant interest in Native American language and culture. Elizabeth Bonaparte, a wondrously beautiful American who had married Napoleon's brother Jérôme in 1803, gave them a brush with social celebrity when they introduced her into diplomatic circles. Napoleon had nullified her marriage and barred her from Europe, and his downfall brought her to Paris in search of the life she had once imagined. A Corsican named Carlo Andrea Pozzo di Borgo became one of Gallatin's most important friends. Pozzo was the Russian minister to France, and his influence with Richelieu's ministry was so great that wags said the French had exchanged the rule of one Corsican for the rule of another. Pozzo even read the dispatches sent home by the French ambassador in Washington, and Gallatin's own dispatches show that Pozzo was an invaluable source of information.[20]

Gallatin's duties as the American minister were relatively undemanding because the Bourbon government had little to offer the United States. Monroe had instructed Gallatin to get indemnities for the American ships that France had seized under Napoleon's restrictive system and to seek a commercial treaty that would eliminate discriminatory French charges on American trade. But Gallatin had scant chance of making headway on either assignment.[21]

The war indemnities imposed by the allies left the French government little room to deal with other claims. Given "the present situation of France," Richelieu politely suggested in his first interview with Gallatin, he had hoped that the United States might not "fill up the measure of [France's] embarrassments" by pressing American claims. It was the most promising response Gallatin ever received. Even after France paid off the allies with huge loans from Baring Brothers, its debt service to the Barings was far more pressing than American claims. In fact, France did not agree to pay the American claims for another fifteen years, and it did not actually pay them until Andrew Jackson threatened to collect by force five years after that. The French government also found it difficult to reduce discriminatory duties on trade because Richelieu's relatively liberal ministry depended on the support of merchants, manufacturers, and bankers who thought the country needed protective measures to rebuild its economy. Only after an ultra-royalist ministry took over in 1821 did the government show real interest in a commercial treaty with the United States. Gallatin helped to bring about the negotiations, but the French ministry chose to entrust them to its ambassador in Washington.[22]

Gallatin did achieve important diplomatic success on a special mission to London in 1818. The commercial treaty with Britain that Gallatin had negotiated after the peace was about to expire, and Adams asked Gallatin to help Richard Rush extend it. Rush, the new American minister to Britain, had been Gallatin's protégé at the Treasury, and the two of them made a strong team in a new round of negotiations with Henry Goulburn and Frederick John Robinson. The new treaty not only extended the expiring commercial treaty but also settled some of the issues left open at Ghent. The British recognized American fishing rights off the Canadian coast. They accepted the 49th parallel as the Canadian boundary from Lake of the Woods (in northern Minnesota) out to the Rocky Mountains, and they agreed that both countries could occupy the contested Oregon territory beyond the Rockies for the next ten years. The British also agreed to arbitrate American claims to compensation for the slaves that British troops had freed during the war. The British wanted to implement the provision in the Treaty of Ghent for cooperation against the slave trade, but Gallatin and Rush insisted that the United States would not give the British navy a right to stop and search American vessels. By settling the issues most likely to spark conflict, however, the new treaty helped to reset Anglo-American relations.[23]

The Gallatins grew so comfortable in Paris that they were reluctant to leave. Washington Irving and George Bancroft found them happily ensconced at their country house outside the city one sunny afternoon in 1821. Irving was America's best-known writer at the time, and Bancroft, who later distinguished himself as a historian and politician, was travelling around Europe after completing his studies at two German universities. Bancroft recorded Gallatin's gaiety as he showed the visitors his garden and the laughter shared during a lively family dinner. The skeptical German philosophers with whom Bancroft had studied came in for their share of good-natured ridicule—along with those writers "who deal in quotations by the hundreds and stud their pages" with footnotes. Writing to John Badollet shortly after his return to the United States, Gallatin reflected that the "seven years I spent in Europe, though not the most useful were the most pleasant of my life." Where you do not stand in anybody's way, "you meet with indulgence...instead of collision and envy." He had not been accustomed to such pleasant treatment, he wrote, and he found that he missed it very much.[24]

༄

It was concern about the future that brought Hannah and Albert Gallatin back to the United States in the summer of 1823. Their three children were young adults, and they needed to find places in American life. Albert Rolaz, who was twenty-three, had gone to New Geneva two years earlier so that his uncle James Nicholson could train him in business. But twenty-seven-year-old James was wasting his time in Paris. And Frances, the clever twenty-year-old daughter of a poor American ambassador, was unlikely to find a suitable match there. Albert Gallatin was sixty-two, and he had begun to worry about how he would live in retirement. What he heard about his business affairs was discouraging. An economic depression triggered by a financial panic in 1819 had shoved many American businesses toward the ditch. Among them were Gallatin's glassworks in New Geneva and some of the banks in which he owned shares, and Gallatin feared they might not survive. He and Hannah Gallatin concluded they would have to retire to the farm at Friendship Hill because they could not afford to live anywhere else. They asked Albert Rolaz to arrange for another addition to the house there, and Gallatin requested a leave of absence from Paris to tend to his business affairs. The family reached New York at the end of June. Then Albert and James set out for New Geneva by way of Washington.[25]

What Gallatin found in New Geneva was a mess. The glassworks had failed entirely, his farm was overgrown with weeds, brush, and vines, and the large stone addition to his house was a vernacular pastiche. "Our house," he wrote to his daughter, "has been built by a new Irish carpenter" in "an Hyberno-teutonic style." The exterior looked like an Irish barracks, the interior like a Dutch tavern, and neither suited "the French marble chimney-pieces, [wall]paper, and mirrors" that the Gallatins had sent over to furnish it. "As to Albert [Rolaz]," continued Gallatin, "he has four guns, a pointer, three boats, two riding-horses, and a pet colt…who feeds on the fragments of my old lilacs." His "clothes adorn our parlor," and his socks provide the pockets for his billiard table. After a few months of trying to sort things out, Gallatin sounded less playful. He pushed Albert Rolaz to study law. He arranged for his family to spend the winter in Baltimore with Hannah Gallatin's sister Maria Montgomery and her husband John, and he confessed to his daughter that "more will remain to be done after our arrival next spring than I would have wished." He sent Monroe a letter of resignation saying that he could not afford to return to Paris.[26]

Gallatin had lost touch with American politics as well as his personal affairs. Treasury secretary William Crawford was the only member of the Monroe administration who had sent him much political news while he was away, and Gallatin had paid relatively little attention to it. "Here you will not immediately see into our political condition which you once understood so well," Jefferson now warned him. "[I]t is not exactly what it seems to be." Others would tell him, said Jefferson, that the Federalist wolves had lain down with the Republican lambs, but the truth was that the old monarchist predators had just wrapped themselves in sheepskins and hidden in the Republican flock. You "will soon see into this disguise." A warning was apt, but the eighty-year-old revolutionary's unshakable Manichean conception of the everlasting struggle for liberty was anachronistic. Gallatin soon found himself involved in a new struggle between political forces that it took him a while to understand.[27]

The jockeying to succeed Monroe in the presidential election of 1824 put those new political forces on display. The Panic of 1819, which had upset Gallatin's own affairs, abruptly ended the economic boom that followed the peace with Britain. Depression followed. The prices of wheat, cotton, and other agricultural exports fell by half. Wages fell by at least that much. The Bank of the United States forced state banks to pay off their notes, and banks throughout the country had to call in their loans to private borrowers. A sharp drop in imports and land sales knocked federal revenues from $48 million in 1816 to $15 million in 1821. Many Easterners objected to spending federal money on roads and canals that would increase the competing agricultural surplus from Western land, and Southern planters and farmers complained that protective tariffs forced them to pay higher prices for the benefit of Northern manufacturers. Treasury secretary Crawford and his so-called Radical Republican supporters in Congress pulled the plug on increased federal spending for the army, navy, and internal improvements, and they argued that Congress should use import duties only to raise revenue and not to protect domestic manufacturers.[28]

Just as the Panic of 1819 began, a fight over whether Missouri could join the Union as a slave state added heat to the arguments over fiscal and trade policy. A New York Republican named James Tallmadge proposed to deny Missouri admission unless it adopted a plan for gradual emancipation. Southern Republicans bridled at this assault on slavery. The federal government had no constitutional right whatever, they said, to interfere with domestic slavery. And since the Union already had as many free states as slave states, the refusal to admit a state simply because it practiced slavery would create an unacceptable precedent. It would condemn the slave states to become a minority and ultimately doom the labor system on which they depended to control their black populations and produce their essential exports. Congress defused the issue with a compromise that admitted Missouri without restriction, admitted the free state of Maine to balance the number of free and slave states, and prohibited slavery in future states to be formed from territory north of Missouri's southern border. But the Missouri crisis irretrievably changed American politics. The sectional debate inflamed financial and economic policy disputes within the Republican party in much the same way that the debate over John Jay's treaty had inflamed fiscal disputes between Federalists and Republicans in the 1790s. And the Missouri Compromise left slavery little room to expand without pushing west into the Mexican province of Tejas.[29]

The economic and political turmoil heightened the American people's distrust of banks and other public institutions. Many believed that the new Bank of the United States had lent irresponsibly—often to insiders—during the boom and then tightened credit after the crash in order to save itself, whatever the cost to everyone else. They were disgusted with the depreciated bank notes forced on them when the banks once again stopped making specie payment after the crash. They thought corporate charters gave the owners of banks and toll roads unfair economic privileges, and they complained that those on the inside—particularly those who had held office too long—were using their political and administrative offices to profit at everyone else's expense. Voter participation in most states rose as more men began to exercise what in practice had become almost universal white male suffrage.[30]

By the time the depression eased in 1822, William H. Crawford, John Quincy Adams, Henry Clay, and a brilliant young War secretary named John C. Calhoun were openly competing for the presidency. Andrew Jackson, an outsider who had become a national hero after the battle of New Orleans, was snipping at their heels. And the hot political question was whether a caucus of the Republican members in Congress—which had chosen their party's candidate in every presidential election since at least 1800—should pick the Republican nominee. When Congress had been the only place where party leaders from the whole country came together, the Republicans had used the caucus to build the broad Republican consensus they needed to defeat Federalist candidates in national elections. But now that the Federalists posed no real threat to the Republican presidential candidate, many Republicans had begun to say that the caucus was just a way for party insiders to take the choice of the president away from the people. "The condition of things is entirely changed," said the moderate *Niles's Weekly Register*, "and so should be the practice." A "nomination by *congress* would be an act of dictation to the *people*." Distrust in established institutions stiffened this objection to the caucus, and most of the candidates agreed.[31]

But Crawford and his supporters did not agree because Crawford had the inside track to nomination by the Congressional caucus. This giant of a man had always been popular with Republicans in Congress, and he had consolidated his hold on their loyalty during his six years at the Treasury through a subtle combination of patronage and fiscal retrenchment. Although he had supported the Bank of the United States and toyed with protective tariffs and internal improvements, his brake on federal spending had endeared him even to old Republicans like Macon and Randolph. A masterful young New York senator named Martin Van Buren was busily organizing support for Crawford because he thought Crawford's election would recommit the Republican party to Jefferson's old principles of limited federal government. One of Van Buren's allies in the effort claimed that those who ridiculed Crawford as "the 'radical' candidate" were the same sort of people who had once called Jefferson "the democratic or jacobinical candidate." But Crawford had a problem. He had suffered a stroke in September that left him partly paralyzed, practically blind, and almost unable to speak. The funny thing was that he remained the frontrunner despite those disabilities. Savvy Republican political observers such as Margaret Bayard Smith, a Washington insider since Jefferson's day, did not even see anything wrong with that.[32]

Gallatin did not yet understand it, but Crawford's candidacy was a metaphor for what had gone wrong with Republican politics while he was away. Confronted with the unavoidable lesson of the war—the need for preparation in peace—party leaders had traded the old Republican mantra of peace, economy, and riddance of public debt for a program built around a national bank, a stronger army, a larger navy, internal improvements, and protection for domestic manufacturing. Although there were rivalries and differences between them from the start, all of the potential presidential contenders had at first supported the program. Crawford found ways to pay for it, Clay became its leading Congressional spokesman, Adams built a strong foreign policy around it, and Calhoun found excuses to implement parts of it as a matter of military necessity.[33]

But the Panic of 1819 had delivered a staggering blow to the Republicans' progressive post-war program. Times were hard, and money was short. Voters grew testy. Crawford and the Radicals reverted to frugal old Republican ways in order to balance the federal budget and retain the support of agrarian voters. They shed the new program and clung to the Republican past. And now many other Republicans in Congress were supporting Crawford's candidacy in order to protect their power and their accustomed way of doing things. Andrew Jackson himself believed in the frugal old Republican values, but the blinkered self-interest of the party insiders appalled him. Could there be any clearer proof that the Republican establishment was corrupt, he fumed, than the nomination of a man who could scarcely walk, read, or speak to be President of the United States?[34]

Crawford's supporters wanted Gallatin to be Crawford's vice presidential running mate. Crawford had courted Gallatin while he was in France, and the two of them shared many of the same views—particularly on fiscal responsibility. Van Buren and the rest of the Crawford crowd thought Gallatin could lend their man the golden aura of the Jeffersonian past, mollify the more progressive Republicans, and deliver the keystone Republican state of Pennsylvania. They took the idea to Gallatin soon after Congress met in December 1823 and invited him to come to Washington to talk about it.[35]

"Ten years is an age in Washington," Albert wrote to Hannah after a reception at the President's House in January. The reception was "as crowded as any Paris rout, and there were several handsome ladies, but most faces of both sexes were new to me." Crawford was "mending slowly." His friends remained uncertain whether he would recover, and they said that was "why I should be made Vice-President. My answer was that I did not want the office," he wrote, "and would dislike to be proposed and not elected." He probably meant that—certainly the last part—but he also knew that he would not refuse the party's call. The Republican caucus nominated Crawford and Gallatin a few weeks later, and Gallatin gave Crawford's managers a detailed memorandum confirming that he was constitutionally eligible to be president. He was indeed eligible despite his foreign birth because the Constitution made an exception for anyone who had been a citizen of the United States at the time the Constitution was adopted.[36]

Gallatin's run for the vice presidency was a washout from the start. Politics had changed more than Crawford's supporters realized, and the aura of the Jeffersonian past meant less than they hoped. "There are not," Gallatin's old friend Macon warned him, "five members of Congress who entertain the opinions which those did who brought Mr. Jefferson into power.... what has lately been called the law of circumstances is an abandonment of principle, and has been the ruin of all free governments." Because Republicans in Congress were worried about popular hostility to the nominating caucus, only 66 of the 230 Republican members showed up when it met. Those who came were the Crawford die-hards, and they cast 62 votes for Crawford and 57 for Gallatin. Only three men from Pennsylvania attended, and two weeks later Pennsylvania Republicans at a convention in Harrisburg overwhelmingly nominated Jackson for president. They also picked Calhoun over Gallatin for vice president by a margin of 87 to 10. The Harrisburg convention marked the beginning of a strong national groundswell for Jackson that surprised even his supporters. And it left Gallatin in an extremely awkward position.[37]

Gallatin thought Jackson had to be stopped, but he did not think he was the man to help Crawford do it. Gallatin and most other establishment Republicans saw Jackson as a military chieftain just as dangerous as the Corsican general who had subverted republican government in France. During the war with Britain and his campaigns against the Native tribes, Jackson had ignored orders, broken the law, and summarily executed British civilians. Whatever "gratitude we owe him for his eminent military services," Gallatin wrote, he "is not fit for the office of first magistrate of a free people and to administer a government of laws." But "as a foreigner, as residuary legatee of the federal hatred, and as one whose old services were forgotten," Gallatin confessed himself a weak opponent for such a man. He had not carried Pennsylvania, and he was a lightning rod for criticism. The Jacksonian newspapers abused him as an alien ineligible for office, a wily Genevan who lived from the public purse, and a frail posthumous bastard of dead King Caucus. "Hie back to your mountains at Geneva," proclaimed a paper in Philadelphia, "and remember that though we have treated you...with all kindness and attention, we are not prepared to summon you to the second, perhaps in the course of nature's frailty to the first office" in the land.[38]

Gallatin wanted to withdraw from the ticket after the Harrisburg convention, but Crawford's managers resisted. As Crawford's prospects slipped throughout the summer, however, Martin Van Buren concluded that Crawford would have to pair himself with one of the other presidential candidates in order to stay in the race. He wanted to get Clay on Crawford's ticket or, failing that, to let Crawford's supporters in each state choose their own vice presidential candidate. Late in September, he clumsily requested Gallatin's withdrawal. Gallatin was glad to step aside, but he worried about how it looked. What was meant to be a sympathetic comment in the leading Republican newspaper struck the very chord that he dreaded. The younger generation, said the *National Intelligencer*, did not properly appreciate Gallatin's long and distinguished service to the country. He had been away too long.[39]

Lafayette was in Washington in February 1825 when the presidential election went to the House of Representative for the second time in America's history. The sixty-seven-year-old Revolutionary hero had accepted President Monroe's invitation to tour the nation on the eve of its fiftieth anniversary, and the ballyhoo that followed him everywhere revealed the depth of the popular patriotism that also fueled Jackson's appeal. None of the four presidential candidates had won a majority in the autumn election, but Jackson had taken the lead. He had significantly more electoral (if not popular) votes than Adams. The two of them had pushed Crawford into third place and eliminated Clay.[40]

The House convened an hour earlier than usual on the day it was to make the election. Snow was falling, but Lafayette found "the long avenue that leads to the Capitol...covered with a large crowd," the halls inside packed with people who could get no further, and the gallery of the House "filled with a large gathering of ladies, citizens and foreigners of distinction." To the crowd's surprise, they did not have to wait long. House Speaker Clay was determined to keep a dangerous military chieftain and a political rival from the West out of the presidency, and he used his influence in the House to get Adams elected. Thirteen of the twenty-four state delegations—including three from states whose electors had gone to Jackson—voted for Adams on the first ballot. As stunned silence gave way to murmurs and ragged applause, Clay ordered the House galleries cleared. Adams and Jackson manfully exchanged a long handshake at a reception the next evening. Five days later—as many expected— Adams appointed Clay to be his Secretary of State. Jackson's supporters took this as proof that the two men had made a "corrupt bargain," and the old warrior himself never forgave Adams, Clay, or anyone else who might have had anything to do with it.[41]

Lafayette's grand tour of the United States brought him to Friendship Hill three months later. Gallatin met the old general and his entourage fifteen miles away in Uniontown, where Gallatin gave a short speech welcoming them to Fayette County. He recalled Lafayette's sacrifices for the cause of liberty in France and America, and he praised the progress of freedom and the rule of law in America since the Revolution. Here, he said, "[r]epresentative government is established in its most simple form, founded on universal suffrage and frequent elections," and the "different branches of government" have only the limited power "necessary to attain their objects." A militia company escorted the two friends back to Gallatin's house, where the private respite Lafayette had expected turned—like so many breaks throughout his tour—into a day of visitation by people from throughout the neighborhood.[42]

A few months after Lafayette's visit, the Gallatin family left western Pennsylvania forever. Hannah Gallatin had never liked living there, and the substantial stone addition to their house was not enough to change her mind. James and Frances felt the same way. They had grown up in Washington, New York, and Paris, and they were—Gallatin told Badollet—"more fit for a court than a wilderness." Only Albert Rolaz enjoyed life in the West, but his father could see that he was not applying himself to business with the necessary "perseverance & steadiness." Gallatin thought that the young man should study law—and that the whole family would be better off in town. "After all," Gallatin explained to Albert Rolaz a few years later, "in the present state of society, we have to choose between obscurity and labour." Although obscure poverty in the country might suit the two of them, it was not a fulfilling way to live because it would not suit "such a woman as from her education can alone be an acceptable and proper companion for life."[43]

The Gallatin family rented a comfortable house on St. Paul Street in Baltimore. The energetic port city was friendly, familiar, and graced by monuments bearing tribute to the recent burst of popular patriotism. A few blocks from the Gallatins' house stood a new marble war memorial—the nation's first—dedicated to those who had died defending the city from the British, and on a high wooded hill above the end of their street rose the country's first monument to George Washington (designed by the same architect who would later create the iconic monument in Washington). Hannah's cousin Joseph Nicholson, the Gallatins' closest friend in Baltimore, had died while they were in Paris. But her brother-in-law John Montgomery was in his second term as mayor of the city, and the Gallatins' son James had just married a twenty-year-old Baltimore woman named Josephine Pascault. Snug in his new study, Gallatin plunged back into the investigation of Native American languages that he had begun with Humboldt's encouragement in Paris. It was with mixed feelings that he accepted John Quincy Adams's nomination to become the American minister to Britain in the spring of 1826.[44]

Gallatin spent most of the next three and a half years absorbed in the issues that he and the other negotiators had left unresolved at Ghent. There were many of them—ranging from a series of boundary disputes through impressment and indemnities to the exclusion of American ships from trade in the British West Indies—and there was still plenty of ill feeling on both sides. Britons had gained enormous self-confidence from their military victory over France and their surging economic power after the war ended, but in the back of their minds they still resented the American Republicans for betraying them during the struggle with Napoleon. At the same time, Americans determined to make their own place in the world resented British naval dominance and the inescapable influence of British capital on American finance, trade, and manufacturing. Americans' anxious Anglophobia spilled out in belligerent speeches in Congress, strident newspaper editorials, and even some bloodshed along the Canadian border. Diplomacy alone could not resolve the tension between the dominant Atlantic power and its scrappy young competitor, but both governments saw the benefit of settling what they could.[45]

Gallatin was in London for only one of the three and a half years he spent on Anglo-American affairs. He got the British government to pay for American slaves freed during the war, to submit to arbitration of the northeastern boundary of Maine, and to continue joint occupation of the Oregon territory. Those agreements were useful, but he saw little prospect of more and neither he nor Hannah Gallatin enjoyed living in London. In the autumn of 1827, he resigned and they came back to New York. The city had always been Hannah's emotional home. She had grown up there and spent most of her summers there even after she moved away. Two of her sisters and their families lived nearby, and her eighty-three-year-old mother in Greenwich was ailing. The Gallatins decided that they would stay, and they rented a house on the northern edge of the city not far from Greenwich. But Albert remained in government harness for two more years to prepare for the northeastern boundary arbitration.[46]

The King of the Netherlands had agreed to arbitrate the Maine boundary, and the State department asked Gallatin and William Preble, a justice of the Maine supreme court, to prepare the American case. It was hard work. Gallatin dug through archives in Boston, Albany, and Washington, drafted the long American argument, and assembled the supporting documents. "I have not worked so hard," he told his wife, "since I was in the Treasury." (Despite his efforts, Gallatin overlooked old maps on which British and American peace negotiators had marked the intended boundary in 1783—along substantially the same line for which the United States was now contending. The oversight did not come to light until 1842 when the United States, having rejected a compromise boundary proposed by the Dutch king, finally negotiated a Maine boundary treaty with Britain.) Gallatin, Preble, and fifteen assistants— including Albert Rolaz Gallatin—spent the last months of 1829 completing the final documents at a hotel in Washington. Gallatin delivered them to the State department on the last business day of the year.[47]

ᏜᎦᎤ

By the time Gallatin completed the arbitration papers, Andrew Jackson was President of the United States. He had swept John Quincy Adams from office a year earlier in what even contemporary observers recognized as an inflection point in American politics. Jackson ran for office as a man of the people dedicated to the reform and retrenchment of the federal government. His supporters scorned Adams as an effete man of privilege who wanted to consolidate federal power, push federal roads and canals through the sovereign states, and spend the public's money on such outlandish things as a national observatory that he called a "light-house of the skies." Adams's first annual message, they snorted, had even urged Congress not to be "palsied by the will of [their] constituents." Most of Crawford's old supporters turned to Jackson because they thought he would keep the federal government small and frugal. Adams hung on to the electoral votes of his native New England and the small coastal states of New Jersey, Delaware, and Maryland. Jackson won everywhere else.[48]

Even Washington insiders thought the enormous crowd that swept into Washington for Jackson's outdoor inauguration was sublime, but the rowdy throng that pressed into the President's House for the reception afterwards bared a grittier reality. There was pushing and shoving, broken glass, marred furniture, and bloody noses. "The noisy and disordered rabble," Margaret Bayard Smith told her sister, brought to mind "the mobs in the Tuileries and Versailles" during the French Revolution. "God grant that one day or other, the People, do not put down all rule and rulers." Jackson promptly spent $45,000 to refurnish the simple public rooms that had served his Republican predecessors, not because the crowd had trashed them but to suit his grandiose tastes. He excoriated his cabinet officers when their wives—like most of Washington society—chose to avoid a young innkeeper's daughter named Peggy O'Neal who had just married Jackson's friend and War secretary John Eaton. And he began to remove many long-serving federal officeholders from their places in order to make room for his own supporters.[49]

Although Gallatin found the new president "very cordial" when they met, there was no place for a man like Gallatin in the new order of things. He was sixty-eight years old, and he had not supported Andrew Jackson. Gallatin hinted to Martin Van Buren—who had swung to Jackson after Crawford's defeat and was now the Secretary of State—that he would accept another stint as the American minister to France, but the appointment went to a thirty-six-year-old Congressman from Virginia instead. Whatever may be "the claims of age and service," Gallatin explained to his wife, "I had none whatever on the present Administration. Age...so advanced as mine is not a recommendation; and we must make room for younger men." But Gallatin could not quite leave it at that. "Perhaps old age makes me querulous," he wrote to Badollet, yet "it seems to me that now and for the last eight years, people and leaders have been much less anxious about the public service & the manner in which it should be performed than by whom the Country should be governed." When he had dinner with Jackson the following year, Gallatin made it a point not to mention "myself, his Cabinet, and the removals" from office.[50]

Gallatin missed a large dinner at the President's House shortly before he completed his work on the arbitration, but Albert Rolaz brought back a full description that Gallatin relayed to his wife. "This was a splendid affair," he told her. The East Room that Adams and his predecessors had left unfinished was, "under our more Republican Administration" adorned with Brussels carpeting, silk curtains, three splendid English crystal chandeliers, and "four immense French looking-glasses, the largest Albert ever saw, and, by the by, not necessary in a dining-room." There were fifty dinner guests, one hundred lamps and candles, masses of new silver, "and for a queen, Peggy O'Neal," led in by the British minister as head of the diplomatic corps and seated between him and the president. "All which I mention," Gallatin told her, that "having had with me your share of the vanities and grandeurs of this world, you may be quite satisfied that we were not indebted for them to any particular merit of ours" and that the "loss of popularity, which we perhaps regret too much...is no more an object of astonishment than the manner in which it is acquired."[51]

Albert Gallatin's departure from Washington in January 1830 marked the end of his public career and the beginning of an extraordinary eighteen years as a private citizen in New York City. By 1830, New York had become the largest and most important city in the United States. The completion of the Erie Canal five years earlier had expanded the city's hinterland across western New York and along the Great Lakes into northern New England, Pennsylvania, Ohio, Indiana, and Michigan. The grain, meat, and other produce of those developing Western regions poured through the city, and its superb harbor drew cargoes of cotton and other Southern produce for brokerage and shipment to Europe. As trade expanded, merchants who had once handled commercial and financial activities of all kinds became increasingly specialized. Importers and exporters grew distinct from wholesalers, commission agents, and auctioneers. Those who succeeded with cotton exports or Chinese imports became notably wealthy. Finance also became a separate and more complicated business. New York supplanted Philadelphia as the main place for trading in bonds and shares, and although the presence of the Bank of the United States kept Philadelphia preeminent in banking for a few more years, the banks in New York grew and proliferated.[52]

Fast growth and great wealth changed life in New York. As traffic in the port increased, lower Manhattan grew denser, noisier, dirtier, and more commercial. The wealthy drifted west and then north along Broadway and into a narrow strip of fashionable suburban blocks on either side of it. There the jumble of houses, offices, warehouses, and worse that filled the lower city gave way to wider streets, a few more trees, small parks, and rows of handsome new Greek Revival townhouses that were comfortable and architecturally sophisticated. Most of the houses had a columned portico mounted above a service level half buried in the ground. The portico sheltered a tall front door painted to imitate expensive hardwood. Behind the door was a long, high-ceilinged side hall that continued to a back courtyard or an ell attached to the rear of the building. To one side of the hall were two large parlors divided by folding or sliding doors. Each had a handsome marble mantel surmounted by a gilt-framed mirror that reached to a wide plaster cornice. Fitted carpets and heavy curtains dampened sound. On the two or three upper floors were six to nine bedrooms to accommodate the several generations of a family that often lived together. Wealthy men kept a library at home and perhaps a separate office elsewhere, and elite women spent significant parts of their day on activities outside the house.[53]

Although they were not very wealthy when they settled in New York, Hannah and Albert Gallatin fit easily into the city's elite. Hannah's family had been well-established in New York since her grandfather settled there before the Revolution, Albert was a distinguished elder statesman, and they could afford to live in the fashionable area along Broadway. They rented five different townhouses over ten years before finally purchasing 57 Bleecker Street in 1838 with part of Hannah's inheritance from her grandfather. Gallatin's old friends introduced him to the new leading men of the city. He joined the Literary Club, an exclusive group of twelve prominent merchants and professionals who dined at a member's house each Friday evening. Among the club's members were the artist and inventor Samuel F. B. Morse, the scholarly lawyer Chancellor James Kent, and a well-to-do former mayor of the city named Philip Hone. When New York celebrated the French people's overthrow of the Bourbon monarchy in 1830, Gallatin and James Monroe—who had come to live with his daughter in New York after his wife died—were the senior dignitaries in the parade.[54]

With the dignity of age came its infirmities, and the Gallatins were growing visibly older. Edward Coles, who had been James Madison's private secretary in Washington, was quick to notice when he visited them in 1832. "Mr. & Mrs. G. are in good health," he reported to Dolley Madison, but "she has become very fleshy, & he much changed in his appearance by wearing an ugly wig." Harriet Martineau, a brilliant young English writer who toured the United States a few years later, was kinder when she wrote about her meeting with Gallatin. While her British readers might not recognize the names Clay or Calhoun, she knew that they would recognize "Mr. Gallatin's name" because he was "everywhere known and welcome." She described him as a "tall...dignified and courteous" man who spoke "with a very slight foreign accent." Her private notes on the meeting etched the lines of that portrait a bit deeper. "Gallatin is tall, bald, toothless, speaks with *burr*, looks venerable and courteous. Opened out and apologized for his [frankness]. Kissed my hand."[55]

Gallatin's old friend John Jacob Astor helped him to greater financial security. Astor was the wealthiest man in the city, probably the wealthiest man in the United States. Although Gallatin had declined Astor's earlier offer to join him in business, Astor came to Gallatin with another proposal in the spring of 1831. Astor was moving the great fortune that he had made in trade into New York real estate and finance, and two years earlier he had invested in a small bank called the National Bank. He wanted Gallatin to run it. The $2,000 salary was modest, but Astor sweetened the offer with a proposal to put Gallatin's two sons into a trading business of their own.[56]

It was an attractive offer. Finance had always held Gallatin's attention in a way that other business did not. James still had no occupation, and Albert Rolaz was too shy to make much headway in the legal profession. So at age seventy Gallatin became president of the National Bank. The bank was at 13 Wall Street, and Gallatin Brothers opened an office on the upper floor of a building several blocks down the street. Gallatin's duties at the bank required only three or four hours a day, so he had ample time for his studies, investments, and other activities. His position at the bank kept him in touch with the business community and public affairs. And although he continued to say that he was not good at making money, Gallatin began to accumulate some. That was important in a city where there was, as visitor Charles Dickens told readers back home in Britain, a growing "spirit of contention in reference to appearances, and the display of wealth and costly living." When a New York journalist began to publish a popular (if unreliable) list of the wealthiest New Yorkers ten years later, Gallatin was on it.[57]

Albert and Hannah Gallatin had a close and indulgent relationship with their children, and their sons were slow to make their own way in the world. Their daughter Frances married a well-off New York importer named Byam Kerby Stevens in the spring of 1830. But her two brothers remained at home. "Though industrious and in business," Gallatin told Badollet, "they do not yet earn enough to sustain a separate establishment." Albert Rolaz finally moved on in 1838 when, at the age of thirty-seven, he married a well-to-do young woman named Mary Lucille Stevens. He and his brother closed their trading business soon afterwards, and James succeeded his father as president of the National Bank. Soon both brothers appeared on the pulp list of the wealthiest New Yorkers. Frances had seven children, James had one, and Albert Rolaz had three. Each of them named his or her first son Albert.[58]

⁘

Andrew Jackson's first annual message to Congress—delivered the month before Gallatin left Washington in 1830—signaled the beginning of a revolution in the American banking and currency system. Banks and currency had not been a major issue during the presidential election campaign, but Jackson's message made them one. Jackson hated banks. He was convinced that bank charters allowed the privileged few who held them to exploit everyone else by issuing bank notes for face value whether or not they actually could redeem the notes with hard money. He said that gold and silver coins were the only safe, constitutional, and democratic currency. And he thought the banks' refusal to pay specie for their notes during the war with Britain proved his point. Jackson particularly hated the Bank of the United States. He said its large capital and its legal monopoly on all federal deposits gave it the power to oppress the state banks and the ordinary people who depended on them for credit to do business. The Bank's decision to contract credit during the Panic of 1819 showed, thought Jackson, how destructive its power could be. So toward the end of his message Jackson reminded Congress that the Bank's charter would expire in five years—and he questioned whether it should be renewed. A "large portion of our fellow-citizens" doubts the constitutionality and the expediency of the Bank, he said, and it had to be admitted that the Bank "has failed in the great end of establishing a uniform and sound currency."[59]

Gallatin had left Washington with Jackson's challenge to the Bank ringing in his ears, and he spent much of his first year in New York preparing an answer. He had done this before. He had defended the first Bank of the United States to Jefferson, and he had tried to convince Congress to re-charter it before the war with Britain. But this time was different. In the past, he had defended the Bank as a fiscal agent that could hold the Treasury's money safely and move it efficiently from one part of the country to another. He had sidestepped controversial questions about the Bank's power over the state banks and its use of that power to control credit and the money supply. Jackson's message made it impossible to avoid those issues, and what raised Gallatin's hackles was the firm conviction that Jackson had everything backwards. Early in the spring of 1830 Gallatin agreed to write an essay about banks and currency for the *American Quarterly Review*. The *Review* was a respected Philadelphia journal, and Nicholas Biddle—the president of the Bank of the United States—had recruited its editor (along with editors throughout the country) to help defend the Bank from Jackson. Gallatin declined Biddle's offers to pay for the essay, but Biddle gave Gallatin significant support. He sent Gallatin financial data, a research assistant (Biddle's nephew), and a flurry of more than twenty letters during the final three months of the project.[60]

Gallatin's essay on banks and currency was long and detailed, but his basic argument was simple. The Bank of the United States was not the problem; it was the solution. The problem with the American currency was the proliferation of notes issued by hundreds of state banks without any central control. Gallatin agreed with Jackson that a pure metallic currency would be better, but he thought it was no longer a feasible alternative. The federal government could not stop the state banks from issuing notes without challenging the states' right to govern their own banks, and the Treasury could not collect taxes efficiently if it refused to take payment in the bank notes that the whole country was using to do business. But by making the state banks repay their notes in specie, the Bank of the United States could limit the amount of paper money in circulation and test whether the banks that issued it were sound. That power—the very power that irked Jackson—enabled the Bank to push the notes of all banks toward a uniform value. By turning a monetary problem into a political confrontation between the many and the few, Jackson was making it impossible to solve the monetary problem.[61]

Committees in both houses of Congress agreed. The Senate committee, chaired by Gallatin's old enemy Samuel Smith, reported that the Bank had skillfully managed the monetary problems arising from the last war and created a paper currency that was "safe for the community, and eminently useful to the Government." The House committee report declared that the question Jackson had raised about the Bank's constitutionality was "forever settled and at rest." It praised the Bank for forcing the state banks to resume specie payment after the war and pronounced the Bank's own notes to be "*a currency of absolutely uniform value in all places.*" Gallatin congratulated a New York member of the committee on the report. Although he was "aware of the objections to a powerful moneyed institution," he wrote, a national bank was as a practical matter the best check against the over-issuance of paper money. Jackson had a more visceral reaction to the Congressional reports. He denounced them as proof that the Bank was using its financial influence to corrupt the political process. And a state banker in Boston made Jackson's populist theme explicit when—after bashing Gallatin's essay and the Congressional reports—he called Jackson "THE PROTECTOR OF THE POOR MAN'S RIGHTS" and "THE RESTORER OF THE TRUE PRINCIPLES OF THE CONSTITUTION."[62]

Jackson vetoed a bill to re-charter the Bank of the United States on the eve of the 1832 presidential election, and his overwhelming victory in the election sealed the Bank's doom. Although its charter ran until 1836, Jackson began to dismantle the Bank in September 1833 by shifting the federal government's deposits into state banks loyal to his administration. The Bank tried to compensate for the loss of deposits and to embarrass Jackson by calling in outstanding loans and restricting new credit. New York banks wobbled under this pressure, and businesses throughout the city found themselves in trouble. When leading New Yorkers called an outdoor public meeting on the banking crisis in February, it drew an enormous crowd that one enthusiastic organizer estimated at ten to twenty thousand people. A committee appointed by the meeting criticized both Jackson and the Bank in a widely circulated report largely written by Albert Gallatin—a man whom the opposition newspapers touted as an even better democrat than Andrew Jackson. The Bank, realizing that it had hurt its own case, backed away from the credit contraction. The Senate censured Jackson for removing the federal deposits, but the House supported him and voted not to re-charter the Bank.[63]

The financial commotion created by the fight over the Bank left the American economy vulnerable, but Gallatin tried to remain calm. He gamely tried to explain to the governor of the Bank of England, who asked for his views, how twenty-four distinct state legislatures could operate a single currency system. To an American correspondent he more frankly admitted that the country's "democratic institutions and habits" simply would not allow a more centralized system. Abolish all of the state banks, he said, and a few of "the wealthiest capitalists" would "engross" the financial business in which thousands of state bank shareholders now participated. But he foresaw that Jackson's destruction of the flywheel on the system—the Bank of the United States—would not end well.[64]

At first business seemed to return to normal after the lame duck Bank of the United States resumed lending, but the economy quickly inflated. British demand for American cotton drove prices sharply higher. British credit allowed the banks to accumulate specie and increase lending. And easy credit fueled speculation that drove the price of cotton land in Georgia, Alabama, and Mississippi to new highs. Gallatin watched these events carefully, but with growing emotional detachment. He could not bring himself to write another essay about banks and currency, he told Badollet, because "the Bank mania has extended itself so widely" that only "a catastrophe" could correct it. Although he knew that the "energy of this nation is not to be controlled," he wondered whether tinsel prosperity based on cheap paper money could really make the people happier. He thought "gradual, slow, & more secure progress" would be better. "I am however an old man; and the young generation has a right to govern itself."[65]

The inflationary bubble started to contract when the Treasury required purchasers of public land to pay for it in specie, British lenders reined in credit, and cotton and commodity prices began to fall. Soon after Martin Van Buren succeeded Jackson as president in the spring of 1837, a financial panic that started among cotton brokers abruptly pricked what remained of the bubble. Prices collapsed, and debtors could not raise the money to repay their loans. Businesses throughout the country failed as one insolvency triggered another. The Panic of 1837 and the severe economic depression that followed it were hard on the common men who had voted for Andrew Jackson.[66]

A second financial policy issue that divided the nation during Jackson's administration was not of the president's own making, and Gallatin's views on it were not so different from Jackson's. The high import duties that Congress had adopted to protect domestic manufacturers after the war with Britain had increased over the years as more industries sought protection, and just before Jackson took office Congress had pushed the average rate to 40 percent in a highly protectionist measure that opponents derided as the "Tariff of Abominations." Merchants who traded in international markets and farmers who produced commodities for export raised a clamor. Some of the strongest objections came from merchants in New York—the country's principal international port—but the shrillest cries came from cotton planters in the Southern states. They claimed that tariffs not only made Americans pay higher prices for manufactured goods but also invited other nations to retaliate by imposing high import duties on cotton and other vital American exports. They insisted that the federal government had no constitutional right to impose import duties except to raise revenue. The South Carolina legislature distributed five thousand copies of an inflammatory *Exposition and Protest* (secretly written by John C. Calhoun) claiming that individual states had the right to stop the enforcement of unconstitutional federal laws. The implicit threat of disunion was foreboding, and although

Jackson vowed to enforce the tariffs in any state that defied them, he favored a compromise reduction in the rates.[67]

Gallatin also favored compromise. In the autumn of 1831, he joined a delegation of prominent New Yorkers to a free trade convention in Philadelphia. Southern planters dominated the meeting, and they wanted it to declare protectionist tariffs unconstitutional. Gallatin objected for two reasons. He said the Constitution allowed Congress to impose taxes for any purpose that it considered to be consistent with the general welfare, and he believed the economic arguments against protective tariffs were more politic than constitutional ones. Gallatin failed to talk the convention out of alluding to the constitutional claim in its declaration to the people. But the convention chose Gallatin to draft its memorial to Congress—knowing that the reasonable voice of a distinguished elder statesman would give the memorial heft.[68]

Gallatin's memorial for the free trade convention was one of his finest pieces of writing. He put his usual exhaustive factual analysis into uncharacteristically resonant prose, and the memorial has the rich, resolute tone of an old bell pealing out a firm, steady call for reason, compromise, and union. Gallatin began with a simple statement of the classic liberal case for free trade. A nation grows wealthy by producing the goods that it can produce most cheaply and then trading its surplus production for goods that other nations produce more cheaply than it could. He then refuted in careful detail the arguments being made for the protection of particular industries. Virtually all citizens agreed, he said, that domestic manufacturing was desirable and important. But the advocates of restrictive tariffs—"whether taking advantage of that general and patriotic feeling, or carried away by it"—were hampering the national development they claimed to promote. There was healthy international demand for the commodities that Americans produced most efficiently, and American workers would never lack employment as long as the country had a supply of cheap land. While there were good non-economic reasons to protect industries needed for national defense, there was no good reason to protect other industries. The import duties needed for revenue alone would average 25 percent. Surely the incidental protection from duties that high was enough to sustain any domestic industry worth having. Even "Mr. Hamilton, so often quoted," had never proposed a protective duty higher than 15 percent.[69]

Gallatin's free trade memorial stung Henry Clay. Clay was the most vocal Congressional proponent of protective tariffs, and a national convention of the Republicans who opposed Andrew Jackson—the National Republicans—had just nominated him to run against Jackson for president in 1832. Clay was staking his presidential bid on the appeal of his "American System," which called for a national bank, federal funding for roads and canals, and tariff protection for domestic manufacturing. Gallatin's memorial squarely challenged a key component of that system. A week after the memorial appeared, Clay defended protective tariffs in a speech to Congress that lasted for three days.[70]

"Free trade! Free trade!" cried Clay. Why the call for free trade was as useless as "the cry of a spoiled child, in its nurse's arms, for the moon or the stars." Free trade never had existed, and it never would exist as long as European nations imposed their mercantile systems. Free trade was nothing but a prescription for recolonizing the United States under "the commercial dominion of Great Britain." Clay therefore was not surprised to find that the leading spokesman for free trade was a foreigner. Although this man had filled "some of the highest offices under this Government, during thirty years," he was "still at heart an alien" without true sympathy for the American people. "Go back to your native Europe," Clay bawled, and teach "her sovereigns your Utopian doctrines of free trade, and when you have prevailed on them" to drop their restrictions on American trade, then "come back and we shall be prepared to believe you."[71]

Gallatin was unruffled. He had gotten into the tariff fight, he told a South Carolina Congressman, only to help preserve the Union. While he believed that free trade was the best policy, he thought both sides should compromise. He urged free traders to stop quibbling over the constitutional principle and to accept high tariffs on some goods. In fact, he told them, lowering the tariffs would not increase cotton and other commodity exports as much as they thought it would. The tariff bill that

Congress passed a few months later did reduce tariffs on most goods to the 25 percent revenue rate. But the new bill failed to prevent a show-down between Jackson and the South Carolina free traders because the South Carolinians strongly objected to the high tariffs kept on iron and cotton textiles. They declared the tariff law null and unenforceable in South Carolina. Jackson's response was firm, and South Carolina finally backed down when Congress adopted a compromise bill that gradually reduced the tariffs on all goods to 20–25 percent over ten years. "I was, as far as I know," Gallatin later told a Pennsylvania Congressman, "the earliest public advocate in America of the principles of free trade, and I have seen no cause to change my opinion." There was no good reason to support "forced, hot-house products" that needed more protection than they got from a revenue tariff.[72]

Gallatin was completely in accord with the Jackson administration on what he saw as a much more vital policy—the repayment of the public debt. Jackson had built his program for government reform and retrenchment around the old Republican claim that public borrowing encouraged wasteful and corruptive government spending. Jackson was determined to extinguish the public debt, and his first inaugural address echoed the democratic argument against it that Republicans had been making for over thirty years. As long as the nation was in debt, Jackson declared, ordinary people could not achieve "real independence" because lenders, bankers, and wealthy investors would effectively control the government. Gallatin did not bash lenders and bankers, but he approved Jackson's commitment to debt repayment. When Jackson's administration paid off the last of the federal debt in January 1835, the event marked the culmination of Gallatin's efforts in political life. "Free from public debt [and] at peace with all the world," Jackson told Congress, the nation could now establish forever the domestic policies "best calculated to give stability to our Republic and secure the blessing of freedom to our citizens." And then, like a good Republican of the previous generation, Jackson reminded them of the "fundamental and sacred" principles of "rigid economy," moderate taxes, and strict limits on the federal government's power. By keeping government cheap and taxes low, Jackson declared, the government would give "all members of our happy Confederacy new motives for patriotic affection and support."[73]

Gallatin did not scramble to claim credit for paying off the public debt, but he did think that his contribution to this great accomplishment had been overlooked. He was grateful when a newspaper opposed to Jackson pointed out to its readers that Gallatin was the man who had put in place the fixed annual debt repayment plan that had extinguished the debt over the previous thirty-three years. Although Gallatin thought that even this newspaper's description failed to do him full justice, his characteristically matter-of-fact complaint to the editors could not disguise his quiet satisfaction. His essential breakthrough, he wrote, had been to replace "the mystifying and useless machinery with which Mr. Hamilton had...encumbered the very simple subject of paying the debt" with a repayment commitment that took priority over all other government spending. The government had repaid the national debt "without any...alteration" to his plan except for increases in the fixed annual payment to cover new debt incurred for the Louisiana purchase and the second war with Britain. Gallatin's quiet letter to the editors was a fitting coda to the financial reports he had written over a political lifetime. It made what had been complicated and contentious seem quite simple.[74]

Although Albert Gallatin never lost interest in national politics, he became deeply absorbed in other projects during his years in New York. Two intellectual projects were particularly important to him. The first was a plan for extending university education to students of all backgrounds. The second was a study of Native American language and culture.[75]

The idea for a great public university dedicated to educating ordinary people for the ordinary business of life was not entirely Gallatin's. The project had begun to take shape when a small group of New York merchants, bankers, clergymen, and other professionals held an organizational meeting in December 1829, shortly before Gallatin finished his work in Washington on the boundary arbitration. These men announced their goal in a prospectus published the following month. The mission of existing American colleges, they said, was to prepare a select number of young men for the learned professions. The colleges operated "in an exclusive spirit" for the benefit of "a privileged class." Their curriculum centered on Greek and Latin literature rather than the affairs of modern life. A great commercial city such as New York needed something more. It needed a university that could extend higher education in *"greater abundance and variety"* and *"at a cheaper rate"* to *"larger numbers of young persons."* The prospectus offered shares in an organization formed to establish such a university. Nine months later, the organizers asked Gallatin to help them arrange a convention of college leaders and other distinguished men from around the country to discuss plans for the new university. And just before the convention met, they elected Gallatin as president of the governing board for what they were calling the University of the City of New York.[76]

It was in a speech to the planning convention that Gallatin laid out his own vision for the new university. The main question at the convention was whether instruction in Greek and Latin was essential to a proper university education. Although the speakers were sympathetic to broadening the curriculum, they generally agreed that the best students should continue to receive a classical education. Gallatin's speech took a step back and then a leap forward. When the classical curriculum had developed centuries ago, he said, it was "adapted to the existing state of society." Most learned texts were written in classical languages, and men who sought knowledge had to learn those languages. But society had changed completely. Great men of letters now wrote in their own languages. Modern civilization depended on branches of knowledge entirely unknown to previous generations. And in a republic, good government depended on giving some of the ordinary people an advanced education. Every branch of learning deserved equal respect, Gallatin said, and students who had neither the means nor the desire to learn classical languages deserved equal access to a university education. The new university must therefore abolish any "invidious distinction" between students in the classical program and students in the sciences and other practical subjects.[77]

In a letter to an old Federalist who presided at Harvard College, Gallatin emphasized that reforming the universities would change the entire educational system. If students no longer needed to know Greek or Latin in order to get into a university, the lower schools could teach more practical subjects and raise the general standard of popular education. Gallatin hoped the schools would teach all of their students mathematics, natural science, history, and English literature. His ultimate aim, Gallatin explained to Badollet, was to foster "a general system of rational & practical education fitted for all & gratuitously opened to all." Democracy depended on bringing "the standard of general education & the mind of the labouring classes nearer to a level with those born under more favorable circumstances."[78]

Gallatin's vision for higher education of the common man was radical. Most Americans had begun to agree that republican government could not succeed unless citizens got an education. Many thought that the state governments should sponsor and pay for better schools. And advanced reformers wanted the states to fund universities that taught practical subjects and provided scholarships to talented students who could not otherwise afford a university education. Thomas Jefferson's plan for the University of Virginia embodied that vision. But implicit in the vision was a meritocratic assumption that higher education would lift talented scholarship students out of their own class. It would improve their lives by giving them access to better occupations, and it would fortify the republican regime by absorbing the most talented citizens into the governing class. Gallatin's vision was different. He thought a modern university should prepare ordinary people to pursue their ordinary occupations with greater skill and success. By giving equal respect to all courses of study, the university would affirm the dignity of the people of all classes and the value of all useful occupations. It also would contribute to the advances in science, commerce, and industry that were driving the country's economic development.[79]

Gallatin's vision was too bold, and by the time the new university in New York opened in the autumn of 1832, he had resigned from the governing board. He gave his health as the reason, but he privately complained that the organizers had fallen away from their aspirations. They had chosen a Dutch Reformed minister named James Mathews as the first chancellor, and he had given the project a sectarian turn. That was only part of the problem. Mathews was a poor businessman and, Gallatin told James Madison, he was "eminent in no science whatever, nor even as a scholar." Mathews committed nearly all of the university's subscription fund to the construction of a grand Gothic Revival building on Washington Square, and he decided not to give university degrees to students outside the classical program. The faculty publicly quarreled with Mathews over those decisions, and although the governing board supported him, they struggled to deal with his financial mismanagement. But New York University—as it soon was called—survived these birth pangs and eventually returned to its original goals. Today, students at its Gallatin School pursue studies shaped around their career goals, and an intranet portal named Albert gives access to the hubbub of modern university life.[80]

Gallatin's study of Native American languages had more immediate results. He had first begun to study Indian languages systematically while he was in Paris, and he continued the project during the brief time he lived in Baltimore. But Gallatin then set the work aside until 1831, when the American Antiquarian Society in Worcester, Massachusetts—which had seen references to his earlier work in a European publication—asked him to contribute an essay to its scholarly journal. At intervals over the next five years, Gallatin prepared a 422-page paper that he called "A Synopsis of the Indian Tribes within the United States East of the Rocky Mountains." It was a bold piece of work, assembling the vocabularies of eighty-one Native American languages that had been collected over more than a century (by Thomas Jefferson among others) and classifying them into twenty-eight language families based on Gallatin's analysis of their linguistic characteristics. In accompanying essays, Gallatin gave an overview of the North American tribes and their histories, a commentary on Native cultures, and an explanation of his philological method. Like others who studied aboriginal languages at the time, Gallatin thought philological analysis could shed light on the geographic and racial origins of the Native tribes, but he considered all of that speculative and his essays said relatively little about it. The society published his paper in 1836 along with a large foldout map on which Gallatin had plotted the distribution of tribes across the continent.[81]

No one had ever produced such a comprehensive study of American aboriginal languages. John Wesley Powell, who pioneered more scientific anthropology in the late nineteenth century when he headed the Smithsonian Institute's Bureau of American Ethnology, saluted Gallatin's work as "the starting point" for all later studies. As Linnaeus was the first to classify living organisms, Powell wrote, Gallatin was "the founder of systematic philology relating to the North American Indians." No scholar before him "had properly adopted comparative methods of research" or absorbed "so large a body of material." Although some of Gallatin's contemporaries criticized the "Synopsis" for giving more attention to vocabulary than to grammatical forms, the paper established Gallatin as a leader in the field. With the help of John Russell Bartlett—a New York bookseller, publisher, and antiquarian—Gallatin used his prestige to assemble others who were interested in aboriginal languages and culture into a new organization that he named the American Ethnological Society. The initial seventy-eight members included the few academics who had studied the subject, but most of the members were missionaries, Indian agents, diplomats, military officers, and armchair scholars in New York. The prominent Prussian scientist Alexander von Humboldt, who had encouraged Gallatin's interest in ethnology when they were both in Paris, was an honorary member. Gallatin wrote an extensive essay on the tribes of Mexico and Central America for the society's first journal. And at the age of eighty-eight, he gave the journal another long essay describing his latest investigations.[82]

But for all his interest in Native languages, Gallatin had little respect for Native cultures. During the years he was writing, the federal government removed over 46,000 Indians from the rich potential cotton lands they occupied in Georgia, Alabama, and Mississippi and forced the survivors to move west of the Mississippi River. Gallatin neither deplored nor approved the Indian removals. He simply considered them inevitable. Agriculture, he wrote in the "Synopsis," was the basis of all civilization, and as long as Native men thought pursuits other than war and hunting were beneath their dignity, the tribes were doomed. Some tribes did raise crops by making their women "slaves and beasts of burden," but the labor of the women alone could not compete with the "energetic industry" of white settlers. "The Indian disappears before the white man," wrote Gallatin, "simply because he will not work." The "laws of nature" required men to support their families, and "no nation, or individual" could avoid the divine decree that declared "labor to be the condition, on which man was permitted to exist."[83]

Gallatin thought that the Indian removals ultimately would accomplish nothing. "Let not the Indians entertain the illusory hope," he warned, "that they can persist in their habits, and remain...quiet possessors of the extensive territory west of the Mississippi lately given to them." White settlers would push farther west in the years ahead, and nations of hunters could not survive the onslaught of an industrious agricultural people. Like most white Americans of his generation, Gallatin thought Native assimilation into white culture was the only workable solution. If Native adult men would not change their ways, which seemed to him almost certain, then the survival of Native populations depended on proper education of the young people. But Gallatin did not bring to this project the same egalitarian notions that he had applied to reformed universities for white students. He did not think it was enough to teach ordinary Native children how to pursue the ordinary business of Native life more industriously. The children instead had to be lifted out of Native life. They should learn the English language so thoroughly, Gallatin wrote, "that they may forget their own." The aboriginal languages that so fascinated him would have to die so that the Native peoples who spoke them could live. Gallatin's ethnological project was essentially antiquarian. Although the seeds that he planted grew into a more scientific discipline, it was in many respects a "salvage ethnology" concerned with the surviving remnants of a civilization for which it held little hope.[84]

⁓

Gallatin's last public speech was his opening salvo in a campaign against impending war with Mexico. It was April 1844, and President John Tyler had just signed a treaty to annex a breakaway Mexican province calling itself the Republic of Texas. Texas was slave country, and since the line drawn in the Missouri Compromise closed most of the American West to slavery, Texas annexation was popular with Southern planters. But annexation would mean war with Mexico because the Mexican government refused to recognize Texas independence. President Jackson and his successor Martin Van Buren had resisted annexation for that reason. They feared that a war for slave territory would split the Republicans who supported them—the Democrats—along sectional lines. Tyler had a different perspective. He had come to office as a member of the Whig party that Henry Clay and the National Republicans formed in opposition to Jackson and Van Buren. But he had lost the party leaders' support, and he thought splitting the Democrats along sectional lines was the only way he could succeed in the 1844 presidential campaign. When Tyler forced the annexation issue, Van Buren took a stand against it, and his supporters in New York City organized a large meeting to oppose ratification of Tyler's treaty.[85]

Three thousand people attended the evening meeting. They crowded into the great circular galleries under the high domed ceiling of the Broadway Tabernacle, four blocks north of City Hall. The dim gaslight from the large fixture hung in the dome scarcely reached the back walls where five hundred of them had to stand. Albert Gallatin presided. He was eighty-three years old, he had shrunk, and when he began to speak, his voice was feeble. But as he warmed to his subject, his voice grew "firm and fervent." The United States, he told the crowd, "had never yet engaged in a disgraceful war for conquest" like the war that annexation would provoke. A radical Democrat named Mike Walsh and his working class hecklers interrupted at this point with cries of "Hurrah for Texas" and curses on Wall Street bankers. When the police restored order, the old man gathered his strength and went on. He said that those who courted war with Mexico in order to gain territory for slavery were endangering peace in their own country. He did not propose interfering with slavery in Texas or anywhere else that it already existed, but he warned that the North would meet those who tried to force the question of its expansion "boldly and unequivocally." Most of the crowd applauded. Gallatin "spoke with more force and more physical strength than one would have anticipated," a young lawyer wrote in his diary that night, "for he's very old and looks very infirm."[86]

Gallatin was growing weak, but his prestige was strong. He was the sole surviving member of the original Republican establishment. Jefferson had died in 1826, Monroe in 1831, and Madison in 1836. When Clay and other National Republicans formed the Whig party and tried to prevent Van Buren's election, Gallatin had remained with the Democrats. Some Democrats proudly pointed to him as living proof that they were the true political heirs of Thomas Jefferson. Others thought Gallatin had effectively deserted them over most of the issues of the day. The populist Democratic *New York Herald* dismissed him and the other organizers of the Tabernacle meeting as a bunch of "stock-jobbers, speculators, financiers, mixed and blended with a few politicians in Wall street" who cared more about the effect war would have on their "paper property" than they did about the nation's future greatness. Yet if anyone had asked Gallatin why he was still a Democrat, he could easily have explained. He thought that politics was a practical business and that men accomplished more when they made some allowances for their political friends. His old friends Thomas Jefferson and Nathaniel Macon had hated banks, but he had worked together with them for years. He did not think, on the other hand, that good politicians should keep silent when they thought their friends were going wrong. So when a relatively unknown Democrat from Tennessee named James Polk got himself elected president by supporting Texas annexation, Gallatin girded to oppose the coming war.[87]

To everyone's surprise, the first threat of war under Polk's administration came from the Oregon territory. Both Britain and the United States still occupied Oregon under the treaty Gallatin had negotiated in 1827, but Polk—who thought the addition of free territory would reduce Northern resistance to the annexation of Texas—threatened to expel the British by force unless they conceded Oregon to the United States. In four newspaper essays, Gallatin drew on his long familiarity with the Oregon problem to point out diplomatic solutions. But a fifth and final essay brought him to a more fundamental point. Nothing the United States could gain in Oregon, he said, was worth what it would cost to fight another war with Britain. Gallatin had contended since the presidency of John Adams that war was a waste of money, but in his usual methodical way, he calculated the projected costs and benefits of this war in enough detail to prove it. The United States and Britain did find a diplomatic solution in Oregon. Britain agreed to extend the Canadian boundary all the way to the Pacific along the 49th parallel that already defined it east of the Rocky Mountains, giving virtually all of the disputed territory to the United States.[88]

But Polk's government made it impossible for Mexico to back down. Polk not only completed the annexation of Texas, he also insisted that the Rio Grande was the new state's southern boundary. That claim pushed Mexican tempers to the breaking point. The Rio Grande was about 150 miles south of the smaller Nueces River that marked the traditional border of the old province of Tejas. Nationalists in the Mexican army overthrew the Mexican government to stop it from receiving an envoy Polk had sent to discuss the subject. Polk ordered American troops into the disputed area along the Rio Grande in April 1846, and the Mexican army attacked them. The maneuver was a trap for Polk's antiwar opponents, and it worked. With sixteen American soldiers killed or wounded, Polk could claim that Mexico had spilled American blood on American soil. Two days later, Congress declared war. Only fourteen representatives and two senators dared to vote against it. One of them was an unbendable seventy-nine-year-old Congressman from Massachusetts named John Quincy Adams.[89]

Gallatin took up his pen a year later when making peace with Mexico had become more difficult than making war. American troops had seized the Mexican provinces of Alta California and Nuevo México, occupied Mexico City, and devastated much of the rest of the country. But Mexico refused to surrender the conquered provinces. What had begun as a war over the Texas border was revealed to be a grab for a chunk of the continent, and continued Mexican resistance now highlighted a contradiction in American policy. A war fought for territory antagonized the people who lived in it, and a democratic political system could not incorporate a hostile alien population without subverting its own political values. The American government hardly dared to deny them political rights, but it neither respected them nor trusted them to be good citizens.[90]

In a pamphlet entitled *Peace with Mexico*, Gallatin traced the problem to its source and called for national repentance. The only just wars were defensive wars, he said, and even they brought on great evils. "What shall we say," therefore, of a war "provoked by ourselves, of a war of aggression, which is now publicly avowed to be one of intended conquest?" Such a war was unworthy of a "representative democratic republic" which had set out to show the world that free men left to govern themselves could live in peace. Indeed, the war had perverted American citizens' most essential virtue—their patriotism—into a means for undoing that great republican vision. Men who would not think of taking their neighbor's farm had been encouraged to seize a neighboring nation's land. In the absence of any decent justification for doing that, they had resorted to the "extraordinary assertion" that Anglo-Saxons were a superior race destined to bring enlightenment and improvement to the "degraded Mexicans." That claim, declared Gallatin, was completely incompatible with the immutable democratic principle "that no one man is born with the right to govern another man." There could be nothing more glorious for the American republic than the abandonment of all conquered lands. A just peace would settle the Texas boundary, set reasonable indemnities for private claims, and leave everything else to be resolved later when passions had cooled.[91]

Although Gallatin called his peace pamphlet mere "seeds thrown to the wind," he worked hard to get ninety thousand copies distributed. He paid for four thousand copies himself, and he solicited support for wider distribution from clergymen and community leaders around the country. "I am persuaded," he told Harvard president Edward Everett, that apart from "money and other worldly considerations," the only thing that "can successfully counteract the spirit of conquest, cupidity, and false glory...is the deep religious feeling which providentially still pervades the whole country." But Gallatin was pessimistic about the strength of morality. *"The weak appeal to justice; the strong appeal to might,"* he told a friend. "Our revolutionary fathers were weak," so "they gloried in the justice of their cause. Now, it is the Mexicans who are weak; and we are glorying in our national strength." So he turned to the persuasive power of money.[92]

Early in 1848, Gallatin published a new pamphlet called *War Expenses* to explain that the rising cost of the war threatened the American economy. He called for an end to the occupation of Mexico, and he berated members of Congress who let themselves be cowed into thinking that "simply because we are at war, we are bound to adopt the views of the President" and give him "all the money and all the men he requires." Britain may have beaten France and won a great empire, he told a Whig Congressman, but the resulting war debt had crippled the ordinary British people. A war to create a great Anglo-Saxon empire "extending from the Atlantic to the Pacific, and from the North Pole to the Equator" would do the same thing to the American people. Manifest destiny was only a disguise for "ambition, cupidity, or silly vanity." "The most important point, if we have peace," he wrote to another Whig Congressman, "is to ascertain the amount of our public debt." But the *New York Herald* dismissed Gallatin's new pamphlet entirely. Mr. Gallatin's tedious views might "have done very well about thirty years ago," it said, "but they are now awfully behind the present age." Surely Mexico could be made to pay "for its own occupation."[93]

Gallatin followed the published debates intently when the Senate began to consider a peace treaty with Mexico just a few months later.

The treaty extended the Texas border to the Rio Grande, ceded Alta California and most of Nuevo México to the United States, and offered indemnities for private claims. Gallatin sent letters of encouragement to senators John C. Calhoun and Thomas Hart Benton, who were working to stop Jefferson Davis and other Southern senators from demanding even more territory. But Gallatin's hands had grown stiff, and he now had to rely on dictation. "I can work only three or four hours a day," he complained to a visitor, "where I could once work twelve." He was relieved when the Senate ratified the peace treaty without major changes.[94]

Albert and Hannah Gallatin spent the summer of 1848 with their daughter Frances Stevens and her family at the Stevens's country place in Astoria, a fashionable exurb across the East River from Manhattan. Even there, Albert found the heat disabling and he often felt too weak to get out of bed. He summoned strength enough to return to his house on Bleecker Street in the autumn, but he fell back into bed during the winter. With his body confined, his mind raced. He found himself "thinking and philosophizing on subjects which occupied my attention years ago," but losing track of "the passing events of the day." He pondered religion. He had always considered himself a Christian, but he had never been as devout as Hannah, Frances, and other members of the Nicholson family. He was too skeptical to accept theological doctrines about the dual nature of Christ and the predestination of human souls. But he tried to climb beyond his doubts to gain peace through repentance and forgiveness. His family invited Presbyterian clergymen to visit him, and they listened anxiously for assurance that he had been saved. "I have no unkind feelings toward any human being," he murmured to one of his nieces. "I was afraid I had some remains of unkindness toward—but I have subdued it all." "By prayer?" she pressed him. "Surely," he said, "by prayer. What could I do of myself?" "*It was deeply impressed on him,*" a visiting minister carefully recorded for his daughter's benefit, "*that we can be saved only by Jesus Christ.*"[95]

Albert was too weak to leave the bed in his library when Hannah Gallatin died in the bedroom next door in May 1849. Her death was a blow from which he could not recover. Mrs. Gallatin's eighty-eight-year-old husband still survives, read her obituary, "a relic of the early days of freedom." But his health "is said to be very precarious, and the death of his wife has militated against his speedy recovery." He could not attend her funeral at St. Thomas Church on upper Broadway or her burial in the Nicholson family vault beside the soaring spire of Trinity Church about a mile and a half down the street. Frances Stevens took him to stay with her in Astoria for the summer. He died there three months later on August 12, 1849. His funeral was at Trinity Church, and he was buried with his wife. Philip Hone, a leading New Yorker who knew Gallatin well, entered a short eulogy in his diary: "This man of many generations, this politician of many parties, this philosopher of many theories, has finished his long and eventful career."[96]

Newspapers of both political parties mourned Gallatin. "His name is linked inseparably with the history of the American republic, almost from its cradle," intoned the Democratic *New York Herald*. Horace Greeley, the Whig editor of the *New-York Tribune*, memorialized him as the "powerful leader of the opposition phalanx in Congress at the end of the eighteenth century," the "last, the only survivor of the cabinets of Jefferson and Madison," and a warm friend of the Whigs. The *Daily Union*, Washington's leading Democratic paper, conceded that "Mr. G. [had] differed in many respects from the democratic party" toward the close of his life, but it applauded the energy with which he had advocated his opinions. He "was a great man," it said, "and we cheerfully express the veneration which is due to his memory." All of the newspapers credited Gallatin for his moderation during the Whiskey Rebellion, but Philip Hone privately reflected that Gallatin's involvement in the insurrection was "a stain to his political character" which he must have regretted.[97]

A finely carved Gothic Revival sarcophagus marks Albert and Hannah Gallatin's tomb on the north side of Trinity Church, and a young shade tree grows nearby. A short walk away in a sunnier spot on the south side of the church, a neoclassical obelisk stands on the grave of Alexander Hamilton.[98]

ACKNOWLEDGMENTS

Anyone who writes about Albert Gallatin is greatly indebted to the editors of *The Papers of Albert Gallatin*, an ambitious microfilm edition sponsored by New York University and the National Historical Publications Commission. My quibbles with the dating of a few documents in the fifty-one-reel project are not meant to detract in the slightest from the editors' enormous accomplishment.

Everyone who studies the Early Republic owes a similar debt to the editors of the George Washington, Alexander Hamilton, Thomas Jefferson, and James Madison papers projects for their well edited and richly annotated letterpress editions and to the National Historic Publications Commission and the University of Virginia Press for putting the material online. Although the Early Access transcriptions in *Founders Online* are unedited drafts, I have cited them when there are no published transcriptions or when they are more accurate than the published transcriptions. *Founders Online* gives the archival location of the original documents.

Many fine libraries have given me gracious assistance. My principal debt is to the Library of Congress and its outstanding librarians, particularly those in the Manuscript Reading Room, the Newspaper and Current Periodical Reading Room, the Law Library, and the Rare Book and Special Collections Reading Room. I also am grateful to the University of Virginia, International Center for Jefferson Studies, New-York Historical Society, New York Public Library, Senator John Heinz History Center, University of Pittsburgh, American Antiquarian Association, Massachusetts Historical Society, Historical Society of Pennsylvania, Library of Virginia, Virginia Historical Society, Duke University, University of Oregon, Huntington Library, University of Michigan, Enoch Pratt Free Library, University of Notre Dame, and the National Park Service's Friendship Hill National Historic Site and Belmont-Paul Women's Equality National Monument.

For the courtesy of illustrations, I am grateful to the New-York Historical Society, Library of Congress, Maryland Historical Society, Pennsylvania Academy of the Fine Arts, Metropolitan Museum of Arts, Indiana Historical Society, Albert and Shirley Small Special Collections Library at the University of Virginia, Smithsonian American Art Museum, Huntington Library, Historical Society of Pennsylvania, and the National Park Service's Independence National Historical Park. For permission to use the excerpt from T. S. Eliot's "Little Gidding" as an epigraph, I thank Houghton Mifflin Harcourt Publishing Company (copyright 1936 by Houghton Mifflin Harcourt Publishing Company; copyright renewed 1964 by T. S. Eliot; copyright 1940, 1942 by T. S. Eliot; copyright renewed 1968, 1970 by Esme Valerie Eliot).

The materials so richly available could not have yielded this book were it not for extremely generous help from several people. David O. Stewart, a longtime friend who has been writing outstanding American history for years, gave me inspiration, plentiful encouragement, and excellent guidance. Peter S. Onuf, who more than deserves his celebrated reputation for wisdom and liberality, asked questions that sent me in the right direction and offered critical reassurance along the way. Andrew Burstein and Nancy Isenberg, whose books on the Early Republic have helped me enormously, were enthusiastic about a new study of Gallatin from the start and kind enough to befriend a poor wanderer who had set out to accomplish it. For the advice, manuscript comments, and friendship of all of them, I am more grateful than I can say.

Others have lent me valuable advice and skillful assistance on this project, and I am very thankful to each one of them. Richard Whatmore kindly read part of the manuscript and shared his exceptional insights into eighteenth-century Geneva. Elizabeth Trapnell Rawlings made English translations that resonate with the original Genevan voices. Megan Kennedy and Julia May brought insight and energy to research projects that required considerable commitment. Kitty Seifert kept me straight about the history of Gallatin's house in western Pennsylvania. David B. Mattern, John Ruston Pagan, and John Ragosta were willing to talk when I needed thoughtful reactions. The participants in the Early American Seminar at the University of Virginia gave me great criticism and great examples. Roger Williams was a firm supporter, a patient teacher, and an excellent literary agent. Alex Novak adeptly shepherded this book to publication, and Elizabeth Kantor edited it with consummate skill, efficiency, and good sense.

For Anna—to whom this book is dedicated—there are not enough syllables in the whole world.

ENDNOTE ABBREVIATIONS

Annals	Annals of Congress: *The Debates and Proceedings of the Congress of the United States.* 42 vols.; Washington, DC: Gales and Seaton, 1834–56; repr., Buffalo, NY: William S. Hein, 2003.
ASP	*American State Papers:* [in 10 classes]. 38 vols.; Washington, DC: Gales and Seaton, 1832–61; repr., Buffalo, NY: William S. Hein, 1998.
CBG	Gayle Thornbrough, ed. *The Correspondence of John Badollet and Albert Gallatin, 1804–1836.* Indianapolis: Indiana Historical Society, 1963.
DHFFE	Merrill Jensen and Robert A. Becker, eds. *The Documentary History of the First Federal Elections, 1788–1790.* 4 vols.; Madison: University of Wisconsin Press, 1976–90.
DHRC	Merrill Jensen et al., eds. *The Documentary History of the Ratification of the Constitution.* 26 vols. to date; Madison: State Historical Society of Wisconsin, 1976–.
DLC	Library of Congress, Washington, DC.
FOL	*Founders Online*, www.founders.archives.gov.
Gibbs, Memoirs	George Gibbs [Jr.], ed. *Memoirs of the Administrations of Washington and John Adams....* 2 vols.; New York, 1846.
JHNP	Joseph Hopper Nicholson Papers, Library of Congress, Washington, DC.
LAG	Henry Adams. *The Life of Albert Gallatin.* 1879; repr., New York: Peter Smith, 1943.
L&B	Andrew Adgate Lipscomb and Albert Ellery Bergh, eds. *The Writings of Thomas Jefferson,* Definitive Edition. 20 vols.; Washington, DC: Thomas Jefferson Memorial Association, 1907.

Laws of Pennsylvania (Dallas Reprint)	*Laws of the Commonwealth of Pennsylvania*. Ed. Alexander James Dallas. 4 vols.; Philadelphia and Lancaster, 1793–1801.
LCRK	Charles R. King, ed. *The Life and Correspondence of Rufus King*. 6 vols.; 1894–1900; repr., New York: Da Capo Press, 1971.
LJCMC	William Parker Cutler and Julia Perkins Cutler, ed. *Life, Journals and Correspondence of Rev. Manasseh Cutler, LL.D.* 2 vols.; 1888; repr., Athens: Ohio University Press, 1987.
LJT	William E. Dodd, ed. "Letters of John Taylor, of Caroline County, Virginia." *John P. Branch Historical Papers of Randolph-Macon College* 2, nos. 3 and 4 (June 1908): 253–353.
LJAB	Maris Stella Connelly, ed. "The Letters and European Travel Journal of James A. Bayard, 1812–1815." Ph.D. diss., Boston University, 2007.
Maclay's Diary	Kenneth R. Bowling and Helen E. Veit, eds. *The Diary of William Maclay and Other Notes on Senate Debates*. Baltimore: Johns Hopkins University Press, 1988.
Minutes of the Committee of the Whole	*Minutes of the Grand Committee of the Whole Convention of the Commonwealth of Pennsylvania...for...Altering and Amending the Constitution...* Philadelphia, [1790].
Minutes of the Convention	*Minutes of the Convention of the Commonwealth of Pennsylvania...for...Altering and Amending the Constitution...* Philadelphia, 1789.
PAG	Carl E. Prince and Helene E. Fineman, eds. *The Papers of Albert Gallatin: Microfilm Edition*. 46 reels; Philadelphia: Historic Publications, 1969.*
PAG-S	Barbara B. Oberg, ed. *Supplement to the Papers of Albert Gallatin: Microfilm Edition*. 5 reels; Wilmington, DE: Scholarly Resources, 1985.

---

* To make references to items in *The Papers of Albert Gallatin* more accessible, these notes often cite reliable published transcriptions, and they occasionally cite other useful transcriptions as versions after giving a citation to the *Papers*. Some of the letters between Albert and Hannah Gallatin survive only as published in Henry Adams's *Life of Albert Gallatin*.

PAH	Harold C. Syrett, ed. *The Papers of Alexander Hamilton.* 27 vols.; New York: Columbia University Press, 1961–87.
PCAB	Mary-Jo Kline and Joanne Wood Ryan, eds. *Political Correspondence and Public Papers of Aaron Burr.* 2 vols.; Princeton, NJ: Princeton University Press, 1983.
Pennsylvania House Journal 1790-91	*Journal of the First House of Representatives of the Commonwealth of Pennsylvania.* Philadelphia, 1790.
Pennsylvania House Journal 1791-92	*Journal of the Second House of Representatives of the Commonwealth of Pennsylvania.* Philadelphia, 1791.
Pennsylvania House Journal 1792-93	*Journal of the Third House of Representatives of the Commonwealth of Pennsylvania.* Philadelphia, 1792.
Pennsylvania House Journal 1794-95	*Journal of the Fifth House of Representatives of the Commonwealth of Pennsylvania.* Philadelphia, 1795.
Pennsylvania Senate Journal 1790-91	*Journal of the Senate of the Commonwealth of Pennsylvania.* Philadelphia, 1790.
PGW-ConS	W. W. Abbot et al., eds. *The Papers of George Washington: Confederation Series.* 6 vols.; Charlottesville: University Press of Virginia, 1992–97.
PGW-PS	Dorothy Twohig et al., eds. *The Papers of George Washington: Presidential Series.* 19 vols.; Charlottesville: University of Virginia Press, 1987–2016.
PJAB	Elizabeth Donnan, ed. "Papers of James A. Bayard, 1796–1815." *Annual Report of the American Historical Association for 1913.* 2 vols.; Washington, DC, 1915.
PJM-CS	William T. Hutchinson et al., eds. *The Papers of James Madison,* Congressional Series. 17 vols.; Chicago: University of Chicago Press, 1962–1977, and Charlottesville: University of Virginia Press, 1977–1991.
PJM-SS	Robert J. Brugger et al., eds. *The Papers of James Madison, Secretary of State Series.* 11 vols. to date; Charlottesville: University of Virginia Press, 1986–.

PJM-PS	Robert A. Rutland et al., eds. *The Papers of James Madison, Presidential Series.* 8 vols. to date; Charlottesville: University of Virginia Press, 1984–.
PJM-RS	David B. Mattern et al., eds. *The Papers of James Madison, Retirement Series.* 3 vols. to date; Charlottesville: University of Virginia Press, 2009–.
PTJ	Julian P. Boyd et al., eds. *The Papers of Thomas Jefferson.* 43 vols. to date; Princeton, NJ: Princeton University Press, 1950–.
PTJ-RS	J. Jefferson Looney et al., eds. *The Papers of Thomas Jefferson, Retirement Series.* 13 vols. to date; Charlottesville: University of Virginia Press, 2004–.
Richardson, Messages and Papers	James D. Richardson, ed. *A Compilation of the Messages and Papers of the Presidents, 1789–1897.* 10 vols.; Washington, DC, 1896–99.
Senate Executive Journal	*Journal of the Executive Proceedings of the Senate of the United States,* [1st through 19th Congresses]. 3 vols.; Washington, DC, 1828.
Statutes at Large	*The Public Statutes at Large of the United States of America.* 17 vols.; Boston: Little, Brown, 1845–73.
SWAG	E. James Ferguson, ed. *Selected Writings of Albert Gallatin.* Indianapolis: Bobbs-Merrill, 1967.
TJW	Merrill D. Peterson, comp. *Thomas Jefferson: Writings.* New York: Library of America, 1984.
WAG	Henry Adams, ed. *The Writings of Albert Gallatin.* 3 vols.; 1879; repr., New York: Antiquarian Press, 1960.
WFA	Seth Ames, ed. *Works of Fisher Ames....* 2 vols.; Boston, 1854.
WJQA	Worthington Chauncey Ford, ed. *Writings of John Quincy Adams.* 7 vols.; New York: Macmillan, 1913–17.
WTJ	Paul Leicester Ford, ed. *The Works of Thomas Jefferson,* Federal Edition. 12 vols.; New York: Putnam, 1904–05.

NOTES

Introduction

1. Philadelphia *Gazette of the United States*, 24 March (letter from New York), 13 and 14 May, 14 October 1801; Boston *Columbian Centinel*, 18 April and 29 July 1801.

2. Lee Soltow, *Distribution of Wealth and Income in the United States in 1798* (Pittsburgh: University of Pittsburgh Press, 1989), 153–55; Allan Kulikoff, "'Such Things Ought Not to Be': The American Revolution and the First National Depression," in *The World of the Revolutionary American Republic: Land, Labor, and the Conflict for a Continent*, ed. Andrew Shankman (New York: Routledge, 2014), 152–53.

3. E. James Ferguson, *The Power of the Purse: A History of American Public Finance, 1776–1790* (Chapel Hill: University of North Carolina Press, 1961), 256–57, 272–86; Thomas M. Doerflinger, *A Vigorous Spirit of Enterprise: Merchants and Economic Development in Revolutionary Philadelphia* (Chapel Hill: University of North Carolina Press, 1986), 310–14; Robert E. Wright, *One Nation under Debt: Hamilton, Jefferson, and the History of What We Owe* (New York: McGraw Hill, 2008), 124, 164, 308 (concentration of federal debt ownership in 1795); Whitney K. Bates, "Northern Speculators and Southern State Debts: 1790," *William and Mary Quarterly*, 3rd Ser., 19, no. 1 (January, 1962): 37–39.

4. [Alexander Hamilton], Federalist Nos. 17 and 34, *The Federalist*, ed. Jacob E. Cooke (Middletown, CT: Wesleyan University Press, 1961), 105, 210, 214; [Hamilton], The Continentalist Nos. IV and V, 30 August 1781 and 18 April 1782, *PAH*, 2:669–74, 3:75–82; Forrest McDonald, *Alexander Hamilton: A Biography* (New York: W. W. Norton, 1979), 38–43; Stanley Elkins and Eric McKitrick, *The Age of Federalism: The Early American Republic, 1788–1800* (New York: Oxford University Press, 1993), 92–123, 750–51; Max M. Edling, *A Revolution in Favor of Government: Origins of the U. S. Constitution and the Making of the*

American State (New York: Oxford University Press, 2003), 222–27. For more critical assessments of Hamilton's policies, see Stephen F. Knott, *Alexander Hamilton and the Persistence of Myth* (Lawrence: University Press of Kansas, 2002), 214–24; Herbert E. Sloan, "Hamilton's Second Thoughts: Federalist Finance Revisited," in *Federalists Reconsidered*, ed. Doron Ben-Atar and Barbara B. Oberg (Charlottesville: University Press of Virginia, 1998), 63–67; Carey Robert, "Alexander Hamilton and the 1790s Economy: A Reappraisal," in *The Many Faces of Alexander Hamilton: The Life and Legacy of America's Most Elusive Founding Father,* ed. Douglas Ambrose and Robert W. T. Martin (New York: New York University Press, 2006), 213–26; Mark Schmeller, "The Political Economy of Opinion: Public Credit and Concepts of Public Opinion in the Age of Federalism," *Journal of the Early Republic* 29, no. 1 (Spring, 2009): 58–60.

5.   Hamilton, Plan for the Support of Public Credit, 9 January 1790, *ASP: Finance,* 1:15–16. Hamilton based his funding system on the British system developed during the eighteenth century. The British Crown and the North American colonial governments both issued short-term tax-anticipation loans that gave holders the right to receive principal and interest from the anticipated revenues of a specific tax in particular years. As a series of wars demanded increasingly large amounts of money, the taxes that the British government thought its population could bear became insufficient to repay the amounts the government needed to borrow. The Crown therefore began to issue so-called funded debt, which was more like a perpetual annuity than a debt obligation. The government pledged to pay interest on the funded debt from specified tax revenues as long as the debt remained outstanding, but the debt had no stated maturity date. John Sinclair, *The History of the Public Revenue of the British Empire,* 3rd ed. (3 vols.; 1803–04; repr. New York: Augustus M. Kelley, 1966), 1:344–79, 2:129, 135–37, 141–42; P. G. M. Dickson, *The Financial Revolution in England: A Study in the Development of Public Credit, 1688–1756* (London: Macmillan, 1967), 50–52.

6.   Hamilton, Plan for the Support of Public Credit, 1:17–18. Hamilton also knew that assumption and funding of state debts would ameliorate the burdensome state taxation that had incited disorder in some heavily indebted states. Hamilton, Objections and Answers respecting the Administration of the Government, 18 August 1792; Hamilton, Defense of the Funding System, July 1795, *PAH,* 12:229–58, 19:89.

7. Act of 4 August 1790, *Statutes at Large* 1 (1845): 138–44; Act of 5 August 1790, ibid., 1:178–79; Act of 10 August 1790, ibid., 1:180–82; Act of 12 August 1790, ibid., 1:186–87. At the time, government obligations with long or indefinite maturities were called "stocks" rather than bonds. This book uses the modern terms "bonds" for long-term government debt and "notes" for short-term government debt.

8. Ferguson, *The Power of the Purse,* 303–04, 326–29.

9. Hamilton, Plan for the Support of Public Credit, 1:22–24; Hamilton, Further Provision for Establishing the Public Credit, 13 December 1790, *ASP: Finance,* 1:64–66; Act of 10 August 1790, *Statutes at Large* 1 (1845): 180–82; Act of 3 March 1791, ibid., 1:199–214; Davis Rich Dewey, *Financial History of the United States,* 9th ed. (New York: Longmans, Green, 1924), 81–83; Max M. Edling and Mark D. Kaplanoff, "Alexander Hamilton's Fiscal Reform: Transforming the Structure of Taxation in the Early Republic," *William and Mary Quarterly,* 3rd Ser., 61, no. 4 (October 2004): 738–42; Frederick Arthur Baldwin Dalzell, "Taxation with Representation: Federal Revenue in the Early Republic" (Ph.D. diss., Harvard University, 1993), 289–97. Hamilton later obtained excises on snuff, refined sugar, auction sales, wine sales, and carriages as well as a stamp tax on legal documents. Those excises did not produce material revenue. Tench Coxe, Report of the Commissioner of the Revenue, 29 February 1796, *ASP: Finance,* 1:386–88, 403.

10. Edwin J. Perkins, *American Public Finance and Financial Services, 1700–1815* (Columbus: Ohio State University Press, 1994), 232–33; Gautham Rao, *National Duties: Custom Houses and the Making of the American State* (Chicago: University of Chicago Press, 2016), 54–69; Patrick K. O'Brien, "The Political Economy of British Taxation, 1660–1815," *Economic History Review,* New Ser., 41, no. 1 (February 1988), 8–17. For discussion of the contemporary belief that indirect or consumption taxes put the tax burden on those best able to bear it, see Clement Fatovic, *America's Founding and the Struggle over Economic Inequality* (Lawrence: University Press of Kansas, 2015), 137–48.

11. Hamilton, Further Provision for Establishing the Public Credit, 1:67–76; Bray Hammond, *Banks and Politics in America from the Revolution to the Civil War* (Princeton, NJ: Princeton University Press, 1957), 48, 77, 144; Donald F. Swanson, "The Origins of Hamilton's Fiscal Policies," *University of Florida Monographs: Social Sciences* 17 (Winter 1963): 11–17, 37–42.

12. Act of 25 February 1791, *Statutes at Large* 1 (1845): 191–96; Act of 2 March 1791, ibid, 1:196–97; Howard Bodenhorn, *State Banking in Early America: A New Economic History* (New York: Oxford University Press, 2003), 130; Edling, *A Revolution in Favor of Government,* 49–55.

13. Elkins and McKitrick, *The Age of Federalism,* 136–52; Lance Banning, *The Sacred Fire of Liberty: James Madison and the Founding of the Federal Republic* (Ithaca, NY: Cornell University Press, 1995), 325–33; Herbert E. Sloan, *Principle and Interest: Thomas Jefferson and the Problem of Debt* (New York: Oxford University Press, 1995), 22–24, 30–32, 126–28, 160–64, 167–68, 171.

14. David J. Siemers, *Ratifying the Republic: Antifederalists and Federalists in Constitutional Time* (Stanford, CA: Stanford University Press, 2002), 108–28; Andrew Burstein and Nancy Isenberg, *Madison and Jefferson* (New York: Random House, 2010), 221–24; E. James Ferguson, "Public Finance and the Origins of Southern Sectionalism," *Journal of Southern History* 28, no. 4 (November 1962): 457–61; Benjamin B. Klubes, "The First Federal Congress and the First National Bank: A Case Study in Constitutional Interpretation," *Journal of the Early Republic* 10, no. 1 (Spring 1990): 23–26.

15. [James Madison], "The Union, Who Are Its Real Friends?" 31 March 1792, *PJM-CS,* 14:274–75; Hamilton to Edward Carrington, 26 May 1792, *PAH,* 11:426–45; Noble E. Cunningham Jr., *The Jeffersonian Republicans: The Formation of Party Organization, 1789–1801* (Chapel Hill: University of North Carolina Press, 1957), 8–32; Rudolph M. Bell, *Party and Faction in American Politics: The House of Representatives, 1789–1801* (Westport, CT: Greenwood Press, 1973), 17–31, 95–131; John F. Hoadley, *Origins of American Political Parties, 1789–1803* (Lexington: University Press of Kentucky, 1986), 107-17; Elkins and McKitrick, *The Age of Federalism,* 703; Siemers, *Ratifying the Republic,* 114–21, 135–63; Gordon S. Wood, *Revolutionary Characters: What Made the Founders Different* (New York: Penguin Press, 2006), 162–65, 231–49; John H. Aldrich, *Why Parties? A Second Look* (Chicago: University of Chicago Press, 2011), 79–94; Douglas Blackburn, "'Parties Are Unavoidable': Path Dependence and the Origins of Party Politics in the United States," in *Practicing Democracy: Popular Politics in the United States from the Constitution to the Civil War,* ed. Daniel Peart and Adam I. P. Smith (Charlottesville: University of Virginia Press, 2015), 31–34.

16. *Annals,* 2nd Cong., 1st Sess., 447–52, 521–25 (William Findley); ibid., 2nd Cong., 2nd Sess., 546–47 (William Branch Giles); Cunningham, *The*

Jeffersonian Republicans: Formation, 67–85; Lance Banning, *The Jeffersonian Persuasion: Evolution of a Party Ideology* (Ithaca, NY: Cornell University Press, 1978), 126–60; Drew R. McCoy, *The Elusive Republic: Political Economy in Jeffersonian America* (Chapel Hill: University of North Carolina Press, 1980), 152–59; Joyce Appleby, *Liberalism and Republicanism in the Historical Imagination* (Cambridge, MA: Harvard University Press, 1991), 291–319.

17. Jefferson, Notes on stockholders in Congress, 23 March 1793, *PTJ,* 25:432–35; [William Findley], *A Review of the Revenue System Adopted by the First Congress...* (Philadelphia, 1794), 48–50; 52–60; Carl E. Prince, *The Federalists and the Origins of the U. S. Civil Service* (New York: New York University Press, 1977), 155; Edling, *A Revolution in Favor of Government,* 59–70; Richard Vernier, "The Fortunes of Orthodoxy: The Political Economy of Public Debt in England and America in the 1780s," in *Articulating America: Fashioning a National Political Culture in Early America,* ed. Rebecca Starr (Lanham, MD: Rowan and Littlefield, 2000), 118–24; Gordon S. Wood, "Rhetoric and Reality in the American Revolution," *William and Mary Quarterly,* 3rd Ser., 23, no. 1 (January 1966): 3–32; John Howe, "Gordon S. Wood and the Analysis of Political Culture in the American Revolutionary Era," ibid., 44, no. 3 (July 1987): 569–75.

18. Jefferson to Madison, 21 September 1795, *PTJ,* 28:475; Cunningham, *The Jeffersonian Republicans: Formation,* 51-54.

19. Jefferson, Notes on Alexander Hamilton's Report on Foreign Loans, [after 4 January 1793] and [about 20 February 1793]; Jefferson, Resolutions on the Secretary of the Treasury, [before 27 February 1793]; Jefferson to Hamilton, 27 March 1793; Jefferson to James Monroe, 5 May 1793, *PTJ,* 25:20–23, 239–43, 292–94, 460–63, 660–63; *Annals,* 2nd Cong., 2nd Sess., 905, 955–63; Elkins and McKitrick, *The Age of Federalism,* 295–302; Richard Sylla, "Financial Foundations: Public Credit, the National Bank, and Securities Markets," in *Founding Choices: American Economic Policy in the 1790s,* ed. Douglas A. Irwin and Richard Sylla (Chicago: University of Chicago Press, 2011), 77–78; Eugene R. Sheridan, "Thomas Jefferson and the Giles Resolutions," *William and Mary Quarterly,* 3rd Ser., 49, no. 4 (October 1992): 600–607. For the further investigation into the Treasury that Hamilton requested, see Madison to Jefferson, 26 March 1794, *PJM-CS,* 15:294–96; Jacob E. Cooke, *Alexander Hamilton* (New York: Charles Scribner's Sons, 1982), 137–39.

20. Madison to Jefferson, 31 January 1796, *PJM-CS*, 16:208–10; Jefferson to Madison, 6 March 1796, *PTJ*, 29:6–8.

21. Albert Gallatin, *A Sketch of the Finances of the United States* (New York, 1796); Gallatin, *Views of the Public Debt, Receipts and Expenditures of the United States* (New York, 1800); Adam Smith, *An Inquiry into the Nature and Causes of the Wealth of Nations*, ed. Edwin Cannan (1789; New York: Modern Library, 1937), 877–81; Emma Rothschild, *Economic Sentiments: Adam Smith, Condorcet, and the Enlightenment* (Cambridge, MA: Harvard University Press, 2001), 55–57, 68 –69; Samuel Fleischacker, *On Adam Smith's* Wealth of Nations: *A Philosophical Companion* (Princeton, NJ: Princeton University Press, 2004), 14–19; Vernier, "Fortunes of Orthodoxy," 94–105, 128–29; Sylla, "Financial Foundations," 74–81.

22. Gallatin, *A Sketch of the Finances*, 84–86, 123–29, 202; Gallatin, *Views of the Public Debt*, 1–29.

23. James McHenry to Charles Carroll, 8 April 1801, James McHenry Papers, Huntington Library; Karen E. Robbins, *James McHenry, Forgotten Federalist* (Athens: University of Georgia Press, 2013), 250–53, 270–72.

24. McHenry to Carroll, 8 April 1801, McHenry Papers, Huntington Library. A more typical Federalist reaction came from Hamilton's friend Robert Troup, who called Gallatin's appointment "a violent outrage on the virtue and respectability of our country; you know his history." Troup to Rufus King, 22 May 1801, *LCRK*, 3:454. For Gallatin's candid recollection of his ambition to lead the Republicans in financial matters, see Gallatin, Autobiographical sketch, [1849], *PAG*, extract in *SWAG*, 12–13.

25. John Taylor to Henry Tazewell, 13 June 1797 (quoted) and 26 May 1798, Tazewell Family Papers, Library of Virginia; Robert E. Shalhope, *John Taylor of Caroline: Pastoral Republican* (Columbia: University of South Carolina Press, 1980), 70–107.

26. Edmund Pendleton, "The Danger Not Over," Richmond *Enquirer*, 20 October 1801, reprinted in David John Mays, ed., *The Letters and Papers of Edmund Pendleton, 1734–1803* (Charlottesville: University Press of Virginia, 1967), 697–98; John Taylor to James Monroe, 26 October 1810 (quoted) and 15 June 1810, LJT, 310, 307–08; John Taylor to Wilson Cary Nicholas, 14 April 1806, David N. Mayer, ed., "Of Principles and Men: The Correspondence of John Taylor with Wilson Cary Nicholas, 1806–1808," *Virginia Magazine of History and Biography* 96, no. 3 (July 1988): 358; John Taylor to James Mercer Garnett, 14 December 1807, John Taylor Papers, Rubenstein Library, Duke University.

27. Jefferson to Gallatin, 11 October 1809, *PTJ-RS*, 1:597–99; Pierce Butler to James Monroe, 27 September 1816, James Monroe Papers, DLC.

28. Jefferson to Pierre Samuel du Pont, 18 January 1802, *PTJ*, 36:390–92; Jean Jacques Rousseau, "A Discourse on Political Economy" (1755), in *The Social Contract and Discourses*, transl. G. D. H. Cole (New York: E. P. Dutton, 1950), 314 ("This cruel alternative of letting the State perish, or of violating the sacred right of property, which is its support, constitutes the great difficulty of just and prudent economy."); Merrill D. Peterson, *The Jeffersonian Image in the American Mind* (New York: Oxford University Press, 1960), 78; Dumas Malone, *Jefferson and His Time*, vol. 4, *Jefferson the President: First Term, 1801–1805* (Boston: Little Brown, 1970), 101; Sloan, *Principle and Interest*, 53–62, 195–200; Andrew Burstein, *The Inner Jefferson: Portrait of a Grieving Optimist* (Charlottesville: University Press of Virginia, 1995), 237–45; James A. Bear Jr. and Lucia C. Stanton, eds., *Jefferson's Memorandum Books: Accounts with Legal Records and Miscellany, 1767–1826* (2 vols.; Princeton, NJ: Princeton University Press, 1997), 1:xviii–xix; Norman K. Risjord, *Jefferson's America, 1760–1815*, 3rd ed. (Lanham, MD: Rowman and Littlefield, 2010), 338–41; Donald F. Swanson, "Thomas Jefferson on Establishing Public Credit: The Debt Plans of a Would-be Secretary of the Treasury?" *Presidential Studies Quarterly* 23, no. 3 (Summer 1993): 502–6; Steven Harold Hochman, "Thomas Jefferson: A Personal Financial Biography" (Ph.D. diss., University of Virginia, 1987), 6, 229, 244–48.

29. Henry Adams to Samuel J. Tilden, 24 January 1883; Henry Adams to Brooks Adams, 18 February 1909, J. C. Levenson et al., eds., *The Letters of Henry Adams* (6 vols.; Cambridge, MA: Harvard University Press, 1982–88), 2:491, 6:227; Henry Adams, *The Life of Albert Gallatin* (1879; repr., New York: Peter Smith, 1943), iii; Henry Adams, *History of the United States during the Administrations of Thomas Jefferson and James Madison* (1889-91; 2 vols.; New York: Library of America, 1986), 1:129–30; Ernest Samuels, *Henry Adams* (Cambridge, MA: Harvard University Press, 1989), 139–43; Edward Chalfrant, *Better in Darkness: A Biography of Henry Adams, His Second Life, 1862–1891* (Hamden, CT: Archon Books, 1994), 345–47, 360–61; J. C. Levenson, *The Mind and Art of Henry Adams* (1957; Stanford, CA: Stanford University Press, 1968), 65; Peterson, *The Jeffersonian Image in the American Mind*, 285; Lois Hughson, "Power and Self in Henry Adams's Art of Biography," *Biography* 7, no. 4 (Fall 1984), 309–24. Henry Cabot Lodge responded

to Adams's biography with a short monograph that critiqued Gallatin from a Hamiltonian perspective. A few years later, a historian related to the Gallatin family wrote a biography for the American Statesmen series that condensed but did not otherwise improve on Adams's work. Henry Cabot Lodge, *Albert Gallatin* (New York, 1879); John Austin Stevens, *Albert Gallatin* (Boston, 1883); Henry Cabot Lodge, "Albert Gallatin," *International Review* 7 (July 1879): 250–66. Gallatin's papers were closed to the public until the late 1940s. Raymond Walters Jr., *Albert Gallatin: Jeffersonian Financier and Diplomat* (New York: Macmillan, 1957), vii.

30. Walters, *Albert Gallatin*, v–vii; Alexander Balinky, *Albert Gallatin: Fiscal Theories and Policies* (New Brunswick, NJ: Rutgers University Press, 1948), 139-53, 207-12, 223-44; Paul Studenski and Herman Edward Kroos, *The Financial History of the United States* (1952; Washington, DC: Beard Books, 2003), 71–72; Curtis P. Nettels, *The Emergence of a National Economy, 1775-1815* (New York: Holt, Reinhart, and Winston, 1962), 318–20; Robert H. Smith, "Albert Gallatin and American Fiscal Policy during Jefferson's First Administration" (Ph.D. diss., Syracuse University, 1953), 230–62; Edwin G. Burrows, *Albert Gallatin and the Political Economy of Republicanism, 1761–1800* (New York: Garland Publishing, 1986), 15–21 (print of Ph.D. diss., Columbia University, 1974). Two recent biographies of Gallatin consider him from the perspective of immigrant exceptionalism. See Nicholas Dungan, *Gallatin: America's Swiss Founding Father* (New York: New York University Press, 2010) and Thomas K. McCraw, *The Founders and Finance: How Hamilton, Gallatin, and Other Immigrants Forged a New Economy* (Cambridge, MA: Harvard University Press, 2012); Richard R. John, "Prophet of Perspective: Thomas K. McCraw," *Business History Review* 89, no. 1 (Spring 2015): 150–53.

31. Gallatin to Marquis de Lafayette, 12 May 1833, *WAG*, 2:473–74; James D. Savage, *Balanced Budgets and American Politics* (Ithaca, NY: Cornell University Press, 1988), 147–50; Robert E. Wright and David J. Cohen, *Financial Founding Fathers: The Men Who Made America Rich* (Chicago: University of Chicago Press, 2006), 87–88; Sheldon D. Pollack, *War, Revenue, and State Building: Financing the Development of the American State* (Ithaca, NY: Cornell University Press, 2009), 197–204, 286–90; McCraw, *Founders and Finance*, 329–65; Mark Blyth, *Austerity: The History of a Dangerous Idea* (New York: Oxford University Press, 2013), 178–226. From recent writing about democracy

and public finance, see James Macdonald, *A Free Nation Deep in Debt: The Financial Roots of Democracy* (New York: Farrar, Straus, and Giroux, 2003), 465–73; David Stasavage, *Public Debt and the Birth of the Democratic State: France and Great Britain, 1688–1789* (Cambridge, UK: Cambridge University Press, 2003), 39–49, 174–80; W. Elliot Brownlee, *Federal Taxation in America: A History*, 3rd ed. (Cambridge, UK: Cambridge University Press, 2016), 37–45; Wright, *One Nation Under Debt*, 172–83; David Stasavage, *States of Credit: Size, Power, and the Development of European Politics* (Princeton, NJ: Princeton University Press, 2011), 72–90, 156-65; William Hogeland, *Founding Finance: How Debt, Speculation, Foreclosures, Protests, and Crackdowns Made Us a Nation* (Austin: University of Texas Press, 2012), 160–85; Bill White, *America's Fiscal Constitution: Its Triumph and Collapse* (New York: Public Affairs, 2014), 45–68, 363–408.

32.   McCoy, *The Elusive Republic*, 185–88, 186n4; Banning, *The Jeffersonian Persuasion*, 273–302, 304–05; Daniel T. Rodgers, "Republicanism: The Career of a Concept," *Journal of American History* 79, no. 1 (June 1992), 11–38; Markus Claudius Cachia-Riedl, "Albert Gallatin and the Politics of the New Nation" (Ph.D. diss., University of California Berkeley, 1998), vi–xii. From the vast literature on political economy in the Early Republic, see John R. Nelson Jr., *Liberty and Property: Political Economy and Policymaking in the New Nation, 1789–1812* (Baltimore: Johns Hopkins University Press, 1987), 100–61; Steven Watts, *The Republic Reborn: War and the Making of Liberal America, 1790–1820* (Baltimore: Johns Hopkins University Press, 1987), 230–31, 235–39, 316–21; Cathy D. Matson and Peter S. Onuf, *A Union of Interests: Political and Economic Thought in Revolutionary America* (Lawrence: University Press of Kansas, 1990), 147–68; Appleby, *Liberalism and Republicanism in the Historical Imagination,* 253-76; Sloan, *Principle and Interest,* 86–124; Carl Lane, *A Nation Wholly Free: The Elimination of the National Debt in the Age of Jackson* (Yardley, PA: Westholme, 2014), 27–44; Sylla, "Financial Foundations," 74–86; John Francis Devanny Jr., "Commerce, Credit, and Currency: Continuity and Differentiation in Jeffersonian Political Economy, 1760–1848" (Ph.D. diss., University of South Carolina, 2000), 72–85, 94–97, 117.

33.   Edling, *A Revolution in Favor of Government*, 163–218; Brian Balogh, *A Government Out of Sight: The Mystery of National Authority in Nineteenth-Century America* (New York: Cambridge University Press, 2009), 120–29; Jerry L. Mashaw, *Creating the Administrative*

Constitution: The Lost One Hundred Years of American Administrative Law (New Haven, CT: Yale University Press, 2012), 81–143; Max M. Edling, *A Hercules in the Cradle: War, Money, and the American State, 1783-1867* (Chicago: University of Chicago Press, 2014), 108–44; Gary Gerstle, *Liberty and Coercion: The Paradox of American Government from the Founding to the Present* (Princeton, NJ: Princeton University Press, 2015), 17–54; James T. Sparrow, William J. Novak, and Stephen W. Sawyer, eds., *Boundaries of the State in U. S. History* (Chicago: University of Chicago Press, 2015), 1–15; Brian Phillips Murphy, *Building the Empire State: Political Economy in the Early Republic* (Philadelphia: University of Pennsylvania Press, 2015), 10–16; Rao, *National Duties,* 4–14, 117–19; Richard R. John, "Governmental Institutions as Agents of Change: Rethinking American Political Development in the Early Republic," *Studies in American Political Development* 11 (1997): 347–80; William J. Novak, "The Myth of the 'Weak' American State," *American Historical Review* 113, no. 3 (June 2008): 752–72; Gautham Rao, "William E. Nelson's *The Roots of American Bureaucracy* and the Resuscitation of the Early American State," *Chicago-Kent Law Review* 89, no. 3 (January 2014): 997–1018.

34.   Adams, *The Life of Albert Gallatin,* 268–69; Charles Sellers, *The Market Revolution: Jacksonian America, 1815–1846* (New York: Oxford University Press, 1994), 39. For assessments by leading historians of the period, see Adams, *History of the United States,* 1:129–30; Henry C. Adams, *Public Debts: An Essay in the Science of Public Finance* (New York, 1887), 268–69; Leonard D. White, *The Jeffersonians: A Study in Administrative History, 1801–1829* (New York: Macmillan Company, 1956), 135–36; Malone, *Jefferson and His Time,* 4:57; Merrill D. Peterson, *Thomas Jefferson and the New Nation* (New York: Oxford University Press, 1970), 660–61; Robert M. Johnstone Jr., *Jefferson and the Presidency: Leadership in the Young Republic* (Ithaca, NY: Cornell University Press, 1978), 88–89; Burstein and Isenberg, *Madison and Jefferson,* 361, 629–30. For Gallatin's own assessment of his importance to the Jefferson and Madison administrations, see Philip S. Klein, ed., "Memoirs of a Senator from Pennsylvania: Jonathan Roberts, 1771–1854," *Pennsylvania Magazine of History and Biography* 62, no. 2 (April 1938), 23. On Gallatin's statue at the Treasury building, see Public Resolution 69–50, *Statutes at Large* 44 (1927): 934; Public Resolution 75–43, ibid., 50 (1937): 260; A. L. Freundlich, *The Sculpture of James Earle Fraser* (n. p.: Universal, 2001), 84–85; James M. Goode, *Washington*

Sculpture: A Cultural History of Outdoor Sculpture in the Nation's Capital (Baltimore: Johns Hopkins University Press, 2008), 461.

35.   Thomas Hart Benton, *Thirty Years' View; or, A History of the Working of the American Government for Thirty Years* (2 vols.; New York, 1854), 1:5 ("a nation wholly free").

Chapter 1: Becoming Republican

1.   Albert Gallatin, Diary, 1 April–19 July 1780, *PAG;* Gallatin to Jean Badollet, 14 September 1780, *LAG,* 27; Marquis de Chastellux, *Travels in North-America in the Years 1780, 1781, and 1782,* 2ⁿᵈ ed. (2 vols., London, 1787), 2:255–56; Robert Middlekauff, *The Glorious Cause: The American Revolution, 1763–1789,* 2ⁿᵈ ed. (New York: Oxford University Press, 2005), 296. Winnisimmet is now part of Chelsea. Nathaniel B. Shurtleff, *A Topographical and Historical Description of Boston* (Boston, 1871), 138–39, 429, 627.

2.   Gallatin, Diary, 1 April–19 July 1780; Gallatin to Badollet, 16 May and 14 September 1780, *LAG,* 23, 27.

3.   Chastellux, *Travels in North-America,* 2:268–69; Benson Bobrick, *Angel in the Whirlwind: The Triumph of the American Revolution* (New York: Simon and Schuster, 1997), 392–404, 447–51.

4.   Gallatin to Jean Badollet, 1 October 1783; John Badollet to Gallatin, 30 January 1792; Gallatin to John Badollet, 29 July 1824; Gallatin to Algernon Sidney Badollet, 23 May 1846, *PAG;* Washington, PA, *Herald of Liberty,* 1 October 1798 ("Letter from a Westmoreland gentleman"); Curtius [John Taylor?], *A Defence of the Measures of the Administration of Thomas Jefferson* (Washington, DC, 1804), 1722; John Russell Bartlett, "Reminiscences of Albert Gallatin," *Proceedings of the New York Historical Society for 1849* (New York, 1849), 283–84; John E. Crowley, *The Privileges of Independence: Neomercantilism and the American Revolution* (Baltimore: Johns Hopkins University Press, 1993), 67–70; Jefferson P. Selth, *Firm Heart and Capacious Mind: The Life and Friends of Etienne Dumont* (Lanham, MD: University Press of America, 1997), 18–27; Richard Whatmore, *Against War and Empire: Geneva, Britain, and France in the Eighteenth Century* (New Haven, CT: Yale University Press, 2012), 157–67, 177–86. For traditional accounts of Gallatin's emigration, see Henry Adams, *The Life of Albert Gallatin* (1879; repr., New York: Peter Smith, 1943), 16–22; Raymond Walters Jr., *Albert Gallatin: Jeffersonian Financier and Diplomat* (New York: Macmillan, 1957), 8–10, 15–16; L. B. Kuppenheimer, *Albert Gallatin's*

Vision of Democratic Stability (Westport, CT: Praeger, 1996), 17; Thomas K. McCraw, *The Founders and Finance: How Hamilton, Gallatin, and Other Immigrants Forged a New Economy* (Cambridge, MA: Harvard University Press, 2012), 182–85. For the first important critique of those accounts, see Edwin G. Burrows, *Albert Gallatin and the Political Economy of Republicanism, 1761–1800* (New York: Garland Publishing, 1986), 15–21 (print of Ph.D. diss., Columbia University, 1974), 11–21, 114–17.

5.   Patrick F. O'Mara, "Geneva in the Eighteenth Century: A Socio-Economic Study of the Bourgeois City-State during Its Golden Age" (Ph.D. diss., University of California, Berkeley, 1954), 19, 93, 121–34; Philip Benedict, *Christ's Churches Purely Reformed: A Social History of Calvinism* (New Haven, CT: Yale University Press, 2002), 89–90, 536–37, 540–41. The procedure for electing syndics resembled the procedure for the election of bishops described in John Calvin's *Institutes,* and the preference for aristocracy over other forms of civil government also found support in the *Institutes.* Calvin, *The Institutes of the Christian Religion,* trans. Henry Beveridge (1559; 2 vols., Edinburgh, 1845), bk. IV, chap. 4, sec. xii and chap. 20, sec. viii. For Gallatin's later description of Geneva's aristocratic government, see Gallatin to Eben[ezer] Dodge, 21 January 1847, *PAG,* version in *WAG,* 2:647–48. Gallatin characterized Calvin as "a great, good, and austere man" to whom he had only one objection: "he was an aristocrat." James W. Alexander, Recollections of Albert Gallatin, 1 July 1850 (conversation of 7 December 1847); James W. Alexander to Mrs. Byam K. Stevens [Frances Gallatin], 1 July 1850 (misdated 1880 by the editors), *PAG.*

6.   Gallatin to Dodge, 21 January 1847, *PAG,* version in *WAG,* 2:647–49; Alexander, Recollections of Albert Gallatin, 1 July 1850, *PAG* (conversations of 7 December 1847 and 27 November 1848); Benedict, *Christ's Churches Purely Reformed,* 85–90, 302–03, 311, 313–14, 319–23; O'Mara, "Geneva in the Eighteenth Century," xiii, 123–24.

7.   Adams, *The Life of Albert Gallatin,* 5–9; Jennifer Powell McNutt, *Calvin Meets Voltaire: The Clergy of Geneva in the Age of Enlightenment, 1685–1798* (Farnham, UK: Ashgate Publishing, 2013), 145–86; Rebecca L. Spang, *Stuff and Money in the Time of the French Revolution* (Cambridge, MA: Harvard University Press, 2015), 23–30; Linda Kirk, "'Going Soft': Genevan Decadence in the Eighteenth Century," in *The Identity of Geneva: The Christian Commonwealth, 1564–1864,* ed. John

B. Roney and Martin I. Klauber (Westport, CT: Greenwood Press, 1998), 148–49.

8. Francis d'Ivernois, *An Historical and Political View of the Constitution and Revolutions of Geneva in the Eighteenth Century,* trans. John Farell (London, 1784); Antoine Lilti, "The Writing of Paranoia: Jean-Jacques Rousseau and the Paradoxes of Celebrity," *Representations* 103, no. 1 (Summer 2008): 55–56, 72.

9. R. R. Palmer, *The Age of Democratic Revolution: A Political History of Europe and America, 1760–1800,* rev. ed. (Princeton, NJ: Princeton University Press, 2014), 83–105; Whatmore, *Against War and Empire,* 54–95.

10. Gallatin to John Badollet, 9 March 1793, *PAG;* Palmer, *The Age of Democratic Revolution,* 84, 105, 270–72, 666-69; Whatmore, *Against War and Empire,* 156–76; O'Mara, "Geneva in the Eighteenth Century," 307–18.

11. "Gallatin á Genève," n. d., Gallatin Family Papers, Small Special Collections Library, University of Virginia; Extrait du Regître des affairs des particuliers de la Republique de Genève, 6 April 1779, *WAG,* 3:593-97; William Plumb Bacon, comp., *Ancestry of Albert Gallatin and of Hannah Nicholson* (New York: Tobias A. Wright, [1916]), 6–7, 12–16; Walters, *Albert Gallatin,* 1–2.

12. Expense accounts with Bourse Gallatin, 1775–79, *PAG;* Gallatin, Autobiographical sketch, [1849], *PAG,* extract in *SWAG,* 7; Burrows, *Albert Gallatin,* 2-11; E. William Monter, "Women in Calvinist Geneva, 1550–1800," *Signs* 6, no. 2 (Winter 1980): 193–94, 198–99, 201.

13. Gallatin to Dodge, 21 January 1847, *PAG,* version in *WAG,* 2:640–47; Thomas Jefferson to John Banister Jr., 15 October 1785, *PTJ,* 8:635-38; George Keate, *A Short Account of the Ancient History, Present Government, and Laws of the Republic of Geneva* (London, 1761), 124–39; John D. Moore, *A View of Society and Manners in France, Switzerland, and Germany,* 2nd ed. (2 vols.; London, 1779), 1:158–59, 162–63; John Delafield, ed., *Journal of the Proceedings of a Convention of Literary and Scientific Gentlemen* (New York, 1831), 180–82 (Gallatin account of Geneva Academy). When Jefferson's grandnephew went to study abroad in 1816, Jefferson directed him to the Geneva Academy. Jefferson to Gallatin, 30 January 1816; Gallatin to Jefferson, 1 April 1816, *PTJ-RS,* 9:413, 620–21. On the proposal to move the Geneva Academy to the United States and the American reputation of the Academy, see François d'Ivernois to Jefferson, 5 September 1794, 11 November 1794;

Jefferson to Wilson Cary Nicholas, 23 November 1794; Jefferson to John Adams, 6 February 1795; Jefferson to François d'Ivernois, 6 February 1795; Jefferson to George Washington, 23 February 1795, *PTJ*, 28:123–33, 189–96, 208–09, 261–62, 262–64, 275–78; Washington to Jefferson, 15 March 1795, *PGW-PS*, 17:654–67; Gallatin to Badollet, 29 December 1794, *LAG*, 144-45; Badollet to Gallatin, 18 June 1795, *PAG*; Jefferson to Marc Auguste Pictet, 14 October 1795, 5 February 1803, *PTJ*, 28:505, 39:456–57; Jennifer Powell McNutt and Richard Whatmore, "The Attempts to Transfer the Genevan Academy to Ireland and to America, 1782–1795," *Historical Journal* 56, no. 2 (June 2013): 345–68.

14.   Alexander, Recollections of Albert Gallatin, 1 July 1850 (conversation of 7 December 1847); Gallatin to Dodge, 21 January 1847, *PAG*, version in *WAG*, 2:641–42, 644; Sven Stelling-Michaud and Suzanne Stelling-Michaud, eds., *Le Livre du Recteur de L'Académie de Genève* (6 vols.; Geneva: Droz, 1959–80), 1:315, 3:390; Michael Heyd, "The Geneva Academy in the Eighteenth Century: A Calvinist Seminary or a Civic University?" in *The University and the City: From Medieval Origins to the Present,* ed. Thomas Bender (New York: Oxford University Press, 1988), 79–99; Hilde de Ridder-Symoens, "Mobility," in *A History of the University in Europe,* vol. 2, *Universities in Early Modern Europe, 1500–1800,* ed. Hilde de Ridder-Symoens (4 vols.; Cambridge, UK: University of Cambridge Press, 1996), 421–24.

15.   Paul-Michel Gallatin to Albert Gallatin, 21 May 1780, *LAG*, 19–22; Alexander, Recollections of Albert Gallatin, 1 July 1850 (conversation of 7 December 1847); Gallatin to Dodge, 21 January 1847, *PAG*, version in *WAG*, 2:641. The expression that Gallatin's guardian used to describe the offer from Gallatin's uncle—*"honnête médiocrité"*—had a heavily nuanced meaning. Deirdre Nansen McCloskey, *Bourgeois Equality: How Ideas, Not Capital or Institutions, Enriched the World* (Chicago: University of Chicago Press, 2016), 239–46.

16.   Albert Gallatin to Jean Badollet, 16 May and 14 September 1780, *LAG*, 23, 27; Gallatin to Robert Morris, 14 June 1782, *PAG*.

17.   Catherine Pictet to Gallatin, 1 October 1787 (quoted), 5 February 1782, 22 July 1785, *LAG,* 65, 38–39, 64. For examples of introductions and assistance, see M. de Chapeaurouge to John Adams, 21 May 1780, Robert J. Taylor et al., eds., *The Papers of John Adams* (18 vols. to date; Cambridge, MA: Harvard University Press, 1977–), 9:332–33; Duchesse d'Enville to Benjamin Franklin, 22 May 1780; Robert Pigott to Benjamin Franklin, 26 November 1782, Leonard W. Labaree et al., eds., *The Papers*

of Benjamin Franklin (42 vols. to date; New Haven: Yale University Press, 1959–), 32:410–1, 38:*359*–60. For examples of Gallatin's self criticism, see Albert Gallatin to Hannah Gallatin, 3 December 1794, 17 January 1797, 8 February 1798, *PAG;* same to same, 25 July 1793, 22 April 1795, 17 January and 31 January 1797, 2 January 1798, *LAG,* 102, 147, 181, 182-83, 189; Albert Gallatin to Maria Nicholson, 12 March 1801; Albert Gallatin to Albert Rolaz Gallatin, 14 May 1827, *PAG.*

18.   Albert Gallatin to Hannah Gallatin, 29 September (quoted) and 29 June 1795, *PAG;* Albert Gallatin to Badollet, 8 March 1790; Albert Gallatin to Hannah Gallatin, 18 January 1799, *LAG,* 73–75, 226; Albert Gallatin, Autobiographical sketch, [1849], *PAG;* J[ames] M. Mathews, *Recollections of Persons and Events, Chiefly in the City of New York…* (New York, 1865), 123–24 (late-life recollections of Catherine Pictet).

19.   Chastellux, *Travels in North-America,* 2:264–65; Abbé [Claude] Robin, *New Travels through North-America in a Series of Letters,* trans. [Philip Freneau] (Philadelphia, 1783), 13 (quoted), 15–17; Gallatin to Badollet, 16 May, 14 September, 29 October 1780, *LAG,* 23, 27–28, 30–34; Edwin G. Burrows, ed., "'Notes on Settling America': Albert Gallatin, New England, and the American Revolution," *New England Quarterly* 58, no. 3 (September 1985), 449–51; Gary B. Nash, *The Urban Crucible: Social Change, Political Consciousness, and the Origins of the American Revolution* (Cambridge, MA: Harvard University Press, 1979), 244–45; John J. McCusker and Russell R. Menard, *The Economy of British America, 1607–1789* (Chapel Hill: University of North Carolina Press, 1985), 358–74; Allan Kulikoff, *From British Peasants to Colonial American Farmers* (Chapel Hill: University of North Carolina Press, 2000), 255–80; Peter H. Lindert and Jeffrey G. Williamson, *Unequal Gains: American Growth and Inequality since 1700* (Princeton, NJ: Princeton University Press, 2016), 84–90; Allan Kulikoff, "'Such Things Ought Not to Be': The American Revolution and the First National Depression," in *The World of the Revolutionary American Republic: Land, Labor, and the Conflict for a Continent,* ed. Andrew Shankman (New York: Routledge, 2014), 147–51.

20.   Gallatin to Badollet, 29 October 1780, 15 September 1782; Henri Serre to Badollet, [29 October 1780], 13 December 1782, *LAG,* 30–34 (quoted at 32), 35, 34–35, 39–42; John McGown, Deposition in favor of Lewis F. Delesdernier, 24 February 1800 (filed by Albert Gallatin, 7 April 1800), *Papers of the War Department, 1784 to 1800,* www.wardepartmentpapers.

org/documents.php?id=38858; E. C. Royle, *Pioneer, Patriot, and Rebel: Lewis Delesdernier of Nova Scotia and Maine, 1752-1838,* 2nd ed. (Hudson Heights, Quebec: n. p., 1976), JMC-1, L-19–L-21. Gallatin and Serre apparently sold some goods to the army in exchange for relatively worthless government warrants, the only currency available to the troops. Gallatin also may have been left temporarily in charge of an army outpost. When resisting expulsion from the United States Senate in 1794, Gallatin therefore claimed he had contributed money and volunteer services to the Revolutionary cause while he was in Maine. Near the end of his life, he conceded that he had exaggerated. *Annals,* 3rd Cong., 1st Sess., 47; Gallatin to John Connell, 9 January 1846, *PAG.*

21.   Gallatin to Robert Morris, 14 June 1782, *PAG;* Pictet to Gallatin, 5 February, 30 November, 26 December 1782; Serre to Badollet, 13 December 1782, *LAG,* 38-39, 39–42.

22.   Pictet to Gallatin, 5 February and 14 November 1782, *LAG,* 38–39; Extract from minutes of the President and Fellows of Harvard College, 2 July 1782; Contract and lists of Harvard French students, 28 August 1782, *PAG;* Boston *Independent Chronicle,* 28 April 1796 (speech by Harrison Gray Otis); Thomas Twining, *Travels in India a Hundred Years Ago with A Visit to the United States,* ed. William H. G. Twining (London, 1893), 375–77 (12 April 1795); William Dunlap, *Diary of William Dunlap* (3 vols.; New York: New York Historical Society, 1930), 2:384 (13 February 1806); Samuel Eliot Morison, *The Life and Letters of Harrison Gray Otis, Federalist, 1765–1848* (2 vols.; Boston: Houghton Mifflin, 1913), 1:55–57, 77; C. Dallett Hemphill, *Bowing to Necessities: A History of Manners in America, 1620-1860* (New York: Oxford University Press, 1999), 79–80, 84–86. It was Pictet's friend Samuel Cooper, the prominent pastor of a congregation filled with American patriots at the Brattle Street Church in Boston, who introduced Gallatin to the authorities at Harvard College.

23.   Wilma A. Dunaway, *The First American Frontier: Transition to Capitalism in Southern Appalachia, 1700-1860* (Chapel Hill: University of North Carolina Press, 1996), 53–59; L. Scott Philyaw, *Virginia's Western Visions: Political and Cultural Expansion on an Early American Frontier* (Knoxville: University of Tennessee Press, 2004), 103–10; William H. Bergmann, *The American National State and the Early West* (New York: Cambridge University Press, 2012), 18–39; John R. Van Atta, *Securing the West: Politics, Public Lands, and the Fate of the Old*

Republic, 1785–1850 (Baltimore: Johns Hopkins University Press, 2014), 33–34.

24. Burrows, "'Notes on Settling America,'" 449–52; Gallatin to Badollet, 14 September and 29 October 1780, *LAG,* 27-28, 30-34; Kulikoff, *From British Peasants to Colonial American Farmers,* 109–17. When living in Paris nine years later—and himself suspended between two worlds—Jefferson would muse about settling his slaves on small farms with German peasants as a possible step toward emancipation. Annette Gordon-Reed and Peter S. Onuf, *"Most Blessed of the Patriarchs": Thomas Jefferson and the Empire of the Imagination* (New York: Liveright Publishing, 2016), 147–50.

25. Gallatin to William Bentley, 11 July 1783, *PAG;* Gallatin to Serre, 22 July 1783; Gallatin to Badollet, 1 October 1783, 29 December 1784, 30 March 1785, *LAG,* 44–45, 47–53, 55–56, 60–61; Gallatin to J. J. Jackson, 1 May 1848, *PAG;* Gallatin to William Maxwell, 15 February 1848, *WAG,* 2:659–60.

26. Abraham Gallatin to Albert Gallatin, 20 June 1785, *LAG,* 64; Thomas Perkins Abernethy, *Western Lands and the American Revolution* (New York: Russell and Russell, 1959), 217–29; Otis K. Rice, *The Allegheny Frontier: West Virginia Beginnings, 1730–1830* (Lexington: University Press of Kentucky, 1970), 124–42; Henry M. Dater, "Albert Gallatin—Land Speculator," *Mississippi Valley Historical Review* 26, no. 1 (June 1939): 21–38. Gallatin and Savary ended their partnership in 1789, but they jointly held significant amounts of land in Virginia, Kentucky, and the Northwest Territory (later Ohio) for many years. Gallatin to Badollet, 4 May 1789, *LAG,* 70-71; Agreements between Gallatin and Jean Savary, 18 and 22 August 1797; Gallatin to Thomas Worthington, 15 August 1801, 27 September 1804; Edward Carrington to Gallatin, 2 July 1804; Agreements between Gallatin and John Savary, 7 April and 14 August 1807; Worthington to Gallatin, 30 December 1807; Gallatin to Robert Alexander, 20 April 1816, *PAG.*

27. [Gallatin], Diary, 11 July–13 November 1783; Note and expense book, 13 November 1783–27 February 1784; Diary, 31 March–25 November 1785; [Savary], Diary, 17 October 1783–6 July 1784; Diary, 1 July 1785–September 1786, *PAG;* Gallatin to Badollet, 29 December 1784, *LAG,* 55; Adams, *The Life of Albert Gallatin,* 46.

28. Gallatin to Badollet, 1 October 1783, *LAG,* 47–53; Whatmore, *Against War and Empire,*167–72; O'Mara, "Geneva in the Eighteenth Century," 307–18.

29. Gallatin to Badollet, 1 October 1783, *LAG,* 47–53; J. Hector St. John Crèvecoeur, *Letters from an American Farmer and Other Essays,* ed. Dennis D. Moore (Cambridge, MA: Harvard University Press, 2013), 14–27 (pleasures of the American farmer), 31–32 ("The American is a new man"), 42–43 (enterprise); Thomas Jefferson, *Notes on the State of Virginia* (London, 1787), 273–75 (Query XIX); Burrows, *Albert Gallatin,* 106–10; Leo Marx, *The Machine in the Garden: Technology and the Pastoral Ideal in America* (1964; New York: Oxford University Press, 2000), 126–44; Andrew Burstein, *Sentimental Democracy: The Evolution of America's Romantic Self-Image* (New York: Hill and Wang, 1999), 156–62; Manuela Albertone, *National Identity and the Agrarian Republic: The Transatlantic Commerce of Ideas between America and France, 1750–1830* (Farnham, UK: Ashgate Publishing, 2014), 13–14, 15–16, 33–37.

30. Washington to Benjamin Harrison, 10 October 1784, *PGW-ConS,* 2:89–98; Eric Hinderaker, *Elusive Empires: Constructing Colonialism in the Ohio Valley, 1673–1800* (Cambridge, UK: Cambridge University Press, 1997), 189–95; John C. Weaver, *The Great Land Rush and the Making of the Modern World, 1650–1900* (Montreal: McGill-Queens University Press, 2003), 152–60; Burrows, *Albert Gallatin,* 126–35; John Lauritz Larson, *Internal Improvement: National Public Works and the Promise of Popular Government in the Early United States* (Chapel Hill: University of North Carolina Press, 2001), 10–20; Douglas R. Littlefield, "Eighteenth-Century Plans to Clear the Potomac River," *Virginia Magazine of History and Biography* 93, no. 3 (July 1985): 291–322; Littlefield, "The Potomac Company: A Misadventure in Financing an Early American Internal Improvement Project," *Business History Review* 58, no. 4 (Winter 1984): 562–85. For Gallatin's encounter with Washington, see Richard Beale Davis, ed., *Jeffersonian America: Notes on the United States of America...by Sir Augustus John Foster* (San Marino, CA: Huntington Library, 1954), 120; Bartlett, "Reminiscences of Albert Gallatin," 288–90; William Beach Lawrence to B[yam] K[erby] Stevens, 14 August 1848, *PAG;* Donald Jackson and Dorothy Twohig, eds., *The Diaries of George Washington* (6 vols.; Charlottesville: University Press of Virginia, 1976–79), 4:39–41, 42n4 (24 September 1784).

31. Memorial to General Irvine, 26 February 1782, quoted in James Patrick McClure, "The Ends of the American Earth: Pittsburgh and the Upper Ohio Valley to 1795" (Ph.D. diss., University of Michigan, 1983), 471;

Ephraim Douglass to James Irvine, 6–11 February 1784, Detre Library, Heinz History Center, Pittsburgh, PA, printed in Franklin Ellis, ed., *History of Fayette County, Pennsylvania* (Philadelphia, 1882), 283–84; Solon J. Buck and Elizabeth Hawthorn Buck, *The Planting of Civilization in Western Pennsylvania* (Pittsburgh: University of Pittsburgh Press, 1939), 204–08; R. Eugene Harper, *The Transformation of Western Pennsylvania, 1770–1800* (Pittsburgh: University of Pittsburgh Press, 1991), 7–16, 18–21.

32. Gallatin to Badollet, 30 March 1785, LAG, 60; Gallatin, Diary, 31 March 1785–25 November 1785, *PAG;* Gallatin, "Introduction to 'Hale's Indians of North-West America,'" *Transactions of the American Ethnological Society* 2 (1848): l; Sarah S. Hughes, *Surveyors and Statesmen: Land Measuring in Colonial Virginia* (Richmond: Virginia Surveyors Foundation, 1979), 38–54, 113–18.

33. Peter S. Du Ponceau to John Jay, 14 May 1786; Jefferson to Jean-Armand Tronchin, 1 August 1786; Jefferson to Jay, 27 January 1786, *PTJ,* 10:184–85 (quoted), 182, 9:233–36; Anne Gallatin to Albert Gallatin, 6 March 1786, *LAG,* 65; Philadelphia *Pennsylvania Gazette,* 3 August 1785 (killed and scalped); Philadelphia *Pennsylvania Packet and Daily Advertiser,* 11, 15, and 18 May, 7 and 12 June 1786 (diplomatic inquiry); Certificate of oath of allegiance, Monongalia County [Virginia] Court, October Session, 1785, *PAG;* Gregory Evans Dowd, *A Spirited Resistance: The North American Indian Struggle for Unity, 1745–1815* (Baltimore: Johns Hopkins University Press, 1992), 90–94; Hinderaker, *Elusive Empires,* 237–44; Patrick Griffin, *American Leviathan: Empire, Nation, and Revolutionary Frontier* (New York: Hill and Wang, 2007), 190–91; Gordon C. Baker, "Thomas Clare," *Journal of the Alleghenies* 16 (1980): 1921; Colin G. Calloway, "Neither White Nor Red: White Renegades on the American Frontier," *Western Historical Quarterly* 17, no. 1 (January 1986): 55–56.

34. "Compte de la fortune de Monsieur Albert Gallatin (Rolaz)," 1786; Gallatin to Badollet, 21 October 1786, *PAG;* Deed to Friendship Hill, Pennsylvania Supreme Executive Council, 26 January 1788, copy at Heinz History Center, Pittsburgh, PA; Gallatin to Badollet, 4 May 1789, *LAG,* 70–71; Harper, *The Transformation of Western Pennsylvania,* 21–29, 41–43, 50. Friendship Hill is now a National Historic Site. On Gallatin's construction of the house there, see Gallatin, Notebook and accounts, 1787 (sketch of gable); Contract between Gallatin and Daniel Duggin, 13 June 1791 (interior woodwork); Gallatin to Thomas Clare, 5 March 1794

(plastering); U. S. Department of the Interior, National Park Service, *Friendship Hill National Historic Site: Historic Structure Report— Architectural Data Section,* comp. John B. Marsh and Scott Jacobs (August 1984), 6–10, and Evolutionary Drawings, Main House, Sheet 2.

35. Gallatin to Badollet, 7 February 1833, 6 June 1804, *CBG,* 309, 28–30; Abraham Trembley to Gallatin, 8 April 1787; Gallatin, Notebook and diary, 1787–88; Gallatin to Badollet, 22 February 1792 (backcountry "does not afford much room for the exercise of the talents we may possess"), *PAG;* Burrows, *Albert Gallatin,* 141–43; Norman B. Wilkinson, *Land Policy and Speculation in Pennsylvania, 1779–1800* (New York: Arno Press, 1979), 107–10; Jennifer J. Baker, *Securing the Commonwealth: Debt, Speculation, and Writing in the Making of Early America* (Baltimore: Johns Hopkins University Press, 2005), 104–06 (analysis of "the main chance"). As late as 1815, Gallatin estimated that the Virginia, Kentucky, and Ohio lands in which he had invested were worth less than $12,000. Gallatin to Josiah Meigs, 4 December 1815, *WAG,* 1:672.

36. On Pennsylvania's political proto-parties and the constitutional ratification debate, see Gordon S. Wood, *The Creation of the American Republic, 1776–1787* (New York: W. W. Norton, 1972), 83–90, 226–37; Jackson Turner Main, *Political Parties before the Constitution* (Chapel Hill: University of North Carolina Press, 1973), 174, 203, 206–11; Thomas M. Doerflinger, *A Vigorous Spirit of Enterprise: Merchants and Economic Development in Revolutionary Pennsylvania* (Chapel Hill: University of North Carolina Press, 1986), 251–80; Lee Soltow, *Distribution of Wealth and Income in the United States in 1798* (Pittsburgh: University of Pittsburgh Press, 1989), 224–25, 274–76; Owen S. Ireland, *Religion, Ethnicity, and Politics: Ratifying the Constitution in Pennsylvania* (University Park: Pennsylvania State University, 1995), 3–33; George David Rappaport, *Stability and Change in Revolutionary Pennsylvania: Banking, Politics, and Social Structure* (University Park: Pennsylvania University Press, 1996), 96–108, 125–27; Saul Cornell, *The Other Founders: Anti-Federalism and the Dissenting Tradition in America, 1788–1828* (Chapel Hill: University of North Carolina Press, 1999), 85–98; Richard Alan Ryerson, "Republican Theory and Partisan Reality in Revolutionary Pennsylvania: Toward a New View of the Constitutionalist Party," in *Sovereign States in an Age of Uncertainty,* ed. Ronald Hoffman and Peter J. Albert (Charlottesville: University Press of Virginia, 1981), 95–133; Roland Milton Baumann, "The

Democratic-Republicans of Philadelphia: The Origins, 1776–1797" (Ph.D. diss., Pennsylvania State University, 1970), 37–43, 50–55; Douglas McNeil Arnold, "Political Ideology and the Internal Revolution in Pennsylvania, 1776–1790" (Ph.D. diss., Princeton University, 1976), 247–49.

37.   David Redick to William Irvine, 24 September 1787, in *The Debate on the Constitution: Federalist and Antifederalist Speeches, Articles, and Letters During the Struggle over Ratification,* comp. Bernard Bailyn (New York: Library of America, 1993), 1:15–16; *DHRC,* 2:58–117, 619–22.

38.   Pauline Maier, *Ratification: The People Debate the Constitution, 1787–1788* (New York: Simon and Schuster, 2010), 59–69, 100–22; Michael J. Farber, "Democratic Anti-Federalism: Rights, Democracy, and the Minority in the Pennsylvania Ratifying Convention," *Pennsylvania Magazine of History and Biography* 138, no. 2 (April 2014): 154–59. Federalists in Congress also had struck proposed amendments to the constitution from the Congressional journal of the debates about referring the document to the states. Maier, *Ratification,* 58.

39.   Address and Reasons of Dissent of the Minority of the Convention, 18 December 1787, *DHRC,* 2:617–39 (signed by all but two of the twenty-three dissenters); Centinel Nos. 1, 2, 4, and 5, October-December 1787, reprinted in John Bach McMaster and Frederick D. Stone, eds., *Pennsylvania and the Federal Constitution, 1787–1788* (1888; Indianapolis: Liberty Fund, 2011), 565-91, 601-14; Max M. Edling, *A Revolution in Favor of Government: Origins of the U. S. Constitution and the Making of the American State* (New York: Oxford University Press, 2003), 180–90.

40.   Pennsylvania Assembly proceedings, *DHRC* 2:720; Cumberland County proceedings and circular letter, 3 July 1788; Tench Coxe to Robert Smith, 5 August 1788, *DHFFE,* 1:239–41, 247–48; Maier, *Ratification,* 316–17, 341–44.

41.   Gallatin to Badollet, 10 February 1788, *PAG;* Certificate of appointment, 18 August 1788, *PAG,* printed in *DHFFE,* 1:252–53; Philip S. Klein, ed., "Memoirs of a Senator from Pennsylvania: Jonathan Roberts, 1771–1854," *Pennsylvania Magazine of History and Biography* 62, no. 2 (April 1938), 238 (Gallatin's foreign birth less an impediment on the frontier); Harper, *The Transformation of Western Pennsylvania,* 111–12, 201–02; Diane E. Wenger, *A Country Storekeeper in Pennsylvania: Creating Economic Networks in Early America, 1790–1807* (University Park:

Pennsylvania State University Press, 2008); Rodger C. Henderson, "John Smilie, Antifederalism, and the 'Dissent of the Minority,' 1787–1788," *Western Pennsylvania Historical Magazine* 71, no. 3/4 (July/October 1988): 237. Nathaniel Breading, who apparently chaired the committee that appointed Gallatin, was a Revolutionary veteran, judge, member of the Pennsylvania Supreme Executive Council, and dissenting member of the Pennsylvania ratification convention. He continued to support Gallatin in the 1790s. Nathaniel Breading to Gallatin, 10 October 1794; *Pittsburgh Gazette,* 26 January, 2 February, and 9 February 1788; Ellis, *History of Fayette County,* 650.

42. Gallatin, Draft resolutions at Harrisburg Convention, [3 September 1788], *PAG,* printed in *DHFFE,* 1:259–60; Report of the proceedings of the Harrisburg Convention, ibid., 1:260–4; Paul Leicester Ford, *The Origin, Purpose, and Result of the Harrisburg Convention of 1788: A Study in Popular Government* (Brooklyn, NY, 1890); Harry Marlin Tinkcom, *The Republicans and Federalists in Pennsylvania, 1790–1801* (Harrisburg: Pennsylvania Historical and Museum Commission, 1950), 23–24; Cornell, *The Other Founders,* 136–42; Terry Bouton, *Taming Democracy: "The People," the Founders, and the Troubled Ending of the American Revolution* (New York: Oxford University Press, 2007), 188–94.

43. Alexander Graydon to Lambert Cadwalader, 7 September 1788, *DHFFE,* 1:265; Richard Peters to Washington, 17 September 1788, *PGW-ConS,* 6:521; Election returns for representatives, *DHFFE,* 1:376–380; William Petriken to John Nicholson, 23 March 1789, ibid., 1:406–7; Roland Baumann, "The Harrisburg Convention and the Creation of a 'Loyal Opposition,'" in *Pennsylvania and the Bill of Rights,* ed. Robert G. Crist (University Park: Pennsylvania Historical Association, 1990), 41–52.

44. Adams, *Albert Gallatin,* 69; Harry M. Ward and Harold E. Greer Jr., *Richmond during the Revolution, 1775–83* (Charlottesville: University Press of Virginia, 1977), 18; Genealogical entries for Sophia Gallatin, www.geni.com/people/Sophia-Gallatin/6000000004594262332 and www.wikitree.com/wiki/Allegre-28.

45. Gallatin to Badollet, 4 May 1789, *LAG,* 69–71.

46. Sophia Gallatin to Jane Allegre, 16 May 1789, AHM Collection, New-York Historical Society, version in *LAG,* 72; Albert Gallatin, Note and expense book, 13 November 1783–27 February 1784; Marriage bond and certificates from Albert Gallatin and Savary de Valcoulon, 14 May 1789, *PAG.*

47. L. K. Evans, *Pioneer History of Greene County, Pennsylvania* (Waynesburg, PA: Waynesburg Republican, 1941), 89 (Gallatin quoted); Badollet to Albert Gallatin, 13 January [1790] (original misdated 1789), *PAG;* Gallatin to Badollet, 8 March 1790, *LAG,* 73–75.

Chapter 2: Political Promise

1. Albert Gallatin to Charles Brown, 1 March 1838, *WAG,* 2:523.
2. Gallatin to Hannah Nicholson, 27 August 1793, *LAG,* 103; James S. Biddle, ed., *Autobiography of Charles Biddle* (Philadelphia, 1883), 219; Thomas Twining, *Travels in India a Hundred Years Ago with A Visit to the United States,* ed. William H. G. Twining (London, 1893), 375–77 (12 April 1795); William Dunlap, *Diary of William Dunlap* (3 vols.; New York: New York Historical Society, 1930), 2:384 (13 February 1806); David A. Wilson, ed., *Peter Porcupine in America: Pamphlets on Republicanism and Revolution* (Ithaca, NY: Cornell University Press, 1994), 237.
3. Ephraim Douglass to Gallatin, 5 October 1794, *PAG;* François Furstenberg, *When the United States Spoke French: Five Refugees Who Shaped a Nation* (New York: Penguin Press, 2014), 27–30; Beth A. Twiss-Garrity, "Double Vision: The Philadelphia Cityscape and Perceptions of It," and Robert J. Gough, "The Philadelphia Economic Elite at the End of the Eighteenth Century," in *Shaping the National Culture: The Philadelphia Experience, 1750–1800,* ed. Catherine E. Hutchins (Winterthur, DE: Winterthur Museum, 1994), 4–8, 16–32; Mary M. Schweitzer, "The Spatial Organization of Federalist Philadelphia, 1790," *Journal of Interdisciplinary History* 24, no. 1 (Summer, 1993): 31–57.
4. Gallatin to Alexander Addison, 7 October 1789; James Marshel to Gallatin, 9 October 1789; David Redick to Gallatin, 9 October, 1789; Gallatin, Memorandum of Fayette County election, [October] 1789, *PAG; Minutes of the Convention,* 7–9, 24, 27, 31; *Minutes of the Committee of the Whole,* 5–7; [Alexander Graydon], *Memoirs of a Life, Chiefly Passed in Pennsylvania...*(Harrisburg, 1811), 317; Russell J. Ferguson, *Early Western Pennsylvania Politics* (Pittsburgh: University of Pittsburgh Press, 1938),101–4; Owen S. Ireland, *Religion, Ethnicity, and Politics: Ratifying the Constitution in Pennsylvania* (University Park: Pennsylvania State University Press, 1995), 212–14; Pennsylvania 1789 Constitutional Convention, Fayette County, *Lampi Collection of American Electoral Returns, 1788–1825* (American Antiquarian Society, 2007) (available at *A New Nation Votes: American Election Returns, 1788–1825,* Tufts

Digital Library). On the same day he was elected to the Constitutional Convention, Gallatin lost his bid for a seat in the legislature to more seasoned men. Pennsylvania 1789 House of Representatives, Fayette County, ibid.

5.   Robert L. Brunhouse, *The Counter-Revolution in Pennsylvania, 1776–1790* (Harrisburg: Pennsylvania Museum and Historical Commission, 1942), 221–27; Gordon S. Wood, *The Creation of the American Republic, 1776–1787* (New York: W. W. Norton, 1972), 438–46; Gary B. Nash, *The Unknown American Revolution: The Unruly Birth of Democracy and the Struggle to Create America* (New York: Viking, 2005), 272–80; Terry Bouton, *Taming Democracy: "The People," the Founders, and the Troubled Ending of the American Revolution* (New York: Oxford University Press, 2007), 51–57; Rodger C. Henderson, "Rural Antifederalists and the Bill of Rights in Pennsylvania, 1787–1791," in *Pennsylvania and the Bill of Rights,* ed. Robert G. Crist (University Park: Pennsylvania Historical Association, 1990), 66.

6.   *Minutes of the Convention,* 3–5; Pennsylvania Constitution of 1776, ch. 1, sec. 5 (reform, alter, or abolish clause), ch. 2, sec. 47 (Council of Censors); Graydon, *Memoirs of a Life,* 315–16; Saul Cornell, "Reflections on 'The Late Remarkable Revolutions in Government': Aedanus Burke and Samuel Bryan's Unpublished History of the Ratification of the Federal Constitution," *Pennsylvania Magazine of History and Biography* 62, no. 1 (January 1988): 115–17; Roland Milton Baumann, "The Democratic-Republicans of Philadelphia: The Origins, 1776–1797" (Ph.D. diss., Pennsylvania State University, 1970), 37–43, 50–55; Douglas McNeil Arnold, "Political Ideology and the Internal Revolution in Pennsylvania, 1776–1790" (Ph.D. diss., Princeton University, 1976), 247–49.

7.   Brunhouse, *The Counter-Revolution,* 221–27; Joseph S. Foster, "The Politics of Ideology: The Pennsylvania Constitutional Convention of 1789–90," *Pennsylvania History* 59, no. 2 (April 1992): 122–26.

8.   Graydon, *Memoirs of a Life,* 324; *Minutes of the Committee of the Whole,* 4–9; *Minutes of the Convention,* 32–37; *Maclay's Diary,* 175–77 (30 December 1789); [William Findley], "William Findley of Westmoreland, Pa.,"*Pennsylvania Magazine of History and Biography* 5 (1881): 445–46 (autobiographical sketch); Stephen Carl Arch, "Writing a Federalist Self: Alexander Graydon's *Memoirs of a Life,*" *William and Mary Quarterly,* 3rd Ser., 52, no. 3 (July 1995): 415–32; Arnold, "Political Ideology and the Internal Revolution," 299–317.

9. Gallatin to Charles Brown, 1 March 1838; Gallatin, Notes on freedom of press, [February] 1790; John Marshall to Gallatin, 3 January 1790, *PAG; Minutes of the Committee of the Whole,* 68–70, 86, 91–93; *Minutes of the Convention,* 117–20, 140–41, 178–83; Graydon, *Memoirs of a Life,* 326.

10. On the other hand, Gallatin's attempt to increase the size of the state senate also failed. Gallatin, "Substance of my first speech in Penns[a] Convention in favor of a larger number of representation in the House," [29 December 1789]; Notes on popular government, [February 1790], *PAG; Minutes of the Committee of the Whole,* 17–18, 27–30; *Minutes of the Convention,* 69–71, 136; Dissent of the Minority of the Convention, *DHRC,* 2:631; Saul Cornell, *The Other Founders: Anti-Federalism and the Dissenting Tradition in America, 1788–1828* (Chapel Hill: University of North Carolina Press, 1999), 147–53; Rosemarie Zagarri, *The Politics of Size: Representation in the United States, 1776–1850* (Ithaca, NY: Cornell University Press, 1987), 84–103. On Madison and more elitist views, see [James Madison], Federalist Nos. 10, 53, 55–57, *The Federalist,* ed. Jacob E. Cooke (Middletown, CT: Wesleyan University Press, 1961), 63, 362–65, 373–78, 379–81, 385–86; Wood, *Creation of the American Republic,* 215–18, 237, 504-05; Jennifer Nedelsky, *Private Property and the Limits of American Constitutionalism: The Madisonian Framework and Its Legacy* (Chicago: University of Chicago Press, 1990), 50–55, 163–70; Jack N. Rakove, *Original Meanings: Politics and Ideas in the Making of the Constitution* (New York: Alfred A. Knopf, 1997), 214–27; Gary J. Kornblith and John M. Murrin, "The Making and Unmaking of an American Ruling Class," in *Beyond the American Revolution: Explorations in the History of American Radicalism,* ed. Alfred F. Young (DeKalb: Northeastern Illinois University Press, 1993), 55–57, 60. For a balancing view on Madison, see Lance Banning, *The Sacred Fire of Liberty: James Madison and the Founding of the Federal Republic* (Ithaca, NY: Cornell University Press, 1995), 208–12, 372; Gordon S. Wood, *Revolutionary Characters: What Made the Founders Different* (New York: Penguin Press, 2006), 147–50.

11. Gallatin, Notes on electors for senators; Gallatin, Notes for speech opposing John [viz., James] Ross, [December 1789/January 1790], *PAG; Minutes of the Committee of the Whole,* 20, 22–23, 27; *Minutes of the Convention,* 71–72, 167, 170–72; Graydon, *Memoirs of a Life,* 318–20; Wood, *The Creation of the American Republic,* 244–51, 446–53. For Madison and Jefferson's views on the Virginia constitution, see Thomas

Jefferson, Third draft of Virginia Constitution, [before June 1776]; Jefferson to Edmund Pendleton, 26 August 1776; Jefferson, Draft of Constitution for Virginia, [May–June 1783] (proposal to replace the 1776 constitution); Madison, Observations on Jefferson's draft of a Constitution for Virginia, [October 1788], *PTJ*, 1:356–65, 503–06, 6:294–308, 6:308–17. On James Wilson's similar views at the Federal Convention, see Nedelsky, *Private Property and the Limits of American Constitutionalism*, 114–17. The Pennsylvania Constitutional Convention's minutes say nothing about a proposal for the election of senators by the lower house described in Ferguson, *Early Western Pennsylvania Politics*, 107; Harry Marlin Tinkcom, *The Republicans and Federalists in Pennsylvania, 1790–1801* (Harrisburg: Pennsylvania Historical and Museum Commission, 1950), 14–15; and Raymond Walters Jr., *Albert Gallatin: Jeffersonian Financier and Diplomat* (New York: Macmillan, 1957), 36.

12. Gallatin, Notes on suffrage, [January] 1790; Gallatin, Notes for state legislature, [January/February] 1790; Gallatin, Notes on general Congress ticket, [January/February] 1790, *PAG; Minutes of the Committee of the Whole*, 49–50, 80–82, 85; *Minutes of the Convention*, 37, 39, 94–95; Nedelsky, *Private Property and the Limits of American Constitutionalism*, 54–55; Donald Ratcliffe, "The Right to Vote and the Rise of Democracy, 1787–1828," *Journal of the Early Republic* 33, no. 2 (Summer 2013): 222–31. Jefferson's draft constitution for Virginia contained a freehold requirement for suffrage; Third draft of Virginia Constitution, [before June 1776]; *PTJ*, 1:356–65. For Jefferson's later statements against the freehold requirement, see Jefferson to Jeremiah Moore, 14 August 1800, ibid., 32:102–03; Jefferson to John Hampden Pleasants, 19 April 1824, *WTJ*, 12:353. Although Gallatin apparently suggested in later years that he had supported suffrage for "freemen" regardless of race, the minutes of the Convention contain no discussion of the issue. [William Beach Lawrence], "Biographical Memoir of Albert Gallatin," *United States Magazine and Democratic Review* 12, no. 60 (June 1843): 4; William Beach Lawrence to B[yam] K[erby] Stevens, 14 August 1848, *PAG;* Julie Winch, "Free Men and 'Freemen': Black Voting Rights in Pennsylvania, 1790–1870," *Pennsylvania Legacies* 8, no. 2 (November 2008): 16.

13. Gallatin, Fayette County election tally, [October] 1790; Gallatin, Fayette County election results, [October] 1791; Gallatin, 1792 election tally, filmed with Alexander Addison to Gallatin, 11 October 1792, *PAG;* Pennsylvania House of Representatives, Fayette County, 1790, 1791, and 1792, *Lampi Collection of American Electoral Returns.* Earlier

biographers, apparently relying on Gallatin's late-life recollections, have said that Gallatin had no opposition in 1791. Henry Adams, *The Life of Albert Gallatin* (1879; repr., New York: Peter Smith, 1943), 84; Walters, *Albert Gallatin*, 38; Thomas K. McCraw, *The Founders and Finance: How Hamilton, Gallatin, and Other Immigrants Forged a New Economy* (Cambridge, MA: Harvard University Press, 2012), 195; Gallatin, Autobiographical sketch, [1849], *PAG*, extract in *SWAG*, 8; Lawrence, "Biographical Memoir of Albert Gallatin," 4.

14. *Maclay's Diary*, 380 (12 February 1791); Steve Rosswurm, "Class Relations, Political Economy, and Society in Philadelphia," in *Shaping the National Culture: The Philadelphia Experience, 1750–1800*, ed. Catherine E. Hutchins (Winterthur, DE: Winterthur Museum, 1994), 56–60; Edwin G. Burrows, *Albert Gallatin and the Political Economy of Republicanism, 1761–1800* (New York: Garland Publishing, 1986), 15–21 (print of Ph.D. diss., Columbia University, 1974), 188–94; Amy Hudson Henderson, "Furnishing the Republican Court: Building and Decorating Philadelphia Houses, 1790–1800" (Ph.D. diss., University of Delaware, 2008), 77–94.

15. Days after he became the Secretary of State in 1795, Timothy Pickering declined an invitation from the Binghams with the candid explanation that he and Mrs. Pickering could not afford to socialize as they did. Robert C. Alberts, *The Golden Voyage: The Life and Times of William Bingham, 1752–1804* (New York: Houghton Mifflin, 1969), 209–13, 238–39, 298–99, 303–11; Albrecht Koschnik, *"Let a Common Interest Bind Us Together": Associations, Partisanship, and Culture in Philadelphia, 1775–1840* (Charlottesville: University of Virginia Press, 2007), 11–40; Furstenberg, *When the United States Spoke French*, 24–31; Clement Fatovic, *America's Founding and the Struggle Over Economic Inequality* (Lawrence: University Press of Kansas, 2015), 22–23; Roland M. Baumann, "John Swanwick: Spokesman for 'Merchant-Republicanism' in Philadelphia, 1790–98," *Pennsylvania Magazine of History and Biography* 97, no. 2 (April 1973): 135–48; David S. Shields and Fredricka J. Teute, "The Court of Abigail Adams," *Journal of the Early Republic* 35, no. 2 (Summer 2015), 229–33.

16. *Maclay's Diary*, 380 (12 February 1791); Biddle, *Autobiography of Charles Biddle*, 255–56; James Hutchinson to Gallatin, 11 June 1790, 17 February 1791, 19 August 1792, and 14 September 1792; John Badollet to Gallatin, 14 December 1793; Membership certificate for Albert Gallatin, American Philosophical Society, 14 February 1791; Membership

certificate for Albert Gallatin, Pennsylvania Society for Promoting the Abolition of Slavery, 3 March 1793, *PAG;* Gallatin to Hannah Nicholson, 2 September 1793, *LAG,* 105–06; *Centennial Anniversary of the Pennsylvania Society for Promoting the Abolition of Slavery* (Philadelphia, 1875), 42 (list of members in 1789); Tinkcom, *Republicans and Federalists,* 53–54; Forrest McDonald, *Alexander Hamilton: A Biography* (New York: W. W. Norton, 1979), 192; Gary B. Nash and Jean R. Soderlund, *Freedom by Degrees: Emancipation in Pennsylvania and Its Aftermath* (New York: Oxford University Press, 1991), 124–25, 130; Nicholas P. Wood, "A 'Class of Citizens': The Earliest Black Petitioners to Congress and Their Quaker Allies," *William and Mary Quarterly,* 3rd Ser., 74, no. 1 (January 2017), 128–31. Gallatin opposed slavery, but not aggressively. At the time he joined the Pennsylvania abolition society, he supported a bill in the Pennsylvania Assembly for the complete abolition of slavery. As a Congressman in later years, he supported a ban on slavery in the Mississippi Territory and backed a petition against the slave trade. Although he spoke of resisting the temptation to use slave labor in Fayette County in the 1790s, he "purchased the time" of a young enslaved African American woman in Philadelphia in 1798 and of another in Fayette County in 1823. Those women, born of enslaved mothers after Pennsylvania had passed its gradual emancipation law, would themselves have remained enslaved until they reached the age of twenty-eight. Gallatin to James W. Nicholson, 5 May 1798; Albert Gallatin to Hannah Gallatin, 6 May 1800 and 5 February 1801, *PAG; Annals,* 5th Cong., 2nd Sess., 1309–10; ibid., 6th Cong., 1st Sess., 237–38; [Gallatin], Pennsylvania House committee report, 23 March 1793, *LAG,* 86; Nash and Soderlund, *Freedom by Degrees,* 111, 173–78, 130–36; Padraig Riley, *Slavery and the Democratic Conscience: Political Life in Jeffersonian America* (Philadelphia: University of Pennsylvania Press, 2016), 56–58; Christopher M. Osborne, "Invisible Hands: Slaves, Bound Laborers, and the Development of Western Pennsylvania, 1780–1820," *Pennsylvania History* 72, no. 1 (Winter 2005): 81.

17.   Alexander J. Dallas to Gallatin, 4 May 1792, 25 September 1792, and 8 November 1793, *PAG;* Albert Gallatin to Hannah Gallatin, 18 December 1793, *LAG,* 113; Raymond Walters Jr., *Alexander James Dallas: Lawyer—Politician—Financier, 1759–1817* (Philadelphia: University of Pennsylvania Press, 1943), 6–13, 18–27, 34–35; Kenneth R. Rossman, *Thomas Mifflin and the Politics of the American Revolution* (Chapel Hill: University of North Carolina Press, 1952), 197–98, 207–08.

18. Gallatin, Autobiographical sketch [1849], *PAG,* extract in *SWAG,* 8; Gallatin, Committee Book for 1790–91, October 1790; Gallatin to Badollet, 7 January 1792, 3 May 1793; Gallatin to Thomas Clare, 9 March 1793, *PAG.*

19. Gallatin, Notes on Pennsylvania finances, [1790] (worksheet for appendices to committee report); Gallatin to Badollet, 22 February 1792; Dallas to Gallatin, 4 May 1792, *PAG;* Gallatin, Autobiographical sketch, [1849], *PAG,* extract in *LAG,* 85; *Maclay's Diary,* 214-15 (8 March 1790); *Pennsylvania House Journal 1790–91,* 162–73; *Laws of Pennsylvania* (Dallas Reprint), 2:256–62 (1785 funding act), 417–22 and 426–28 (1786 funding system); *Annals,* 1st Cong., 3rd Sess., 1885 (Pennsylvania creditors' petition); Pelatiah Webster, *Political Essays on the Nature and Operation of Money, Public Finances, and Other Subjects* (Philadelphia, 1791), 269–305 (critique of Pennsylvania funding system replaced by plan in Gallatin's report); Anon., *A View of the Principles, Operation and Probable Effects of the Funding System of Pennsylvania* (Philadelphia, 1788), 10–12; [William Findley], *A Review of the Revenue System Adopted by the First Congress…* (Philadelphia, 1794), 31 (need for inducement to state creditors); E. James Ferguson, *The Power of the Purse: A History of American Public Finance, 1776-1790* (Chapel Hill: University of North Carolina Press, 1961), 277–80, 330–31; McDonald, *Alexander Hamilton,* 190, 226–27.

20. Norman B. Wilkinson, *Land Policy and Land Speculation in Pennsylvania, 1779–1800* (New York: Arno Press, 1979), 126 (quoting the cornerstone); *Pennsylvania House Journal 1790–91,* 215–17, 226–31, 238, 242, 247–48, 333–36; *Pennsylvania House Journal 1791–92,* 157–62, 188, 256–59, 297–98; *Laws of Pennsylvania* (Dallas Reprint), 3:31–32, 51–55, 55–57, 62–63, 63–65, 67 (1791 reform acts); Anthony M. Joseph, *From Liberty to Liberality: The Transformation of the Pennsylvania Legislature, 1776–1820* (Lanham, MD: Lexington Books, 2012), 87; Raymond Walters Jr., "The Making of a Financier: Albert Gallatin in the Pennsylvania Assembly," *Pennsylvania Magazine of History and Biography* 70, no. 3 (July 1946): 260–62, 264–67; Roland M. Baumann, "'Heads I Win, Tails You Lose': The Public Creditors and the Assumption Issue in Pennsylvania, 1790–1802," *Pennsylvania History* 44, no. 3 (July 1977): 212–222.

21. Gallatin, "Calculation in favour of 1st amendment proposed by Congress in 1789 to Constitution," [1798]; Gallatin, Notes on debt service, [1796]; Gallatin, Notes on exports, [January 1798); Albert Gallatin to Hannah

Gallatin, 29 January 1801, *PAG;* Gallatin to Jefferson, [14–15 November] and 15 November 1801, *PTJ,* 35:622–24, 626–30; Gallatin to Eben[ezer] Dodge, 21 January 1847, *PAG,* version in *WAG,* 2:643; Jerry E. Mueller, ed., *Autobiography of John Russell Bartlett, 1805–1889* (Providence, RI: John Carter Brown Library, 2006), 27.

22. Gallatin to Robert Walsh Jr., 2 August 1830, *WAG,* 2:429–30; Gallatin to William Duane, 5 July 1801 (takes no general view on a subject "until all the facts & minutiae are familiar"); William Beach Lawrence to B[yam] K[erby] Stevens, 14 August 1848, *PAG* (life sketch reviewed by Gallatin); Gallatin to J[oseph] R[eed] Ingersoll, 25 March 1846, *WAG,* 2:628 ("It may be otherwise with men more sagacious or bolder than I am, but if I have ever produced anything perspicuous and useful, it has uniformly been the result of long experience or of arduous and persevering labor.").

23. Gallatin, Autobiographical sketch [1849], *PAG,* extract in *LAG,* 85. On a similar but unsuccessful proposal to protect Massachusetts state creditors from the interest rate cut that came with federal assumption, see Christopher Gore to Rufus King, 24 January 1790, *LCRK,* 1:385–86; Paul Goodman, *The Democratic-Republicans of Massachusetts: Politics in a Young Republic* (Cambridge, MA: Harvard University Press, 1964), 34–35.

24. [Pelatiah Webster], *An Essay on Credit in Which the Doctrine of Banks Is Considered…* (Philadelphia, 1786), 9, 24–27; [Findley], *Review of the Revenue System,* 81–82. Gallatin and Savary had boarded with Pelatiah Webster, an articulate advocate for the Bank of North America, during the summer of 1783. *Annals,* 3rd Cong., 1st Sess. 59 (Webster deposition). On the early debates over banking, see Bray Hammond, *Banks and Politics in America from the Revolution to the Civil War* (Princeton, NJ: Princeton University Press, 1957), 48–64, 116–17, 144; Stanley Elkins and Eric McKitrick, *The Age of Federalism: The Early American Republic, 1788–1800* (New York: Oxford University Press, 1993), 229–30; Robert E. Wright, *Origins of Commercial Banking in America, 1750–1800* (Lanham, MD: Rowman and Littlefield, 2001), 149–52; Howard Bodenhorn, *State Banking in Early America: A New Economic History* (New York: Oxford University Press, 2003), 125–28; Barbara Weill, "Democracy and Revolution: Democratic and Leveling Movements in Pennsylvania, 1776–1790" (Ph.D. diss., New School for Social Research, 1977), 134–39.

25. *Pennsylvania House Journal 1792–93,* 156–57; *Laws of Pennsylvania* (Dallas Reprint), 3:323–35; Philadelphia *General Advertiser,* 14, 16, and 18 February 1793; Bodenhorn, *State Banking,* 141–48; Howard Bodenhorn, *A History of Banking in Antebellum America: Financial Markets and Economic Development in an Era of Nation-Building* (Cambridge, UK: Cambridge University Press, 2000), 35–37; Joseph, *From Liberty to Liberality,* 87–90, 117–18; Baumann, "Democratic-Republicans of Philadelphia," 325–41. Although Gallatin as mover of the committee report received credit for the bank proposal, its principal backer in the House seems to have been the prominent Republican merchant John Swanwick. Baumann, "John Swanwick: Spokesman for 'Merchant-Republicanism,'" 153–54. Louis Hartz's classic work treats the Bank of Pennsylvania as a harbinger of the use of mixed public-private corporations for economic development. Hartz, *Economic Policy and Democratic Thought: Pennsylvania, 1776–1860* (Cambridge, MA: Harvard University Press, 1948), 82–83. On the bank's architecturally striking headquarters, see Talbot Hamlin, *Benjamin Henry Latrobe* (New York: Oxford University Press, 1955), 152–57.

26. Gallatin to Badollet, 22 February 1792, 7 and 21 January 1792, 9 March 1793; Ephraim Douglass to Gallatin, 3 April 1791; John Nevill to Gallatin, 6 July 1791; Badollet to Gallatin, 30 January 1792; Gallatin to Clare, 18 December 1792, 9 March 1793, *PAG;* Tinkcom, *Republicans and Federalists,* 113–33.

27. Albert Gallatin, Report of the Secretary of the Treasury on the Subject of Public Roads and Canals, Senate Print (Washington, DC, 1808), 59, reprinted in *ASP: Miscellaneous,* 1:738; *Pennsylvania House Journal 1791–92,* 232–33; *Laws of Pennsylvania* (Dallas Reprint), 3:246–58; Philadelphia *General Advertiser,* 7 April 1791; Gallatin to Badollet, 3 May 1793; Badollet to Gallatin, 6 June and 8 July 1793, *PAG;* Charles I. Landis, "History of the Philadelphia and Lancaster Turnpike," *Pennsylvania Magazine of History and Biography* 42, no. 2 (1918): 127–40; William A. Hunter, "John Badollet's 'Journal of the Time I Spent in Stony Creek Glades,' 1793–1794," *Pennsylvania Magazine of History and Biography* 104, no. 2 (April 1980): 162–65.

28. Philadelphia *American Daily Advertiser,* 10 February 1792; Philadelphia *General Advertiser,* 8 and 9 February 1792; *Pennsylvania House Journal 1791–92,* 31–32, 35, 69–70, 75–76, 279–80; *Laws of Pennsylvania* (Dallas Reprint), 3:209–14. To get the land act passed, Gallatin finally supported a compromise that would allow absentee investors to buy land

if they arranged for others to settle it. Speculators were able to circumvent the settlement requirement, however, by relying on a waiver available when Native American violence prevented settlement. Resulting litigation clouded land titles for years. In the 1798 election, Gallatin's supporters had to defend him from the not entirely unjust charge that he was partly responsible for the mess. Washington, PA, *Herald of Liberty,* 1 October 1798; Gallatin to Jefferson, 28 November 1807, *FOL*—Early Access (recalling speculators' abuses); Wilkinson, *Land Policy and Speculation in Pennsylvania, 1779–1800,* 129–34; M. Ruth Reilly Kelly, "'Rightfully Theirs and Valid in Law': Western Pennsylvania Land Wars, 1792–1810," *Pennsylvania History* 71, no. 1 (Winter 2004): 25–49.

29. *Pennsylvania House Journal 1790–91,* 372–73, 452, 497–98, 543, 553–54; *Pennsylvania House Journal 1791–92,* 29, 44–45, 57–58, 63, 166, 169, 243, 252, 298, 303, 311; *Pennsylvania House Journal 1792–93,* 104–06, 120-21, 190–91, 217–21; Jacob Cox Parsons, ed., *Extracts from the Diary of Jacob Hiltzheimer* (Philadelphia, 1893), 186 (14 December 1792); Deposition of Thomas Stokely, [January 1794]; Gallatin to Clare, 9 March 1793; Gallatin to Badollet, 9 March 1793, *PAG; Annals,* 3rd Cong., 1st Sess., 58–60; *Maclay's Diary,* 365 (20 January 1791); Tinkcom, *Republicans and Federalists,* 145–53.

30. Jefferson to William Short, 3 January 1793, *PTJ,* 25:14–17; Eugene Perry Link, *Democratic-Republican Societies, 1790–1800* (New York: Columbia University Press, 1942), 10-12, 80-81; Philip S. Foner, ed., *The Democratic-Republican Societies, 1790–1800: A Documentary Sourcebook* (Westport, CT: Greenwood Press, 1976), 7–8, 64–71; Elkins and McKitrick, *The Age of Federalism,* 308–11, 330–31; Matthew Q. Dawson, *Partisanship and the Birth of American's Second Party, 1796–1800: "Stop the Wheels of Government"* (Westport, CT: Greenwood Press, 2000), 6–12; Gordon S. Wood, *Empire of Liberty: A History of the Early Republic, 1789–1815* (New York: Oxford University Press, 2009), 174–89; Harry Ammon, "The Genêt Mission and the Development of American Political Parties," *Journal of American History* 52, no. 4 (March 1966): 718–32; Baumann, "The Democratic-Republicans of Philadelphia," 406–14.

31. *Annals,* 3rd Cong., 1st Sess., 9–10, 19, 24, 27–29, 42-44, 47–62; Motion of Aaron Burr, 10 January 1794; Motion of John Taylor, 10 January 1794; Gallatin to [Burr], [January/February 1794]; [Gallatin], Notes for speeches, 21 and 27 February 1794, *PAG;* Albert Gallatin to Hannah Gallatin, 3, 6, 11, 15, 18, 20 December 1793, *LAG,* 111-14; James

Monroe to Jefferson, 3 March 1794, *PTJ*, 28:29–31; Gallatin to Walter
Lowrie, 19 February 1824, *WAG*, 2:283–87; Gallatin to J[oseph] Gale
Jr., 30 June 1826, AHM Collection, New-York Historical Society; Editors'
note and documents, *PCAB*, 1:160–74; U. S. Senate Historical Office,
*United States Senate Election, Expulsion and Censure Cases, 1793–
1990*, by Anne M. Butler and Wendy Wolff, Senate Doc. 103-33 (1995),
3–5.

32. *Annals*, 3rd Cong., 1st Sess., 25–26, 29–30, 34–36; Gallatin, "Resolution
that Sec. of Treasury has violated law," December, 1793 (draft); Hamilton
to John Adams, 22 February 1794 (copy), *PAG;* Hamilton to John Adams,
6 February and 22 February 1794, *PAH*, 16:9–12, 47–49; Noble E.
Cunningham Jr., *The Jeffersonian Republicans: The Formation of a Party
Organization, 1789–1801* (Chapel Hill: University of North Carolina
Press, 1957), 51–53; Elkins and McKitrick, *The Age of Federalism*,
295–302. Days after Hamilton's letters to the Senate, William Branch
Giles carried new resolutions in the House to begin an investigation of
Treasury accounts that Hamilton had demanded as he began to plan his
return to private life. *Annals*, 3rd Cong., 1st Sess., 464–66; McDonald,
Alexander Hamilton, 286.

33. Gallatin to Badollet, 3 May 1793; Gallatin to Clare, 3 May 1793; Gallatin
to Badollet, 31 July 1793, 1 February 1794, *PAG;* Charles Peirce, *A
Meteorological Account of the Weather of Philadelphia from January 1,
1790, to January 1, 1847* (Philadelphia, 1847), 109; James Grant Wilson,
ed., *The Memorial History of the City of New-York* (4 vols.; New York,
1892–93), 3:152 (1799 tax assessment of Nicholson house); Byam Kerby
Stevens, comp., *Genealogical-Biographical Histories of the Families of
Stevens, Gallatin, and Nicholson* (New York: National Americana
Society, 1911), 38–39; Robert D. Arbuckle, *Pennsylvania Speculator and
Patriot: The Entrepreneurial John Nicholson, 1757–1800* (University
Park: Pennsylvania State University Press, 1975), 44, 47, 54–60; Alfred
F. Young, *The Democratic Republicans of New York: The Origins,
1763–1797* (Chapel Hill: University of North Carolina Press, 1967), 285,
373, 414.

34. Hannah Nicholson to James W. Nicholson, 21 February and 6 March
1792; Gallatin to James Nicholson, 20 July 1793; James Nicholson to
Gallatin, 24 July 1793 (draft and final versions), *PAG;* John Ramage,
Portrait of Catherine Nicholson (later Catherine Few), watercolor on
ivory, 1787, Metropolitan Museum of Art; James Sharples, Portrait of
Albert Gallatin, pastel on paper, c. 1796, Metropolitan Museum of Art;

[unknown artist], Silhouette of Hannah Gallatin, c. 1806, Gallatin Family Papers, Small Special Collections Library, University of Virginia, reproduced in Albert Eugene Gallatin, *Gallatin Iconography* (Boston, privately pub., 1934), 44; Susan E. Klepp, *Revolutionary Conceptions: Women, Fertility, and Family Limitation in America, 1760-1820* (Chapel Hill: University of North Carolina Press, 2009), 50, 295, 298; Carrie Rebora Barratt and Lori Zabar, *American Portrait Miniatures in the Metropolitan Museum of Art* (New Haven, CT: Yale University Press, 2010), 40.

35. Gallatin to Hannah Nicholson, 25 July, 25 August, 29 August, 2 September, 4 September 1793, *LAG*, 102-07; Gallatin to Badollet, 1 February 1794, ibid., 107–10. Konstantin Dierks, *In My Power: Letter Writing and Communications in Early America* (Philadelphia: University of Pennsylvania Press, 2009), 141–77; Sarah Knott, *Sensibility and the American Revolution* (Chapel Hill: University of North Carolina Press, 2009), 122–30, 149–51, 230–34.

36. Albert Gallatin to Maria Nicholson, 1 March 1799; Albert Gallatin to Hannah Gallatin, 15 January 1801; Albert Gallatin, Notes on career of Commodore Nicholson, [before August] 1849, *PAG;* Thomas Paine to Jefferson, 15 September 1789, *PTJ*, 15:429–30 (compliments to Nicholson family); Statement of administration of Thomas Witter estate, [1833], Nicholson Family Papers, Box 1, Folder 1, New-York Historical Society; William Plumb Bacon, comp., *Ancestry of Albert Gallatin and of Hannah Nicholson* (New York: Tobias A. Wright, [1916]), 35–39; Nathan Miller, *Sea of Glory: A Naval History of the American Revolution* (Charleston: Nautical and Aviation Publishing, 1974), 213–14; J. Jefferson Looney and Ruth L. Woodward, *Princetonians: A Biographical Dictionary, 1791– 1794* (Princeton, NJ: Princeton University Press, 1991), 81 (sketch of James Witter Nicholson, who attended Princeton before Columbia); Arthur Irving Bernstein, "The Rise of the Democratic-Republican Party in New York City, 1789–1800" (Ph.D. diss., Columbia University, 1964), 9–13.

37. Gallatin to Badollet, 31 July 1793, 1 February 1794, *PAG;* Rosemarie Zagarri, *Revolutionary Backlash: Women and Politics in the Early American Republic* (Philadelphia: University of Pennsylvania Press, 2007), 88–93; Klepp, *Revolutionary Conceptions*, 107–08, 113–14, 251–53; Jan Lewis, "The Republican Wife: Virtue and Seduction in the Early Republic," *William and Mary Quarterly*, 3rd Ser., 44, no. 4 (October 1987): 697–702.

38. Albert Gallatin to Hannah Gallatin, 15, 18, and 20 December 1793, 7 and 19 April 1794, *LAG,* 112–14, 121–22; Albert Gallatin to Clare, 5 March 1794, *PAG.*

Chapter 3: Gallatin's Insurrection

1. [Alexander Hamilton], Federalist Nos. 12 and 35, *The Federalist,* ed. Jacob E. Cooke (Middletown, CT: Wesleyan University Press, 1961), 75, 216–17; Hamilton, Plan for the Support of Public Credit, 9 January 1790, *ASP: Finance,* 1:22–23; Hamilton, Further Provision for Establishing the Public Credit, 13 December 1790, ibid., 1:64–66; John Brewer, *The Sinews of Power: War, Money, and the English State, 1688–1783* (New York: Alfred A. Knopf, 1989), 100–13; Max M. Edling, *A Revolution in Favor of Government: Origins of the U. S. Constitution and the Making of the American State* (New York: Oxford University Press, 2003), 176; John V. C. Nye, *War, Wine, and Taxes: The Political Economy of Anglo-French Trade, 1689–1900* (Princeton, NJ: Princeton University Press, 2007), 68–88. James Madison professed to prefer direct taxes, but he supported Hamilton's proposal, saying that he felt public and legislative opinion favored excises. *Annals,* 1ˢᵗ Cong., 3ʳᵈ Sess., 1791, 1894–1900; Philadelphia *American Daily Advertiser,* 14 January 1791; Madison to Hamilton, 19 November 1789; Madison to Edmund Pendleton, 2 January 1791, *PJM-CS,* 12:449–50, 13:342–45.
2. U. S. Bureau of the Census, *Population of States and Counties of the United States, 1790–1990,* ed. Richard L. Forstall, PB96–119060 (March 1996), 137–39 (1790 census); R. Eugene Harper, *The Transformation of Western Pennsylvania, 1770–1800* (Pittsburgh: University of Pittsburgh Press, 1991), xvii–xviii, 15, 29–43; Andrew Shankman, *Crucible of American Democracy: The Struggle to Fuse Egalitarianism and Capitalism in Jeffersonian Pennsylvania* (Lawrence: University Press of Kansas, 2004), 55–56; Mary K. Bonsteel Tachau, "A New Look at the Whiskey Rebellion," in *The Whiskey Rebellion: Past and Present Perspectives,* ed. Steven R. Boyd (Westport, CT: Greenwood Press, 1985), 99–100. For an important study questioning how much the excise actually burdened Western distillers, see David O. Whitten, "An Economic Inquiry into the Whiskey Rebellion of 1794," *Agricultural History* 49, no. 3 (July 1975), 491–504.
3. *Pennsylvania House Journal 1790–91,* 108–11, 124, 142–49; *Pennsylvania Senate Journal 1790–91,* 92; Act of 3 March 1791, *Statutes at Large* 1 (1845): 199–214; Jacob E. Cooke, "The Whiskey Rebellion:

A Re-evaluation," *Pennsylvania History* 30, no. 3 (July 1963), 335–346; William D. Barber, "'Among the Most Techy Articles of Civil Police': Federal Taxation and the Adoption of the Whiskey Excise," *William and Mary Quarterly,* 3rd Ser., 25, no. 1 (January 1968), 80–2; Roger V. Gould, "Patron-Client Ties, State Centralization, and the Whiskey Rebellion," *American Journal of Sociology* 102, no. 2 (Sept. 1996), 400–29; Dorothy E. Fennell, "From Rebelliousness to Insurrection: A Social History of the Whiskey Rebellion, 1765–1802" (Ph.D. diss., University of Pittsburgh, 1981), 50–54, 98–140.

4. Congressmen received $6 per day, while Pennsylvania Assemblymen received only $3. *Maclay's Diary,* 385 (17 February 1791) (quoted), 356, 366–67, 375–77, 388–89; Anthony M. Joseph, *From Liberty to Liberality: The Transformation of the Pennsylvania Legislature, 1776–1820* (Lanham, MD: Lexington Books, 2012), 47.

5. William Pencak, "A Historical Perspective," in *Riot and Revelry in Early America,* ed. William Pencak, Matthew Dennis, and Simon P. Newman (University Park: Pennsylvania State University Press, 2002), 8–11; Paul A. Gilje, *Rioting in America* (Bloomington: Indiana University Press, 1996), 51–59; Barbara Clark Smith, *The Freedoms We Lost: Consent and Resistance in Revolutionary America* (New York: New Press, 2010), 134–210; Seth Cotlar, *Tom Paine's America: The Rise and Fall of Transatlantic Radicalism in the Early Republic* (Charlottesville: University of Virginia Press, 2011), 170–88; Gary J. Kornblith and John M. Murrin, "The Making and Unmaking of an American Ruling Class" and Alfred F. Young, "How Radical Was the American Revolution?" in *Beyond the American Revolution: Explorations in the History of American Radicalism,* ed. Alfred F. Young (DeKalb: Northern Illinois University Press, 1993), 60–61, 335–36.

6. John Adams to William Stephens Smith, 14 March 1791, Adams Family Papers: Electronic Archive, Massachusetts Historical Society; John Nevill to Albert Gallatin, 6 July 1791, *PAG;* William Findley, *History of the Insurrection in the Four Western Counties of Pennsylvania…* (Philadelphia, 1796), 78–82; Carl E. Prince, *The Federalists and the Origins of the U. S. Civil Service* (New York: New York University Press, 1977), 138–39; Thomas P. Slaughter, *The Whiskey Rebellion: Frontier Epilogue to the American Revolution* (New York: Oxford University Press, 1986), 152–53; Cooke, "The Whiskey Rebellion: A Re-evaluation," 336–42; Gould, "Patron-Client Ties, State Centralization, and the Whiskey Rebellion," 410–11.

7. James Marshel to Gallatin, 16 July 1791, *PAG;* Alexander Hamilton to George Washington, 5 August 1794, *PAH,* 17:27–28; Hugh H. Brackenridge, *Incidents of the Insurrection in the Western Parts of Pennsylvania*...(Philadelphia, 1795), 3:9-10, 16-18; *Pennsylvania House Journal 1790–91,* 147–49 (separate statement of Thomas Ryerson); Philadelphia *American Daily Advertiser,* 17 August 1791; Russell J. Ferguson, *Early Western Pennsylvania Politics* (Pittsburgh: University of Pittsburgh Press, 1938), 28–29, 44; Harper, *The Transformation of Western Pennsylvania,* 17–18, 50, 108, 112; Fennell, "From Rebelliousness to Insurrection," 46–48. The Pennsylvania excise on spirits was a tax on sales, not a tax on production like the federal excise. Robin L. Einhorn, *American Taxation American Slavery* (Chicago: University of Chicago Press, 2006), 287n16; Whitten, "Economic Inquiry into the Whiskey Rebellion," 493. Gallatin had registered a still under the Pennsylvania excise law at least in 1786 and 1789. Franklin Ellis, ed., *History of Fayette County, Pennsylvania* (Philadelphia, 1882), 768.
8. Minutes of the first meeting at Pittsburgh, 7 September 1791, *Pennsylvania Archives,* 2nd Ser., ed. John B. Linn and William H. Egle (19 vols.; Harrisburg, 1896), 4:16–18; Findley, *History,* 267 ("improper for a meeting convened for the express purpose of preparing a petition...to avail themselves of that opportunity to censure the measures of government"). Gallatin did not include this call for popular nullification when he later listed the protest actions that had gone too far. Albert Gallatin, *The Speech of Albert Gallatin...on...the Validity of the Elections Held in the Four Western Counties*...(Philadelphia, 1795), 6–7.
9. Gordon S. Wood, *The Radicalism of the American Revolution* (New York: Alfred A. Knopf, 1992), 256–70; Saul Cornell, *The Other Founders: Anti-Federalism and the Dissenting Tradition in America, 1788–1828* (Chapel Hill: University of North Carolina Press, 1999), 213–17; Terry Bouton, *Taming Democracy: "The People," the Founders, and the Troubled Ending of the American Revolution* (New York: Oxford University Press, 2007), 145–63; Christian G. Fritz, *American Sovereigns: The People and America's Constitutional Tradition Before the Civil War* (New York: Cambridge University Press, 2008), 9–116; Robert W. T. Martin, *Government by Dissent: Protest, Resistance, and Radical Democratic Thought in the Early American Republic* (New York: New York University Press, 2013), 21–81; Michael J. Farber, "Democratic Anti-Federalism: Rights, Democracy, and the Minority in the Pennsylvania Ratifying Convention," *Pennsylvania Magazine of History and Biography*

138, no. 2 (April 2014), 145, 160–61. On the Pennsylvania excise, the remonstrance against it, and its repeal, see Philadelphia *American Daily Advertiser,* 30 September 1791; Philadelphia *General Advertiser,* 30 September 1791; *Pennsylvania House Journal 1790–91,* 464, 475, 480, 528; Dall W. Forsyth, *Taxation and Political Change in the Young Nation, 1781–1833* (New York: Columbia University Press, 1977), 43. On resistance to federal excise collection outside Pennsylvania, see Hamilton, Report on the Difficulties in the Execution of the Act Laying Duties on Distilled Spirits, 5 March 1792, *PAH,* 11:77–106; Mary K. Bonsteel Tachau, "The Whiskey Rebellion in Kentucky: A Forgotten Episode of Civil Disobedience," *Journal of the Early Republic* 2, no. 3 (Autumn 1982): 239–59.

10. Bouton, *Taming Democracy,* 159–66; Alan Taylor, "Agrarian Independence: Northern Land Rioters after the Revolution," in *Beyond the American Revolution,* 224–28; Michael Lienesch, "Reinterpreting Rebellion: The Influence of Shays's Rebellion on American Political Thought," in *In Debt to Shays: The Bicentennial of an Agrarian Rebellion,* ed. Robert A. Gross (Charlottesville: University Press of Virginia, 1993), 168–75; Fennell, "From Rebelliousness to Insurrection," 5–43.

11. Resolutions of Pittsburgh meeting, 22 August 1792, *PAG* (broadside), printed in *Pennsylvania Archives,* 2nd Ser., 4:25–26; Petition to Congress, [22 August 1792], *PAG* (broadside); Draft petition to Congress, [August] 1792, *PAG* (different petition in Gallatin's handwriting), printed in *WAG,* 1:2–4.

12. Hamilton to John Adams, 25 June 1792; *PAH,* 11:559; Hamilton to Tench Coxe, 1 September 1792; Hamilton to Washington, 1, 9, and 11 September 1792; Washington to Hamilton, 26 August and 17 September 1792, *PAH,* 12:305–10, 311–12, 347-50, 366, 276–78, 390; Washington, Proclamation, 15 September 1792, *PGW-PS,* 11:122–24; Richard H. Kohn, "The Washington Administration's Decision to Crush the Whiskey Rebellion," *Journal of American History* 59, no. 3 (December 1972), 569–71.

13. Hamilton to John Jay, 3 September 1792; Edmund Randolph to Hamilton, 8 September 1792, *PAH,* 12:316–17, 337. Hamilton had a similar exchange with new Attorney General William Bradford early in 1794, when the Democratic Society of Washington County sent a remonstrance against the excise tax to Washington. Robert M. Chesney, "Democratic-Republican Societies, Subversion, and the Limits of Legitimate Political

Dissent in the Early Republic," *North Carolina Law Review* 82, no. 5 (2004), 1554–55.

14. Philadelphia *General Advertiser,* 28 September 1792; Gallatin to Thomas Clare, 18 December 1792; Gallatin to John Badollet, 18 December 1792, *PAG;* George Clymer to Hamilton, 28 September, 4 October, and 10 October, 1792, *PAH,* 12:495–97, 517–22, 540–42; James Tagg, *Benjamin Franklin Bache and the Philadelphia Aurora* (Philadelphia: University of Pennsylvania Press, 1991), 210–12. William Findley, who had not attended either Pittsburgh meeting, later wrote that the resolutions "disgusted" members of Congress and "offended the citizens at large." Findley, *History,* 45.

15. Alexander J. Dallas to Gallatin, 25 September 1792; James Hutchinson to Gallatin, 14 September, 25 September, 24 October 1792; James Lang to Gallatin, 19 September 1792; William Findley to Gallatin, 27 September 1792; Andrew Gregg to Gallatin, 27 September 1792; Alexander Addison to Gallatin, 11 October 1792, *PAG;* Randolph to Washington, 10 September 1792, *PGW–PS,* 11:107 (convictions for the assault on a revenue officer will encourage Gallatin's and Smilie's friends to disavow the Pittsburgh resolutions); Harry Marlin Tinkcom, *The Republicans and Federalists in Pennsylvania, 1790–1801* (Harrisburg: Pennsylvania Historical and Museum Commission, 1950), 51–68; Noble E. Cunningham Jr., *The Jeffersonian Republicans: The Formation of Party Organization, 1789–1801* (Chapel Hill: University of North Carolina Press, 1957), 38–45; Raymond Walters Jr., "The Origins of the Jeffersonian Party in Pennsylvania," *Pennsylvania Magazine of History and Biography* 66, no. 4 (October 1942), 454–56; Roland Milton Baumann, "The Democratic-Republicans of Philadelphia: The Origins, 1776–1797" (Ph.D. diss., Pennsylvania State University, 1970), 354–86.

16. Gallatin to Clare, 18 December 1792; Gallatin to Badollet, 18 December 1792, *PAG.*

17. Findley to Thomas Mifflin, 21 November 1792, *Pennsylvania Archives,* 2nd Ser., 4:41; Gallatin to Badollet, 18 December 1792, *PAG;* Gallatin, *The Speech on Validity of Elections,* 43–44, 49–50. The government later withdrew the indictments against the two men on the basis of exculpatory affidavits. Hamilton to Washington, 5 August 1794, *PAH,* 17:42–43.

18. Gallatin, *The Speech on Validity of Elections,* 7; Gallatin to Badollet, 3 May 1793, 1 February 1794; Gallatin to Clare, 5 March and 10 April 1794; Gallatin to Clare, 9 March 1793, *PAG* (hopes for excise law repeal). Gallatin and his friend John Badollet apparently talked about the need

for militia training in early 1794, Badollet to Gallatin, 24 March 1794, ibid., but their conversation probably reflected the prevailing concern about threats from Europe that had led Pennsylvania Governor Thomas Mifflin to urge enforcement of the militia laws a few days earlier; Mifflin to Judges of Pennsylvania Supreme Court, 21 March 1794, *Pennsylvania Archives,* 2nd Ser., 4:50.

19.   Washington, Proclamation, 24 February 1794, *PGW-PS,* 15:275–77; *Pittsburgh Gazette,* 15 February 1794; Leland D. Baldwin, *Whiskey Rebels: The Story of a Frontier Uprising,* rev. ed. (Pittsburgh: University of Pittsburgh Press, 1968), 99–104.

20.   Hamilton to Washington, 5 August 1794, *PAH,* 17:53–57; Declaration of Fayette County Township Committees, 10 September 1794, Whiskey Rebellion Collection, DLC; Brackenridge, *Incidents,* 1:39–70; 3:25–27; Baldwin, *Whiskey Rebels,* 95-96, 113-20, 141-71; Eugene Perry Link, *Democratic-Republican Societies, 1790-1800* (New York: Columbia University Press, 1942), 67–68, 146–47; Jeffrey A. Davis, "Guarding the Republican Interest: The Western Pennsylvania Democratic Societies and the Excise Tax," *Pennsylvania History* 67, no. 1 (Winter 2000), 47–48, 57–58.

21.   Hamilton to Washington, 2 August, 5 August, and 2 September 1794, *PAH,* 17:15-19, 24–58, 180–190; Philadelphia *American Daily Advertiser,* 21 August 1794 (names redacted).

22.   Findley to Mifflin, 21 November 1792, *Pennsylvania Archives,* 2nd Ser., 4:41, 43; William Bradford to Washington, [5] August 1794 (treason) and 17 August 1794 (Senator Ross says "any man who would openly recommend obedience to the excise laws would be in danger of assassination"), *PGW-PS,* 16:472–78, 568–71; Brackenridge, *Incidents,* 1:32 ("There was but a moment between treason on the one hand and popular odium on the other, popular odium which might produce personal injury."), 3:22–24, 41–61 (dissertation on treason); Findley, *History,* 267–68, 303–09; Cornell, *Other Founders,* 200–18; Larry D. Kramer, *The People Themselves: Popular Constitutionalism and Judicial Review* (New York: Oxford University Press, 2004), 105–14; Jason Frank, *Constituent Moments: Enacting the People in Postrevolutionary America* (Durham, NC: Duke University Press 2010), 82–100.

23.   James Ross, J[asper] Yeates, and William Bradford to Randolph, 17 August 1794, Whiskey Rebellion Collection, DLC (describing three parties at the Parkinson's Ferry meeting); Alexander Addison to Henry Lee, 23 November 1794, Boyd, ed., *Whiskey Rebellion,* 54; Brackenridge,

Incidents, 1:88; Baldwin, *Whiskey Rebels,* 172–82; Joseph J. Ellis, *After the Revolution: Profiles of Early American Culture* (New York: W. W. Norton, 1979), 89–92, 103–106; John Caldwell, *William Findley from West of the Mountains: Congressman, 1791–1821* (Gig Harbor, WA: Red Apple, 2002), 110–11.

24. Brackenridge, *Incidents,* 1:87–100 (quoted at 91); Findley, *History,* 113–17; Gallatin, *The Speech on Validity of Elections,* 13–16, 53-54 (compares Marshel's proposed resolutions to those actually adopted by the Parkinson's Ferry meeting); Henry Adams, *The Life of Albert Gallatin* (1879; repr., New York: Peter Smith, 1943), 133.

25. Washington, Proclamation, 7 August 1794, *PGW–PS,* 16:531–37; *Report of the Commissioners…to Confer with the Insurgents in the Western Counties of Pennsylvania* (Philadelphia, 1794), 3-12; Baldwin, *Whiskey Rebels,* 181, 190–99.

26. *Kline's Carlisle Weekly Gazette,* 20 August 1794, reprinted in Philadelphia *General Advertiser,* 10 September 1794; Fritz, *American Sovereigns,* 24–29; Smith, *The Freedoms We Lost,* 200–201 (Samuel Adams opposes popular resistance); Carol Berkin, *A Sovereign People: The Crisis of the 1790s and the Birth of American Nationalism* (New York: Basic Books, 2017), 8–9. William Findley put the problem in more practical terms after the second Pittsburgh meeting. Although Congress had the right to levy excises, he said, "the People's prejudices" against them are among the "questions of serious importance to government." Findley to Mifflin, 21 November 1792, *Pennsylvania Archives,* 2nd Ser., 4:43.

27. Tully Nos. 2, 3, and 4, 16 August, 28 August, and 2 September 1794, *PAH,* 17:148–50, 159–61, 175–80; Alexander Addison, *Charges to Grand Juries of the Counties of the Fifth Circuit of the State of Pennsylvania* (1800; Philadelphia, 1883), 465–66; James P. Martin, "When Repression Is Democratic and Constitutional: The Federalist Theory of Representation and the Sedition Act of 1798," *University of Chicago Law Review* 66, no. 1 (Winter 1999), 142, 155, 161–65; Linda Myrsiades, "A Tale of a Whiskey Rebellion Judge: William Paterson, Grand Jury Charges, and the Trials of the Whiskey Rebels," *Pennsylvania Magazine of History and Biography* 140, no. 2 (April 2016): 143–45.

28. John Boreman et al. to Federal Commissioners, 11 September 1794; Gallatin to Federal Commissioners, 16 September 1794, Whiskey Rebellion Collection, DLC; Henry Purviance to Gallatin, 7 September 1794, *PAG;* Declaration of Fayette County Township Committees, 10 September 1794, Whiskey Rebellion Collection, DLC (final document in

Gallatin's handwriting); Fayette County Declaration, 10 September 1794,
PAG (signed draft in Gallatin's handwriting); Findley, *History*, 130–34.

29.   Declaration of Fayette County Township Committees, 10 September
1794, Whiskey Rebellion Collection, DLC, redacted in *WAG*, 1:4–9;
Philadelphia *General Advertiser*, 25 September 1794 (Richmond
correspondent). The Fayette County declaration contains echoes of the
charge Pennsylvania judge Alexander Addison gave to a grand jury in
Pittsburgh on September 1. Philadelphia *General Advertiser*, 13 September
1794, reprinted in Addison, *Charges to Grand Juries*, 450–57.

30.   *Report of the Commissioners...to Confer with the Insurgents*, 14–15;
General Henry Lee to General William Irvine, 9 November 1794,
Pennsylvania Archives, 2nd Ser., 4:376–77; Gallatin to Badollet, 20 May
1795; Gallatin to Clare, 30 May 1795, *PAG*; Elizabeth Bradford to
Washington, 10 December 1794, 22 January 1795, Whiskey Rebellion
Collection, DLC; Baldwin, *Whiskey Rebels*, 230–58.

31.   Albert Gallatin to Hannah Gallatin, 3 December 1794; Clare to Albert
Gallatin, 14 December 1794, *PAG*; Randolph to Washington, 18 August
1792, *PGW–PS*, 16:579 (warns against appearing to target Gallatin);
Alexander J. Dallas to Maria Dallas, 23 October 1794, George Mifflin
Dallas, *Life and Writings of Alexander James Dallas* (Philadelphia, 1871),
42–43; Nathaniel Breading to Gallatin, 10 October 1794; Gallatin to
Clare, [after 14 October] 1794, 7 November 1794; Badollet to Gallatin,
14 December 1794, *PAG*; Robert Patterson Jr. to William Canon, 24
October 1794, Swann Galleries (NY) Catalog, 17 September 2015 Sale,
Lot 286 (traveler passing through federal troops ordered back for
examination by judge); Brackenridge, *Incidents*, 2:56–57; Findley,
History, 228–230, 239–40, 242–43, 245–46; [William Findley], *A
Review of the Revenue System Adopted by the First
Congress...*(Philadelphia, 1794), 44–62, 118; Caldwell, *William Findley:
Congressman*, 86–96.

32.   Gallatin to Clare, [after 14 October], 7 November 1794; James W.
Alexander, Recollections of Albert Gallatin, 1 July 1850; James W.
Alexander to Mrs. Byam K. Stevens [Frances Gallatin], 1 July 1850
(misdated 1880 by the editors), *PAG*; Dwight Raymond Guthrie, *John
McMillan: The Apostle of Presbyterianism, 1752–1833* (Pittsburgh:
University of Pittsburgh Press, 1952), 166–72; Ronald W. Long, "The
Presbyterians and the Whiskey Rebellion," *Journal of Presbyterian
History (1962–1985)* 43, no. 1 (March 1965): 32–33; Pennsylvania 1794
Congress, District 12, *Lampi Collection of American Electoral Returns,*

1788–1825 (American Antiquarian Society, 2007) (available at *A New Nation Votes: American Election Returns, 1788–1825*, Tufts Digital Library).

33. "Speech of the President," Philadelphia *Gazette of the United States,* 19 November 1794; Washington to Burgess Ball, 25 September 1794, *PGW–PS,* 16:723. From its outset Washington had called the Western Insurrection the "fruit" of the Democratic Republican Societies. Washington to Randolph, 11 April 1794; Washington to Henry Lee, 26 August 1794, *PGW–PS,* 15:571, 16:601–602. James Marshel and David Bradford were principal officers of the Democratic Society in Washington County. Five other members of that society took substantial parts in the insurrection. Link, *Democratic-Republican Societies,* 146; Philip S. Foner, ed., *The Democratic-Republican Societies, 1790–1800: A Documentary Sourcebook* (Westport, CT: Greenwood Press, 1976), 129–30 (a footnote here incorrectly describes Brackenridge as a member of the Washington County society); William Miller, "The Democratic Societies and the Whiskey Insurrection," *Pennsylvania Magazine of History and Biography* 62, no. 3 (July 1938): 342–48. The Democratic Republican Societies scrambled to distance themselves from the insurrection, but they generally did not survive Washington's denunciation. Philadelphia *American Daily Advertiser,* Dec. 22, 1794 (letter from Democratic Society of Philadelphia); Albrecht Koschnik, *"Let a Common Interest Bind Us Together": Associations, Partisanship, and Culture in Philadelphia, 1775–1840* (Charlottesville: University of Virginia Press, 2007), 37–38; Matthew Schoenbachler, "Republicanism in the Age of Democratic Revolution: The Democratic-Republican Societies of the 1790s," *Journal of the Early Republic* 18, no. 2 (Summer 1998), 254–58.

34. *Annals,* 3rd Cong., 2nd Sess., 794–95, 899–949; James Madison to Thomas Jefferson, 30 November 1794; Madison to James Monroe, 4 December 1794, *PJM-CS,* 15:396–98, 405–9; Jeffrey Alan Davis, "The Democratic-Republican Societies of Pennsylvania, 1793–1796" (Ph.D. diss., Washington State University, 1996), 67. For a discussion of Washington's reversion to the same theme in his 1796 farewell address, see Richard Hofstadter, *The Idea of a Party System: The Rise of Legitimate Opposition in the United States, 1780–1840* (Berkeley: University of California Press, 1972), 96–102. Jefferson emphatically rejected Washington's position at the time, Jefferson to Madison, 28 December 1794, *PJM–CS,* 15:426–27, but during his own presidency he questioned

the use of citizen committees "unknown to the constitution," Jefferson to William Duane, 24 July 1803, *PTJ*, 41:107.

35.　*Pennsylvania House Journal 1794–95*, 7, 34 (quoted), 47, 58–59, 61–72, 75–81, 170, 174, 181; Fisher Ames to Thomas Dwight, 12 December 1794, *WFA*, 1:155; Albert Gallatin to Hannah Gallatin, 7 December 1794; Clare to Albert Gallatin, 14 December 1794; Badollet to Gallatin, 14 December 1794; Gallatin to James Nicholson, 26 December 1794; Gallatin to Badollet, 10 January 1795; Gallatin to Clare, 5 March 1795, *PAG;* Madison to Jefferson, 21 December 1794, *PJM–CS*, 15:420; Brackenridge, *Incidents,* 2:44; Tinkcom, *The Republicans and Federalists,* 109–11; Baldwin, *Whiskey Rebels,* 218–19.

36.　Gallatin, *The Speech on Validity of Elections,* 4–6 (quoted at 4); Gallatin, Notes on validity of elections, [about 5 January] 1795, *PAG; Pennsylvania House Journal 1794–95*, 63–81; Edwin G. Burrows, *Albert Gallatin and the Political Economy of Republicanism, 1761–1800* (New York, 1986), 309–26. On the procedure that the Pennsylvania legislature had used in earlier contested elections, see Jacob Cox Parsons, ed., *Extracts from the Diary of Jacob Hiltzheimer* (Philadelphia, 1893), 186–87.

37.　Gallatin, *The Speech on Validity of Elections,* 7, 27, 31; Findley to Addison, 9 January 1795, Alexander Addison Papers, Darlington Digital Library, University of Pittsburgh.

38.　Albert Gallatin to Hannah Gallatin, 12, 15, 18 and 19, 25 May, 1 June 1795; Albert Gallatin to Badollet, 20 May 1795; Gallatin to Clare, 30 May 1795, *PAG;* William Rawle, Copy of charges, Whiskey Rebellion, [May] 1795, ibid.; *United States v. Insurgents,* 2 U. S. (2 Dallas) 335 (U. S. Circuit Court, District of Pennsylvania 1795) (jury pool challenged); Brackenridge, *Incidents,* 3:36, 136–39 (Rawle's notes from interview with Gallatin about the Parkinson's Ferry meeting); Baldwin, *Whiskey Rebels,* 262–264; Slaughter, *The Whiskey Rebellion,* 219–20. William Rawles was the United States district attorney who prosecuted the insurgents.

39.　John Adams to Jefferson, 30 June 1813; Jefferson to Adams, 15 June 1813, Lester J. Cappon, ed., *The Adams-Jefferson Letters: The Complete Correspondence Between Thomas Jefferson and Abigail and John Adams* (Chapel Hill, NC, 1959), 2:346, 331; John A. Schutz and Douglass Adair, eds., *The Spur of Fame: Dialogues of John Adams and Benjamin Rush, 1805–1813* (San Marino, CA: Huntington Library, 1966), 230, 240–41. Adams's correspondence at the time of the Western Insurrection suggests that he did not then regard Gallatin as the leading culprit. John Adams to Abigail Adams, 4 January [1795], Adams Family Papers: Electronic

Archive, Massachusetts Historical Society (calling the insurgents "Bradfords Rebels").

40. James Roger Sharp, *American Politics in the Early Republic: The New Nation in Crisis* (New Haven, CT: Yale University Press, 1993), 73–74, 151; Gilje, *Rioting in America,* 57–58; Martin, *Government by Dissent,* 16, 34.

Chapter 4: Opposition Leader

1. Alfred F. Young, *The Democratic Republicans of New York: The Origins, 1763–1797* (Chapel Hill: University of North Carolina Press, 1967), 449–53; Todd Estes, *The Jay Treaty Debate, Public Opinion, and the Evolution of Early American Political Culture* (Amherst: University of Massachusetts Press, 2006), 71–103; Jeffrey S. Selinger, *Embracing Dissent: Political Violence and Party Organization in the United States* (Philadelphia: University of Pennsylvania Press, 2016), 55–67.

2. Albert Gallatin to Hannah Gallatin, 6 September 1795, *LAG,* 152–32; Hannah Gallatin to Albert Gallatin, 3 August 1795, *PAG;* John Beckley to James Madison, 25 May 1795, *PJM-CS,* 16:9–13; James Nicholson to Alexander Hamilton, 20 July 1795, *PAH,* 18:471–72; Milton Halsey Thomas, "Alexander Hamilton's Unfought Duel of 1795," *Pennsylvania Magazine of History and Biography* 78, no. 3 (July 1954): 342–352. Gallatin's friend Alexander Dallas, who had published attacks on the treaty, withdrew from the controversy after the president ratified it in late summer. [Alexander J. Dallas], *Features of Mr. Jay's Treaty* (Philadelphia, 1795); Raymond Walters Jr., *Alexander James Dallas: Lawyer— Politician—Financier, 1759–1817* (Philadelphia: University of Pennsylvania Press, 1943), 66–74.

3. Alexander Hamilton, Plan for the Support of Public Credit, 9 January 1790; Further Plan for Support of Public Credit, 4 March 1790; Further Provision for Establishing the Public Credit [additional taxes], 13 December 1790; Further Provision for Establishing the Public Credit [Bank of the United States], 13 December 1790; Plan for the Further Support of Public Credit, 16 January 1795, *ASP: Finance,* 1:15, 43, 64, 67, 320; Hamilton to George Washington, 9 September 1792, *PAH,* 12:347–50; Fisher Ames to Hamilton, 31 July and 15 August 1791, ibid., 8:589–91, 9:55–59; Ames to Thomas Dwight, 12 December 1794; Ames to Christopher Gore, 24 February 1795, *WFA,* 1:154, 167; P. G. M. Dickson, *The Financial Revolution in England: A Study in the Development of Public Credit, 1688–1756* (London: Macmillan, 1967),

9–12, 205–14, 243–45; Forrest McDonald, *Alexander Hamilton: A Biography* (New York: W. W. Norton, 1979), 163–210, 303–05; Max M. Edling, *A Hercules in the Cradle: War, Money, and the American State, 1788–1867* (Chicago: University of Chicago Press, 2014), 50–107; Patrick K. O'Brien, "The Political Economy of British Taxation, 1660–1815," *Economic History Review,* New Ser., 41, no. 1 (February 1988), 17–28; Herbert Sloan, "Hamilton's Second Thoughts," in *Federalists Reconsidered,* ed. Doron Ben-Atar and Barbara B. Oberg (Charlottesville: University Press of Virginia, 1998), 67–76.

4. [Robert R. Livingston], *Considerations on the Nature of a Funded Debt...*(New York, 1790), 1-6; [George Logan,] *Five Letters Addressed to the Yeomanry of the United States...*(Philadelphia, 1792), 6; [John Beckley and James Monroe], *An Examination of the Late Proceedings in Congress...*(Richmond, 1793); [John Taylor], *An Enquiry into the Principles and Tendencies of Certain Public Measures* (Philadelphia, 1794), 7–47, 65–85; [John Taylor], *A Definition of Parties...*(Philadelphia, 1794), 14–16; [William Findley], *A Review of the Revenue System Adopted by the First Congress...*(Philadelphia, 1794), 44–62; Thomas Jefferson to Washington, 23 May and 9 September 1792, *PTJ,* 23:535–41, 24:351–60; Madison to Jefferson, 11 May 1794, 26 January, and 15 February 1795, *PJM-CS,* 15:327–28, 454–55, 474–75; Fisher Ames to George Richards Minot, 20 January 1795, *WFA,* 1:164–65; Richard Buel Jr., *Securing the Revolution: Ideology in American Politics, 1789–1815* (Ithaca, NY: Cornell University Press, 1972), 8–27; Lance Banning, *The Jeffersonian Persuasion: Evolution of a Party Ideology* (Ithaca, NY: Cornell University Press, 1978), 161–206; Drew R. McCoy, *The Elusive Republic: Political Economy in Jeffersonian America* (Chapel Hill: University of North Carolina Press, 1980), 136–65, 186–88; Edwin J. Perkins, *American Public Finance and Financial Services, 1700–1815* (Columbus: Ohio State University Press, 1994), 220–21; Mark Schmeller, "The Political Economy of Opinion: Public Credit and Concepts of Public Opinion in the Age of Federalism," *Journal of the Early Republic* 29, no. 1 (Spring 2009): 51–58; John Francis Devanny Jr., "Commerce, Credit, and Currency: Continuity and Differentiation in Jeffersonian Political Economy, 1760–1848" (Ph.D. diss., University of South Carolina, 2000), 73–104.

5. Andrew Shankman, *Crucible of American Democracy: The Struggle to Fuse Egalitarianism and Capitalism in Jeffersonian Pennsylvania* (Lawrence: University Press of Kansas, 2004), 58–63, 233–46; J. M.

Opal, "Natural Rights and National Greatness: Economic Ideology and Social Policy in the American States, 1780s–1820s," in *The World of the Revolutionary American Republic: Land, Labor, and the Conflict for a Continent,* ed. Andrew Shankman (New York: Routledge, 2014), 301–05. For early Republican party formation, see James Hutchinson to Gallatin, 11 June 1790 and 25 September 1792; William Findley to Gallatin, 27 September 1792; [Gallatin], List of committees of correspondence, [autumn 1794], *PAG;* Ames to Minot, 30 November 1791, *WFA,* 1:104–05; Jefferson, Notes on the letter of Christoph Ebeling, [after 15 October 1795]; Jefferson to Madison, [13 May 1793], *PTJ,* 28:506–10, 26:25–27 (describing Republican and Federalist constituencies); [Madison], "Parties," Philadelphia *National Gazette,* 23 January 1792; "The Union: Who Are Its Real Friends?" ibid., 31 March 1792; and "A Candid State of Parties," ibid., 22 September 1792, reprinted in *PJM-CS,* 14:197–98, 274–75, 370–72. For works from the vast literature on party formation that shed particular light on Gallatin's early experiences, see Young, *The Democratic Republicans of New York,* 231–56; Joyce Appleby, *Capitalism and a New Social Order: The Republican Vision of the 1790s* (New York: New York University Press, 1984), 74–75; James Roger Sharp, *American Politics in the Early Republic: The New Nation in Crisis* (New Haven, CT: Yale University Press, 1993), 60–68; Lawrence A. Peskin, *Manufacturing Revolution: The Intellectual Origins of Early American Industry* (Baltimore: Johns Hopkins University Press, 2003), 81, 91–92, 109–12; Jeffrey L. Pasley, *The First Presidential Contest: 1796 and the Founding of American Democracy* (Lawrence: University Press of Kansas, 2013), 1–15; Reeve Huston, "Rethinking the Origins of Partisan Democracy," in *Practicing Democracy: Popular Politics in the United States from the Constitution to the Civil War,* ed. Daniel Peart and Adam I. P. Smith (Charlottesville: University of Virginia Press, 2015), 53–55; Roland M. Baumann, "Philadelphia's Manufacturers and the Excise Taxes of 1794: The Forging of the Jeffersonian Coalition," *Pennsylvania Magazine of History and Biography* 106, no. 1 (January 1982): 3–39; Roland Milton Baumann, "The Democratic-Republicans of Philadelphia: The Origins, 1776–1797" (Ph.D. diss., Pennsylvania State University, 1970), 574–87.

6. Albert Gallatin to Hannah Gallatin, 22 April 1795, *LAG,* 147; Albert Gallatin to John Badollet, 22 February 1792, *PAG;* Walters, *Alexander James Dallas,* 32-51. On the roots of differences between politics in New York and Pennsylvania, see Alan Tully, *Forming American Politics:*

Ideals, Interests, and Institutions in Colonial New York and Pennsylvania (Baltimore: Johns Hopkins University Press, 1994), 372–89, 398–413.

7. Jefferson to Madison, 3 and 11 August 1793, *PTJ*, 26:606–07, 651–54; Albert Gallatin to Hannah Gallatin, 25 August 1793, *LAG*, 103–04; Alexander J. Dallas to Gallatin, 8 November 1793, *PAG;* Samuel Flagg Bemis, *Jay's Treaty: A Study in Commerce and Diplomacy,* rev. ed. (New Haven, CT: Yale University Press, 1962), 183–200; Appleby, *Capitalism and a New Social Order,* 57; Stanley Elkins and Eric McKitrick, *The Age of Federalism: The Early American Republic, 1788–1800* (New York: Oxford University Press, 1993), 330–65; Herbert E. Sloan, *Principle and Interest: Thomas Jefferson and the Problem of Debt* (New York: Oxford University Press, 1995), 167–69, 190–94; Matthew Q. Dawson, *Partisanship and the Birth of American's Second Party, 1796–1800: "Stop the Wheels of Government"* (Westport, CT: Greenwood Press, 2000), 6–7; Gordon S. Wood, *Empire of Liberty: A History of the Early Republic, 1789-1815* (New York: Oxford University Press, 2009), 177–81; John R. Howe Jr., "Republican Thought and the Political Violence of the 1790s," *American Quarterly* 19, no. 2 (Summer 1967): 147–65.

8. Jerald A. Combs, *The Jay Treaty: Political Battleground of the Founding Fathers* (Berkeley: University of California Press, 1970), 116–36, 160–61; Buel, *Securing the Revolution,* 54–71; McCoy, *The Elusive Republic,* 140–44, 146–47; Elkins and McKitrick, *The Age of Federalism,* 375–96, 417–20.

9. Hamilton to Senate, 18 November 1791, *ASP: Commerce and Navigation,* 1:34–35; Jefferson to Washington, 9 September 1792, *PTJ,* 24:353–54; Ames to Thomas Dwight, 3 February 1795, *WFA,* 1:166; Albert Gallatin to Hannah Gallatin, 29 June 1795, *LAG,* 151; Oliver Wolcott Jr. to Jedediah Morse, 16 July 1795, Gibbs, *Memoirs,* 1:212; Doron Ben-Atar, *The Origins of Jeffersonian Commercial Policy and Diplomacy* (New York: St. Martin's Press, 1993), 137–51; John E. Crowley, *The Privileges of Independence: Neomercantilism and the American Revolution* (Baltimore: Johns Hopkins University Press, 1993), 156–68; Estes, *The Jay Treaty Debate,* 36–70; Susan B. Carter et al., eds., *Historical Statistics of the United States: Earliest Times to Present,* Millennial Ed. (5 vols.; New York: Cambridge University Press, 2006), 5:510 (Table Ee424–430), 5:534 (Table Ee533–550), 5:540 (Table Ee551–568).

10. John F. Hoadley, *Origins of American Political Parties, 1789–1803* (Lexington: University Press of Kentucky, 1986), 125–40; Kenneth C. Martis, ed., *The Historical Atlas of Political Parties in the United States*

Congress, 1789–1989 (New York: Macmillan, 1989), 24; Estes, *The Jay Treaty Debate*, 71–103.

11. Jefferson to Madison, 21 September 1795, *PTJ*, 28:475–77; Madison to Jefferson, 13 December 1795; Madison to James Monroe, 20 December 1795, *PJM-CS*, 16:163, 170; Chauncey Goodrich to Oliver Wolcott Sr., 12 January and 21 February 1796, Gibbs, *Memoirs,* 1:298, 303; Albert Gallatin to Hannah Gallatin, 24 January 1797, *PAG*.

12. In the last year of his life, Gallatin vividly remembered how ambitious he had been when he entered the House of Representatives. He found that the "financial depart.m in the House was quite vacant, so far at least as the Opposition was concerned," and he soon "made myself complete master of the subject, and occupied that field almost exclusively." Gallatin, Autobiographical sketch, [1849], *PAG,* extract in *SWAG,* 12–13.

13. Hamilton, Plan for the Support of Public Credit, 1:24. Gallatin did not attack the use of a funding system to refinance Revolutionary War debts, but only the extension of the funding system to finance new deficits. Some Federalist members of the House, who were accustomed to hearing loose Republican cant about the funding system, did not notice the distinction. For Hamilton's own explanation of the distinction, see [Hamilton], Fact No. 1, 11 September 1792, *PAH*, 12:361–65.

14. *Annals,* 4ᵗʰ Cong., 1ˢᵗ Sess., 841–56, 883–84, 909–10, 914–38 (quoted at 854, 856, 932, 909); ibid., 4ᵗʰ Cong., 2ⁿᵈ Sess., 2128–30.

15. *Annals,* 4ᵗʰ Cong., 1ˢᵗ Sess., 1398–99, 1475–96 (quoted at 1492, 1476); ibid., 4ᵗʰ Cong., 2ⁿᵈ Sess., 2039–40 (specific appropriations language), 2341–42, 2349–51 (same), 2358–61 (same); ibid., 5ᵗʰ Cong., 2ⁿᵈ Sess., 826–27, 1316–17, 1436–38; Acts of March 3, 1797, *Statutes at Large* 1 (1845): 498, 508 ("the following sums be respectively appropriated; that is to say:"); Leonard D. White, *The Federalists: A Study in Administrative History* (New York: Macmillan, 1956), 328–29. On the Federalist Treasury's looser interpretation of appropriations, see Oliver Wolcott [Jr.], *An Address to the People of the United States…* (Boston, 1802), 23–25; Jefferson to Gallatin, 19 February 1804, L&B, 11:12–13; Gerhard Casper, "Appropriations of Power," *University of Arkansas at Little Rock Law Journal* 13, no. 1 (Fall 1990): 8–15.

16. *Annals,* 4ᵗʰ Cong., 1ˢᵗ Sess., 152, 158, 159, 165; ibid., 4ᵗʰ Cong., 2ⁿᵈ Sess., 1668; Oliver Wolcott Jr. to Hamilton, 5 April 1798, *PAH,* 21:396–99; Goodrich to Oliver Wolcott Sr., 21 February 1796, Gibbs, *Memoirs,* 1:304 (Republicans on Ways and Means not constructive); Madison to Jefferson, 26 March and 31 March 1794, *PJM–CS,* 15:294–96, 299;

Oliver Wolcott Jr. to Oliver Wolcott Sr., 20 Feb 1797, Gibbs, *Memoirs,* 1:443 (Treasury's loss of influence); Theodore Sedgwick to Rufus King, 11 May 1800, *LCRK,* 3:236 (10 May 1800 statute requiring annual estimates from Treasury secretary meant to redress balance); Gallatin to Jefferson, [by 16 November] 1801, *PTJ,* 35:630–36 (questions special statutes for direct Treasury reports to Congress); David J. Siemers, *Ratifying the Republic: Antifederalists and Federalists in Constitutional Time* (Stanford, CA: Stanford University Press, 2002), 187; Patrick J. Furlong, "The Origins of the House Committee of Ways and Means," *William and Mary Quarterly,* 3rd Ser., 25, no. 4 (October 1968): 587–604.

17. *Annals,* 4th Cong., 1st Sess., 254–65; U. S. Constitution, art. 1, sec, 7, cl. 1. During the autumn of 1795, the Virginia General Assembly had debated whether the Constitution also gave the House of Representatives jurisdiction over any treaty provision that affected commerce. Norman K. Risjord, *Chesapeake Politics, 1781–1800* (New York: Columbia University Press, 1978), 457–59.

18. Peter Porcupine [William Cobbett], *The Political Censor, or Monthly Review for March 1796* (Philadelphia, 1796), 9–16; Donald Dewey, *The Art of Ill Will: The Story of American Political Cartoons* (New York: New York University Press, 2007), 4–5. For various renditions of the cartoon ridiculing Gallatin, see Porcupine, *The Political Censor, or Monthly Review* . . . (2nd and 3rd eds., Philadelphia, April 1796), frontispiece; Porcupine, *The Political Censor, or Monthly Review* . . . (Philadelphia, May 1796), frontispiece. Contemporaries sometimes spelled Gallatin's name "Gallatine," which suggests a rhyme with "guillotine."

19. Philadelphia *Porcupine's Gazette,* 2 December 1797 (Quaker petition); *Annals,* 4th Cong., 1st Sess., 468, 918, 923; ibid., 5th Cong., 2nd Sess., 656–70, 945–46, and 1032–33 (Quaker petition), 895, 905, and 1112 ("wheels of government"); *Pittsburgh Gazette,* 4 June 1796 (letter from Carlisle); Oliver Wolcott Jr. to Oliver Wolcott Sr., 18 April 1796, Gibbs, *Memoirs,* 1:327; Abigail Adams to Cotton Tufts, 8 June 1798, quoted in Page Smith, *John Adams* (Garden City, NY: Doubleday, 1962), 2:967; John Adams to Oliver Wolcott Jr., 24 September 1798, *FOL*—Early Access; [Fisher Ames], Laocoon No. 2, April 1799, *WFA,* 2:126 (Jay Treaty contest "stopped the wheels of government"); Christopher Caustic [Thomas Green Fessenden], *Democracy Unveiled, or, Tyranny Stripped of the Garb of Patriotism,* 3rd ed. (2 vols.; New York, 1805–6), 2:140 ("To Stop of government 'de vell'!"). Some Federalists took a calmer view.

Oliver Wolcott Jr.'s brother-in-law, for example, believed the Republicans with whom he served in Congress were loyal men simply misguided by "an unreasonable prejudice against past expense." Chauncey Goodrich to Oliver Wolcott Sr., 10 February 1797, Gibbs, *Memoirs,* 1:442. For the cartoon of Gallatin pulling back on the wheels of government, see [anon.], "The Times: A Political Portrait," c. 1796, New-York Historical Society; Anthony Aufére, *A Warning to Britons against French Perfidy and Cruelty: or, A Short Account of the Treacherous and Inhuman Conduct of the French Officers and Soldiers...* (London, 1798); William Cobbett and Anthony Aufrére, *The Cannibals' Progress; or the Dreadful Horrors of French Invasion...* (New London, CT, 1798); Noble E. Cunningham Jr., *The Image of Thomas Jefferson in the Public Eye: Portraits for the People, 1800–1809* (Charlottesville: University Press of Virginia, 1981), 112; Rachel Hope Cleves, "On Writing the History of Violence," *Journal of the Early Republic* 24, no. 4 (Winter 2004): 655–56. Shaking off his own contemporaneous encounter with American nativism, Talleyrand famously remarked that in "every part of America through which I have travelled, I have not found a single Englishman who did not feel himself an American; not a single Frenchman who did not find himself a stranger." Charles Maurice de Talleyrand-Périgord, *Memoir Concerning the Commercial Relations of the United States with England* (1797; transl., London, 1806), 18.

20. Robert R. Livingston to Edward Livingston, 30 October 1795, quoted in Combs, *The Jay Treaty,* 175; *Annals,* 4th Cong., 1st Sess., 426–28; George Dangerfield, *Chancellor Robert R. Livingston of New York, 1746–1813* (New York: Harcourt, Brace, 1960), 278–80; Rudolph M. Bell, *Party and Faction in American Politics: The House of Representatives, 1789–1801* (Westport, CT: Greenwood Press, 1973), 145–49.

21. Jefferson to Madison, 27 March 1796, *PTJ,* 29:51–52; Ames to Christopher Gore, 11 March 1796, *WFA,* 1:189; Madison to Jefferson, 27 December 1795 and 23 April 1796, *PJM–CS,* 16:173–74, 335–36; Goodrich to Oliver Wolcott Sr., 23 April 1796, Gibbs, *Memoirs,* 1:331; *Annals,* 4th Cong., 1st Sess., 464–74, 487–94; Philadelphia *Aurora General Advertiser,* 14 March 1796; David O. Stewart, *Madison's Gift: Five Partnerships That Built America* (New York: Simon & Schuster, 2015), 162–64; Jack N. Rakove, "The Political Presidency: Discovery and Invention," in *The Revolution of 1800: Democracy, Race, and the New Republic,* ed. James Horn, Jan Ellen Lewis, and Peter S. Onuf (Charlottesville: University of Virginia Press, 2002), 43–49; Amanda C.

Demmer, "Trick or Constitutional Treaty? The Jay Treaty and the Quarrel over Diplomatic Separation of Power," *Journal of the Early Republic* 35, no. 4 (Winter 2015), 582, 593–95.

22. Jay to Washington, 18 April 1796, Henry P. Johnston, ed., *The Correspondence and Public Papers of John Jay* (4 vols.; New York: G. P. Putnam's Sons, 1890–93), 4:208; John Beckley to Monroe, 2 April 1796, Gerald W. Gawalt, ed., *Justifying Jefferson: The Political Writings of John James Beckley* (Washington, DC: Library of Congress, 1995), 114; *Annals,* 4ᵗʰ Cong., 1ˢᵗ Sess., 759–60; Estes, *The Jay Treaty Debate,* 162–70. Gallatin made a more definitive statement on the Congressional appropriation power as a check on the executive's foreign policy powers in a later debate over salaries for foreign ministers. *Annals,* 5ᵗʰ Cong., 2ⁿᵈ Sess., 1118–43. The speech circulated as a pamphlet and provoked a persuasive response from one of Gallatin's opponents in the Western Country. Alexander Addison, *Observations on the Speech of Albert Gallatin... on the Foreign Intercourse Bill* (Washington, PA, 1798); Robert W. Smith, "The Foreign Intercourse Bill of 1798 and the Debate over Early American Foreign Relations," *Journal of the Early Republic* 36, no. 1 (Spring 2016): 146–47. Toward the end of his life, Gallatin still maintained that it was doubtful whether the treaty power trumped the power of the purse, and doubts still linger. The Bricker Amendment proposed in the 1950s would have prevented treaties from becoming law without enabling legislation, and Congress continues to wield the denial of funding as a weapon against unpopular international agreements. Gallatin to Edward Everett, January 1835, *WAG,* 2:479; Kate Stith, "Congress' Power of the Purse," *Yale Law Journal* 97, no. 7 (1988): 1360–63; Nelson Richards, "The Bricker Amendment and Congress's Failure to Check the Inflation of the Executive's Foreign Affairs Powers, 1951–54," *California Law Review* 94, no. 1 (January 2006): 75–213.

23. *Pittsburgh Gazette,* 12 March, 19 March, and 21 May 1796 (petitions); Combs, *The Jay Treaty,* 184-87; John Grenier, *The First Way of War: American War Making on the Frontier, 1607–1814* (New York: Cambridge University Press, 2005), 193–202.

24. Hugh Henry Brackenridge to Addison, 30 April 1796, Alexander Addison Papers, Darlington Digital Library, University of Pittsburgh; John McMillan to Gallatin, 5 May 1796; Badollet to Gallatin, 18 May 1796, *PAG; Annals,* 4ᵗʰ Cong., 1ˢᵗ Sess., 940–75, 976, 1183–1202, 1291, 1296–98; Gallatin, *The Oregon Question* (New York, 1846), App. on "War Expenses," reprinted in *WAG,* 3:553 (recollection about Republican

caucus); Dwight Raymond Guthrie, *John McMillan: The Apostle of Presbyterianism, 1752–1833* (Pittsburgh: University of Pittsburgh Press, 1952), 166–72; John Caldwell, *William Findley from West of the Mountains: Congressman, 1791–1821* (Gig Harbor, WA: Red Apple Publishing, 2002), 161–67. South Carolina Senator Pierce Butler (who had been a Federalist until 1795) later criticized Gallatin's objectives in the caucus as self-interested and unpatriotic. Pierce Butler to Monroe, 27 September 1816, James Monroe Papers, DLC.

25. *Pittsburgh Gazette,* 28 May, 4 June, and 20 August 1796; Election broadside, Washington County, PA, [before 9 November] 1796, *PAG.*
26. Oliver Wolcott Jr. to Oliver Wolcott Sr., 18 April 1796, Gibbs, *Memoirs,* 1:327; Boston *Independent Chronicle,* 28 April 1796; Porcupine [Cobbett], *The Political Censor* (May 1796), 182–83, 193–94; "Political Investigation" and A Federal Republican, Boston *Columbian Centinel,* 27 April 1796; Correspondences, ibid., 7 May 1796 (third item); Badollet to Gallatin, 25 July 1796, *PAG* (fears Gallatin has challenged Otis to duel); Samuel Eliot Morison, *The Life and Letters of Harrison Gray Otis: Federalist, 1765–1848* (2 vols.; Boston: Houghton Mifflin, 1913), 1:56; Ralph Ketcham, *James Madison: A Biography* (1971; Charlottesville: University Press of Virginia, 1990), 362–65; Estes, *The Jay Treaty Debate,* 160–61. For a plain Massachusetts republican's satire of Otis's "second shirt" speech, see William Manning, "The Key of Liberty" (1797, revised 1799), in Michael Merrill and Sean Wilentz, eds., *The Key of Liberty: The Life and Democratic Writings of William Manning, 'A Laborer,' 1747–1814* (Cambridge, MA: Harvard University Press, 1993), 151.
27. Gallatin, Autobiographical sketch, [1849], *PAG,* extract in *SWAG,* 11-12; David M. Erskine to Thomas M. Erskine, 1 January 1799, Patricia Holbert Menk, ed., "D. M. Erskine: Letters from America, 1798–1799," *William and Mary Quarterly,* 3rd Ser., 6, no. 2 (April 1949): 281–82.
28. John Thomson, *The Letters of Curtius* (1798; Richmond, 1804), 50; Julian Ursyn Niemcewicz, *Under Their Vine and Fig Tree: Travels through America in 1797–1799, 1805,* trans. and ed. Metchie J. E. Budka (Elizabeth, NJ: Grassman Publishing, 1965), 60; [William Duane], The Treasury Nos. I and II, Philadelphia *Aurora General Advertiser,* 20 and 21 December 1810; Noble E. Cunningham Jr., *The Jeffersonian Republicans: The Formation of Party Organization, 1789–1801* (Chapel Hill: University of North Carolina Press, 1957), 123–24; Edwin G. Burrows, *Albert Gallatin and the Political Economy of Republicanism, 1761–1800* (New York: Garland, 1986), 274–308; Edward A. Wyatt IV,

"John Thomson, Author of 'The Letters of Curtius'...," *William and Mary Quarterly,* 2ⁿᵈ Ser., 16, no. 1 (January 1936): 19–23; Dennis Golladay, "John Nicholas: Virginia Congressman, New York Quid," *New York History* 60, no. 1 (January 1979): 9–12.

29. Madison to Jefferson, 31 January 1796, *PJM–CS,* 16:208–10; Jefferson to Madison, 6 March 1796, *PTJ,* 29:6–8; James Nicholson to James W. Nicholson, 4 July 1796; Badollet to Gallatin, 25 July 1796, *PAG.* Among those who read Gallatin's book were Jefferson, Madison, Hamilton, Wolcott, and a British bibliophile who enthusiastically sent Gallatin other books on public finance. Jefferson to Madison, 17 December 1796, *PTJ,* 29:223-24; Oliver Wolcott Jr. to Hamilton, [8 December 1796], *PAH,* 20:435–37; Samuel Paterson to Gallatin, 12 March 1799, *PAG.*

30. Albert Gallatin, *A Sketch of the Finances of the United States* (New York: William A. Davis, 1796), 70–71; John Taylor to Henry Tazewell, 13 June 1797, 26 May 1798, Tazewell Family Papers, Library of Virginia; *Annals,* 4ᵗʰ Cong., 1ˢᵗ Sess., 1514 (Gallatin's dispassionate quantitative argument left William Loughton Smith "at a loss to discover [his] motives"); William Letwin, *The Origins of Scientific Economics: English Economic Thought, 1660–1776* (London: Methuen, 1963), 221–28; John R. Nelson Jr., *Liberty and Property: Political Economy and Policymaking in the New Nation, 1789–1812* (Baltimore: Johns Hopkins University Press, 1987), 102–6; Richard Vernier, "The Fortunes of Orthodoxy: The Political Economy of Public Debt in England and America in the 1780s," in *Articulating America: Fashioning a National Political Culture in Early America,* ed. Rebecca Starr (Lanham, MD: Rowan and Littlefield, 2000), 94–105, 128–29. Gallatin may not have known until later that Hamilton had shifted the money intended to repay foreign loans to the repayment of bank loans that he had used to bid up the price of federal securities during speculative price collapses in 1791 and 1792. Everett Somerville Brown, ed., *William Plumer's Memorandum of Proceedings in the United States Senate, 1803–1807* (New York: Macmillan Company, 1923), 632 (28 February 1807) (Gallatin said Hamilton's disputed payments were not correctly recorded in Treasury's books); Richard Sylla, "Financial Foundations: Public Credit, the National Bank, and Securities Markets," in *Founding Choices: American Economic Policy in the 1790s,* ed. Douglas A. Irwin and Richard Sylla (Chicago: University of Chicago Press, 2011), 77.

31. Gallatin, *A Sketch of the Finances,* 97, 110–1, 127–32; Gallatin, Autobiographical sketch, [1849], *PAG* ("not quite so orthodox...as my

Virginia friends"); Jefferson to Monroe, 12 June 1796, *PTJ*, 29:123–24; Banning, *The Jeffersonian Persuasion*, 185–207.

32. Gallatin, *A Sketch of the Finances*, 49–67, 82–87, 96–99, 102–03, 108–11; William W. Story, ed., *Life and Letters of Joseph Story* (2 vols.; Boston, 1851), 2:504 (Story recalled Gallatin saying "[s]tatistic figures are far weightier and more useful than figures of speech").

33. Gallatin, *A Sketch of the Finances*, 123–34. Gallatin's summary of his view on public debt and government spending in *Sketch*, 123–29, paraphrases a passage in Adam Smith's *Inquiry into the Nature and Causes of the Wealth of Nations*, ed. Edwin Cannan (1789; New York: Modern Library, 1937), 877–81. For examples of Jefferson's acceptance of Smith's views and his own use of Smith's *Wealth of Nations*, see Jefferson to John Novell, 14 June 1807, L&B, 11:223; Jefferson to John W. Eppes, 11 September 1813 and 6 November 1813, *PTJ-RS*, 6:490–99, 578–94. See also Thomas Paine, *The Decline and Fall of the English System of Finance* (1796), in Moncure Daniel Conway, ed., *The Writings of Thomas Paine* (4 vols.; New York: G. P. Putnam's Sons, 1894–96), 3:286–312 (similar attack on the British funding system); Livingston, *Considerations on the Nature of a Funded Debt*, 4–6 (earlier Republican tract saying that public debt obligations could create working capital).

34. Gallatin, *A Sketch of the Finances*, 96, 99–108, 115–16, 122, 137–39, App. B. For a modern assessment of the amount by which Hamilton's program increased the public debt, see E. James Ferguson, *The Power of the Purse: A History of American Public Finance, 1776–1790* (Chapel Hill: University of North Carolina Press, 1961), 329–30. For summary figures on the size of the Federalist deficits, see Adam Seybert, *Statistical Annals of the United States* (1818; repr., New York: Augustus M. Kelley, 1970), 727; Davis Rich Dewey, *Financial History of the United States*, 9th ed. (New York: Longmans, Green, 1924), 110–13; Paul Studenski and Herman Edward Kroos, *The Financial History of the United States* (1952; Washington, DC: Beard Books, 2003), 55–56.

35. Gallatin, *A Sketch of the Finances*, 67–87, 134–42.

36. Gallatin, *A Sketch of the Finances*, 10–14, 149–64. Gallatin's *Sketch* confidently explained how to distinguish direct taxes from indirect taxes for constitutional purposes (relying on analysis in Adam Smith's *Wealth of Nations*), but then struggled to apply the distinction. Ibid., 12–14, 44–46; Smith, *Wealth of Nations*, 777, 821. The meaning of the distinction still remains deeply contested. Bruce Ackerman, "Taxation and the Constitution," *Columbia Law Journal* 99, no. 1 (January 1999):

1–58; Joseph M. Dodge, "What Federal Taxes Are Subject to the Rule of Apportionment Under the Constitution?" *University of Pennsylvania Journal of Constitutional Law* 11, no. 4 (April 2009): 839–956.

37. Gallatin, *A Sketch of the Finances*, 142–49.

38. Albert Gallatin to Hannah Gallatin, 26 September and 12 October 1796, *LAG*, 176–77; Gallatin, Washington County election returns, [after 9 November] 1796, *PAG;* Pennsylvania 1796 Congress, District 12, *Lampi Collection of American Electoral Returns, 1788–1825* (American Antiquarian Society, 2007) (available at *A New Nation Votes: American Election Returns, 1788–1825*, Tufts Digital Library); Martis, *Historical Atlas of Political Parties*, 24. On the birth of James Gallatin, see William Plumb Bacon, ed., *Ancestry of Albert Gallatin…* (New York: Tobias A. Wright, 1916), 18. Hannah Gallatin apparently had earlier miscarriages. Badollet to Gallatin, 21 January 1794; Gallatin to Clare, 30 May 1795, *PAG*.

39. Albert Gallatin to Hannah Gallatin, 24 January 1797, *LAG*, 182; Charles Peirce, *A Meteorological Account of the Weather of Philadelphia from January 1, 1790, to January 1, 1847* (Philadelphia, 1847), 11; Nathaniel C. Green, "'The Focus of the Wills of Converging Millions': Public Opposition to the Jay Treaty and the Origins of the People's Presidency," *Journal of the Early Republic* 37, no. 3 (Fall 2017): 439–42.

40. Stephen G. Kurtz, *The Presidency of John Adams: The Collapse of Federalism, 1795–1800* (Philadelphia: University of Pennsylvania Press, 1957), 114–33, 285–90; Alexander De Conde, *The Quasi-War: The Politics and Diplomacy of the Undeclared War with France, 1797–1801* (New York: Charles Scribner's Sons, 1966), 30–34, 124–30; Elkins and McKitrick, *The Age of Federalism*, 502-04, 537-39, 546-47; Hoadley, *Origins of American Political Parties*, 144–57, 207–9; Doran S. Ben-Atar, *The Origins of Jeffersonian Commercial Policy and Diplomacy* (New York: St. Martin's Press, 1993), 140-42; Dawson, *Partisanship and the Birth of American's Second Party*, 29–39; Pasley, *The First Presidential Contest*, 349–64, 366–69, 372–74. Wolcott privately alleged that Gallatin and William Findley had abetted French agents sent into the American West, but those allegations apparently did not become public at the time. Memoranda, 19 and 21 May 1796, Gibbs, *Memoirs*, 1:350–2; Ezekiel Bacon to Gallatin, 26 July 1846; Gallatin to Bacon, 20 August 1846, *PAG;* James Morton Smith, *Freedom's Fetters: The Alien and Sedition Laws and American Civil Liberties* (1956; Ithaca, NY: Cornell University Press, 1966), 165–69.

41. *Annals,* 5th Cong., 1st Sess., 330–31 (quoted), 378–79; ibid., 6th Cong., 1st Sess., 360; ibid., 5th Cong., 2nd Sess., 1542–44; ibid., 4th Cong., 2nd Sess., 2128–30. From both the internal evidence and the absence of external evidence, it appears unlikely that Gallatin wrote a pamphlet criticizing the Adams administration's policy toward France that some have attributed to him. Citizen of Pennsylvania (pseud.), *Examination of the Conduct of the Executive of the United States Towards the French Republic* (Philadelphia, 1797) [Evans, 32172].

42. Sedgwick to King, 9 April 1798, *LCRK,* 2:310; James Nicholson to Albert Gallatin, 29 May 1797; Albert Gallatin to Hannah Gallatin, 5 July 1797, 6 March 1798, *PAG;* same to same, 30 January 1798, *LAG,* 190; Jefferson to Elbridge Gerry, 13 May 1797; Jefferson to Horatio Gates, 30 May 1797; Jefferson to Aaron Burr, 17 June 1797, *PTJ,* 29:361–66, 407, 437–40; Jefferson to Edmund Pendleton, 14 February 1799, ibid., 31:36–39 (British spoliations exceed those of the French, "[y]et not a word of these things is said officially to the legislature"); Oliver Wolcott Jr. to Hamilton, 5 April 1798, *PAH,* 21:396–99; Elkins and McKitrick, *The Age of Federalism,* 581–82.

43. Smith, *Freedom's Fetters,* 15 (newspaper quote); Abigail Adams to Mary Cranch, 22 April 1798, Stewart Mitchell, ed., *New Letters of Abigail Adams, 1788–1801* (Boston: Houghton Mifflin, 1947), 161; *Annals,* 5th Cong., 2nd Sess., 1357–71, 1473; Kenneth Roberts and Anna M. Roberts, eds. and trans., *Moreau de St. Méry's American Journey, 1793–1798* (Garden City, NY: Doubleday, 1947), 240, 252–53; Menk, "D. M. Erskine: Letters from America, 1798–1799," 259; Niemcewicz, *Under Their Vine and Fig Tree,* 68; De Conde, *The Quasi-War,* 74–89, 92; Michael Durey, *Transatlantic Radicals and the Early American Republic* (Lawrence: University Press of Kansas, 1997), 221–51; David A. Wilson, *United Irishmen, United States: Immigrant Radicals in the Early Republic* (Ithaca, NY: Cornell University Press, 1998), 39–57; François Furstenberg, *When the United States Spoke French: Five Refugees Who Shaped a Nation* (New York: Penguin Press, 2014), 371–74; Catherine A. Hebert, "The French Element in Pennsylvania in the 1790s: The Francophone Immigrants' Impact," *Pennsylvania Magazine of History and Biography* 108, no. 2 (October 1984): 456-458; Rogers M. Smith, "Reconstructing American National Identity: Strategies of the Federalists," in *Federalists Reconsidered,* 36–40.

44. Abigail Adams to Mary Cranch, 22 April 1798, Mitchell, *New Letters,* 161; Smith, *Freedom's Fetters,* 22–111; Jeffrey L. Pasley, *"The Tyranny*

of Printers:" Newspaper Politics in the Early American Republic
(Charlottesville: University Press of Virginia, 2001), 118–24; Douglas
Blackburn, *The Citizenship Revolution: Politics and the Creation of the
American Union, 1774–1804* (Charlottesville: University of Virginia
Press, 2009), 148–50, 155–56, 162–64.

45. *Annals,* 5th Cong., 2nd Sess., 1357–71, 1473, 2064-65 (Otis quoted), 1568
(Harper quoted); Editors' note, *PCAB,* 1:363–66 (proposed constitutional
amendment).

46. Gallatin to James W. Nicholson, 18 May 1798, *PAG;* Robert Troup to
King, 10 June 1798, *LCRK,* 2:345; Jefferson, Thoughts on lotteries, 20
January 1826, *FOL*—Early Access; Jefferson to Madison, 26 April 1798;
Jefferson to John Taylor, 4 June 1798, *PTJ,* 30:299-302, 387-90; John
Taylor to Henry Tazewell, 1 July 1798, Tazewell Family Papers, Library
of Virginia; Jefferson to William Duane, 28 March 1811, *PTJ-RS,* 3:506-
07; Albert Gallatin to Hannah Gallatin, 13 February 1798, *PAG;* same
to same, 21 December 1798, *LAG,* 224-24; John Swartwout to Gallatin,
7 January 1799, *PAG;* Gallatin to Samuel Breck, 20 June 1843, *WAG,*
2:604; Dice Robins Anderson, *William Branch Giles: A Study in the
Politics of Virginia and the Nation from 1790 to 1830* (1914; repr.,
Gloucester, MA: Peter Smith, 1965), 57-59.

47. Albert Gallatin to Hannah Gallatin, 14 June 1797, 3 February 1798,
LAG, 184 (quoted), 190-91; *Annals,* 4th Cong., 1st Sess., 918, 923; ibid.,
4th Cong., 2nd Sess., 2275-77, 2281-84; ibid., 5th Cong., 2nd Sess., 1508,
1515–16, 1996–97; ibid., 5th Cong., 3rd Sess., 2534–36; Albert Gallatin
to Hannah Gallatin, 19 December 1797; Albert Gallatin to Maria
Nicholson, 15 June 1798; *PAG;* Albert Gallatin to Lewis F. Delesdernier,
25 May 1798, *WAG,* 1:16; Joseph W. Cox, *Champion of Southern
Federalism: Robert Goodloe Harper of South Carolina* (Port Washington,
NY: National University Publications, 1972), 90–97, 131–32.

48. "Though a Genevese," recalled a Pennsylvania politician of the next
generation, Gallatin "appear'd in everything a Frenchman." Philip S.
Klein, ed., "Memoirs of a Senator from Pennsylvania: Jonathan Roberts,
1771–1854," *Pennsylvania Magazine of History and Biography* 62, no.
2 (April 1938), 238. *Annals,* 4th Cong., 1st Sess., 918; 5th Cong., 2nd Sess.,
1473 (quoted), 1547, 1552 (Livingston quoted); Joyce Appleby, *Inheriting
the Revolution: The First Generation of Americans* (Cambridge, MA:
Harvard University Press, 2000), 28; William B. Hatcher, *Edward
Livingston: Jeffersonian Republican and Jacksonian Democrat* (1940;
repr., Gloucester, MA: Peter Smith, 1970), 2–8, 36–37; Durey,

Transatlantic Radicals, 221–57; Jason Frank, *Constituent Moments: Enacting the People in Postrevolutionary America* (Durham, NC: Duke University Press, 2010), 177–79; Seth Cotlar, *Tom Paine's America: The Rise and Fall of Transatlantic Radicalism in the Early Republic* (Charlottesville: University of Virginia Press, 2011), 82–111; Paul Goodman, "Social Status of Party Leadership: The House of Representatives, 1797–1804," *William and Mary Quarterly,* 3rd Ser., 25, no. 3 (July 1968): 465–74; Edmund Philip Willis, "Social Origins of Political Leadership in New York City from the Revolution to 1815" (Ph.D. diss., University of California, Berkeley, 1967), 324–33; Charles Brockden Brown, *Wieland, or The Transformation* (1798), in *Charles Brockden Brown: Three Gothic Novels,* comp. Sydney J. Krause (New York: Library of America, 1998), 46–50, 62–64; Bryan Waterman, "The Bavarian Illuminati, the Early American Novel, and Histories of the Public Sphere," *William and Mary Quarterly,* 3rd Ser., 62, no. 1 (January 2005): 9–30.

49. Philadelphia *Porcupine's Gazette,* 28 and 29 March 1798; *Annals,* 5th Cong., 1st Sess. 326–31, 378–86; ibid., 5th Cong., 2nd Sess., 822–27, 1327–30, 1437–38, 1545-47; ibid., 5th Cong., 3rd Sess., 2823–32, 2837 and 2849 (quoted), 2862–70; Jefferson to Madison, 30 January and 5 February 1799, *PTJ,* 30:665–67, 31:9; Jefferson to Burr, 11 February 1799, ibid., 31:22–23; *Pittsburgh Gazette,* 9 June 1798; De Conde, *The Quasi-War,* 124–25; Elkins and McKitrick, *The Age of Federalism,* 595–618. Radical English émigré Thomas Cooper published a cost-benefit analysis of war preparations along the lines of Gallatin's argument. "Political Arithmetic Nos. I and II," in Thomas Cooper, *Political Essays,* 2nd ed. (1800; repr., Bristol, UK: Thoemmes Press, 2001), 32–50. Some Republicans feared that Federalists wanted the troops to deal with insurrections by slaves or republican radicals in the South, and there may have been some basis for those fears. Oliver Wolcott Jr. to Hamilton, 31 March 1797; Wolcott to Washington, 19 April 1797, Gibbs, *Memoirs,* 1:486, 496.

50. *Annals,* 3rd Cong., 1st Sess., 623, 625; Oliver Wolcott Sr. to Oliver Wolcott Jr., 23 April 1790; Goodrich to Oliver Wolcott Jr., 28 May, 1790; Goodrich to Oliver Wolcott Sr., 12 January 1797, Gibbs, *Memoirs,* 1:44, 45, 298; Hamilton to Oliver Wolcott Jr., 6 and 8 June 1797, *PAH,* 21:98–101, 103–04; Oliver Wolcott Jr., Direct Taxes, *ASP: Finance,* 1:414–65 (14 December 1796); Oliver Wolcott Jr., Apportionment of Direct Tax, ibid., 1:588–90 (25 May 1798); Act of 14 July 1798, *Statutes at Large* 1

(1845): 598; Ferguson, *The Power of the Purse*, 290–92; Clement Fatovic, *America's Founding and the Struggle Over Economic Inequality* (Lawrence: University Press of Kansas, 2015), 48, 153–60; Frederick Arthur Baldwin Dalzell, "Taxation with Representation: Federal Revenue in the Early Republic" (Ph.D. diss., Harvard University, 1993), 313–17, 321–28, 335–36.

51. *Annals*, 4th Cong., 2nd Sess., 1852–54, 1885–89, 1891–95, 1908–09, 1941–42; ibid., 5th Cong., 2nd Sess., 1595–1604; Madison to Jefferson, 31 January 1796, 15 January 1797, and 5 February 1797, *PJM-CS*, 16:208–10, 455–57, 483–84; Albert Gallatin to Hannah Gallatin, 24 January 1797, *PAG* (consulting with Wolcott on direct tax proposal in 4th Congress); Gallatin, *A Sketch of the Finances*, 151, 161–64; *Hylton v. United States*, 3 U. S. (3 Dall.) 171, 176–77 (1796) (Constitution intended the apportionment clause to favor the Southern states). On the separate assessment of houses, see Ames to Gore, 27 January 1797, *WFA*, 1:213; Jefferson to St. George Tucker, 28 August 1797; Jefferson to Madison, 7 June 1798; Jefferson to Gerry, 26 January 1799; Burr to Jefferson, 3 February 1799, *PTJ*, 29:519–20, 30:393–95, 645–53, 31:4–5; [Alexander Graydon], *Memoirs of a Life, Chiefly Passed in Pennsylvania…* (Harrisburg, 1811), 388–90. The final vote on the direct tax bill was not along pary lines. But afterwards, some Federalists did claim that Republicans had supported direct taxation to alienate Federalists from their agrarian supporters, and Republican polemicist John Taylor ascribed the Republican ascendency to "taxes imposed and removed." *Annals*, 7th Cong., 1st Sess., 606–07 (James Bayard); Taylor to Monroe, 15 January 1809, LJT, 299; Bell, *Party and Faction*, 112–15; Robin L. Einhorn, *American Taxation American Slavery* (Chicago: University of Chicago Press, 2006), 184–94.

52. Gallatin to Maria Nicholson, 15 June 1798, *PAG;* Jefferson to John Taylor, 26 November and 4 June 1798, *PTJ*, 30:588–90, 387–90; Petition [to Gallatin] from constituents, 22 September 1798, *PAG* (approving Gallatin's votes against taxes and increased military spending); Washington, PA, *Herald of Liberty*, 15 April 1799 (Gallatin's speech about tax burden); *Annals*, 5th Cong., 2nd Sess., 1616–21, 2052–60, 2066–67; ibid., 5th Cong., 3rd Sess., 2868. Treasury secretary Wolcott's original proposal had classified houses by value and imposed a fixed amount of tax on all houses within each class. After Gallatin showed that the resulting tax rates were not progressive, the final bill substituted progressive *ad valorem* rates. *Annals*, 5th Cong., 2nd Sess., 848–53, 1866,

2049–53; Henry Carter Adams, *Taxation in the United States, 1789–1816* (Baltimore, 1884), 54–56. Thirty-five years later, Gallatin claimed that even *ad valorem* taxes hit rural houses more heavily than urban houses because the rental income from rural houses was lower in proportion to their value. Gallatin to Marquis de Lafayette, 12 May 1833, *WAG,* 2:473.

53. Philadelphia *Porcupine's Gazette,* 13 September 1798.

54. *Pittsburgh Gazette,* 11 and 25 August 1798, 1, 8, and 29 September 1798; Washington, PA, *Herald of Liberty,* 1 and 22 October 1798; "Address of the Voters of Washington County," 22 September 1798, in Philadelphia *Aurora General Advertiser,* 10 November 1798; John B. C. Lucas to Gallatin, 5 June 1798; Gallatin to James W. Nicholson, 16 August 1798; John Israel to Gallatin, 23 September 1798; [Gallatin], Election returns, [October] 1798, *PAG;* Albert Gallatin to Hannah Gallatin, 14 December 1798, 18 January 1799, *LAG,* 179, 226; Hannah Gallatin to Maria Nicholson, 23 January 1799, *PAG; Annals,* 5th Cong., 3rd Sess., 2985–3017; Jefferson to Madison, 26 February 1799, *PTJ,* 31:63–65; Claude Milton Newlin, *The Life and Writings of Hugh Henry Brackenridge* (Princeton, NJ: Princeton University Press, 1932), 198–207; Carl E. Prince, "John Israel: Printer and Politician on the Pennsylvania Frontier, 1798–1805," *Pennsylvania Magazine of History and Biography* 91, no. 1 (January 1967), 49; Pennsylvania 1798 Congress, District 12, *Lampi Collection of American Electoral Returns.*

55. Articles of Agreement between James W. Nicholson, Louis Bourdillon, Anthony C[harles] Cazenove, John Badollet, and Albert Gallatin, 17 September 1795, Fayette County (Pennsylvania) Deed Book B, 342–43; Articles of Agreement between George Kramer et al., 20 September 1797 (glassworks); Articles of Agreement between Thomas Mifflin and Albert Gallatin, 5 February 1799 (muskets), *PAG;* Certificate of Plan of New Geneva, 28 October 1797, Fayette County Deed Book C, 1131-34; Albert Gallatin to Hannah Gallatin, 6 September 1795, *LAG,* 152–53; Badollet to Gallatin, 15 March and 10 May 1797, 17 January 1798; Bourdillon to Gallatin, 21 December 1798; Gallatin to Bourdillon, 30 July 1799; Gallatin to James W. Nicholson, 24 November 1797, 9 March, 16 and 24 November, and 1 and 28 December 1798, 18 January and 1, 8, and 15 February 1799, 4 April, 2 May, and 12 June 1800, 19 February 1802; Albert Gallatin to Hannah Gallatin, 1 February 1799; Clement Biddle to Gallatin, 24 November 1801, *PAG;* Washington, PA, *Herald of Liberty,* 12 February 1798 (advertising glassworks in full operation); Gallatin to

Matthew Lyon, 7 May 1816, *WAG,* 1:701; Franklin Ellis, ed., *History of Fayette County, Pennsylvania* (Philadelphia, 1882), 695–96, 698–99, 700–01, 768–69; Furstenberg, *When the United States Spoke French,* 208; William Bining, "The Glass Industry in Western Pennsylvania, 1797–1857," *Western Pennsylvania Historical Magazine* 19, no. 4 (December 1936): 255–68; John Askling, ed., "Autobiographical Sketch of Anthony-Charles Cazenove: Political Refugee, Merchant, and Banker, 1775–1852," *Virginia Magazine of History and Biography* 78, no. 3 (July 1970): 301–3; Michael E. Albert, "Albert Gallatin and the Beginning of Industry in the 'Western Country'" (unpub. MS, 1984), Friendship Hill National Historic Site, Point Marion, PA; Ronald C. Carlisle, "Products and Markets of Albert Gallatin Sawmill, Georges Creek, Fayette County, Pennsylvania" (unpub. MS, 1996), Heinz History Center Library, Pittsburgh, PA. Gallatin also investigated the possibility of selling muskets to the federal government. James McHenry to Gallatin, 8 October 1799; Gallatin to James W. Nicholson, 30 November 1799; Isaac Craig to Gallatin, 20 January 1800, *PAG.*

56.   Gallatin to Maria Nicholson, 15 June 1798, 10 May 1800; Albert Gallatin to Hannah Gallatin, 4 January 1799, *PAG;* Raymond Walters Jr., *Albert Gallatin: Jeffersonian Financier and Diplomat* (New York: Macmillan, 1957), 133–39.

57.   Gallatin to Lewis F. Delesdernier, 25 May 1798, *WAG,* 1:13–17; Statement of real property sold at auction to settle affairs of Albert Gallatin & Co., 20 May 1803; Gallatin to James W. Nicholson, 8 June and 26 October 1804; James W. Nicholson to Thomas Meason, 24 July 1808, *PAG;* J. Jefferson Looney and Ruth L. Woodward, *Princetonians: A Biographical Dictionary, 1791–1794* (Princeton, NJ: Princeton University Press, 1991), 81–84.

58.   Albert Gallatin to Hannah Gallatin, 7 December 1798 (quoted), 4 January 1799, *PAG;* same to same, 19 April 1794, 31 July 1795, 14 December 1796, *LAG,* 122, 152, 179; Robert Morris to Albert Gallatin, 10 December 1798; Gallatin to Henry Middleton, 13 November 1834 (Morris note unpaid); Gallatin to J. D. D. Rosset and Jonathan Casto, 5 June 1847 (details of unpaid Morris note), *PAG;* Ryan K. Smith, *Robert Morris's Folly: The Architectural and Financial Failures of an American Founder* (New Haven, CT: Yale University Press, 2014), 154–63; [François d'Ivernois], *Authentic History of the Origins and Progress of the Late Revolution in Geneva* (Philadelphia, 1794); Richard Whatmore, *Against War and Empire: Geneva, Britain, and France in the Eighteenth*

Century (New Haven, CT: Yale University Press, 2012), 248–56; Patrick F. O'Mara, "Geneva in the Eighteenth Century: A Socio-Economic Study of the Bourgeois City-State during Its Golden Age" (Ph.D. diss., University of California, Berkeley, 1954), 388–453.

Chapter 5: Republican Triumph

1.   John Israel to Albert Gallatin, 6 October and 20 October 1799; Isaac Griffin to Gallatin, 19 December 1799, *PAG*; [Alexander Graydon], *Memoirs of a Life, Chiefly Passed in Pennsylvania...* (Harrisburg, 1811), 395; Sanford W. Higginbotham, *The Keystone in the Democratic Arch: Pennsylvania Politics, 1800–1816* (Harrisburg: Pennsylvania Historical and Museum Commission, 1952), 25–27; G. S. Rowe, *Thomas McKean: The Shaping of an American Republicanism* (Boulder: Colorado Associated University Press, 1978), 303–14; James Roger Sharp, *The Deadlocked Election of 1800: Jefferson, Burr, and the Union in the Balance* (Lawrence: University Press of Kansas, 2010), 82–83.

2.   Albert Gallatin to Hannah Gallatin, 18 January and 1 March 1799, *LAG*, 226, 227–28; Albert Gallatin to James Nicholson, 30 January 1799, *PAG*; Thomas Jefferson to Edmund Pendleton, 14 February 1799, *PTJ*, 31:36-39; John Adams to James McHenry, 22 October 1798, *FOL*—Early Access ("there is no more prospect of seeing a French army here, than there is in Heaven"); John Taylor to James Monroe, 15 January 1809, *LJT*, 299; Graydon, *Memoirs of a Life*, 393–95; Stanley Elkins and Eric McKitrick, *The Age of Federalism: The Early American Republic, 1788–1800* (New York: Oxford University Press, 1993), 706–11; Max M. Edling, *A Revolution in Favor of Government: Origins of the U.S. Constitution and the Making of the American State* (New York: Oxford University Press, 2003), 216; Paul Douglas Newman, *Fries's Rebellion: The Enduring Struggle for the American Revolution* (Philadelphia: University of Pennsylvania Press, 2004), 79–111, 142–64. For Pennsylvania German objections to the Alien Acts and Gallatin's overtures to the German-speaking community, see Solomon Myers to Gallatin, 24 March and 25 May 1799; Gallatin to Myers, 4 April 1799, *PAG*.

3.   Oliver Wolcott Jr. to Fisher Ames, 29 December 1799, Gibbs, *Memoirs*, 2: 313–17; Theodore Sedgwick to Rufus King, 15 November and 12 December 1799, *LCRK*, 3:146, 155–56; Forrest McDonald, *Alexander Hamilton: A Biography* (New York: W. W. Norton, 1979), 342–52; William B. Skelton, *An American Profession of Arms: The Army Officer*

Corps, 1784–1861 (Lawrence: University Press of Kansas, 1992), 95–98; Elkins and McKitrick, *The Age of Federalism,* 726–43.

4.   *Annals,* 6ᵗʰ Cong., 1ˢᵗ Sess., 28–32, 49, 62–63, 65–67, 68–96, 117–19, 121–24, 126–46, 176–77, 691–97, 710, 713; William Bingham to Rufus King, 6 August 1800, *LCRK,* 3:284; Dumas Malone, *The Public Life of Thomas Cooper, 1783–1839* (1926; New York: AMS Press, 1979), 114–19; Higginbotham, *The Keystone in the Democratic Arch,* 28–30; James Morton Smith, *Freedom's Fetters: The Alien and Sedition Laws and American Civil Liberties* (1956; Ithaca, NY: Cornell University Press, 1966), 288–306; Rowe, *Thomas McKean,* 314–17; Nigel Little, *Transoceanic Radical, William Duane: National Identity and Empire, 1760–1835* (London: Pickering and Chatto, 2008), 148–50; Sharp, *The Deadlocked Election,* 87–88; James E. Lewis Jr., "'What Is to Become of Our Government?' The Revolutionary Potential of the Election of 1800," in *The Revolution of 1800: Democracy, Race, and the New Republic,* ed. James Horn, Jan Ellen Lewis, and Peter S. Onuf (Charlottesville: University of Virginia Press, 2002), 11–12.

5.   Matthew L. Davis to Gallatin, 29 March, 15 April, 1 May (quoted), and 5 May 1800, *PAG;* Jefferson to Monroe, 12 January 1800; Jefferson to James Madison, 4 March 1800, *PTJ,* 31:300–1, 407–11; Timothy Pickering to King, 7 May 1800, *LCRK,* 3:232; Alexander Hamilton to John Jay, 7 May 1800, *PAH,* 24:464–67; Washington, PA, *Herald of Liberty,* 19 May 1800 (proclaiming New York City election made Jefferson's victory certain); Nancy Isenberg, *Fallen Founder: The Life of Aaron Burr* (New York: Viking, 2007), 196–200; Sharp, *The Deadlocked Election,* 83–87; Brian Phillips Murphy, "'A Very Convenient Instrument': The Manhattan Company, Aaron Burr, and the Election of 1800," *William and Mary Quarterly,* 3ʳᵈ Ser., 65, no. 2 (April 2008): 260–06; Arthur Irving Bernstein, "The Rise of the Democratic-Republican Party in New York City, 1789–1800" (Ph.D. diss., Columbia University, 1964), 390–414; Jeffrey L. Pasley, "Matthew Livingston Davis's Notes from the Political Underground: The Conflict of Political Values in the Early American Republic" (unpub. paper, 1996, www.pasleybrothers.com/jeff/writings/davisv2.htm). For other examples of Gallatin's Burrite connections, see Gallatin to James Nicholson, 30 January 1799 (proposing possible contributors to payment of Matthew Lyon's fine for violating the Sedition Act); John Swartwout to Gallatin, 7 January 1799, 16 September 1801; David Gelston to Gallatin, 17 February 1800, 14 April, 13 July, and 4 September 1801; Aaron Burr to Gallatin, 16 January 1801, *PAG;*

Burr to Jefferson, 25 May 1801, *PTJ*, 34:178–79 (nominates Commodore Nicholson as Commissioner of Loans for New York).

6. Albert Gallatin to Hannah Gallatin, 6 May 1800, *PAG*; Richard R. John, *Spreading the News: The American Postal System from Franklin to Morse* (Cambridge, MA: Harvard University Press, 1995), 42–43.

7. John Taylor to Henry Tazewell, 8 December 1796, Tazewell Family Papers, Library of Virginia (Virginia electors believed votes for Burr in 1796 would prevent Jefferson's election); John P. Kaminski, *George Clinton: Yeoman Politician of the New Republic* (Madison, WI: Madison House, 1993), 247–52; Isenberg, *Fallen Founder*, 105–06, 141–54.

8. James Nicholson to Gallatin, 6 May 1800, *PAG*. Nicholson's misspelling of Hamilton's name was as engrained as his contempt for the man. After seeing Hamilton at an election meeting two years earlier, Nicholson had described him to Gallatin as the "Devil…in the shape of a small man" who allowed himself to be "frequently insulted without [making any] reply." Nicholson to Gallatin, 20 April 1798, ibid.

9. James Nicholson to Gallatin, 7 May 1800, *PAG*; Hannah Gallatin to Albert Gallatin, 7 May (quoted) and 12 May 1800, *LAG*, 243. It emerged a few years later that Nicholson had overstated George Clinton's declination of the vice presidential nomination, although Clinton never complained. Carl Becker, "A Letter of James Nicholson, 1803," *American Historical Review* 8, no. 3 (April 1903): 511–13; Milton Lomask, *Aaron Burr: The Years from Princeton to Vice President, 1756–1805* (New York: Farrar Straus Giroux, 1979), 247–55; Editors' note, *PCAB*, 1:432–33; Kaminski, *George Clinton*, 253–55, 262–63; Joanne B. Freeman, *Affairs of Honor: National Politics in the New Republic* (New Haven, CT: Yale University Press, 2001), 235–36, 241–44. On the effort to prevent Southern Republicans from throwing electoral votes away from Burr, see David Gelston to Madison, 8 October 1800; Madison to Monroe, [21 October] 1800; Gelston to Madison, 21 November 1800, *PJM-CS*, 17:418–19, 426, 438; Madison to John Francis Mercer, 23 October 1800, *PJM-SS*, 8:538–39.

10. Fisher Ames to Christopher Gore, 29 December 1800, *WFA*, 1:288; Jeffersoniad Nos. VII and XIII, Boston *Columbia Centinel*, 26 July (quoted) and 27 August 1800; Albert Gallatin, *Views of the Public Debt, Receipts and Expenditures of the United States* (New York: M. L. and W. A. Davis, 1800), 1-29, 35-47; Philadelphia *Aurora General Advertiser*, 22 August, 14 October, 18 October, 5 November 1800; Washington, PA, *Herald of Liberty*, 15 September 1800; Burr to William Eustis, 15 July

1800, *PCAB,* 1:439; John Beckley to Monroe, 26 August 1800, Gerald W. Gawalt, ed., *Justifying Jefferson: The Political Writings of John James Beckley* (Washington, DC: Library of Congress, 1995), 191; Roger Griswold to House of Representatives, 8 May 1800, *ASP: Finance,* 1:657–78; Edmund Berkeley and Dorothy Smith Berkeley, *John Beckley: Zealous Partisan in a Nation Divided* (Philadelphia: American Philosophical Society, 1973), 201, 206. Demand for Gallatin's book after the election prompted a reprinting in Philadelphia. Matthew Carey to Gallatin, 31 December 1800, 28 January 1801, *PAG.*

11.   Jefferson to Madison, 19 December (quoted), 26 December 1800; Jefferson to Thomas Mann Randolph, 9 January 1801 (lamenting absence of Gallatin, Edward Livingston, Joseph Nicholson, and other Republican members), *PTJ,* 32:321–24, 358–59, 417–19; John Randolph to Joseph H. Nicholson, 16 December and 17 December 1800, JHNP. The Republican newspaper in Gallatin's district had a sprightlier response to the election result: "Yankee doodle, keep it up / Let us all be friskey, / The Democrats have beat the Rats / Push about the whiskey." If Federalists think Burr is not a Republican, argued the next issue, let them ask Hamilton—who will say Burr is "not only a republican, but a Democrat." Washington, PA, *Herald of Liberty,* 29 December 1800, 5 January 1801.

12.   Albert Gallatin to Hannah Gallatin, 15 January, 5 February 1801 (quoted); Hannah Gallatin to Albert Gallatin, 8 and 22 January, 5 February 1801; Albert Gallatin to Maria Nicholson, 11 July 1799, 12 March 1801; Gallatin to James W. Nicholson, 10 January 1800 (birth of second son, Albert Rolaz), *PAG; Annals,* 6th Cong., 2nd Sess., 906 (Gallatin seated 12 January 1801); Virginia K. Bartlett, *Keeping House: Women's Lives in Western Pennsylvania, 1790–1850* (Pittsburgh: University of Pittsburgh Press, 1994), 23–24, 37; Rosemarie Zagarri, "The Family Factor: Congressmen, Turnover, and the Burden of Public Service in the Early American Republic," *Journal of the Early Republic* 33, no. 2 (Summer 2013): 289-96; Charles Morse Stotz, *The Early Architecture of Western Pennsylvania* (1936; Pittsburgh: University of Pittsburgh Press, 1995), 45, 169 (paneling in Friendship Hill addition); U. S. Department of the Interior, National Park Service, *Friendship Hill National Historic Site: Historic Structure Report—Architectural Data Section,* comp. John B. Marsh and Scott Jacobs (August 1984), 9–10, and Evolutionary Drawings, Main House, Sheet 3; Pennsylvania 1800 Congress, District 12, *Lampi Collection of American Electoral Returns, 1788–1825*

(American Antiquarian Society, 2007) (available at *A New Nation Votes: American Election Returns, 1788–1825,* Tufts Digital Library).

13. Albert Gallatin to Hannah Gallatin, 15 January 1801, *PAG;* Gouverneur Morris to Princess de la Tour et Taxis, 14 December 1800, Anne Cary Morris, ed., *The Diary and Letters of Gouverneur Morris* (2 vols.; New York, 1888), 2:394; John Melish, *Travels Through the United States of America, in the Years 1806 and 1807, 1809, 1810, and 1811* (London, 1818), 144; Constance McLaughlin Green, *Washington: Village and Capital, 1800–1878* (Princeton, NJ: Princeton University Press, 1962), 23–30, 78; James Sterling Young, *The Washington Community, 1800–1828* (New York: Columbia University Press, 1966), 41–48; Catherine Allgor, *Parlor Politics: In Which the Ladies of Washington Help Build a City and a Government* (Charlottesville: University Press of Virginia, 2000), 4–10; Richard Mannix, "Albert Gallatin in Washington, 1801–1813," *Records of the Columbia Historical Society, Washington, D.C.* 71–72 (1971–72), 60–65.

14. Gordon S. Wood, *Empire of Liberty: A History of the Early Republic, 1789-1815* (New York: Oxford University Press, 2009), 278–85. For citations to the many excellent accounts of the 1801 election in the House of Representatives, see Thomas N. Baker, "'An Attack Well Directed': Aaron Burr Intrigues for the Presidency," *Journal of the Early Republic* 31, no. 4 (Winter 2011), 554n1. On the constitutional flaw that gave rise to the crisis, see Tadahisa Kuroda, *The Origins of the Twelfth Amendment: The Electoral College in the Early Republic, 1787–1804* (Westport. CT: Greenwood Press, 1994), 73–105; Bruce Ackerman, *The Failure of the Founding Fathers: Jefferson, Marshall, and the Rise of Presidential Democracy* (Cambridge, MA: Harvard University Press, 2005), 1–108; Joanne B. Freeman, "The Election of 1800: A Study in the Logic of Political Change," *Yale Law Journal* 108, no. 8 (June 1999): 1969–82, 1990–94.

15. Albert Gallatin to Hannah Gallatin, 15 January 1801, *PAG;* Nathaniel Macon to Andrew Jackson, 12 January 1801, Daniel Feller et al., eds., *The Papers of Andrew Jackson* (10 vols. to date; Knoxville: University of Tennessee Press, 1980–), 1:238; John Randolph to Joseph H. Nicholson, 1 January 1801; Caesar A. Rodney to Nicholson, 3 January 1801, JHNP. Gallatin almost certainly knew that Aaron Burr had told Samuel Smith—who boarded with Gallatin and Jefferson at Conrad and McMunn's—that he would neither seek nor refuse election. Even the Philadelphia and New

York newspapers had reported the gist of the meetings between Smith and Burr. Editors' note, *PCAB,* 1:483-84.

16. Albert Gallatin to Hannah Gallatin, 22 January [1801] (original misdated 1800), *PAG;* Harrison Gray Otis to Sally Foster Otis, 1 February 1801, Samuel Eliot Morison, *The Life and Letters of Harrison Gray Otis: Federalist, 1765–1848* (2 vols.; Boston: Houghton Mifflin, 1913), 1:148.

17. Albert Gallatin to Hannah Gallatin, 29 January 1801, *PAG;* Gallatin, Plan of balloting for Jefferson and Burr, [before 29 January], 1801, *WAG,* 1:18-23; Ackerman, *The Failure of the Founding Fathers,* 80–85, 87. The more excitable Edward Livingston—who also had returned to Congress late—believed that the Federalists were supporting Burr to block an election by the House and open the way to appointing an executive by statute. Edward Livingston to Robert L. Livingston, 29 January 1801, quoted in *PCAB,* 1:504n2; William B. Hatcher, *Edward Livingston: Jeffersonian Republican and Jacksonian Democrat* (1940; repr., Gloucester, MA: Peter Smith, 1970), 68–71, 87–92. A few historians have pointed to a letter that Gallatin wrote to Burr on 3 February 1801 as evidence that Gallatin supported Burr rather than Jefferson. Gallatin's letter has not survived, but Burr's reply pointedly rejected both "Usurpation" and "timid temporizing projects." Those historians conclude from Burr's letter that Gallatin had proposed such tactics. But given the context in which Gallatin wrote the missing letter, it seems more likely that Gallatin was asking Burr to make it known that he would not accept the presidency if the Federalists used such tactics to install him. Burr to Gallatin, 12 February 1801, *PCAB,* 1:500-1; Roger G. Kennedy, *Burr, Hamilton, and Jefferson: A Study in Character* (New York: Oxford University Press, 2000), 167-68; Bernard A. Weisberger, *America Afire: Jefferson, Adams, and the First Contested Election* (New York: HarperCollins, 2000), 269-71. Some Republicans did consider extra-constitutional actions. Madison, for example, thought that Jefferson and Burr should jointly call an early meeting of the next Congress to resolve the stalemate. Jefferson seems to have considered a new constitutional convention. Gallatin's balloting plan does not mention either idea, and Gallatin later claimed never to have heard of the second one. Madison to Jefferson, 10 January 1801, *PJM-CS,* 17:453–57; Samuel Smith to Burr, 11 January 1801, *PCAB,* 1:487–89; Jefferson to Monroe, 15 February 1801; Jefferson to Madison, 18 February 1801, *PTJ,* 32:594, 33:16–17; Gallatin to Henry A. Muhlenberg, 8 May 1848, *WAG,* 2:663; James

Roger Sharp, *American Politics in the Early Republic: The New Nation in Crisis* (New Haven, CT: Yale University Press, 1993), 275.

18. Albert Gallatin to Hannah Gallatin, 5 February 1801, *PAG*; Ebenezer Mattoon to Samuel Henshaw, 10 and 17 February 1801, Swann Galleries (NY) Catalog, 17 September 2015 Sale, Lot 295 (demonstrators); John Randolph to St. George Tucker, 11 February 1801, quoted in William Cabell Bruce, *John Randolph of Roanoke, 1773–1833* (2 vols.; New York: G. P. Putnam's Sons, 1922), 1:168; Albert Gallatin to James Nicholson, 14 February 1801, *PAG; Annals,* 6th Cong., 2nd Sess., 987, 1008–11; Gaillard Hunt, ed., *The First Forty Years of Washington Society* (New York: Charles Scribner's Sons, 1906), 23–24; Elkins and McKitrick, *The Age of Federalism,* 749; Scott S. Sheads, "Joseph Hopper Nicholson: Citizen-Soldier of Maryland," *Maryland Historical Magazine* 98, no. 2 (Summer 2003): 137–38.

19. Albert Gallatin to Hannah Gallatin, 12 and 17 February 1801; Albert Gallatin to James Nicholson, 16 February 1801; John Beckley to Gallatin, 15 February 1801; Alexander J. Dallas to Gallatin, 15 February 1801, *PAG;* Gallatin to Dallas, 11, 12, 13, 16, 17, and 18 February 1801, George Mifflin Dallas, *Life and Writings of Alexander James Dallas* (Philadelphia, 1871), 112–13; Morton Borden, *The Federalism of James A. Bayard* (New York: Columbia University Press, 1955), 88–93.

20. Gilbert Stuart, Portrait of Samuel Smith, oil on canvas, c. 1800, National Portrait Gallery; Rembrandt Peale, Portrait of Samuel Smith, oil on canvas, c. 1816, Maryland Historical Society; Frank A. Cassell, *Merchant Congressman in the Young Republic: Samuel Smith of Maryland, 1752–1839* (Madison: University of Wisconsin Press, 1971), 5–6, 38–41.

21. Burr to Samuel Smith, 16, 17, 24, and 29 December 1800; Smith to Burr, 11 January [1801]; Burr to Smith, 16 January, 4 February 1801, *PCAB,* 1:471, 472, 475, 478–79, 487–89, 493, 497; Burr to Gallatin, 16 January, 12 and 25 February, 1801, *PCAB,* 1:492, 500, 509; James Bayard to Richard Bassett, 16 and 17 February 1801; Bayard to Allan McLane, 17 February 1801, PJAB, 2:126–27, 127, 127–29; Cassell, *Merchant Congressman,* 96–102; John Pancake, *Samuel Smith and the Politics of Business, 1752–1839* (Tuscaloosa: University of Alabama Press, 1972), 53–58; Freeman, *Affairs of Honor,* 248–50; Isenberg, *Fallen Founder,* 217–18; David O. Stewart, *American Emperor: Aaron Burr's Challenge to Jefferson's America* (New York: Simon and Schuster, 2011), 24–25.

22. Gallatin to Henry A. Muhlenberg, 8 May 1848, *WAG,* 2:664–65; Joseph George Henrich, "The Triumph of Ideology: The Jeffersonians and the

Navy, 1779–1807" (Ph.D. diss., Duke University, 1971), 168–74. Samuel
Smith had insinuated to Burr that Jefferson should not nominate Gallatin
to be Treasury secretary because Gallatin was a foreigner. Burr said that
was a "frivolous & absurd" objection that no one had raised against the
immigrant Hamilton when Washington nominated him to the Treasury.
Burr to Samuel Smith, 17 December 1800, *PCAB,* 1:472.

23. James McHenry to Charles Carroll, 8 April 1801, James McHenry Papers,
Huntington Library; James Bayard to Andrew Bayard, 9 January 1802,
PJAB, 2:145; Philadelphia *Aurora General Advertiser,* 18 March 1801
(plan to thwart Gallatin confirmation); Washington, PA, *Herald of
Liberty,* 6 April 1801; [Fisher Ames], Falkland No. IV, February 1801,
WFA, 2:141–42; George Cabot to King, 30 March 1801; Robert Troup
to King, 22 May 1801, *LCRK,* 3:417, 454; Lucius Junius Brutus [pseud.],
*An Examination of the President's Reply to the New-Haven
Remonstrance* (New York 1801), 40–41, 46, 52. Gallatin had criticized
James McHenry for his poor financial management of the War
department. *Annals,* 5th Cong., 2nd Sess., 1399; Julian Ursyn Niemcewicz,
*Under Their Vine and Fig Tree: Travels through America in 1797–1799,
1805,* trans. and ed. Metchie J. E. Budka (Elizabeth, NJ: Grassman
Publishing, 1965), 60.

24. Albert Gallatin to Hannah Gallatin, 19 February (two letters; one
quoted), 29 January, 26 February, 12 March 1801, *PAG;* same to same,
23 February (quoted), 5 March 1801, *LAG,* 263–64, 265; Jefferson to
Madison, 9 November 1800; Jefferson to Thomas Mann Randolph, 25
November 1800, *PTJ,* 32:250, 259; Madison to Jefferson, 11 November
1800, *PJM-CS,* 17:437.

25. Gallatin to Jefferson, 14 March, 23 April 1801 (quoted); Jefferson to
Madison, 12 March 1801; Jefferson to Samuel Smith, 13 March 1801,
PTJ, 33:275–77, 637, 255–56, 271–72; Gallatin to Maria Nicholson, 12
March 1801; Gallatin to [Joseph?] Boone, 12 March 1801, *PAG.* President
Adams had called the Senate of the next Congress into special session,
but absences and late elections left the session with a Federalist majority
likely hostile to Gallatin's nomination. Albert Gallatin to Hannah
Gallatin, 5 February 1801, *PAG;* Philadelphia *Aurora General Advertiser,*
18 March 1801. Gallatin took the oath of office in May 1801, and the
new Senate approved his recess appointment the following year in its first
regular session. William Cranch, Oath of office certificate, 14 May 1801,
PAG; Senate Executive Journal, 7th Cong., 1st Sess., 400, 405 (26 January
1802).

Chapter 6: Debt and Democracy

1. U. S. Treasury Department, Roll of the Officers, Civil, Military, and Naval, of the United States, 12 February 1802, *ASP: Miscellaneous,* 1:260–319; Philadelphia *Gazette of the United States,* 23 September 1801; Leonard D. White, *The Jeffersonians: A Study in Administrative History, 1801–1829* (New York: Macmillan, 1956), 137–40; Noble E. Cunningham Jr., *The Process of Government under Jefferson* (Princeton, NJ: Princeton University Press, 1978), 97–98, 325–26; Pamela Scott, *Fortress of Finance: The United States Treasury Building* (Washington, DC: Treasury Historical Association, 2010), 15–23. On the Treasury fire, see Albert Gallatin to Hannah Gallatin, 29 January 1801; John Beckley to Albert Gallatin, 4 February 1801, *PAG;* Washington, PA, *Herald of Liberty,* 2 February 1801; *Annals,* 6ᵗʰ Cong., 2ⁿᵈ Sess., 1020–21; Report on Books and Papers Destroyed, 23 February 1801; Report on Causes of the Late Fires, 28 February 1801, *ASP: Miscellaneous,* 1:241–43, 247-52; Edmund Berkeley and Dorothy Smith Berkeley, *John Beckley: Zealous Partisan in a Nation Divided* (Philadelphia: American Philosophical Society, 1973), 211–15.

2. Thomas Jefferson to Elbridge Gerry, 26 January 1799; Jefferson, First Inaugural Address, 4 March 1801; Jefferson to Gideon Granger, 13 August 1800 ("economical government"), *PTJ,* 30:645–53, 33:148–52, 32:95-97; Dumas Malone, *Jefferson and His Time,* vol. 4, *Jefferson the President: First Term, 1801–1805* (Boston: Little Brown, 1970), 99–104; Merrill D. Peterson, *Thomas Jefferson and the New Nation: A Biography* (New York: Oxford University Press, 1970), 660–61, 687–89, 692; see Introduction, pp. xxvi–xxvii.

3. Edward Thornton to [Robert Jenkinson], Lord Hawkesbury, 2 June 1801, U. K. National Archives, FO 5/32/32; Robert Troup to Rufus King, 2 October 1798, *LCRK,* 2:432 ("Madison seems to be in a tomb; we hear nothing of him."); Gallatin to Maria Nicholson, 12 March 1801, *PAG.*

4. *Annals,* 12ᵗʰ Cong., 2ⁿᵈ Sess., 562 (Josiah Quincy); Jefferson, Circular to Heads of Department, 6 November 1801; Gallatin to Jefferson, 9 November 1801; Jefferson to Gallatin, 10 November 1801, *PTJ,* 35:576–78, 586–88, 595–96; Gallatin to Jefferson, 15 March 1804, *PAG,* extract in *WAG,* 1:179–80; Jefferson to James Madison, 9 April 1804, *PJM-SS,* 7:25–26; Jefferson to Antoine Destutt de Tracy, 26 January 1811, *PTJ-RS,* 3:334–39; Peterson, *Thomas Jefferson and the New Nation,* 660–61; Ralph Ketcham, *James Madison: A Biography* (1971; Charlottesville: University Press of Virginia, 1990), 391–407; Cunningham, *The Process*

of Government under Jefferson, 63–65; Robert M. Johnstone Jr., *Jefferson and the Presidency: Leadership in the Young Republic* (Ithaca, NY: Cornell University Press, 1978), 88–90; Everett Lee Long, "Jefferson and Congress: A Study of the Jeffersonian Legislative System, 1801–1809" (Ph.D. diss., University of Missouri, 1966), 75–80. On leadership in Revolutionary Virginia, see A. G. Roeber, *Faithful Magistrates and Republican Lawyers: Creators of Virginia Legal Culture, 1680–1810* (Chapel Hill: University of North Carolina Press, 1981), 145–59, 163–71; Daniel P. Jordan, *Political Leadership in Jefferson's Virginia* (Charlottesville: University of Virginia Press, 1983), 21–25; Emory G. Evans, *A "Topping People": The Rise and Decline of Virginia's Old Political Elite, 1680–1790* (Charlottesville: University of Virginia Press, 2009), 177–202. On Jefferson, Madison, and Gallatin as a triumvirate, see Henry Adams, *The Life of Albert Gallatin* (1879; repr., New York: Peter Smith, 1943), 269; Henry Adams, *History of the United States during the Administrations of Thomas Jefferson and James Madison* (1889–91; 2 vols., New York: Library of America, 1986), 1:129–30; Raymond Walters Jr., *Albert Gallatin: Jeffersonian Financier and Diplomat* (New York: Macmillan, 1957), 145; Malone, *Jefferson and His Time,* 4:57, 446; Thomas K. McCraw, *The Founders and Finance: How Hamilton, Gallatin, and Other Immigrants Forged a New Economy* (Cambridge, MA: Harvard University Press, 2012), 181.

5.   [Joseph?] Boone to Gallatin, 12 March 1801; Gallatin to Maria Nicholson, 12 March 1801; Gallatin to James W. Nicholson, 3 and 19 June 1801, *PAG;* Margaret Bayard Smith to Susan B. Smith, 26 May 1801; Margaret Bayard Smith to Maria Bayard, 28 May 1801, Gaillard Hunt, ed., *The First Forty Years of Washington Society* (New York: Charles Scribner's Sons, 1906), 27–28, 29; Irving Brant, *James Madison,* vol. 4, *James Madison: Secretary of State, 1800–1809* (Indianapolis: Bobbs-Merrill, 1953), 42–43; William E. Ames, *A History of the National Intelligencer* (Chapel Hill: University of North Carolina Press, 1972), 4–12; Richard Mannix, "Albert Gallatin in Washington, 1801–1813," *Records of the Columbia Historical Society, Washington, D.C.* 71 and 72 (1971–72), 63, 68–69, 75–77; Cassandra Good, "'Transcript of My Heart': The Unpublished Diaries of Margaret Bayard Smith," *Washington History* 17, no. 1 (Fall/Winter 2005): 77.

6.   Gallatin to James W. Nicholson, 14, 21, and 26 August 1801, 11 and 18 September 1801, 1 October 1802; Daniel C. Brent to Gallatin, 15 August 1801; Gallatin to Jefferson, 18 and 24 August 1801; Adden Nicholson to

James W. Nicholson, 18 January, 1803; Robert Sewall to Gallatin, 6 October 1807 (lowers rent to $400), *PAG;* William Russell Birch, *View of the Capitol of Washington before It Was Burnt Down by the British*, watercolor, 1800, Prints and Photographs Division, DLC (perspective southwest from 1st Street and Constitution Avenue, N. E.); White, *The Jeffersonians,* 401–02. The Gallatins' house became the headquarters of the National Woman's Party in 1929, and the National Park Service now operates it as the Belmont-Paul Women's Equality National Monument. U. S. Department of the Interior, National Park Service, Historic American Buildings Survey, "Sewall-Belmont House," comp. Scott G. Schultz, HABS DC-821 (1998), 6–9. For references to the Gallatin's servants and the leasing of enslaved servants in Washington, see Gallatin to James W. Nicholson, 5 May 1798; Albert Gallatin to Hannah Gallatin, 6 May 1800, 5 February 1801, 6 June 1804; Albert Gallatin to Maria Nicholson, 10 May 1800, 28 May 1808; Anthony C. Cazenove to Gallatin, 11 March 1814, *PAG;* Frances Few, Journal, 21 December 1808, Ad Hoc Collections, *Georgia's Virtual Vault: Digital Treasures from the Georgia Archives,* printed in Noble E. Cunningham Jr., ed., "The Diary of Frances Few, 1808–1809," *Journal of Southern History* 29, no. 3 (August 1963): 354; Nathaniel Macon to Joseph H. Nicholson, 16 January 1811, JHNP; Margaret Bayard Smith to Jane Kirkpatrick, 21 July 1801, Hunt, *The First Forty Years,* 32; Constance McLaughlin Green, *Washington: Village and Capital, 1800–1878* (Princeton, NJ: Princeton University Press, 1962), 20–22, 98–99; Bob Arnebeck, *Through a Fiery Trial: Building Washington, 1790-1800* (Lanham, MD: Madison Books, 1991), 374, 392; Stephanie Cole, "Changes for Mrs. Thornton's Arthur: Patterns of Domestic Service in Washington, DC," *Social Science History* 15, no. 3 (Autumn 1991): 369–73.

7.   Philip S. Klein, ed., "Memoirs of a Senator from Pennsylvania: Jonathan Roberts, 1771–1854," *Pennsylvania Magazine of History and Biography* 62, no. 2 (April 1938): 239 (Roberts entered Congress in 1811); Frances Few to Maria Nicholson, 29 January 1809, *PAG;* Few, Journal, 1 October, 21 December, and 26 December 1808, in Cunningham, "Diary of Frances Few," 348, 354, 355–56; Kenneth C. Martis, *The Historical Atlas of Political Parties in the United States Congress, 1789–1989* (New York: Macmillan, 1989), 24; Rosemarie Zagarri, *Revolutionary Backlash: Women and Politics in the Early American Republic* (Philadelphia: University of Pennsylvania Press, 2007), 62–68, 75–81 ("female politicians").

8. Macon to Jefferson, 20 April 1801 (listing plain Republican measures); Jefferson to Macon, 14 May 1801, *PTJ*, 33:620–1, 34:109–10; Macon to Joseph H. Nicholson, 31 January, 12 March, and 15 April 1806; John Randolph to Nicholson, 1 January and 18 July 1801, JHNP; Gallatin to Randolph, 31 March and 13 April 1802; Randolph to Gallatin, [3 March], 9 April and 10 April 1803, 3 December 1804, [28 January] 1805, 11 February 1807, *PAG;* William E. Dodd, *The Life of Nathaniel Macon* (Raleigh, NC: Edwards and Broughton, 1903), 172–74; Robert Dawidoff, *The Education of John Randolph* (New York: W. W. Norton, 1979), 164–97; David Johnson, *John Randolph of Roanoke* (Baton Rouge: Louisiana State University Press, 2012), 54–58, 64; Stephen J. Barry, "Nathaniel Macon: The Prophet of Pure Republicanism, 1758–1837" (Ph.D. diss., State University of New York at Buffalo, 1996), 65–66, 78, 88–90.
9. Gallatin to Nicholson, 13 March 1801, 3 April and 27 April 1802, 27 March 1805, 17 April 1806, JHNP; Nicholson to Gallatin, 7 July 1801, *PAG;* Few, Journal, 1 October 1808, in Cunningham, "Diary of Frances Few," 348; Macon to Nicholson, 30 January 1813, JHNP; Charles Balthazar Julien Févret de Saint-Mémin, Portrait of Joseph Hopper Nicholson, engraving, 1806, Maryland Historical Society; Betty Wood, ed., *Mary Telfair to Mary Few: Selected Letters, 1802–1844* (Athens: University of Georgia Press, 2007), 14, 28, 32, 68–69; Scott S. Sheads, "Joseph Hopper Nicholson: Citizen-Soldier of Maryland," *Maryland Historical Magazine* 98, no. 2 (Summer 2003), 132–51.
10. Gallatin to Jefferson, 26 March 1804, *PAG;* Gallatin to Jefferson, 3 January 1802; Jefferson to Gallatin, 23 August and 9 November 1803, *PTJ,* 36:270, 41:243–33, 689–90; Gallatin to Samuel L. Mitchill, 3 January 1805; Gallatin to Jefferson, 25 November 1806, *WAG*, 1:219–26, 322–24; Albert Gallatin to Hannah Gallatin, 30 October 1807, *LAG,* 363; Cunningham, *The Process of Government under Jefferson,* 188–213; Johnstone, *Jefferson and the Presidency,* 73, 140–41; Merry Ellen Scofield, "The Fatigues of His Table: The Politics of Presidential Dining during the Jefferson Administration," *Journal of the Early Republic* 26, no. 3 (Fall 2006): 449–69; Long, "Jefferson and Congress," 166–78, 223–27; Alexander B. Lacy Jr., "Jefferson and Congress: Congressional Method and Politics, 1801–1809" (Ph.D. diss., University of Virginia, 1964), 121–44. Dumas Malone describes Gallatin as the principal connection between the executive triumvirate of Jefferson, Madison, and Gallatin and a legislative triumvirate of Macon, Randolph, and Nicholson.

James Sterling Young treats Gallatin's house on Capitol Hill as a vector between the separate Congressional and executive precincts that he postulated. But Gallatin was not the only cabinet member who lived on Capitol Hill; the secretaries of the War and Navy departments, Henry Dearborn and Robert Smith, also lived there. Malone, *Jefferson and His Time*, 4:446; Young, *The Washington Community, 1800–1828* (New York: Columbia University Press, 1966), 166; Thom M. Armstrong, *Politics, Diplomacy, and Intrigue in the Early Republic: The Cabinet Career of Robert Smith, 1801–1811* (Dubuque, IA: Kendall/Hunt Publishing, 1991), 8; Richard Alton Erney, "The Public Life of Henry Dearborn" (Ph.D. diss., Columbia University, 1957), 43, 184–85.

11. Albert Gallatin to Hannah Gallatin, 15 January 1801 (quoted); Albert Gallatin to James W. Nicholson, 17 July 1801; Albert Gallatin to Jefferson, 18 August 1801; Hannah Gallatin to Albert Gallatin, 5 July 1807; Albert Gallatin to James Gallatin, 19 February 1825, *PAG;* Few, Journal, 21 December 1808, in Cunningham, "Diary of Frances Few," 354 (Gallatin's hours); Jefferson to Gabriel Duval, 5 November 1802, *PTJ*, 38:639–40 (Treasury's regular office hours are 9:00 a.m. to 3:00 p.m.); Nicholas King, *View of Blodgett's Hotel in Washington*, watercolor, c. 1799–1801, Huntington Library (perspective west from C Street at 6th Street, N. W.); Wilhelmus Bogart Bryan, *A History of the National Capital* (2 vols.; New York: Macmillan, 1914-16), 1:149n1; Don A. Hawkins, "The City of Washington in 1800: A New Map," *Washington History* 12, no. 1 (Spring/Summer 2000): 74–77.

12. Everett Somerville Brown, ed., *William Plumer's Memorandum of Proceedings in the United States Senate, 1803–1807* (New York: Macmillan, 1923), 634–35 (1 March 1807) (quoted), 193–94 (10 November 1804) (Jefferson receives in soiled, threadbare clothes), 212 (3 December 1804) (Jefferson dines in new, clean clothes), 333 (29 November 1805) (Jefferson's slippers ragged and hair disheveled); Philadelphia *Gazette of the United States*, 6 May 1802 (from Charleston *Daily Advertiser*, 14 April 1802); Klein, "Memoirs of a Senator from Pennsylvania: Jonathan Roberts, " 238–39 (Gallatin's cigars and bad teeth); Troup to King, 9 April 1802, *LCRK*, 4:103; Barnabas Bidwell to Mary Bidwell, 28 November 1805, Barnabas Bidwell Papers, Miscellaneous Manuscripts Collection, DLC (Gallatin's appearance); Macon to Joseph H. Nicholson, 22 May 1809, JHNP (gift of plain Carolina cloth); same to same, 15 December 1816, William E. Dodd, ed., "Nathaniel Macon Correspondence," *John P. Branch Historical Papers*

of Randolph-Macon College 3, no. 1 (June 1909): 73–74 (political equality depends on economy and simplicity); Richard Beale Davis, ed., *Jeffersonian America: Notes on the United States of America…by Sir Augustus John Foster* (San Marino, CA: Huntington Library, 1954), 9–10; Joanne B. Freeman, *Affairs of Honor: National Politics in the New Republic* (New Haven, CT: Yale University Press, 2001), 265-74; Michael Zakin, *Ready-Made Democracy: A History of Men's Dress in the American Republic, 1760–1860* (Chicago: University of Chicago Press, 2003), 27–32; Maurizio Valsania, *Jefferson's Body: A Corporeal Biography* (Charlottesville: University of Virginia Press, 2017), 48–49, 53–55; David Waldstreicher, "Why Thomas Jefferson and African Americans Wore Their Politics on Their Sleeves," in *Beyond the Founders: New Approaches to the Political History of the Early American Republic,* ed. Jeffrey L. Pasley, Andrew W. Robertson, and David Waldstreicher (Chapel Hill: University of North Carolina Press, 2004), 83–87; Donald R. Hickey, "The United State Army versus Long Hair: The Trials of Colonel Thomas Butler, 1801–1805," *Pennsylvania Magazine of History and Biography* 101, no. 4 (October 1977): 463–66.

13.	Jefferson to Gallatin, 1 April 1802, *PTJ,* 37:15–59; Manasseh Cutler to Joseph Dana, 5 December 1801; Cutler to Joseph Torrey, 4 January 1802, *LJCMC,* 2:46, 65–66; Edwin J. Perkins, *American Public Finance and Financial Services, 1700–1815* (Columbus: Ohio State University Press, 1994), 220–1; Max M. Edling, *A Hercules in the Cradle: War, Money, and the American State, 1763–1867* (Chicago: University of Chicago Press, 2014), 104–7; Herbert E. Sloan, "Hamilton's Second Thoughts: Federal Finance Revisited," in *Federalists Reconsidered,* ed. Doran Ben-Atar and Barbara B. Oberg (Charlottesville: University of Virginia Press, 1998), 69–76; Donald F. Swanson and Andrew P. Trout, "Alexander Hamilton's Hidden Sinking Fund," *William and Mary Quarterly,* 3rd Ser., 49, no. 1 (January 1992): 108–116.

14.	Albert Gallatin, Report on Public Debt, 31 March 1802, *ASP: Finance,* 1:748; *Annals,* 6th Cong., 1st Sess., 359–60; ibid., 4th Cong., 1st Sess., 846–49 (Gallatin speeches); Albert Gallatin, *A Sketch of the Finances of the United States* (New York, 1796), 138–42; Albert Gallatin, *Views of the Public Debt, Receipts and Expenditures of the United States* (New York, 1800), 1, 27–29, 35; Jefferson to Gallatin, 1 April 1802, *PTJ,* 37:157–59 (comments on Gallatin's Report on Public Debt); Gallatin to Randolph, 28 December 1805, *ASP: Finance,* 2:162; Gallatin to Gales and Seaton, 5 February 1835, *WAG,* 2:501. Gallatin suspected that the

Federalists had sabotaged even their loose commitment to pay money into the sinking fund. Gallatin to Jefferson, 10 April 1802, *PTJ*, 37:198; John Steele to Secretary of the Treasury, [1799], H. M. Wagstaff, ed., *The Papers of John Steele* (2 vols.; Raleigh, NC: Edwards and Broughton, 1924), 2:856–58 (internal Treasury memorandum about restricting payments to the sinking fund).

15. Gallatin to Jefferson, [15 November], [by 16 November], and 19 November 1801, *PTJ*, 35:623–24, 627, 693. For an earlier exercise in calculating a schedule for debt repayment, see Gallatin, Notes on debt repayment, [1796], *PAG* (dated 1796–1806 by editors).

16. Gallatin to Jefferson, [by 16 November] 1801; Gallatin, Remarks to Jefferson on draft annual message, [by 16 November] 1801, *PTJ*, 35:628–29, 633; Gallatin, State of the Finances, 18 December 1801; Gallatin to Randolph, 31 March 1802, *ASP: Finance*, 1:701–17, 746–50; Gallatin, *Views of the Public Debt*, App. 3; Adam Seybert, *Statistical Annals of the United States of America* (1818; repr., New York: Augustus M. Kelley, 1970), 712–15; Davis Rich Dewey, *Financial History of the United States*, 9th ed. (New York: Longmans, Green, 1924), 111; Richard H. Kohn, *Eagle and Sword: The Beginnings of the Military Establishment in America* (New York: Free Press, 1975), 299–302; Paul Studenski and Herman Edward Krooss, *Financial History of the United States* (1952; Washington, DC: Beard Books, 2003), 54, 66. Historians differ over whether the Jefferson administration's modest cuts in the already diminished army aimed to shrink and Republicanize the officer corp. Theodore J. Crackel, *Mr. Jefferson's Army: Political and Social Reform of the Military Establishment, 1801–1809* (New York: New York University Press, 1987), 44–45; William B. Skelton, *An American Profession of Arms: The Army Officer Corps, 1784–1861* (Lawrence: University Press of Kansas, 1992), 25–26, 99, 368n32.

17. Jefferson to Gallatin, 14 November and 14 December 1801, 1 April 1802, *PTJ*, 35:622, 36:107–08, 37:157–59; Gallatin to Jefferson, Report on collection of internal revenue, 28 July 1801, ibid., 34:651–55; Gallatin to Jefferson, 12 June 1801; [15 November], [by 16 November], [13 December] 1801, ibid., 34:318–19; 35:623, 35:627–28, 36:101–04; Gallatin, Remarks to Jefferson on draft annual message, [by 16 November] 1801, ibid., 35:631-32; Malone, *Jefferson and His Time*, 4:100–101.

18. Joseph Hale to King, 19 December 1801, *LCRK*, 4:39; Jefferson, First Annual Message, 8 December 1801; Jefferson to John Dickerson, 19 December 1801, *PTJ*, 36:60–61, 165–66; Theodore Sedgwick to King,

14 December 1801 and 20 February 1802, *LCRK*, 4:36, 73–74; Cutler to Torrey, 4 January 1802, *LJCMC*, 2:64–65; Robert Smith to Randolph, 30 January 1802, *PAG*; Randolph, Report on Internal Duties, 8 March 1802, *ASP: Finance*, 1:734–35; *Annals*, 7th Cong., 1st Sess. 1017–74; Act of 6 April 1802, *Statutes at Large* 2 (1845): 148–50 (internal taxes repealed); Randolph, Report on Public Debt, 9 April 1802, *ASP: Finance*, 1:746–50; Gallatin to Randolph, 13 April 1802, *PAG*; Act of 29 April 1802, *Statutes at Large* 2 (1845): 167–70 (debt redemption); Gallatin to Jefferson, 21 September 1802, *PTJ*, 38:416–18.

19. Gallatin, Remarks to Jefferson on draft annual message, [by 16 November] 1801, *PTJ*, 35:635; Jefferson, First Annual Message, 8 December 1801, ibid., 36:61; Jefferson to Gallatin, 1 April 1802, ibid., 37:157–59; Acts of 1 May 1802, *Statutes at Large* 2 (1845): 178, 183 (sums for the army and navy are "respectively appropriated...that is to say:"); Act of 1 May 1802, *ibid.*, 2:184 (civilian appropriations); Joseph H. Nicholson to Gallatin, 7 July 1801; Gallatin to Nicholson, 19 January, 3 April, and 27 April 1802, *PAG; Annals*, 7th Cong., 1st Sess., 1157, 1251, 1255–85; Nicholson, Report on Application of Public Money, 29 April 1802, *ASP: Finance*, 1:752–821; Oliver Wolcott [Jr.], *An Address to the People of the United States on the Subject of the Report of a Committee of the House of Representatives...* (Boston, 1802), 1–10, 23–27, 70; Robert Smith to Gallatin, 24 February 1802, 6 May and 21 May 1802, *PAG;* Fisher Ames to King, 20 December 1801, *LCRK*, 4:40; Cunningham, *The Process of Government*, 114–15. For Gallatin's continued insistence that everyone who spent money for the War and Navy departments should account directly to the Treasury, see Macon to Gallatin, 6 April 1816; Gallatin to Macon, 23 April 1816, *PAG*. Congress adopted that requirement in 1817. Act of 3 March 1817, *Statutes at Large* 3 (1846): 366–68. Gallatin did not tell Jefferson that the Treasury investigations vindicated Alexander Hamilton. Some historians have claimed otherwise on the basis of a passage in James Hamilton's reminiscences in which he defends his famous father's reputation. James Hamilton wrote that Gallatin had reported to Jefferson that the investigation revealed "the most perfect system ever formed" and that "Hamilton made no blunders, committed no frauds. He did nothing wrong." James Hamilton claimed that Gallatin repeated those statements to him during a private conversation in 1829 (when the Jackson administration in which James Hamilton was serving began its attack on the Bank of the United States). James A. Hamilton, *Reminiscences of James A. Hamilton...* (New York, 1869), 23; Ron

Chernow, *Alexander Hamilton* (New York: Penguin, 2004), 647; McCraw, *Founders and Finance*, 232, 413n11. Gallatin may have reassured James Hamilton that he did not believe Hamilton's father had committed fraud. He also may have told James Hamilton that he had rejected Jefferson's proposal to simplify and reduce the Treasury staff in Washington. Jefferson to Gallatin, 1 April 1802, *PTJ*, 37:157-59; Cunningham, *The Process of Government*, 99. But James Hamilton's account is scant and lonely evidence for the proposition that Gallatin found no fault with Alexander Hamilton's management of the Treasury. For some of Gallatin's copious complaints to Jefferson about the disorder and subterfuge that he found in Alexander Hamilton's Treasury, see Gallatin to Jefferson, 24 August 1801, [15 November] 1801, [by 16 November] 1801, and 10 April 1802, *PTJ*, 35:133, 622–23, 626–27, 37:198; Gautham Rao, *National Duties: Custom Houses and the Making of the American State* (Chicago: University of Chicago Press, 2016), 119.

20.   [Alexander Hamilton], The Examination Nos. 1–4, 9, 11, and 18, *New-York Evening Post*, 17 December 1801–8 April 1802, reprinted in *PAH*, 25:453-74 (quoted at 453), 500–506 (quoted at 501), 514–20 (quoted at 515), 589–97 (quoted at 597); John Quincy Adams to King, 18 January 1802, *WJQA*, 3:4; William Plumer to John Norris, 20 December 1802, quoted in Lynn W. Turner, *William Plumer of New Hampshire, 1759–1850* (Chapel Hill: University of North Carolina Press, 1962), 101. For similar criticisms from the leading Federalist newspaper in Philadelphia and the Federalist newspaper in Gallatin's old Congressional district, see Philadelphia *Gazette of the United States*, 17 September 1801; *Pittsburgh Gazette*, 17 September 1802. For a contemporary Federalist satire on the Illuminist origins of Jeffersonian democracy that traces its roots to Rousseau and Genevan republicanism, see Christopher Caustic [Thomas Green Fessenden], *Democracy Unveiled, or, Tyranny Stripped of the Garb of Patriotism*, 3rd ed. (2 vols.; New York, 1805–06), 1:17–85, 105n74.

21.   Gallatin, *A Sketch of the Finances*, 123–37; Gallatin, State of the Finances, 18 December 1801, *ASP: Finance*, 1:703–04; Adam Smith, *An Inquiry into the Nature and Causes of the Wealth of Nations*, ed. Edwin Cannan (1789; New York: Modern Library, 1937), 872, 877–81, 681–89; Jean-Baptiste Say, *A Treatise of Political Economy, or the Production, Distribution, and Consumption of Wealth*, trans. C. R. Prinsep, ed. Clement C. Biddle (Philadelphia, 1847), 124–25, 201, 412–14, 443, 477–79 (first French edition published 1803); [Antoine] Destutt de Tracy, *A Treatise on Political Economy*, trans. [Thomas Jefferson] (1817; repr.,

New York: Augustus M. Kelley, 1970), 196–97, 233–44; David Ricardo, *On the Principles of Political Economy, and Taxation,* 3rd ed. (1821), in *The Works and Correspondence of David Ricardo,* ed. Piero Sraffa and M. H. Dobb (11 vols., Cambridge, UK: Cambridge University Press, 1951–73), 1:152-53, 244–49; Thomas Cooper, *Lectures on the Elements of Political Economy,* 2nd ed. (1830; repr., New York: Augustus M. Kelley, 1971), 271–72.

22. John Taylor, *An Enquiry into the Principles and Tendencies of Certain Public Measures* (Philadelphia, 1794), 7, 11, 19–20, 35–40, 66–68; Jefferson to Gallatin, 11 April and 18 May 1816; Jefferson to John W. Eppes, 24 June 1813; Jefferson to John Taylor, 28 May 1816; Jefferson to [Samuel Kercheval], 12 July 1816; Jefferson to William Plumer, 21 July 1816, *PTJ-RS,* 9:663–64, 10:66, 6:220–26, 10:86–87, 224–25, 260–61; Jefferson to Gallatin, 26 December 1820, *WTJ,* 12:186; William Letwin, *The Origins of Scientific Economics: English Economic Thought, 1660–1776* (London: Methuen, 1963), 225; John Brewer, *The Sinews of Power: War, Money, and the English State, 1688–1783* (New York: Alfred A. Knopf, 1989), 206–10; Max M. Edling, *A Revolution in Favor of Government: Origins of the U.S. Constitution and the Making of the American State* (New York: Oxford University Press, 2003), 63–66. American writers on public finance echoed this democratic critique of funded debt throughout the nineteenth century. Hamilton had been alert to these arguments, and he had conceded that the government should not issue funded debt without imposing taxes sufficient to repay the principal. Hamilton, Plan for the Support of Public Credit, 9 January 1790, *ASP: Finance,* 1:24; Henry C. Adams, *Public Debt: An Essay in the Science of Finance* (New York, 1887), 22–38, 240–47. On Jefferson's notions about funded public debt and the need to repay it, see Jefferson to Thomas Leiper, 25 May 1808, L&B, 12:65–66; Jefferson to James Monroe, 28 January 1809, *WTJ,* 11:96; Jefferson to William Short, 28 November 1814, *PTJ-RS,* 8:107–11; Donald F. Swanson, "Thomas Jefferson on Establishing Public Credit: The Debt Plans of a Would-be Secretary of the Treasury?" *Presidential Studies Quarterly* 23, no. 3 (Summer 1993): 499–508.

23. Jefferson to Eppes, 11 September 1813; Jefferson to [Samuel Kercheval], 12 July 1816, *PTJ-RS,* 6:496–97, 10:225–26; Smith, *Wealth of Nations,* 863, 881–82; John Taylor, *An Inquiry into the Principles and Policy of the Government of the United States* (1814; Indianapolis: Bobbs-Merrill, 1969), 227, 233; Herbert E. Sloan, *Principle and Interest: Thomas*

Jefferson and the Problem of Debt (New York: Oxford University Press, 1995), 97–103.

24. William Ioor, *Independence; or Which Do You Like Best, the Peer or the Farmer?* (Charleston, 1805), 12; Jefferson to William Plumer, 21 July 1816, *PTJ-RS,* 10:261 ("I...place economy among the first and most important of republican virtues, and public debt as the greatest of the dangers to be feared."); Bruce H. Mann, *Republic of Debtors: Bankruptcy in the Age of American Independence* (Cambridge, MA: Harvard University Press, 2002), 6–33, 130-39; Kate Haulman, *The Politics of Fashion in Eighteenth-Century America* (Chapel Hill: University of North Carolina Press, 2011), 201–02; Clement Fatovic, *America's Founding and the Struggle Over Economic Inequality* (Lawrence: University Press of Kansas, 2015), 8–9; Charles S. Watson, "Jeffersonian Republicanism in William Ioor's 'Independence,' the First Play of South Carolina," *South Carolina Historical Magazine* 69, no. 3 (July 1968): 198–99. The visceral connection between political freedom and freedom from debt positively pulsates through Jefferson's famous argument that "the earth belongs in usufruct to the living"—that natural justice prevents one generation from creating debts that will burden a future generation. Jefferson to Madison, 6 September 1789, *PTJ,* 15:392-98; Jefferson to Eppes, 24 June 1813, *PTJ-RS,* 6:220–26; Sloan, *Principle and Interest,* 50–62, 204–05, 354n18. The notion of voter independence also has deep resonance in classical republican political thought. The belief that ordinary citizens should be independent enough to vote in their own self-interest was a modern inversion of the much older belief that only men of standing, means, and education had independence enough to govern a republic in the public interest. J. G. A. Pocock, *The Machiavellian Moment: Florentine Political Thought and the Atlantic Republican Tradition* (1975; Princeton, NJ: Princeton University Press, 2003), 517–24.

25. [Hamilton], Federalist Nos. 6 and 8, *The Federalist,* ed. Jacob E. Cooke (Middletown, CT: Wesleyan University Press, 1961), 33 (quoted), 41; Michael Howard, *War and the Liberal Conscience* (New Brunswick, NJ: Rutgers University Press, 1978), 25–30; Karl-Friedrich Walling, *Republican Empire: Alexander Hamilton on War and Free Government* (Lawrence: University Press of Kansas, 1999), 176–85; Richard Whatmore, *Against War and Empire: Geneva, Britain, and France in the Eighteenth Century* (New Haven, CT: Yale University Press, 2012), 274–76; Jasper M. Trautsch, "'Mr. Madison's War' or the Dynamic of Early American Nationalism?" *Early American Studies* 10, no. 3 (Fall

2012), 635–38. The belief that self-governing people are less warlike than kings courses through the Republicans' running debate with Federalists in the 1790s about the need for legislative participation in the conduct of foreign affairs. *Annals,* 4th Cong., 1st Sess., 464–74 (Gallatin on Jay's treaty), 5th Cong., 2nd Sess., 1118–1143 (Gallatin on foreign intercourse bill); [Madison], Helvidius No. 1, 24 August 1793, *PJM-CS,* 15:66–74; John Zvesper, *Political Philosophy and Rhetoric: A Study in American Party Politics* (Cambridge, UK: Cambridge University Press, 1977), 160–62.

26. [Madison], "Universal Peace," Philadelphia *National Gazette,* 31 January 1792, reprinted in *PJM-CS,* 14:206–09; Macon to Joseph H. Nicholson, 31 January 1806, JHNP; Jefferson to Henry Middleton, 8 January 1813, *PTJ-RS,* 5:546; Taylor, *Inquiry into the Principles and Policy of the Government of the United States,* 217–18, 220; Jefferson, First Inaugural Address, 4 March 1801, *PTJ,* 33:150; Gallatin to Jefferson, 12 September 1805, *WAG,* 1:246–47; Walter Jones to [Constituents], 24 April 1806, *PAG,* printed in Noble E. Cunningham Jr., *Circular Letters of Congressmen to Their Constituents, 1789–1829* (3 vols.; Chapel Hill: University of North Carolina Press, 1978), 1:466–69 (arguing that war creates larger armies, a stronger executive, increased debt, and more money in the hands of rich creditors); Jefferson to Thaddeus Kosciuszko, 16 April 1811; Jefferson to Eppes, 24 June and 11 September 1813, *PTJ-RS,* 3:565–67, 6:220–26, 490–1; Brown, *Plumer's Memorandum,* 470 (2 April 1806); Robert W. Tucker and David C. Hendrickson, *Empire of Liberty: The Statecraft of Thomas Jefferson* (New York: Oxford University Press, 1990), 43–44, 180–2, 318–21n9; Sloan, *Principle and Interest,* 86–87, 90–4; Garrett Ward Sheldon and C. William Hill Jr., *The Liberal Republicanism of John Taylor of Caroline* (Madison, NJ: Fairleigh Dickinson University Press, 2008), 94–95, 107–12; Armin Mattes, *Citizens of a Common Intellectual Homeland: The Transatlantic Origins of American Democracy and Nationhood* (Charlottesville: University of Virginia Press, 2015), 107–14.

27. *Annals,* 5th Cong., 3rd Sess., 2870; Gallatin to Jefferson, [by 16] November 1801, *PTJ,* 35:628; Albert Gallatin to Hannah Nicholson, 25 August 1793, *LAG,* 103–4; White, *The Jeffersonians,* 266–67.

28. Philadelphia *Gazette of the United States,* 20 July 1802; John Taylor to Wilson Cary Nicholas, 5 September 1801, Coolidge Collection of Thomas Jefferson Manuscripts, Massachusetts Historical Society; [John Beckley], Andrew Marvel Nos. I and II, Philadelphia *Aurora General Advertiser,*

8 and 14 September 1802, reprinted in Gerald W. Gawalt, ed., *Justifying Jefferson: The Political Writings of John James Beckley* (Washington, DC: Library of Congress, 1995), 252–66; Algernon Sydney [Gideon Granger], *A Vindication of the Measures of the Present Administration* (Hartford, CT, 1803), 13. For Jefferson's later reflections on the repeal of internal taxes, see Jefferson to Pierre Samuel du Pont, 15 April 1811, *PTJ-RS*, 3:559–61, and for the repeal as an example of the Republicans' agrarian tendencies, see Doran S. Ben-Atar, *The Origins of Jeffersonian Commercial Policy and Diplomacy* (New York: St. Martin's, 1993), 156–61; Robert F. Haggard, "The Politics of Friendship: Du Pont, Jefferson, Madison, and the Physiocratic Dream for the New World," *Proceedings of the American Philosophical Society* 153, no. 4 (December 2009): 432–37. The internal revenue service was not completely dismantled until 1808 when it had finished collecting most of the unpaid taxes. Gallatin to Jefferson, 3 September 1808, *FOL*—Early Access.

29. Jefferson to Madison, 21 June 1792, *PTJ*, 24:106; Sloan, *Principle and Interest*, 113–203, 315n144; Brewer, *The Sinews of Power*, 89–91, 95–101; David Stasavage, *Public Debt and the Birth of the Democratic State: France and Great Britain, 1688-1789* (Cambridge, UK: Cambridge University Press, 2003), 93–98; Edling, *A Hercules in the Cradle*, 94; W. Elliot Brownlee, *Federal Taxation in America: A History*, 3rd ed. (Cambridge, UK: Cambridge University Press, 2016), 32, 51n17; Patrick K. O'Brien, "The Political Economy of British Taxation, 1660–1815," *Economic History Review*, New Ser., 41, no. 1 (February 1988), 3, 6–8. For examples of the European liberal economic critique that influenced Republican thinking about taxes and government spending during the Jeffersonian period, see Smith, *Wealth of Nations*, 777–858, 865–87; John Sinclair, *The History of the Public Revenue of the British Empire*, 3rd ed. (3 vols.; 1803-04; repr. New York: Augustus M. Kelley, 1966), 1:365–79, 3:66–90; Say, *A Treatise of Political Economy*, 446–77; Destutt de Tracy, *A Treatise on Political Economy*, 227–32, 241–44.

30. Jefferson to Kosciuszko, 2 April 1802; Jefferson to Thomas Cooper, 29 November 1802; Jefferson to Gallatin, 3 August 1802, *PTJ*, 37:67–68, 39:83–84, 38:156–58; John Beckley to Tench Coxe, 28 March 1802, Gawalt, *Justifying Jefferson*, 246; Dumas Malone, *The Public Life of Thomas Cooper* (New Haven, CT: Yale University Press, 1926), 164–68; Edward P. Alexander, "Jefferson and Kosciusko: Friends of Liberty and of Man," *Pennsylvania Magazine of History and Biography* 92, no. 1 (January 1968): 90–97. Postmaster General Gideon Granger said the

Federalists deserved no credit for the revenue system, which they had just adopted from British practice. [Granger], *Vindication of the Measures of the Present Administration*, 8.

31. Jefferson to Craven Peyton, 8 October 1801; Jefferson, Notes on the Bank of the United States and Internal Revenue, [10 November] 1801; Jefferson to Gallatin, 11 November 1801, *PTJ*, 35:412–14, 602–04, 606. For Jefferson's views on the banking system and the Bank of the United States, see Jefferson to Washington, 23 May 1792; Jefferson, Agenda to reduce the government to true principles, [11 July 1792]; Jefferson to Pierre Samuel DuPont, 18 January 1802, *PTJ*, 23:538, 24:215–17; 36:390–92; Sloan, *Principle and Interest*, 171–75, 182–84. Investors in the federal debt did not expect Jefferson and a Republican Congress to repudiate it. Soon after Jefferson's election, the price of federal bonds exceeded their price before the electoral crisis. Clement Biddle to Gallatin, 31 July, 13 August, and 25 October 1801, *PAG*.

32. Gallatin to Jefferson, 18 June 1802, *PTJ*, 37:616-17; Gallatin to Thomas Willing, 9 June and 27 June 1801; Gallatin to the Bank of Columbia, 31 October 1801, *PAG*. Soon after Gallatin took charge of the Treasury, a well-established Philadelphia merchant with whom he had done business assured him that the "Bank of the United States depend so much on our Government, that you can command their Aid at all times & I will give you remarks on this subject occasionaly." Biddle to Gallatin, 20 March 1801, ibid.

33. Jefferson to Gallatin, 13 December 1803, L&B, 10:436–39; Gallatin to Jefferson, [after 13] December 1803, *WAG*, 1:171–72; Jefferson to Gallatin, 19 June and 7 October 1802, *PTJ*, 37:620–21, 38:459; Jefferson to Gallatin, 12 July 1803, *WTJ*, 10:15–16; Gallatin to Jefferson, 12 April 1804; Jefferson to Gallatin, 17 April 1804, *PAG*; Jefferson to Madison, 17 April 1804, *PJM-SS*, 7:73.

34. Gallatin to Robert Walsh Jr., 27 April 1830; Gallatin to G[ulian] C. Verplanck, 22 May 1830, *WAG*, 2:426–27, 428; Fritz Redlich, *The Molding of American Banking: Men and Ideas* (1951; 2 parts; repr., Mansfield Center, CT: Martino Publishing, 2012), 1:96–100; Noble E. Cunningham Jr., *The Jeffersonian Republicans in Power: Party Operation, 1801–1809* (Chapel Hill; University of North Carolina Press, 1963), 64–65; Richard H. Timberlake Jr., *The Origins of Central Banking in the United States* (Cambridge, MA: Harvard University Press, 1978), 8–10; Stuart Bruchey, *Enterprise: The Dynamic Economy of a Free People* (Cambridge, MA: Harvard University Press, 1990), 171–72;

Perkins, *American Public Finance and Financial Services*, 249–50; Edward S. Kaplan, *The Bank of the United States and the American Economy* (Westport, CT: Greenwood Press, 1999), 28–29; Carl Wennerlind, *Casualties of Credit: The English Financial Revolution, 1620–1720* (Cambridge, MA: Harvard University Press, 2011), 108–22, 169–89. For Gallatin's guidance to the Bank of the United States during liquidity events, see Gallatin to Thomas Willing, 27 October and 13 November 1804, 4 February and 5 March 1805; Gallatin to David Lennox, 5 November 1808, *PAG*. Hamilton supported the Bank of New York, which he helped found, with federal deposits in 1792–93. Bruchey, *Enterprise*, 126–27; Richard Sylla, Robert E. Wright, and David J. Cowen, "Alexander Hamilton, Central Banker: Crisis Management during the U. S. Financial Panic of 1792," *Business History Review* 83, no. 1 (Spring 2009).

35. Jefferson to William Wirt, 3 May 1811, *PTJ-RS*, 3:603; Gallatin to John M. Botts, 14 June 1841, *WAG*, 2:551–52. For Jefferson's late-life views on banking and the Bank of the United States, see Jefferson to John Adams, 24 January 1814; Jefferson to John Taylor, 28 May 1816, *PTJ-RS*, 7:149–50, 10:86 and 89. Gallatin lived to see other presidents implement Jefferson's inchoate banking proposals: Andrew Jackson removed the federal government's deposits from the Bank of the United States and gave them to politically supportive state banks in 1833, and Martin Van Buren and James Polk shifted the government's money to an independent Treasury in 1840 and 1846. Timberlake, *The Origins of Central Banking*, 43, 50–1, 64.

36. Jefferson to Granger, 29 March 1801; Jefferson, Notes on cabinet meetings, 8 March and 9 March 1801, *PTJ*, 33:492–94, 219–20 and 232–33; Richard E. Ellis, *The Jeffersonian Crisis: Courts and Politics in the Young Republic* (New York: Oxford University Press, 1971), 32–35, Carl E. Prince, *The Federalists and the Origins of the U. S. Civil Service* (New York: New York University Press, 1977), 2–15, 268–79; Noble E. Cunningham Jr., *In Pursuit of Reason: The Life of Thomas Jefferson* (Baton Rouge: Louisiana State University, 1987), 239–44; Peter S. Onuf, *Jefferson's Empire: The Language of American Nationhood* (Charlottesville: University Press of Virginia, 2000), 98–107; Andrew Burstein and Nancy Isenberg, *Madison and Jefferson* (New York: Random House, 2010), 362–67; Barbara B. Oberg, "A New Republican Order, Letter by Letter," *Journal of the Early Republic* 25, no. 1 (Spring 2005): 12–15.

37. Jefferson, First Inaugural Address, 4 March 1801, *PTJ*, 33:148–52; George Cabot to King, 20 March 1801, *LCRK*, 3:408; William Branch Giles to Jefferson, 16 March 1801; Jefferson to Giles, 23 March 1801; Monroe to Jefferson, 3 March 1801; Jefferson to Monroe, 7 March 1801; Jefferson to William Findley, 24 March 1801, *PTJ*, 33:310–12, 413–15, 126–28, 208–09, 427–28; Ames to Theodore Dwight, 19 March 1801, *WFA*, 1:292; Sedgwick to King, 24 March 1801; Troup to King, 27 May 1801, *LCRK*, 3:456, 461.

38. The list of federal employees that Gallatin delivered to the president a year after he took office showed about 3,000 positions in the civilian service. About 900 of those were in the postal service and about 1,900 in the rest of the Treasury. U. S. Treasury Department, Roll of the Officers, Civil, Military, and Naval, of the United States, 1:260–319; Richard R. John, *Spreading the News: The American Postal System from Franklin to Morse* (Cambridge, MA: Harvard University Press, 1995), 51.

39. John M. Taylor to Gallatin, 29 July 1801 (Gallatin annotation quoted); Matthew Lyon to Gallatin, 15 March 1801; David Gelston to Gallatin, 14 April 1801; Aaron Burr to Gallatin, 13 March, 21 April, 24 April, 6 June, 28 June, and 9 October 1801; Samuel Smith to Gallatin, 3 July 1801; Alexander Boyd to Gallatin, 17 March, 2 June, 21 October, 28 October 1801, 20 August 1802; John G. Jackson to Gallatin, 18 June 1801; James Tilton to Isaac Griffin, 30 March 1801, *PAG*; Burr to Jefferson, after 17 March 1801, *PCAB*, 1:532–45; Editors' notes, ibid., 2:673 (on John M. Taylor); Tench Coxe to Jefferson, 19 April 1801; Gallatin to Jefferson, [16 June 1801], *PTJ*, 33:612–14, 34:354–55; John Beckley to Coxe, 18 February and 21 May 1801, Gawalt, *Justifying Jefferson*, 234, 250.

40. Alexander J. Dallas to Gallatin, 14 June 1801, *PAG*; Gallatin to Jefferson, 27 December 1801, *PTJ*, 36:210–14; Gallatin to Jefferson, 12 February 1802, *ASP: Miscellaneous*, 1:260–61; Cunningham *The Process of Government*, 23–25.

41. Jefferson to Granger, 29 March 1801; Remonstrance of the New Haven Merchants, 18 June 1801, *PTJ*, 33:492–94, 34:381–84; Cunningham, *The Jeffersonian Republicans in Power*, 19–25; David Waldstreicher and Stephen R. Grossbart, "Abraham Bishop's Vocation; or, the Mediation of Jeffersonian Politics," *Journal of the Early Republic* 18, no. 4 (Winter 1998): 617–57.

42. Jefferson, Reply to the Remonstrance of the New Haven Merchants, 12 July 1801, *PTJ*, 34:554–58; Lucius Junius Brutus [pseud.], *An Examination of the President's Reply to the New-Haven Remonstrance*

(New York, 1801), 15, 40, 52 (quoted); Jefferson to Levi Lincoln, 26 August 1801, *PTJ*, 35:145–47; Troup to King, 8 August 1801; Ames to King, 27 October 1801, *LCRK*, 3:495, 4:5. Gallatin found Samuel Bishop to be a less than effective customs collector. About two years later, he died and was replaced with his son. Gallatin to Samuel Bishop, 1 August 1801, 10 February 1803, *PAG*; Gallatin to Jefferson, 13 August and 20 August 1803; Jefferson to Gallatin, 23 August and 30 August 1803, *PTJ*, 41:194, 232–33, 243–44, 288–89.

43. Gallatin to Jefferson, 25 July 1801, *PTJ*, 34:635-36 (quotes from enclosure); Act of 31 July 1789, sec. 5, *Statutes at Large* 1 (1845): 37; White, *The Jeffersonians*, 148-49, 401–03; Sidney H. Aronson, *Status and Kinship in the Higher Civil Service: Standards of Selection in the Administrations of John Adams, Thomas Jefferson, and Andrew Jackson* (Cambridge, MA: Harvard University Press, 1964), 3–7; Prince, *The Federalists and the Origins of the U. S. Civil Service*, 21–23, 45–46, 74, 105; William E. Nelson, "Officeholding and Powerwielding: An Analysis of the Relationship between Structure and Style in American Administrative History," *Law and Society Review* 10, no. 2 (Winter 1976): 203–06.

44. Jefferson to Gallatin, 26 July 1801, *PTJ*, 34:644–45. The summer after his response to the New Haven merchants, Jefferson called another merchants' remonstrance against the removal of a Federalist collector "impudently malignant" and refused to answer it. Two years later, he proposed to tell a Federalist holdover that he was being removed for his "active opposition to the national will." Jefferson to Gallatin, 20 August 1802, *PTJ*, 38:259–60; same to same, 30 May 1804, *WTJ*, 8:303–04 (quoted); Gallatin to Jefferson, 30 May 1804, *WAG*, 1:193–94.

45. Gallatin to Jefferson, 10 August (quoted) and 17 August 1801, *PTJ*, 35:52–57, 100–2; Thomas Leiper to Gallatin, 17 March 1801; Henry Dearborn to Gallatin, 8 August 1801, *PAG*.

46. Jefferson to Gallatin, 14 August and 21 August 1801, *PTJ*, 35:84–86, 117-18; Jefferson, Key to the Arrangement of Interim Nominations, [before 6 January 1802]; Jefferson to Senate, 6 January 1802; Jefferson to Gallatin, 28 October 1802, ibid., 36:328–330, 331–36, 38:590–91; Jefferson to Gallatin, 8 September 1804, *WTJ*, 10:101; Gallatin to Jefferson, 18 September 1804, *WAG*, 1:208–9; John Steele to Gallatin, 25 November 1802, Wagstaff, *The Papers of John Steele*, 1:332–33; Cunningham, *The Process of Government*, 170-77; Johnstone, *Jefferson and the Presidency*, 112; Carl Prince, "The Passing of the Aristocracy:

Jefferson's Removal of the Federalists, 1801–1805," *Journal of American History* 57, no. 3 (December 1970): 563–75. Gallatin also maintained that it was his policy not to interfere in the collectors' appointments of their subordinates. Gallatin to Jefferson, 11 December 1806, *FOL*—Early Access (one of multiple letters of the same date).

47. Gallatin to James W. Nicholson, 7 December 1799; Michael Leib to Gallatin, 14 May 1801; John Kean to Gallatin, 17 June 1801, *PAG;* Thomas McKean to Jefferson, 21 July 1801; Jefferson to McKean, 24 July 1801, *PTJ*, 34:612–13, 625–27; Sanford W. Higginbotham, *The Keystone in the Democratic Arch: Pennsylvania Politics, 1800–1816* (Harrisburg: Pennsylvania Historical and Museum Commission, 1952), 29-31; Ellis, *The Jeffersonian Crisis,* 31–32; G. S. Rowe, *Thomas McKean: The Shaping of an American Republicanism* (Boulder: Colorado Associated University Press, 1978), 313–14, 318–24; David A. Wilson, *United Irishmen, United States: Immigrant Radicals in the Early Republic* (Ithaca, NY: Cornell University Press, 1998), 11; Jeffrey L. Pasley, *"The Tyranny of Printers": Newspaper Politics in the Early American Republic* (Charlottesville: University Press of Virginia, 2001), 176–95; Nigel Little, *Transoceanic Radical, William Duane* (London: Pickering and Chatto, 2008), 143–45; Kim Tousley Phillips, "William Duane, Revolutionary Editor" (Ph.D. diss., University of California, Berkeley, 1968), 68-76, 118-30.

48. William Duane, List of government clerks, [August] 1801; Gallatin to Duane, 5 July 1801, Duane to Gallatin, 12 September and 13 December 1801, *PAG;* Duane to Jefferson, 10 May and 10 June 1801, *PTJ*, 34:71, 296–300; Jefferson to Duane, 23 May 1801, ibid., 34:169–70; Duane to Madison, 10 May 1801, *PJM-SS,* 1:152–54.

49. Gallatin to Jefferson, 10 August, 18 August, 14 September, and 15 December 1801, *PTJ*, 35:52–57, 107–09, 284–89, 36:120–22; Jefferson to Gallatin, 14 August 1801, ibid., 35:84–85; Ames, *History of the National Intelligencer,* 31–32; Berkeley and Berkeley, *John Beckley,* 231–33; Cunningham, *The Process of Government,* 181–82, 328–29; Michael Durey, *Transatlantic Radicals and the Early American Republic* (Lawrence: University Press of Kansas, 1997), 259, 265–67; Pasley, *The Tyranny of Printers,* 259, 286–90; Jay C. Heinlein, "Albert Gallatin: A Pioneer in Public Administration," *William and Mary Quarterly,* 3rd Ser., 7, no. 1 (January 1950), 91–93. Jefferson eventually appointed one of Duane's informants to be American consul in Demerara (Guyana) and the other to be an ensign in the army. Carl Russell Fish, *The Civil Service*

and the Patronage (Cambridge, MA: Harvard University Press, 1920), 47.

50. Raymond Walters Jr., *Alexander James Dallas: Lawyer—Politician—Financier, 1759–1817* (Philadelphia: University of Pennsylvania Press, 1943), 119–32; Higginbotham, *The Keystone in the Republican Arch*, 40–43; Aronson, *Status and Kinship in the Higher Civil Service*, 8–14, 85–93; Johnstone, *Jefferson and the Presidency*, 227–31; Ronald Schultz, *The Republic of Labor: Philadelphia Artisans and the Politics of Class, 1720–1830* (New York: Oxford University Press, 1993), 151–60; Pasley, *The Tyranny of Printers*, 291–99; Andrew Shankman, *Crucible of American Democracy: The Struggle to Fuse Egalitarianism and Capitalism in Jeffersonian Pennsylvania* (Lawrence: University Press of Kansas, 2004), 74–84, 96–98.

51. Gallatin to Jefferson, 14 September 1801; Leiper to Jefferson, 26 August 1802; Duane to Jefferson, 18 October 1802, *PTJ*, 35:284–89, 38:292–95, 511–14; Duane to Pierce Butler, 12 November 1801, Worthington C. Ford, ed., "Letters of William Duane," *Proceedings of the Massachusetts Historical Society* 20 (May–June 1906): 271–73; *Pittsburgh Gazette*, 27 August 1802 ("The Pigs Squeaking"); Kim T. Phillips, "William Duane, Philadelphia's Democratic Republicans, and the Origins of Modern Politics," *Pennsylvania Magazine of History and Biography* 101, no. 3 (July 1977): 366–72; Jeffrey L. Pasley, "'A Journeyman, Either in Law or Politics': John Beckley and the Social Origins of Political Campaigning," *Journal of the Early Republic* 16, no. 4 (Winter 1996): 560–5.

52. Burr, Memorandum on appointments, [after 17 March 1801], *PCAB*, 1:541; Jefferson, Notes on New York patronage, [after 17 February 1801], *PTJ*, 33:11–12; Gallatin to Jefferson, 21 May 1801 (enclosing recommendations for Davis); Burr to Gallatin, 28 June and 8 September 1801, 25 March 1802; Gelston to Gallatin, 4 September 1801, *PAG*; Troup to King, 27 May and 8 August 1801, *LCRK*, 3:460, 495; Editors' note, *PCAB*, 1:532-40; Nancy Isenberg, *Fallen Founder: The Life of Aaron Burr* (New York: Viking, 2007), 226–31; Jerome Mushkat, "Matthew Livingston Davis and the Political Legacy of Aaron Burr," *New-York Historical Society Quarterly* 59, no. 2 (April 1975): 127–30; Jeffrey L. Pasley, "Matthew Livingston Davis's Notes from the Political Underground: The Conflict of Political Values in the Early American Republic" (unpub. paper), 1996, www.pasleybrothers.com/jeff/writings/davisv2.htm.

53. John Armstrong to Gallatin, 7 May 1801; DeWitt Clinton to Gallatin, 21 July 1801; Gelston to Gallatin, 28 July 1801, *PAG;* Johnstone, *Jefferson and Presidency,* 225–27; C. Edward Skeen, *John Armstrong, Jr., 1758–1843: A Biography* (Syracuse, NY: Syracuse University Press, 1981), 44–45.

54. James Nicholson to Gallatin, 10 August 1801, *PAG;* Samuel Osgood to Madison, 24 April 1801, *PJM-SS,* 1:113–14; Marinus Willett to Jefferson, 4 May 1801; Gallatin to Jefferson, 14 September 1801, *PTJ,* 34:36–37, 35:284–89; Alan Taylor, "'The Art of Hook & Snivey': Political Culture in Upstate New York during the 1790s," *Journal of American History* 29, no. 4 (March 1993): 1374–80; John L. Brooke, "'King George Has Issued Too Many Pattents for Us': Property and Democracy in Jeffersonian New York," *Journal of the Early Republic* 33, no. 2 (Summer 2013): 195-203. On Commodore Nicholson's appointment as Commissioner of Loans (the officer who disbursed payments to federal debt holders), see Albert Gallatin to Hannah Gallatin, 15 January 1801; John Swartwout to Gallatin, 16 September 1801; Gelston to Albert Gallatin, 17 September 1801; James Nicholson to Gallatin, 15 October 1801; Jefferson, Commission to James Nicholson, 19 November 1801, *PAG;* DeWitt Clinton to Jefferson, 14 September 1801, *PTJ,* 35:283–84; Burr to Jefferson, 25 May and 23 September 1801, *PCAB,* 1:587, 2:628–31; Jefferson to Senate, 6 January 1802, *PTJ,* 36:331-36 (interim appointments); Gallatin to Jefferson, 11 December 1806, *FOL*—Early Access (embarrassed that Hannah Gallatin's uncle was the only applicant for the Chestertown, Maryland collectorship). When Nicholson became fatally ill in 1804, his son-in-law William Few succeeded him as loan commissioner. Gallatin to Jefferson, 11 May 1804, *WAG,* 1:192; Jefferson to Madison, 29 May 1804, *PJM-SS,* 7:263; Gallatin to James W. Nicholson, 8 June 1804, *PAG.*

55. Gallatin to Jefferson, 12 September and 14 September 1801, *PTJ,* 35:272–75, 284–89.

56. Boston *Columbian Centinel,* 3 October 1801; Jefferson to Gallatin, 18 September 1801; Jefferson to Burr, 18 November 1801, *PTJ,* 35:314–15, 687–88; Jefferson to George Clinton, 17 May 1801; Jefferson, Notes on conversation with Robert R. Livingston, 4 June 1801, ibid., 34:127–28, 256; Duane to Abraham Bishop, 28 August 1802, Ford, "Letters of William Duane," 276; Cunningham, *The Jeffersonian Republicans in Power,* 39–44; Valsania, *Jefferson's Body,* 83. Gallatin continued to worry that Jefferson's alienation from Burr left him politically exposed

and compromised Republican strength in New York. Gallatin to Jefferson, 21 September 1802, *PTJ*, 38:416–18.

57. Samuel Mitchill to Gallatin, [26] May 1801; Thomas Cooper to Gallatin, 27 May 1801; John Kean to Gallatin, 17 June 1801, *PAG*; Gallatin to Jefferson, 7 September 1801; Jefferson to Gallatin, [by 5 March 1802]; Gallatin, Comments on list of federal officeholders, [about 11 July] 1803; Jefferson to Gallatin, 20 August 1803, *PTJ*, 35:226–30, 37:10–1, 41:23–25, 232–33; Editors' note, ibid., 41:12–14; Gallatin to Jefferson, 9 November 1807; 4 February 1809, *PAG;* Aronson, *Status and Kinship in the Higher Civil Service*, 175–99. Matthew Livingston Davis was not the only unpolished Republican political operative slighted by the administration. John Beckley—who had lost his job as clerk of the House of Representatives in 1797 for doing the Republicans' political chores—got nothing but his old job and a meager supplement to his salary for serving as the first Librarian of Congress. Jefferson to Beckley, 22 October 1801; Beckley to Jefferson, 22 January 1802, *PTJ*, 35:479, 36:415; Berkeley and Berkeley, *John Beckley*, 226–27; Pasley, "'A Journeyman, Either in Law or Politics,'" 556, 565.

58. Jefferson to Gallatin, 13 January 1807, *WAG*, 1:328; Linda K. Kerber, *Women of the Republic: Intellect and Ideology in Revolutionary America* (Chapel Hill: University of North Carolina Press, 1980), 274–85; John, *Spreading the News*, 140–1; Valsania, *Jefferson's Body*, 175–78; David E. Paterson, "Jefferson's Mystery Woman Identified," *Common-place* 15, no. 4 summer 2015), http://common-place.org/book/jefferson's-mystery-woman-identified/.

59. Gallatin to James W. Nicholson, 18 May 1798; Gallatin to Thomas Worthington, 20 October and 8 November 1800; Worthington to James W. Nicholson, 12 February 1801; Worthington to Gallatin, 21 April 1805, *PAG*; Gallatin to John Badollet, 7 February 1833, *CBG*, 309; Malcolm J. Rohrbough, *The Trans-Appalachian Frontier* (New York: Oxford University Press, 1978), 89–91; Drew R. McCoy, *The Elusive Republic: Political Economy in Jeffersonian America* (Chapel Hill: University of North Carolina Press, 1980), 13–47, 67–75. On Jefferson and Madison's scant personal experience in the West, see Madison to Jefferson, 24 October 1787, *PJM-CS*, 10:218–19; Jefferson to C. F. de C. Volney, 8 February 1805, *TJW*, 1154; Peterson, *Thomas Jefferson and the New Nation*, 6, 576–89; Ketcham, *James Madison*, 154–56, 323–26; Donald Jackson, *Thomas Jefferson and the Stony Mountains: Exploring the West from Monticello* (1981; Norman: University of Oklahoma Press, 1993),

xii–xiii, 66–71. On the infrequency of Gallatin's returns to the West while he was Treasury Secretary, see Gallatin to James W. Nicholson, 15 September 1802, 6 May 1803, and 16 June 1806, *PAG;* Gallatin to Jefferson, 19 May 1806, *WAG,* 1:299.

60.   Hamilton, Plan for Disposing of the Public Lands, *ASP: Public Lands,* 1:4–5; Gallatin, *A Sketch of the Finances,* 142–49; Paul W. Gates, *History of Public Land Law Development* (Washington, DC: Public Land Review Commission, 1968), 124–26, 128–31; Rudolph M. Bell, *Party and Faction in American Politics: The House of Representatives, 1789–1801* (Westport, CT: Greenwood Press, 1973), 82–89; Malcolm J. Rohrbough, *The Land Office Business: The Settlement and Administration of American Public Lands, 1789–1837* (New York: Oxford University Press, 1968), 13–29; McCoy, *The Elusive Republic,* 68; Joyce Appleby, *Liberalism and Republicanism in the Historical Imagination* (Cambridge, MA: Harvard University Press, 1992), 271–73; Allan Kulikoff, *The Agrarian Origins of American Capitalism* (Charlottesville: University of Virginia, 1992), 43–45, 129–51, 217–23; Peter S. Onuf, *Jefferson's Empire: The Language of American Nationhood* (Charlottesville: University of Virginia Press, 2000), 41–46, 70–79; John R. Van Atta, *Securing the West: Politics, Public Lands, and the Fate of the Old Republic, 1785–1850* (Baltimore: Johns Hopkins University Press, 2014), 47–49, 62–67; Fatovic, *America's Founding and the Struggle over Economic Inequality,* 166–73; Farley Grubb, "U. S. Land Policy: Founding Choices and Outcomes, 1781–1802," in *Founding Choices: American Economic Policy in the 1790s,* ed. Douglas A. Irwin and Richard Sylla (Chicago: University of Chicago Press, 2011), 266–81.

61.   *Annals,* 4th Cong., 1st Sess., 339–43, 404–07, 409–15 (quoted at 411), 858–68; ibid., 6th Cong., 1st Sess., 537–38, 651–52; Act of 18 May 1796, *Statutes at Large* 1 (1845): 464–69; Curtius [John Taylor?], *A Defence of the Measures of the Administration of Thomas Jefferson* (Washington, DC, 1804), 22; Gallatin, Report of the Secretary of the Treasury on the Subject of Public Roads and Canals, Senate Print (Washington, DC, 1808), 71, reprinted in *ASP: Miscellaneous,* 1:741; [Gallatin], *Laws, Treaties, and Other Documents Having Operation and Respect to the Public Lands* (Washington, DC, [1811]), reprinted in *WAG,* 3:207–29.

62.   Gallatin to Randolph, 13 January 1803, in *Annals,* 7th Cong., 2nd Sess., 1332; Gallatin to Thomas Worthington, 10 June and 16 July 1801, *PAG;* Act of 10 May 1800, *Statutes at Large* 2 (1845): 7378; Alfred Byron Sears, *Thomas Worthington: Father of Ohio Statehood* (Columbus: Ohio State

University Press, 1958), 39–43; Gates, *History of Public Land Law Development*, 132; Van Atta, *Securing the West*, 77–83.

63. Gallatin to Joseph H. Nicholson, 2 January 1804; Nicholson to Gallatin, 1 December 1803, *ASP: Public Lands*, 1:183–84, 182. Gallatin previously had supported credit sales. Gallatin, *A Sketch of the Finances*, 145–49.

64. Act of 26 March 1804, *Statutes at Large* 2 (1845): 277–83; Edward Tiffin to President of Senate, 4 January 1813, *ASP: Public Lands*, 2:732–34 (table of land sales); White, *The Jeffersonians*, 513–15; Gates, *History of Public Land Law Development*, 131–36; Rohrbough, *The Land Office Business*, 26-50; Brain Balogh, *A Government Out of Sight: The Mystery of National Authority in Nineteenth-Century America* (New York: Cambridge University Press, 2009), 180–3; Van Atta, *Securing the West*, 69–70. A land officer in Ohio who was a particular friend of Gallatin wrote the following year that "not one half the purchasers of publick lands in this district…will be able to pay up. I am more firmly fixed in the opinion than ever that the present system of sales ought to be altered." Thomas Worthington to Gallatin, 8 May 1805, *PAG*. Congress did not stop selling public land on credit until 1820.

65. Jerry L. Mashaw, *Creating the Administrative Constitution: The Lost One Hundred Years of American Administrative Law* (New Haven, CT: Yale University Press, 2012), 119 (quoted), 124–43; White, *The Jeffersonians*, 518–24; Gates, *History of Public Land Law Development*, 126-27.

66. Jared Mansfield to Gallatin, 27 November 1807, quoted in Rohrbough, *The Land Office Business*, 46; Rohrbough, op. cit., 30–32, 36–37, 45; Worthington to Gallatin, 2 April 1811; Gallatin to Worthington, 10 June and 16 July 1801; Gallatin to George Washington Campbell, 4 February 1809; R…M…to Gallatin, 22 February 1811, *PAG*; Sears, *Thomas Worthington*, 40–42, 159–60; Jay Clare Heinlein, "The Administrative Theory and Practice of Albert Gallatin" (Ph.D. diss., University of Chicago, 1948), 256–73. On John Badollet's appointment and his complaints, see Gallatin to Jefferson, 28 March 1804, *WAG*, 1:181–82; Gallatin to Badollet, 7 April 1804; Badollet to Gallatin, 25 April 1804, 21 December 1807, 24 June 1810; William Henry Harrison to Gallatin, 29 August 1809; Gallatin to Harrison, 27 September 1809, *CBG*, 25–26, 26–28, 88–96, 151–59, 107–13, 113–14; Robert M. Owens, *Mr. Jefferson's Hammer: William Henry Harrison and the Origins of American Indian Policy* (Norman: University of Oklahoma Press, 2007), 108–15, 144–50, 188–94; Patrick Bottiger, "Stabbed in the Back:

Vincennes, Slavery, and the Indian 'Threat,'" *Indiana Magazine of History* 107, no. 2 (June 2011): 94, 104–05.

67. King to Madison, 31 October and 20 November 1801; King to Robert R. Livingston, 12 July 1802, *LCRK*, 4:6–7, 15-16, 146; Lyon to Gallatin, 16 February 1803, *PAG;* James E. Lewis Jr., *The American Union and the Problem of Neighborhood: The United States and the Collapse of the Spanish Empire, 1783–1829* (Chapel Hill: University of North Carolina Press, 1998), 14–32; Peter J. Kastor, *The Nation's Crucible: The Louisiana Purchase and the Creation of America* (New Haven, CT: Yale University Press, 2004), 36–45; Peter S. Onuf, *The Mind of Thomas Jefferson* (Charlottesville: University of Virginia Press, 2007), 106.

68. Madison to Robert R. Livingston and James Monroe, 2 March 1803, *PJM-SS*, 4:364–79; Jefferson to John Breckinridge, 12 August 1803; Jefferson to Andrew Jackson, 19 September 1803, *PTJ*, 41:185–86, 395; Alexander De Conde, *This Affair of Louisiana* (New York: Charles Scribner's Sons, 1976), 147–72.

69. Jefferson to Thomas Paine, 10 August 1803; Jefferson to Wilson Cary Nicholas, 7 September 1803, *PTJ*, 41:175–77, 346–48; Jefferson to Madison, [July] 1803 and 24 August 1803; Madison to Jefferson, [July] 1803 (two items), James Morton Smith, ed., *The Republic of Letters: The Correspondence between Jefferson and Madison, 1776–1826*, (3 vols.; New York: W. W. Norton, 1995), 2:1269–70; David N. Mayer, *The Constitutional Thought of Thomas Jefferson* (Charlottesville: University Press of Virginia, 1994), 244–51; Kastor, *The Nation's Crucible*, 45–52; Jon Kukla, *A Wilderness So Immense: The Louisiana Purchase and the Destiny of America* (2003; New York: Random House, 2004), 284–309; Onuf, *The Mind of Thomas Jefferson*, 131–33; Jeremy David Bailey, "Executive Prerogative and the 'Good Officer' in Thomas Jefferson's Letter to John B. Colvin," *Presidential Studies Quarterly* 34, no. 4 (December 2004): 732–54.

70. Gallatin to Jefferson, 13 January 1803; Jefferson to Gallatin, 13 January 1803; Gallatin to Jefferson, 14 March 1803; Gallatin to Jefferson, [13] April 1803, *PTJ*, 39:324–26, 327–28; 40:59–60, 173–74; James E. Lewis Jr., *The Louisiana Purchase: Jefferson's Noble Bargain?* (Charlottesville, VA: Thomas Jefferson Foundation, 2003), 52–53, 69–73.

71. Gallatin, Draft of money article for Louisiana treaty, [February 1803], *PAG* (dated by editors to April 1803); Gallatin to Madison, 28 February 1803; Madison to Livingston and Monroe, 2 March 1803, *PJM-SS*, 4:352–55, 4:375; Ralph W. Hidy, *The House of Baring in American Trade*

and Finance: English Merchant Bankers at Work, 1763–1861 (Cambridge, MA: Harvard University Press, 1949), 33–35; George Dangerfield, *Chancellor Robert R. Livingston of New York, 1746–1813* (New York: Harcourt, Brace, 1960), 374–75, 380–83; Philip Ziegler, *The Sixth Great Power: Barings, 1762–1929* (London: Collins, 1988), 70–72.

72. John Taylor to Monroe, 12 November 1803, LJT, 289; Madison to Monroe, 30 July 1803, *PJM-SS*, 5:248–50; Gallatin to Jefferson, 18 August 1803, *PTJ*, 41:214–17; King to Christopher Gore, 12 August, 20 August, and 24 October 1803, *LCRK*, 4:293, 294, 317; Gallatin to Ezekiel Bacon, 25 February and 2 April 1812, *ASP: Finance*, 2:554, 555 (corruption in French settlement of the American claims); Stuart Gerry Brown, ed., *The Autobiography of James Monroe* (Syracuse, NY: Syracuse University Press, 1959), 189–90.

73. Gallatin to Jefferson, 31 August 1803, *PTJ*, 41:296–301; Gallatin, State of the Finances, 25 October 1803, *ASP: Finance*, 2:48–49; Gallatin to Jefferson, 11 January 1804; Gallatin, Remarks on Presidential message, [29] October 1804, *WAG*, 1:172, 213; Gallatin to Thomas Willing, 26 March and 6 April 1805, *PAG*; Gallatin to Joseph H. Nicholson, 27 March 1805, JHNP; Gallatin to Jefferson, 28 March, 1 July, and 21 November 1805, *WAG*, 1:228, 235, 262; Jefferson to Gallatin, 3 April 1805, ibid., 1:229; Randolph to Gallatin, 12 October 1805, *PAG*; Jefferson, Fifth Annual Message, 3 December 1805, Richardson, *Messages and Papers*, 1:387–88; Gallatin to Armstrong, 1 November 1810, *PAG*; Gallatin to Gales and Seaton, 5 February 1835, *WAG*, 1:502; Act of 10 November 1803, secs. 4–5, *Statutes at Large* 2 (1845): 246–47 (authorized purchase bonds and increased appropriation for debt repayment); Act of 10 November 1803, ibid., 247–48 (authorized claims payments).

74. Gallatin to Giles, 13 February 1802, *WAG*, 1:76-79 (Gallatin later endorsed his copy of this letter with "Origin of [the] National Road"); Smith, *Wealth of Nations*, 681–89; Destutt de Tracy, *A Treatise on Political Economy*, 155, 233–34.

75. Jefferson, Second Inaugural Address, 4 March 1805, Richardson, *Messages and Papers*, 1:379; Jefferson to Gallatin, 13 October 1802, 21 April 1803, *PTJ*, 38:486–87, 40:250–51; John Lauritz Larson, *Internal Improvement: National Public Works and the Promise of Popular Government in the Early United States* (Chapel Hill: University of North Carolina Press, 2001), 53–58.

76. Jefferson, Second Inaugural Address, Richardson *Messages and Papers*, 1:379; Jefferson, Sixth Annual Message, ibid., 2 December 1806,

1:409–10; Jefferson to Gallatin, 29 May 1805; Gallatin to Jefferson, 16 and 22 November 1806, 2 November 1808; Jefferson to Gallatin, 23 November 1806, *WAG,* 1:232, 319–20, 425, 320–21, 321; Jefferson to Joel Barlow, 10 December 1807, *WTJ,* 10:529-30; Balogh, *A Government Out of Sight,* 122-25; Joseph H. Harrison Jr., "'Sic et Non': Thomas Jefferson and Internal Improvement," *Journal of the Early Republic* 7, no. 4 (Winter 1987): 338–41.

77. Gallatin to Jefferson, 12 February 1808; Jefferson to Gallatin, 14 July 1806; Gallatin to Jefferson, 13 April 1807, 27 July 1808, *WAG,* 1:370, 304–05, 334–35, 395–96; Jefferson to Gallatin, 6 August 1808, L&B, 12:118–19; Jefferson to Congress, 19 February 1808, *ASP: Miscellaneous,* 1:714-15; Gallatin, Memorandum on Cumberland Road (with sketch of route), April 1802; Gallatin to Badollet, 3 May 1804, *PAG;* Carter Goodrich, *Government Promotion of American Canals and Railroads, 1800–1890* (New York: Columbia University Press, 1960), 24–26, 38; Harry Ammon, *James Monroe: The Quest for National Identity* (1971; Charlottesville: University Press of Virginia, 1990), 387–92; Phillips, "William Duane," 262.

78. Brown, *Plumer's Memorandum,* 628–29 (24 February 1807); *Annals,* 9ᵗʰ Cong., 2ⁿᵈ Sess., 33–35, 55–60, 79–87, 88–90, 92–93, 95–97; Gallatin to James W. Nicholson, 1 March 1803; Worthington to Gallatin, 21 April 1805, *PAG;* Gallatin to Jefferson, 25 November 1806, *WAG,* 1:321–24; Goodrich, *Government Promotion,* 26–27; Sears, *Thomas Worthington,* 124–28; Lynn Hudson Parsons, *John Quincy Adams* (Madison, WI: Madison House, 1998), 83; Larson, *Internal Improvement,* 59.

79. Gallatin, *Report of the Secretary of the Treasury on the Subject of Public Roads and Canals,* Senate Print (Washington, DC, 1808), 7–8, reprinted in *ASP: Miscellaneous,* 1:724-25.

80. Gallatin, Report on Roads and Canals, 66–69 (quoted at 69), 79–123 (Latrobe and Fulton reports); Talbot Hamlin, *Benjamin Henry Latrobe* (New York: Oxford University Press, 1955), 292–96, 360-61, 545-49.

81. Gallatin, Report on Roads and Canals, 69–73 (quoted at 73); Goodrich, *Government Promotion,* 19–21, 28–35; John R. Nelson Jr., *Liberty and Property: Political Economy and Policymaking in the New Nation, 1789–1812* (Baltimore: Johns Hopkins University Press, 1987), 125–26; Balogh, *A Government Out of Sight,* 125–27; Lawrence G. Hines, "The Early 19ᵗʰ Century Internal Improvements Reports and the Philosophy of Public Investment," *Journal of Economic Issues* 2, no. 4 (October 1968): 384–86; Hines, "Precursors to Benefit-Cost Analysis in Early United

States Public Investment Projects," *Land Economics* 49, no. 3 (August 1973): 310–14; Michael J. Hostetler, "The Early American Quest for Internal Improvements: Distance and Debate," *Rhetorica: Journal of the History of Rhetoric* 29, no. 1 (Winter 2011): 60–63.

82. William Tatham to Gallatin, 24 July 1810, *PAG;* On Canals—No. III, Philadelphia *Aurora General Advertiser,* 17 July 1810; Gallatin to H. M. Ridgely, 6 January 1812, *ASP: Miscellaneous,* 2:179; *Annals,* 12ᵗʰ Cong., 1ˢᵗ Sess., 1078–80; J. C. A. Stagg, *Mr. Madison's War: Politics, Diplomacy, and Warfare in the Early American Republic, 1783-1830* (Princeton, NJ: Princeton University Press, 1983), 81–83; G. Melvin Herndon, "The 1806 Survey of the North Carolina Coast, Cape Hatteras to Cape Fear," *North Carolina Historical Review* 49, no. 3 (July, 1972): 242–253; Lee W. Formwalt, "Benjamin Henry Latrobe and the Revival of the Gallatin Plan of 1808," *Pennsylvania History* 48, no. 2 (April 1981): 111–25.

83. Goodrich, *Government Promotion,* 32–48; McCoy, *The Elusive Republic,* 248–52; Lynton K. Caldwell, *The Administrative Theories of Hamilton and Jefferson: Their Contribution to Thought on Public Administration,* 2ⁿᵈ ed. (New York: Holmes and Meier, 1988), 164–67; Mayer, *The Constitutional Thought of Thomas Jefferson,* 218–20; Larson, *Internal Improvement,* 62–69; Burstein and Isenberg, *Madison and Jefferson,* 591–93.

84. On Jefferson's view, see Jefferson to Leiper, 25 May 1808, L&B, 12:65–66; to du Pont, 15 April 1811; to Kosciusko, 16 April 1811; to Elizabeth Trist, 10 May 1812, *PTJ-RS,* 3:559–61, 565–67, 5:26–27; Jefferson to Gallatin, [before 6 June] 1817, *PTJ-RS,* 11:410–11; Jefferson to Madison, 24 December 1825 (enclosing draft Declaration and Protest of the Commonwealth of Virginia); Madison to Jefferson, 28 December 1825 (enclosing draft letter to Thomas Ritchie), Smith, *The Republic of Letters,* 3:1943–46, 1947–51; Jefferson to Giles, 26 December 1825, *TJW,* 1509–11; Peterson, *Thomas Jefferson and the New Nation,* 855–60, 1002–03. On the old Republican view generally, see Macon to Bartlett Yancey, 8 March and 15 April 1818, Edwin Mood Wilson, ed., "The Congressional Career of Nathaniel Macon," *James Sprunt Historical Monographs* 2 (University of North Carolina, 1900), 47, 48 ("I must ask you to examine the Constitution of the U. S. . . . and then tell me if Congress can establish banks, make roads and canals, whether they cannot free all the slaves in the U. S."); *Annals,* 18ᵗʰ Cong., 1ˢᵗ Sess., 1307–08 (similar statement by John Randolph); Norman K. Risjord, *The Old Republicans: Southern*

Conservatism in the Age of Jefferson (New York: Columbia University Press, 1965), 237–43; Balogh, *A Government Out of Sight,* 128–45; Pamela L. Baker, "The Washington National Road Bill and the Struggle to Adopt a Federal System of Internal Improvement," *Journal of the Early Republic* 22, no. 3 (Autumn 2002): 438–40; Daniel M. Mulcare, "Restricted Authority: Slavery Politics, Internal Improvements, and the Limitation of National Administrative Capacity," *Political Research Quarterly* 61, no. 4 (December 2008): 678–79.

85.   Hannah to Albert Gallatin, 5 June 1804, *PAG;* Albert Gallatin to Jefferson, 9 September 1802, *PTJ,* 38:372–74; Boston *Columbian Centinel,* 3 October 1801; Gallatin to Jefferson, 21 September 1801, 30 April, 17 July, and 24 August 1802, *PTJ,* 35:329–30, 37:377–78, 38:87–89, 286; Jefferson to Gallatin, 18 September 1801, 3 August, 23 August, and 30 August 1802, ibid., 35:314–15, 38:156–58, 277–78, 317–18; Gallatin to Jefferson, 18 September 1804, *WAG,* 1:208–9; Gallatin to James W. Nicholson, 17 July 1801, 30 April 1802, 27 July, 23 August, and 31 August 1803, 16 August and 5 September 1804, 15 July and 20 September 1805, 22 July 1806, 21 April 1808; Gallatin to Frances Nicholson, 27 May 1805; Gallatin to Maria Nicholson, 16 April 1808, *PAG;* Macon to Joseph H. Nicholson, 18 April 1808, JHNP; King to Gore, 20 August 1803, *LCRK,* 4:294 (Gallatin comment on lack of progress in building the city of Washington); Philadelphia *Gazette of the United States,* 23 September 1801; William Plumb Bacon, comp., *Ancestry of Albert Gallatin and of Hannah Nicholson* (New York: Tobias A. Wright, [1916]), 19; Barbara G. Carson, *Ambitious Appetites: Dining, Behavior, and Patters of Consumption in Federal Washington* (Washington, DC: American Institute of Architects Press, 1990), 2–6. From deep in the Virginia countryside one summer, John Randolph described Washington as a place "where the wretched exile is cut off from all information, society, or amusement & where common necessaries of life can be procured not without difficulty, & the most enormous expence." Randolph to Gallatin, 28 June 1805, *PAG.*

86.   Gallatin to James W. Nicholson, 15 September 1802; Albert Gallatin to Hannah Gallatin, 6 June 1804; Hannah Gallatin to Albert Gallatin, 5 June 1804, *PAG.*

Chapter 7: Frugality's Price

1.   Thomas Jefferson, Second Inaugural Address, 4 March 1805, Richardson, *Messages and Papers,* 1:379; Albert Gallatin, State of the Finances, 19

November 1804; Gallatin, Report on Public Debt, 9 April 1808, *ASP: Finance,* 2:108–09, 287; James Nicholson to Gallatin, 28 April 1803; Gallatin to James W. Nicholson, 26 October 1804, *PAG;* Curtius [John Taylor?], *A Defence of the Measures of the Administration of Thomas Jefferson* (Washington, DC, 1804), 17–22, 40–55; Charles Wilson Peale to Reuben Peale and others, 19 January, 30 January, and 4 February 1805, Lillian B. Wilson et al., eds., *The Selected Papers of Charles Willson Peale and His Family* (5 vols.; New Haven, CT: Yale University Press, 1983–2000), 2:2:793–94, 797, 799; Rembrandt Peale, Portrait of Albert Gallatin, oil on canvas, February 1805, Independence National Historical Park, Philadelphia; Doris Devine Fanelli and Karie Deithorn, *History of the Portrait Collection, Independence National Historical Park, and Catalog of the Collection* (Philadelphia: American Philosophical Society, 2001), 142; Noble E. Cunningham Jr., *The Jeffersonian Republicans in Power: Party Operation, 1801–1809* (Chapel Hill; University of North Carolina Press, 1963), 103–08; Kenneth C. Martis, *The Historical Atlas of Political Parties in the United States Congress, 1789–1989* (New York: Macmillan, 1989), 24. Jefferson and Madison famously wrote almost nothing about the Burr-Hamilton duel. Gallatin—who remained sympathetic to Burr—said more than either of them when he ended a letter to his brother-in-law with this short appraisal: "Much real sympathy and sincere regret have naturally been excited by that catastrophe. But unquenchable hatred of Burr and federal policy have continued in producing an artificial sensation much beyond what might have been expected; and a majority of both parties seem disposed at this moment to deify Hamilton and to treat Burr as a murderer. The duel, for a duel, was certainly fair; yet the coroner's jury have sat already six days & not yet agreed on their verdict." Gallatin to James W. Nicholson, 19 July 1804; Gallatin to Jefferson, 18 July 1804, *PAG;* Theodosia Alston [Theodosia Burr] to Gallatin, 9 March 1811, Matthew L. Davis, ed., *The Private Journal of Aaron Burr* (2 vols.; New York, 1858), 2:155–56; Nancy Isenberg, *Fallen Founder: The Life of Aaron Burr* (New York: Viking, 2007), 223–56, 262–82.

2. Gallatin, State of the Finances, 18 December 1801, 16 December 1802, 25 October 1803, 19 November 1804, *ASP: Finance,* 1:701–12, 2:5–9, 47–58, 107–13; Gallatin to Jefferson, 3 May 1804 and 28 May 1805; Jefferson to Gallatin, 29 May 1805, *WAG,* 1:190–91, 231–32, 232–33; Davis Rich Dewey, *Financial History of the United States,* 9th ed. (New York: Longmans, Green, 1924), 110–11, 123–25; Paul Studenski and

Herman Edward Krooss, *Financial History of the United States* (1952; Washington, DC: Beard Books, 2003), 54, 66–68.

3. Albert Gallatin to Hannah Gallatin, 6 June 1804; Albert Gallatin to Frances Nicholson, 27 May 1805, *PAG;* Jefferson to Larkin Smith, 26 November 1804; Jefferson to John Dickinson, 13 January 1807, *TJW,* 1148, 1169–70.

4. John Quincy Adams to Rufus King, 8 October 1802, *WJQA,* 3:9; John Taylor to Wilson Cary Nicholas, 14 April 1806, David N. Mayer, ed., "Of Principles and Men: The Correspondence of John Taylor of Caroline with Wilson Cary Nicholas, 1806–1808," *Virginia Magazine of History and Biography* 96, no. 3 (July 1988): 358.

5. Thomas Rodney to Caesar A. Rodney, 31 October 1804, Simon Gratz, ed., "Thomas Rodney," *Pennsylvania Magazine of History and Biography* 44, no. 1 (January 1920): 68; same to same, 2 May 1809, ibid., 45, no. 2 (April 1921): 180; David Gelston to Gallatin, 11 April 1804, *PAG.* On the property dispute behind the closure of the Sandy Hook lighthouse, see Gallatin to Jefferson, 28 November 1801, *PTJ,* 35:738; Gallatin to Jefferson, 15 November 1805, 12 March 1806, Thomas Jefferson Papers, DLC; Jefferson to Gallatin, 16 November and 15 December 1805, *PAG.*

6. Act of 2 September 1789, sec. 2, *Statutes at Large* 1 (1845): 65–66; Gallatin to Jefferson, [14–15] November, [by 16] November, and 13 December 1801, *PTJ,* 35:622–24, 630-36, 36:101–04; Gallatin, Memorandum on reporting of expenses, [by 16 November] 1801, ibid., 35:636-38; Jefferson to Gallatin, 14 December 1801, ibid., 36:107-08; Leonard D. White, *The Federalists: A Study in Administrative History* (New York: Macmillan, 1956), 118-19; Leonard D. White, *The Jeffersonians: A Study in Administrative History, 1801-1829* (New York: Macmillan, 1956), 140-42.

7. White, *The Jeffersonians,* 162–65; Noble E. Cunningham Jr., *The Process of Government under Jefferson* (Princeton, NJ: Princeton University Press, 1978), 99–107.

8. Jefferson to James Madison, 19 February 1799; Jefferson to Gallatin, 19 February 1804, *PTJ,* 31:44–46, 42:508–10; Alexander De Conde, *The Quasi-War: The Politics and Diplomacy of the Undeclared War with France, 1797–1801* (New York: Scribners, 1966), 136–40; Ronald Angelo Johnson, *Diplomacy in Black and White: John Adams, Touissaint Louverture, and Their Atlantic World Alliance* (Athens: University of Georgia Press, 2014), 68–86, 165–67. Gallatin and other Republicans had opposed the Adams administration's diplomatic overtures to

Saint-Domingue; *Annals,* 5ᵗʰ Cong., 3ʳᵈ Sess., 2750–53, 2769–70, 2774–76; Donald R. Hickey, "America's Response to the Slave Revolt in Haiti, 1791–1806," *Journal of the Early Republic* 2, no. 4 (Winter 1982): 368–69; Tim Matthewson, "Jefferson and Haiti," *Journal of Southern History* 61, no. 2 (May 1995): 209–48.

9. Gallatin to Jefferson, 21 February 1804; Jefferson to Gallatin, 22 February 1804, *PTJ,* 42:523, 529; Jefferson to Gallatin, 9 June 1804, *WAG,* 1:196. From among the many letters on Stevens's case, see Madison to Stevens, 17 April 1802; Richard Harrison to Madison, 24 and 27 December 1803 and 7 January 1804; Madison to Harrison, 9 January 1804; Madison to Jefferson, 20 April 1804, *PJM-SS,* 3:134, 6:209-10, 236, 315, 326, 7:81-90; Gallatin to Jefferson, 31 March 1804, *PAG;* same to same, 11 June 1804, *WAG,* 1:196–98; Jefferson to Gallatin, 12 June 1804, *PAG.* Years later, Gallatin authorized the payment of expenses to Joel Poinsett, consular agent to Buenos Aires, based on merely verbal assurances from the Secretary of State; see Gallatin to James Monroe, 3 July 1811, *PAG.*

10. Frances Few, Journal, 1 and 11 October 1808, Ad Hoc Collections, *Georgia's Virtual Vault: Digital Treasures from the Georgia Archives,* printed in Noble E. Cunningham Jr., ed., "The Diary of Frances Few, 1808–1809," *Journal of Southern History* 29, no. 3 (August 1963): 348, 352; Charles Balthazar Julien Févret de Saint-Mémin, Portrait of Robert Smith, engraving, 1803, Maryland Historical Society; Frank A. Cassell, *Merchant Congressman in the Young Republic: Samuel Smith of Maryland, 1752–1839* (Madison: University of Wisconsin Press, 1971), 105–07; John Pancake, *Samuel Smith and the Politics of Business, 1752-1839* (Tuscaloosa: University of Alabama Press, 1972), 60–2; Thom M. Armstrong, *Politics, Diplomacy, and Intrigue in the Early Republic: The Cabinet Career of Robert Smith, 1801–1811* (Dubuque, IA: Kendall/Hunt Publishing, 1991), 5–9.

11. White, *The Federalists,* 159; White, *The Jeffersonians,* 266–67; Francis D. Cogliano, *Emperor of Liberty: Thomas Jefferson's Foreign Policy* (New Haven, CT: Yale University Press, 2014), 152–61; Michael Kitzen, "Money Bags or Cannon Balls: The Origins of the Tripolitan War, 1795–1801," *Journal of the Early Republic* 16, no. 4 (Winter 1996): 601–24.

12. Gallatin to Jefferson, 18 January 1803, *PTJ,* 39:346; Jefferson to Elbridge Gerry, 26 January 1799; Jefferson, Notes on cabinet meeting, 15 May 1801; Jefferson to Gallatin, 14 November 1801; Gallatin to Jefferson, 6 October 1803, ibid., 30:646; 34:114–15, 35:622, 41:477; John Randolph

to St. George Tucker, 15 January 1802, quoted in Norman K. Risjord, *The Old Republicans: Southern Conservatism in the Age of Jefferson* (New York: Columbia University Press, 1965), 22 (war with Tripoli was utterly incompatible with repeal of internal taxes). For a kinder assessment of Robert Smith's management during the Tripolitan War, see Paul A. C. Koistinen, *Beating Plowshares into Swords: The Political Economy of American Warfare, 1606–1865* (Lawrence: University Press of Kansas, 1996), 54.

13.   Gallatin to Jefferson, 16 and 24 August, 9 and 21 September 1802, 21 March 1803, *PTJ*, 38:229–33, 286, 372-74, 416–18, 40:91–92; *Annals, 5th Cong., 3rd Sess.*, 2831, 2862–78; [Enos Bronson?], *An Address to the People of the United States on the Policy of Maintaining a Permanent Navy* (1802; repr., Tarrytown, NY: William Abbatt, 1921), 18, 29–35; Curtius [John Taylor?], *Defence of the Measures of the Administration*, 71–87; Craig L. Symonds, *Navalists and Antinavalists: The Naval Policy Debate in the United States, 1785–1827* (Newark: University of Delaware Press, 1980), 40–49; Alexander Balinky, "Albert Gallatin: Naval Foe," *Pennsylvania Magazine of History and Biography* 82, no. 3 (July 1958): 293–304; Joseph George Henrich, "The Triumph of Ideology: The Jeffersonians and the Navy, 1779–1807" (Ph.D. diss., Duke University, 1971), 69–73, 77–81, 106–13, 281–83.

14.   Henry Adams, *History of the United States during the Administrations of Thomas Jefferson and James Madison* (1889–91; 2 vols.; New York: Library of America, 1986), 1:397; Jefferson to Gallatin, 8, 13, and 20 September 1802, *PTJ*, 38:365, 390–91, 410–11; Symonds, *Navalists and Antinavalists*, 95.

15.   Gallatin to Jefferson, 30 May 1805, *WAG*, 1:233-34; Robert Smith to Gallatin, 7 June 1805, *PAG*.

16.   Randolph to Gallatin, 28 June 1805, *PAG*; Gallatin to Jefferson, 12 September 1805; Gallatin to Madison, 6 August 1805, *WAG*, 1:252–54, 238; Gallatin to Jefferson, 16 August 1802, *WAG*, 1:88 ("Eight years hence we shall, I trust, be able to assume a different tone [than the naval response he suggests at the beginning of the Tripolitan War]; but our exertions at present consume the seeds of our greatness and retard to an indefinite time the epoch of our strength."); Richmond *Enquirer*, 30 September, 3, 7, and 10 October 1806 (reprinting pieces on naval policy from Washington *National Intelligencer*). Jefferson's 1805 annual message drew Congress's attention to the need for naval construction. Jefferson, Fifth Annual Message, 3 December 1805, Richardson, *Messages*

and Papers, 1:383. For the somewhat restrained view of naval power that Jefferson expressed to a leading Republican merchant months later, see Jefferson to Jacob Crowninshield, 13 May 1806, *WTJ*, 10:266–67. And for the reflections on naval spending that Jefferson shared with John Adams late in life, see Jefferson to Adams, 27 May 1813, *PTJ-RS*, 6:137-39; same to same, 1 November 1822, *WTJ*, 12:268–70.

17. Jefferson to Gallatin, 17 October 1807, *WAG*, 1:357; Gallatin to Robert Smith, 2 November (draft) and 21 November 1805, 12 May 1806; Smith to Gallatin, 18, 20, and 27 November 1805, 9 May 1806, 20, 21, and 27 October 1807; Gallatin to Joseph H. Nicholson, 12 September and 21 October 1805, *PAG;* Gallatin to Jefferson, 21 November 1805, 21 October 1807, *WAG*, 1:262-63, 364; Jefferson to Gallatin, 3 July 1806, 24 October 1807; Gallatin to Joseph B. Varnum, 28 October 1807, *PAG;* Smith to Jefferson, 10 September 1805, *FOL*—Early Access (arguing for larger navy); Acts of 31 January 1804, 25 January 1805, and 25 November 1807, *Statutes at Large* 2 (1845): 249, 310, 450.

18. Gallatin, Remarks on annual message, 29 October 1804, *PAG;* Gallatin to Jefferson, 8 February 1807, *WAG*, 1:328–31; Cunningham, *The Process of Government*, 119–20; Symonds, *Navalists and Antinavalists*, 108; Spencer C. Tucker, *The Jeffersonian Gunboat Navy* (Columbia: University of South Carolina Press, 1993), 26–32; Gene A. Smith, *"For Purposes of Defense": The Politics of the Jeffersonian Gunboat Program* (Newark: University of Delaware Press, 1995), 11–14.

19. [Washington Irving et al.], Salmagundi No. XIII, 14 August 1807, reprinted in Bruce I. Granger et al., eds., *Washington Irving: History, Tales and Sketches* (New York: Library of America, 1983), 239; Jefferson to Gallatin, 9 February 1807, L&B, 11:153–54; Jefferson to Congress, 10 February 1807, *ASP: Naval Affairs*, 1:163–64; Jefferson, Third, Fourth, and Fifth Annual Messages, 17 October 1803, 8 November 1804, 3 December 1805, Richardson, *Messages and Papers*, 1:359, 372, 385; Jonathan Williams, *Letter from Col. Jonathan Williams, on the Subject of Fortifying and Protecting the Harbour of New-York* (New York, 1807), 12 (torpedoes); Robert Smith to Samuel L. Mitchill, 20 November 1807; Smith to Thomas Blount, 30 November 1807, *ASP: Naval Affairs*, 1:168, 169–70; Act of 18 December 1807, *Statutes at Large* 2 (1845): 451; Henry Dearborn, Report on Fortifications, 6 January 1809, *ASP: Military Affairs*, 1:236–39; Dumas Malone, *Jefferson and His Time*, vol. 5, *Jefferson the President: Second Term, 1805–1809* (Boston: Little Brown, 1974), 497–506; Smith, *"For Purposes of Defense,"* 48–56.

20. Dewey, *Financial History,* 112, 123; Studenski and Krooss, *Financial History,* 54, 68.
21. Anna C. Clauder, *American Commerce as Affected by the Wars of the French Revolution and Napoleon, 1793–1812* (1932; repr., Clifton, NY: Augustus M. Kelley, 1972), 67–79; Gautham Rao, *National Duties: Custom Houses and the Making of the American State* (Chicago: University of Chicago Press, 2016), 119–31; Lester H. Woolsey, "Early Cases on the Doctrine of Continuous Voyages," *American Journal of International Law* 4, no. 4 (October 1910): 823–47; Claudia D. Goldin and Frank D. Lewis, "The Role of Exports in American Economic Growth during the Napoleonic Wars, 1793–1807," *Explorations in Economic History* 17, no. 1 (January 1980): 6–25; Donald R. Adams Jr., "American Neutrality and Prosperity, 1793–1808: A Reconsideration," *Journal of Economic History* 40, no. 4 (December 1980): 713–37.
22. Jefferson to Robert R. Livingston, 4 June 1801, *PTJ,* 34:251–54; [James Madison], *Examination of the British Doctrine, Which Subjects to Capture a Neutral Trade Not Open in Time of Peace* ([Philadelphia, 1806]).
23. [John Baker Holroyd], Lord Sheffield, *Strictures on the Necessity of Inviolably Maintaining the Navigation and Colonial System of Great Britain* (London, 1804), 16–26; Bradford Perkins, *Prologue to War: England and the United States, 1805–1812* (Berkeley: University of California Press, 1961), 3–30; Burton Spivak, *Jefferson's English Crisis: Commerce, Embargo, and the Republican Revolution* (Charlottesville: University Press of Virginia, 1979), 7–12.
24. Gallatin to Samuel Smith, 17 January 1804, *PAG* (printed and misdated in *WAG,* 1:236); Gallatin to Jefferson, 28 May 1805; Jefferson to Gallatin, 29 May 1805, *WAG,* 1:231–32, 232–33; [James Stephen], *War in Disguise; or, The Frauds of the Neutral Flags* (London, 1805), 7–10, 39–41; Perkins, *Prologue to War,* 77–84; Spivak, *Jefferson's English Crisis,* 12-30; Clifford L. Egan, *Neither Peace Nor War: Franco-American Relations, 1803–1812* (Baton Rouge: Louisiana State University Press, 1983), 67–72; Doran S. Ben-Atar, *The Origins of Jeffersonian Commercial Policy and Diplomacy* (New York: St. Martin's, 1993), 162–65; Paul A. Gilje, *Free Trade and Sailors' Rights in the War of 1812* (New York: Cambridge University Press, 2013), 149–54; Cogliano, *Emperor of Liberty,* 215–24; Bradford Perkins, "Sir William Scott and the *Essex,*" *William and Mary Quarterly,* 2nd Ser., 13, no. 2 (April 1956): 169–83; Joshua J. Wolf, "'The Misfortune to Get Pressed':

The Impressment of American Seamen and the Ramifications on the United States, 1793–1812" (Ph.D diss., Temple University, 2015), 31–32, 45–63.

25. Gallatin to Jefferson, 21 November 1805; Jefferson to Gallatin with enclosure, 26 November 1805, *WAG,* 1:262, 266–75; Jefferson, Fifth Annual Message, 3 December 1805, Richardson, *Messages and Papers,* 1:383–84; Jefferson to Joseph B. Varnum, 9 December 1805, *FOL*—Early Access; Madison, Notes on neutral trade, [14 September 1805], *PJM-SS,* 10:326–35; Samuel Smith to unknown, 16 December 1805, Samuel Smith Letterbook, Samuel Smith Family Papers, DLC; Perkins, *Prologue to War,* 150; Spivak, *Jefferson's English Crisis,* 68–69.

26. Richard Beale Davis, ed., *Jeffersonian America: Notes on the United States of America...by Sir Augustus John Foster* (San Marino, CA: Huntington Library, 1954), 236 (Gallatin's epithet for Gregg); *Annals,* 9th Cong., 1st Sess., 851 (Randolph quoted), 412–13, 430, 449–51, 537–74, 592–98, 777, 877, 240; Gallatin to Nathaniel Macon, 16 January 1806, *ASP: Finance,* 2:169–79; George Washington Campbell to Moses Fiske, 11 April 1806, Noble E. Cunningham Jr., *Circular Letters of Congressmen to Their Constituents, 1789–1829* (3 vols.; Chapel Hill: University of North Carolina Press, 1978), 1:432; Spivak, *Jefferson's English Crisis,* 32–46; Gilje, *Free Trade and Sailors' Rights,* 151–52; Brian Schoen, "Calculating the Price of Union: Republican Economic Nationalism and the Origins of Southern Sectionalism," *Journal of the Early Republic* 23, no. 2 (Summer 2003): 184–86.

27. *Annals,* 9th Cong., 1st Sess., 258–62, 409–13, 415; Gallatin to Jefferson, [3 December 1805]; Gallatin to Joseph H. Nicholson, 7 December 1805; Jefferson to Gallatin, 7 December 1805, *WAG,* 1:278–81, 282, 282; Nicholson to Gallatin, 8 December 1805, *PAG;* Jefferson to Barnabas Bidwell, 5 July 1806, *TJW,* 1164–66; John Taylor to Monroe, 27 February 1806, LJT, 291; Taylor to Wilson Cary Nicholas, 10 June 1806 and 5 February 1808, Mayer, "Of Principles and Men," 361–63, 376; Decius [John Randolph], Richmond *Enquirer,* 15 August and 18 November 1806; Jefferson to William A. Burwell, 17 September 1806, *WTJ,* 10:286–91; Gerard W. Gawalt, ed., "'Strict Truth': The Narrative of William Armistead Burwell," *Virginia Magazine of History and Biography* 101, no. 1 (January 1993): 121–24; Russell Kirk, *John Randolph of Roanoke: A Study in American Politics* (Chicago: Henry Regnery, 1964), 98–126; Risjord, *The Old Republicans,* 33–71; Peter Magrath, *Yazoo: Law and Politics in the New Republic—The Case of* Fletcher v. Peck (Providence,

RI: Brown University Press, 1966), 20–49; Alexander De Conde, *This Affair of Louisiana* (New York: Charles Scribner's Sons, 1976), 229–35; Robert Dawidoff, *The Education of John Randolph* (New York: W. W. Norton, 1979), 169–88; John F. Devanny Jr., "'A Loathing of Public Debt, Taxes, and Excises': The Political Economy of John Randolph of Roanoke," *Virginia Magazine of History and Biography* 109, no. 4 (2001): 392–406; Alexander B. Lacy Jr., "Jefferson and Congress: Congressional Method and Politics, 1801–1809" (Ph.D. diss., University of Virginia, 1964), 157–66.

28. John Randolph to St. George Tucker, 15 January 1802 ("Every day, every hour increases my respect for the judgment, talents, & disinterestedness of Mr. Gallatin."), quoted in Everett Lee Long, "Jefferson and Congress: A Study of the Jeffersonian Legislative System, 1801–1809" (Ph.D. diss., University of Missouri, 1966), 223; Randolph to Gallatin, 14 October 1804 and 24 February 1806, *PAG;* William Cabell Bruce, *John Randolph of Roanoke, 1773–1833* (2 vols.; New York: G. P. Putnam's Sons, 1922), 1:227–31; Dawidoff, *The Education of John Randolph,* 145–60. Gallatin was one of the commissioners who proposed the Yazoo settlement to Congress, and he personally lobbied Randolph to support the $2 million appropriation for West Florida. Decius [John Randolph], Richmond *Enquirer,* 15 August 1806; Magrath, *Yazoo,* 35-36, 47. For Gallatin's active participation in the attempt to purchase West Florida, see Jefferson, Notes on cabinet meeting, 12 November 1805, *WTJ,* 1:387; Gallatin to Jefferson, 12 September, 21 November, 3 December (letter), 3 December (memorandum) 1805, 12 February 1806, *WAG,* 1:242–43, 263, 275-77, 278–80, 290–91; Gallatin to Joseph H. Nicholson, 7 December 1805, ibid., 1:262; Nicholson to Gallatin, 8 December 1805; Jefferson to Gallatin, 7 December 1805; Randolph to Gallatin, 24 February 1806, *PAG;* Gallatin to Madison, 1 March 1806, *WAG,* 1: 291–92.

29. *Annals,* 9th Cong., 1st Sess., 561 (quoted), 564–65, 771, 430–31, 984–85; Dawidoff, *The Education of John Randolph,* 188–97; David Johnson, *John Randolph of Roanoke* (Baton Rouge: Louisiana University Press, 2012), 107–12, 115; David A. Carson, "That Ground Called Quiddism: John Randolph's War with the Jefferson Administration," *Journal of American Studies* 20, no. 1 (April 1986): 71–92.

30. Everett Somerville Brown, ed., *William Plumer's Memorandum of Proceedings in the United States Senate, 1803–1807* (New York: Macmillan, 1923), 444 (6 March 1806) (quoted), 446 (8 March 1806), 600 (12 February 1807); Alexander J. Dallas to Gallatin, 19 March 1806,

PAG; Samuel Smith to unknown, 5, 14, and 17 March 1806, Samuel Smith Letterbook, Samuel Smith Family Papers, DLC; Gallatin to Jefferson, 4 April 1806, *FOL*—Early Access (with Jefferson annotation); Gallatin to George Clinton Jr., 5 April 1806; Clinton to Gallatin, 10 April 1806 (with Gallatin annotation); Gallatin to Speaker of the House, 15 April 1806, *WAG,* 1:295–97, 297-98, 298–99; Walter Jones to [Constituents], 24 April 1806, *PAG,* printed in Cunningham, *Circular Letters of Congressmen,* 1:466–69; Jones to Gallatin, 26 April [1806] (misdated 1807 by editors); Gallatin to Jones, 26 April 1806, *PAG; Annals,* 9ᵗʰ Cong., 1ˢᵗ Sess., 988, 993, 995, 1028; Risjord, *The Old Republicans,* 77–78; Merry Ellen Scofield, "The Fatigues of His Table: The Politics of Presidential Dining during the Jefferson Administration," *Journal of the Early Republic* 26, no. 3 (Fall 2006): 467.

31.   Randolph to Joseph H. Nicholson, 21 July 1807, 3 April 1806; Gallatin to Nicholson, 17 April 1806, JHNP; Macon to Nicholson, 10, 15, and 17 April 1806; Randolph to Nicholson, 10, 17, and 21 April, 24 June, and 10 December 1806, JHNP; Randolph to Gallatin, 11 February 1807, *PAG;* Albert to Hannah Gallatin, 30 October 1807, *LAG,* 363–64; Jefferson to William Wirt, 3 May 1811, *PTJ-RS,* 3:601–04; Henry Adams to Hugh Blair Grigsby, 29 September 1877, J. C. Levenson et al., eds., *The Letters of Henry Adams* (6 vols.; Cambridge, MA: Harvard University Press, 1982–88), 2:321–22. Six months after Joseph Nicholson left the House, Jefferson offered him the lucrative post of customs collector for Baltimore, which he declined. Jefferson to Gallatin, 12 October 1806, *WTJ,* 11:126–27; Nicholson to Gallatin, 15 October 1806, *PAG;* Malone, *Jefferson and His Time,* 5:111–12.

32.   William Duane to Jefferson, 12 March 1806, Worthington C. Ford, ed., "Letters of William Duane," *Proceedings of the Massachusetts Historical Society* 20 (May–June 1906): 282; Thomas Leiper to Jefferson, 23 March 1806, *FOL*—Early Access; Dallas to Gallatin, 16 October 1804, 26 January and 4 April 1805; Gallatin to James W. Nicholson, 26 October 1804, *PAG;* John Beckley to Madison, 5 May 1803, Gerald W. Gawalt, ed., *Justifying Jefferson: The Political Writings of John James Beckley* (Washington, DC: Library of Congress, 1995), 267; Gallatin to John Badollet, 25 October 1805, *CBG,* 51–52; Philadelphia *Aurora General Advertiser,* 9 October 1804 ("To the Democrats"), 9, 10, and 23 September 1806; Sanford W. Higginbotham, *The Keystone in the Democratic Arch: Pennsylvania Politics, 1800–1816* (Harrisburg: Pennsylvania Historical and Museum Commission, 1952), 43–45, 58–73,

116; Jacob E. Cooke, *Tench Coxe and the Early Republic* (Chapel Hill: University of North Carolina Press, 1978), 436–44; Jeffrey L. Pasley, *"The Tyranny of Printers:" Newspaper Politics in the Early American Republic* (Charlottesville: University Press of Virginia, 2001), 291–312; Andrew Shankman, *Crucible of American Democracy: The Struggle to Fuse Egalitarianism and Capitalism in Jeffersonian Pennsylvania* (Lawrence: University Press of Kansas, 2004), 96–160.

33. Duane to Jefferson, 12 March 1806; Duane to Henry Dearborn, 3 July 1810, Ford, "Letters of William Duane," 282 (quoted), 335; Jefferson to William Wirt, 3 May 1811, *PTJ-RS,* 3:601; Philadelphia *Aurora General Advertiser,* 30 September 1806 ("Mr. Gallatin has just passed through this city"), 30 August 1816 ("The Ruling Party"); Kim Tousley Phillips, "William Duane, Revolutionary Editor" (Ph.D. diss., University of California, Berkeley, 1968), 158–90.

34. Gallatin to Jefferson, 11 August 1803 (quoted), 21 March 1803, and [11 July] 1803 (comments on list of federal officeholders); Jefferson to Gallatin, 28 March, 25 July, and 18 August 1803; Jefferson to Duane, 24 July 1803 (draft not sent); Joseph H. Nicholson to Jefferson, 10 May 1803; Jefferson to Nicholson, 13 May 1803; Jefferson to Madison, 29 August 1803, *PTJ,* 41:178–79, 40:91–92, 41:23–25, 40:111, 41:114–14, 213, 108, 40:347, 371–72, 41:286; Dallas to Gallatin, 30 March 1803, *PAG.*

35. Jefferson to Duane, 22 March 1806, *WTJ,* 10:241–43. For Jefferson's more candid acknowledgment to others that there was disharmony in the cabinet, see Jefferson to Madison, 9 April 1804, *PJM-SS,* 7:25–26. For his comments on the several schisms in the Republican party, see his letters to Gideon Granger, 14 April 1804; Robert Smith, 28 August 1804; Wilson Cary Nicholas, 26 March 1805; George Logan, 11 May 1805; Michael Leib, 12 August 1805; Andrew Ellicott, 1 November 1806; and James Sullivan, 19 June 1807, *WTJ,* 10:74, 97, 137, 141, 143, 299, 420.

36. Philadelphia *Aurora General Advertiser,* 30 September 1806; Richmond *Enquirer,* 7 October (quoted), 29 April 1806, 12 September 1806 (Zeno [pseud.] to Gallatin); Randolph to Gallatin, 25 October 1805, *PAG;* Charles Henry Ambler, *Thomas Ritchie: A Study in Virginia Politics* (Richmond: Bell Book, 1913), 34–36, 46–47; Irving Brant, *James Madison,* vol. 4, *James Madison: Secretary of State, 1800–1809* (Indianapolis: Bobbs-Merrill, 1953), 434–36; Harry Ammon, *James Monroe: The Quest for National Identity* (1971; Charlottesville: University Press of Virginia, 1990), 254–57, 270–73; John P. Kaminski,

George Clinton: Yeoman Politician of the New Republic (Madison, WI: Madison House, 1993), 278–89; Phillips, "William Duane," 245–52.

37. Jefferson to Gallatin, 12 October 1806; Gallatin to Jefferson, 13 October 1806, *FOL*—Early Access (final letter); Gallatin to Jefferson, 13 October 1806, *PAG* (draft letter), version in *WAG*, 1:310–11; Gallatin to Maria Nicholson, 27 October 1806, *LAG*, 347.

38. Jefferson to Henry Middleton, 8 January 1813, *PTJ-RS*, 5:546; Jefferson to Jean, Count Diodati, 29 March 1807, *FOL*—Early Access; Jefferson to John Dickinson, 13 January 1807, *TJW*, 1170; Stephen L. Mitchill to Catherine Mitchill, 13 February 1807, "Dr. Mitchill's Letters from Washington: 1801–1813," *Harper's New Monthly Magazine* 58, no. 347 (April 1879): 752; Brown, *Plumer's Memorandum*, 453 (16 March 1806), 601–02 (4 February 1807); Jefferson to John W. Eppes, 11 September 1813, *PTJ-RS*, 6:491 ("this happy consummation"); Perkins, *Prologue to War*, 135–39; Malone, *Jefferson and His Time*, 5:9-14; Spivak, *Jefferson's English Crisis*, 60–67; Andrew Burstein, *The Inner Jefferson: Portrait of a Grieving Optimist* (Charlottesville: University Press of Virginia, 1995), 246–48; Gilje, *Free Trade and Sailor's Rights*, 154–55; Francis D. Cogliano, *Thomas Jefferson: Reputation and Legacy* (Charlottesville: University of Virginia Press, 2006), 1–2; Maurizio Valsania, *The Limits of Optimism: Thomas Jefferson's Dualistic Enlightenment* (Charlottesville: University of Virginia Press, 2011), 9, 33, 57; Donald R. Hickey, "The Monroe-Pinkney Treaty of 1806: A Reappraisal," *William and Mary Quarterly*, 3rd Ser., 44, no. 1 (January 1987): 65–88.

39. Jefferson to Gallatin, 25 June 1807, *WAG*, 1:336; Albert Gallatin to Hannah Gallatin, 28 June 1807, *PAG*; James Barron to Robert Smith, 23 June 1807, *ASP: Foreign Relations*, 3:18–19; Jefferson, Proclamation against the *Leander*, 3 May 1806, Richardson, *Messages and Papers*, 1:402–04.

40. Jefferson to Gallatin, 1 July 1807, *WAG*, 1:337; Jefferson, Notes on cabinet meetings, 2, 4 (quoted), 5, and 7 July 1807, *FOL*—Early Access; Gallatin to Jefferson, 29 June 1807, *WAG*, 1:336; Jefferson, Proclamation against British armed vessels, 2 July 1807, Richardson, *Messages and Papers*, 1:422–24; Jefferson to Thomas Cooper, 9 July 1807; Jefferson to Bidwell, 11 July 1807, *WTJ*, 10:451, 456; Joseph H. Nicholson to Gallatin, 14 July 1807, *PAG*; Robert Smith to Jefferson, 17 July 1807, *FOL*—Early Access.

41. Albert Gallatin to Hannah Gallatin, 4 and 10 July 1807; Hannah Gallatin to Albert Gallatin, 5 July 1807, *PAG;* Albert Gallatin to Hannah Gallatin, 14 July 1807, *LAG,* 359; Jefferson to Albert Gallatin, 10 July 1807, *WTJ,* 10:452–53.

42. Gallatin to Joseph H. Nicholson, 17 July 1807, *PAG,* version in *WAG,* 1:338–40; Robert Smith to Thomas Blount, 16 November 1807, *ASP: Naval Affairs,* 1:168–69; White, *The Jeffersonians,* 213, 267–68; Russell F. Weigley, *History of the United States Army,* enl. ed. (Bloomington: Indiana University Press, 1984), 109; Jonathan R. Dull, *American Naval History, 1607–1865: Overcoming the Colonial Legacy* (Lincoln: University of Nebraska Press, 2012), 52–53.

43. Max M. Edling, *A Hercules in the Cradle: War, Money, and the American State, 1783–1867* (Chicago: University of Chicago Press, 2014), 120-26; Henry C. Adams, "American War-Financiering," *Political Science Quarterly* 1, no. 3 (September 1886): 355–58.

44. Gallatin to Joseph H. Nicholson, 17 July 1807, *WAG,* 1:339; Gallatin to Jonathan Burrall, 18 and 21 July 1807; Gallatin to George Simpson, 21 and 27 July 1807; Samuel Smith to Gallatin, 19, 26, and 27 July 1807; Baring Brothers to Gallatin, 25 August 1807, *PAG;* Gallatin, State of the Finances, 5 November 1807, *ASP: Finance,* 2:248–49.

45. Gallatin to Jefferson, 25 July 1807, *WAG,* 1:340–53 (quoted at 343); Albert Gallatin to Hannah Gallatin, 10 July 1807, *LAG,* 358; Dearborn to Jefferson, 3 July 1807; Robert Smith to Jefferson, 7, 17, and 20 July 1807, *FOL*—Early Access.

46. Jefferson to Dearborn, 7, 13, 17, and 29 July and 7 August 1807, *FOL*—Early Access; Jefferson to Pierre Samuel du Pont, 14 July 1807; Jefferson to Marquis de Lafayette, 14 July 1807; Jefferson to Madison, 9 August 1807, *WTJ,* 10:460–61, 465, 474–75. On warning ships in the Indian Ocean, see Robert Smith to Jefferson, 29 August 1807, 3 and 4 September 1807; Gallatin to Jefferson, 2 and 8 September 1807; Jefferson to Robert Smith, 3 and 4 September 1807, *FOL*—Early Access. Jefferson made unauthorized purchases of naval stores in reaction to the *Chesapeake* crisis, which drew criticism when Congress returned. *Annals,* 10th Cong., 1st Sess., 818–30.

47. Macon to Gallatin, 2 August 1807; Joseph H. Nicholson to Gallatin, 14 July (quoted) and 10 September 1807, *PAG;* Gallatin to Madison, 15 August 1807, *WAG,* 1:353.

48. Albert Gallatin to Hannah Gallatin, 30 October 1807, *LAG,* 364; Jefferson to Albert Gallatin, 5 November 1807; Gallatin to Jefferson, 21

October 1807, *WAG,* 1:366 (quoted), 358–59; Macon to Joseph H. Nicholson, 3 August 1807, JHNP; Jefferson to Thomas Mann Randolph, 26 October 1807, *FOL*—Early Access.

49. Jefferson, Seventh Annual Message, 27 October 1807, Richardson, *Messages and Papers,* 1:425–29; *Annals,* 10th Cong., 1st Sess., 795–98, 806–15, 1039–56, 1064, 1084–72; Gallatin to Jefferson, 2, 3, and 5 December 1807, *PAG;* Jefferson to Gallatin, 3 December 1807, *WAG,* 1:367; Gallatin to Thomas Newton, 5 December 1807, *ASP: Commerce and Navigation,* 1:699; Perkins, *Prologue to War,* 147–49; Spivak, *Jefferson's English Crisis,* 97–101; Richard James Mannix, "The Embargo: Its Administration, Impact, and Enforcement" (Ph.D. diss., New York University, 1975), 47–56. The non-importation act of 1806 came into force a few days before Jefferson called for an embargo, and Congress amended it two months after the embargo to deal with the problems Gallatin had identified. Act of 27 February 1808, *Statutes at Large* 2 (1845): 469.

50. Jefferson, Report on Commerce, 16 December 1793, *ASP: Foreign Relations,* 1:300–304; unknown to Gallatin, 7 December 1799, *PAG* (well-developed earlier Republican argument for a ban on exports and imports instead of military preparations); Louis Martin Sears, *Jefferson and the Embargo* (1927; New York: Octagon, 1966), 4-26; Ralph Ketcham, *James Madison: A Biography* (1971; Charlottesville: University Press of Virginia, 1990), 456–57; Robert W. Tucker and David C. Hendrickson, *Empire of Liberty: The Statecraft of Thomas Jefferson* (New York: Oxford University Press, 1990), 35–37, 39; Stanley Elkins and Eric McKitrick, *The Age of Federalism: The Early American Republic, 1788–1800* (New York: Oxford University Press, 1993), 378–84; Peter Onuf and Nicholas Onuf, *Federal Union, Modern World: The Law of Nations in an Age of Revolution, 1776–1814* (Madison, WI: Madison House, 1993), 103–08, 154-63; Cogliano, *Emperor of Liberty,* 118–19.

51. Madison to James Monroe and William Pinkney, 20 May 1807, *ASP: Foreign Relations,* 3:171–72; Jefferson to Leiper, 25 May 1808, L&B, 12:65–66; Perkins, *Prologue to War,* 150–53; Adam Seybert, *Statistical Annals of the United States* (1818; repr., New York: Augustus M. Kelley, 1970), 92, 94–95, 112–13, 152; Douglass C. North, *The Economic Growth of the United States, 1790–1860* (Englewood Cliffs, NJ: Prentice-Hall, 1961), 40–41, 231; Sears, *Jefferson and the Embargo,* 276–301; Reginald C. Stuart, *The Half-Way Pacifist: Thomas Jefferson's View of*

War (Toronto: University of Toronto Press, 1978), 42–47; Drew R. McCoy, *The Elusive Republic: Political Economy in Jeffersonian America* (Chapel Hill: University of North Carolina Press, 1980), 209–23; Gilje, *Free Trade and Sailors' Rights,* 155-59; Cogliano, *Emperor of Liberty,* 236–40; Sven Beckert, *Empire of Cotton: A Global History* (New York: Alfred A. Knopf, 2015), 103–04, 118–20; Mannix, "The Embargo," 59–68.

52. Spivak, *Jefferson's English Crisis,* 10711; Mannix, "The Embargo," 14–17, 47.

53. Gallatin to Jefferson, 18 December 1807; Jefferson to Gallatin, 18 December 1807, *WAG,* 1:368, 369. Gallatin's opposition to the embargo became no secret. The "feds have a story by the handle which they wield most dexterously," James Madison's brother-in-law reported to Dolley Madison shortly before the 1808 presidential election. It "is that Sec. Smith declared...that the President & M[adison] urged the embargo against the opinion of his great self Gallatin & Co." John G. Jackson to Dolley Madison, 8 October 1808, David B. Mattern and Holly C. Shulman, eds., *The Selected Letters of Dolley Payne Madison* (Charlottesville: University of Virginia Press, 2003), 89.

54. Jefferson to Congress, 18 December 1807, Richardson, *Messages and Papers,* 1:433; Jefferson to Gallatin, 24 (quoted) and 29 December 1807, *PAG; Annals,* 10th Cong., 1st Sess., 50–51, 1216–23; Acts of 22 December 1807 and 9 January 1808, *Statutes at Large* 2 (1845): 451–53, 453–54; Gallatin, Treasury Circular, 22 December 1807; Gallatin to Jefferson, 23 and 31 December 1807; Gallatin to David Gelston, 30 December 1807; Gallatin to Allen McLane, 30 December 1807, *PAG.*

55. Washington *National Intelligencer,* 23 (quoted), 25, and 28 (quoted) December 1807, 4 and 18 January 1808; Brant, *James Madison,* 4:402–03.

56. Jefferson to John Taylor, 6 January 1808; Jefferson to Gideon Granger, 22 January 1808; Thomas Cooper to Jefferson, 4 December 1808, *FOL—Early Access.* Some historians have accepted the Jefferson administration's claim that coercive motivations were secondary when it first asked for the embargo. But a supplementary ban on exports by land across the inland frontiers enacted a few months later clearly had no purpose other than coercion. Jefferson's letters to Gallatin throughout the spring of 1808 expressly justified enforcement decisions by reference to the law's coercive intent. And as the presidential election approached in the autumn, Postmaster General Gideon Granger published a fuller defense of the

embargo in which he frankly defended its coercive as well as its precautionary purposes. Jefferson's final annual message to Congress focused on the embargo's failure to change the belligerents' policies. Act of 12 March 1808, *Statutes at Large* 2 (1845): 473–75; Jefferson to Gallatin, 23 March, 8 April, 6 May, and 20 May 1808, *FOL*—Early Access; Algernon Sydney [Gideon Granger], *An Address, to the People of New-England* (n. p.: 1808), 4; Jefferson, Eight Annual Message, 8 November 1808, Richardson, *Messages and Papers*, 1:451-53; Spivak, *Jefferson's English Crisis*, 105–19.

57. Dallas to Gallatin, 23 December 1807, *PAG;* Timothy Pickering to King, 19 (quoted) and 28 January 1808, *LCRK*, 5:64, 69; Civis [pseud.], *Remarks on the Embargo Law...*(New York, 1808), 2–10, 13 (quoted); James M. Banner Jr., *To the Hartford Convention: the Federalists and the Origins of Party Politics in Massachusetts, 1789–1815* (New York: Alfred A. Knopf, 1970), 40–46; Linda K. Kerber, *Federalists in Dissent: Imagery and Ideology in Jeffersonian America* (1970; Ithaca, NY: Cornell University Press, 1980), 185–88.

58. King to Pickering, 24 January and 5 February 1808, *LCRK*, 5:65 (quoted), 69–70; Albert Gallatin to Hannah Gallatin, 29 June 1808, *LAG,* 373; Fabius, *Pittsburgh Gazette*, 20 July 1808; Rao, *National Duties*, 139–40.

59. William Bentley, *The Diary of William Bentley, D.D.* (4 vols.; Salem, MA: Essex Institute, 1905–14), 3:402; Gallatin to Jefferson, 31 December 1807, 21 March 1808; Jefferson to Gallatin, 31 March 1808, *FOL*—Early Access; Jefferson to Gallatin, 6 May 1808, *WAG,* 1:385–86; Acts of 9 January 1808, 12 March 1808, 22 April 1808, and 25 April 1808, *Statutes at Large* 2 (1845): 453–54, 473–75, 490, 499–502; White, *The Jeffersonians*, 426–32; Jerry L. Mashaw, *Creating the Administrative Constitution: The Lost One Hundred Years of American Administrative Law* (New Haven, CT: Yale University Press, 2012), 99–101.

60. Dallas to Gallatin, 30 July 1808; Silas Lee to Gallatin, 3 January 1812; Gallatin to Dallas, 12 December 1815, *PAG;* White, *The Jeffersonians*, 139, 153-58; Mashaw, *Creating the Administrative Constitution*, 108–12; Rao, *National Duties*, 102, 133-54; Douglas Lamar Jones, "'The Caprice of Juries': The Enforcement of the Jeffersonian Embargo in Massachusetts," *American Journal of Legal History* 24, no. 4 (October 1980): 310–14; Mashaw, "Reluctant Nationalists: Federal Administration and Administrative Law in the Republican Era, 1801–1829," *Yale Law Journal* 116, no. 8 (June 2007): 1660–74.

61.   Gallatin, Circular to Collectors, 28 April 1808, *PAG;* Gallatin to
      Jefferson, 16 March, 5 May, 23 May, 15 July 1808; Jefferson to Gallatin,
      16 May 1808, *WAG,* 1:377–79, 384, 390–92, 394, 389–90; Jefferson to
      Gallatin, 27 May 1808, L&B, 12:66–67; *Ex parte Gilchrist,* 10 F. Cas.
      355 (C. C. D. S. C. 1808); Act of 25 April 1808, sec. 11, *Statutes at Large*
      2 (1845): 501; White, *The Jeffersonians,* 431, 438–42; Mashaw, *Creating
      the Administrative Constitution,* 101, 107–08. Federal judicial
      interference with embargo enforcement confirmed Jefferson's suspicions
      about the Federalist-dominated courts, but the courts' rulings on the
      embargo actually were much more principled than Jefferson was willing
      to admit. It was a Federalist judge in Massachusetts, for example, who
      rejected the claim that the entire embargo was unconstitutional. *In re The
      William,* 28 F. Cas. 614 (D. Mass. 1808) (Davis, J.); Richard E. Ellis, *The
      Jeffersonian Crisis: Courts and Politics in the Young Republic* (New
      York: Oxford University Press, 1971), 25–35; Mashaw, *Creating the
      Administrative Constitution,* 105–08; Jones, "The Caprice of Juries,"
      321–29.
62.   Gallatin to Phineas Manning, 13 April 1808; Lewis F. Delesdernier to
      Gallatin, 8 June 1808; Gallatin to Delesdernier, 7 March, 29 March, and
      7 April 1808; Gallatin to Jefferson, 14 February 1808; Gallatin to David
      Gelston, 7 March 1808, *PAG;* Gallatin to Jefferson, 6, 9, and 17 August
      1808, *WAG,* 1:401–02, 402–05, 405–07; Nathaniel Atcheson, *American
      Encroachment on British Rights...* (London, 1808), xv–xvii (American
      smuggling in Passamaquoddy Bay); Sears, *Jefferson and the Embargo,*
      167–71; Leonard W. Levy, *Jefferson and Civil Liberties: The Darker Side*
      (Cambridge, MA: Harvard University Press, 1963), 93–120; Joshua M.
      Smith, *Borderland Smuggling: Patriots, Loyalists, and Illicit Trade in the
      Northeast, 1783–1820* (Gainesville: University Press of Florida, 2006),
      22–23, 43–45, 49–65; Rao, *National Duties,* 144, 154; E. C. Royle,
      *Pioneer, Patriot, and Rebel: Lewis Delesdernier of Nova Scotia and
      Maine, 1752–1838,* 2nd ed. (Hudson Heights, Quebec: n. p., 1976), L-22,
      L-26.
63.   Gallatin to Jefferson, 29 July 1808, *WAG,* 1:398–99; Albert Gallatin to
      Hannah Gallatin, 7 July 1802, *LAG,* 304; White, *The Jeffersonians,*
      461–62.
64.   Jefferson to Gallatin, 11 August 1808, *WTJ,* 11:41; Gallatin to Jefferson,
      28 December 1808, *WAG,* 1:447–48; Levy, *Jefferson and Civil Liberties,*
      121–41; Tucker and Hendrickson, *Empire of Liberty,* 222–24. Madison,

who had pushed for the embargo, kept his distance from the ugliness of enforcing it. Madison to Gallatin, 31 August 1808, *FOL*—Early Access.

65. Ezekiel Bacon to Gallatin, 22 August, 1808; Dallas to Gallatin, 30 July 1808, *PAG;* Ammon, *James Monroe,* 264–77; Ketcham, *James Madison,* 466-68; Andrew Burstein and Nancy Isenberg, *Madison and Jefferson* (New York: Random House, 2010), 457–63; David O. Stewart, *Madison's Gift: Five Partnerships That Built America* (New York: Simon and Schuster, 2015), 192–202, 222–25.

66. Gallatin to Madison, 9 September 1808, *FOL*—Early Access; Gallatin to Joseph H. Nicholson, 18 October 1808, JHNP; Gallatin, State of the Finances, 10 December 1808, *ASP: Finance,* 2:307, 310–13; Seybert, *Statistical Annals,* 146–47, 256–57, 454; Dewey, *Financial History of the United States,* 126; Sears, *Jefferson and the Embargo,* 397–452; Jeffrey A. Frankel, "The 1807–1808 Embargo against Great Britain," *Journal of Economic History* 42, no. 2 (June 1982): 294-308. "The [American] embargo," crowed a leading British proponent of trade restrictions, "has most effectually re-established our carrying trade, and it has, more especially, forwarded the re-establishment of our navigation and colonial system." Lord Sheffield, *The Orders in Council and the American Embargo…*(London, 1809), 38.

67. Gallatin to Jefferson, 15 November 1808, *WAG,* 1:428; Jefferson to Monroe, 28 January 1809, *WTJ,* 11:96; Jefferson, Eighth Annual Message, 8 November 1808, Richardson, *Messages and Papers,* 1:451–53; Jefferson to Levi Lincoln, 13 November 1808; Jefferson to Charles Thomson, 25 December 1808, *WTJ,* 11:77–75, 84; Jefferson to George Logan, 27 December 1808; Jefferson to Leiper, 21 January 1809, L&B, 12:219–20, 237; Malone, *Jefferson and His Time,* 5:622–26, 629–32.

68. Gallatin to Charles Pinckney, 24 October 1808 (contains phrases later used in Campbell's Report); Gallatin, Draft of Campbell's Report, [before 22 November 1808], *PAG;* Gallatin, State of the Finances, 16 December 1808, *ASP: Finance,* 2:307–16; Robert Smith to Jefferson, 1 November 1808 (for war), *FOL*—Early Access; Brant, *James Madison,* 4:470–72.

69. George Washington Campbell [written by Gallatin], Report on Foreign Relations (known as "Campbell's Report"), 22 November 1808, *ASP: Foreign Relations,* 3:259–62 (quoted at 261); Gallatin, State of the Finances, 16 December 1808, 2:308-09.

70. Macon to Joseph H. Nicholson, 4 December 1808, JHNP; Gallatin to Nicholson, 29 December, 1808, *WAG,* 1:449; James Bayard to Andrew Bayard, 19 January 1809, PJAB, 2:174–75; William Branch Giles to

Gallatin, 12 and 14 November 1808, *PAG;* Gallatin to Giles, 24 November 1808, *WAG,* 1:428–35; *Annals,* 10ᵗʰ Cong., 2ⁿᵈ Sess., 231–36, 241–98, 310–19, 514–895, 903–04, 910–12; C[harles] B[rockden] Brown to Gallatin, 12 January 1809, *PAG;* [Charles Brockden Brown], *An Address to the Congress of the United States on the Utility and Justice of Restrictions upon Foreign Commerce* (Philadelphia, 1809), 28–37 (criticizes Campbell's Report); Spivak, *Jefferson's English Crisis,* 177–80.

71.　On the naval deployment bill, see *Annals,* 10ᵗʰ Cong., 2ⁿᵈ Sess., 238–39, 304–05, 306, 328–29, 336–37, 1031–40 (cost estimate, 1033), 1042–54, 1095–96, 1184–88, 1191–92; Robert Smith to Roger Nelson, 7 December 1808; Smith to Giles, 16 December 1808, *ASP: Naval Affairs,* 1:184–86, 186; Act of 31 January 1809, *Statutes at Large* 2 (1845): 514; Smith to Gallatin, 10 February 1809, *PAG.* On repeal of the embargo, see *Annals,* 345, 353–87, 1172, 1230–40, 1426–29, 1523–36; Gallatin, Memorandum on repeal of embargo, [January 1809]; Gallatin, Notes on political situation, February 1809; Gallatin, Notes on embargo modification [embargo replacement], February 1809; [Madison], Draft resolution on repeal of embargo (with Gallatin's annotations), 9 February 1809, *PAG.* Gallatin reacted to the naval deployment bill by renewing his old proposal to make the army and navy settle their accounts directly with the Treasury rather than separate auditors in the War and Navy departments. But Robert Smith sent Giles a long letter claiming that Gallatin's proposal was impractical, Giles published the letter as a report to the Senate, and the Congress allowed the army and navy to continue settling their own accounts. Gallatin to George Washington Campbell, 4 February 1809, *PAG; Annals,* 10ᵗʰ Cong., 2ⁿᵈ Sess., 437, 443, 450–55, 461, 1575; Smith to Giles, 25 February 1809, *ASP: Finance,* 2:348–50; Act of 3 March 1809, *Statutes at Large* 2 (1845): 535–37.

72.　*Annals,* 10ᵗʰ Cong., 2ⁿᵈ Sess., 1249 (Orchard Cook; quoted), 1475-87 (Campbell), 1487-92 (Macon); Jefferson to Thomas Mann Randolph, 7 February 1809, *FOL*—Early Access; Act of 1 March 1809, sec. 19, *Statutes at Large* 2 (1845): 533; Weymouth T. Jordan, *George Washington Campbell of Tennessee: Western Statesman* (Tallahassee: Florida State University Press, 1955), 76–86; Spivak, *Jefferson's English Crisis,* 192; Richard Buel Jr., *America on the Brink: How the Political Struggle over the War of 1812 Almost Destroyed the Young Republic* (New York: Palgrave Macmillan, 2005), 61–72, 79–87.

73.　Gallatin, List of "The Navy Coalition of 1809," [January 1809], *PAG,* printed in *LAG,* 387–88; Gallatin to Maria Nicholson, 31 January 1809,

PAG; Gallatin to Madison, 18 May 1809, *PJM-PS,* 1:191; Robert Smith to Jefferson, 10 September 1805, *FOL*—Early Access (arguing for full deployment of the navy).

74. Few, Journal, 11 October 1808, in Cunningham, "Diary of Frances Few," 351 ("Mr. Madison the President-elect is a small man quite devoid of dignity in his appearance—he bows very low and never looks at the person to whom he is bowing but keeps his eyes on the ground"); Brant, *James Madison,* 4:419–26; Ketcham, *James Madison,* 466–69; Malone, *Jefferson and His Time,* 5:643–49; Robert Allen Rutland, *The Presidency of James Madison* (Lawrence: University Press of Kansas, 1990), 5–18; Burstein and Isenberg, *Madison and Jefferson,* 476–79.

75. Giles to Madison, [about 15] February and 27 February 1809; John Quincy Adams to John Adams, 24 December 1804, *FOL*—Early Access; Thomas Hart Benton, *Thirty Years' View; or, A History of the Working of the American Government for Thirty Years* (2 vols.; New York, 1854), 1:683 (describes Giles); Dice Robins Anderson, *William Branch Giles: A Study in the Politics of Virginia and the Nation from 1790 to 1830* (1914; repr., Gloucester, MA: Peter Smith, 1965), 146–49; Ketcham, *James Madison,* 481–82; Mary A. Giunta, "The Public Life of William Branch Giles, Republican, 1790–1815" (Ph.D. diss., Catholic University, 1980), 98–110.

76. John Randolph to Monroe, 1 January 1809, James Monroe Papers, DLC; Wilson Cary Nicholas to Madison, 3 March 1809, *PJM-PS,* 1:10–11; Robert Smith, *Address to the People of the United States* (Baltimore, 1811), 37; Irving Brant, *James Madison,* vol. 5, *James Madison: The President, 1809–1812* (Indianapolis: Bobbs-Merrill, 1956), 23-25; Cassell, *Merchant Congressman,* 144–47; Egan, *Neither Peace Nor War,* 134–35; Armstrong, *Politics, Diplomacy, and Intrigue,* 93–96; John S. Pancake, "The 'Invisibles': A Chapter in the Opposition to President Madison," *Journal of Southern History* 21, no. 1 (February 1955), 27–28; Stephen J. Barry, "Nathaniel Macon: The Prophet of Pure Republicanism, 1758–1837" (Ph.D. diss., State University of New York at Buffalo, 1996), 134–35.

77. Few, Journal, 25 February 1809 ("squeeze"), in Cunningham, "Diary of Frances Few," 360; Margaret Bayard Smith to Susan Bayard Smith, 26 February 1809, Gaillard Hunt, ed., *The First Forty Years of Washington Society* (New York: Charles Scribner's Sons, 1906), 56–57; Barbara G. Carson, *Ambitious Appetites: Dining, Behavior, and Patterns of Consumption in Federal Washington* (Washington, DC: American

Institute of Architects Press, 1990), 124–30; Catherine Allgor, *Parlor Politics: In Which the Ladies of Washington Help Build a City and a Government* (Charlottesville: University Press of Virginia, 2000), 64–82.

78. Few, Journal, 21 December 1808 (frequent visitors), in Cunningham, "Diary of Frances Few," 354–55; Gallatin to Jefferson, 11 November 1809, *PTJ-RS,* 1:664–66; Albert Gallatin to Hannah Gallatin, 23 May 1829, *LAG,* 633 ("Was I not postponed to make room for Robert Smith, even when in my prime and with Mr. Jefferson and Mr. Madison to sustain me?").

79. Gallatin to Joseph H. Nicholson, 23 March (quoted), 11 May (quoted), 24 March, 8 April, 20 April 1809; Gallatin to Thomas Worthington, 18 April 1809; Nicholson to Gallatin, 4 May and 16 October 1809; Worthington to Gallatin, 2 May 1809; Gallatin to John Montgomery, 6 April 1809; Dallas to Gallatin, 19 October 1809; Gallatin to Maria Montgomery [Maria Nicholson], 28 October 1809, *PAG.*

80. Gallatin to John Badollet, 12 May 1809, *CBG,* 106.

Chapter 8: Republicans at War

1. Thomas Jefferson to James Madison, 17 August 1809 (quoted); Madison to Jefferson, 16 and 23 August 1809; Jefferson to William Thornton, 24 August 1809, *PTJ-RS,* 1:441, 437–39, 464, 465–66; Margaret Bayard Smith's account of a visit to Monticello, [29 July–2 August] 1809, ibid., 1:386–401; Albert Gallatin to John Montgomery, 12 July 1809, *PAG;* Jack McLaughlin, *Jefferson and Monticello: The Biography of a Builder* (New York: Henry Holt, 1988), 209–13, 354–55; Catherine Allgor, "Margaret Bayard Smith's 1809 Journey to Monticello and Montpelier: The Politics of Performance in the Early Republic," *Early American Studies* 10, no. 1 (Winter 2012): 30–68.

2. Gallatin to Jefferson, 19 May 1806, *WAG,* 1:299; Adden Nicholson to Maria Nicholson, 19 May 1806, *PAG;* Jefferson to Martha Randolph, 16 June 1806, Edwin Morris Betts and James A. Bear Jr., eds., *The Family Letters of Thomas Jefferson* (Columbia: University of Missouri Press, 1966), 284-85; Anne Cary Randolph to Jefferson, 4 July 1806, *FOL –* Early Access; Gallatin to Joseph H. Nicholson, 23 and 24 March, 8 and 20 April, 11 May 1809, JHNP; Gallatin to Montgomery, 6 April 1809; Nicholson to Gallatin, 14 May 1809; Gallatin to Thomas Worthington, 9 September 1809; Alexander J. Dallas to Gallatin, 19 October 1809, *PAG;* Gallatin to Madison, 11 September 1809, *PJM-PS,* 1:371-72.

3. Jefferson to Gallatin, 11 October 1809, *PTJ-RS*, 1:597–99. Jefferson expected Gallatin to show his letter to members of Congress as a testament of Jefferson's support and confidence. The following summer, a writer to the Philadelphia *Aurora* complained that Gallatin had gone to see Jefferson only because "he knew very well that Mr. Jefferson would advise him to remain" at the Treasury. Philadelphia *Aurora General Advertiser,* 8 August 1810 (Zeno); Joanne B. Freeman, *Affairs of Honor: National Politics in the New Republic* (New Haven, CT: Yale University Press, 2001), 114-16. But Jefferson's expressed hope that Madison and Gallatin could repay the public debt was an honest extension of the unconsummated longing for "peace, economy, and riddance of public debt" with which he had ended his own administration. Jefferson to John W. Eppes, 11 September 1813, *PTJ-RS*, 6:491.

4. By the time Gallatin replied to Jefferson's letter, workmen were already refreshing the plaster, paint, and wallpaper at his rented house on Capitol Hill. Hannah Gallatin to Frances Few, 9 November 1809, *PAG*.

5. Gallatin to Jefferson, 11 November 1809, *PTJ-RS*, 1:664–66.

6. John Taylor to James Monroe, 15 January 1809, LJT, 299; Gallatin, State of the Finances, 5 November 1807, 16 December 1808, and 7 December 1809, *ASP: Finance*, 2:248–49, 309, 373–74.

7. Madison, Proclamation, 19 April 1809, *PJM-PS*, 1:125–26; Jefferson to Madison, 27 April 1809, *PTJ-RS*, 1:168–70; Matthew Lyon to Gallatin, 13 September 1809, *PAG* ("I think our Cabinet has out witted Poor Erskine"); Irving Brant, *James Madison*, vol. 5, *James Madison: The President, 1809–1812* (Indianapolis: Bobbs-Merrill, 1956), 34–50; Bradford Perkins, *Prologue to War: England and the United States, 1805–1812* (Berkeley: University of California Press, 1961), 103–04, 210–20.

8. Rufus King to Jonathan Trumbull Jr., 24 April 1809, quoted in Perkins, *Prologue to War*, 218–19. The British government published Erskine's dispatches, one of which said Gallatin had insinuated that the new administration was more open to compromise because Madison—unlike Jefferson—was not an Anglophobe. Gallatin sent the *National Intelligencer* a letter denying that he had implied what Erskine reported, but William Duane's *Aurora* kept mentioning Erskine's statement throughout the summer of 1810. By August, Jefferson felt obliged to reassure Gallatin that Erskine's statement had not affected their relationship. David M. Erskine to George Canning, 4 December 1808, U. K. National Archives, FO 5/58; Gallatin to National Intelligencer, 21 April

1810, Washington *National Intelligencer,* 18 July 1810; Philadelphia *Aurora General Advertiser,* 14 June, 20, 23, 24, 27, 28, 30, and 31 July, 1 and 6 August 1810; Richmond *Enquirer,* 24 July 1810; Jefferson to Gallatin, 16 August 1810, *PTJ-RS,* 3:30–32.

9. Gallatin to Montgomery, 27 July 1809, *PAG;* Gallatin to Madison, 24, 26, and 31 July 1809; Madison to Gallatin, 28 and 30 July 1809; Madison to Jefferson, 16 August 1809, *PJM-PS,* 1:299, 306, 313, 309–10, 311, 437-39; Madison, Proclamation, 9 August 1809, ibid., 1:320–21; Gallatin, Treasury Circular, 9 August 1809, *ASP: Foreign Affairs,* 3:304; Robert Smith to Erskine, 9 August 1809; Erskine to Smith, 14 August 1809; Gallatin to Erskine, 13 August 1809; Erskine to Gallatin, 15 August 1809, ibid., 3:304–05, 305–06, 307, 307–08.

10. Nathaniel Macon to Joseph H. Nicholson, 23 May (first of two letters) and 23 June 1809, JHNP; Frank A. Cassell, *Merchant Congressman in the Young Republic: Samuel Smith of Maryland, 1752–1839* (Madison: University of Wisconsin Press, 1971), 147–53, 162–64; Thom M. Armstrong, *Politics, Diplomacy, and Intrigue in the Early Republic: The Cabinet Career of Robert Smith, 1801–1811* (Dubuque, IA: Kendall/ Hunt Publishing, 1991), 97–102; John S. Pancake, "The 'Invisibles': A Chapter in the Opposition to President Madison," *Journal of Southern History* 21, no. 1 (February 1955): 17–37; J. C. A. Stagg, "James Madison and the 'Malcontents': The Political Origins of the War of 1812," *William and Mary Quarterly,* 3rd ser., 33, no. 4 (October 1976): 561–64.

11. Gallatin to Samuel Smith, 29 June 1809; Broadside, "General Smith's Bills of Exchange Exposed," [30 June 1809], *PAG;* Thomas Cooper, *Lectures on the Elements of Political Economy,* 2nd ed. (1830; repr., New York: Augustus M. Kelley, 1971), 187–88 (bills of exchange); Bruce H. Mann, *Republic of Debtors: Bankruptcy in the Age of American Independence* (Cambridge, MA: Harvard University Press, 2002), 11–12.

12. Joseph H. Nicholson to Gallatin, 14 May and 21 June 1809; Gallatin to John Randolph, 26 and 27 June 1809, *PAG;* Macon to Nicholson, 23, 24, 25, and 27 May, 2, 6, 20, and 23 June 1809, JHNP; Alexander J. Dallas to Gallatin, 1 January 1810, *PAG; Annals,* 11th Cong., 1st Sess., 63-73, 448; Cassell, *Merchant Congressman,* 151–52; John Pancake, *Samuel Smith and the Politics of Business, 1752–1839* (Tuscaloosa: University of Alabama Press, 1972), 93–94.

13. Robert Smith to [Gallatin?], 28 June 1809; Samuel Smith to Gallatin, 26 June 1809; Gallatin to Samuel Smith, 29 June 1809, *PAG;* Samuel Smith

to Jefferson, 23 July 1809; William Burwell to Jefferson, 16 February 1810, *PTJ-RS*, 1:361, 2:224–25.

14. Gallatin, Report on the Bank of the United States, 2 March 1809, *ASP: Finance*, 2:351–53; Cassell, *Merchant Congressman*, 165–70; James O. Wettereau, "New Light on the First Bank of the United States," *Pennsylvania Magazine of History and Biography* 61, no. 3 (July 1937): 269, 279–82; Wettereau, "The Branches of the First Bank of the United States," *Journal of Economic History* 2, Suppl. (December 1942): 91, 96–98. On Gallatin's decision to sell shares in the Bank of the United States to Barings, see Minutes of the commissioners of the sinking fund, 7 June 1802; Gallatin, Report on the sinking fund, 3 February 1803, *ASP: Finance*, 2:9, 23-24; Gallatin to Thomas Willing, 12 June 1802; Gallatin to King, 17 June 1802, *PAG*. The Bank had petitioned for re-charter in the spring of 1808 despite Gallatin's warning not to raise the issue until after the autumn presidential election. Gallatin to Thomas Willing, 25 November 1807, *PAG*; Samuel Breck to Congress, 20 April 1808 (date delivered), *ASP: Finance*, 2:301.

15. George Harrison to Samuel Smith, 19 March (quoted) and 10 March 1810; Smith to Harrison, 11, 13, and 15 March 1810; Adam Seybert and Edward Livingston to Smith, 10 April 1810; Gabriel Duvall to Smith, 16 April 1810; Joseph Story to Smith, 18 April 1810, Samuel Smith Family Papers, General Correspondence, 1801–14, DLC.

16. Stuart Bruchey, *Enterprise: The Dynamic Economy of a Free People* (Cambridge, MA: Harvard University Press, 1990), 171–74; Edwin J. Perkins, *American Public Finance and Financial Services, 1700-1815* (Columbus: Ohio State University Press, 1994), 272–76; Robert E. Wright, *Origins of Commercial Banking in America, 1750–1800* (Lanham, MD: Rowman and Littlefield, 2001), 149–66; Howard Bodenhorn, *State Banking in Early America: A New Economic History* (New York: Oxford University Press, 2003), 13–18, 45–62; Brian Phillips Murphy, *Building the Empire State: Political Economy in the Early Republic* (Philadelphia: University of Pennsylvania Press, 2015), 76–109; Andrew Shankman, "'A New Thing on Earth': Alexander Hamilton, Pro-Manufacturing Republicans, and the Democratization of American Political Economy," *Journal of the Early Republic* 23, no. 3 (Autumn 2003): 340–41. Gallatin later estimated that the state banks' capital in 1811 was only $42.6 million. Albert Gallatin, *Considerations on the Currency and Banking System of the Unites States* (Philadelphia, 1831), reprinted in *WAG*, 3:285–86.

17. Samuel Smith to Madison, 8 August 1810; Madison to Gallatin, 14 August 1810; Gallatin to Madison, 21 August 1810; Madison to Smith, 29 August 1810, *PJM-PS*, 2:470-72, 483, 499, 514–15; Gautham Rao, *National Duties: Custom Houses and the Making of the American State* (Chicago: University of Chicago Press, 2016), 81–84.

18. Gallatin, Report on the Bank of the United States, 2:351–53; Erick Bollman, *Paragraphs on Banks*, 2nd ed. (Philadelphia, 1811), 59, 89–106, 116–17; Mathew Carey, *Desultory Reflections upon the Ruinous Consequences of a Non-Renewal of the Charter of the Bank of the United States* (Philadelphia, 1810); Carey, *Nine Letters to Dr. Adam Seybert...*, 2nd ed. (Philadelphia, 1811); Wettereau, "New Light on the First Bank," 268; Edward C. Carter II, "The Birth of a Political Economist: Mathew Carey and the Recharter Fight of 1810–1811," *Pennsylvania History* 33, no. 3 (July 1966): 274–88; Lester B. McAllister Jr., "Monetary and Banking Theories of Albert Gallatin" (Ph.D. diss., University of Oregon, 1953), 234–65.

19. Gallatin, Report on the Bank of the United States, 3 April 1810, *ASP: Finance*, 2:417–18; Gallatin to Montgomery (chair, House committee on Bank petition for re-charter), 12 February 1810, *PAG;* Macon to Worthington, 9 April 1810, Miscellaneous Manuscripts, Small Special Collections Library, University of Virginia; David Lenox (President, Bank of the United States) to Congress, 10 December 1810; Condy Raguet (Philadelphia Chamber of Commerce) to Congress, 24 December 1810; M[atthew] Clarkson (President, Bank of New York) to Congress, 8 January 1811, *ASP: Finance*, 2:451–52, 453–54, 460; Fritz Redlich, *The Molding of American Banking: Men and Ideas* (1951; 2 parts; repr., Mansfield Center, CT: Martino Publishing, 2012), 1:100; Richard H. Timberlake Jr., *The Origins of Central Banking in the United States* (Cambridge, MA: Harvard University Press, 1978), 8-11; Edward S. Kaplan, *The Bank of the United States and the American Economy* (Westport, CT: Greenwood Press, 1999), 28–33; John H. Wood, *A History of Central Banking in Great Britain and the United States* (New York: Cambridge University Press, 2005), 13–30, 123–55.

20. Washington *Daily National Intelligencer,* 29 November 1814 ("conscientiously opposed"); *Annals,* 11th Cong., 3rd Sess., 488–93, 580–95.

21. Macon to Joseph H. Nicholson, 28 January (quoted), 16, 17, and 18 January 1811, JHNP; William Duane to Henry Dearborn, 3 July 1810, Worthington C. Ford, ed., "Letters of William Duane," *Proceedings of*

the *Massachusetts Historical Society* 20 (May–June 1906): 337; The Treasury Nos. I–IX, Philadelphia *Aurora General Advertiser*, 20–31 December 1810; The Bank Charter and Gallatin Nos. I-III, ibid., 13–15 February 1811; Resolution of Pennsylvania General Assembly, 11 January 1811; Resolution of Virginia General Assembly, 22 January 1811, *ASP: Finance*, 2:467, 470; *Annals*, 11ᵗʰ Cong., 3ʳᵈ Sess., 618–25, 680–85, 700–05, 779–86, 805–07, 824, 826; Brant, *James Madison*, 5:265–70; Norman K. Risjord, *The Old Republicans: Southern Conservatism in the Age of Jefferson* (New York: Columbia University Press, 1965), 110–16; Robert Allen Rutland, *The Presidency of James Madison* (Lawrence: University Press of Kansas, 1990), 68–70; Kim Tousley Phillips, "William Duane, Revolutionary Editor" (Ph.D. diss., University of California, Berkeley, 1968), 329–35. Gallatin mistakenly believed that Robert Smith wrote many of the newspaper attacks on him. James A. Bayard, European Diary, 13 November 1813, PJAB, 2:484–85.

22.   William H. Crawford to Gallatin, 29 January 1811; Gallatin to Crawford, 30 January 1811, *ASP: Finance*, 2:480, 481; Chase C. Mooney, *William H. Crawford, 1771–1834* (Lexington: University Press of Kentucky, 1974), 2–13.

23.   *Annals*, 11ᵗʰ Cong., 3ʳᵈ Sess., 122, 134–50 (quoted at 149 and 142).

24.   *Annals*, 11ᵗʰ Cong., 3ʳᵈ Sess., 209–19 (quoted at 210, 217, 211, 218), 361; Bernard Mayo, *Henry Clay: Spokesman of the New West* (Boston: Houghton Mifflin, 1937), 374–78; Robert V. Remini, *Henry Clay: Spokesman for the Union* (New York: W. W. Norton, 1991), 12–13, 68–71.

25.   Macon to Joseph H. Nicholson, 28 January (quoted), 14, and 20 February 1811, JHNP; Samuel Taggart to John Taylor, 4 February 1811, George H. Haynes, ed., "Letters of Samuel Taggart: Representative in Congress from 1803 to 1814, Part II, 1808–1814," *Proceedings of the American Antiquarian Society*, [New Ser.] 33 (October 1923): 354; King to Timothy Pickering, 24 February 1811, *LCRK*, 5: 241; *Annals*, 11ᵗʰ Cong., 3ʳᵈ Sess., 346–47; John P. Kaminski, *George Clinton: Yeoman Politician of the New Republic* (Madison, WI: Madison House, 1993), 289–90. Twenty years later, Gallatin attributed the Bank's defeat to "the *personal* opposition to Mr. Madison or myself of the Clintons, the Maryland Smiths, Leib, and Giles." He claimed the state banking system was not then well enough developed to account for the passionate opposition to the Bank, and he laid no blame on Madison. Gallatin to Nicholas Biddle, 14 August 1830; Gallatin to Robert Porter, 3 December 1830, *WAG*,

2:435, 441. Madison's most exhaustive biographer attributes Madison's failure to give the Bank his open support to his "lifelong unwillingness to make a public display of political inconsistency." A recent study of Madison's serial revisions to his notes on the federal constitutional convention exposes the depths of this obsession. Brant, *James Madison,* 5:269; Madison to Charles J[ared] Ingersoll, 25 June 1831, M. St. Clair Clarke and D.A. Hall, eds., *Documentary and Legislative History of the Bank of the United States* (Washington, DC, 1832), 779 (refutes charge of "inconsistency" on the Bank question); Mary Sarah Bilder, *Madison's Hand: Revising the Constitutional Convention* (Cambridge, MA: Harvard University Press, 2015).

26.   Robert Smith to [Samuel Smith], 12 March 1811, Samuel Smith Family Papers, General Correspondence, 1801–14, DLC; *Baltimore Whig,* 6 March 1811; Joseph H. Nicholson to Gallatin, 6 March 1811, *PAG;* Gabriel Duval to Gallatin, 7 January 1811; Gallatin to Joseph B. Varnum, 20 February 1811 (Leghorn report), *PAG;* John W. Eppes to Samuel Smith, 7 February 1811, Samuel Smith Family Papers, General Correspondence, 1801–14, DLC; *Annals,* 11th Cong., 3rd Sess., 464–65, 467, 982; J. H. Powell, *Richard Rush* (Philadelphia: University of Pennsylvania Press, 1942), 14–15; Brant, *James Madison,* 5:273–83.

27.   Randolph to Joseph H. Nicholson, 17 February (quoted) and 14 February (two letters) 1811; Crawford to Nicholson, 1 March 1811; Macon to Nicholson, 9 February, 1811, JHNP; Nicholson to Gallatin, 4 and 5 March 1811, *PAG; Annals,* 11th Cong., 3rd Sess., 464–65, 467, 982; Ralph Ketcham, *James Madison: A Biography* (1971; University Press of Virginia, 1990), 483–90. Gallatin drafted a resignation letter, but Madison's surviving papers contain no copy of it. Gallatin probably never sent it. He and Madison often spoke in person about contentious matters that he and Jefferson would have handled in writing. Gallatin to Madison, [4 March 1811] (draft), *PAG,* printed in *WAG,* 1:495–96 and *PJM-PS,* 3:208–09 (where dated c. 7 March 1811).

28.   John Taylor to Monroe, 21 March (quoted) and 24 March 1811, LJT, 320–21, 321–24; Richard Brent to Monroe, [8–12 March] 1811; Monroe to Brent, 18 March 1811, Daniel Preston, ed., *The Papers of James Monroe: Selected Correspondence and Papers* (6 vols. to date; Santa Barbara, CA: Greenwood, 2003-), 5:797, 800–801; Brent to Gallatin, 22 March 1811 (enclosing Monroe to Brent, 18 March 1811), *WAG,* 1:496–98; Randolph to Joseph H. Nicholson, 16 March 1811, JHNP; Madison to Monroe, 20 March 1811, *PJM-PS,* 3:226–27; Risjord, *The Old*

Republicans, 116–19; Harry Ammon, *James Monroe: The Quest for National Identity* (1971; Charlottesville: University Press of Virginia, 1990), 277–88; David O. Stewart, *Madison's Gift: Five Partnerships That Built America* (New York: Simon and Schuster, 2015), 230, 238–40.

29. Philadelphia *Aurora General Advertiser*, 8 April (quoted) and 3 April 1811; Taggart to John Taylor, 23 April 1811, Haynes, "Letters of Samuel Taggart," 359; Gallatin to Joseph H. Nicholson, 30 May 1811, JHNP; Madison, Memorandum on Robert Smith, [11] April 1811, *PJM-PS*, 3:255–65; John Smith [senator from New York] to Gallatin, 15 April 1811, *PAG*; Robert Smith, *Address to the People of the United States* (Baltimore, 1811). Jefferson warned Duane that his attacks on Gallatin were damaging the Republican party, and he tried to relieve the financial hardship that stoked Duane's hostility. But Madison finally told Jefferson his efforts were useless. On the subject of Gallatin, wrote Madison, Duane "seems to be incorrigible." Jefferson to Duane, 28 March and 30 April 1811; Jefferson to Gallatin, 24 April 1811; Jefferson to Madison, 24 April 1811; Jefferson to William Wirt, 30 March and 3 May 1811; Madison to Jefferson, 7 June 1811, *PTJ-RS*, 3:506–09, 591–94, 584; 585–86, 515, 601–04, 638–39; Brant, *James Madison*, 5:291–96, 307; Andrew Burstein and Nancy Isenberg, *Madison and Jefferson* (New York: Random House, 2010), 496–98; Phillips, "William Duane," 335–44.

30. Frank A. Updyke, *The Diplomacy of the War of 1812* (1915; repr., Gloucester, MA: Peter Smith, 1965), 111–16; Anna C. Clauder, *American Commerce as Affected by the Wars of the French Revolution and Napoleon, 1793–1812* (1932; repr., Clifton, NY: Augustus M. Kelley, 1972), 182–88; Perkins, *Prologue to War*, 242–60; Paul A. Gilje, *Free Trade and Sailors' Rights in the War of 1812* (New York: Cambridge University Press, 2013), 164–65.

31. Ketcham, *James Madison*, 502–06; Roger H. Brown, *The Republic in Peril: 1812* (New York: Columbia University Press, 1964), 23–25; Richard Buel Jr., *American on the Brink: How the Political Struggle over the War of 1812 Almost Destroyed the Young Republic* (New York: Palgrave Macmillan, 2005), 108–11. Gallatin was outraged to discover years later, when he was the American minister to France, that Napoleon had secretly authorized the sale of American ships detained in French ports (under the so-called Trianon Decree) at the same time he was making the apparently conciliatory offer in the Cadore letter. Gallatin to John Quincy Adams, 15 September 1821, *WAG*, 2:197–99; Perkins, *Prologue to War*, 247–48.

32.   Dall W. Forsythe, *Taxation and Political Change in the Young Nation, 1781–1833* (New York: Columbia University Press, 1977), 67–68; Gary M. Walton and James F. Shepherd, *The Economic Rise of Early America* (New York: Cambridge University Press, 1979), 182–98; Eliga H. Gould, *Among the Powers of the Earth: The American Revolution and the Making of a New World Empire* (Cambridge, MA: Harvard University Press, 2012), 119–26.

33.   Alexander Hamilton, Report on the Subject of Manufacturers, 5 December 1791; Editors' note, *PAH,* 10:230–340, 1–15; John C. Miller, *Alexander Hamilton: Portrait in Paradox* (New York: Harper and Brothers, 1959), 282–95, 298; Forrest McDonald, *Alexander Hamilton: A Biography* (New York: W. W. Norton, 1979), 232–36; Jacob E. Cooke, *Alexander Hamilton* (New York: Charles Scribner's Sons, 1982), 98–102; Stanley Elkins and Eric McKitrick, *The Age of Federalism: The Early American Republic, 1788–1800* (New York: Oxford University Press, 1993), 258–63; Stanley Karl-Friedrich Walling, *Republican Empire: Alexander Hamilton on War and Free Government* (Lawrence: University Press of Kansas, 1999), 198–208; Brian Balogh, *A Government Out of Sight: The Mystery of National Authority in Nineteenth-Century America* (New York: Cambridge University Press, 2009), 102–03.

34.   Gallatin to Jefferson, 2 November 1808, *WAG,* 1:423; Gallatin to Thomas Newton, 2 June 1809, *PAG; Annals,* 11th Cong., 1st Sess., 235–37; Louis Martin Sears, *Jefferson and the Embargo* (1927; New York: Octagon, 1966), 143–38; Douglass C. North, *The Economic Growth of the United States, 1790–1860* (Englewood Cliffs, NJ: Prentice-Hall, 1961), 56; Curtis P. Nettels, *The Emergence of a National Economy* (New York: Holt, Reinhart and Winston, 1962), 274–76; Sidney Ratner, James H. Soltow, and Richard Sylla, *The Evolution of the American Economy: Growth, Welfare, and Decision Making,* 2nd ed. (New York: Macmillan Publishing, 1993), 184–85; Lawrence A. Peskin, *Manufacturing Revolution: The Intellectual Origins of Early American Industry* (Baltimore: Johns Hopkins University Press, 2003), 49–55, 89–92, 133–38; Sven Beckert, *Empire of Cotton: A Global History* (New York: Alfred A. Knopf, 2015), 158.

35.   Jefferson, *Notes on the State of Virginia* (London, 1787), 273–75 (Query XIX); Drew R. McCoy, *The Elusive Republic: Political Economy in Jeffersonian America* (Chapel Hill: University of North Carolina Press, 1980), 13–15, 223–33; Charles Sellers, *The Market Revolution: Jacksonian America, 1815–1846* (New York: Oxford University Press,

1991), 34–40; Peskin, *Manufacturing Revolution,* 188–206; Andrew Shankman, *Crucible of American Democracy: The Struggle to Fuse Egalitarianism and Capitalism in Jeffersonian Pennsylvania* (Lawrence: University Press of Kansas, 2004), 40–73; Peter S. Onuf, *The Mind of Thomas Jefferson* (Charlottesville: University of Virginia Press, 2007), 23–27; Manuela Albertone, *National Identity and the Agrarian Republic: The Transatlantic Commerce of Ideas between America and France, 1750–1830* (Farnham, UK: Ashgate Publishing, 2014), 72–83; Caroline Winterer, *American Enlightenments: Pursuing Happiness in the Age of Reason* (New Haven, CT: Yale University Press, 2016), 209–22; Shankman, "A New Thing on Earth," 323–52. For Jefferson's growing acceptance of domestic manufacturing under the pressures of trade sanctions and war, see Jefferson to Jean-Baptiste Say, 1 February 1804, *TJW,* 1143–44; to Pierre Samuel du Pont, 15 April 1811; to Say, 2 March 1815; to Benjamin Austin, 9 January 1816, *PTJ-RS,* 3:559–61, 8:303–08, 9:333–37. For treatments of Gallatin's report on manufacturing by his modern biographers, see Raymond Walters Jr., *Albert Gallatin: Jeffersonian Financier and Diplomat* (New York: Macmillan, 1957), 235; Thomas K. McCraw, *The Founders and Finance: How Hamilton, Gallatin, and Other Immigrants Forged a New Economy* (Cambridge, MA: Harvard University Press, 2012), 261–63. The agrarian myth deluded Alexander Balinky—whose flawed critique of Gallatin's fiscal policies nevertheless remains useful—into claiming that Gallatin himself was an agrarian whose "interests and sympathies lay with the landed classes." Alexander Balinky, *Albert Gallatin: Fiscal Theories and Policies* (New Brunswick, NJ: Rutgers University Press, 1948), 74–75.

36. Gallatin to House of Representatives, 24 January 1804; Gallatin, State of the Finances, 7 November 1807 and 16 December 1808, *ASP: Finance,* 2:78, 248, 309.

37. Gallatin to Jefferson, 18 December 1807, *WAG,* 1:368; Gallatin to Madison, 28 November 1810, *PJM-PS,* 3:32–33; Gallatin to Jefferson, [19-21 November] 1802, *PTJ,* 39:18–19; same to same, 2 November 1808, *WAG,* 1:423; Macon to Joseph H. Nicholson, 21 April 1810, JHNP.

38. Gallatin, Report on Manufactures, 17 April 1810, *ASP: Finance,* 2:425–39. After receiving Gallatin's report on domestic manufactures, Congress authorized him to compile additional information as part of the 1810 census and then (when lack of funding made that impossible) to hire a third party to compile the information. Gallatin retained Tench Coxe—a Philadelphian who had worked on Hamilton's report when he was a

Federalist and remained one of the most vocal advocates for domestic manufacturing after he became a Republican—to compile the information. The Treasury finally delivered the report to Congress in 1814. Act of 1 May 1810, sec. 2, *Statutes at Large* 2 (1845): 605; Resolution of 19 March 1812, *Annals*, 12ᵗʰ Cong., 1ˢᵗ Sess., 2362–63; Gallatin to Tench Coxe, 26 June 1812, *PAG;* Digest of Manufactures, 13 January 1814, *ASP: Finance,* 2:666–812; Jacob E. Cooke, *Tench Coxe and the Early Republic* (Chapel Hill: University of North Carolina Press, 1978), 497–502; Peskin, *Manufacturing Revolution,* 156–59.

39. Gallatin, Report on Manufactures, 2:430. For the best comparative analysis of the Hamilton and Gallatin reports on manufacturing, see John R. Nelson Jr., *Liberty and Property: Political Economy and Policymaking in the New Nation, 1789–1812* (Baltimore: Johns Hopkins University Press, 1987), 3751, 150–61.

40. Gallatin, Report on Manufacturers, 2:430; Adam Smith, *An Inquiry into the Nature and Causes of the Wealth of Nations,* ed. Edwin Cannan (1789; New York: Modern Library, 1937), 420–39, 472–88; Norman Sydney Buck, *The Development of the Organization of Anglo-American Trade, 1800–1850* (1925; repr., Newton Abbot, UK: David and Charles, 1969), 104–17; Elkins and McKitrick, *The Age of Federalism,* 261. For a contrary argument that Hamilton's Report on Manufactures was at least as liberal as it was neomercantilist, see John E. Crowley, *The Privileges of Independence: Neomercantilism and the American Revolution* (Baltimore: Johns Hopkins University Press, 1993), 146–54.

41. John Rodgers to Paul Hamilton, 23 May 1811; Augustus J. Foster to Monroe, 4 September 1811; Monroe to Foster, 10 June 1812, *ASP: Foreign Relations,* 3:497–98, 472–76, 464–68; Madison, Proclamation, 24 July 1811; Madison to Gallatin, 14 September 1811, *PJM-PS,* 3:392–93, 460; Troy Bickham, *The Weight of Vengeance: The United States, the British Empire, and the War of 1812* (New York: Oxford University Press, 2012), 28–36; Joshua J. Wolf, "'The Misfortune to Get Pressed': The Impressment of American Seamen and the Ramifications on the United States, 1793–1812" (Ph.D. diss., Temple University, 2015), 267–97.

42. John Badollet to Gallatin, 6 August, 15 October, 13 and 19 November, 4 December 1811, *CBG,* 184, 197, 205–06, 207–08, 209–10; William Henry Harrison to William Eustis, 18 November and 4 December 1811, *ASP: Indian Affairs,* 1:776–80; [Badollet] to Oliver Oldschool [pseud. writer in Philadelphia *Port Folio*], 19 January 1815, *PAG;* Reginald Horsman, *The Causes of the War of 1812* (1962; New York: A. S. Barnes,

1962), 204–16; Richard White, *The Middle Ground: Indians, Empires, and Republics in the Great Lakes Region, 1650–1815* (1991; New York: Cambridge University Press, 2011), 476–517; Gregory Evans Dowd, *A Spirited Resistance: The North American Indian Struggle for Unity, 1745–1815* (Baltimore: Johns Hopkins University Press, 1992), 118–47; Anthony F. C. Wallace, *Jefferson and the Indians: The Tragic Fate of the First Americans* (Cambridge, MA: Harvard University Press, 1999), 306–17; Robert M. Owens, *Mr. Jefferson's Hammer: William Henry Harrison and the Origins of American Indian Policy* (Norman: University of Oklahoma Press, 2007), 199–223; Patrick Bottiger, "Stabbed in the Back: Vincennes, Slavery, and the Indian 'Threat,'" *Indiana Magazine of History* 107, no. 2 (June 2011): 115–18.

43. Perkins, *Prologue to War,* 282–92; Brown, *The Republic in Peril,* 44–66; Victor A. Sapio, *Pennsylvania and the War of 1812* (Lexington: University Press of Kentucky, 1970), 4, 128–31, 133–37; Gilje, *Free Trade and Sailors' Rights,* 190–96; Lawrence B. A. Hatter, "Party Like It's 1812: The War at 200," *Tennessee Historical Quarterly* 71, no. 2 (Summer 2012): 93–102.

44. Gallatin to Worthington, 22 October 1811; Worthington to Gallatin, 16 October 1811, *PAG;* Macon to Joseph H. Nicholson, 14 April 1812, JHNP; David Hackett Fischer, *The Revolution of American Conservatism: The Federalist Party in the Era of Jeffersonian Democracy* (New York: Harper and Row, 1965), 172–79; Buel, *American on the Brink,* 126–35; Donald R. Hickey, "The Federalists and the Coming of the War, 1811–1812," *Indiana Magazine of History* 75, no. 1 (March 1979): 70–88.

45. Gallatin to Madison, [1 November] 1811, *PJM-PS,* 3:535–36; Philip S. Klein, ed., "Memoirs of a Senator from Pennsylvania: Jonathan Roberts, 1771–1854," *Pennsylvania Magazine of History and Biography* 62, no. 2 (April 1938), 231; Ketcham, *James Madison,* 523–33; Brown, *The Republic in Peril,* 30–33; Norman K. Risjord, "1812: Conservatives, War Hawks, and the Nation's Honor," *William and Mary Quarterly,* 3rd Ser., 18, no. 2 (April 1961): 196–210; Roger H. Brown, "The War Hawks of 1812: An Historical Myth," *Indiana Magazine of History* 60, no. 2 (June 1964): 137–51; Norman K. Risjord, "The War Hawks and the War of 1812," ibid., 155–58.

46. *Annals,* 10th Cong., 2nd Sess., 1112 (Quincy); James A. Bayard to Andrew Bayard, 25 January 1812, PJAB, 2:189–90; Gallatin to Madison, [1

November] 1811, *PJM-PS,* 3:538; Donald R. Hickey, *The War of 1812: A Forgotten Conflict* (Urbanna: University of Illinois Press, 1989), 40.

47.   Gallatin, State of the Finances, 22 November 1811, *ASP: Finance,* 2:497; Gallatin, State of the Finances, 5 November 1807, 16 December 1808, and 7 December 1809, ibid., 2:248–49, 309, 374–75; James A. Bayard to Caesar A. Rodney, 27 February 1812, *Bulletin of the New York Public Library* 4, no. 7 (July 1900): 235 ("Congress has more respect for the people's money now than…in the time of John Adams.").

48.   E[zekiel] Bacon to Gallatin, 9 December 1811; Gallatin to Bacon, 10 January 1812, *ASP: Finance,* 2:523, 523–27; Klein, "Memoirs of a Senator from Pennsylvania: Jonathan Roberts," 237. As the administration prepared for war in the spring of 1812, Gallatin and Alexander Dallas considered a scheme for inducing foreign shareholders of the Bank of the United States to lend the federal government the money they would receive as the Bank liquidated. Dallas to Gallatin, 21 March 1812; Thomas W. Francis to Gallatin, 22 March 1812, *PAG.*

49.   *Annals,* 12th Cong., 1st Sess., 47-51 (Giles); Randolph to Joseph H. Nicholson, 17 January 1812, JHNP; James A. Bayard to Andrew Bayard, 25 January 1812, PJAB, 2:190; Madison to Jefferson, 7 February and 6 March 1812, *PJM-PS,* 4:168–70, 228–29; Andrew Jackson to Felix Grundy, 12 February 1812, Daniel Feller et al., eds., *The Papers of Andrew Jackson* (10 vols. to date; Knoxville: University of Tennessee Press, 1980–), 2:283–85. Several members who were opposed to war tried unsuccessfully to have Gallatin's report to the Ways and Means committee printed for circulation outside the House. *Annals,* 12th Cong., 1st Sess., 846–47, 1633–37, 1680–82.

50.   Philadelphia *Aurora General Advertiser,* 30 January 1812 ("The Rat—in the Treasury!"), 1 February 1812 (Mercator), 7 March, 25 and 28 January, 11 February, and 11 March 1812.

51.   Baltimore *Weekly Register,* 1 February 1812, reprinted in H[ezekiah] Niles, ed., *The Weekly Register,* 3rd ed. (1816), 1:408; *New-York Evening Post,* 23 January 1812 (*"The Budget opened at last"*); London *Times,* 22 February 1812. On Hezekiah Niles's attitudes toward Britain and war, see Nicole Eustace, *1812: War and the Passions of Patriotism* (Philadelphia: University of Pennsylvania Press, 2012), 23–24, 27–28.

52.   Madison to Congress, 9 March 1812, *ASP: Foreign Relations,* 3:545–54; Madison to Jefferson, 9 March 1812; Monroe to Jefferson, 9 March 1812, *PTJ-RS,* 4:541, 542; Edouard de Crillon to Gallatin, 16 March 1812; Gallatin to de Crillon, [March 1812]; de Crillon to Gallatin, [March 1812]

(two letters), *PAG;* Buel, *America on the Brink,* 139–41; Lawrence A. Peskin, "Conspiratorial Anglophobia and the War of 1812," *Journal of American History* 98, no. 3 (December 2011): 658–60, 663–64.

53. Gallatin to Jefferson, 10 March 1812, *PTJ-RS,* 4:547; Richard Bache [Jr.] to Gallatin, 21 February 1812; Dallas to Gallatin, 2 March 1812, *PAG.*

54. James A. Bayard to Rodney, 9 March 1810, LJAB, 41; David Parish to Gallatin, 26 December 1811; John Jacob Astor to Gallatin, 11 June 1812, *PAG;* J. C. A. Stagg, *Mr. Madison's War: Politics, Diplomacy, and Warfare in the Early American Republic, 1783-1830* (Princeton, NJ: Princeton University Press, 1983), 107–10.

55. Madison to Congress, 1 June 1812, *PJM-PS,* 4:432–39; Brant, *James Madison,* 5:470–78; J. C. A. Stagg, *The War of 1812: Conflict for a Continent* (New York: Cambridge University Press, 2012), 18–22; Jon Latimer, *1812: War with America* (Cambridge, MA: Harvard University Press, 2007), 33–34; Gilje, *Free Trade and Sailor's Rights,* 195.

56. Monroe to Gallatin, 1 June 1812, *WAG,* 1:520–21; *Annals,* 12th Cong., 1st Sess., 1546–54, 1629–38, 1679–83, 265–98; Brown, *The Republic in Peril,* 116–20; Leland R. Johnson, "The Suspense Was Hell: The Senate Vote for War in 1812," *Indiana Magazine of History* 65, no. 4 (December 1969): 247–67.

57. *Annals,* 12th Cong., 1st Sess., 1637, 297; Astor to Gallatin, 27 June 1812; Rodney to Gallatin, 30 June 1812; Joseph H. Nicholson to Gallatin, 30 June 1812, *PAG;* Monroe to John Taylor, 13 June 1812, Stanislaus Murray Hamilton, ed., *The Writings of James Monroe* (7 vols.; New York: G. P. Putnam's Sons, 1898–1903), 5:205–12; Samuel Smith to Michael Leib, 14 October 1812, Samuel Smith Family Papers, General Correspondence, 1801–14, DLC; Brown, *The Republic in Peril,* 131–57; Stagg, *Mr. Madison's War,* 111–12, 114–15; Hickey, "Federalists and the Coming of the War of 1812," 80–81; Rudolph M. Bell, "Mr. Madison's War and Long-Term Congressional Voting Behavior," *William and Mary Quarterly,* 3rd Ser., 36, no. 3 (July 1979): 373–95.

58. Gallatin to Joseph H. Nicholson, 26 June 1812; Macon to Nicholson, 10 April 1812, JHNP; Langdon Cheves to Gallatin, 9 June 1812; Gallatin to Cheves, 10 June 1812, *ASP: Finance,* 2:614; same to same, 23 June 1812, *ASP: Commerce and Navigation,* 1:931. William Duane later claimed that Gallatin's report had disguised the real cost of war so that Congress would not shrink from declaring it. Philadelphia *Aurora General Advertiser,* 31 August 1816 ("The Ruling Party").

59.   Gallatin to Bacon, 24 June 1812, *ASP: Finance*, 2:569; *Annals*, 12th
      Cong., 1st Sess., 1128–55, 1128–55, 1280–1314, 1333, 1431–32, 1493–
      1510, 1511–32, 1544–46, 1554–59; Acts of 14 March, 30 June, 1 July,
      and 6 July 1812, *Statutes at Large* 2 (1845): 694–95, 766–68, 768–69,
      784; Albert Gallatin, *The Oregon Question* (New York, 1846), App. on
      "War Expenses," reprinted in *WAG*, 3:539, 543; Albert Gallatin, *War
      Expenses* (New York, 1848), 14; Albert Gallatin, "War Expenses: The
      Subject of Capital," *Niles' National Register*, 12 February 1848, reprinted
      in Jeremiah Hughes, ed., *Niles' National Register* (Baltimore, 1848),
      73:380–83; Rafael A. Bayley, *The National Loans of the United States
      from July 4, 1776 to June 30, 1880* (Washington, DC, 1881), 48–49;
      P. G. M. Dickson, *The Financial Revolution in England: A Study in the
      Development of Public Credit, 1688–1756* (London: Macmillan, 1967),
      341-92; Klein, "Memoirs of a Senator from Pennsylvania: Jonathan
      Roberts," 237–39; Raymond W. Champagne Jr. and Thomas J. Rueter,
      "Jonathan Roberts and the 'War Hawk' Congress of 1811–1812,"
      Pennsylvania Magazine of History and Biography 104, no. 4 (October
      1980): 440–42.
60.   Gallatin to Cheves, 14 May 1812; Gallatin to Bacon, 24 June 1812;
      Gallatin, State of the Finances, 1 December 1812; Gallatin to Madison,
      22 January 1813, *ASP: Finance*, 2: 564–68, 569, 580, 600–601;
      anonymous to Gallatin, 2 May 1812, *PAG* (Boston Federalists urging
      lenders not to subscribe); Bayley, *The National Loans of the United States*,
      48; Buel, *American on the Brink*, 186.
61.   For the sustained scholarly criticism of Republican war finance, see Henry
      C. Adams, *Public Debts: An Essay in the Science of Public Finance* (New
      York, 1887), 111–26; Davis Rich Dewey, *Financial History of the United
      States*, 9th ed. (New York: Longmans, Green, 1924), 128–42; Paul
      Studenski and Herman Edward Kroos, *The Financial History of the
      United States* (1952; Washington, DC: Beard Books, 2003), 75–81;
      Nettels, *Emergence of a National Economy*, 331–34; Balinky, *Albert
      Gallatin: Fiscal Theories and Policies*, 165–212; Timberlake, *The Origins
      of Central Banking*, 13–18, 22; James D. Savage, *Balanced Budgets and
      American Politics* (Ithaca, NY: Cornell University Press, 1988), 97–99;
      Ratner, Soltow, and Sylla, *The Evolution of the American Economy*, 163,
      168–69; Perkins, *American Public Finance and Financial Services*, 324–
      48; Paul A. C. Koistinen, *Beating Plowshares into Swords: The Political
      Economy of American Warfare, 1606-1865* (Lawrence: University Press
      of Kansas, 1996), 59–60; Murray N. Rothbard, *A History of Money and*

Banking in the United States: The Colonial Era to World War II (Auburn, AL: Ludwig von Mises Institute, 2005), 72–78; Steven A. Bank, Kirk J. Stark, and Joseph J. Thorndike, *War and Taxes* (Washington, DC: Urban Institute Press, 2008), 15–20; Sheldon D. Pollack, *War, Revenue, and State Building: Financing the Development of the American State* (Ithaca, NY: Cornell University Press, 2009), 199-203; Lisa R. Morales, "The Financial History of the War of 1812" (Ph.D. diss., University of North Texas, 2009), 5–8. For an important recent reappraisal, see Max M. Edling, *A Hercules in the Cradle: War, Money, and the American State, 1783-1867* (Chicago: University of Chicago Press, 2014), 119–44.

62. Gallatin, State of the Finances, 22 November 1811, *ASP: Finance,* 2:497 ("In time of peace, [a revenue dependent on commerce] is almost sufficient to defray the expenses of a war; in time of war, it is hardly competent to support the expenses of a peace establishment."); King to Christopher Gore, 17 July 1812, *LCRK,* 5:273; Gallatin to Cheves, 9 February 1813, *ASP: Finance,* 2:613. In a response to the Ways and Means committee, Gallatin underestimated the time required to reconstruct arrangements for collecting internal revenue. Gallatin to Cheves, 12 February 1813, ibid., 614.

63. Stagg, *Mr. Madison's War,* 3, 130; Dewey, *Financial History of the United States,* 123–25; Hickey, *The War of 1812,* 90–91; Koistinen, *Beating Plowshares into Swords,* 60–62; Wade G. Dudley, *Splintering the Wooden Wall: The British Blockade of the United States, 1812–1815* (Annapolis, MD: Naval Institute Press, 2003), 38–39; Jeremy Black, *The War of 1812 in the Age of Napoleon* (Norman: University of Oklahoma Press, 2009), 11–33.

64. Gallatin to Joseph H. Nicholson, 26 June 1812, JHNP; Nicholson to Gallatin, 30 June 1812, *PAG;* Edling, *A Hercules in the Cradle,* 125–27.

65. John Taylor to Monroe, 10 May 1812, LJT, 337; *New-York Evening Post,* 28 April 1812 ("The Gallatin Loan"); Donald H. Kagan, "Monetary Aspects of the Treasury Notes of the War of 1812," *Journal of Economic History* 44, no. 1 (March 1984): 72–76.

66. Henry Clay to Thomas Bodley, 18 December 1813, James F. Hopkins et al., eds., *The Papers of Henry Clay* (11 vols.; Lexington: University of Kentucky Press, 1959–92), 1:842; Madison to Gallatin, 8 August 1812, *PJM-PS,* 5:129; Hickey, *The War of 1812,* 72–73; Rutland, *The Presidency of James Madison,* 110–11; Latimer, *1812,* 30–31; Alan Taylor, *The Civil War of 1812: American Citizens, British Subjects, Irish Rebels, and Indian Allies* (New York: Alfred A. Knopf, 2010), 132–40;

Clifford L. Egan, "The Origins of the War of 1812: Three Decades of Historical Writing," *Military Affairs* 38, no. 2 (April 1974): 772–73; J. C. A. Stagg, "Enlisted Men in the United States Army, 1812–1815: A Preliminary Survey," *William and Mary Quarterly*, 3rd Ser., 43, no. 4 (October 1986): 615–45; Stagg, "Soldiers in Peace and War: Comparative Perspectives on the Recruitment of the United States Army, 1802-1815," ibid., 57, no. 1 (January 2000): 79–120; Hatter, "Party Like It's 1812," 95–99.

67.   Jefferson to Duane, 4 August 1812, *PTJ-RS*, 5:293–94; Leonard D. White, *The Jeffersonians: A Study in Administrative History, 1801–1829* (New York: Macmillan Company, 1956), 528–36; Dumas Malone, *Jefferson and His Time*, vol. 5, *Jefferson the President: Second Term, 1805–1809* (Boston: Little Brown, 1974), 512–16; Richard H. Kohn, *Eagle and Sword: The Beginnings of the Military Establishment in America* (New York: Free Press, 1975), 279–83; Russell F. Weigley, *History of the United States Army,* enlarged ed. (Bloomington: Indiana University Press, 1984), 101–05, 109; David Alan Martin, "Mr. Jefferson's Army in Mr. Madison's War: Atrophy, Policy, and Legacy in the War of 1812" (M. A. thesis, University of Southern Mississippi, 2016), 114–22. The administration's newspaper soon acknowledged that militia "are not precisely the species of force on which to rely for carrying on war, however competent they may be to repel invasion." Washington *National Intelligencer,* 22 December 1812.

68.   Albert Gallatin to Hannah Gallatin, 31 August 1812, *LAG,* 468; Harry L. Coles, *The War of 1812* (Chicago: University of Chicago Press, 1965), 44–57; Hickey, *The War of 1812,* 80–84; Taylor, *The Civil War of 1812,* 153–66.

69.   John Jacob Astor to Gallatin, 8 and 30 June 1812; Astor to William Eustis, 8 June 1812; Daniel Sheldon to Alexander J. Dallas, 12 May 1813, *PAG;* Gallatin, "Astor and communications by the Treasury to collectors before the declaration of war," [1815?], *WAG,* 1:678–80; Gallatin to Madison, 13 August 1812, *PJM-PS,* 5:152; Duane to Jefferson, 14 February 1813, *PTJ-RS,* 5:634–38; Gallatin to Astor, 5 August 1835; Gallatin to Daniel Jackson, 23 August 1836, *WAG,* 2:503–05, 506–11; John Armstrong [Jr.], *Notices of the War of 1812* (2 vols.; New York, 1836), 1:47–48; John Wesley Jarvis, Portrait of John Jacob Astor, oil on canvas, c. 1825, National Portrait Gallery, Washington, DC; John Denis Haeger, *John Jacob Astor: Business and Finance in the Early Republic* (Detroit: Wayne State University Press, 1991), 144–47; R. W. B. Lewis

and Nancy Lewis, *American Characters: Selections from the National Portrait Gallery* (New Haven, CT: Yale University Press, 1999), 38. When Astor sent Gallatin a letter offering to explain a questionable exportation of specie, Gallatin succinctly noted on the back: "I believe that his only explanation will be that he made money by it." Astor to Gallatin, 2 December 1810, *PAG*. For other glimpses at their early relationship, see Astor to Gallatin, 8 February 1808, 16 May 1809, 2 and 21 April 1810, 12 and 16 December 1811; Gallatin to William Jones, 10 August 1808, *PAG;* Gallatin to Jefferson, 18 November 1808, *FOL*—Early Access; Gallatin to Madison, 5 September 1801, 5 January 1811, 17 December 1811, *PJM-PS*, 2:526, 3:100, 4:70; Madison to Gallatin, 12 September 1810, ibid., 2:536; Philadelphia *Aurora General Advertiser,* 11 February 1812 ("INFATUATION"); Alexander Emmerich, *John Jacob Astor and the First Great American Fortune* (Jefferson, NC: McFarland, 2013), 65–55, 72, 77, 86.

70. Daniel Tompkins to New York Senate and Assembly, 3 November 1812, Hugh Hastings, ed., *Public Papers of Daniel D. Tompkins* (3 vols.; New York and Albany, 1898–1902), 3:180; Gallatin to Madison, 21 June, [12] July, and 13 August 1812, *PJM-PS*, 4:494, 5:13, 151–52; Montgomery to Gallatin, 21 June 1812, *PAG;* Hickey, *The War of 1812,* 90–93; Dudley, *Splintering the Wooden Wall,* 38–39, 48, 65–78.

71. John K. Mahon, *The War of 1812* (Gainesville: University of Florida Press, 1972), 57–59; Craig L. Symonds, *Navalists and Antinavalists: The Naval Policy Debate in the United States, 1785–1827* (Newark: University of Delaware Press, 1980), 172–74; Hickey, *The War of 1812,* 93–98; Kenneth Ross Nelson, "Socio-Economic Effects of the War of 1812 on Britain" (Ph.D. diss., University of Georgia, 1972), 30–43, 91–95.

72. Gallatin to Jefferson, 18 December 1812, *PTJ-RS*, 5:493; Hickey, *The War of 1812,* 86–90; Rutland, *The Presidency of James Madison,* 105–07, 120; Roger H. Brown, "Who Bungled the War of 1812?" *Reviews in American History* 19, no. 2 (June 1991): 183–87.

73. Gallatin to Monroe, 26 December 1812; Gallatin, "Notes on Army General Staff Plan," [December] 1812; Monroe to Gallatin, 5 and 13 January 1813; Gallatin to Monroe, [14] January 1813; Gallatin, Draft act for General Staff, [before March 1813], *PAG;* Samuel Smith to Leib, 14 October 1812, Samuel Smith Family Papers, General Correspondence 1801–14, DLC; Stagg, *Mr. Madison's War,* 278–80; Hickey, *The War of 1812,* 75–76, 90.

74. Benjamin Stoddert to John Steele, 3 September 1812, H. M. Wagstaff, ed., *The Papers of John Steele* (2 vols.; Raleigh, NC: Edwards and Broughton, 1924), 2:682; Benjamin Henry Latrobe to Benjamin Henry Latrobe Jr., 14 January 1813, quoted in Talbot Hamlin, *Benjamin Henry Latrobe* (New York: Oxford University Press, 1955), 386; Henry Clay to Rodney, 29 December 1812, Hopkins, *Papers of Henry Clay*, 1:750-51; Rodney to Gallatin, 30 June 1812, *PAG*.

75. King to Gore, 19 September 1812, *LCRK*, 5:278; Ketcham, *James Madison*, 544–45; Hickey, *The War of 1812*, 104–05; Kenneth C. Martis, ed., *The Historical Atlas of Political Parties in the United States Congress, 1789–1989* (New York: Macmillan, 1989), 24; Steven Edwin Siry, "The Sectional Politics of 'Practical Republicanism': De Witt Clinton's Presidential Bid," *Journal of the Early Republic* 5, no. 4 (Winter 1985): 441–62.

76. Gallatin, State of the Finances, 7 December 1812, *ASP: Finance*, 2:580–81; William Jones, State of the Finances, 2 June 1813, ibid., 2:623 (prepared by Gallatin).

77. Gallatin to Madison, 13 and 19 August 1812, *PJM-PS*, 5:151–52, 168–69; anonymous to Madison, 14 October 1812 (complaint about enforcement with Gallatin annotations), *PAG*; Acts of 1 March 1809, 1 May 1810, 2 March 1811, and 6 July 1812, *Statutes at Large* 2 (1845): 528–33, 605–06, 651–52, 778–81.

78. William Branch Giles to Wilson Cary Nicholas, 10 December 1812, Papers of the Randolph Family of Edgehill and Wilson Cary Nicholas, Box 2:97, Small Special Collections Library, University of Virginia; Gallatin to Madison, 1 November 1812, *PJM-PS*, 5:425; Madison, Annual Message to Congress, 4 November 1812, ibid., 5:427-35; Gallatin, "Notes on Mr Dallas's Opinion," November 1812; Josiah Quincy to Gallatin, 22 January 1813; Gallatin to Quincy, 13 February 1813; Gallatin to Collectors, 16 February 1813; Gallatin to Henry A. S. Dearborn, 21 February 1813; Dearborn to Gallatin, 1 March 1813; James Lloyd to Gallatin, 19 February 1813; Gallatin to Joseph H. Nicholson, 1 March 1813; Nicholson to Gallatin, 5 March 1813; Treasury Department Circular to District Attorneys, 3 March 1813, *PAG;* Klein, "Memoirs of a Senator from Pennsylvania: Jonathan Roberts," 244-45; *Annals,* 12th Cong., 2nd Sess., 28, 31–33, 90, 100, 198–99, 217–63, 267–404, 441–43, 450–51, 1124–26; Act of 2 January 1813, *Statutes at Large* 2 (1845): 789–90.

79. Gallatin to Madison, [about 19 November 1812], 17 February 1813, *PJM-PS,* 5:460, 6:34; Gallatin to Cheves, 5 and 8 January 1813; Gallatin to Monroe, [14] January 1813; Gallatin to President of the Miami Exporting Company, 26 March 1813, *PAG;* James A. Bayard to Rodney, 17 January 1813, *Bulletin of the New York Public Library* 4, no. 7 (July 1900): 239; Cheves to House of Representatives, 15 February 1813, *ASP: Finance,* 2:613–14; Bayard to James Canby, 21 February 1813, LJAB, 68, 75; *Annals,* 12ᵗʰ Cong., 2ⁿᵈ Sess., 893–908, 75; Act of 8 February 1813, *Statutes at Large* 2 (1845): 798–99.

80. Astor to Gallatin, 14 February 1813, *PJM-PS,* 6:29; *New-York Evening Post,* 18 March 1813 (from *New-York Gazette and General Advertiser*); Gallatin to William Jones, 10 January 1813; Astor to Gallatin, 6 and 18 February, 20 March 1813; Gallatin, Treasury Circular to Presidents of Banks, 24 February 1813, *PAG;* Gallatin to Madison, 17 February and 5 March 1813, *PJM-PS,* 6:34, 90–91; James P. Ronda, *Astoria and Empire* (Lincoln: University of Nebraska Press, 1990), 266–71, 305–15; Philip G. Walters and Raymond Walters Jr., "The American Career of David Parish," *Journal of Economic History* 4, no. 2 (November 1944): 159–61; J. Mackay Hitsman, "David Parish and the War of 1812," *Military Affairs* 26, no. 4 (Winter 1962–63): 172–75.

81. W[illiam] Jones to Joseph H. Nicholson, 11 November 1816, JHNP; Gallatin, Treasury Circular, 18 March 1813, *ASP: Finance,* 2:625–26; Dallas to Gallatin, 29 July 1812 (Girard's earlier interest in lending); Gallatin to Dallas, 19 March 1813; Astor to Gallatin, 20 March 1813; Dallas to Gallatin, 23 March 1813; Dallas to Collectors, 8 April 1813, *PAG;* William Jones to House of Representatives, 15 June 1813, *ASP: Finance,* 2:638–44; Raymond Walters Jr., *Alexander James Dallas: Lawyer—Politician—Financier, 1759-1817* (Philadelphia: University of Pennsylvania Press, 1943), 170–74, 179–81; Donald R. Adams Jr., *Finance and Enterprise in Early America: A Study of Stephen Girard's Bank, 1812–1831* (Philadelphia: University of Pennsylvania Press, 1978), 26–34; George Wilson, *Stephen Girard: The Life and Times of America's First Tycoon* (Conshohocken, PA: Combined Books, 1995), 247–52, 266–68, 272–78, 280–81; Kenneth L. Brown, "Stephen Girard's Bank," *Pennsylvania Magazine of History and Biography* 66, no. 1 (January 1942): 29–55; Thomas M. Doerflinger, "Capital Generation in the New Nation: How Stephen Girard Made His First $735,872," *William and Mary Quarterly,* 3ʳᵈ Ser., 72, no. 4 (October 2015): 624–25.

82. William Jones, State of the Finances, 2 June 1813 (report prepared by
     Gallatin); Jones to Madison, 28 July 1813, *ASP: Finance,* 2:624, 646–47;
     David Parish and Stephen Girard to Gallatin, 5 April, [6 April], and 8
     April 1813; Astor to Gallatin, 5 April 1813; Gallatin to Parish and Girard,
     7 April 1813; Girard and Parish to Gallatin, 8 April 1813, *PAG;* U. S.
     House of Representatives, Ways and Means Committee, Report on the
     Bank of the United States, 13 April 1830, reprinted in M. St. Clair Clarke
     and D.A. Hall, eds., *Documentary and Legislative History of the Bank
     of the United States* (Washington, DC, 1832), 744–45; Gallatin to
     G[ulian] C. Verplanck, 22 May 1830, *WAG,* 2:427–28; Perkins, *American
     Public Finance,* 330-33; Edling, *A Hercules in the Cradle,* 137–40.
83. Andrei Dashkov to Nikolai Rumyantsev, [1] and 17 March 1813; Dashkov
     to Monroe, 8 March 1813, Nina N. Bashkina et al., eds., *The United
     States and Russia: The Beginning of Relations, 1765–1815* (Washington,
     DC: U. S. Government Printing Office, 1980), 931–32, 940–41, 933–34;
     Daniel L. Schlafly Jr., "The First Russian Diplomat in America: Andrei
     Dashkov on the New Republic," *Historian* 60, no. 1 (Fall 1997): 39–57.
84. John Quincy Adams to Monroe, 30 September [1812], *ASP: Foreign
     Relations,* 3:625; Madison to Jefferson, 10 March 1813; Madison to John
     Nicholas, 2 April 1813, *PJM-PS,* 6:100–01, 175–76; Eugene Tarle,
     Napoleon's Invasion of Russia, 1812 (New York: Oxford University
     Press, 1942), 9–13, 51–56, 399–403; Alfred W. Crosby Jr., *America,
     Russia, Hemp, and Napoleon: American Trade with Russia and the
     Baltic, 1783–1812* (Columbus: Ohio State University Press, 1965), 53–54,
     255–61, 270; Norman E. Saul, *Distant Friends: The United States and
     Russia, 1763–1867* (Lawrence: University Press of Kansas, 1991), 72;
     Cathal J. Nolan, "Detachment from Despotism: US Responses to Tsarism,
     1776-1865," *Review of International Studies* 19, no. 4 (October 1993):
     351–56. On Madison's and Jefferson's perceptions that Emperor
     Alexander was friendly to the United States, see Madison to Jefferson, 19
     April and 22 September 1804, *PJM-SS,* 7:79–80, 8:77–78; John C. Hildt,
     Early Diplomatic Negotiations of the United States with Russia
     (Baltimore: Johns Hopkins Press, 1906), 36–57; Francis D. Cogliano,
     Emperor of Liberty: Thomas Jefferson's Foreign Policy (New Haven, CT:
     Yale University Press, 2014), 1–5.
85. Monroe to Dashkov, 11 March 1813; Monroe to American
     Commissioners, 15 April 1813, *ASP: Foreign Relations,* 3:624–25, 700;
     King, Memorandum on Gallatin's mission, 25–27 June 1813; King to
     Gore, 29 August 1813, *LCRK, 5:320,* 342–45; Morton Borden, *The*

Federalism of James A. Bayard (New York: Columbia University Press, 1955), 165–68, 186–96.

86. Dashkov to Rumyantsev, 16 March 1813, Bashkina, *United States and Russia,* 938–39; Gallatin to James W. Nicholson, 5 May 1813; Gallatin to William Few, 9 May 1813, *PAG.* Gallatin had been thinking for some months about whether he should resign from the Treasury. Astor to Gallatin, 31 August and 16 November 1812, ibid.

87. Henry Adams, *History of the United States during the Administrations of Thomas Jefferson and James Madison* (1889–91; 2 vols.; New York: Library of America, 1986), 2:593; Gallatin to Madison, 7 January (quoted) and 4 January 1813, *PJM-PS,* 5:557, 552; Bayard to Rodney, 17 January 1813, *Bulletin of the New York Public Library* 4, no. 7 (July 1900): 239; Armstrong to Duane, 16 March [1813], *Historical Magazine,* 2nd Ser., 4, no. 2 (August 1868): 61; Gallatin to Few, 9 May 1813; Gallatin to James W. Nicholson, 5 May 1813; Gallatin to Worthington, 8 May 1813, *PAG;* Irving Brant, *James Madison,* vol. 6, *James Madison: Commander in Chief, 1812–1836* (Indianapolis: Bobbs-Merrill, 1961), 126–29; C. Edward Skeen, *John Armstrong, Jr., 1758–1843: A Biography* (Syracuse, NY: Syracuse University Press, 1981),115–25; Stagg, *Mr. Madison's War,* 58–63, 66, 72, 282–84, 310–11; Phillips, "William Duane: Revolutionary Editor," 371–79.

88. Astor to Albert Gallatin, 6 April (quoted), 8 April, 19 June, and 17 July 1813; Astor to Hannah Gallatin, 8 April and [15] July 1813; Girard to Albert Gallatin, 4 May 1813; Adrian Bentzon to Gallatin, 27 July 1813, *PAG;* Madison to Gallatin, 5 April 1813; Madison, Commission to Gallatin, Bayard, and John Quincy Adams, 17 April 1813; Madison to William Jones, 20 April 1813, *PJM-PS,* 6:177–78, 209–10, 216–17; Nikolai Koslov to Rumyantsev, 22 April 1813; Dashkov to Rumyantsev, 16 April 1814, Bashkina, *United States and Russia,* 955, 1063; Madison to Senate, 3 June 1813, *ASP: Miscellaneous,* 2:206; Jesse Bledsoe to Isaac Shelby, 21 July 1813, *PAG;* King, Memorandum on Gallatin's mission, 5:319–20; Klein, "Memoirs of a Senator from Pennsylvania: Jonathan Roberts," 361–62.

89. Armstrong to Duane, 21 March 1813, *Historical Magazine,* 2nd Ser., 4, no. 2 (August 1868): 61–62; Gallatin to Armstrong, 17 April 1813 (three letters); Gallatin to William Jones, 20 April 1813, *PAG;* Gallatin to Madison, 17 April 1813, *PJM-PS,* 6:205–08; *Annals,* 12th Cong., 2nd Sess., 1114, 1120–23; Act of 27 February 1813, *Statutes at Large* 2 (1845):

804 (extra session of Congress); Powell, *Richard Rush,* 27–28, 43–44; Skeen, *John Armstrong,* 133.

90.   Richard Rush to John Adams, 6 June 1813; Adams to Rush, 13 June 1813, *FOL*—Early Access.

91.   Bledsoe to Shelby, 21 July 1813, *PAG;* Latrobe to Duane, 27 June 1813, quoted in Hamlin, *Benjamin Henry Latrobe,* 394.

Chapter 9: Redemption

1.   Albert Gallatin to James A. Bayard, 29 April 1813; Gallatin to James Monroe, 29 April and 1 May 1813; Monroe to Gallatin, 1 May 1813; Monroe to Gallatin and Bayard, 3 May 1813; Gallatin, Memorandum on voyage to St. Petersburg, 11 May 1813, *PAG;* James A. Bayard, European Diary, 9–11 May 1813, PJAB, 2:385–86; Baltimore *Weekly Register,* 1 and 15 May 1813, reprinted in H[ezekiah] Niles, ed., *The Weekly Register,* 3ʳᵈ ed. (1816), 4:150–51, 177, 184; Wade G. Dudley, *Splintering the Wooden Wall: The British Blockade of the United States, 1812–1815* (Annapolis, MD: Naval Institute Press, 2003), 84–85, 90–91.

2.   Morton Borden, *The Federalism of James A. Bayard* (New York: Columbia University Press, 1955), 158 (quoting William Plumer), 5, 8; Bayard, European Diary, 29 May 1813; Gallatin to Bayard, 12 March 1812; Bayard to Gallatin, 12 March 1812, PJAB, 2:391, 193–95, 195; Adden Nicholson to James W. Nicholson, 18 January 1803; Charles Pettit to Gallatin, 21 February 1802; Bayard to Gallatin, 7 February 1807, *PAG.*

3.   Gallatin, Memorandum on voyage to St. Petersburg, 21 June and 9 May 1813, *PAG;* Bayard, European Diary, 20–21 June 1813, PJAB, 2:395–97; Gallatin to Monroe, 22 April 1813; Alexander J. Dallas to Gallatin, 8 May 1813; Hannah Gallatin to Albert Gallatin, 1 December 1814, *PAG;* Bayard to Caesar Rodney, 27 June 1813, LJAB, 155; James Madison to Gallatin, 24 and 26 April 1813, *PJM-PS,* 6:231, 237. Very few of the personal letters that Albert Gallatin wrote during the peace mission have survived. James Gallatin may have kept a diary, but the only evidence for it is a counterfeit text—so enticing that some scholars still use it— published by his grandson at the centennial of the Treaty of Ghent. Count Gallatin [James Francis Gallatin], ed., *A Great Peace Maker: The Diary of James Gallatin: Secretary to Albert Gallatin, 1813–1827* (New York: Charles Scribner's Sons, 1914); Raymond Walters Jr., "The James Gallatin Diary: A Fraud?" *American Historical Review* 62, no. 4 (July 1957): 878–85.

4. Gallatin to Baring Brothers, 22 June 1813, *WAG*, 1:546; Peter E. Austin, *Baring Brothers and the Birth of Modern Finance* (London: Routledge, 2007), 18–19.

5. Alexander Baring to Gallatin, 22 July 1813; Gallatin to Baring, 27 August 1813, *WAG*, 1:547–48, 564–65. On the British ministry's rejection of mediation, see Khristofor Lieven to Nikolai Rumyantsev, 5 January and 25 May 1813, Nina N. Bashkina et al., eds., *The United States and Russia: The Beginning of Relations, 1765–1815* (Washington, DC: U. S. Government Printing Office, 1980), 912–13, 963; [Robert Stewart], Lord Castlereagh to [William], Lord Cathcart, 14 July and 27 September 1813; Cathcart to Castlereagh, 5 August 1813, C[harles] K. Webster, ed., *British Diplomacy, 1813–1815: Selected Documents Dealing with the Reconstruction of Europe* (London: G. Bell and Sons, 1921), 14–15, 31–34, 16; Philip Ziegler, *The Sixth Great Power: Barings, 1762–1929* (London: Collins, 1988), 73–74.

6. Norman E. Saul, *Distant Friends: The United States and Russia, 1763–1867* (Lawrence: University Press of Kansas, 1991), 55–59, 70–72, 75; Eugene Tarle, *Napoleon's Invasion of Russia, 1812* (New York: Oxford University Press, 1942), 17, 37; Adam Zamoyski, *Moscow 1812: Napoleon's Fatal March* (New York: HarperCollins, 2004), 24, 71–72, 122–25, 248.

7. Charles Francis Adams, ed., *The Memoirs of John Quincy Adams* (12 vols.; Philadelphia, 1874–77), 2:478–82 (22 June 1813), 2:509–18, 520 (19, 24, and 26 August 1813); John Quincy Adams to Monroe, 26 June 1813, *ASP: Foreign Relations*, 3:627; Gallatin to Baring, 27 August 1813, *WAG*, 1:564; Bayard, European Diary, 29-30 September, 1 October, and 25 December 1813, PJAB, 2:469, 469–70, 495; Adams to Monroe, 5 February 1814, *WJQA*, 5:15–18; Frank A. Updyke, *The Diplomacy of the War of 1812* (1915; repr., Gloucester, MA: Peter Smith, 1965), 154–64; Bradford Perkins, *Castlereagh and Adams: England and the United States, 1812–1823* (Berkeley: University of California Press, 1964), 20–22; Saul, *Distant Friends,* 75; Jon Latimer, *1812: War with America* (Cambridge, MA: Harvard University Press, 2007), 222.

8. Gallatin to James W. Nicholson, 5 May 1813; Gallatin to Thomas Worthington, 8 May 1813; Albert Gallatin to Hannah Gallatin, 30 August 1813, *PAG*; Albert Gallatin to Baring, 27 August 1813, *WAG*, 1:567; Adams, *Memoirs*, 2:535–36 (19 and 25 October 1813); Bayard, European Diary, 20 October 1813, PJAB, 2:476; Act of 13 February 1795, *Statutes at Large* 2 (1845): 415.

9.   Thomas Hart Benton to Andrew Jackson, 15 June 1813, Daniel Feller et al., eds., *The Papers of Andrew Jackson* (10 vols. to date; Knoxville: University of Tennessee Press, 1980–), 2:406; Monroe to Thomas Jefferson, 28 June 1813, *PTJ-RS*, 6:241–42; James Madison to Albert Gallatin, 2 August 1813, *PJM-PS*, 6:491–92; John Jacob Astor to Hannah Gallatin, [15] July 1813; Monroe to Albert Gallatin, 5 and 6 August 1813; Dallas to Albert Gallatin, 14 February 1814, *PAG;* Dolley Madison to Hannah Gallatin, 29 July 1813, David B. Mattern and Holly C. Shulman, eds., *The Selected Letters of Dolley Payne Madison* (Charlottesville: University of Virginia Press, 2003), 179; Rufus King, Notes of a speech against Gallatin's appointment, [May/June 1813], *LCRK*, 5:313–18; *Annals,* 13th Cong., 1st Sess., 83–87; Irving Brant, *James Madison*, vol. 6, *James Madison: Commander in Chief, 1812–1836* (Indianapolis: Bobbs-Merrill, 1961), 182–94; Andrew Burstein and Nancy Isenberg, *Madison and Jefferson* (New York: Random House, 2010), 524–25. William Branch Giles published a long diatribe against Gallatin's dual appointments in one of Virginia's Republican newspaper. *New-York Evening Post,* 30 November and 2 December 1813 (from *Virginia Argus*). Federalists claimed that Gallatin was a foreigner unfit to represent the United States in diplomatic negotiations, but Hezekiah Niles's moderate Republican paper defended him. An American, *Porcupine Revived, or An Old Thing Made New* (New York, 1813), 17–24; *New-York Evening Post,* 16 August 1813 (advertising *Porcupine Revived*); Baltimore *Weekly Register,* 10 April 1813 ("Of Foreigners"), reprinted in *Weekly Register* [1813], 4:99–100.

10.   Jesse Bledsoe to Isaac Shelby, 21 July 1813; Astor to Albert Gallatin, 9 August 1813, *PAG;* Hannah Gallatin to Dolley Madison, 15 August 1813; Dolley Madison to Hannah Gallatin, 29 July and 30 August 1813, Mattern and Shulman, *The Selected Letters of Dolley Payne Madison,* 181, 179, 181; James Madison to Albert Gallatin, 2 August 1813, *PJM-PS,* 6:491–92; Worthington to Hannah Gallatin, 19 July 1813; Dallas to Hannah Gallatin, 22 July and 14 August 1813; Richard Rush to Albert Gallatin, 4 August 1813, *PAG;* Andrei Dashkov to Rumyantsev, 7 August 1813, Bashkina, *United States and Russia,* 995; *Annals,* 13th Cong., 1st Sess., 87–90. Senator Bledsoe had voted for the resolution declaring that the duties of Treasury secretary and peace envoy were incompatible, and his letter to Kentucky governor Shelby about the final vote on Gallatin's nomination was an attempt to justify himself. There also were false insinuations that Gallatin's dual appointment gave him two salaries,

which made Gallatin's youngest sister-in-law bristle. "I wish I did not feel so warmly" about them, she told her mother, "but I love Mʳ Gallatin too well to hear such abominable lies with any patience." A[dden] Chrystie to Frances Nicholson, 26 June 1813, Nicholson Family Papers, Box 1, Folder 9, New-York Historical Society.

11.   Bayard and Gallatin to Lloyd Jones, 25 October 1813; American Commissioners to Monroe, 21 November 1813, LJAB, 299, 317–19; Adams, *Memoirs,* 2:540–44, 553-68 (3 November 1813 and 1–27 January 1814); Rumyantsev to Emperor Alexander, 3 November 1813; Levett Harris to Bayard, 17 January 1814; Rumyantsev to Adams and Bayard, 17 January 1814; Adams and Bayard to Rumyantsev, 19 January 1814; Gallatin to Rumyantsev, 25 January 1814, Bashkina, *United States and Russia,* 1023, 1040–42, 1042–43, 1044–45, 1045–46; Bayard, European Diary, 11–12 November and 6 December 1813, 25 January 1814, PJAB, 2:483–84, 492, 497. The British ambassador to Russia had sent his government's final refusal of mediation to Karl Nesselrode in September 1813, but Nesselrode did not inform Rumyantsev. Confronted with the slight, Rumyantsev retired—as Nesselrode and Emperor Alexander must have intended—in February 1814. Adams to Monroe, 5 February 1814, *WJQA,* 5:12–18; Updyke, *Diplomacy of the War of 1812,* 163–64.

12.   James A. Bayard to Adams, 6 March 1814; James A. Bayard to Andrew Bayard, 19 March 1814; Bayard, European Diary, 25 January–5 March 1814, PJAB, 2:276, 281–82, 497–502; Adams to Monroe, 15 April 1814, *WJQA,* 5:34–38; Hannah Gallatin to James W. Nicholson, 22 May 1814, *PAG;* Joel R. Poinsett, Diary, March 1807, Bashkina, *United States and Russia,* 471–73. For a vividly detailed account of Louisa Catherine Adams's journey over a similar route one year later, see Michael O'Brien, *Mrs. Adams in Winter: A Journey in the Last Days of Napoleon* (New York: Farrar, Straus and Giroux, 2010), 43, 54–55, 60–65.

13.   Colonel Henry Torrens to Major General Sir George Murray, 14 April 1814, Arthur Richard Wellesley, Duke of Wellington, ed., *Supplementary Despatches, Correspondence and Memoranda of Field Marshall Arthur, Duke of Wellington* (14 vols.; London, 1858–72), 9:58; Gallatin to Crawford, 21 April 1814 (quoted); Bayard and Gallatin to Monroe, 6 May 1814, *WAG,* 1:602–03, 611–13; Hannah Gallatin to Dolley Madison, 15 May 1814 (quoting Albert Gallatin to Hannah Gallatin, 9 March 1814), Mattern and Shulman, *The Selected Letters of Dolley Payne Madison,* 184–85; William H. Crawford to American Commissioners, 8 April 1814;

Bayard to Henry Clay and Jonathan Russell, 20 April 1814, James F. Hopkins et al., eds., *The Papers of Henry Clay* (10 vols.; Lexington: University of Kentucky Press, 1959–92), 1:872–73, 881–83; Bayard to Monroe, 16 March 1814, LJAB, 387–89; Hannah Gallatin to Dallas, 2 July 1814 (quoting Albert Gallatin to Hannah Gallatin, 9 May 1814), *PAG;* Nathaniel Atcheson, *A Compressed View of the Points to be Discussed, in Treating with the United States of America* (London, 1814), 24–26; Perkins, *Castlereagh and Adams,* 83–84; Jeremy Black, *The War of 1812 in the Age of Napoleon* (Norman: University of Oklahoma Press, 2009), 147–50. For the agreement to hold direct negotiations in Gothenburg, see Castlereagh to Monroe, 4 November 1813; Cathcart to Karl Nesselrode, 1 September 1813; Monroe to Cathcart, 5 January 1814, *ASP: Foreign Relations,* 3:621, 621–22, 622–23; Monroe, Views respecting the rejection of the mediation of Russia, [January 1814], Stanislaus Murray Hamilton, ed., *The Writings of James Monroe* (7 vols.; New York: G. P. Putnam's Sons, 1898–1903), 5:277–81.

14.	Gallatin to Clay, 22 April 1814; Clay to Gallatin, 2 May 1814, Hopkins, *The Papers of Henry Clay,* 1:883–84, 892–93; *Annals,* 13th Cong., 2nd Sess., 600, 625, 629, 633; *Senate Executive Journal,* 13th Cong., 2nd Sess., 470–71 (8 and 9 February 1814); Dolley Madison to Hannah Gallatin, 21 January 1814, Mattern and Shulman, *The Selected Letters of Dolley Payne Madison,* 183–84; *New-York Evening Post,* 24 and 27 January, 10 February 1814; Brant, *James Madison,* 6:241.

15.	Gallatin to Marquis de Lafayette, 21 April 1814, *WAG,* 1:605; Harris to Adams, 21 June 1814, Bashkina, *United States and Russia,* 1078; Gallatin to Crawford, 21 April 1814; Gallatin to Clay, 22 April 1814; Bayard and Gallatin to Adams, Clay, and Russell, 17 May 1814; Bayard and Gallatin to Monroe, 23 May 1814; Lafayette to Gallatin, 25 and 26 May 1814; Gallatin to Monroe, 3 June 1814; Gallatin to Emperor Alexander, [19] June 1814; Gallatin to Monroe, 20 June 1814 and 30 November 1815, *WAG,* 1:602–05, 606–08, 617–18, 618–19, 620–21, 623–24, 625–26, 629–31, 632–33, 668–69; American Commissioners to Monroe, 11 July 1814, LJAB, 451-53; Monroe to American Commissioners, 11 August 1814, Bashkina, *United States and Russia,* 1085; Henry Kissinger, *A World Restored: Metternich, Castlereagh, and the Problems of Peace, 1812–1822* (1957; London: Phoenix Press, 2000), 141–44, 147–49. For Alexander's poor relationship with the British ministry when he visited London, see Charles Webster, *The Congress of Vienna, 1814–1815* (1919; London: Thames and Hudson, 1963), 66–67. For a more generous assessment of Emperor Alexander's interest in Anglo-American peace, see Saul, *Distant Friends*, 78–79.

16.   Nathaniel Macon to Joseph H. Nicholson, 4 and 18 February 1814, JHNP; Gallatin to Monroe, 13 June 1814, *WAG,* 1:627–29; William Jones, State of the Finances, 2 June 1813 (prepared by Gallatin); John W. Eppes, Report on Increase of Revenue, 10 June 1813; William Jones, State of the Finances, 10 January 1814, *ASP: Finance,* 2:623, 627–28, 651–52; Acts of 24 July 1813, *Statutes at Large* 3 (1846): 35, 39, 40, 42, 44; Acts of 29 July and 2 August 1813, ibid., 49, 53, 72, 77, 82.

17.   Gallatin to Castlereagh, 9 June 1814, LJAB, 436–37; Gallatin to Monroe, 13 and 20 June 1814, *WAG,* 1:627–29, 632; Bayard, European diary, 27–28 June, 6 July, 6 August 1814, PJAB, 2:513–14; John Quincy Adams to Abigail Adams, 30 June 1814, *FOL*—Early Access; Rear Admiral George Cockburn to Monroe, 8 July 1814; Monroe to Castlereagh, 11 July 1814; American Commissioners to Monroe, 11 July and 12 August 1814; Bayard to Robert Goodloe Harper, 19 August 1814, LJAB, 450, 451, 451–53, 471–72, 496; Fred L. Engelman, *The Peace of Christmas Eve* (London: Rupert Hart-Davis, 1962), 120–25; Donald R. Hickey, *The War of 1812: A Forgotten Conflict* (Urbanna: University of Illinois Press, 1989), 126–58, 182–83, 194–96; Alan Taylor, *The Internal Enemy: Slavery and War in Virginia, 1772–1832* (New York: W. W. Norton, 2013), 265–73.

18.   Castlereagh to Cathcart, 27 September 1813; Memorandum of Cabinet, 26 December 1813, Webster, *British Diplomacy,* 31–34, 126; Gallatin to Monroe, 2 June 1814, *WAG,* 1:625; Castlereagh to British Commissioners, 28 July and 14 August 1814, Charles William Vane, Marquess of Londonderry, ed., *Correspondence, Despatches, and Other Papers of Viscount Castlereagh* (12 vols.; London, 1848–53), 10:67–72, 86–91; Henry Goulburn to [Henry], Lord Bathurst, 9 August 1814; [Robert Jenkinson], Lord Liverpool to Castlereagh, 2 September 1814, Wellington, *Supplementary Despatches,* 9:177–79, 214; Monroe to American Commissioners, 11 August 1814, Bashkina, *United States and Russia,* 1086; Crawford to Clay, 26 September 1814, Hopkins, *The Papers of Henry Clay,* 1:980; Perkins, *Castlereagh and Adams,* 58–67; J. C. H. Blom and E. Lamberts, eds., *History of the Low Countries,* new ed. (New York: Berghahn Books, 2009), 36–37, 40, 250–51, 258; Latimer, *1812,* 360–61, 401; Mark Jarrett, *The Congress of Vienna and Its Legacy: War and Great Power Diplomacy after Napoleon* (London: I. B. Tauris, 2016), 70–72, 87, 89–91, 94; Brian E. Vick, *The Congress of Vienna: Power and*

Politics after Napoleon (Cambridge, MA: Harvard University Press, 2014), 10–14. For a different conclusion about the relative importance of an American peace to the Liverpool ministry, see Troy Bickham, *The Weight of Vengeance: The United States, the British Empire, and the War of 1812* (New York: Oxford University Press, 2012), 234–36.

19.   Bernard Mayo, *Henry Clay: Spokesman of the New West* (Boston: Houghton Mifflin, 1937), 471–78; Borden, *The Federalism of James A. Bayard*, 193–97; Greg Russell, *John Quincy Adams and the Public Virtues of Diplomacy* (Columbia: University of Missouri Press, 1995), 16–17, 28–31, 39–40; Twila Muriel Linville, "The Public Life of Jonathan Russell" (Ph.D. diss., Kent State University, 1971), 167–69.

20.   John Quincy Adams to Louisa Catherine Adams, 30 September 1814, *FOL*—Early Access; same to same, 9 September, 28 October, and 16 December 1814, *WJQA*, 5:120–21, 174–75, 239; Goulburn to Bathurst, 23 August and 2, 5, 16, and 23 September 1814, Wellington, *Supplementary Despatches*, 9:190, 217, 221–22, 265, 278; Adams, *Memoirs*, 3:25 and 30 (1 September 1814), 105 (12 December 1814); James A. Bayard to Richard Henry Bayard, 27 October 1814, PJAB, 2:350; Russell to Crawford, 23 December 1814, "Letters Relating to the Negotiations at Ghent, 1812–14," *American Historical Review* 20, no. 1 (October 1914), 128; Engelman, *The Peace of Christmas Eve*, 197; Perkins, *Castlereagh and Adams*, 59–61; Brian Jenkins, *Henry Goulburn, 1784–1856: A Political Biography* (Montreal: McGill–Queen's University Press, 1996), 81–85, 86–87; Wilbur Devereux Jones, ed., "A British View of the War of 1812 and the Peace Negotiations," *Mississippi Valley Historical Review* 45, no. 3 (December 1958): 482–83, 485–87 (Goulburn's memoirs).

21.   American Commissioners to Monroe, 12 August 1814, *ASP: Foreign Relations*, 3:705–08 (with protocols of meetings); Adams, *Memoirs*, 3:4–13 (8–11 August 1814); Goulburn to Bathurst, 9 August 1814, Wellington, *Supplementary Despatches*, 9:177-79.

22.   James A. Bayard to Andrew Bayard, 6 August 1814, PJAB, 2:312-13; British Commissioners to American Commissioners, 19 August 1814, *ASP: Foreign Relations*, 3:710; Adams, *Memoirs*, 3:17–20 (19 August 1814); Castlereagh to Bathurst, 4 October 1814, Francis Bickley, ed., *Report on the Manuscripts of Earl Bathurst* (London: H. M. Stationery Office, 1923), 296; Atcheson, *Compressed View*, 2–5; J. C. A. Stagg, *Mr. Madison's War: Politics, Diplomacy, and Warfare in the Early American Republic, 1783–1830* (Princeton, NJ: Princeton University Press, 1983),

35–42; Black, *The War of 1812*, 46–49; Alan Taylor, *The Civil War of 1812: American Citizens, British Subjects, Irish Rebels, and Indian Allies* (New York: Alfred A. Knopf, 2010), 158–61, 170–72, 300–317.

23. Bathurst to George Prevost, 3 June 1814, in *The War of 1812: Writings from America's Second War of Independence*, ed. Donald R. Hickey (New York: Library of America, 2013), 430–31; John Quincy Adams to Louisa Catherine Adams, 27 September 1814, *WJQA*, 5:147; Treaty of Peace, United States–Great Britain [Treaty of Paris], 3 September 1783, arts. 2 and 8; Treaty of Amity, Commerce, and Navigation, United States–Great Britain [Jay's Treaty], 19 November 1794, arts. 4 and 5; Explanatory Article, United States–Great Britain [re. Jay's Treaty, art. 5], 15 March 1798, Charles I. Bevans, ed., *Treaties and Other International Agreements of the United States of America, 1776–1949* (13 vols.; Washington, DC: U. S. Government Printing Office, 1968-76), 12:10, 12, 16, 17, 36–37. The idea of a Native buffer zone was not new. In 1792, the British government had instructed its first minister to the United States to raise the idea with the Washington Administration, but Alexander Hamilton warned him not to pursue it. Stanley Elkins and Eric McKitrick, *The Age of Federalism: The Early American Republic, 1788–1800* (New York: Oxford University Press, 1993), 255.

24. Dashkov to Rumyantsev, 20 March 1813, Bashkina, *United States and Russia*, 942; Jefferson to Germaine de Staël, 28 May 1813, 3 July 1815, *PTJ-RS*, 6:140–45; 8:576–77; Monroe to American Commissioners, 28 January 1814, *ASP: Foreign Relations*, 3:701–02 (published text) and PJAB, 2:263–65 (confidential paragraphs); Gallatin to Monroe, 20 August 1814, *WAG*, 1:637–40; Madison to Jefferson, 10 October 1814; Jefferson to Madison, 15 October 1814, *PJM-PS*, 8:297–98, 308–11; James A. Bayard to Andrew Bayard, 26 October 1814, PJAB, 2:348; Madison to Jefferson, 12 March 1815, *PTJ-RS*, 8:338–40; [Alexander J. Dallas], *An Exposition of the Causes and Character of the Late War with Great Britain* (Washington, DC, 1815), 4–19; Updyke, *The Diplomacy of the War of 1812*, 175–82; Bradford Perkins, *The First Rapprochement: England and the United States, 1795–1805* (1955; Berkeley: University of California Press, 1967), 60–91; Robert W. Tucker and David C. Hendrickson, *Empire of Liberty: The Statecraft of Thomas Jefferson* (New York: Oxford University Press, 1990), 249–52; Bickham, *The Weight of Vengeance*, 243–49.

25. Goulburn to Bathurst, 23 August 1814; Duke of Wellington to Lieutenant Colonel Chapman, 1 September 1814; Liverpool to Castlereagh, 2

September 1814; Major General Hudson Lowe to Major General Bunbury, 17 October 1814; Lieutenant Colonel S. R. Chapman, Memorandum respecting [defense of] the Netherlands, 27 January 1815, Wellington, *Supplementary Despatches*, 9:189–90, 196–97, 214, 349–50, 518; Adams, *Memoirs*, 3:30 (1 September 1814), 42 (27 September 1814); John Quincy Adams to Louisa Catherine Adams, 9 September and 28 October 1814; John Quincy Adams to Crawford, 14 September 1814, *WJQA*, 5:120–21, 174–75, 140; John Quincy Adams to Louisa Catherine Adams, 16 September and 30 September 1814, *FOL*—Early Access; James A. Bayard to Richard Henry Bayard, 27 October 1814, PJAB, 2:350; Baltimore *Niles's Weekly Register*, 24 December 1814, reprinted in H[ezekiah] Niles, ed., *Niles's Weekly Register* [1815], 7:269; Engelman, *The Peace of Christmas Eve*, 118–19. Jonathan Russell soon felt uncomfortable around the other, more accomplished American commissioners, and at the end of September he moved from their shared house into the hotel where their secretaries lodged. Adams, *Memoirs*, 3:44–45, 58–60.

26. Adams, *Memoirs*, 3:21 (21 August 1814) (quoted), 39–42 (22–25 September 1814), 51–53 (10–13 October 1814); John Quincy Adams to Louisa Catherine Adams, 27 September 1814, *WJQA*, 5:146–47; Paul C. Nagel, *John Quincy Adams: A Public Life, A Private Life* (New York: Alfred A. Knopf, 1997), 217–20; Lynn Hudson Parson, *John Quincy Adams* (Madison, WI: Madison House, 1998), 117.

27. John Quincy Adams to Louisa Catherine Adams, 9 September 1814, *FOL*—Early Access ("extent and copiousness"); same to same, 16 December and 27 September 1814, *WJQA*, 5:238 ("extraordinary combinations"), 147–48 ("keeps and increases"); Adams, *Memoirs*, 3:37–38 (20 September 1814) ("playfulness"); Gallatin to John Badollet, 29 July 1824, *CBG*, 266. Gallatin offered his assessment of Adams at a time when he and William H. Crawford were running against Adams in the 1824 presidential election; see Chapter 10, pp. 276–78.

28. Adams, *Memoirs*, 3:45 (1 and 2 October 1814); Baltimore *Niles's Weekly Register*, 27 August 1814, reprinted in *Niles's Weekly Register* [1814], 6:442–44; Anthony S. Pitch, *The Burning of Washington: The British Invasion of 1814* (Annapolis, MD: Naval Institute Press, 1998), 30–31, 72–85, 100–104, 105–11, 117–22, 124–25, 131, 143–44, 163–65.

29. Hannah Gallatin to Dolley Madison, 29 October 1813; Dallas to Albert Gallatin, 14 February 1814; Ann E. Van Ness to Frances Gallatin, 27 February 1814; Anthony Charles Cazenove to Albert Gallatin, 11 March

and 11 May 1814; Dallas to Hannah Gallatin, 1 August 1815, *PAG;* Dolley Madison to Hannah Gallatin, 12 November 1813, [6] and 17 August 1814; Hannah Gallatin to Dolley Madison, 14 January and 9 August 1814: Dolley Madison to Hannah Gallatin, 17 August 1814, Holly C. Shulman, ed., *The Dolley Madison Digital Edition* (Charlottesville: University of Virginia Press, Rotunda, 2004); John K. Mahon, *The War of 1812* (Gainesville: University of Florida Press, 1972), 301; Latimer, *1812,* 316; Black, *The War of 1812,* 174. The fire set by the British troops probably did not completely destroy the Gallatin house. The greatly altered house on the site today may contain some of the walls and interior fabric from the original building. Lewis Salomon to Gallatin, 14 September 1814, *PAG* (fire obliged owner to quit his house for two months); Robert Henry Goldsborough to Senate, 25 January 1819, *ASP: Claims,* 670 (report on petition for compensation from Robert Sewall, owner of the house); U. S. Department of the Interior, National Park Service, Historic American Buildings Survey, "Sewall-Belmont House," comp. Scott G. Schultz, HABS DC-821 (1998), 4, 8-9.

30.   Hannah Gallatin to James W. Nicholson, 22 May 1814; Joseph H. Nicholson to Hannah Gallatin, 4 September 1814; Cazenove to Hannah Gallatin, 19 September 1814; Hannah Gallatin to Albert Gallatin, 1 December 1814; Salomon to Albert Gallatin, 3 December 1814, *PAG.*

31.   Gallatin to de Staël, 4 October 1814, *LAG,* 532; Goulburn to Clay, 3 October 1814; Clay to Crawford, 17 October 1814, Hopkins, *The Papers of Henry Clay,* 1:982, 988–89; John Payne Todd to Madison, 9 October 1814, *PJM-PS,* 8:294–95; Germaine de Staël, *Ten Years of Exile,* trans. Avriel H. Goldberger (DeKalb: Northern Illinois University Press, 2000), lii–liii; Richmond Laurin Hawkins, *Madame de Staël and the United States* (Cambridge, MA: Harvard University Press, 1930), 38–39, 53–55; Hickey, *The War of 1812,* 129–30; Bickham, *The Weight of Vengeance,* 166; Steven D. Kale, "Women, Salons and Sociability as Constitutional Problems in the Political Writings of Madame de Staël," *Historical Reflections* 32, no. 2 (Summer 2006): 309–38.

32.   Isaac Munroe to "his Friend in Boston," 17 September 1814, *The War of 1812: Writings,* 541–43; Maria Montgomery to James W. Nicholson, 19 September and 4 November 1814, James Witter Nicholson Family Letters, Special Collections, Hesburgh Libraries, University of Notre Dame; Liverpool to Castlereagh, 21 October 1814, Wellington, *Supplementary Despatches,* 9:367; Mahon, *The War of 1812,* 305–28; Pitch, *The Burning of Washington,* 207, 221; Hickey, *The War of 1812,* 202–04,

189–94; Taylor, *The Civil War of 1812*, 214–17; Scott S. Sheads, "Joseph Hopper Nicholson: Citizen-Soldier of Maryland," *Maryland Historical Magazine* 98, no. 2 (Summer 2003): 144–48.

33. Goulburn to Bathurst, 21 October 1814, Wellington, *Supplementary Despatches*, 9:366; Adams to Crawford, 6 November 1814, *WJQA*, 5:181; James A. Bayard to Andrew Bayard, 26 October 1814; James A. Bayard to Rodney, 28 October 1814, PJAB, 2:348–49, 596.

34. Crawford to Adams, 10 November 1814, "Letters Relating to the Negotiations at Ghent, 1812–1814," *American Historical Review* 20, no. 1 (October 1914): 125; Macon to Joseph H. Nicholson, 29 November 1814, JHNP; American Commissioners to Monroe, 25 October 1814, *ASP: Foreign Relations*, 3:710–11; Gallatin to Monroe, 26 October 1814, *WAG*, 1:640–43; Clay to Monroe, 26 October 1814, Hopkins, *The Papers of Henry Clay*, 1:995–96. On Crawford's important role as a source of information for the American negotiators, see Chase C. Mooney, *William H. Crawford, 1771–1834* (Lexington: University Press of Kentucky, 1974), 67–71.

35. Webster, *The Congress of Vienna*, 118–23; Perkins, *Castlereagh and Adams*, 106–11; Black, *War of 1812*, 160–64, 176–88; Jarrett, *The Congress of Vienna*, 52, 87, 96–119; Vick, *The Congress of Vienna*, 15–16, 278–81; Kenneth Ross Nelson, "Socio-Economic Effects of the War of 1812 on Britain" (Ph.D. diss., University of Georgia, 1972), 135–45.

36. Liverpool to Castlereagh, 14, 21, and 28 October, 2 and 18 November 1814; Liverpool to Wellington, 4 and 26 November 1814; Bathurst to Wellington, 4 November 1814; Wellington to Liverpool, 9 November 1814; Liverpool to George Canning, 28 December 1814, Wellington, *Supplementary Despatches*, 9:343, 367, 382, 402, 438, 405–07, 455–56, 416–17, 425–26, 513–15; Castlereagh to Wellington, 25 October 1814, Londonderry, *Correspondence*, 10:173–75.

37. Gallatin to Monroe, 26 December (quoted) and 26 October 1814, *WAG*, 1:645, 640–43; Monroe to American Commissioners, 27 June and 11 August 1814, *PAG*, extracted in *ASP: Foreign Relations*, 3:704, 705; Updyke, *Diplomacy of the War of 1812*, 269–76, 283–93; Paul A. Gilje, *Free Trade and Sailors' Rights in the War of 1812* (New York: Cambridge University Press, 2013), 258. For the devastating effect of the war and the peace treaty on Native American peoples, see Daniel Walker Howe, *What Hath God Wrought: The Transformation of America, 1815–1848* (New

York: Oxford University Press, 2007), 75–76, 125–26, 136; Taylor, *The Civil War of 1812*, 426–39.

38. American Commissioners to British Commissioners, 10 November 1814, *ASP: Foreign Relations*, 3:733–40; Adams, *Memoirs*, 3:60–69 (29 October–10 November 1814); Engelman, *The Peace of Christmas Eve*, 240–47; David S. Heidler and Jeanne T. Heidler, *Henry Clay: The Essential American* (New York: Random House, 2010), 116–17. Before peace negotiations even began, Congress had passed a statute that would keep British subjects from serving on American ships after the war. The administration believed the statute would undercut sympathy for British maritime pretensions and provide a basis for resolving impressment in a peace treaty. Act of 3 March 1813, *Statutes at Large* 2 (1845): 809-11; Stagg, *Mr. Madison's War*, 295–97, 305; Gilje, *Free Trade and Sailors' Rights*, 250–51, 289.

39. British Commissioners, Marginal notes on American treaty *projet*, 26 November 1814, *ASP: Foreign Relations*, 3:735 (Article 1); John Quincy Adams to Louisa Catherine Adams, 2 December 1814, 29 November 1814, *FOL—Early Access*; same to same, 23 December 1814, *WJQA*, 5:246; British Commissioners to American Commissioners, 26 November 1814, *ASP: Foreign Relations*, 3:740–41; Goulburn to Bathurst, 25 November 1814, Wellington, *Supplementary Despatches*, 9:452–54; Adams, *Memoirs*, 3:70–77 (27–29 November 1814); Bayard to Harris, 6 December 1814, LJAB, 607–08; Francis M. Carroll, *A Good and Wise Measure: the Search for the Canadian-American Boundary, 1783–1842* (Toronto: University of Toronto Press, 2001), 38–40; Joshua M. Smith, *Borderland Smuggling: Patriots, Loyalists, and Illicit Trade in the Northeast, 1783–1820* (Gainesville: University Press of Florida, 2006), 19–20.

40. Liverpool to Castlereagh, 23 December 1814; Goulburn to Bathurst, 10 and 30 December 1814, Wellington, *Supplementary Despatches*, 9:495, 472, 516–17; Adams, *Memoirs*, 3:96–97, 98, 112 (10 and 12 December 1814); Bathurst to Anthony St. John Baker, 31 December 1814, Londonderry, *Correspondence*, 10:231–32; Treaty of Peace and Amity, United States–Great Britain [Treaty of Ghent], 24 December 1814, Bevans, *Treaties and Other International Agreements*, 12:41–48; Updyke, *The Diplomacy of the War of 1812*, 323–55. For the American statutes against slave trading, see Acts of 22 March 1794, 10 May 1800, and 2 March 1807, *Statutes at Large* 1 (1845): 347, ibid. 2 (1845): 70, 426. The slave trade article in the Treaty of Ghent did not authorize the

British Navy to board and search American ships suspected of slave trading. Howard Jones, *To the Webster-Ashburton Treaty: A Study in Anglo-American Relations, 1783–1843* (Chapel Hill: University of North Carolina Press, 1977), 70–72; Matthew Mason, *Slavery and Politics in the Early American Republic* (Chapel Hill: University of North Carolina Press, 2006), 92–94; Eliga H. Gould, *Among the Powers of the Earth: The American Revolution and the Making of a New World Empire* (Cambridge, MA: Harvard University Press, 2012), 170–71.

41.   Adams, *Memoirs*, 3:126–27 (24 December 1814); Bathurst to British Commissioners, 26 December 1814, Londonderry, *Correspondence,* 10:228–29; John Quincy Adams to Louisa Catherine Adams, 27 December 1814, *WJQA*, 5:253–54; Engelman, *The Peace of Christmas Eve*, 285–86. Amédée Forestier's familiar centennial painting of the signing of the Treaty of Ghent shows the British commissioners in diplomatic uniform and the Americans in civilian suits. Contemporary accounts do not say what the parties wore, but the depiction is probably accurate. Monroe, Gallatin, and Bayard had designed a uniform for the mission that resembled the British uniforms in the painting—high-collared dark blue coats with gold braid, white breeches, and white stockings—but the American commissioners seem rarely to have worn it after they left St. Petersburg. Gallatin to Monroe, 22 April 1813; Monroe to Gallatin, 23 and 24 April 1813, *PAG;* Bayard to Monroe, 29 April 1813, LJAB, 112; Bayard, European Diary, 11 and 12 October 1813, PJAB, 2:472–73; Adams, *Memoirs,* 3:138 (5 January 1815); Amédée Forestier, *Signing of the Treaty of Ghent, Christmas Eve, 1814*, oil on canvas, 1914, Smithsonian American Art Museum; Robert Ralph Davis, "Manners and Diplomacy: A History of American Diplomatic Etiquette and Protocol during the Early National Period" (Ph.D. diss., Michigan State University, 1967), 178–79.

42.   Albert Gallatin to Hannah Gallatin, 25 December 1814, *PAG;* John Quincy Adams to Abigail Adams, 24 December 1814, *WJQA*, 5:248; Russell to Crawford, 23 December 1814, quoted in Updyke, *The Diplomacy of the War of 1812,* 368; Clay to Monroe, 25 December 1814, Hopkins, *The Papers of Henry Clay*, 1:1007; James A. Bayard to Andrew Bayard, 24 December 1814, PJAB, 2:364; Clay to Crawford, 25 December 1814, Hopkins, *The Papers of Henry Clay*, Supp. vol., 44 (treaty "not perhaps dishono[rable] under existing circumstances"). For Russell's later attack on John Quincy Adams, which was intended to help Clay defeat

Adams in the 1824 presidential election, see Nagel, *John Quincy Adams,* 283–85; Linville, "Public Life of Jonathan Russell," 224–39.

43. Gallatin to Monroe, 25 December 1814, *PAG,* version in *WAG,* 1:645–46. Bayard came to a similar conclusion: "The war has raised our reputation in Europe and it excites astonishment that we should have been able for one campaign to have fought Great Britain single handed. The peace we have made will add to the consideration in which we are held as it proves that Great Britain expected nothing from a continuance of the contest." James A. Bayard to Richard Henry Bayard, 26 December 1814, PJAB, 2:366. Adams took a more jaundiced view. John Quincy Adams to Louisa Catherine Adams, 27 January 1815, *WJQA,* 5:275.

44. Goulburn to Bathurst, 30 December 1814, Wellington, *Supplementary Despatches,* 9:516; John Quincy Adams to Louisa Catherine Adams, 24 January 1815, *WJQA,* 5:272–73; Adams, *Memoirs,* 3:58, 113 (26 October and 12 December 1814), 137–39 (2–5 January 1815); Christopher Hughes to Clay, 12 June 1827, Hopkins, *The Papers of Henry Clay,* 6:675; Peter Van Huffel, Sketch of Albert Gallatin [1815], photographic copy, 1915, Prints and Photographs Division, DLC; Albert Eugene Gallatin, *Gallatin Iconography* (Boston, privately pub., 1934), 20; Editor's note, PJAB, 2:9–10; Andrew Oliver, *Portraits of John Quincy Adams and His Wife* (Cambridge, MA: Harvard University Press, 1970), 50–57.

45. John Quincy Adams to Louisa Catherine Adams, 13 January 1815, *WJQA,* 5:267; Albert Gallatin to Hannah Gallatin, 25 December 1814, *PAG;* James A. Bayard to Andrew Bayard, 25 December 1814 and 28 February 1815; American Commissioners to British Commissioners, 28 December 1814, PJAB, 2:365–66, 377–78, 367; O'Brien, *Mrs. Adams in Winter,* 7–9; Linville, "Public Life of Jonathan Russell," 190–91, 195.

46. Gouverneur Morris to Rufus King, 27 December 1813, *LCRK,* 5:359; Jefferson to William Duane, 24 November 1814; Jefferson to LeRoy, Bayard & McEvers, 7 April 1816, *PTJ-RS,* 8:105, 9:646; Douglass C. North, *The Economic Growth of the United States, 1790–1860* (Englewood Cliffs, NJ: Prentice-Hall, 1961), 57–62; Curtis P. Nettels, *The Emergence of a National Economy, 1775–1815* (New York: Holt, Reinhart, and Winston, 1962), 396; Margaret G. Myers, *A Financial History of the United States* (New York: Columbia University Press, 1970), 75–82; Hickey, *The War of 1812,* 167–73; Sidney Ratner, James H. Soltow, and Richard Sylla, *The Evolution of the American Economy: Growth, Welfare, and Decision Making,* 2nd ed. (New York: Macmillan Publishing, 1993), 197; Stuart D. Brandes, *Warhogs: A History of War*

Profits in America (Lexington: University Press of Kentucky, 1997), 56–58; Skeen, *1816*, 18–19.

47. John W. Eppes to House of Representatives, 10 October 1814, *ASP: Finance*, 2:854; King to Morris, 13 October 1814, *LCRK*, 5:418; Baltimore *Niles's Weekly Register*, 10 September 1814, reprinted in *Niles's Weekly Register*, 7:10; Bray Hammond, *Banks and Politics in America from the Revolution to the Civil War* (Princeton, NJ: Princeton University Press, 1957), 227–29; Richard H. Timberlake Jr., *The Origins of Central Banking in the United States* (Cambridge, MA: Harvard University Press, 1978), 14–16; Stuart Bruchey, *Enterprise: The Dynamic Economy of a Free People* (Cambridge, MA: Harvard University Press, 1990), 174; Edwin J. Perkins, *American Public Finance and Financial Services, 1700–1815* (Columbus: Ohio State University Press, 1994), 339–42; Murray N. Rothbard, *A History of Money and Banking in the United States: The Colonial Era to World War II* (Auburn, AL: Ludwig von Mises Institute, 2005), 73–74; Jamie Karmel, "The Market Moment: Banking and Politics in Jeffersonian Pennsylvania, 1810–1815," *Pennsylvania History* 70, no. 1 (Winter 2003): 55–80; Warren E. Weber, "Early State Banks in the United States: How Many Were There and When Did They Exist?" *Journal of Economic History* 66, no. 2 (June 2006): 443. A concentration of specie in New England exacerbated the fear of bank failure elsewhere. New England banks had more specie than the banks in the rest of the country because New Englanders lent less money to the war effort, suffered relatively less from the British blockade, and enjoyed a large illegal trade with Canada. Baltimore *Niles's Weekly Register*, 3 December 1814, reprinted in *Niles's Weekly Register*, 7:194–95; Walter Buckingham Smith and Arthur Harrison Cole, *Fluctuations in American Business, 1790–1860* (Cambridge, MA: Harvard University Press, 1935), 28–29. Thomas Jefferson and John Adams denounced banks and banking during the war in letters that are often quoted out of context; see Adams to Jefferson, 15 November 1813; Jefferson to Adams, 24 January 1814, Lester J. Cappon, ed., *The Adams-Jefferson Letters: The Complete Correspondence Between Thomas Jefferson and Abigail and John Adams* (Chapel Hill, NC, 1959), 1:401–02, 424–25.

48. Gallatin, State of the Finances, 25 November 1811; Dallas to Eppes, 2 December 1814, 24 February 1815, *ASP: Finance*, 2:496, 878–79, 916–17; Baring to Gallatin, 15 and 29 November, 2 December 1814; Gallatin to Baring, 18 and 24 November 1814, *PAG;* Gallatin to Dallas, 24 December 1814, *WAG*, 1:644; Ralph W. Hidy, *The House of Baring in American*

Trade and Finance: English Merchant Bankers at Work, 1763–1861 (Cambridge, MA: Harvard University Press, 1949), 51–52. Calculations of the public debt at the end of the War of 1812 vary slightly. Davis Rich Dewey, *Financial History of the United States*, 9th ed. (New York: Longmans, Green, 1924), 125, 138; Paul Studenski and Herman Edward Kroos, *The Financial History of the United States* (1952; Washington, DC: Beard Books, 2003), 78–79; Susan B. Carter et al., eds., *Historical Statistics of the United States: Earliest Times to Present,* Millennial Ed. (5 vols.; New York: Cambridge University Press, 2006), 5:5–80 (Table Ea584–587).

49. Asa Briggs, *The Age of Improvement, 1783–1867* (1959; London: Longman, 1971), 169–72, 204; John H. Wood, *A History of Central Banking in Great Britain and the United States* (New York: Cambridge University Press, 2005), 9, 46–47, 127; Richard Cooper, "William Pitt, Taxation, and the Needs of War," *Journal of British Studies* 22, no. 1 (Autumn 1982): 96–103.

50. William Jones, State of the Finances, 8 January 1814; George Washington Campbell, State of the Finances, 23 September 1814; Eppes to House of Representatives, 10 October 1814, *ASP: Finance,* 2:651–53, 840–43 and 846–48, 854–55; Acts of 17 January, 24 March, and 10, 15, 21, and 23 December 1814, *Statutes at Large* 3 (1846): 94, 112, 148, 148, 152, 159; Acts of 9 and 18 January, 4, 8, and 27 February 1815, ibid., 3:164, 180, 186, 201, 205, 216–17.

51. Astor to Gallatin, 14 February 1813, *PJM-PS,* 6:29; Adam Seybert, *Statistical Annals of the United States* (1818; repr., New York: Augustus M. Kelley, 1970), 561–63, 657–63; Stagg, *Mr. Madison's War,* 504–06; Paul A. C. Koistinen, *Beating Plowshares into Swords: The Political Economy of American Warfare, 1606–1865* (Lawrence: University Press of Kansas, 1996), 62–69; Dudley, *Splintering the Wooden Wall,* 82–84, 103–04, 106–07.

52. Monroe to Jefferson, 21 December 1814, Hamilton, *The Writings of James Monroe,* 5:305; Campbell to Madison, 4 May 1814; Dallas to Madison, 15 November 1814, *PJM-PS,* 7:454–55, 8:381–83; King to Christopher Gore, 24 May 1814, *LCRK,* 5:395; Campbell, State of the Finances, 23 September 1814, *ASP: Finance,* 2:651–53, 840–43 and 846–48; Jacob Barker, Petition, 22 December 1821, *ASP: Claims,* 828–29; Acts of 4 and 24 March 1814, *Statutes at Large* 3 (1846): 100, 111; Rafael A. Bayley, *The National Loans of the United States from July 4, 1776 to June 30, 1880* (Washington, DC, 1881), 51–52; Max M. Edling,

A Hercules in the Cradle: War, Money, and the American State, 1783-1867 (Chicago: University of Chicago Press, 2014), 131–32, 138–39.

53. Charles J. Ingersoll, *Historical Sketch of the Second War between the United States of America and Great Britain* (2 vols.; Philadelphia, 1845–49), 2:253 (quoting Abner Lacock to Edward Coles); Campbell, State of the Finances, 23 September 1814, *ASP: Finance,* 2:843; Raymond Walters Jr., *Alexander James Dallas: Lawyer—Politician—Financier, 1759–1817* (Philadelphia: University of Pennsylvania Press, 1943), 182–89; Sanford W. Higginbotham, *The Keystone in the Democratic Arch: Pennsylvania Politics, 1800–1816* (Harrisburg: Pennsylvania Historical and Museum Commission, 1952), 272–73, 308–11; Weymouth Jordan, *George Washington Campbell of Tennessee: Western Statesman* (Tallahassee: Florida State University, 1955), 129–31; Sidney Homer and Richard Sylla, *A History of Interest Rates,* 4th ed. (Hoboken, NJ: John Wiley and Sons, 2005), 291, 293.

54. John W. Eppes to House of Representatives, 10 October 1814, *ASP: Finance,* 2:854–55; Jefferson to Eppes, 24 June, 11 September, and 6 November 1813; *PTJ-RS,* 6:220–26, 490–99, 578–94. A year after giving Eppes his Treasury note proposal, Jefferson also began urging it on Monroe and Madison. Jefferson to Monroe, 3 August and 24 September 1814, ibid., 7:510–11, 699–700, enclosing Jefferson to Joseph C. Cabell, 17 January and 23 September 1814, ibid., 7:133–35, 689–91; Jefferson to Madison, 24 September and 15 October 1814, ibid., 7:691–93, 8:26–29. Jefferson's letters to Eppes about the plan are familiar to historians for a different reason. It is in these letters that Jefferson elaborated his argument that each generation must pay its own debts—that no generation has a right to bind succeeding generations because the earth "belongs in usufruct to the living." When Jefferson was the American minister to Paris, some French revolutionaries had made this argument to justify a proposal—rejected by the National Assembly—for repudiating the old royal government's debts. The argument resonated with an American revolutionary burdened by his personal inheritance of debt and slavery. Jefferson to Madison, 6 September 1789, *PTJ,* 15:392–98; Herbert E. Sloan, *Principle and Interest: Thomas Jefferson and the Problem of Debt* (New York: Oxford University Press, 1995), 62–70, 205–10; Peter S. Onuf, *The Mind of Thomas Jefferson* (Charlottesville: University of Virginia Press, 2007), 215–18; Manuela Albertone, *National Identity and the Agrarian Republic: The Transatlantic Commerce of Ideas between America and France, 1750–1830* (Farnham, UK: Ashgate

Publishing, 2014), 93–98; Rebecca L. Spang, *Stuff and Money in the Time of the French Revolution* (Cambridge, MA: Harvard University Press, 2015), 52–55, 61–72.

55.   Dallas to Eppes, 17 October 1814, *ASP: Finance*, 2:866; Gallatin to Monroe, 26 October 1814, *WAG*, 1:642–43; Adam Smith, *An Inquiry into the Nature and Causes of the Wealth of Nations*, ed. Edwin Cannan (1789; New York: Modern Library, 1937), 276–86; John Sinclair, *The History of the Public Revenue of the British Empire*, 3rd ed. (3 vols.; 1803–04; repr. New York: Augustus M. Kelley, 1966), 2:319–39; Erik Bollman, *Plan of an Improved System of Money-Concerns of the Union* (Philadelphia, 1816), 12–13, 19–20; David Ricardo, *On the Principles of Political Economy, and Taxation*, 3rd ed. (1821), in *The Works and Correspondence of David Ricardo*, ed. Piero Sraffa and M. H. Dobb (11 vols., Cambridge, UK: Cambridge University Press, 1951–73), 1:356–63. Monroe embraced Jefferson's paper money scheme despite Gallatin's warning. Madison, on the other hand, pointed out to Jefferson that Treasury notes would not sell for par unless they bore interest and that Treasury notes bearing interest were just like any other public debt. But Jefferson was not deterred. In a letter to Gallatin a year later, he was still denouncing banks and rhapsodizing that Treasury notes could carry the country "thro' the longest war...without knowing the want of a dollar." Jefferson to Gallatin, 16 October 1815, *PTJ-RS*, 9:94–97; Monroe to Jefferson, 21 December 1814, Hamilton, *The Writings of James Monroe*, 5:305; Madison to Jefferson, 10 and 23 October 1814, *PJM-PS*, 8:297–98, 319–20; Jefferson to William Short, 28 November 1814, *PTJ-RS*, 8:107–11.

56.   Dallas to Eppes, 17 October 1814, *ASP: Finance*, 2:866–69; Walters, *Alexander James Dallas*, 190–94; Fritz Redlich, *The Molding of American Banking: Men and Ideas* (1951; 2 parts; repr., Mansfield Center, CT: Martino Publishing, 2012), 1:103–04; Edward S. Kaplan, *The Bank of the United States and the American Economy* (Westport, CT: Greenwood Press, 1999), 49–52.

57.   Dallas to William Jones, 29 January 1815, quoted in Hickey, *The War of 1812*, 251; Madison to Senate, 30 January 1815, *PJM-PS*, 8:541–43; Acts of 10, 15, 21, and 23 December 1814, *Statutes at Large* 3 (1846): 148, 148, 152, 159; Acts of 9 and 18 (two acts) January and 4, 8, and 27 (two acts) February 1815, ibid., 164, 180, 186, 201, 205, 216, 217; Stagg, *Mr. Madison's War*, 442–52. Prominent members of both political parties feared the people could not pay the heavy new taxes. Morris to King, 1

November 1814, *LCRK,* 5:433 ("The Project of putting a world on an Elephant's Back to stand on a Tortoise and he on nothing will have the Success to be expected from so rational a Device, Immediate Peace, or the Destruction of Money Capital. Take your Choice."); Jefferson to Duane, 24 November 1814, *PTJ-RS,* 8:105 ("I dread a tax of 21. million on a people who cannot get half a dollar a bushel for their wheat, & pay 12.D. a bushel for salt. the taxgatherer too will be in the height of his collection while the election of a new President will be going on.").

58. George Ticknor to Edward T. Channing, 22 January 1815, George S. Hillard et al., eds., *Life, Letters, and Journals of George Ticknor* (2 vols.; Boston, 1876), 1:31 (quoted), 2:186; Astor to Gallatin, 22 December (quoted) and 22 March 1814, 17 July 1814, *PAG;* Dallas to Eppes, 17 January 1815, *ASP: Finance,* 2:885–88; David B. Tyack, *George Ticknor and the Boston Brahmins* (Cambridge, MA: Harvard University Press, 1967), 36–38; Edling, *A Hercules in the Cradle,* 133.

59. Philip S. Klein, ed., "Memoirs of a Senator from Pennsylvania: Jonathan Roberts, 1771–1854," *Pennsylvania Magazine of History and Biography* 62, no. 3 (July 1938), 378; Mahon, *The War of 1812,* 368; William Seale, *The President's House: A History* (2 vols.; Washington, DC: White House Historical Association, 1986), 1:136–37; Latimer, *1812,* 369–88; Black, *War of 1812,* 194–203; J. C. A. Stagg, *The War of 1812: Conflict for a Continent* (New York: Cambridge University Press, 2012), 154–55. On the more mixed British reception of the treaty, see Updyke, *The Diplomacy of the War of 1812,* 369–77; Latimer, *1812,* 398–99; Bickham, *The Weight of Vengeance,* 264–66.

60. *Annals,* 13th Cong., 3rd Sess., 1161, 1159 (Charles Jared Ingersoll); Madison to Congress, 18 February 1815, *PJM-PS,* 8:599; Ingersoll, *Historical Sketch of the Second War between the United States of America and Great Britain;* Perkins, *Castlereagh and Adams,* 150–55; Steven Watts, *The Republic Reborn: War and the Making of Liberal America, 1790–1820* (Baltimore: Johns Hopkins University Press, 1987), 283–89; Nicole Eustace, *1812: War and the Passions of Patriotism* (Philadelphia: University of Pennsylvania Press, 2012), 215–20; Gilje, *Free Trade and Sailors' Rights,* 280–85.

61. Jonathan Roberts to Matthew Roberts, 17 February 1815, quoted in Roger H. Brown, *The Republic in Peril: 1812* (New York: Columbia University Press, 1964), 190–91; Matthew Lyon to Gallatin, 27 October 1815, *PAG;* Samuel Taggart to Manasseh Cutler, 19–20 February 1815, *LJCMC,* 2:334, 332.

62. Macon to Joseph H. Nicholson, 22 November 1814, JHNP; Madison to Wilson Cary Nicholas, 26 November 1814, *PJM-PS*, 401–02; Timothy Dwight, *History of the Hartford Convention* (New York, 1833), 377–78 (resolutions); James M. Banner Jr., *To the Hartford Convention: The Federalists and the Origins of Party Politics in Massachusetts, 1789–1815* (New York: Alfred A. Knopf, 1970), 314–45; Stagg, *Mr. Madison's War*, 478–84; Hickey, *War of 1812*, 232; Richard Buel Jr., *Securing the Revolution: Ideology in American Politics, 1789–1815* (Ithaca, NY: Cornell University Press, 1972), 219–35.

63. Hector Benevolus [pseud.], *The Hartford Convention in an Uproar! and the Wise Men of the East Confounded!... Being the First Book of the Chronicles of the Children of Disobedience* (Windsor, VT, 1815), 20; Harrison Gray Otis to Sally Foster Otis, 23 February 1815, quoted in Samuel Eliot Morison, *The Life and Letters of Harrison Gray Otis, Federalist, 1765–1848* (2 vols.; Boston: Houghton Mifflin, 1913), 2:168; Jefferson to Gallatin, 29 October 1822, 8 September 1816, 15 February 1818, *WAG*, 2:259, 6, 57; Mathew Carey, *The Olive Branch: or Faults on Both Sides...*(Philadelphia, 1814), 99–105; Shaw Livermore Jr., *The Twilight of Federalism: The Disintegration of the Federalist Party, 1815–1830* (Princeton, NJ: Princeton University Press, 1962), 23–24, 265–73; David Hackett Fischer, *The Revolution of American Conservatism: The Federalist Party in the Era of Jeffersonian Democracy* (New York: Harper and Row, 1965), 179–81; C. Edward Skeen, *1816: America Rising* (Lexington: University Press of Kentucky, 2003), 19–27; Richard Buel Jr., *America on the Brink: How the Political Struggle over the War of 1812 Almost Destroyed the Young Republic* (New York: Palgrave Macmillan, 2005), 229–31; Edward C. Carter II, "Mathew Carey and 'The Olive Branch,' 1814–1818," *Pennsylvania Magazine of History and Biography* 89, no. 4 (October 1965): 399–415; Brian Schoen, "Calculating the Price of Union: Republican Economic Nationalism and the Origins of Southern Sectionalism, 1790–1828," *Journal of the Early Republic* 23, no. 2 (Summer 2003): 173-206; Philip J. Lampi, "The Federalist Party Resurgence, 1808–1816: Evidence from the New Nation Votes Database," ibid., 33, no. 2 (Summer 2013): 275–80.

64. Albert Gallatin to Hannah Gallatin, 25 December 1814; Adams, Passport for Albert Gallatin, 11 January 1815; Crawford, Passport for Albert Gallatin, 16 January 1815, *PAG*.

65. James McHenry to Charles Carroll, 8 April 1801, James McHenry Papers, Huntington Library; Philadelphia *Porcupine's Gazette*, 29 March 1798;

Washington, PA, *Herald of Liberty,* 6 April 1801; George Linen, *Portrait of James Gallatin,* oil on wood panel, 1837, Fogg Art Museum, Harvard University; Henry Adams, *The Life of Albert Gallatin* (1879; repr., New York: Peter Smith, 1943), 547; Gallatin, *Gallatin Iconography,* 45 (miniature of James Gallatin, c. 1822); de Staël, *Ten Years of Exile,* 60–62, 85–86, 103–06; Richard Whatmore, *Against War and Empire: Geneva, Britain, and France in the Eighteenth Century* (New Haven, CT: Yale University Press, 2012), 239–42, 267; Theodore E. Stebbins and Melissa Renn, *American Paintings at Harvard: Volume One: Paintings, Watercolors, and Pastels by Artists Born before 1826* (New Haven, CT: Yale University Press, 2014), 640–41; Angelica Goodden, *Madame de Staël: The Dangerous Exile* (Oxford, UK: Oxford University Press, 2008), 33–35, 119–20, 154, 182–83; Julian Swann, *Exile, Imprisonment, or Death: The Politics of Disgrace in Bourbon France, 1610–1789* (Oxford: Oxford University Press, 2017), 429–31, 450–54.

66.   De Staël to Gallatin, 31 July 1814, *LAG,* 531; Webster, *The Congress of Vienna,* 153; Whatmore, *Against War and Empire,* 268–70, 282–83; R. R. Palmer, *The Age of Democratic Revolution: A Political History of Europe and America, 1760–1800,* rev. ed. (Princeton, NJ: Princeton University Press, 2014), 668–69; Jarrett, *The Congress of Vienna,* 136–38.

67.   Gallatin to Eben[ezer] Dodge, 21 January 1847, *PAG,* version in *WAG,* 2:647–48; Raymond Walters Jr., *Albert Gallatin: Jeffersonian Financier and Diplomat* (New York: Macmillan, 1957), 289–90; Whatmore, *Against War and Empire,* 274–89. Gallatin's papers contain correspondence with his relatives in Geneva throughout his life, and his requests for genealogical information from Geneva—which yielded a mound of material—suggest that he began to take greater interest in documenting his origins after about 1809. James W. Alexander, Recollections of Albert Gallatin, 1 July 1850 (conversation of 7 December 1847); James W. Alexander to Mrs. Byam K. Stevens [Frances Gallatin], 1 July 1850 (misdated 1880 by editors), *PAG.* There is a family story that Gallatin, although no reader of novels, reread Sir Walter Scott's *The Antiquarian* every year in his later life. The novel tells the story of a poor young man of uncertain origin who arrives unannounced in an obscure part of the Scottish highlands where trying circumstances eventually bring to light his sterling merit and aristocratic birth. John Austin Stevens, *Albert Gallatin* (Boston, 1883), 396n1.

68. Adams, *Memoirs,* 3:165, 169, 171, 175–76, 183, 205–06 (7, 13, 18, and 20 March, 5 April, and 29 May 1815); Crawford, Passport for Gallatin, 24 March 1815; Gallatin to Baring, 27 March 1815, *PAG;* John Quincy Adams to John Adams, 24 April 1815, *WJQA,* 5:305–08.

69. Goulburn to Gallatin, 14 April and 23 May 1815; Castlereagh to Gallatin, 15 April 1815; Gallatin and Clay to Reuben G. Beasley, 18 April 1815, *PAG;* Clay to Bayard, 3, 15, and 28 April, 13 and 17 May 1815; Clay to Russell, 10 May 1815, Hopkins, *The Papers of Henry Clay,* 2:17, 18–19, 21–22, 28–29, 29–30, 24–25; Clay and Gallatin, Minutes of conversation with Castlereagh, 16 May 1815; Clay and Gallatin to Monroe, 18 May 1815; American Plenipotentiaries to Monroe, 3 July 1815, *ASP: Foreign Relations,* 4:19, 8, 11; Adams, *Memoirs,* 3:208–12 (6–7 June 1815); Gilje, *Free Trade and Sailors' Rights,* 262–75; Elizabeth Jones-Minsinger, "'Our Rights Are Getting More & More Infringed Upon': American Nationalism, Identity, and Sailors' Justice in British Prisons during the War of 1812," *Journal of the Early Republic* 37, no. 3 (Fall 2017): 474–77, 480–81, 503. James Bayard probably suffered from avascular necrosis, a circulatory failure—often associated with heavy drinking—that leads to the death of bone tissue. Editor's note, LJAB, 9–10.

70. Gallatin to Adams, 21 June 1815; Gallatin to Frederick Robinson, 1 July 1815; Gallatin, Outline of negotiations, 3 July 1815, *PAG;* American Plenipotentiaries to Monroe, 3 July 1815, *ASP: Foreign Relations,* 4:11–18 (with attachments); Adams to Russell, 10 October and 14 December 1815, *WJQA,* 5:413–16, 442–43; Adams, *Memoirs,* 3:240, 243, 246 (1, 2, and 3 July 1815); Convention on Commerce and Navigation, United States–Great Britain, 3 July 1815, Bevans, *Treaties and Other International Agreements,* 12:49–53; Updyke, *The Diplomacy of the War of 1812,* 388–95; Perkins, *Castlereagh and Adams,* 168–70. The American negotiators took their cue from a statute, adopted shortly after Congress got word of peace with Britain, that provided for the reciprocal repeal of discriminating duties. Congress expected that otherwise British countervailing duties would damage American shipping interests. American Plenipotentiaries to Monroe, 3 July 1815, *ASP: Foreign Relations,* 4:11; *Annals,* 13th Cong., 3rd Sess., 263–66; Act of 3 March 1815, *Statutes at Large* 3 (1846): 224; Lawrence A. Peskin, *Manufacturing Revolution: The Intellectual Origins of Early American Industry* (Baltimore: Johns Hopkins University Press, 2003), 210–11.

71. Gallatin to Madison, 4 September 1815; Madison to Gallatin, 11 September 1815; Gallatin to Monroe, 25 November 1815, *WAG,* 1:650,

652–53, 662–65; John Quincy Adams to Monroe, 7 October 1815; John
Quincy Adams to John Adams, 9 October 1815; John Quincy Adams to
Abigail Adams, 27 December 1815, *WJQA,* 5:405, 408–10, 453. On
American trade with the British West Indies, see Gallatin to Thomas R.
Gold, 19 March 1816, *WAG,* 1:691; Stagg, *Mr. Madison's War,* 512–17.
For the provisions on trade with Britain and the British East Indies in
earlier Anglo-American treaties, see Jay's Treaty, articles 13 and 15,
Bevans, *Treaties and Other International Agreements,* 12:23–24;
Monroe-Pinkney Treaty, 31 December 1806, arts. 3–5, *ASP: Foreign
Relations,* 3:148.

72. Adams, *Memoirs,* 3:182, 249 (5 April and 4 July 1815); Dallas to Albert
Gallatin, 14 February 1814; Beasley to Albert Gallatin, 23 May 1815;
Hannah Gallatin to James W. Nicholson, 7 April 1815; John Quincy
Adams, Passport for Albert Gallatin, James Gallatin, and suite, 1 July
1815; Crawford to Hannah Gallatin, 16 August 1815; Monroe to Richard
Harrison, 6 November 1815, *PAG;* Crawford to Albert Gallatin, 5 April
1815, *WAG,* 1:648–50; Clay to Todd, 6 July 1815, Hopkins, *The Papers
of Henry Clay,* 2:59–60; Adams to Hughes, 18 July 1815, *WJQA,* 5:326–
27; *Senate Executive Journal,* 13th Cong., 3rd Sess., 623–24 (27–28
February 1815).

73. Dallas to Hannah Gallatin, 1 August 1815; Lloyd Jones to Hannah
Gallatin, 7 August 1815; Crawford to Hannah Gallatin, 16 August 1815,
PAG; Dallas to James Madison, 29 July, 1 and 3 August, *FOL*—Early
Access; Dolley Madison to Hannah Gallatin, [7] and 12 August 1815;
Hannah Gallatin to Dolley Madison, 13 August 1815, Mattern and
Shulman, *The Selected Letters of Dolley Payne Madison,* 203, 204,
204–05; A. R[ichardson] to Hannah Pennock, 9 August 1815, LJAB,
652–53; Borden, *The Federalism of James A. Bayard,* 200–201 (misdates
Bayard's death to 8 March rather than 8 August 1815).

74. *New-York Evening Post,* 6 September (quoted), 25 August, 1 and 2
September 1815; King to Gore, 29 August 1815, *LCRK,* 5: 488–89;
Dallas to Madison, 5 September 1815, *FOL*—Early Access; James Grant
Wilson, ed., *The Memorial History of the City of New-York* (4 vols.; New
York, 1892–93), 3:201–02; Gustavus Myers, *The History of Tammany
Hall,* 2nd ed. (New York: Boni and Liveright, 1917), 31–32, 35–36; Jerome
Mushkat, *Tammany: The Evolution of a Political Machine, 1789–1865*
(Syracuse, NY: Syracuse University Press, 1971), 44–45, 53; George J.
Lankevich, *New York City: A Short History* (New York: New York
University Press, 2002), 60–61.

Chapter 10: Republican Rebirth

1. Albert Gallatin to Richard Bache [Jr.], 24 September 1815 (draft); Gallatin to James W. Nicholson, 22 November 1815; Gallatin to Anthony Charles Cazenove, 10 May 1815, *PAG;* Plat of Frances Nicholson's Greenwich property, n.d.; Inventory of Frances Nicholson's estate, 16 October 1832; Statement of administration of Thomas Witter estate, [1833], Nicholson Family Papers, Box 1, Folders 8, 7, and 1, New-York Historical Society; William Bridges, "Map of the City of New York and Island of Manhattan as laid out by the commissioners appointed…1807" (New York, 1811); Thomas H. Poppleton, "Plan of the City of New York" (New York, 1817); Edwin G. Burrows and Mike Wallace, *Gotham: A History of New York City to 1898* (New York: Oxford University Press, 1999), 447–48, 475; New York City Landmarks Preservation Commission, Greenwich Village Historic District Designation Report (1969), 1:12–16.

2. Alexander J. Dallas to James Madison, 5 September 1815, *FOL*—Early Access; Gallatin to Thomas Jefferson, 6 September (quoted) and 27 November 1815; Jefferson to Gallatin, 16 October 1815, *PTJ-RS,* 9:9, 202, 95; Hannah Gallatin to Dolley Madison, 9 August 1814, 18 January 1815; Dolley Madison to Hannah Gallatin, 6 August 1814, 14 January, [5 March] and 19 March 1815; Catherine Maria Frances Smith to Dolley Madison, 5 September 1815, Holly C. Shulman, ed., *The Dolley Madison Digital Edition* (Charlottesville: University of Virginia Press, Rotunda, 2004); Hannah Gallatin to James W. Nicholson, 7 April 1815; James Monroe to Albert Gallatin, 12 May 1815, *PAG;* Albert Gallatin to James Madison, 4 September 1815, *WAG,* 1:650–51.

3. Cazenove to Gallatin, 4 November 1815; John Jacob Astor to Gallatin, 9 and 10 October 1815; Bache to Gallatin, 23 September 1815; Dallas to Gallatin, 23 March 1805, *PAG;* Sanford W. Higginbotham, *The Keystone in the Democratic Arch: Pennsylvania Politics, 1800–1816* (Harrisburg, PA: Pennsylvania Historical and Museum Commission, 1952), 309, 312; John Denis Haeger, *John Jacob Astor: Business and Finance in the Early Republic* (Detroit: Wayne State University Press, 1991), 172; Harold W. Hurst, *Alexandria on the Potomac: The Portrait of an Antebellum Community* (Lanham, MD: University Press of America, 1991), 22–24; François Furstenberg, *When the United States Spoke French: Five Refugees Who Shaped a Nation* (New York: Penguin Press, 2014), 113–14, 208; John Askling, ed., "Autobiographical Sketch of Anthony-Charles Cazenove: Political Refugee, Merchant, and Banker, 1775–1852,"

Virginia Magazine of History and Biography 78, no. 3 (July 1970): 301–03.

4.   Gallatin to Madison, 23 November 1815; Gallatin to Monroe, 23 November 1815, *WAG,* 1:657–59, 659; Gallatin to Bache, 24 September 1815 (draft), *PAG,* version in *WAG,* 1:653–54; Gallatin to James W. Nicholson, 22 November 1815; Cazenove to Gallatin, 25 November 1815, *PAG.*

5.   Monroe to Gallatin, 4 and 16 December (quoted) 1815, [27] January and 13 February 1816; Gallatin to Monroe 26 December 1815, 2 February 1816, *WAG,* 1:672–73, 676, 683–84, 689, 677, 688. For Monroe's unsuccessful effort to increase diplomatic salaries, see Henry Clay to Monroe, 5 April 1816; William Crawford to Monroe, 5 April 1816; Monroe to William Lowndes, 5 April 1816, *PAG.*

6.   Gallatin to Thomas Worthington, 29 February 1816; Gallatin to James W. Nicholson, 12 April and 4 May 1816; Nicholson to Gallatin, 24 April 1816, *PAG;* Gallatin to Jefferson, 1 April 1816; Jefferson to Gallatin, 11 April 1816, *PTJ-RS,* 9:620–21, 663; Gallatin to Matthew Lyon, 7 May 1816; Gallatin to Madison, 2 June 1816, *WAG,* 1:700–701, 706.

7.   Gallatin to Monroe, 26 December 1815, *WAG,* 1:677; Jefferson to William Short, 28 November 1814, *PTJ-RS,* 8:107–11; Rufus King to Charles King, 11 February 1815, *LCRK,* 5:466.

8.   John Quincy Adams to William Crawford, 14 September 1814; John Quincy Adams to William Plumer, 5 October 1815, *WJQA,* 5:140–41, 400; John Quincy Adams to John Adams, 29 May 1816, ibid., 6:38 ("An efficient revenue and a growing navy, these are the pillars of my peace."); Steven Watts, *The Republic Reborn: War and the Making of Liberal America, 1790–1820* (Baltimore: Johns Hopkins University Press, 1987), 317–18.

9.   Madison to Congress, 5 December 1815, Richardson, *Messages and Papers,* 1:564–68; Ralph Ketcham, *James Madison: A Biography* (1971; Charlottesville: University Press of Virginia, 1990), 602–06, 609–10; Daniel Walker Howe, *What Hath God Wrought: The Transformation of America, 1815–1848* (New York: Oxford University Press, 2007), 80–81. Even Jefferson confessed that the changes brought about by the war with Britain had convinced him of the need to protect and encourage American manufacturing. Jefferson to Benjamin Austin, 9 January 1816, *PTJ-RS,* 9:933–37.

10. Acts of 1, 5, 9, and 22 February, 5 March, and 9, 19, and 26 April 1816, *Statutes at Large* 3 (1846): 253–56, 264, 291–94, 302–06 (internal taxes);

Act of 10 April 1816, ibid., 266–77 (Bank of the United States); Act of 24 April 1816, ibid., 297–99 (army staff); Act of 27 April 1816, sec. 1, paras. 3–5, ibid., 310–11 (protective duties); Act of 29 April 1816, ibid., 321 navy ships); *Annals,* 14th Cong., 1st Sess., 107–11, 148, 300; ibid., 14th Cong., 2nd Sess., 1059–62 (internal improvements); George Dangerfield, *The Awakening of American Nationalism* (New York: Harper Torchbooks, 1965), 5–20; Watts, *The Republic Reborn,* 305–11, 318–19; Robert V. Remini, *Henry Clay: Spokesman for the Union* (New York: W. W. Norton, 1991), 135–43; C. Edward Skeen, *1816: America Rising* (Lexington, KY: University Press of Kentucky, 2003), 53–75, 115–20, 138–49.

11. Nathaniel Macon to Joseph H. Nicholson, 25 March, 15 December, and 3 March 1816, JHNP; John Randolph to James Mercer Garnett, 2 February 1816, quoted in David Johnson, *John Randolph of Roanoke* (Baton Rouge: Louisiana State University Press, 2012), 173; Norman K. Risjord, *The Old Republicans: Southern Conservatism in the Age of Jefferson* (New York: Columbia University Press, 1965), 159–68; Stephen J. Barry, "Nathaniel Macon: The Prophet of Pure Republicanism, 1758–1837" (Ph.D. diss., State University of New York at Buffalo, 1996), 163–69.

12. Gallatin to Thomas R. Gold, 19 March 1816, *WAG,* 1:689–91; Norman Sydney Buck, *The Development of the Organization of Anglo-American Trade, 1800–1850* (1925; repr., Newton Abbot, UK: David and Charles, 1969), 135–38; John Lauritz Larson, *Internal Improvement: National Public Works and the Promise of Popular Government in the Early United States* (Chapel Hill: University of North Carolina Press, 2001), 63–69; Sam W. Haynes, *Unfinished Revolution: The Early American Republic in a British World* (Charlottesville: University of Virginia Press, 2010), 133–35.

13. Gallatin to Monroe, 26 December 1815; Gallatin to Madison, 7 June 1816, *WAG,* 1:677, 707; Gallatin to Joseph H. Nicholson, 26 October and 3 November (quoted) 1815, JHNP; Gallatin to Jefferson, 6 September and 27 November 1815, *PTJ-RS,* 9:8, 202–03; [Isaac?] Bronson to Gallatin, 18 January 1816; Miscellaneous banking data, [January 1816] (dated by editors to January 1815); Gallatin, Notes on specie data, [after 1 January 1816]; Gallatin to Macon, 23 April 1816, *PAG;* Grant Morrison, "Isaac Bronson and the Search for System in American Capitalism, 1789–1838" (Ph.D. diss., City University of New York, 1973), 178–79, 189–90. Gallatin opposed suggestions that the banks could

redeem their notes with Treasury notes as a step toward full resumption of specie payments and that bank notes would not even need to be redeemable in specie if the country had a strong national bank to regulate the currency. Macon to Gallatin, 18 April 1816, *PAG;* Gallatin to Macon, 23 April 1816, *WAG,* 1:697–98; Erik Bollman to Gallatin, 20 January 1816, *PAG;* Erik Bollman, *Plan of an Improved System of Money-Concerns of the Union* (Philadelphia, 1816), 2–20. Congress increased the pressure on the banks to resume specie payment by adopting a resolution in April 1816 that required the Treasury to collect all federal revenue in hard money after 20 February 1817. *Annals,* 14th Cong., 1st Sess., 369-71; Dallas to John C. Calhoun, 6 April 1816; Dallas, State of the Finances, 20 September 1816, *ASP: Finance,* 3:116–17, 130–33.

14.   Clay to Gallatin, 5 December 1815; Dallas to Gallatin, 18 December (quoted), 22 September, and 19 October 1815, 12 February and 26 March 1816; Gallatin to Clay, 23 November 1815; Gallatin to Dallas, 9 February 1816, *PAG;* Gallatin to Dallas, 25 September and 12 December 1815, *WAG,* 1:654–57, 673–75; Louis Salomon to Gallatin, 16 May and 6 July 1816; Gallatin to Joseph Nourse, 4 June 1816; Nourse to Gallatin, 7 June 1816, *PAG;* Gallatin to Madison, 4 June 1816, ibid., extract in *WAG,* 1:706; Dolley Madison to Hannah Gallatin, 26 May 1816, David B. Mattern and Holly C. Shulman, eds., *The Selected Letters of Dolley Payne Madison* (Charlottesville: University of Virginia Press, 2003), 208–09.

15.   Joseph H. Nicholson to Gallatin, 13 April 1816, *PAG;* Gallatin to Madison, 18 April 1816; Madison to Gallatin, 12 April 1816, *WAG,* 1:694–95, 694; Dallas to Madison, 8 April 1816, George Mifflin Dallas, *Life and Writings of Alexander James Dallas* (Philadelphia, 1871), 451–52; Gallatin to Nicholson, 19 April 1816, JHNP.

16.   Crawford to Gallatin, 6 and 10 May 1816; Gallatin to Madison, 7 June 1816, *WAG,* 1:699–700, 702–04, 707; Crawford to George W. Erving, 14 May 1816; Crawford to William Lee, 19 May 1816, *PAG;* Irving Brant, *James Madison,* vol. 6, *James Madison: Commander in Chief, 1812–1836* (Indianapolis: Bobbs-Merrill, 1961), 412; Harry Ammon, *James Monroe: The Quest for National Identity* (1971; Charlottesville, VA: University Press of Virginia, 1990), 352–56; Chase C. Mooney, *William H. Crawford, 1771–1834* (Lexington, KY: University Press of Kentucky, 1974), 90–91. For an account that treats Gallatin, Clay, and Adams as Monroe's candidates for Secretary of State but discounts Gallatin's interest in the job, see Samuel Flagg Bemis, *John Quincy Adams and the*

Foundations of American Foreign Policy (New York: Alfred A. Knopf, 1965), 244–45.

17. Gallatin to Monroe, 1 June (quoted), 30 April, and 7 June 1816; Gallatin to Lyon, 7 May 1816 (quoted), *PAG;* Gallatin to John Badollet, 8 May 1816, *CBG,* 256; Gallatin to Madison, 2 and 7 June 1816, *WAG,* 1:706, 707; Hannah Gallatin to Dolley Madison, 2 June 1816, Mattern and Shulman, *The Selected Letters of Dolley Payne Madison,* 210; Watts, *The Republic Reborn,* 317; Nicole Eustace, *1812: War and the Passions of Patriotism* (Philadelphia: University of Pennsylvania Press, 2012), x–xiii.

18. The Gallatins' landlord was the Duc de Cambacérès, Napoleon's Arch-Chancellor and justice minister, who had bought the house to replace a grander place that he had sold when he fled France after Waterloo. Lease between Louis Charles Thibon (as agent for Jean Jacques Régis de Cambacérès) and Albert Gallatin, 9 August 1816; Receipts from Nast, Père et Fils, 2 and 28 August, 12 October 1816, *PAG;* Hannah Gallatin to Dolley Madison, 12 August 1816, Mattern and Shulman, *The Selected Letters of Dolley Payne Madison,* 211; Albert Gallatin to James Madison, 12 August and 14 September 1816, *FOL*—Early Access; Guillaume de Bertier de Sauvigny, *The Bourbon Restoration,* trans. Lynn M. Case (Philadelphia: University of Pennsylvania Press, 1966), 257–64, 328–32; Philip Mansel, *Paris between Empires: Monarchy and Restoration, 1814–1852* (New York: St. Martin's Press, 2001), 83–140; Stefan Brönnimann and Daniel Krämer, *Tambora and the "Year Without a Summer" of 1816: A Perspective on Earth and Human Systems Science* (Bern: Geographica Bernensia, 2016), 34. The counterfeit diary of James Gallatin published in 1914 gives interesting descriptions of the Gallatins' years in Paris; see p. 456n3.

19. Albert Gallatin to Albert Rolaz Gallatin, 27 February 1827, *PAG;* Ammon, *James Monroe,* 358–59; Donald Ratcliffe, *The One-Party Presidential Contest: Adams, Jackson, and 1824's Five-Horse Race* (Lawrence: University Press of Kansas, 2015), 59. Clay was miffed when Monroe offered him the War department instead of State, and he refused to take it. Remini, *Henry Clay,* 150–51.

20. Albert Gallatin to Hannah Gallatin, 6 June 1804; Marquis de Lafayette to Albert Gallatin, 13 and 14 July, 3 September 1816, *PAG;* Jefferson to Gallatin, 24 April 1815, *PTJ-RS,* 8:437; Gallatin to Madison, 12 August and 14 September 1816, *FOL*—Early Access; Germaine de Staël to Jefferson, 12 February 1817; Gallatin to Jefferson, 17 July 1817, *PTJ-RS,*

11:116–18, 540; Gallatin to John Quincy Adams, 18 October 1826, *WAG,* 2:332; Phoebe Warren Tayloe, *In Memoriam: Benjamin Ogle Tayloe* (Washington, DC, 1872), 15–16; Mansel, *Paris between Empires,* 52–53, 76, 80, 109–10, 119–20, 125, 129, 144. On de Staël's salon, see J. Christopher Herold, *Mistress of an Age: A Life of Madame de Staël* (Indianapolis: Bobbs-Merrill, 1958), 449–50, 459–61, 468–71. On Humboldt and Gallatin, see Laura Dassow Walls, *The Passage to Cosmos: Alexander von Humboldt and the Shaping of America* (Chicago: University of Chicago Press, 2009), 103, 114–15. On Elizabeth Bonaparte—who was a niece of the wife of Gallatin's old political enemy Samuel Smith—see Charlene M. Boyer Lewis, *Elizabeth Patterson Bonaparte: An American Aristocrat in the Early Republic* (Philadelphia: University of Pennsylvania Press, 2012), 13, 55–57, 93–96, 103–04, 199; Carol Berkin, *Wondrous Beauty: The Life and Adventures of Elizabeth Patterson Bonaparte* (New York: Alfred A. Knopf, 2014), 102–05. On Pozzo di Borgo, see Gallatin to John Quincy Adams, 10 August, 5 November, and 10 December 1818, 19 January and 26 October 1819, 24 January 1823, *WAG,* 2:74, 75, 91, 94, 125, 272; Philip Mansel, *Louis XVIII,* rev. ed. (Stroud, Gloucestershire: Sutton Publishing, 1999), 264, 307.

21.   Linda K. Kerber, "Albert Gallatin as Minister to France: A Study in Diplomacy" (M. A. thesis, New York University, 1961), chap. 5 (deposited Klingenstein Library, New-York Historical Society).

22.   Gallatin to Monroe, 12 September 1816; Monroe to Gallatin, 15 April and 7 May 1816; Gallatin to Monroe, 3 May 1816; Gallatin to Adams, 23 October and 13, 16, and 24 November 1821, *PAG;* Gallatin to Adams, 29 July 1822, 13 November 1822, 27 February 1823; Crawford to Gallatin, 26 June 1822; Gallatin to Clay, 29 June 1826; Gallatin to Edward Everett, 5 January and [n. d.] January 1835, *WAG,* 2:254, 260–61, 265–66, 246–49, 311, 474–76, 478–501; Charles Francis Adams, ed., *The Memoirs of John Quincy Adams* (12 vols.; Philadelphia, 1874–77), 5:262–63, 273–74, 282, 295–97 (5, 13, 16, and 24 February 1821); Convention on Navigation and Commerce, United States–France, 24 June 1822, Charles I. Bevans, ed., *Treaties and Other International Agreements of the United States of America, 1776–1949* (13 vols.; Washington, DC: U.S. Government Printing Office, 1968–76), 7:822–25; Nora E. Hudson, *Ultra-Royalism and the French Restoration* (Cambridge, UK: University Press, 1936), 95–101; Bemis, *John Quincy Adams and the Foundations of American Foreign Policy,* 451–56; Sauvigny, *The Bourbon Restoration,*

154–55, 226–30; Peter E. Austin, *Baring Brothers and the Birth of Modern Finance* (London: Routledge, 2007), 12–14; Pamela Pilbeam, "The 'Impossible Revolution': The Left and the Revolutionary and Napoleonic Legacies," in *Napoleon's Legacy: Problems of Government in Restoration Europe,* ed. David Laven and Lucy Riall (Oxford, UK: Berg, 2000), 187–88; Robert Charles Thomas, "Andrew Jackson Versus France: American Policy toward France, 1834-36," *Tennessee Historical Quarterly* 35, no. 1 (Spring 1976): 51–64; Lloyd Clay Dotson, "The Diplomatic Mission of Baron Hyde de Neuville to the United States, 1816–1822" (Ph.D. diss., University of Georgia, 1986), 121–43.

23. Gallatin and Richard Rush to Adams, 20 October 1818; Adams to Gallatin and Rush, 2 November 1818, *ASP: Foreign Relations,* 4:380–83, 400–401; Convention on Fisheries, Boundaries, and Restoration of Slaves, United States–Great Britain, 20 October 1818, Bevans, *Treaties and Other International Agreements,* 12:57-60; Frank A. Updyke, *The Diplomacy of the War of 1812* (1915; repr., Gloucester, MA: Peter Smith, 1965), 407–09, 443–49, 469–71; Bradford Perkins, *Castlereagh and Adams: England and the United States, 1812–1823* (Berkeley: University of California Press, 1964), 260–76.

24. M. A. DeWolfe Howe, *The Life and Letters of George Bancroft* (2 vols.; New York: Charles Scribner's Sons, 1908), 1:106–09 (20 June 1821); Gallatin to Badollet, 29 July 1824, *CBG,* 264–65; Washington Irving to William Irving, 22 September 1820, Pierre M. Irving, ed., *The Life and Letters of Washington Irving* (3 vols.; New York: G. P. Putnam, 1862–63), 2:19; Henry Adams, *The Life of Albert Gallatin* (1879; repr., New York: Peter Smith, 1943), 565; Raymond Walters Jr., *Albert Gallatin: Jeffersonian Financier and Diplomat* (New York: Macmillan, 1957), 300.

25. James W. Nicholson to Gallatin, 3 November 1821, *PAG;* Gallatin to Monroe, 13 November 1822; Gallatin to Adams, 28 February, 18 April, and 24 June 1823, *WAG,* 2:262, 267, 267–68, 270–72; Elizabeth Bonaparte to William Patterson, 6 May and 9 November 1823, Eugene L. Didier, *The Life and Letters of Madame Bonaparte,* 3rd ed. (London, 1879), 147, 157–59; Gallatin to Jefferson, 29 June 1823, *FOL*—Early Access; Gallatin to Badollet, 29 July 1824, *CBG,* 264; Walters, *Albert Gallatin,* 315–17; Murray N. Rothbard, *The Panic of 1819: Reactions and Politics* (1962; Auburn, AL: Ludwig von Mises Institute, 2007), 19–25.

26. Albert Gallatin to Frances Gallatin, 17 September and 15 October 1823, *LAG,* 589–90; Monroe to Albert Gallatin, 15 October 1823; Gallatin to

Monroe, 26 October 1823, *WAG*, 2:274, 274–75; Walters, *Albert Gallatin*, 317–18, 323, 326; U. S. Department of the Interior, National Park Service, *Friendship Hill National Historic Site: Historic Structure Report—Architectural Data Section*, comp. John B. Marsh and Scott Jacobs (August 1984), 10–14.

27. Jefferson to Gallatin, 2 August 1823 (quoted), 29 October 1822; Crawford to Gallatin, 24 July 1819, 13 May and 26 June 1822, 26 May 1823, *WAG*, 2:273–74, 258-60, 112–17, 242–43, 248–49, 269–70. For the old Republican perspective on the growth of federal power during the decade after the War of 1812, see John Taylor, *Tyranny Unmasked* (1822; Indianapolis: Liberty Fund, 1992) (protective tariffs), and John Taylor, *New Views of the Constitution of the United States* (1823; Washington, DC: Regnery Publishing, 2000) (federal consolidation); Garrett Ward Sheldon and C. William Hill Jr., *The Liberal Republicanism of John Taylor of Caroline* (Madison, NJ: Fairleigh Dickinson University Press, 2008), 159–206.

28. Davis Rich Dewey, *Financial History of the United States*, 9th ed. (New York: Longmans, Green, 1924), 168–71; Rothbard, *The Panic of 1819*, 19–24; Howe, *What Hath God Wrought*, 142–47; Clyde A. Haulman, *Virginia and the Panic of 1819: The First Great Depression and the Commonwealth* (London: Pickering and Chatto, 2008), 10–15, 25–30; Lynn Hudson Parsons, *The Birth of Modern Politics: Andrew Jackson, John Quincy Adams, and the Election of 1828* (New York: Oxford University Press, 2009), 59; Ratcliffe, *The One-Party Presidential Contest*, 28.

29. Sean Wilentz, *The Rise of American Democracy: Jefferson to Lincoln* (New York: W. W. Norton, 2005), 222–40, 251–52; Matthew Mason, *Slavery and Politics in the Early American Republic* (Chapel Hill: University of North Carolina Press, 2006), 177–212; Padraig Riley, *Slavery and the Democratic Conscience: Political Life in Jeffersonian America* (Philadelphia: University of Pennsylvania Press, 2016), 207–28.

30. Jefferson to Gallatin, 26 December 1820, *WAG*, 2:176–77; Bray Hammond, *Banks and Politics in America from the Revolution to the Civil War* (Princeton, NJ: Princeton University Press, 1957), 251–62, 279–85; Rothbard, *The Panic of 1819*, 15–19; Parsons, *The Birth of Modern Politics*, 60-61; Ratcliffe, *The One-Party Presidential Contest*, 14–17, 275; Donald Ratcliffe, "The Right to Vote and the Rise of Democracy, 1787–1828," *Journal of the Early Republic* 33, no. 2 (Summer 2013): 219–54. Some historians have traced the rise in voter participation to the popular outcry over Congress's 1816 decision to give itself a pay

raise. That outcry arose before Gallatin left for Paris, but Gallatin— already losing touch with American politics—did not understand Jefferson's clear allusion to it in a letter Gallatin received shortly before he sailed. An unprecedented number of Congressmen lost their seats in the next election. Jefferson to Gallatin, 18 May and 8 September 1816; Gallatin to Jefferson, 7 June 1816, *PTJ-RS*, 10: 66–67, 379, 154; Skeen, *1816*, 77–95.

31. Baltimore *Niles's Weekly Register*, 31 May 1823, reprinted in H[ezekiah] Niles, ed., *Niles's Weekly Register* (1823), 24:195; Astor to Gallatin, 18 October 1822, *LAG*, 584; Richard P. McCormick, *The Second American Party System: Party Formation in the Jacksonian Era* (Chapel Hill: University of North Carolina Press, 1966), 26–29; Skeen, *1816*, 216–20; Parsons, *The Birth of Modern Politics*, 77–79; Jeffrey L. Pasley, *The First Presidential Contest: 1796 and the Founding of American Democracy* (Lawrence: University Press of Kansas, 2013), 202-03; Ratcliffe, *The One-Party Presidential Contest*, 10–13, 149–50;

32. Erastus Root to Martin Van Buren, 3 January 1823, quoted in Wilentz, *The Rise of American Democracy*, 241; Margaret Bayard Smith to Anna Boyd, 19 December 1823; Smith to Jane Kirkpatrick, 28 June 1824, Gaillard Hunt, ed., *The First Forty Years of Washington Society* (New York: Charles Scribner's Sons, 1906), 162–63, 165–66; Risjord, *The Old Republicans*, 248–55; Mooney, *William H. Crawford*, 151–72, 249–68; Donald B. Cole, *Martin Van Buren and the American Political System* (Princeton, NJ: Princeton University Press, 1984), 116–17, 135–36; Charles Sellers, *The Market Revolution: Jacksonian America, 1815–1846* (New York: Oxford University Press, 1991), 181; Ratcliffe, *The One-Party Presidential Contest*, 25–32, 40–44.

33. McCormick, *The Second American Parry System*, 330; Mooney, *William H. Crawford*, 148–55; Remini, *Henry Clay*, 137–39; Noble E. Cunningham Jr., *The Presidency of James Monroe* (Lawrence, KS: University Press of Kansas, 1996), 45–53; Lynn Hudson Parsons, *John Quincy Adams* (Madison, WI: Madison House, 1998), 133–63.

34. Mooney, *William H. Crawford*, 155–66; Robert V. Remini, *Andrew Jackson*, vol. 2, *Andrew Jackson and the Course of American Freedom, 1822–1832* (New York: Harper and Row, 1981), 13–27; Ratcliffe, *The One-Party Presidential Contest*, 256–57. Andrew Jackson personally detested William Crawford because Crawford was among the members of Monroe's cabinet who had wanted to discipline Jackson for disobeying orders during his campaign against the Natives after the War of 1812.

Andrew Burstein, *The Passions of Andrew Jackson* (New York: Alfred
A. Knopf, 2003), 130; Parsons, *The Birth of Modern Politics*, 70.

35.　Crawford to Gallatin, 26 May 1823, *WAG,* 2:269; J[esse] B[urgess]
Thomas to Gallatin, 5 January 1824; Thomas W. Cobb to Macon, [before
16 January] 1824; Macon to Gallatin, 16 January 1824; Walter Lowrie
to Gallatin, 10 February 1824, *LAG,* 592–95. Thomas and Lowrie were
Crawfordite senators from Illinois and Pennsylvania, and Cobb was a
Crawfordite Congressman from Georgia.

36.　Albert Gallatin to Hannah Gallatin, 24 January 1824, *LAG,* 594; Albert
Gallatin to Lowrie, 19 February 1824, *PAG* (draft), version in *WAG,*
2:283–87; U. S. Constitution, art. 2, sec. 1, cl. 5.

37.　Macon to Gallatin, 13 February (quoted) and 14 February 1824; Lowrie
to Gallatin, 10 February 1824, *LAG,* 596, 597, 595; Philip Shriver Klein,
Pennsylvania Politics, 1817–1832: A Game without Rules (Philadelphia:
Historical Society of Pennsylvania, 1940), 155–65; James A. Kehl, *Ill
Feeling in the Era of Good Feeling: Western Pennsylvania Political
Battles, 1817–1825* (Pittsburgh; University of Pittsburgh Press, 1956),
212-30; Ronald Schultz, *The Republic of Labor: Philadelphia Artisans
and the Politics of Class, 1720–1830* (New York: Oxford University
Press, 1993), 230–33; Ratcliffe, *The One-Party Presidential Contest,*
119–20, 128–29, 152–55; Kim T. Phillips, "The Pennsylvania Origins of
the Jackson Movement," *Political Science Quarterly* 91, no. 3 (Autumn
1976): 489–508.

38.　Gallatin to Lowrie, 22 May 1824, *WAG,* 2:289; Gallatin to Badollet, 29
July 1824, *CBG,* 266; "Wyoming," Philadelphia *Columbian Observer,*
6 September 1824, quoted in Robert P. Hay, "The Pillorying of Albert
Gallatin: The Public Response to His 1824 Vice-Presidential Nomination,"
Western Pennsylvania Historical Magazine 65, no. 3 (July 1962): 193–94;
Burstein, *The Passions of Andrew Jackson,* 120–33. The *Columbian
Observer* was founded as a Jackson campaign organ, and the "Wyoming"
letters that it published in 1823—written by Jackson's friend John
Eaton—attracted wide attention and appeared as a pamphlet in 1824.
[John H. Eaton], *The Letters of Wyoming* (Philadelphia, 1824); Robert
P. Hay, "The Case for Andrew Jackson in 1824: Eaton's 'Wyoming
Letters,'" *Tennessee Historical Quarterly* 29, no. 2 (Summer 1970):
139–151.Gallatin believed that Jefferson and Madison backed Crawford
and disapproved of Jackson's candidacy, but their own surviving
statements about the candidates are circumspect. Jefferson to Rush, 5

June 1824, *WTJ,* 12:355; Jefferson to Crawford, 15 February 1825, *FOL*—Early Access; Brant, *James Madison,* 6:441–42; Dumas Malone, *Jefferson and His Time,* vol. 6, *The Sage of Monticello* (Boston: Little, Brown, 1981), 436–37.

39. Lowrie to Gallatin, 10 March 1824, *PAG;* Gallatin to B[enjamin] Ruggles, 16 May 1824; Lowrie to Gallatin, 25 September 1824; Gallatin to Lowrie, 2 and 7 October 1824; Gallatin to Martin Van Buren, 2 October 1824, *WAG,* 2:288, 292–93, 294–96, 300, 297–99; Gallatin to Badollet, 29 July 1824, *CBG,* 266; Washington *Daily National Intelligencer,* 21 October 1824; Robert V. Remini, *Martin Van Buren and the Making of the Democratic Party* (New York: Columbia University Press, 1961), 66–68; Alvin Kass, *Politics in New York State, 1800–1830* (Syracuse, NY: Syracuse University Press, 1965), 120–21, 131–32; Ratcliffe, *The One-Party Presidential Contest,* 167. Ruggles, a senator from Ohio who had supported Crawford but later switched to Clay, organized the Republican caucus. Van Buren remained a leading organizer for Crawford until Crawford was defeated.

40. [Frances Milton] Trollope, *Domestic Manners of the Americans* (1832; Barre, MA: Imprint Society, 1969), 261; Andrew Burstein, *America's Jubilee: How in 1826 a Generation Remembered Fifty Years of Independence* (New York: Alfred A. Knopf, 2001), 8–33; Ratcliffe, *The One-Party Presidential Contest,* 19–21, 232–53; 280–81 (App. 1); Robert P. Hay, "The American Revolution Twice Recalled: Lafayette's Visit and the Election of 1824," *Indiana Magazine of History* 69, no. 1 (March 1973): 43–62. Lafayette toured the United States from August 1824 until September 1825.

41. Auguste Levasseur, *Lafayette in America in 1824 and 1825: Journal of a Voyage to the United States,* trans. Alan R. Hoffman (Manchester, NH: Lafayette Press, 2006), 283–87 (quoted at 283); Margaret Bayard Smith, Notebook, February 1825, Hunt, *The First Forty Years,* 186–87; Remini, *Andrew Jackson,* 2:86–99; Burstein, *The Passions of Andrew Jackson,* 155–57; Parsons, *The Birth of Modern Politics,* 104, 111.

42. Levasseur, *Lafayette in America,* 455-67 (quoted at 461); Gallatin, Speech Welcoming Lafayette to Uniontown, PA, 27 May 1825, *PAG-S.*

43. Albert Gallatin to Badollet, 29 July 1824, *CBG,* 264; Albert Gallatin to Albert Rolaz Gallatin, 14 May 1827, *PAG.*

44. *Senate Executive Journal,* 19th Cong., 1st Sess., 537–38 (9–10 May 1826); Walters, *Albert Gallatin,* 325–29; *Biographical Directory of the United States Congress, 1774 to 2005* (Washington, DC: U. S. Government

Printing Office, 2005), 1604–05 (John Montgomery); Cindy Kelly, *Outdoor Sculpture in Baltimore: A Historical Guide to Public Art in the Monumental City* (Baltimore: Johns Hopkins University Press, 2011), 58–59, 82–83.

45.　Updyke, *The Diplomacy of the War of 1812,* 404, 421–29; Perkins, *Castlereagh and Adams,* 174–79, 229–38; Francis M. Carroll, *A Good and Wise Measure: The Search for the Canadian-American Boundary, 1783–1842* (Toronto: University of Toronto Press, 2001), 197–99; Haynes, *Unfinished Revolution,* 108–13, 133–41, 161–65.

46.　Gallatin to John Quincy Adams, 20 and 30 June 1826; Adams to Gallatin, 26 June 1826, 20 May 1827, *WAG,* 2:307, 319–20, 307–08, 364–68; Albert Gallatin to James Gallatin, 13 January 1827; Adams to Albert Gallatin, 12 December 1827, *LAG,* 622, 627–29; Albert Gallatin to Madison, 27 February 1828, *FOL*—Early Access; Gallatin to Badollet, 26 March 1829, 7 February 1833, *CBG,* 285, 312; Convention on Claims, United States–Britain, 13 November 1826; Convention on Boundaries, United States–Britain, 6 August 1827; Convention on Commerce and Navigation, United States-Britain, 6 August 1827; Convention on Submission to Arbitration, United States–Britain, 29 September 1827, Bevans, *Treaties and Other International Agreements,* 12:61–73, 74–75, 75–77, 78–81; Frederick Merk, *Albert Gallatin and the Oregon Problem: A Study in Anglo-American Diplomacy* (Cambridge, MA: Harvard University Press, 1950), 66–82; Walters, *Albert Gallatin,* 342; Bemis, *John Quincy Adams and the Foundations of American Foreign Policy,* 530–32; Carroll, *A Good and Wise Measure,* 149–53.

47.　Albert Gallatin to Hannah Gallatin, 16 December 1828, 2 and 23 May, 8 November 1829, *LAG,* 630, 632–33; Albert Gallatin to C. P. Van Ness, 22 March 1829; Gallatin to W[illiam] P[itt] Preble, 22 March 1829; Gallatin to William C. Bradley, 22 March 1829, *WAG,* 2:406–08, 408–09, 409–10; William Preble and Albert Gallatin, *Statement on the Part of the United States of the Case Referred…to…the King of the Netherlands…* (Washington, DC, 1829); Preble and Gallatin, *Definitive Statement on the Part of the United States…* (Washington, DC, 1829); Albert Gallatin, *A Memoir on the North-Eastern Boundary, in Connexion with Mr. Jay's Map* (New York, 1843); *New York Herald,* 16 and 17 April 1843; Bemis, *John Quincy Adams and the Foundations of American Foreign Policy,* 476–81; Howard Jones, *To the Webster-Ashburton Treaty: A Study in Anglo-American Relations, 1783–1843* (Chapel Hill: University of North Carolina Press, 1977), 14–15, 104–13;

Carroll, *A Good and Wise Measure,* 154–57, 187-94, 289, 297, 301. Gallatin's old friend Alexander Baring, then Lord Ashburton, came to Washington to negotiate the 1842 northeastern boundary treaty, and he went to New York after the negotiations to visit Gallatin. Ashburton to Gallatin, 12 April 1842; Gallatin to Ashburton, 20 April 1842, *WAG,* 2:594–95, 596–97; Ashburton to Gallatin, 23 August 1842; Ashburton to Morgan Lewis, Gallatin, et al., 30 August 1842, *PAG.*

48. John Quincy Adams, First Annual Message, 6 December 1825, Richardson, *Messages and Papers,* 2:313, 316; Parsons, *The Birth of Modern Politics,* 127–29; Johnson, *John Randolph of Roanoke,* 206–07, 215; Howe, *What Hath God Wrought,* 275–76, 280–83; Barry, "Nathaniel Macon," 264–70.

49. Margaret Bayard Smith to Jane Kirkpatrick, 11 March 1829, Hunt, *The First Forty Years,* 296; Leonard D. White, *The Jacksonians: A Study in Administrative History, 1829–1861* (New York: Macmillan, 1954), 307–09; Sidney H. Aronson, *Status and Kinship in the Higher Civil Service: Standards of Selection in the Administrations of John Adams, Thomas Jefferson, and Andrew Jackson* (Cambridge, MA: Harvard University Press, 1964), 15–21, 193–98; Remini, *Andrew Jackson,* 2:161–63, 173–78, 203–13; Robert V. Remini, *Andrew Jackson,* vol. 3, *Andrew Jackson and the Course of American Democracy* (New York: Harper and Row, 1984), 392; William Seale, *The President's House: A History* (2 vols.; Washington, DC: White House Historical Association, 1986), 1:179, 184–87; Burstein, *The Passions of Andrew Jackson,* 173–80; Jerry L. Mashaw, *Creating the Administrative Constitution: The Lost One Hundred Years of American Administrative Law* (New Haven, CT: Yale University Press, 2012), 175–77; Kirsten E. Wood, "'One Woman So Dangerous to Public Morals': Gender and Power in the Eaton Affair," *Journal of the Early Republic* 17, no. 2 (Summer 1997): 244–63.

50. Albert Gallatin to Hannah Gallatin, 23 May 1829, 8 November 1829, *LAG,* 633, 633–34; Albert Gallatin to Badollet, 26 March 1829, *CBG,* 286; Gallatin to Van Buren, 4 March 1829, *WAG,* 2:405–06; Madison to Gallatin, 13 July 1829, *FOL*—Early Access (introducing William Cabell Rives, Jackson's new minister to France); Badollet to Gallatin, 14 August 1829, *CBG,* 289–91, 296; Remini, *Martin Van Buren,* 104, 115, 120, 123–25.

51. Albert Gallatin to Hannah Gallatin, 29 November 1829, *LAG,* 634. Gallatin's description of the East Room was accurate. Seale, *The President's House,* 1:186–87; Remini, *Andrew Jackson,* 3:389–91.

52.   Douglas T. Miller, *Jacksonian Aristocracy: Class and Democracy in New York: 1830–1860* (New York: Oxford University Press, 1967), 22; J. T. W. Hubbard, *For Each, the Strength of All: A History of Banking in the State of New York* (New York: New York University Press, 1995), 72–77; Burrows and Wallace, *Gotham,* 431–32, 435–39, 443–46; Howard Bodenhorn, *State Banking in Early America: A New Economic History* (New York: Oxford University Press, 2003), 95–122, 155–91; John Lauritz Larson, *The Market Revolution in America: Liberty, Ambition, and the Eclipse of the Common Good* (New York: Cambridge University Press, 2010), 46–52; Clifton Hood, *In Pursuit of Privilege: A History of New York's Upper Class and the Making of a Metropolis* (New York: Columbia University Press, 2017), 91–93. On the earlier and more traditional distinctions between small- and large-scale merchants, see Gallatin to Madison, 30 July 1810, *PJM-PS,* 2:454.

53.   Trollope, *Domestic Manners of the Americans,* 268–69; Miller, *Jacksonian Aristocracy,* 76; Edward Pessen, *Riches, Class, and Power: America before the Civil War,* rev. ed. (New Brunswick, NJ: Transaction Publishers, 1990), 172–79; Burrows and Wallace, *Gotham,* 456–59, 463–67; Hood, *In Pursuit of Privilege,* 109–12, 115–18, 122–23.

54.   Edward Coles to Dolley Madison, 22 February 1832, Shulman, *The Dolley Madison Digital Edition;* [Thomas Longworth, ed.,] *Longworth's American Almanac, New-York Register, and City Directory* (New York, 1829), 241; (1830), 276; (1832), 308; (1833), 273; (1834), 302; (1835), 271; (1836), 267; (1837), 258; (1838), 264; Bayard Tuckerman, ed., *The Diary of Philip Hone, 1828–1851* (2 vols.; New York, 1889), 1:17 (10 April 1830), 24 (27 November 1830); Walters, *Albert Gallatin,* 346–48; Ammon, *James Monroe,* 569; Thomas Bender, *New York Intellect: A History of Intellectual Life in New York City, from 1750 to the Beginnings of Our Own Time* (New York: Alfred A. Knopf, 1987), 134–35; Mansel, *Paris between Empires,* 258–68.

55.   Coles to Dolley Madison, 22 February 1832, Shulman, *The Dolley Madison Digital Edition;* Harriet Martineau, *Retrospect of Western Travel* (3 vols.; London, 1838), 1:50–52; Maria Weston Chapman, ed., *Harriet Martineau's Autobiography,* 2nd ed. (3 vols.; London, 1877), 3:114–15 (24 September 1834). Edward Coles, who had moved to Illinois and been elected governor, was about to settle in Philadelphia. A year earlier, he had reported to James Madison that the Gallatins were "retaining their looks in a wonderful manner." Coles to James Madison, 16 January 1831, *FOL*—Early Access; Suzanne Cooper Guasco,

Confronting Slavery: Edward Coles and the Rise of Antislavery Politics in Nineteenth-Century America (DeKalb, IL: Northern Illinois University Press, 2013), 100–107, 156–57, 165–67.

56. Astor to Gallatin, 7 March 1827, *PAG;* Gallatin to Badollet, 26 March 1829; Badollet to Gallatin, 14 August 1829, *CBG,* 284-85, 291-92; Haeger, *John Jacob Astor,* 278, 281; Burrows and Wallace, *Gotham,* 448–49.

57. Charles Dickens, *American Notes* (1842; London: Everyman's Library, 1970), 94–95; Coles to Dolley Madison, 22 February 1832, Shulman, *The Dolley Madison Digital Edition; Longworth's American Almanac, New-York Register, and City Directory* (New York, 1832), 67, 308; [Moses Y. Beach, ed.], *Wealth and Pedigree of Wealthy Citizens of New York City,* 4th ed. (New York, 1842), 11; [Beach], *Wealth and Biography of the Wealthy Citizens of New York City,* 6th ed. (New York, 1845), 11; [Beach], *Wealth and Biography...,* 10th ed. (New York, 1846), 12; Walters, *Albert Gallatin,* 341, 347; Edward Pessen, "Moses Beach Revisited: A Critical Examination of His Wealthy Citizens Pamphlets," *Journal of American History* 58, no. 2 (September 1971): 415–26. Gallatin left an estate valued at $100,000, which his children divided equally. Division of Albert Gallatin's estate, [1850], *PAG* (unsigned document dated by editors to 1849).

58. Albert Gallatin to Badollet, 3 September 1836, 7 February 1833, 3 February [1835], *CBG,* 323, 311–12, 318–19; Albert Gallatin to Albert Rolaz Gallatin, 27 February 1827, *PAG;* [Beach,] *Wealth and Biography,* 6th ed., 11; ibid., 10th ed., 12; ibid., 12th ed. (New York, 1855), 32; Tuckerman, *The Diary of Philip Hone,* 1:16; William Plumb Bacon, comp., *Ancestry of Albert Gallatin and of Hannah Nicholson* (New York: Tobias A. Wright, [1916]), 18–20; Walters, *Albert Gallatin,* 326, 341, 346–48.

59. Andrew Jackson, First Annual Message, 8 December 1829, Richardson, *Messages and Papers,* 2:462; Hammond, *Banks and Politics,* 373-75; Marvin Meyers, *The Jacksonian Persuasion: Politics and Belief* (Stanford, CA: Stanford University Press, 1957), 17–20; Remini, *Andrew Jackson,* 2:200.

60. Robert Walsh Jr. to Gallatin, 22 April, 3 and 11 May 1830, 13 February 1831; Nicholas Biddle to Gallatin, 9 and 11 September 1830, *PAG;* Gallatin to Walsh, 27 April and 2 August 1830, 16 February 1831; Gallatin to Biddle, 14 August and 8 December 1830, *WAG,* 2: 425–27, 429–31, 447, 431–40, 443–44; Biddle to Gallatin, 11 and 28 October, 4,

9, 10, 11, 15, 17, 19, 24, 26, 27, 29, and 30 November, 6, 13, and 28 December 1830, 1 January, 3 and 22 February 1831; Gallatin to Biddle, 17 February 1831, *PAG;* Biddle to William B. Lawrence, 8 February 1831; Biddle to Joseph Hemphill, 10 February 1831; Biddle to Joseph Gales, 2 March 1831; Biddle to James Hunter, 4 May 1831, Reginald C. McGone, ed., *The Correspondence of Nicholas Biddle Dealing with National Affairs, 1807–1844* (Boston: Houghton Mifflin, 1919), 123–24, 124, 125–26, 126–27. Nicholas Biddle's financial support for the journals and newspapers that defended the Bank of the United States drew withering criticism from the Bank's enemies. Thomas Payne Govan, *Nicholas Biddle: Nationalist and Public Banker, 1786–1844* (Chicago: University of Chicago Press, 1959), 132–33, 188–89; William E. Ames, *A History of the National Intelligencer* (Chapel Hill: University of North Carolina Press, 1972), 199–203, 215–20.

61.   [Albert Gallatin,] "Banks and Currency," *American Quarterly Review* 8, no. 16 (December 1830): 441-528; Gallatin to Robert Porter, 3 December 1830, *WAG,* 2:440–42; Fritz Redlich, *The Molding of American Banking: Men and Ideas* (1951; 2 parts; repr., Mansfield Center, CT: Martino Publishing, 2012), 1:171; Richard H. Timberlake Jr., *The Origins of Central Banking in the United States* (Cambridge, MA: Harvard University Press, 1978), 32–34; Stuart Bruchey, *Enterprise: The Dynamic Economy of a Free People* (Cambridge, MA: Harvard University Press, 1990), 184–88; Lester B. McAllister Jr., "Monetary and Banking Theories of Albert Gallatin" (Ph.D. diss., University of Oregon, 1953), 54–75, 115–59, 234–65. An expanded version of Gallatin's essay appeared a month later as a separate pamphlet. Gallatin, *Considerations on the Currency and Banking System of the United States* (Philadelphia, 1831), reprinted in *WAG,* 3:231–488 (see especially 3:332–35, 345–46). For the similar views of a Republican political economist of the time, see George Tucker, *The Theory of Money and Banks Investigated* (1839; repr., New York: Greenwood Press, 1968), 275–77, and for the more Jacksonian views of another who nevertheless defended the Bank, see Thomas Cooper, *Lectures on the Elements of Political Economy,* 2ⁿᵈ ed. (1830; repr., New York: Augustus M. Kelley, 1971), 163, 178–80; Dumas Malone, *The Public Life of Thomas Cooper* (New Haven, CT: Yale University Press, 1926), 376-81. While Gallatin thought a purely metallic currency was no longer realistic, he did advise Jackson's Treasury secretary—a Pennsylvania manufacturer named Samuel D. Ingham—on how to increase the amount of specie in circulation by adjusting the

amount of silver that the Mint paid for gold. But he warned that an increase in the relative price of gold would not increase the hard money supply enough to stop the over-issuance of bank notes. Congress raised the Mint's gold-to-silver-ratio in 1834. Gallatin to Ingham, 4 August, 27 September, and 31 December 1829, *WAG,* 2:410–25; Murray N. Rothbard, *A History of Money and Banking in the United States: The Colonial Era to World War II* (Auburn, AL: Ludwig von Mises Institute, 2005), 104–06; David A. Martin, "Bimetallism in the United States before 1850," *Journal of Political Economy* 76, no. 3 (May-June 1968): 432–37.

62. M. St. Clair Clarke and D. A. Hall, eds., *Documentary and Legislative History of the Bank of the United States* (Washington, DC, 1832), 776 (Senate report), 738 and 747 (House report); Gallatin to G[ulian] C. Verplanck, 22 May 1830, *WAG,* 2:428; [David Henshaw], *Remarks upon the Bank of the United States* (Boston, 1831), 47; Verplanck to Gallatin, 27 May 1830, *PAG;* Hammond, *Banks and Politics,* 379; Sellers, *The Market Revolution,* 322–23; Wilentz, *The Rise of American Democracy,* 364. For Samuel Smith's checkered relationship with the second Bank of the United States, see Frank A. Cassell, *Merchant Congressman in the Young Republic: Samuel Smith of Maryland, 1752–1839* (Madison: University of Wisconsin Press, 1971), 223–26. On Gallatin's relationship with Gulian Verplanck, see Bender, *New York Intellect,* 135–39.

63. *New-York Spectator,* 12 and 17 February, 24 March 1834; New York *Evening Post,* 12 February 1834; Washington *United States Telegraph,* 27 and 29 March 1834; *Report of the "Union Committee"* (New York, 1834); Tuckerman, *The Diary of Philip Hone,* 1:91–93 (7 and 11 February 1834); Walters, *Albert Gallatin,* 363–64; Remini, *Andrew Jackson,* 3:105–07, 110–11, 151–52, 166–67.

64. Gallatin to [John] Horsley Palmer, 1 May 1833; Gallatin to Frederick Beasley, 3 September 1836; Gallatin to Leonard Maison, 20 December 1836, *WAG,* 2:461, 513, 514; J. K. Horsefield, "The Opinions of Horsley Palmer: Governor of the Bank of England, 1830–33," *Economica,* New Ser., 16, no. 62 (May 1949): 150–52.

65. Gallatin to Badollet, 3 September 1836, *CBG,* 324; Peter Temin, *The Jacksonian Economy* (New York: W. W. Norton, 1969), 120–47; Jane Knodell, "Rethinking the Jacksonian Economy: The Impact of the 1832 Bank Veto on Commercial Banking," *Journal of Economic History* 66, no. 3 (September 2006): 541–74; Ta-Chen Wang, "Banks, Credit Markets, and Early American Development: A Case Study of Entry and

Competition," ibid., 68, no. 2 (June 2008): 438–61. Gallatin did publish another 124-page essay on banking and currency after the banks again stopped specie payments in 1839. Gallatin, *Suggestions on the Banks and Currency of the Several United States...* (New York, 1841), reprinted in *WAG*, 3:365–488.

66.   Temin, *The Jacksonian Economy*, 114–20; Burrows and Wallace, *Gotham*, 603–18; Larson, *The Market Revolution*, 92–97; Jessica M. Lepler, *The Many Panics of 1837: People, Politics, and the Creation of a Transatlantic Crisis* (New York: Cambridge University Press, 2013), 3–6, 45–61, 100-22; Peter L. Rousseau and Richard Sylla, "Emerging Financial Markets and Early U.S. Growth," *Explorations in Economic History* 42, no. 1 (January 2005): 10.

67.   [John C. Calhoun], *Exposition and Protest, Reported by the Special Committee of the House of Representatives, on the Tariff* (Columbia, SC, 1829), 32–40; Cooper, *Lectures on the Elements of Political Economy*, 217–46; Malone, *The Public Life of Thomas Cooper*, 331–35; Howe, *What Hath God Wrought*, 274, 395–400.

68.   *The Journal of the Free Trade Convention...and Their Address to the People of the United States* (Philadelphia, 1831), 21, 23, 25–27, 33–34, 62–64, 66; Tuckerman, *The Diary of Philip Hone*, 1:35, 38 (8 September and 10 October 1831).

69.   Albert Gallatin, *Memorial of the Committee Appointed by the "Free Trade Convention"* (New York, 1832), 30 and 47 (both quoted), 8–13, 16–17, 80.

70.   Remini, *Henry Clay*, 386–91; Michael F. Holt, *The Rise and Fall of the American Whig Party: Jacksonian Politics and the Onset of the Civil War* (New York: Oxford University Press, 1999), 2, 17; Howe, *What Hath God Wrought*, 270–73.

71.   *Register of Debates in Congress* (14 vols.; Washington, DC: Gales and Seaton, 1825–37), 22nd Cong., 1st Sess., 266–67; Badollet to Gallatin, [20 January 1833], *CBG*, 307; Haynes, *Unfinished Revolution*, 142–48. Clay published his speech as a campaign pamphlet. Henry Clay, *Speech of Henry Clay in Defence of the American System against the British Colonial System*, 11 (Washington, 1832).

72.   Gallatin to J[oseph] R[eed] Ingersoll, 25–30 March 1846; Gallatin to William Drayton, 7 April 1832; Gallatin to Robert Y. Hayne, 7 February 1832, *WAG*, 2:628–29, 450–58, 449–50; Gallatin to Badollet, 7 February 1833, *CBG*, 313; Howe, *What Hath God Wrought*, 401–08.

73.   Jackson, First Inaugural Address, 4 March 1829, Richardson, *Messages and Papers*, 2:437; Jackson, Sixth Annual Message, 1 December 1834,

ibid., 3:108; Remini, *Andrew Jackson*, 3:222–25; Max M. Edling, *A Hercules in the Cradle: War, Money, and the American State, 1783–1867* (Chicago: University of Chicago Press, 2014), 142–43; Carl Lane, *A Nation Wholly Free: The Elimination of the National Debt in the Age of Jackson* (Yardley, PA: Westholme, 2014), 155–69.

74. Gallatin to Gales and Seaton, 5 February 1835, *WAG*, 2:501–02; Washington *Daily National Intelligencer*, 17 January and 3 February 1835; Ames, *A History of the National Intelligencer*, 162–67, 176–78, 222–23. An anonymous writer to another opposition newspaper claimed that neither Gallatin nor any other Democrat deserved credit for repaying the national debt; he said Alexander Hamilton's sinking fund had done it. Washington *United States Telegraph*, 29 January 1835.

75. A leading historian of intellectual life in New York sets the stage for discussing Gallatin's contributions by calling him "the most accomplished and distinguished of New York's citizens in 1830." Bender, *New York Intellect*, 99.

76. [Jonathan Mayhew Wainwright?], *Considerations upon the Expediency and the Means of Establishing a University in the City of New-York* (New York, 1830), 5, 6; [John Delafield, secretary], *Journal of the Proceedings of a Convention of Literary and Scientific Gentlemen* (New York, 1831), 5; Tuckerman, *The Diary of Philip Hone*, 1:27 (2 February 1831); Theodore Francis Jones, *New York University, 1832–1932* (New York: New York University Press, 1933), 12–27; Bender, *New York Intellect*, 92–100; Caroline Winterer, *The Culture of Classicism: Ancient Greece and Rome in American Intellectual Life, 1780–1910* (Baltimore: Johns Hopkins University Press, 2002), 29–36, 44–55; John Albert Leuenberger, "Albert Gallatin: Educational Interests" (Ph.D. diss., Case Western Reserve University, 1968), 98–104.

77. Delafield, *Journal of the Proceedings*, 170–80 (quoted at 172, 178); Leuenberger, "Albert Gallatin: Educational Interests," 107–12. Gallatin's speech also described the Geneva Academy of his youth, and the published version prompted an inquiry from Ebenezer Dodge (later president of a college that became Colgate University) that led Gallatin to write a much fuller description of the Geneva Academy. Gallatin to Eben[ezer] Dodge, 21 January 1847, *PAG*, version in *WAG*, 2:640-47.

78. Gallatin to Badollet, 7 February 1833, *CBG*, 312-13; Gallatin to Josiah Quincy, 9 December 1830, *WAG*, 2:445-46; Bender, *New York Intellect*, 100-02.

79. Bender, *New York Intellect*, 102. In describing his initial post-Revolutionary plan for public education in Virginia, Jefferson spoke of

scholarships as a means for raking "the best geniuses" up from "the rubbish." And he conceived of the United States Military Academy and the University of Virginia as schools for future leaders. Thomas Jefferson, *Notes on the State of Virginia* (London, 1787), 244 (Query XIV); Jefferson to John Bazier, 24 August 1819, *TJW*, 1423–25 (value of classical education); Merrill D. Peterson, *Thomas Jefferson and the New Nation* (New York: Oxford University Press, 1970), 964–66, 973, 980–81, 986–87; Malone, *Jefferson and His Time*, 6:237–40, 417; Theodore J. Crackel, *Mr. Jefferson's Army: Political and Social Reform of the Military Establishment, 1801–1809* (New York: New York University Press, 1987), 61–62, 71–73; Jennings L. Wagoner Jr., *Jefferson and Education* (Charlottesville, VA: Thomas Jefferson Foundation, 2004), 86–87, 128–31, 138; Peter S. Onuf, *The Mind of Thomas Jefferson* (Charlottesville: University of Virginia Press, 2007), 191–92; Susan Dunn, *Dominion of Memories: Jefferson, Madison, and the Decline of Virginia* (New York: Basic Books, 2007), 61–84; Jennings L. Wagoner Jr. and Christine Coalwell McDonald, "Mr. Jefferson's Academy: An Educational Interpretation," in *Thomas Jefferson's Military Academy: Founding West Point*, ed. Robert M. S. McDonald (Charlottesville, VA: University of Virginia Press, 2004), 131–34; Richard A. Samuelson, "Consistent in Creation: Thomas Jefferson, Natural Aristocracy, and the Problem of Knowledge," in *Light and Liberty: Thomas Jefferson and the Power of Knowledge*, ed. Robert M. S. McDonald (Charlottesville, VA: University of Virginia Press, 2012), 86–88.

80. Gallatin to Madison, 9 April 1831, *FOL*—Early Access; J[ames] M. Mathews, *Recollections of Persons and Events, Chiefly in the City of New York* (New York, 1865), 195, 206, 212, 251–52; Gallatin to Badollet, 7 February 1833, *CBG*, 312–13; Professors of the Faculty, *History of the Controversy in the University of the City of New York* (New York, 1838), 4–8; Jones, *New York University*, 28–31, 36, 40–52; Joan Marans Dim and Nancy Murphy Cricco, *The Miracle on Washington Square: New York University* (Lanham, MD: Lexington Books, 2001), 26–27; Louise L. Stevenson, "Preparing for Public Life: The Collegiate Students at New York University, 1832–1881," in *The University and the City from Medieval Origins to the Present*, ed. Thomas Bender (New York: Oxford University Press, 1988), 150–57; Leuenberger, "Albert Gallatin: Educational Interests," 114–25. James Mathews was a member of the Literary Club to which Gallatin belonged. Mathews, *Recollections*, 122.

81. Albert Gallatin, "A Synopsis of the Indian Tribes within the United States East of the Rocky Mountains, and in the British and Russian Possessions in North America," *Archaeologia Americana: Transactions and Collections of the American Antiquarian Society* 2 (1836): 1–422; Gallatin to Verplanck, 26 February 1831, *PAG;* Robert E. Bieber, *Science Encounters the Indian, 1820–1880: The Early Years of American Ethnology* (Norman: University of Oklahoma Press, 1986), 29–35; Anthony F. C. Wallace, *Jefferson and the Indians: The Tragic Fate of the First Americans* (Cambridge, MA: Harvard University Press, 1999), 325–26. For Gallatin's use of the War department's Indian agents to collect vocabulary when he was in Baltimore, see Cameron Strong, "Scientific Instructions and Native American Linguistics in the Imperial United States: The Department of War's 1826 Vocabulary," *Journal of the Early Republic* 37, no. 3 (Fall 2017): 413–25. On the continuing use of linguistics to investigate human origins, see Robert Blust, "New Perspectives in Southeast Asian and Pacific Prehistory," in *Historical Linguistics and Archaeology: An Uneasy Alliance*, ed. Philip J. Piper et al. (Acton, Australia: ANU Press, 2017), 275–92; Christopher Ehret, "Linguistic Archaeology," *African Archaeological Review* 29, nos. 2 and 3 (September 2012): 109–30.

82. J[ohn] W[esley] Powell, "Indian Linguistic Families of America North of Mexico," *Seventh Annual Report of the Bureau of Ethnology...1885–'86* (Washington, DC: U. S. Government Printing Office, 1891), 9–10; Albert Gallatin, "Notes on the Semi-Civilized Nations of Mexico, Yucatan, and Central America," *Transactions of the American Ethnological Society* 1 (1845): 1–352; Gallatin, "Introduction to 'Hale's Indians of North-West America,'" ibid., 2 (1848): xxv–clxxxviii; John Russell Bartlett, "Reminiscences of Albert Gallatin," *Proceedings of the New York Historical Society for 1849* (New York, 1849), 281–83; Jerry E. Mueller, ed., *Autobiography of John Russell Bartlett, 1805–1889* (Providence, RI: John Carter Brown Library, 2006), 25–27; Robert Lawrence Gunn, *Ethnology and Empire: Languages, Literature, and the Making of the North American Borderlands* (New York: New York University Press, 2015), 42–44, 148–55; Sean P. Harvey, *Native Tongues: Colonialism and Race from Encounter to the Reservation* (Cambridge, MA: Harvard University Press, 2015), 169, 194–204, 215–18; Richard B. Woodbury and Nathalie F. S. Woodbury, "The Rise and Fall of the Bureau of American Ethnology," *Journal of the Southwest* 41, no. 3 (autumn 1999): 284–88; D. Leedom Shaul, "Linguistic Natural History: John Wesley

Powell and the Classification of American Languages," ibid.: 297–310; John Duncan Haskell Jr., "John Russell Bartlett (1805–1886): Bookman" (Ph.D. diss., George Washington University, 1977), 95–110. Gallatin and John Russell Bartlett also worked together to revive the New-York Historical Society, and Gallatin served as the society's president for six years. Gallatin, "Inaugural Address of the Hon. Albert Gallatin on Taking the Chair as President of the New-York Historical Society" (New York, 1843); R. W. G. Vail, *Knickerbocker Birthday: A Sesqui-Centennial History of the New-York Historical Society, 1804–1954* (New York: New York Historical Society, 1954), 89–93; Mueller, *Autobiography of John Russell Bartlett,* 22–23.

83.   Gallatin, "A Synopsis of the Indian Tribes," 108, 142–59 (quoted at 151, 154, 158). Writing to Jefferson thirty years earlier, Gallatin had claimed that the greatest obstacle to the improvement of Native culture was "licentiousness…and the consequent want of the social institutions which establish and secure *property* and *marriage.*" Gallatin to Jefferson, [12 February 1805], *WAG,* 1:227. A jingle from the Indian removal era in Georgia captured the competing urges of white males: "All I want in this creation / Is a pretty little wife and a big plantation / Away up yonder in the Cherokee nation." Howe, *What Hath God Wrought,* 414–23, quoting Joel Chandler Harris, *Stories of Georgia* (New York, 1896), 216; Jason Edward Black, *American Indians and the Rhetoric of Removal and Allotment* (Jackson: University Press of Mississippi, 2015), 37–58; S. Charles Bolton, "Jeffersonian Indian Removal and the Emergence of Arkansas Territory," *Arkansas Historical Quarterly* 62, no. 3 (Autumn 2003): 259–70.

84.   Gallatin, "A Synopsis of the Indian Tribes," 158–59; Brian W. Dippie, *Catlin and His Contemporaries: The Politics of Patronage* (Lincoln: University of Nebraska Press, 1990), 55–58, 61–64, 71–73; Philip J. Deloria, *Playing Indian* (New Haven: Yale University Press, 1998), 90–91; Steven Conn, *History's Shadow: Native Americans and Historical Consciousness in the Nineteenth Century* (Chicago: University of Chicago Press, 2004), 86–99; John P. Bowes, *Land Too Good for Indians: Northern Indian Removal* (Norman: University of Oklahoma Press, 2016), 211–13. For the classic treatment of Republican policies for Native American assimilation and removal, see Bernard W. Sheehan, *Seeds of Extinction: Jeffersonian Philanthropy and the American Indian* (Chapel Hill: University of North Carolina Press, 1973), 119–81, 243–75. Thirty years after Gallatin wrote the "Synopsis," a federal commission on

pacification of the Western tribes recommended that "their barbarous dialects should be blotted out and the English language substituted" in order to stamp out their tribal identities. "Uniformity of language will do this," the commission concluded, "nothing else will." Report to the President by the Indian Peace Commission, 7 January 1868, U. S. Department of the Interior, *Annual Report of the Commissioner of Indian Affairs, 1868* (Washington, DC: U. S. Government Printing Office, 1868), 44.

85. Sellers, *The Market Revolution*, 412–13; Holt, *The Rise and Fall of the American Whig Party*, 168–70; Charles W. McCurdy, *The Anti-Rent Era in New York Law and Politics, 1839–1865* (Chapel Hill: University of North Carolina Press, 2001), 141–44; Howe, *What Hath God Wrought*, 679–81; David A. Clary, *Eagles and Empire: The United States, Mexico, and the Struggle for a Continent* (New York: Bantam Books, 2009), 33–61; Haynes, *Unfinished Revolution*, 239–49; John Craig Hammond, "The 'High-Road to a Slave Empire': Conflict and the Growth and Expansion of Slavery on the North American Continent," in *The World of the Revolutionary American Republic: Land, Labor, and the Conflict for a Continent*, ed. Andrew Shankman (New York: Routledge, 2014), 346–69.

86. New York *Evening Post*, 25 April 1844; Allan Nevins and Milton Halsey Thomas, eds., *The Diary of George Templeton Strong, 1835–1875* (4 vols.; New York: Macmillan, 1952), 1:229 (24 April 1844); *New York Herald*, 25 April 1844; Tuckerman, *The Diary of Philip Hone*, 2:214–15 (25 April 1844); Theodore Sedgwick, *Thoughts on the Proposed Annexation of Texas to the United States… Together with the Address of Albert Gallatin, LL.D. Delivered at the Tabernacle Meeting…*, 2nd ed. (New York, 1844), 53–56; Susan Hayes Ward, *The History of the Broadway Tabernacle Church* (New York: privately pub., 1901), 28–29, 94; Wilentz, *The Rise of American Democracy*, 534–35, 564–68, 572; U. S. Department of the Interior, National Park Service, "Gaslight in America: A Guide for Historic Preservation," Plate 16, www.nps.gov/parkhistory/online_books/hcrs/myers/plate2.htm.

87. *New York Herald*, 26 April 1844; John Russell Bartlett, Diary extracts, 12 September 1848– [26] October 1849, *PAG* (undated entry headed "Mr Gallatin's Political Principles," probably written in connection with Bartlett's reminiscences of Gallatin for the New-York Historical Society); Holt, *The Rise and Fall of the American Whig Party*, 25–29. James Polk's vice president, George Mifflin Dallas, visited Gallatin soon after the

election. He was the son of Alexander Dallas, and he had accompanied Gallatin as a secretary on his peace mission in 1813. *New York Herald,* 10 January 1845.

88.   Washington *Daily National Intelligencer,* 22, 24, 27, and 29 January and 14 February 1846, reprinted as Albert Gallatin, *Letters of Albert Gallatin on the Oregon Question* (Washington, DC, 1846) (without appendix on war expenses), and Gallatin, *The Oregon Question* (New York, 1846) (with appendix), reprinted in *WAG,* 3:489–553; Howe, *What Hath God Wrought,* 715–22; Haynes, *Unfinished Revolution,* 251–66.

89.   John H. Schroeder, *Mr. Polk's War: American Opposition and Dissent, 1846–1848* (Madison: University of Wisconsin Press, 1973), 8–18; Wilentz, *The Rise of American Democracy,* 582–83; Amy S. Greenberg, *A Wicked War: Polk, Clay, Lincoln, and the 1846 U. S. Invasion of Mexico* (New York: Alfred A. Knopf, 2012), 99–108.

90.   Schroeder, *Mr. Polk's War,* 121–49; Greenberg, *A Wicked War,* 192–93, 210–11, 222, 233.

91.   Albert Gallatin, *Peace with Mexico* (New York, 1847), reprinted in *WAG,* 3:555–91 (quoted at 583, 584, 581, 585, and 586); Ezekiel Bacon to Gallatin, 5 December 1847, *PAG* (Whig opposition to the war palsied by "the *Ghost of the Hartford convention*"). Gallatin's *Peace with Mexico* appeared in varied editions and various newspapers. Gallatin, "Address on War with Mexico," Baltimore *Niles' National Register,* 11 December 1847, reprinted in Jeremiah Hughes, ed., *Niles' National Register* [1848] 73:235–39; Mueller, *Autobiography of John Russell Bartlett,* 27–28. On racism in the war with Mexico, see Greenberg, *A Wicked War,* 133, 213, 222, 233, 263.

92.   Gallatin to Garrett Davis, 16 February 1848; Gallatin to Edward Everett, 16 December 1847, *WAG,* 2:661, 656; James W. Alexander, Recollections of Albert Gallatin, 1 July 1850, *PAG* (conversation of 7 December 1847); Gallatin to Thomas M. Ward, 10 December 1847, *WAG,* 2:653–56; Jonathan Roberts to Gallatin, 17 December 1847; Everett to Gallatin, 20 December 1847; Gallatin to John Quincy Adams, 22 December 1847; Theodore Dwight to Gallatin, 22 December 1847; Adams to Gallatin, 29 December 1847, *PAG.*

93.   Albert Gallatin, *War Expenses* (New York, 1848), 17; Gallatin to Davis, 16 February 1848; Gallatin to John A. Rockwell, 8 May 1848, *WAG,* 2:661–62, 666; *New York Herald,* 7 February 1848; Gallatin, "War Expenses: The Subject of Capital," *Niles' National Register,* 12 February 1848, reprinted in *Niles' National Register* 73:380-83 (main body of the

pamphlet printed in New York); Amy S. Greenberg, *Manifest Manhood and the Antebellum American Empire* (New York: Cambridge University Press, 2005), 8–11; Edling, *A Hercules in the Cradle,* 150–66.

94. Alexander, Recollections of Albert Gallatin, 1 July 1850 (conversation of 7 December 1848); Gallatin to John C. Calhoun, 3 March 1848; Calhoun to Gallatin, 13 March 1848; Thomas Hart Benton to Gallatin, 6 March 1848, *PAG;* Gallatin to Francis Brooke, 4 March 1847, printed in Washington *Daily Union,* 15 August 1849; Treaty of Peace, Friendship, Limits, and Settlement, United States–Mexico [Treaty of Guadalupe Hidalgo], 2 February 1848, Bevans, *Treaties and Other International Agreements,* 9:791–806; Wilentz, *The Rise of American Democracy,* 611-13.

95. Bartlett, Diary extracts, 12 September 1848–[26] October 1849 (quoted from entry for 17 January 1849); Frances Stevens, Copy of Mary Few's note on conversation with Albert Gallatin, 11 December 1848; Alexander, Recollections of Albert Gallatin, 1 July 1850 (quoted from conversation of 27 November 1848); James W. Alexander to Mrs. Byam K. Stevens [Frances Gallatin], 1 July 1850 (misdated 1880 by editors), *PAG;* Frances Chrystie [Frances Few] to Thomas Chrystie, [14 December] 1848, James Witter Nicholson Family Letters, Special Collections, Hesburgh Libraries, University of Notre Dame; Mueller, *Autobiography of John Russell Bartlett,* 27. Frances Stevens and her family also had a house on Lafayette Place in the same fashionable strip along upper Broadway where her parents lived. [John Doggett, ed.], *Doggett's New-York City Directory for 1847 and 1848,* 6ᵗʰ ed. (New York, 1847), 388.

96. *New York Herald,* 16 May (quoted) and 17 May 1849; Tuckerman, *The Diary of Philip Hone,* 2:363 (13 August 1849); Alexander, Recollections of Albert Gallatin, 1 July 1850, *PAG* (conversation of 16 May 1849); New York *Evening Post,* 13 and 15 August 1849. On the two Episcopal churches along Broadway, see Burrows and Wallace, *Gotham,* 459, 717. The spire of Trinity Church made it the tallest building in the United States at the time.

97. *New York Herald,* 14 August 1849; *New-York Daily Tribune,* 14 August 1849; Washington *Daily Union,* 15 August 1849; Tuckerman, *The Diary of Philip Hone,* 2:363 (13 August 1849).

98. The Nicholson vault in which the Gallatins were buried originally lay at the southwest corner of Trinity Church within sight of Alexander

Hamilton's grave, but in 1964 it was moved to the northwest corner to make way for construction. "James Nicholson Vault," Vault records of Trinity Church, 64–65 (29 March 1885–25 July 1964), Trinity Church–Wall Street Archives.

INDEX